Lecture Notes in Computer Science 2739

Edited by G. Goos, J. Hartmanis, and J. van Leeuwen

T0189940

Springer
Berlin
Heidelberg
New York
Hong Kong
London
Milan
Paris
Tokyo

Roland Traunmüller (Ed.)

Electronic Government

Second International Conference, EGOV 2003
Prague, Czech Republic, September 1-5, 2003
Proceedings

 Springer

Series Editors

Gerhard Goos, Karlsruhe University, Germany
Juris Hartmanis, Cornell University, NY, USA
Jan van Leeuwen, Utrecht University, The Netherlands

Volume Editor

Roland Traunmüller
University of Linz
Institute of Applied Computer Science
Altenbergerstr. 69, 4040 Linz, Austria
E-mail: traunm@ifs.uni-linz.ac.at

Cataloging-in-Publication Data applied for

A catalog record for this book is available from the Library of Congress.

Bibliographic information published by Die Deutsche Bibliothek
Die Deutsche Bibliothek lists this publication in the Deutsche Nationalbibliografie;
detailed bibliographic data is available in the Internet at <http://dnb.ddb.de>.

CR Subject Classification (1998): K.4, K.6.5, K.5, K.3, C.2, H.5, H.4

ISSN 0302-9743
ISBN 3-540-40485-2 Springer-Verlag Berlin Heidelberg New York

Springer-Verlag Berlin Heidelberg New York
a member of BertelsmannSpringer Science+Business Media GmbH

http://www.springer.de

© Springer-Verlag Berlin Heidelberg 2003
Printed in Germany

Typesetting: Camera-ready by author, data conversion by PTP-Berlin GmbH
Printed on acid-free paper   SPIN: 10929179   06/3142   5 4 3 2 1 0

Preface

The EGOV Conference Series intends to assess the state of the art in e-Government and to provide guidance for research and development in this fast-moving field. The annual conferences bring together leading research experts and professionals from all over the globe. Thus, EGOV 2003 in Prague built on the achievements of the 1st EGOV Conference (Aix-en-Provence, 2002), which provided an illustrative overview of e-Government activities. This year the interest even increased: nearly 100 contributions, and authors coming from 34 countries. In this way EGOV Conference 2003 was a reunion for professionals from all over the globe.

EGOV 2003 brought some changes in the outline and structure of the conference. In line with the broadening of the field and a growing number of submissions it became necessary to decentralize the reviewing process. So reviewing was done via stream chairs who deserve high praise for their dedicated work. In addition, a workshop part was included to cover some subjects of emerging significance, such as dissemination, networking, and regional developments. Further, a subtitle of the conference was chosen that would mirror the expansion of e-Government to e-Governance. Consequently, in this year's conference governance, democratic deliberation and legal issues occupied a growing share. Last, but not least, GIS was incorporated as a topic due to the increasing importance of geographical information systems for planning and operations.

An annual conference bears a message as well. e-Government is at a crossroads; there is progress and success, yet at the same time obstacles and hindrances are mounting. How can we close the gap between the vision of e-Government and the reality we live in? This issue was treated in an introduction statement by the editor.

The set of themes covered was rich in several streams. The following list of issues covered by the 2nd EGOV Conference gives an illustration:

- e-Governance tools for policymaking in governments and in policy networks;
- Government communication and transactions with citizens and enterprises over the Internet: one-stop government, joined-up government;
- Frameworks and guidelines for e-Government and e-Governance;
- Electronic service delivery and Web services;
- International and regional projects, case studies and best practice;
- Strategies, implementation policies and change management;
- Models and methodology of e-Government research;
- e-Democracy strategies, citizen participation in local public affairs;
- Sustaining processes, collaborative activities, legal interpretation and administrative decision making in a virtual space;
- Trust and security: legal and organizational provisions, technical instruments, citizen cards, digital signatures;
- Knowledge management and GIS (geographical information systems);

- Standards for information interchange and processes, interoperability and semantic standardization;
- Institutional changes and new organizational arrangements: ad hoc co-operation, public-private-partnerships;
- Legal, societal and cultural aspects of e-Government.

Many people worked to form the conference and to prepare the program and proceedings. The significance of the work of the stream chairs has been acknowledged above; special credit has to go to them, and to the members of the Program Committee. Also the work of Gabriela Wagner heading the DEXA organization deserves acknowledgment. In particular, the editor expresses thanks to Ute Holler; her exceptionally engaged assistance in preparing both the program and the proceedings was decisive for success.

September 2003   Roland Traunmüller

Program Committee

Program Chair

Roland Traunmüller, University of Linz, Austria

Stream Chairs

e-Governance	Ann Macintosh
e-Democracy	Thomas F. Gordon
Change Management	Jeremy Millard
Electronic Service Delivery	Ronald Leenes
Web Services	Maddalena Sorrentino
	Francesco Virili
Models and Methodology of e-Government Research	Åke Grönlund
Trust and Security	Thomas Menzel
Knowledge Management	Maria Wimmer
	Tom M. van Engers
Geographical IS	Mário Jorge Leitão
Legal Aspects	Fernando Galindo
Global Relations and Regional Development	Gerald Quirchmayr

Program Committee Members

Kim Viborg Andersen, Copenhagen Business School, Denmark
Chris Bellamy, Nottingham Trent University, United Kingdom
Trevor Bench-Capon, University of Liverpool, United Kingdom
Hinrich E.G. Bonin, Fachhochschule Nordostniedersachsen, Germany
Jean-Loup Chappelet, IDHEAP Lausanne, Switzerland
Wichian Chutimaskul, King Mongkut's University of Technology,
Thonburi, Thailand
Nicolae Costake, Consultant, Romania
Arthur Csetenyi, Budapest University of Economic Sciences, Hungary
Freddie Dawkins, GOPA Cartermill International, Belgium
Margrit Falck, Fachhochschule für Verwaltung und Rechtspflege Berlin,
Germany
Herbert Fiedler, Universität Bonn, Lehrstuhl für Juristische Informatik,
Germany
Fernando Galindo, Universidad de Zaragoza, Spain

Additional Reviewers

Ademar Manuel Aguiar, University of Porto, Portugal
Alexander Boer, University of Amsterdam, The Netherlands
Vincent M.F. Homburg, Erasmus University, The Netherlands
Jennifer Rowley, Edge Hill University College, United Kingdom
Jörgen Svensson, University of Twente, The Netherlands
Radboud Winkels, University of Amsterdam, The Netherlands

Table of Contents

Introduction

e-Governance

e-Democracy

Change Management

Electronic Service Delivery

Web Services

Models and Methodology of e-Government Research

Trust and Security

Knowledge Management

Geographical Information System (GIS)

Technical Systems

Legal Aspects

Workshop: Global Relations and Regional Development

E-Government at a Decisive Moment: Sketching a Roadmap to Excellence

Roland Traunmüller and Maria A. Wimmer

University of Linz
Altenbergerstr. 69, 4040 Linz, Austria
{traunm,mw}@ifs.uni-linz.ac.at

1 Progress of E-Government at Crossroads

e-Government has become both: a vision and the world we live in. With information as the lifeblood of modern society, the enabling potential of information technology is recognised sufficiently in its full extent. So e-Government has become a guiding vision that provides a comprehensive view of citizen demands and their fulfilment in administrative processes. Moreover, Government has turned into e-Government: thus all – agencies, citizen and enterprises – draw heavily on increased use of information, on more sophisticated service provision, on a creative and thorough redesign of existing administrative processes, and on innovative forms in assisting governance.

All in all, e-Government has turned into a broad wave spreading to all levels of Government and every single agency. The breakers have reached all countries as well. Just to take the EGOV Conference as an example: this year's conference covers one hundred contributions with authors coming from 34 countries – reaching from Brazil to China, from Belarus to Qatar.

Seen from afar, e-Government looks like the perfect success story; yet there is another side as well. Although powerful and ambitious systems have been produced, users - intern and extern to the governmental realm – seem to be dissatisfied. In part, dissatisfaction is linked to the ambitions. A prevailing discomfort exists stemming from the fact that most of the „easy" things had already been done earlier and the more complicated issues approached now fall short of heightened expectations. Also, a grumbling below the surface of all success stories can be recognised; both, officials and clients are dissatisfied with existing applications, their usability and the limitations of the systems in use.

Discarding the arguments and saying discontent is only a consequence of hyped expectations would not be enough. One has to take the arguments serious. It is a matter of fact that users now are much more willing to be disapproving. Formerly the majority of the users were either sceptical towards technology, or terrified by it, or over-awed by it; now they will not accept when the technology lets them down in one way or another, they are far more prepared to be critical.

There is a challenge from critical questions arising about whether the systems we use are adequate and user-friendly. It is a fact that anticipations have become high as people are used from their every day life to expect a smooth running technology. It is

R. Traunmüller (Ed.): EGOV 2003, LNCS 2739, pp. 1–14, 2003.

not tolerable when administrative systems will not meet the expectations persons have from experiences with commercial systems. Discontent has to spur our ambitions. So the task is twofold: it is not only about recognising problems and limitations for not raising unrealistic expectations; more it is about making happen that vision and reality will come close.

In this respect, our contribution will first investigate the vision and expectations of e-Government (section 2). In section 3, current problems of fragmentation and isolated views are investigated. As a consequence of analysing these problems, we then provide a framework for action (section 4) and dig into engineering and change management as the prerequisites for successfully implementing e-Government (section 5).

2   Vision and Expectations of E-Government

First of all, expectations focus on advanced instruments of governments to improve service provision to all types of clients: individual citizens, communities, commercial and non-profit organisations as well as public authorities themselves. Its overall vision implies:

- Modernisation of the whole machinery of governments including reorganising and restructuring of public organisations,
- Re-engineering of administrative processes to provide public services via modern access means,
- Citizen- and customer-centred service provision including a more active participation in government and democracy, and
- Integrating tools and connecting organisations and people over time and distances to implement seamless government and to reach the eEurope policies [2] [3].

Massive usage of modern information technology (IT) is seen as the enabler of this vision to access governmental services and knowledge resources. IT provides the basic means for collaboration over time and distance between the different actors across borders of various kinds. Modern information technology has also become the driving force to modernise authorities and other institutions of public governance and service provision. The expectations imply as well efficient and transparent possibilities for more active participation, a higher level for the control of public affairs and of those to whom people invest their trust.

With the usage of modern media, new roles and opportunities of human consultation and of citizen/customer-to-government relations emerge. E-government addresses also government-to-government relations within the executive body of administrations and functions of management and of policymaking that cannot always be neatly separated from policy implementation. The important role which knowledge plays in enhancing the work of both, the executive branch of government and governance, must not be neglected.

E-government is a multidimensional and multidisciplinary field, where many mutually interdependent factors impact its success and acceptance. Among others, the multiplicity of e-government refers to a wide range of IT systems and architectures, different access channels and devices, distinct process structures, many parties involved (authorities and customers, citizens, the general public) and various knowledge sources combined in governmental work. From these multiple aspects one can easily deduce that developments in the field have always technical, economic, social, organisational and cultural impact.

The multi-facets of e-government strongly call for a holistic approach to implement e-government following the focus of *humans using IT and modern media systems to serve people for their comfort and convenience.* Yet with current developments in the field, we still have to investigate and learn a lot to reach such ambient and convivial information systems.

3   Current Problems of Fragmentation and Isolated Developments

During the last few years, e-government has received much attention. Many investigations have been made bringing to bear various developments. Yet, the landscape is very fragmented and many issues are rather neglected, are developed in isolation or focus on single aspects. The implementations are treated independently instead of integrating them. As a result, current developments do not reach the maturity and success they should embody. Consequently, expectations [1] originally connected with e-government have not been met satisfactorily.

According to recent studies [6] [5], up to now, online access to public services is not used by citizens and business partners as expected. Experiences show that this is due to a number of factors among which the following loom particularly large:

- Neglect of stakeholder expectations and focus, so resulting in limited take-up of e-Services
- Neglect of the specifics of the Governmental realm and the business processes at Stake
- Neglect of interoperability and integration on various levels
- Limited views impeding progress
- The tricky business of transferring e-Commerce solutions
- Lack of genuine e-Government strategies, clear goals and common effort

In the following sub-sections, these obstacles and weaknesses are detailed.

3.1   Neglect of Stakeholder Expectations and Focus Resulting in Limited Take-Up of E-Services

Low user take-up of e-services has to ring the alarm bell. Resistance to change includes many obstacles and one has to answer the question: What has gone wrong with e-Government projects? This question is strongly linked with the expectations of the different actors (governments, administrations, mediators and intermediaries, citizens and business). What are the needs of users and how can e-services be designed to fit their needs and to bring benefit and comfort to them? Severe deficiencies have been revealed in investigations and the list of shortcomings resulting in low uptake is long:

- a general lack in targeting the audience;
- fragmented solutions without integration not really providing added value to the user of e-services:
- an inadequate and inconsistent design lacking of comments and adequate examples;
- a sloppiness in maintenance showing unreliable and outdated pieces of information.

Going to in-depth analyses of interaction processes provides some insight on weaknesses of currently available solutions:

- impossibility to cope with the logic of administrative thinking;
- users not comprehending the administrative jargon;
- clients piloting helplessly through the jungle of legal information.

Inadequacies may appear at various stages and levels, they may be caused by history or by ingrained behaviour. Sometimes these are characteristic of entire application areas. As a matter of fact, obstacles and opportunities are encountered by all the different actors in building e-Government. And there are manifold occasions where they are perceived: in defining e-Government strategies; in implementing a particular project; in working with application systems as civil servant; in seeking web-information as a citizen.

No wonder that for Government the demands for more quality in e-service provision are claiming for urgent improvements.

3.2 Neglect of the Specifics of the Governmental Realm and the Business Processes at Stake

Governance and government activity is not oriented towards making benefit but cares about our individual life securing a well-organised, safe and comfortable life in our society. In comparison to the private sector, many limitations are systemic in nature of the public sector:

- There are many features that cannot be changed because they are inherent to Government: the extraordinarily complex goal structure in the public sector; legal norms dominating administrative work; transparency and safeguarding legal validity etc.
- An important point is Public Administration mostly works via a complex tissue of cooperation so involving quite many acting entities. This is a way quite contrary to the private sector where streamlining would forbid this. The involvement of many actors has diverse causes: sometimes, the complexity of the subject matter is the reason; other cases may need checks and balances of the experts, independent parties, etc.
- Another example is process reengineering that has its limitations by legal norms for protecting privacy and safeguarding legality.
- Further peculiarities of Government are rooted in bureaucratic attitudes – both on the level of the institution and the individual.

Apart from that, historically grounded evolution of European administrative systems bears some hindrances:

- Generally, administrative systems are very diverse which does not ease a harmonised approach on e-Government.
- Another hindrance is the actual distribution of legal and constitutional competences among agencies, an issue that has to be rethought seriously.
- Further hindrance is a lack of consideration of market principle. One has to learn something from private sector experiences where customising services to the right target group is already practised with success.

Government activity consists not only of simple and well-structured types of processes. To a major part, individual case processing and negotiation processes with a strong binding to legal grounding are characteristic. When providing public services, the specific situation of individual citizens and businesses has to be taken into consideration. This requires some discretionary power of the public servants bringing in their expertise as well. Current e-Government solutions do not support such complex case processing and decision-making processes.

There are many requests that have to be mirrored in planning the architecture. System architectures have to cope with a new relation between front offices and back offices. They also have to cater for the needs of specific interest groups such as the jobless, the elderly, self-employed professionals etc.

3.3 Neglect of Interoperability and Integration on Various Levels

Up to now, a parochial avoidance of interagency co-operation is practised. For this reason, the huge potential which *organisational* integration encompasses is not exploited at all. However, cross-organisational integration would enable new ways of governmental activities through e.g. public-private partnerships, cross-organisational (between different levels of government and within them) and cross-border collaboration as well as one-stop government. The basic requirement to implement such options is a strong commitment from the political side, from governance and from the strategic management.

Putting organisational integration into practice calls for integrated *business process structures*. Yet, current process developments rather reflect local needs and do not equally pay attention to the two sides of government activity, namely the customers' view and the administrations' view. Inter-organisational workflows, cross-border process standardisation of public services and process models integrating the external (service oriented) view of customers with the internal (competence oriented) view of public administrations are among the requirements to implement integration on the process level.

Common, interchangeable data standards are basic to enable inter-organisational co-operation. Despite of that, data and process knowledge, legal knowledge grounding governmental activity, case-bases and human expertise of public servants have to be neatly integrated. Up to now, only few efforts are made towards integration of *data resources, legal and process knowledge*. A much stronger - common - effort is required to advance first approaches towards European standardisation, knowledge ontologies and reference architectures suitable to describe governmental activity, data and knowledge resources.

Even on the technical level, *access media and IT systems* are designed for local needs and specific purposes. Current developments chiefly concern portal developments for electronic service delivery as a part of government practice which is highly visible and where a promise exists of alleviating administrative burdens put on enterprises and on the general public. The negligence of back-office developments integrated with the front-office, of overall system and media interoperability, of module integration (digital IDs, electronic signatures, payment, service application, service delivery, etc.) in all phases of service delivery (information - communication - transaction - aftercare) leads to large investments that do not pay back and that hamper the overall vision of e-government.

3.4   Limited Views Impeding Progress

As a consequence of recent software and technology focus, many systems development approaches to e-government continue to be rather technology-driven. They suffer from the *negligence of a multidisciplinary approach and a holistic view*.

Limited views are a severe obstacle and they have to be overcome. Having only a limited, single-issue focused concept of e-Government is a common problem of many running projects. It is the deeper cause of many inertial forces. Thus changing mindsets has priority and it has to start with those persons who are in charge. This makes convincing and encouraging politicians and senior officials a main concern. As a consequence, those who define objectives and frameworks for e-Government and who allocate funds, need proper understanding on an overall scale. Such decision-makers need to be prepared for taking the right decisions. They have to comprehend the essentials: e-Government is not solely about deploying technology – it is more about modernising administration. Further, e-transformation means inducing some rather radical changes.

3.5   The Tricky Business of Transferring E-Commerce Solutions

When looking from afar, striking correspondences appear between e-Government and e-Commerce. To list four important ones:
- both are rooted in telecooperation;
- both involve reengineering and integrating flows of information, of money and of goods;
- both started with customer interface improvements;
- both now concentrate on digging deeper into an effort to overhaul the businesses in question completely.

However, as Wallace Sayre expressed it in a saying: "public and private management are fundamentally alike in all unimportant respects". Therefore, specific attention is to be put on the differences that exist in many important respects. We have discussed these in [8]. Feasibility of transferring concepts and systems is to be investigated for each individual case. Sometimes, even minor distinctions may exert essential influence on design and, hence, need to be treated properly. Reproducing concepts and systems from the commercial domain has to be done with thoughtfulness and sensitivity.

3.6   Lack of Genuine E-Government Strategies and Common Effort

Clear strategies and views are a prerequisite for any successful development. Surely, technology sets the pace and creates opportunities for more efficient and transparent treatment of public affairs. Yet, e-Government takes place in a socio-cultural and socio-technical environment. Thus, e-Government strategies and long term goals have to reflect non-technical change requests as well. Since Governments and Public Administrations are in charge of "managing" society and its evolution, common effort and economic thinking must not be neglected. Equally, this effort must be balanced with the characteristics and specific duties of governmental activity. However, many current e-government strategies do neglect these interdependencies or they completely lack of feasible strategies targeting the society goals.

Setting common strategies to manoeuvring a huge machinery of government is difficult. Also, eliciting the impact of (local) change to a largely structured, interdependent net of governmental agencies is no simple task. But up to now, we don't even approximate such impacts of developments.

In short and long term planning, setting goals and determining criteria for success is crucial. Due to ever-faster change and evolution, these have to adapt dynamically. An example is e-Service provision where the demands on quality of service have increased considerably. Another example is the request for having a more holistic strategy. As a consequence, plans have to change: becoming less technology focused; turning out to be more open; leaving more room for manoeuvre.

An inherent bias in e-Government developments is the lack of common effort and missing exchange of lessons learnt. In the last years, many initiatives have been established furthering innovation and advanced developments. Yet, the lack of coordinated effort has led to redundant developments being not interoperable and waste of huge amounts of money. A change in culture and minds is urgent, spurring exchange of findings, transparency of (also local) developments and lessons learnt thereby building ground for joint innovation and faster reach of success.

4   Framework for Actions: Sketching a Roadmap

As pointed out before, e-Government is not an objective per se but an advanced instrument of the organisation of governments and public governance in order to better serving individual citizens, communities, commercial and non-profit organisations as well as public authorities themselves. Thereby, technology creates more efficient and transparent possibilities for more participation, a higher level for the control of public affairs and of those to whom people invest their trust. To reach this high level of quality in governmental services, e-Government calls for a socio-cultural and socio-technical balance in its developments, where new roles and opportunities of human consultation and of citizen/customer - administration relations emerge. As stated in the chapter before, it has to be developed in close correlation with the development of non-technical change requests.

Above all, the development of e-Government has to be based on feasible and reasonable change of governments. This is a strong argument in favour of a holistic approach to work-processes and work-situations in government, which are highly knowledge-intensive and which continue to rely on close forms of interaction between humans and IT. Human actors using "machines serving people for their comfort and convenience" is thus a top priority.

With current developments in e-Government and as the obstacles listed in the chapter before clearly demonstrate, we still have to investigate and learn a lot to reach such ambient and convivial information systems.

The challenges of the next years are to learn from above listed weaknesses and to shift to an integrating approach. Recognizing the way to success needs above all a point of view that offers global perspectives. Of course, not all can be implemented in one single initiative. Instead, a list of urgent action points sets the roadmap to direct developments towards the achievement of fully integrated, seamless government:

- Considerations have to start with deeply understanding the user needs. Stakeholder needs have to be put into the centre of interest: who are the users and which are the services they ask for? What are hindrances and obstacles that users don't take-up services offered online?
- Next, the whole machinery of Government comes under scrutiny: providing administrative services, running work processes, and modes of cooperative work have to be defined in a new way without neglecting the core responsibilities and duties of government action. All these redesign efforts - public services, processes, cooperation and knowledge management – will lead up to rethinking the institutional structures of government.
- Taking a holistic approach is another urgent concern. This means integrating several aspects: users, technology, organisation, law, knowledge, culture, society and politics.
- Hand in hand with a sound engineering approach goes a strong focus on harmonisation, standardisation and interoperability. This is a broad claim so let us mention just two key requests: developing standards and building a secure and reliable infrastructure.
- Competent change management and improving the innovative capacity of the public sector is a must.

4.1 Putting Focus on the User Needs

Addressing the specific needs of different user groups not only refers to a superficial distinction of target groups such as citizens, businesses and governments. To better serve the users, electronic public services have to be developed in strong relation with the specific target groups such as public servants at one-stop service encounters, intermediaries (notaries, architects, lawyers, tax consultants), students, unemployed, families, pensioners, accounting staff of companies, etc.

Usability concerns, human-computer interfaces, socio-linguistic problems, education and know-how transfer (e.g. through network-supported dialogues and discussions as well as intelligent online help on demand) within virtual self-service shops need to be addressed. Usability can be improved in several ways. One is building on past experiences (and common sense as well). Some example that even plain rules will benefit are expressed below:

- The prime obligation is: "Stress usability - not alone visibility".

- "Less is more" and "Keep it straight and simple" are sayings that can be applied to design. They will match because overloaded or too complicated presentations are a nuisance.

- Further on it may be wise neglecting a drive to perfection. Designers have to avoid the widespread mistake of shifting too much burden to the client.

- In addition design will be successful when using more analogies.

Nothing against folks wisdom and common sense, but there are complicated interaction processes needing a deeper analysis. Citizens contacting agencies for advice in complex cases is such an issue needing closer inspection. Often the concrete situation is so that rather conflicting demands have to be resolved:

1. the citizen's requests are commonly posed in a rather urgent situation,
2. there may occur need for an in-depth explanation in an unambiguous way,
3. the explanatory capabilities of the system are limited,
4. interactions are connected with a high translation effort (i.e. transforming client demands of the everyday-world in the legal-administrative jargon of public administration and vice versa).

Several means are to be used to support the governmental work systems: programmes for clarifying dialogues, illustrative scenarios. Also detailed knowledge (on both, the field in question and the interaction) can be embodied in software agents. All this can actively help users in accomplishing their tasks. Finally, more advanced future systems will result in intelligent multi-lingual and multi-cultural personal assistants being integrated in electronic public service portals.

4.2 Government and Service Provision under Scrutiny

4.2.1 Reorganising Traditional Processes and Integrating Front- and Back-Office

Portals for delivering services to business, individual citizens and communities reflect a view from outside and have recently been considered of prime concern. However, portals are only the tip of the iceberg, as the entire scope of administrative action has to be regarded. Back-office reorganisation and modernisation has to have an equal significance.

Specifications of service delivery systems have to be elaborated with great care. A new type of organisational architecture is particularly apt at reaping the benefits of communication over distance. Through a separation of back offices (where a service is produced) from the front office (where it is handed over to the citizen or customer) it is possible to concentrate the production of a service while at the same time bringing the service closer to its recipient. The merits of such architectures are increasingly being recognised. The integration of front- and back-office is a key factor for the success of the next generation of e-Government systems.

In designing electronic service delivery one has to regard processes from two sides: the standpoint of the citizen and that of the producer of the service. There are typically five stages - with some parallel to commercial services - which have to be looked at. Seen from the citizen or customer point of view these are:

- Information (pre-informing the citizen about the service or product and about ways to obtain it, in a language which he or she understands)

- Intention (establishing the contact with the service provider, i.e. matching demand with available services)
- Contracting (clarifying conditions, setting the stage, negotiation and settling of the contract or the administrative act) while keeping track of the back office process
- Settlement (product /service vs. money)
- Aftercare (evaluation, customer feedback, complaints).

Such a stage model clarifies several functions in the interaction process that accompanies any service delivery. Of particular importance is addressing the needs of target groups such as professionals, taxpayers, the elderly etc. In that way allowing for a multi-channel choice of access is a must. The user has to decide the medium of choice: one-stop shop, online, letter, fax, citizen counter, etc. Not to forget that for online one-stop Government usability is a must. So design has to take into account service complexity varying according to the categories of business processes supported. Just in line goes the provision of the required level of security including user identification, authentication, cancellation and non-repudiation. For this a data protection policy and transparency measures are required.

Online One-stop Government requires that external service structures are adequately mapped to the internal process structures of public authorities. Therefore, the addressee's perspectives have to be complemented by a restructuring of the business processes. Process design has to break new ground by taking into account several aspects:

- Different locations of service production and delivery
- Organisational front office / back office connection
- Combining processes according to life situations
- Including distinct processes from strict workflows to collaborative decision-making

The last aspect is particularly important, since it is often neglected by concepts of BPR imported from the private sector. The view of BPR follows the model of industrial engineering: a strict coordination of the single steps in these processes is required to make them reliable and efficient. Most administrative work-situations include as well less formal modes of cooperative work. For different types of administrative processes, IT support will rather be dissimilar. So a categorisation of the main types is given here:

- Recurrent and well-structured processes
- Processing of cases: individualised decision-making
- Negotiation processes and consensus finding
- Weakly structured processes in the field of policy-making

Process structure is not the only perspective when discussing the changes. Two complementary perspectives are of equal importance: cooperation and knowledge. This leads to the next two sub-sections.

4.2.2 Strengthening a Broad Cooperation View

The cooperation view is of special importance to those activities that are related to higher order administrative work. Among others, they include negotiation, consensus finding, planning and policy formulation. Especially for the higher ranks of bureaucrats, such mode of work becomes prevalent. However, not only intra-governmental activities need extensive co-operation. When communicating with citizens, such modes of work occur as well: negotiating with citizens, giving advice in complex questions, mediation – they all have to be seen as cooperative settings.

So, what has to be sustained is cooperation in the broad. Support of computer-mediated cooperation in a comprehensive sense means sophisticated tools, multi media and video-contact become a must. To give a flavour of the capabilities, some illustrations are added:

– Meeting as well as related activities take hold of a substantial part of administrative work. Many occurring activities are cooperative in nature and claim for IT-support.

– First, the meeting activity per se may be performed via video techniques – so economizing on travel costs and time.

– Next, many activities associated with meetings can be largely improved by tools using multimedia. Examples are: clarifying procedural questions; scheduling of meetings and implied sub-activities; supporting the agenda setting and spotting experts, supporting brainstorming sessions, structuring issues etc.

– For the illustration of advanced system using multimedia, we regard the future scenario "citizen advice for solving complex questions": A citizen may go to mediating persons at the counter of public one-stop service shops. The mediators will use the system with its diverse repositories. In case the issue is too complex, it is possible to invoke further expertise from distant experts via a multimedia link between the service outlet and back-offices: dialogue becomes trialogue.

As the accessed expert himself may use knowledge repositories, finally, human and machine expertise becomes intensely interwoven. So this example leads to the next issue: knowledge enhanced government.

4.2.3 Knowledge Enhanced Government
In a novel concept of governance, the role of knowledge becomes dominant. Building a modern administration with novel patterns of cooperation is tantamount to changing the distribution of knowledge. Redistribution of knowledge is to be designed and orchestrated carefully. Managing knowledge becomes a major responsibility for officials. All these facts point to the concept "knowledge enhanced Government".

Prospects for knowledge management in Government are remarkable from the point of demand: nearly all administrative tasks are informational in nature, decision making is a public official's daily bread. For any agency, its particular domain knowledge is an asset of key importance. Such a new direction will engender considerable progress:

– The focus of attention is shifted away from a discussion of structures and processes towards issues of content and reaches the very heart of administrative work: making decisions.

– In some aspect, a regained focus on decision-making will help to propagate comprehensive systems thinking.

– Eventually, a better management of knowledge will lead to a form of "smart government". Knowledge derived from previous action or gained through policy evaluation will be fed back to policymaking to better target policies.

- Management of legal and administrative domain knowledge is a critical factor in governance.
- In addition, a deeper understanding of the connections between processes and knowledge will improve design.

In the public agencies of the future, human and software expertise will become intensely interwoven - smart government will be reached.

4.3   Selecting a Holistic Approach

Of critical importance are the methodologies used in developing new systems. Since e-Government, is such a complex, multidisciplinary domain with strategic, development and runtime shape, a traditional systems development approach will not suffice. Instead, *holistic development methodologies* and an overall e-Government framework are required. e-Government is a matter of research, development and application. An iterative exchange of findings, developments and needs / feedback / lessons learnt among these three is important.

The engineering approach has to support in a good balance of the various aspects of e-Government: users, technology, organisation, law, knowledge, culture, society and politics [7].

Planning calls for cooperative efforts of a wide range of actors from administration and software industry. Commonly, the more it comes to details, the more the IT profession is defied. Although enormous progress has been achieved during the last years, application development as a whole is nevertheless marked by substantial insufficiency. Thus, improvement of design is a high priority. There is a claim for improvement and building new and better systems.

5   Engineering and Change Management: Prerequisites for Success

5.1   Engineering Needs Improved Tools: Interoperability and Standards

Comparing the public and the commercial domain, both, communalities as well as differences can be recognised. Similarities exist mainly at the technical level. Differences appear more at the application level. Standards for applications become an issue in its complexity significantly surmounting the private sector. Further on, standardisation has to be seen with a broad focus including several subjects. They reach from the conceptual level (establishing a shared understanding of processes, building on common administrative concepts, including a feasible administrative domain ontology) to basic problems (guaranteeing interoperable platforms and defining formats for data interchange). Standardisation is a huge task. Yet in the long run, all partners involved such as public agencies, software industry and private companies will benefit. There are already some advanced fields such as e-procurement; however, the core administrative processes are still far away from that.

Standards enclosing sophisticated domain knowledge have to be achieved. A common governmental mark-up language has to be developed acting as a means for defining governance-specific content. Among others, this is a prerequisite for the transport of data from back offices and from the distributed information repositories serving them, to both (virtual and physical) front offices, which deliver the services produced elsewhere. Especially for cross-border e-Government having such definitions is a must! These standards will be built on standard exchangeable and interoperable technology combined with domain ontologies. For domain ontologies, a rich kit of methods for knowledge representation already exists (taxonomies, semantic nets, semantic data models, hyper links etc.). Reaching commonly agreed standards and interoperability is currently a topic of highest priority (e.g. in the FP 6 [4] of the EC). To achieve the objectives of eEurope 2005 [2] and of smart government, the lack of commitment to such agreements and common efforts in regards to standards must be overcome beforehand.

5.2   A conditio sine qua non: Safeguarding Trust, Security, and Privacy

Quite similar to last section, differences occur at the higher level. Requests are more strict, as the e-identity is needed in all administrative transactions and as wrong passports may have more serious consequences than bouncing cheques. In addition, taking the point of the users informational guarantees and the trust in the system becomes crucial. Delivering electronic services will largely depend upon the trust and confidence of citizens. For this aim, means have to be developed to achieve the same quality and trustworthiness of public services as provided by the traditional way. Regarding the level of systems design, fundamental request have to be met:

– Identification of the sender of a digital message
– Authenticity of a message and its verification
– Non-repudiation of a message or a data-processing act
– Avoiding risks related to the availability and reliability
– Confidentiality of the existence and content of a message.

5.3   Change Management Has to Get Priority

First, a dictum that has to be taken literally: Change Management is the key to success. Proactive Change Management calls for cooperative efforts of a wide range of actors from administration and software industry. A quantum leap in the innovative capacity of the public sector is asked.

Change Management has to start on the top. In that way *"Good Governance"* becomes an issue and reference has to be made. Further, strategic thinking is an important issue at the political level. For this aim still existing deficiencies in management style and knowledge development have to be cleared.

Next come concrete actions: creating infrastructures and defining ground-breaking projects. This paves the way for making use of best practice. This implies considerable tasks: it means evaluations, dissemination of know-how and last but not least boiling down experiences to guidelines. Thus, competent Change Management also includes empowerment of staff that means starting a remarkable qualification initiative. Other critical success factors include cultural change and setting up new attitudes. Joined-up government is a request in order to break compartmentalisation; yet it will be only achieved after the old egotistic behaviour of shielding information, knowledge and process know-how has been cast off. Eventually, a new way of thinking will emerge with information sharing and cooperation as guiding stars.

6 Our Attitude Is Important: Vision and Determination

Those, who travel the road, have to overcome many obstacles: bureaucratic postures and historical legacies, inertial institutions and impeding regulations, time and budget constraints. Yet those travelling the roads will be rewarded, when they closely perceive the impending e-transformation of society; for them the journey might become an overwhelming experience. There is chance and opportunity – we have to take advantage of the kairos of the moment.

References

1. eEUROPE 2002. Action Plan prepared by the Commission for the European Council of Santa Maria de Feira. Brussels, 14 June 2000.
   http://europa.eu.int/information_society/eeurope/ action_plan/pdf/actionplan_en.pdf
2. eEUROPE 2005. An information Society for all. Brussels 28 May 2002
   http://europa.eu.int/information_society/eeurope/news_library/documents/eeurope2005/
   eeurope2005_en.pdf
3. ERA objectives of the EC: Towards a European Research Area:
   http://www.cordis.lu/rtd2002/era-debate/era.htm
4. IST Workprogramme 2003-2004 "Integrating and strengthening the European Research Area (2002-2006)", http://www.cordis.lu/fp6/sp1_wp.htm
5. RONAGHAN, S. A., "Benchmarking e-Government: a Global Perspective – Assessing the Progress of the UN Member States", Final Report of the Global Survey of e-Government by UN and the American Society for Public Administration, May 2002,
   http://www.unpan.org/e-government/Benchmarking%20E-gov%202001.pdf
6. WAUTERS, P., KERSCHOT, H., Web-based Survey on Electronic Public Services. Summary Report, European Commission, Directorate General Information Society, 2002,
   http://europa.eu.int/information_society/eeurope/benchmarking/list/2002/index_en.htm
7. WIMMER, M.: Integrated service modelling for online one-stop Government, in: EM – Electronic Markets, special issue on e-Government, vol. 12(3):2002, pp. 1–8
8. WIMMER, M., TRAUNMÜLLER, R., LENK, K., Electronic Business Invading the Public Sector: Considerations on Change and Design. Proceedings of the 34th Hawaii International Conference on System Sciences (HICSS–34), Hawaii, 2001

E-Society Accessibility: Identifying Research Gaps

Annika Andersson and Åke Grönlund

Department of Informatics (ESI), Örebro University
701 82 Örebro, Sweden
{annika.andersson,ake.gronlund}@esi.oru.se

Abstract. This paper draws on a literature study on research on accessibility. The first part categorizes the literature found according to different approaches, focused on where one accentuates the solutions. The second part briefly discusses some implications of the findings with respect to e-government and e-democracy, and gaps in current research that should be filled. The paper concludes that in order to further the discussion of the accessibility topic in view of the electronic government agenda, there is a need for making the discussion of "accessibility" more sophisticated so as to distinguish availability (physical access) from approachability (mental access) for the reason of not by default taking progress in one field (typically availability), integrating research from several fields to bring more nuances to the different issues and including research on organizational perspectives to complement the current focus on technology and government regulation.

1 Introduction and Motivation

Accessibility has been the focus of considerable attention over the past few years and is addressed by a large amount of articles. Accessibility is about making sure that, as many users as possible are included in the information society. In particular this means integrating users with disabilities or "ordinary" users that find the information society impairing in some way.[1] The term accessibility has also been used in the context of social and economic access to computers and the Internet, mostly addressed as the digital divide. A strong indicator of society's interest in the subject matter can be found in the European Action plans[2] which both emphasize inclusion, participation and *that special attention should be given to disabled people and the fight against "info-exclusion"*. Accessibility is a broad concept and here we take a wide perspective in order to get a good overview of what kind of research one actually places under the label accessibility. Still, we only deal with accessibility related to the Information Society. Suggested solutions are analysed on the basis of a triangle-model labelled *User, Technology* and *Environment*. There are two main purposes of this study. First, to give an overview to a large amount of literature in the research area. Second, to map and categorize different solutions suggested to the addressed problems. The combined result can then, in turn, serve as a guide for future work. In this article, however, the centre of attention is on the mapping of solutions.

---

[1] EUROPA – the European Union On-Line.
[2] Ibid.

R. Traunmüller (Ed.): EGOV 2003, LNCS 2739, pp. 15–20, 2003.

2 Method

This paper is based on a literature study conducted during Fall 2002, using a multitude of online databases. We looked for literature from 1995 up until present date. The search found about 300 articles, and the categorization in this paper draws on close reading of 100 of those selected by title and abstract as representative for the whole set.

2.1 Concepts

The literature was sorted on basis of the problems they concentrate on and then clustered under assigned labels. One immediate finding was that authors typically do not separate physical accessibility from intellectual or mental accessibility – the ability to understand and use digital content once you have physical access to it. This should be a major concern for the uptake of web use, not least in the e-government area as it is imperative that people understand public services and as the complexity of many such services makes it likely that electronic provision will lead to problems in this respect for many people. Therefore, in this paper we use terms as follows:

Availability = Physical access to computers and Internet, i.e. that you have a computer at home, in your school and that you have a connection to the Internet.

Approachability = Mental access to computer and Internet, i.e. that you comprehend and receive information in a way that you can easily interact with it.

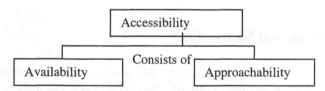

Fig. 1. Distinction between physical and mental access

2.2 Generation of Categories for the Solutions

From the studied papers it appeared solutions typically were related to the type of research and the research community that proposed them. Solutions were typically of one single kind, e g a software product or a government regulation, rather than a combination of several actions. This finding led us to categorize the solutions in that same fashion. *User* and *technology* are typically considered two counterparts in the literature – many tend to look for new computer support or user education as solutions to problems. As Human-Computer Interaction is arguably the currently most salient field in IT research, the previous focus on organizational uses of IT has tended to withdraw into the background. But clearly many issues involved in providing good services to users, and making them accessible, have to do more with the production process – the organization(s) involved in providing and mediating services, and the environments – physical, economic, legal, technical, social etc. – in which they operate. In the following review of the findings we somewhat carelessly lump all this together under the label *environment*. The purpose is simply to point to general gaps in current research. So, we find solutions focused on technology, the user, or the environment.

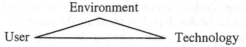
Fig. 2. Model used for showing focus in suggested solutions

3 Mapping the Solutions

We sorted the papers under five general categories, two of which concern availability alone, one approachability alone, and two a mix:
1. Internet approachability for the disabled.
2. Availability of computer aided support for the disabled
3. Divergence between the disabled and the not disabled in availability to computers and the Internet
4. Divergence in availability and approachability to computers and the Internet
5. Availability and approachability to democratic processes using the Internet

3.1 Category 1, Internet Approachability for the Disabled

Contains literatures concerning prospects for the disabled to interact with the Internet. The literature in this category does not address the problems of getting hold of a computer or having physical access to the Internet but rather, when the prior is accomplished, how to be able to understand and get some meaning from the information offered. Most articles here discuss problems with "normal" web design and solutions are mostly found in technical matters such as guidelines, special browsers and software. The guidelines mentioned are developed by an organisation called WAI[3] and the guidelines are designed to make the web accessible to people with disabilities. You will find the majority of solutions in the guidelines or in technological solutions. A few authors, however, stress the need for educating the web designers and the problem with the initial training costs ("Environment").

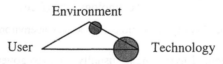
Fig. 3. Majority of solutions are focused on technological aspects.

It was somewhat discouraging to find such a strong technical focus in this category. In the e-Government field, one popular information model has been "life-events", presenting information ordered by perceived user situations rather than institutional (production) arrangements. It would appear that approachability would be enhanced

---
[3] Website, www.w3.org

rather by measures in information organization and design than by technical delivery mechanisms, but we found little research on such things. Also within a technical focus we lacked solutions dealing more with contents than with delivery. For instance, software agents could be developed to facilitate the encounter between a complex and distributed content and a user that is not so knowledgeable in the organization and terminology of government. Such research with a focus on the field of e-government was also lacking.

3.2 Category 2, Availability of Computer Aided Support for the Disabled.

The methods used for the most part include some sort of innovation building and thus gives solutions like handheld computers, electronic assistants, and robot arms. Other suggested ways of meeting the problem include legislation (printing rights), distance learning, supporting personal search strategies by, e g, personalization of web sites, and such.

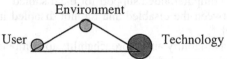

Fig. 4. Majority of solutions are focused on technological aspects

3.3 Category 3, Divergence Between the Disabled and the Not Disabled in Availability to Computers and the Internet

The results show that there definitely is a difference (to the disadvantage of the disabled) and the suggested solutions mainly concern government's financial support to the disabled, schools, libraries, information etc. A few authors emphasize the need for a better interface.

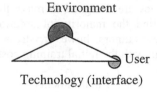

Fig. 5. Majority of solutions are focused on environmental aspects

In this category, then, "Environment" usually refers to government.

3.4 Category 4, Divergence in Availability and Approachability to Computers and the Internet

Among various groups of society (hence this category is wider than category 3 as it is not limited to comparisons with disabled people). The literature in this category addresses both the problems of getting hold of a computer or having physical access to the Internet and the problems of understanding the computers and Internet once you have physical access to it. The solutions are mostly based on economical and legal factors, for example: even out economical differences, suggesting different agreements between nations and making sure all schools have computers. Some authors suggest innovations such as computers designed for illiterates.

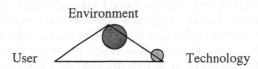

Fig. 6. Majority of solutions are focused on environmental aspects

In this category, "Environment" is most often taken to mean "government", as improved education and other government-organized arrangements are in focus. Less focused are the implementations of such measures. There are indeed studies of IT use in education, but usually focus is on improving skills in computer use or general efficiency in education rather than the contents of it. That is, focus is indeed on availability of the tool – a computer – rather than the potential improvements in approachability of knowledge as contained in digital information, for instance understanding of how government works.

3.5   Category 5, Availability and Approachability to Democratic Processes Using the Internet

Addresses both the availability and the approachability of using the Internet as a tool for democratic processes. Case studies and surveys are made and the results are innovations made to facilitate participation. Focus is heavily on technology. There is, however, a small stream of research on "Teledemocracy" delivering guidelines on how to organize the processes of democracy (but there, the term accessibility is not used).

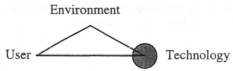

Fig. 7. Majority of solutions are focused n technological aspects

This was perhaps the most confusing finding. One of the most striking differences is that between category 4 and category 5. Clearly, category 5 can be seen as a subunit of category 4 – approachability of e-democracy processes is a part of the general approachability of Internet as many elements of understanding an using are clearly the same (usability and Internet emerging standards, for instance). But whereas category 4 research clearly addresses approachability issues, democratic processes (category 5) are researched as a technical issue exclusively. It appears that this difference stems not from the issues researched but rather from the communities researching the issues, which leads us to some concluding remarks.

4 Conclusions and Future Work

The above review points to a lack of distinction between different aspects of "accessibility". We have here chosen to distinguish between availability (physical) and approachability (mental and intellectual). But it also points to a possible problem of detached research that perhaps should take advantage of some integration. For instance, categories 1,2 and 5 contain issues that are mainly researched by people from various disciplines related to the IS field, such as informatics. Categories 3 and 4, on the contrary, are typically researched by people from sociology and related disciplines. Our findings seem to well illustrate the old saying, "when you have got a hammer, everything looks like a nail": In categories 1, 2 and 5 the solution is most likely a computer tool, in categories 3 and 4 it is government action.

We have also pointed to the fact that the production system linking contents to users – organizations acting as service producers or intermediaries – is little researched. Solutions are typically considered to be found either in technology itself or in government regulation. Much research in information systems has pointed to the importance of organizational arrangements, and in the current situation where organizational arrangements are very much under debate – and indeed real change – in the government/governance field, it appears a great problem that organizational research is largely absent.

References

1. EUROPA – the European Union On-Line, Downloaded 2002-12-19
   http://europa.eu.int/information_society/topics/citizens/accessibility/dfa/index_en.htm
2. EUROPA – the European Union On-Line. eEurope2002 Action Plan – "An information society for all" & eEurope2005 Action Plan – "An information society for all",
   http://europa.eu.int/information_society/eeurope/action_plan/index_en.htm
3. http://www.w3.org/TR/1999/WAI-WEBCONTENT-19990505/

For references used in the literature survey that this paper draws on ask for appendix from Annika Andersson at annika.andersson@esi.oru.se.

The New Citizen Society:
Considerations and Measures for Developing E-Governance in China

Chengyu Xiong

Tsinghu University
Beijing, China

Abstract. The demographic characters of the Internet user make the group worthy paying attention to. This is not only because they have great possibility to be the nucleus of the society and play an important role in social development and decision-making, but also because the growth of this social group is beneficial to the formation of a citizen society – a power which Chinese traditional social system is lack of.

1 Social Configuration

By January 2003, the number of Internet user in China has reached 59,100,000. The figure has been growing rapidly although it just accounts for a very small part of the total population of 1,300,000,000. In this user group, 54.7% of the people have got the degrees of junior college, university or above; 82% are the youth below the age of 35; 84.5% are from the mid or low income class whose salary is below 2,000 RMB per month, which also plays a large part in the group. That is because mainly the university students compose the group. This low-income class nowadays will be the main power and consuming group in the coming few years.

The demographic characters of the Internet user make the group worthy paying attention to. This is not only because they have great possibility to be the nucleus of the society and play an important role in social development and decision-making, but also because the growth of this social group is beneficial to the formation of a citizen society—a power which Chinese traditional social system is lack of.

Citizen society is often called as "civil society". It is a kind of social power between citizens and government. It always maintains the principles of "equity, rationality, justice" through the power of public opinion to fight against the hegemony of politics and the commercial logic. At the same time, the citizen society, especially the existence of a certain amount of citizens who have the ability of distinguishing and decision-making, can provide suitable conditions for carrying out the market economy and democratic politics.

Because of the limitation of the political and cultural traditions and some other reasons, citizen society has little influence on the theory and practice of social structure in China. This is also one of the reasons, which restricts the development of market economy and democratic politics in China.

R. Traunmüller (Ed.): EGOV 2003, LNCS 2739, pp. 21–24, 2003.

The coming of the information society provides great possibility to change this situation. In the circumstance of Internet, the cost of getting information has been depreciated a lot, the quantity and quality of getting information has been increased. In short, citizens' ability to know the public affairs has been greatly improved. Nay, Various public forums have emerged because of the mutual character of Internet. They provide places for the people to comment on public affairs as well as exchange ideas. With the increase ability of knowing and commenting on public affairs, the degree that they involve in the process of social life and social decision-making is getting deeper and deeper. Whereas, this involvement encourages people to know more about public affairs. Under this situation, the emergence of the visual community related with e-government would conform the public will.

The development of Internet brings the prosperity of the citizen society and the public sphere. While the relationship between citizen society and government are interrelated and reciprocal. To induct and integrate the public sphere or indifferent to its development are two completely different kinds of choices and will lead to different results. There is no doubt that adopting suitable ways to induct citizen society in the process of developing and constructing the information society is the advisable choice.

Three main stanchions of the modern society are democratic politics, market economy and mass media. In the information society, we need to consider the two main bodies of government and citizens in a general way, pay more attention to the existence of public benefit, citizen society and public sphere. Guided by the basic, far-sighted and strategic principles, with the adequate use of available resources, we will promote the development of China towards a modern society, which will greatly fit for the current situation of China.

2 Situations in China

Although the number of the Internet user in China keeps a steady increase, the current number 59,100,000 is still too low compared with the total population of the country. From the point of the commercial practice, a media can make profit only when its rate of popularization is over 25%. But as the e-government is concerned, the rate will be over 50% if it wants to embody the principles of equity and reasonableness. So, to some extent, building up E-Governance widely and completely is a kind of advance action. But this precession is very necessary. Because constructing e-government and developing e- governmental affairs will greatly accelerate the reform of the political system and economic system. It is propitious to improve the efficiency of government, promote the role of government and make the government connected with the international new system.

In this situation, we have to consider one problem clearly: whether the Internet users are the bases of Chinese society, in what extent can they represent. This is the question need to be discussed further. It should be clarified that e-government is the government of all the people, not only for the Internet users; the convenient service of E-Governance should overcome the limitation of digital gap and reach every corners of the society.

But according to the Stat. number from CNNIC in Jan. 2003, 73.3% of the Internet users are from eastern provinces of China. The people from farming, foresting, herding and fishing occupation and unemployed group only take up 5.0%.[1] The western area, which keeps a large gap with eastern area, the peasants and paupers who still stay at the bottom of the society pyramid, they are all in great need for the information resources more than other areas. For them, a piece of information can bring the opportunity to the development of the district economy and provide chance to change individual's life.

On the one hand, the current conditions limit some of the citizen from getting information; on the other hand, the laggard areas and groups are eager to get needed information. This is the contradiction we are facing in the process of constructing e-government.

Considering the general low level of information development and imbalance distribution among districts and classes in China, the basic principles of constructing e-government and opening E-Governance should pay attention to moral caring as well as efficiency, try to eliminate digital gap inside the society. Under this guideline, we should give much emphasis on the E-Governance management, services object and spreading channels.

For the current provisions, the e-government and affairs will not solely rely on Internet as its terminal. We have various ways, such as the informational home electrics of i-TVs, e-families, top box on TV and so on, even cell-phone or house phone can be considered as the terminal of the E-Governance. This is because the E-Governance' function covers all areas. The areas are not only including information issuing and acquiring, but also including the personal revenue report forms, identity register, drivers' license file and customs reporting of export and import. It is better to use the terminal based on internet for the affairs needed to keep in secret or operated with complexity, but for getting normal information about production and daily life such as information of traveling or of buying and selling, we can use the terminal of informational home electrics, cell-phone and house phone. If the government can stand out to exploit systematically the needed information of citizens from all professions, and pass this information via all kinds of terminals to the citizens who need it, no doubt it will be a good plan for solving the problem that E-Governance serves for only a small group of people. This plan does not only stimulate the social information and make it increment, but also shows the servicing consciousness of e-government, and it must implant deep into the hearts of people.

3 Countermeasure and Considerations

In early 2002, national informalization leaders group brought pointed out that the keystone of national informalization of China in this year is E-Governance. This shows that the informalizational construction of China has moved from productivity to the regulation of productive relationship. In the phrase "E-Governance", "e" is the tool; the core is still the governmental affairs and the concept of government management. We stress the application of new technology in it, but we cannot neglect the other core meaning "governmental affairs". Electronic, which is the new tool, will make the government explore the efficient and reasonable management mode. In reverse, only with the support of scientific management concept, advanced technical facility can be made the best use.

E-governmental affairs and government-online are two different concepts. It is the "primary concept" of E-Governance to let the citizens take their rights of knowing the inside story. The deeper theme behind it is to make procedures fair, open and transparent and intrigue citizens actively involve social affairs. On the base of scientific management concept, we must distinct the two main bodies of E-Governance: government and citizen, consider the two functions of E-Governance: service and management.

At present, our E-Governance concept shows much concerns on single body and single dimensionality: considering too much of the main body of government while lack of attention to the citizen; paying too much attention to the function of administration while lack of service consciousness. In fact, government and citizen are two supporting main bodies; service and administration are the two basic functions of the governments, which supplement each other.

On the base of the clarification for the main body, we should also give a clear definition to the function of e-government affairs, which means fractionizing the definition and widen its extension, so that we can apply it better in practice. According to this, we should realize that government is the biggest owner and user of information resource, so E-Governance is the key tache of national economy and social informalization. Developing E-Governance will definitely accelerate the process of national economy and social informalization.

E-governmental affairs can enable the government to know the situation of society, the will of people in time and collect the brightness of the people efficiently. Thus promotes the democratic and scientific development of decision-making. At the same time, it is beneficial to improve the working styles and strengthen the relationship between government and people.

E-governmental affairs are the information container and developing center. Where lots of information is collected, through filtering, sorting, integrating and inducing, it becomes the reference materials to the government. At the same time, integrated information will be helpful to the realization of sharing resources and it is convenient for enterprises and society to make best use of it, such as comprehending the government policy, items of the laws, request of environment protection and the admittance to the market. It is also helpful to strengthen the government function of guiding and service, and bring the social benefit and economic benefit into play completely.

In general, we should absorb all kinds of valuable resources and establish the most advanced administration concept, concentrate on both government and citizen, emphasize service as well as administration, and make it clear what the function extension of the E-Governance is, which are the basic principles that we should obey in the process of constructing e-government and implementing the E-Governance.

References

1. C.f. CNNIC: Statistics of China Internet (2003/1) http://www.cnnic.net.cn/develst/2003-1/

From E-Government to E-Governance: A Survey of the Federal and Cantonal E-Policies in Switzerland

Olivier Glassey and Jean-Loup Chappelet

Swiss Graduate School of Public Administration (IDHEAP)
Route de la Maladière 21
1022 Chavannes, Switzerland
{Olivier.Glassey,Jean-Loup.Chappelet}@idheap.unil.ch

Abstract. In this paper we discuss the eGovernment strategies and the eGovernance policies of the Federal Government, of the Cantons and of the largest cities in Switzerland. While some of the cantons have already developed strategic documents that serve as a basis for the implementation of eGovernment, others are currently defining their policies and some do not have their own approach as they follow the recommendations of the Swiss federal government. This paper compares the existing strategies and policies in order to try to identify the overall directions of the Swiss ePolicies.

1 Introduction

The Swiss Federal Government started to consider information society policies in 1996 within the G7 Framework and subsequently ordered a study [1] from a specially appointed reflection group. The latter constituted the foundation for several reports written by the Information Society Coordination Group in 1999, 2000, 2001 and 2002 for the Federal Council (Swiss Government). The latest of these documents [2] defined a detailed roadmap for an information society in Switzerland, covering many important aspects, from infrastructure to education and from eBusiness to eDemocracy. These policies are presented in section 2. There are many other interesting texts that contribute to the establishment of ePolicies at various levels in Switzerland. This literature is virtually unknown although quite interesting. It is presented in section 3. Most of the documents discussed in this paper can be found at http://www.infosociety.ch or at http://www.ippol.org.

2 Federal Policies

As stated in [2], an information society is characterized by the strong interrelations of technology, communication and content in all aspects of the economic and professional world and of everyday life. The Federal Council decided to monitor the transformations brought by information technology and to accordingly define a policy framework for eGovernance in Switzerland. Following the recommendations of different working groups, it defined eight priority domains: education, economic

R. Traunmüller (Ed.): EGOV 2003, LNCS 2739, pp. 25–30, 2003.

development, electronic commerce, electronic government, new forms of culture, security, scientific studies and legal aspects. During 2001 and 2002, several projects were initiated in the domains of education, eGovernment and eCommerce, some of which are presented below. The Swiss federal Government also pushed forward the legal recognition of digital signatures to provide a favourable environment for the development of innovative electronic applications. The Federal Council also decided to set up a scientific follow-up group whose mission it is to evaluate all activities regarding information society. This group published a first report in March 2002 [3] and came to the conclusions that the Federal eGovernance policies provided a solid basis for the development of information society although they also contained some weaknesses. Completing this scientific assessment, another report [4] was published in 2002, containing detailed statistical information on ICT use and on potential ICT developments in Switzerland.

In addition to these more general ePolicies, the federal government defined a strategy for its own activities and all levels of government projects related to eGovernance in Switzerland. The IT strategic unit of the Confederation was mandated to prepare a four-year action plan [5] to integrate ICT in governmental activities and to modernise administrative services. This plan is based on three strategic goals: "creation of basics", "service optimisation" and "networks development". The first goal is to create appropriate conditions for eGovernment regarding organisational perspectives, technology and security. This involves a necessary work of standards' definition in order to enable electronic collaboration between different public administrations and different departmental levels. The second goal is to facilitate the access to electronic services to all actors of the public and private sectors and therefore to reorganise internal processes of the administration so that they support electronic transactions. The last strategic goal of this plan is to create fully interconnected networks between all administrative units (at the federal, cantonal and communal levels) and their different partners, public or private. An example of such a network is the private-public partnership developed by the Confederation, the Cantons and private companies in order to give access to the Internet to all primary and secondary schools of the country (http://www.ppp-sin.ch).

A first and important step towards this interconnection has been taken in February 2003 with the public opening of the first version of the www.ch.ch portal. This project entitled "Guichet virtuel" (virtual counter) is based on the cooperation between the federal, cantonal and communal structures of the Swiss public sector. It was designed in order to respect the complicated distribution of competencies between these levels. This portal provides citizens (but not businesses) with a single point access to all public services, with a thematic organisation articulated around eight domains: private life, society, work, health and social security, mobility and environment, security, fiscal and political matters, economy.

In parallel with the development of the "Guichet virtuel", the eCH organisation has been founded in 2002 to work on the definition of eGovernment standards for Switzerland (http://www.ech.ch). In order to take into account the specific needs of the different actors involved in eGovernment and to closely study relevant international work, it set up several working groups made of members of public administrations, professional associations, research centres and private companies. Their preliminary investigations and conclusions on different topics (security, processes and data, communication, etc.) are due at the end of 2003.

Up to here, we spoke about eSociety and eAdministration policies, but let us not forget that Switzerland has a strong tradition of grass-root democratic participation and that it could therefore be a favourable ground for eDemocracy. In 2001 the Federal Council decided to carefully study the implications of electronic voting on the Swiss political and civil life. In his report on the feasibility of e-voting [6], the Federal Council identified several risks that were considered too important for a rapid introduction of e-voting. It consequently opted for a prudent strategy and decided to proceed step by step, with thorough tests and evaluation of different electronic participation stages. In order to do so, three pilot projects were financed, in the Cantons of Geneva, Neuchâtel and Zurich. The first trials were conducted in Geneva where the citizens of the town of Anières were able to vote via Internet on 19th January 2003, to decide whether to accept a credit of renovation or not (http://www.geneve.ch/ge-vote). This was the first time in the world that a politically binding vote was made electronically although there were previous experiences for elections. The results were encouraging, as 323 citizens chose to vote online, 370 voted by postal mail and only 48 went to the polling station. The authorities were able to count the electronic ballots in 73 seconds. Further tests will take place in Neuchâtel and Zurich in 2003 and 2004, experimenting different technical solutions. The Federal Chancellery announced however that the generalization of e-voting at the federal level was not to be expected before 2010, believing that the technical, organisational and political problems surrounding the e-vote should be levelled by that time.

Table 1. Main eGovernance documents at the Swiss Federal level

Key Institutions	Secondary Institutions
eGovernment projects of the Federal Chancellery (or Government General Secretary) http://www.admin.ch/ch/d/egov/ Portal to Swiss administrations at federal, cantonal and communal levels http://www.ch.ch/ IT Strategy Unit of the Confederation http://www.isb.admin.ch/egov/	Infosociety.ch provides documentary resources on the information society in Switzerland. http://www.isps.ch/ Directory of official websites of the Swiss public sector http://www.gov.ch/ eCH is a non-profit organisation that aims towards the definition of eGovernment standards in Switzerland http://www.ech.ch/
Key Policy Documents	**General Interest Reports**
eGovernment Strategy of the Confederation http://www.isb.admin.ch/egov/ 4 reports of the Information Society Coordination Group (1999, 2000, 2001, 2002) http://www.admin.ch/ch/d/egov/ Report on eVoting: Opportunities, risks and feasibility http://www.admin.ch/ch/d/egov/	Federal Activities for an Information Society: Critical Assessment - Experts' Reports http://www.isps.ch Information Society in Switzerland: Inventory and Perspectives http://www.statistik.admin.ch/ Keppeler report on Information Society in Switzerland (it provided the basis for the Swiss Federal strategy for eGovernment) http://www.isps.ch/

3 Regional Policies

Most Cantons in Switzerland do not have their own ePolicies, as they can count on the Federal ones. However some larger Cantons, such as Zurich, Basle-Town, St.Gallen or Geneva prepared and made publicly available their eGovernment strategies. We will come back to these further on. Other Cantons (Argovia or Neuchâtel) published overall reports about eGovernment. Several Cantons (Jura, Lucerne, Nidwalden, Zug) are currently preparing their own ePolicies and most of them should be available before the end of 2003. We believe that this shows a growing political interest in eGovernance. One the other hand none of the large Swiss cities, with the exception of the City of Zurich, do have any policies or strategic documents in that field, although several of them work in close cooperation with the Canton where they are located. This is more notable in the "Canton-Cities" such as Basle-Town or Geneva, but they are other examples like Neuchâtel where the Canton and the town share their IT resources. There is also a close co-operation between the State of Vaud and its capital city Lausanne through a working group established by the canton in which both webmasters take part.

The first Canton to have a complete document supporting eGovernance [7] was Basle-Town, where a group of experts developed a complete strategy and action plan for eGovernment. They clearly identified the tasks and limitations of an electronic public administration and they outlined several conceptual principles for an administrative One-stop-shop on the Internet. This document also proposes a framework for technical developments, a strong orientation for document and process management, as well as a legal ground for electronic procedures. Moreover, it defines a technical and style guide for the Internet portal of the Canton and it also took great care in the organisational and logistic needs of eGovernment projects. Although this strategy was published in 2001, we think it is to be considered currently as a "best-practice" at the Cantonal level. In 2002, the Canton of St.Gallen also published its own eGovernment strategy [8] that was more focused on infrastructure and networks. A roadmap for the necessary work of "creation of the basics", as termed in the Federal strategy, is clearly defined in this document. Another of its interesting aspects is the integration of the communes and of different external institutions in a true eGovernance spirit enabling public-private partnerships for the development of eGovernment in that Canton. The St.Gallen strategy also provided some ideas and examples of tools or instruments that can be used for monitoring the progress of eGovernment. Whereas Basle-Town and St.Gallen developed their ePolicies internally, under the authority of the State Chancellery, the Canton of Zurich chose to establish a special working group called *wif!* that worked in cooperation with the consulting firm Arthur Andersen to define its eGovernment vision and the necessary foundations for such a project. *wif!* is the acronym for Result Oriented Management. In accordance with this title, [9] presents an interesting blueprint for eGovernment projects in Zurich, containing general definitions, "market" and cost analysis, a general architecture for the cantonal portal as well as the definition of several priority projects (tax, procurement, building permits, social help, etc.). It also advocates the creation of a special competence centre for the coordination of these projects. While developing this report, the authors also took into account the users' perspectives, by conducting interviews of key civil servants and by setting up workshops on strategy.

In this section we saw that, out of the 26 Cantons and the largest cities, less than one third of them developed true eGovernance instruments although they are in possession of most administrative competencies, Switzerland being a confederal state. Two main explanations can be advanced. First, many Cantons are too small and do not have the necessary resources to develop strategies for eGovernment. Second, the Confederation's ePolicies take into account the needs of the Cantons and of the communes that can rely on the Federal policy framework. However we also mentioned that there is a growing interest in eGovernance on the side of the Cantons and we believe more and more of them will turn to eGovernance.

Table 2. Swiss Cantonal eGovernment strategies, as acknowledged by the Cantons in a survey conducted in February 2003.

Canton	Key Policy Documents
Canton of Argovia http://www.ag.ch/	Intermediary Report on eGovernment, November 2002 (not available online)
Canton of Basle-Town http://www.bs.ch/ http://www.e-gov.bs.ch/	eGovernment in Canton Basle-Town: Strategy and action plan http://www.e-gov.bs.ch/bericht.pdf
Canton of Bern http://www.be.ch/	eGovernment Strategy (not available online)
Canton of Geneva http://www.ge.ch/	eGovernment: the vision of Canton Geneva http://www.ge.ch/chancellerie/e-government/doc/confRHInternet_010423.pdf eSociety Framework http://www.geneve.ch/obstech/referentiel/ref-e-soc/ref-e-soc.html
Canton Graubünden http://www.gr.ch/	eGovernment im Kanton Graubünden http://www.gr.ch/e-gov/e-gov-strategie.pdf
Canton of Jura http://www.ju.ch/	eGovernment strategy announced for Q3 2003 IT Blueprint XXI http://www.ju.ch/rapports/schema.pdf
Canton of Neuchâtel http://www.ne.ch/	General information on eGovernment projects in Neuchâtel http://www.ne.ch/neat/site/jsp/rubrique/rubrique.jsp?StyleType=marron&DocId=7573
Canton of St.Gall http://www.sg.ch/	eGovernment Strategy of Canton St.Gall http://www.sg.ch/media/egov(3).pdf
Canton of Ticino http://www.ti.ch/	eGovernment Strategy (not available online)
Canton of Vaud http://www.vd.ch/	Report on eGovernment to the State Council, February 2002 (not available online) Blueprint for eGovernment in preparation Report on the update and development of the City of Lausanne website http://www.lausanne.ch/view.asp?DocID=1841
Canton of Zurich http://www.zh.ch/ http://www.e-gov.zh.ch/	Final Report on the Electronic Government Project http://www.e-gov.zh.ch/internet/sk/e-gov/de/informationen/downloads.html eGovernment-Vision of the City of Zürich http://www.stzh.ch/egov/pdf/vision.pdf

4 Conclusions

All these public authorities policies for eGovernment (ePolicies) slowly lead Switzerland to a gradual transformation of its government internal and external processes through the use of ICT, in particular through the provision of Internet-based services. In other word, Switzerland is entering the age of eGovernance like many other countries.

The repartition of competencies between the different political and administrative levels in Switzerland is complex, but we think that the federal authorities managed to take them into account to define their eGovernance policies. Indeed, they created rather complete strategies and they also realized the importance of standards in eAdministration. These federal ePolicies were well accepted by many Cantons and communes that also use them as eGovernance instruments. Furthermore they are put into application through the implementation of many eGovernment projects, the most interesting of them probably being the "guichet virtuel" and the e-voting tests that we mentioned earlier. However these ePolicies are still at a relatively infant stage, and we believe there is much work to do yet, especially in comparison of other initiatives at national and European levels. Indeed we think Switzerland should follow carefully the work being done by its neighbours and particularly the eEurope action plans, in order to be compliant with eGovernment projects being led at the continental scale.

References

1. Kappeler, B. & al.: Rapport du Groupe de Réflexion: La Suisse et la société de l'information. (1997)
2. Groupe de Coordination Société de l'Information: 4ᵉ rapport du GCSI à l'intention du Conseil Fédéral. (2002)
3. Center for Science and Technology Studies: A Critical Assessment of the Activities of the Swiss Federal Government for the Information Society. (2002)
4. Office Fédéral de la Statistique, Groupement de la Science et de la Recherche, Office Fédéral de la Communication: La société de l'information en Suisse: Etats des lieux et perspectives. (2002)
5. Unité de la stratégie informatique de la Confédération: L'activité gouvernementale à l'heure de la société de l'information – Stratégie de la confédération en matière de cyberadministration. (2002)
6. Conseil Fédéral: Rapport sur le vote électronique – Chances, risques et faisabilité (2002)
7. Staatskanzlei des Kantons Basel-Stadt: e-Government im Kanton Basel-Stadt – Strategie und Aktionsplan, Information und Öffentlichkeitsarbeit. (2001)
8. Staatskanzlei des Kantons St.Gallen: e-Government – Strategie des Kantons St.Gallen. (2001)
9. Arthur Andersen: Schlussbericht Vorprojekt eGovernment, Wirkungsorientierte Führung der Verwaltung des Kantons Zurich. (2001)

"How to Create Things with Words"
Symbolic Power and MIS in the Health Care Sector

Kåre Lines

Nord Trøndelag University College
N-7600 Levanger, Norway
kare.lines@hint.no

Abstract. This paper is concerned with institutional change and the role of IT in public reforms. Specifically, we analyze a historical case concerning the development of a MIS in a local health-care organization in Norway. We use the concept "symbolic power" constructed by Bourdieu to investigate the problem of legitimization during the process of developing the MIS. We illustrate how the use of symbolic power within different logics and conflict of interest has influenced the MIS development. Despite this, we also observe a process which to a great extent has been harmonious. We argue that it is because these logics, interests and values have gained the status of symbolic capital; i.e., are recognized as legitimate competencies and knowledge, that the political dimensions are unrecognized. Our conclusion is that MIS development faces a serious challenge in making it legitimate to define issues of IT as political.

1 Introduction

This paper addresses issues concerned with institutional change and the role of IT as an aspect of the modernization of public governance structure [1]. Specifically, we analyze a historical case (1987-2000) concerning the development of a MIS (management information system) in a local health-care organization in Norway.

Within the IT academic field it has been thoroughly demonstrated, analytically as well as empirically, how MIS development gets caught up in a host of organizational issues. It is, indeed, becoming somewhat of a cliché, spawning efforts to press the argument further by analyzing more specific aspects such as: development of theoretical notions (structuration theory, actor-network theory, activity theory), the alignment with strategy formation, collaborative aspects, or user participation [see 6]. Our longitudinal case study of the development of a MIS in a local health care organization in Norway similarly analyzes one dimension of this socio-technical interplay, namely how the MIS gets embedded in a symbolic and ritualistic power play within a broader framework of public reforms. We analyze how the MIS project develops interactively with ideas from new public management and local practices; i.e., differing logics, values and interests.

Our analytical approach uses the concept of "symbolic power" developed by Bourdieu [3] to investigate the problem of legitimization during the process of developing the MIS. We explore how the MIS, through its development and use, is

R. Traunmüller (Ed.): EGOV 2003, LNCS 2739, pp. 31–36, 2003.
© Springer-Verlag Berlin Heidelberg 2003

translated into symbolic capital; i.e., capital which is recognized as valuable and legitimate and thus becomes an asset in the power play.

2 Theoretical Framework

Bourdieu states two conditions of symbolic power [3]. As any form of performative discourse, symbolic power has to be based on symbolic capital; i.e., capital that the various species of capital, economic cultural and social capital, assume when they are perceived and recognized as legitimate by the actors in a certain field[1]. Secondly, symbolic efficacy depends on the degree to which the vision proposed is founded in reality. The theory effect is all the more powerful in accordance with the adequacy of the theory. Thus we assert that the tendencies to oppose rational and political perspectives and to treat them separately tend to conceal the relational link between them [8, 10]. Symbolic power, then, is to create things with words. Within these conditions, the power to impose a vision (old or new) upon others with social divisions depends on the social authority acquired in previous struggles. We use this approach to investigate the circumstances under which the MIS came into being, the theory guiding it and how the theory effect during the process of development and change affected the way the system developed.

According to Bourdieu [5], cultural capital may exist in three forms: in the embodied state; i.e., in the form of long lasting dispositions of the mind and body; in the objectified state, in the form of cultural goods (pictures, instruments, machines and books) and in its institutional state. Institutionalized cultural capital is a form of objectification that confers entirely original properties to the cultural capital, which it is presumed to guarantee. Examples of this might be a formally stated job title such as "nurse" or a particular management position in the health-care organization. Within this framework, a MIS as cultural capital in its objectified state is a technical artifact of relevance in relation to the objective structure of the field. Secondly, using the system presupposes that the actors have reached a certain level of mastery over the technology; i.e., they are equipped with embodied cultural capital enabling them to effectively use it. Thirdly, the system becomes an element of a process of institutionalization which means that it becomes a stake in the field (symbolic capital). This means that the MIS is a contested technological artifact and is recognized as having a legitimate position in the field.

3 The Health Care Field

Heterogeneous functions, tasks, professions, client groups, and organizational cultures are key features of public health-care services at the local governmental level in Norway. The heterogeneity is reflected in field logic in which different organizational principles operate simultaneously. This combination makes it possible to strike a fragile balance between differing interests and values, but at the same time it creates

---

[1] According to Bourdieu [4] a field refers to a social space in which actors are in competition and conflict with each other about values that all the actors more and less tacitly agree have a legitimate status in the field.

dilemmas and contradictions between democratic, administrative and professional rationalities. Institutional values, such as the right to participate in critical decision-making issues (a democratic logic), must compete with the necessity to manage and control the organization (an administrative logic) and the professional's claim for autonomy within his or her domain (a professional logic).

The clients represent a shared legitimating base for those elected by popular vote, the administrative management and professionals. Moreover, national legislation regulates the field to a great extent defining citizen rights as clients. Accordingly, the state bureaucracy is the main symbolic force in the regulation of the field. Every actor must play the game of bureaucracy. But this regulation also creates tensions between the level of service in accordance with national bureaucratic standards and available economic capital controlled by the local authorities. Restricted by economic resources, citizens' rights are balanced on a juridical logic trying to set standards, but with a high level of discretion. Accordingly, human judgment is an important element. This judgment gives rise to difficult discussions and negotiation about how to prioritize and what criteria will be used. It is a complex mixture between professional, administrative and political judgments and represents high stakes in the field.

4 The Development of the MIS

In the case being analyzed, the MIS came into being within a broader reform effort in which a MBO project (management by objectives) played a dominant role. The idea of a MIS corresponded theoretically with MBO; i.e., a system that should produce statistical information about clients to be used to formulate output objectives and the evaluation of results. We state that because MBO as a theory was not sufficiently rooted in the realities of this organization's practice, the results were quite different than expected. The MBO project and the MIS development took unanticipated turns. The MIS in its first phase turned out to be a failure, but a failure that did not die. We characterize it as an ongoing failure. It was too one-sidedly constructed to satisfy the interests of the top administration in their need for statistical knowledge. However, as an ongoing failure, relative to the expectation at the outset, it had entered the field as cultural capital in its objectified state. Instead of being an instrument to be used in the effort to modernize the health-care organization, it became a contested object of development.

The direction of the development of the MIS changed when a nurse manager formulated a theoretical diagnosis of the situation. She stated and managed to get support for the idea that if the managers and the employees in the service production units were to use IT, they should have a system that corresponded to their interests. This seemingly simplistic diagnosis cannot be underestimated. We interpret it as a theoretical analysis which was inherently political although it was not perceived as such by the actors and, as we shall see, its symbolic power was strong.

The outcome of the ongoing failure was a new MIS that retained the module for producing statistical information about clients, but in addition, was to function as a coordinating device in the service production unit and a professional planning module for the nurses. A system then was constructed that clearly reflected the different logic, interests and values in field.

The new system was piloted and achieved technical approval. The idea was that this strategy of implementation should be carried out throughout the organization. The problem, however, was that the theory guiding the pilot project was too biased toward technical dimensions of the system. Organizational problems arose, and conflicts between the project leader and the participants led to a break down of this strategy of implementation. The effects were twofold: the technical closure of the system and a break-down of the implementation strategy.

In the wake of the collapse of the pilot project and the technical closure of the MIS, a top-down strategy was chosen. This change in strategy led to conflicts which paradoxically strengthened the legitimacy of the system. The top administration used the dispute as an opportunity to get support for the system from the politicians. This was accomplished by going back to the initial idea of the theoretically stated need for statistical data to be used in the decision-making processes. The politicians strongly supported this and the problematic situation was resolved. It became legitimate to invest in a comprehensive educational program so the employees could learn to use the system. Through the technical training the employees were to learn to use the constructed system, a system that was biased towards administrative logic, interests and values. These investments in cultural capital were successful. The system became implemented on large scale. It finally turned into an obligatory passage point [9]. It has become a necessity in the day-to-day activity in the service production unit, although it is still contested.

5 Discussion

Economic capital in the health care field is a question of transforming economic capital into cultural capital. The MIS was to be an instrument within such a process of transformation. Theoretically, it was guided by an economic logic within the language of MBO and in a broader sense modern public management. But instead of being a rather straightforward instrument which should contribute to efficiency and effectiveness, the development of the system qua system turned out to be a time-consuming process. From 1987 to 2000, a huge number of work hours were used during the process of development. Such an investment in cultural capital tends to go unnoticed within the logic centered on efficiency and effectiveness. In hindsight, we observe how unrealistic and exaggerated the expectations were at the outset. Firmly embedded in a rational logic, partly economic and partly bureaucratic, the project created its own dynamic. We state that although the project turned out to be unrealistic with unforeseen consequences, the rational theory guiding the project exerted a theory effect. Norms of rationality are present in everyone's habitus and the actors are disposed to act according to the demands of the authority structure. However, the use of symbolic power within the language of MBO, and based on the formal authority in the leadership structure is only partial. As this case illustrates, there are other sources of authority. Professionals have a legitimized right to autonomy which cannot be ignored. Moreover, the direction of the process of development clearly illustrates the heterogeneity of the authority structure and the contradictory interests and values at work. The planning module to be used by the surgery nurses has not been used at all. Additionally, the statistical data produced is used in an improvised manner and not systematically as expected at the outset.

One important observation is that in spite of the up and down character of the process, the surprises and unforeseen problems, it has also been rather harmonious. Given that there were several logics and relatively stable norms and values in the organizational field, we should expect politics to be pervasive. Obviously that has been the case. The process of development has been characterized by conflicts of interest and contradictory values. These have been evidenced in the processes of structuration [7] and have influenced the process of development. Despite this, we observe a process which to a great extent has been harmonious. This implies that although there may be strong elements of politics and conflicts of interests in the development and use of the MIS, they are not stated as such explicitly. It is precisely because these logics have gained the status of symbolic capital; i.e., are recognized as legitimate competencies and knowledge, that the political dimensions go underground or are unrecognized. How can this observation be interpreted?

The explanation must be found in the way symbolic capital operates. The fact that something is recognized as a legitimate competence; i.e., has gained the status of symbolic capital, creates a social context that hides the obvious: that the actors are involved in a game of power within a structure of domination in which every actor has a legitimate position. The MIS analyzed in this case developed slowly both as cultural capital in its objectified state and in its embodied state, but the form and content of the system became highly biased toward administrative logic, values and interests.

Public administrative reforms in Norway have been characterized by a strong focus on the necessity to get a clear boundary between what is defined as politics and what are administrative responsibilities. Such a classification implies that politics within the administrative and professional domains gains an illegitimate status. We assert that this partly explains the problem of dealing with issues that are inherently political. Because the values and interests inherent in administrative logic and professional logic are not recognized as capital; i.e., that they are about exchange and negotiations, the problem-solving process is biased towards rational mean-ends arguments. How decisions made are affected by the structure of domination and how it effects the distribution of gains and losses cannot be legitimately discussed.

6 Concluding Remarks

A normative implication of the invisibility of politics (in the sense that they are not explicitly recognized as conflicts of interest, along with the lack of recognition of the political dimensions), is the impediment of constructive improvements within IT development. In that respect, politics if explicitly recognized as such by the actors, could represent an emancipating discursive force which could contribute to solutions not only within an already established power game, but has the potential to change the power game itself in a positive direction; i.e., a more human way of dealing with the collective action problem and a more just distribution of capital. However, those who have the upper card in such a game deny such a proposal in its very intention because it threatens their privileges. And more paradoxically, those who are in a dominated position will also tend to deny it because they are disposed to think and act in accordance with objective structures of the field. Within their habitus, the actors tend to perceive as evident the privileged positions of the dominant and to hold a sense of obviousness about their own unprivileged position.

Another implication of this analysis is that when put into use, a MIS becomes a legitimized element in the field's power play. This means that it becomes a stake; i.e., it is not a neutral tool objectively defined, although it may be perceived as such by the actors. Moreover even if it is perceived as a tool, it is not neutral but a controversial element in organizational practice. How it is used, how shortcomings in the system are handled, and who is without access to it must be considered elements in the power play. Those who provide the machines with the necessary input have their own interests, and they use their own judgment. Moreover, the information produced will be interpreted and translated within a theoretical frame of reference. The economic consultant will have a different habitus and act in his peculiar way in accordance with his position in the structure. This is not a problem of opportunism but a problem of how each of the actors manages to cope with the interests and values that are at work in the field in with which they are expected to cope. It must be legitimate to act "opportunistically", both in the processes of developing the system and in using it. Thus the question is how we deal with the construction of IT through a process of competition and conflict and how we cope with the fact that technology structures the political processes we are involved in.

References

1. Bellany C. and Taylor J. 1998. Governing in the Information Age. Buckingham: Open University Press
2. Bourdieu, P. 1977. Outline of a theory of practice. Cambridge: Cambridge University Press.
3. Bourdieu, P. 1990. In other words – essays towards a reflexive sociology. Cambridge: Polity Press.
4. Bourdieu, P. 1992. An Invitation to Reflexive Sociology. University of Chicago, Polity Press
5. Bourdieu. P.1986. Forms of Capital. In J. Richardson (ed.) Handbook of Theory and Research for the Sociology of Education. New York Greenwood Press.
6. Currie, W.L. and Galliers, B. (1999). Rethinking Management Information Systems. Oxford, Oxford University Press.
7. Giddens, A. 1981. Agency, Institution, and Time-Space Analysis. Advances in Social Theory and Methodology. Boston: London and Henley: 161–174.
8. Heeks, R. 2001. Explaining Success and Failure of e-Government. Trinity College Dublin; Proceedings: European Conference on e-Government.
9. Latour, B. (1999). Pandora's Hope. Cambridge, Harvard University Press
10. Robey, D. and Markus M. L. 1984. Rituals in Information System Design. MIS Quarterly

Language and Technology Literacy Barriers to Accessing Government Services

Etienne Barnard[1], Laurens Cloete[2], and Hina Patel[2]

[1] University of Pretoria
ebarnard@eng.up.ac.za
[2] CSIR, PO Box 395, 0001, South Africa
{jcloete,hpatel}@csir.co.za

Abstract. The paper presents research aimed at overcoming barriers to citizens' ability to access electronic government services. Our concern is specifically 'non-connectivity' barriers to electronic service delivery including cultural background, language, literacy and level of technology experience. These issues are investigated and solutions researched in a developing world context. The project on which the paper is based aims to develop a service delivery framework and technology where service delivery is personalised to citizen's unique circumstances taking into account the means by which they will have access to government services and individual characteristics such as language preference. In order to develop appropriate technological interventions, a number of field experiments are done to gain an improved understanding of the extent to which citizens' exposure to technology and home language affect their ability to access electronic services. These experiments will influence technology development on the project that will be incorporated in a technology demonstrator.

1 Introduction

The "Government to citizen e-governance" project is a three-year research and development project aimed at developing technology to enable effective electronic service delivery to citizens in a developing world context. The project is being undertaken by the Council for Scientific and Industrial Research (CSIR) in South Africa and the Fraunhofer-Gesellschaft: Research Institute for Open Communication Systems (FOKUS) in Germany. FOKUS has developed the Enago Open Services Platform [1], which is an advanced, standards-based, distributed, object-oriented application integration middleware platform. CSIR has experience in technological innovation aimed at developing and adapting technology to developing world conditions such as those existing in South Africa.

In Section 2 we sketch the context within which the research is being done. In section 3 we detail factors that will influence the design of such services, and motivate the choice of telephone services for conducting initial experiments. Thereafter we discuss some of the usability issues that will be considered during development (Section 4). In Section 5, we describe our experimental approach, and Section 6 provides initial conclusions on the work undertaken so far.

R. Traunmüller (Ed.): EGOV 2003, LNCS 2739, pp. 37–42, 2003.

2 Context

The demand for e-government services in South Africa results from requirements to: improve the efficiency and quality of government services, ensure that government services are delivered to all levels of society at the most convenient times and locations, grow government's portfolio of services, create government service transparency, and provide citizen with feedback mechanisms. In support of these requirements the focus of the project is primarily on the innovative re-use of current or established technologies and integration of such technologies into an effective service delivery platform accessible through different devices under South African conditions and applied in a South African context. Two basic assumptions behind the project are:

• Effective electronic service delivery has to enable citizens to access government services in different ways and
• Government services have to be presented to citizens in an integrated, citizen-centric manner.

The Enago technology provides functionality that will enable service delivery given these assumptions. The main research challenge of this project is to extend this technology to the demands of a developing world context. Factors such as language, culture, economic means, geographical location, literacy and previous exposure to technology are considered. The goals of the "Government to citizen e-governance" project therefore are to:

• Improve knowledge about how citizens interact with government services through electronic means and improve our understanding of how different user populations interact with electronic government services
• Develop technology and methodologies for application development that will allow for improved government to citizens interaction.
• Demonstrate the potential for citizens to interact with government via electronic means through a practical demonstrator built on existing and new technology

3 Factors to Consider in Designing E-Government Services in the Developing World

The deployment of e-government services is far less advanced in the developing world than in countries with sophisticated infrastructure [2], therefore one of the goals is to build on learning from the developing world. The success of such services is likely to depend on the interactions between four groups of factors: cultural background, literacy levels, technological medium and the nature of the service.

In a developing context cultural factors are particularly important for the successful deployment of most electronic services. One reason is the relative lack of accommodation between many traditional cultures and modern electronic media. Whereas popular culture has already adapted to technologies such as the Internet in most developed countries (and has in turn shaped those technologies), the cultures of developing nations need more careful consideration when these technologies are to be employed. Because of the mass media play a smaller role in the developing world, cultures tend to be less homogenized, increasing the importance of explicit consideration of cultural factors.

In the developing world, functionally illiterate citizens are often a significant fraction of the population. This constrains the delivery of electronic services, which usually require fluent literacy as well as a technological sophistication that builds on such literacy.

A third factor to consider in the developing world is the relative scarcity of financial resources and general infrastructure. This implies that the delivery media for e-government services are typically required to be even more cost-effective than in the developed world – and cannot assume that citizens will have access to tools such as Internet-connected workstations.

These factors will play a substantial role in determining the nature of the services that can be deployed successfully and could place limitations on the nature of services that can be provided electronically in developing countries. By taking proper account of these factors, we can deliver services that address the most salient user concerns, which are directly expressed in concepts such as access, control, content, and equity. Our principal concern will be to understand how these subjective user goals can be reached through an understanding of the objective characteristics of user, task, and technology.

3.1 The Telephone as Preferred Carrier

The factors described above suggest a multi-dimensional grid of possibilities that should be considered in developing appropriate e-government services. To simplify this grid, we will initially limit our attention to telephone-based service delivery. This medium strongly suggests itself in the developing world, because of the rapid growth in the availability of telephone connections in many countries [3].

A further advantage of telephone-based services is the relatively low levels of infrastructure and user sophistication at which such services can operate. We believe that useful services can be delivered to citizens equipped with nothing but a normal telephone (mobile or fixed-line), and requiring no more than the ability to understand and respond to spoken commands. Such a verbal interface is highly appropriate from a cultural perspective in many developing countries, where a strong oral tradition exists amongst a pre-literate or semi-literate population. Thus, telephone-based services place a very direct focus on the role of Human Language Technologies (HLT) in the developing world, and will hopefully assist in drawing resources for the development of such resources.

We therefore envisage services that citizens will access by calling a central toll-free number; they will be given a menu of choices, and be able to obtain or provide information over the telephone. The exact mode of information input raises a number of intriguing research issues – for example, will technologically unsophisticated users fare better using speech recognition or keypresses as input to an automated system? Or, how should prompting be structured to assist a user who has no mental model of the functioning of a computer system? It is likely that good answers to such questions will assist us in developing interfaces that can help bridge the digital divide – not just in e-government, but also in other walks of life.

4 Usability Issues

Graphical user interfaces have been studied intensively in the past two decades, and there has been tremendous progress in determining how to develop usable solutions with such interfaces. Much of that information can be generalized to spoken interfaces. In particular principles crucial for any user interface, regardless of modality include: careful user modelling, thorough understanding of the task domain, and the characteristics of the underlying technologies.

Another principle that holds equally true for graphical and spoken interfaces is the importance of usability testing: by involving trial users (outside the design team) throughout the design process, an improved product can be developed in a reduced amount of time.

These principles will go some way in assisting us with the development of user interfaces for the services we wish to develop. However, the specific nature of the spoken interface – especially for users with limited literacy and technological experience – is certain to introduce issues that have not been considered before in the delivery of services for e-government. (For example, we need to understand how requirements for trust and accountability are satisfied with a telephone-based interface). We will therefore develop a programme of carefully designed experiments to study usability issues when a spoken (telephone-based) interface is used to deliver e-government services.

4.1 The Influence of Culture

The South African context provides a good example of the cultural issues that should be addressed when developing user interfaces for e-government service delivery in the developing world. The people of South Africa speak 11 distinct languages, and there are wide disparities within and between the various language groups in socio-economic standing and literacy [4][5]. Before 1994 a racially selective elite ruled the country in non-democratic fashion, and this history has fostered a deep mistrust in government. Compensating for these historical injustices requires particular attention to the needs of citizens who are functionally illiterate, do not speak a "world language" (such as English), and have been denied access to the benefits of modern technology.

This situation calls for the development of services that explicitly take into account the variables that will influence the user's interaction with the service. These variables include: Language of choice, Age group, Gender, Level of functional literacy, and Mean family income. We intend to investigate the role of these variables in user access to e-government services. Our initial analysis suggests that a useful ordering principle is to make a primary distinction based on geography – in South Africa, citizens' style of access will be largely determined by whether they reside in an urban environment, the rural countryside, or in an informal peri-urban settlement.

5 Experimental Approach

The issues raised above clearly require inputs from experts in a variety of disciplines. To gain access to such expertise, we have initiated a series of workshops with specialists on topics such as human-computer interfaces, cultural factors, and government services. These workshops have provided us with a wide range of opinions on the interface approaches we should attempt, the user populations we should investigate, and the evaluation criteria for assessment of the various approaches.   Below, we describe the application that was targeted for our development, and initial results obtained.

5.1 Application Selection

To investigate the HCI issues, a practical service delivery application was selected, based on a few criteria. The application had to be complex enough to explore the issues raised above. It also had to be feasible with a telephone-only interface, and be practically relevant for non-specialized users. We decided to implement a system that would make it possible for telephone users to obtain information on, and apply for, the Unemployment Insurance Fund (which is currently of much interest to the South African Department of Labour [6]).

5.2 Design and Implementation of Speech and DTMF Systems

User interfaces using DTMF (keypresses) and speech recognition have been designed that allow the various issues to be probed. A working version of the DTMF system was implemented, as well a "wizard-of-oz" mock-up of a speech-recognition system. Wizard of Oz refers to an approach that is commonly used in developing and prototyping speech recognition systems [7]. In a Wizard of Oz a human operator imitates the working of the recognition component. The results of the experiments will be analyzed in terms of transaction completion and user satisfaction, stratified across the various user and technology variables introduced in the study.

We have performed an initial analysis of the DTMF-based system, using the methodology of Heuristic Evaluation [8]. This evaluation demonstrates the complexity of designing such interfaces: although the system was broadly judged to be successful, it was found to be lacking in unexpected ways by users from specific cultural backgrounds. For example:

- Certain evaluators found terms such as "valid" or "menu" to be confusing.
- Commands such as "to do X, press Y" were judged too authoritarian in certain cultural settings; evaluators preferred "If you would like to do X, press Y".
- Even though the system cannot be used to obtain money directly, some evaluators felt that it was not sufficiently "secure" or "private".

We are currently expanding our evaluation to include "naïve" users from various population groups; these groups will also be exposed to the speech-based system. This will allow us to understand these issues quantitatively.

6 Conclusion and Outlook

The rewards from successful service delivery to citizens of the developing world are potentially huge: in South Africa alone, millions of citizens stand to gain access to facilities which are currently either impossible or highly inconvenient for them to use. However, there are significant challenges to effecting truly usable service delivery, caused by lack of literacy, limited resources, and lack of knowledge on how to deliver services in culturally and socially appropriate ways. We have embarked on a program to investigate these issues in the context of a telephone-based solution. Two test platforms (for DTMF and speech-based input) have been developed, and we are in the process of performing a more extensive analysis of the properties of these classes of interfaces.

References

1. enago OSP (Open Service Platform), http://www.ikv.de/content/Produkte/osp_e.htm
2. Richard Heeks, *"eGovernment in Africa: Promise and Practice"*, Institute for Development Policy and management, University of Manchester, UK, iGovernment Working Paper Series, Paper No. 13, 2002.
3. Mike Jensen, *"Information and Communication Technologies (ICTs) in Africa – A Status Report"*, Presented to third task force meeting, UN ICT Task Force, 30 September 2002.
4. "Language use and language interaction in South Africa", Final report on a national sociolinguistic survey, PANSALB, Pretoria, March 2001.
5. http://www.pansalb.org.za/
6. Living Standards Measure, The South African Advertising Research Foundation, http://www.saarf.co.za/
7. South African Department of Labour, http://www.labour.gov.za/
8. Dey, Anind, Lara Catledge, Gregory D. Abowd and Colin Potts. *"Developing Voice-only Applications in the Absence of Speech Recognition Technology,"* GVU Center, Georgia Institute of Technology, Technical Report, GIT-GVU-97-06, February 1997.
9. Jakob Nielsen and Robert L. Mack, eds. *"Usability Inspection Methods"*, John Wiley & Sons, New York, NY, 1994.

Evaluation of an E-Democracy Platform for European Cities

Efthimios Tambouris and Stelios Gorilas

Archetypon S.A.
236 Sygrou Ave., Kallithea
176 72 Athens, Greece
{tambouris,sgorilas}@archetypon.gr
http://www.archetypon.gr

Abstract. In this paper the experiences from evaluating an e-democracy platform in two European cities are presented. The e-democracy platform under evaluation consisted of three main applications, mainly tele-voting for realising opinion poll petitions, tele-consultation and e-Forums. In this paper, the trials performed in Barcelona and Brent borough of London are outlined. The specification, development and trials evaluation of the e-democracy platform were carried out within the IST EURO-CITI project. The main purpose of the evaluation within the project was to prove the robustness of the technological platform. However, the evaluation also provided some interesting results with regards to the use of Internet in order to increase citizens' participation. Although the purpose of the evaluation was not to study the current state and potential of e-democracy, the lessons learnt could nevertheless be useful to researchers and practitioners in the field.

1 Introduction

Electronic government and e-democracy are becoming increasingly important in Europe [1][2]. The benefits of both e-government and e-democracy are now well understood by local authorities worldwide that launch relevant initiatives [3][4]. In particular, the potential of e-democracy to increase citizens' participation [5] is one of the main reasons behind its wide spread.

The aim of this paper is to present the results from evaluating an e-democracy platform in two European cities, namely Barcelona and Brent Borough of London. This evaluation was carried out within EURO-CITI [6][7], a research project partially funded by the European Commission under the IST programme [8].

This paper is organized as follows. In section 2, a general overview of the EURO-CITI e-democracy platform and its services is given. In section 3, some details of the evaluation are outlined while in sections 4 and 5 the trials at Barcelona and Brent are presented. Finally, in section 6 the conclusions and future work are given.

R. Traunmüller (Ed.): EGOV 2003, LNCS 2739, pp. 43–48, 2003.
© Springer-Verlag Berlin Heidelberg 2003

2   The EURO-CITI Platform

The EURO-CITI platform is constituted by two sets of applications. These are:
1. **Applications for the Citizen**. These include:
   - Tele-voting application
   - E-forums application
   - Tele-consulting application
2. **Applications for the Operator at the Local Authority**. These include:
   - Tele-voting Management application
   - E-forums Management application
   - Tele-consulting Management application
   - Configuration and User Administration

In this paper the focus is on applications for the citizens thus the applications for operators are no longer discussed.

The EURO-CITI Tele-Voting service was used for opinion poll petitions. In that context, three tele-voting scenarios have been identified by the participating local authorities as particularly important:

- **"Local Voting"**. In this case, a voting issue is posted in one EURO-CITI server and eligible voters are citizens who are registered in that server.
- **"Local Voting with European Scope"**. In this case, a voting issue is posted in one EURO-CITI server (termed *initiator*). Here, eligible voters consist of citizens who are registered in the initiator as well as citizens from other cities. These cities however must have been invited by the initiator and accepted that invitation.
- **"Network Voting"**. In this case, a voting issue is proposed by one EURO-CITI server (termed *initiator*) and is posted in all servers (i.e. cities) that have accepted to participate in that voting. Here, eligible voters for each server are the citizens who are registered in that server.

In Tele-Consultation both "Local consultation" and "Local consultation with European Scope" scenarios are supported, where these scenarios have the same scope as in Tele-Voting. However, in e-Forums only "Local" scenarios are supported.

3   The Evaluation Method

The evaluation of the applications was performed by two groups of users. The first group was comprised by citizens from the three participating municipalities (Athens, Barcelona and Brent) and the second one by operators who are employees at the local municipalities (mainly IT stuff). The three trials sites were replicates and each citizen or operator used and evaluated his local installation.

For collecting and assessing the feedback of the operators, the GQM methodology was used. An on line tool was also used, which provided the environment for using GQM in collaborative and user-friendly manner. For the case of citizens an on-line questionnaire was used, which was available to the Internet through the EURO-CITI tele-consulting application.

Due to space limitation, in this paper only the results for the case of citizens from Barcelona and Brent are presented.

The evaluation period was almost three months from the beginning of July to the end of August 2002.

4 Trials in Barcelona

The first stage of the trials at Barcelona was the selection of citizens. Barcelona decided to select "Poble Sec", a historical neighbourhood of Barcelona, for performing the trials.

In order to disseminate the trials, the Barcelona City Council designed and distributed leaflets and posters. 10,000 leaflets were sent to citizens (almost all the families of the neighbourhood) and 1,000 posters were hung in almost all the shops of the neighbourhood. The aim of this task was twofold: on one hand, user involvement in the trials (the leaflets and the posters informed of the process and explained how to participate in the trials). On the other hand, e-democracy awareness was generated in the neighbourhood. The process was enhanced by media coverage: a press conference was organised and some newspapers talked about the EURI-CITI trials.

Interested citizens were requested to fill a web questionnaire or to call the Department of Citizen Participation to register. One lesson that the Barcelona City Council learnt is the high effort needed to achieve citizen participation. Among the group of around 30,000 people that was exposed to the direct publicity of the trials (leaflets and trials), only around 200 expressed their initial interest and registered to join the trials (less than 1%). A login and password were generated for each one of them, and the materials (smart card readers, smart cards) were assigned in a first-come first-served basis.

Three public PCs were enabled to allow citizens without computer at home to participate in the trials. One of them was installed in a Public Library, another in a Cultural Centre and the last one in the Coordination Office of Citizen Associations.

Two consultation and two voting issues were launched every week (one on Tuesday and one on Thursday) and they were open for one week. Some consultations were opened to guest users.

It was decided that the issues to be launched would belong to three different categories: specific issues of the services of the neighbourhood, evaluation of the strategic plan and suggestions of the participants. The intention was to have an adaptive approach and react to the people's feedback in the new participation issues.

A portal was created to integrate the EURO-CITI services into the website of the Barcelona City Council. The user guides for the smart card readers were translated into Catalan and were included in the website, as well as some other relevant information.

The citizens that had registered were invited to an event on June 25 2002 where a presentation of the applications was given and the materials were delivered to them. About half of the registered citizens attended (95). 24 were given a smart card reader plus a smart card with digital certificate; 23 were given a smart card reader plus a smart card with user and password stored (Drag & Drop Smart Card); 20 were given a smart card (with digital certificate) to vote in public PCs; the rest were given a user name and a password.

The trials consisted on 17 voting issues, 17 consultation issues and 1 forum. The consultations contained an average of 6 questions each.

All 17 consultations were answered. The participation rate has been increasing steadily since the first consultation, which was about accessibility and mobility in the neighbourhood (9 participants), until 23 July 2002, when a consultation about General Aspects of the Local Services Survey was launched. It was the consultation with the highest participation rate (34 participants). From this date on, the participation decreased regularly – probably because of the holidays. The evaluation consultation (26 July 2002) was answered by 24 people.

The experience of the trials has been extremely positive, as it has provided the Barcelona City Council with very useful knowledge of the potential problems.

The main lessons that the Barcelona City Council has learnt with the trials can be grouped in three categories: lessons regarding to the participation rate, lessons regarding to the usability of the applications and lessons regarding to the stability of the applications

Lessons Regarding the Participation Rate

The main message that the Municipality of Barcelona has received is that it is very difficult to achieve a high participation rate. It is very difficult to involve citizens: in the case of the Barcelona trials, where a considerable effort was invested to disseminate the trials, only 34 out of the 30,000 citizens that were exposed to the dissemination activities were participating actively.

One of the reasons may be that there is not still a "participation culture" among the population. In addition, there is not still a real "Internet culture" either, at least in all the age ranges. Thus, much work has to be done to make citizen participation, Internet, and citizen participation through Internet belongs to the everyday life of citizens.

Another message is the need of a very stable platform. If the platform is not very stable, the few users that would use it are likely to loose their motivation and don't use the applications again. Similarly, the application must be very easy to use, because the citizens are not supposed to be IT skilled and, if they are not able to use them without effort, they give up using the applications.

Finally, valuable information has been gained concerning the temporalisation. One obvious reason for the low participation period has been the fact that the experience has been held in the summer, in the usual vacation term. It's clear that in other months the results would be better, so it is important to keep it in mind for future trials. On the other hand, the duration of the consultations (1 week) has revealed to be too short, while the frequency of them (twice a week) has revealed too high.

Lessons Regarding the Ease of Use

If a high participation rate is wanted, it is obvious that some additional effort should be done in order to make it the easiest for the citizens. e-Government applications should be specially usable, as the people that use them are not supposed to be IT skilled, and no education should be required. The message can be summed us as "the easier it is, the more citizens will participate".

Some technologies don't seem to be mature enough for their use with common citizens. For example, Smart card reader installation and SC operation are not still easy enough to allow inexperienced citizens to use them. In addition, using smart cards in kiosks is not practical at all, because a prior registration of each certificate in the kiosk is needed.

5 Trials in London Borough of Brent

The Consultation department carefully selected 100 citizens from a pool of volunteers.

Unfortunately, trials coincided with the summer period and only 50% were available and willing to participate by the time trials started. Finally, 44 citizens were set up in the system.

Citizens were notified of two-different kick-off meetings where a pack containing instructions, expectations, smart card, smart-card reader, PIN number, username / password and contact details was issued.

There were fears amongst the attendees that the technology was going to be too difficult to understand. Re-assurance was given that everything was explained step-by-step in the manual and a smart-card reader was installed during the meeting for illustration purposes.

Although a hotline was meant to be set up, the low number of participants indicated that there was not a need for this. Instead, direct line phone numbers of IT operators and emails were given as well as a feedback form. Emails were the preferred means of contact by citizens.

The feedback forms were not returned in most of the cases. Feedback was mostly collected through emails and comments that were extracted from telephone conversations. It took a lot of persuasion to finally make citizens to fill up the official online feedback form as it was considered long and it did not always allow the citizen to express particular points that they had in their minds.

All in all, all the different parts involved in Brent EURO-CITI trials learnt valuable lessons, being the main ones:

- The IT unit gained technical expertise in Digital Certificates, Java Web Servers and XML. A valuable lesson was that non-technical users may find non-standard applications frightening and difficult to use. Therefore, higher attention to design of user interfaces should be paid.

- The Consultation department learnt that new technical methods of collecting information such as tele-consulting are easy to use, being quicker and cheaper to set up than traditional surveys. However, tele-consulting was seen as an extra channel for capturing information and not as a replacement of traditional mechanisms.

Councilors learnt that the public is ready to communicate with them in different ways if they are given convenient tools to do so, tools that meet citizens' needs and meet the expectations of democratic representatives.

6 Conclusions and Future Work

The EURO-CITI platform equips local authorities with an integrated eDemocracy platform that includes three important tele-democracy services: tele-voting for realizing opinion poll petitions, tele-consultations and eForums.

The evaluation phase of EURO-CITI besides proving the technological competence of the platform provided some interesting results of general use.

e-democracy platforms are in their first only steps. Both public servants and citizens have to familiarise themselves with using Internet as a tool for active participation.

The platforms have to be technologically very stable and robust. The main emphasis should be put into the usability of the platform. Citizens want the best possible quality and will not compromise with anything less than that.

Trials have to be carefully planned and executed. Issues that have to do with the time and duration of trials may have an impact on the citizens' participation.

Overall, e-democracy is a challenging field with a potential to increase citizens participation in democratic processes. However, technology itself is not a panacea that will automatically increase participation rates. Therefore, a lot of way has to be traveled before this potential if fully realized.

Acknowledgments. The work presented in this paper was carried out as a part of the EURO-CITI project [7]. The EURO-CITI project (EURO-CITI IST-1999-21088) is partially funded by the European Commission under the IST programme [8].

References

1. European Commission: Public Sector Information: A Key Resource for Europe, Green paper on Public Sector Information in the Information Society, ftp.echo.lu/pub/info2000/publicsector/gppublicen.doc (1999).
2. eEurope2002: An Information Society For All, Action Plan of the European Commission, available at http://europa.eu.int/information_society/international/candidate_countries/doc/eEurope_june2001.pdf.
3. Caldow J.: Cinderella Cities, Institute for Electronic Government, IBM Report (2002).
4. Telecities home page, 2002, http://www.telecities.org.
5. Macintoch A. and Smith E.: Citizen Participation in Public Affairs, Proceeding of the 1st International Conference in E-Government within DEXA Conference, LNCS 2456, pp. 256–263.
6. Tambouris E.: An Integrated Platform for Tele-Voting and Tele-Consulting within and across European cities: The EURO-CITI project, Proceeding of the 1st International Conference in E-Government within DEXA Conference, LNCS 2456, pp. 350–357.
7. EURO-CITI project, http://www.euro-citi.org.
8. IST Home page, http://www.cordis.lu/ist.

Internet NGOs: Legitimacy and Accountability

Anton Vedder

Tilburg University, Faculty of Law
P.O. Box 90 153, 5000 LE Tilburg, Netherlands
anton.vedder@uvt.nl

Abstract. As the power and influence of nongovernmental organizations (NGOs) in international debates on social and moral matters increases, questions concerning their legitimacy and accountability become all the more challenging. Some starting points are given for a defensible account of the legitimacy and accountability of internationally operating NGOs. Special attention is given to the use of new information and communication technologies by NGOs and to the ways in which legitimacy and accountability circumscribe the ways in which NGOs are structured and organized.

1 Introduction

It is one of the striking characteristics of our age that, after a long relatively stable period in which politically and legally sovereign states were the *loci* of control, the role and influence of national governmental authorities is declining. International and supranational authorities fill up part of the space that is thus created. Nevertheless, the exponential growth of the global trade, the transboundary traffic and technologies has created open spaces: spaces where neither national governments nor supranational or international governmental authorities play a role.[1] Internationally operating nongovernmental organizations (NGOs) are increasingly inclined to fill up such empty spaces. (Multinationals do so as well, but for reasons of conciseness, I will leave these out of consideration.) The activities with which NGOs fill up this space can be located somewhere on a scale that ranges from speaking up in public debates, through lobbying and organizing campaigns for creating public awareness, raising funds, organizing protests and boycotts, planning and implementing concrete action programs, e.g. for protection of the environment, help with food and medicine, education, to developing public policies independently or in cooperation with enterprises or governmental authorities, etcetera. Although at first sight this role of NGOs seems to be not much more than a matter of bare necessity, it is sometimes thought that it is to be preferred above a further expansion of international or supranational authorities. In this contribution, I will not develop a positive argument of such a kind for the efforts of NGOs in these fields. Instead, I will put into perspective the legitimacy of the activities of NGOs, specifically of those among them that are mainly active through and on the Internet.

One might wonder why I find the legitimacy of NGOs at all a topic worthy of debate. Are non-state actors not to be considered as merely private actors whose role, like any private person's, does not stand in need of legitimization? First of all, it

R. Traunmüller (Ed.): EGOV 2003, LNCS 2739, pp. 49–54, 2003.

might be good to keep in mind that although with regard to private persons we normally do not tend to speak of legitimacy or legitimate actions, this does not mean that certain requirements associated with legitimacy do not even in a very broad sense also apply to private persons. Indeed, in democratic societies private persons are granted all kinds of freedom to speak up, to interfere in debates, to undertake action, etcetera. At the same time, however, these freedoms are not absolute, unconditioned or unrestricted. Private persons can be held accountable for what they say and do. The bigger the impact of what they say and do and the more risk their words and deeds imply for others, the more likely they are indeed to be held accountable and the more stringent will be the requirements regarding their responsibility. This accountability constitutes a kind of bottom line legitimacy that applies to the organizations of private persons, such as NGOs and MNEs as well. There is, however, an extra reason to discuss the legitimacy of non-state actors. As I stated earlier on, NGOs are increasingly inclined to fill up the space left open by national, international, and supranational governmental authorities. In this way, they gradually come to fulfill public roles that in a traditional state are mostly performed by governmental authorities. From the fact that they take up similar roles, I do not simply want to infer that they must conform to similar requirements regarding their legitimacy. Non-state actors just and simply are not governmental authorities. Nevertheless, to the degree that they fill up the void, left open by governments, their power and the effective use of their power increase. And exactly the growth in power and the possibly far-reaching consequences thereof call for consideration in terms of legitimacy. Simply put: power implies responsibility and readiness to legitimate one's role. As the activities of non-state actors can have ever further reaching consequences their ability to legitimate their activities becomes ever more important.

Now, let me narrow the focus. Are NGOs the appropriate organizations for influencing and forming policies regarding moral and social issues? In the debate on globalization, the role of NGOs is often taken for granted. First, there is the empty space for which no governmental authority – national nor international or supranational – is qualified but which nevertheless has to be filled up. Second, there is a certain tendency to consider NGOs as the only type of players in the field that can act as counterbalancing power against the supposedly overwhelming power of MNEs that also try to influence policies and policy formation. Nonetheless, from a morally normative perspective, the self-imposed role of NGOs is all but natural. As I have argued elsewhere, many internationally operating NGOs lack democratic legitimization. They mostly interfere in the lives of people, who are not represented in their organizations. Because they are single issue-organizations they are not very well fit to deal with normative conflicts occur (situations in which one justified normative claim, e.g., to improve the economic well-being of people, can only be met by going against another justified normative claim, e.g., to protect the environment), while the international debate on social and moral issues are almost without exception about these kinds of conflicts. [1]

2 Legitimacy

Michael Edwards observes that the issue of legitimacy is seldom brought up in the literature on NGOs.[2] Even in the literature, in which these questions are brought to the fore explicitly, however, a clear concept of legitimacy and legitimization is mostly lacking. There are persistent tendencies in this context to use 'legitimacy' either as a primarily moral notion or as a predominantly legal one. Furthermore, it is often not clear whether the notion is used to refer to the legitimacy of the organization and the activities of an NGO on the whole, on the one hand, or to the legitimacy of a particular activity of an NGO, on the other. We may label these two kinds of legitimacy as overall legitimacy and occasional legitimacy, respectively. The distinction between the two is of some interest, because failing to distinguish them makes it difficult to understand how certain organizations can in itself and on the whole act legitimately, whereas particular activities of theirs can be illegitimate.

I would like to elucidate the notion of legitimacy with help of some elements of David Beetham's theory of the legitimacy of state governments.[3] I do not consider Beetham's views as the ultimate answer to all questions regarding the definition of legitimacy. Neither do I take his views to be representative for the whole of political theory. I only invoke his account, because some reflection on his conception of legitimacy may help us to come to terms with the difference between legitimacy when applied to NGOs and legitimacy when applied to state governments. Legitimacy has three important aspects. These could be referred to as respectively the legal, the morally normative, and the sociological aspect. According to Beetham, legitimacy is a matter of conformity to rules (legal aspect), which can be justified in terms of shared beliefs (morally normative aspect), while the organization rests on expressed consent (sociological aspect).

Direct application of Beetham's concept of legitimacy to NGOs would be reckless. First and foremost, Beetham's concept is exclusively and explicitly tailored to national governments. A national government seeks support for its activities concerning almost all aspects of the lives of its citizens, except certain parts of the personal sphere. An NGO, by contrast, seeks merely permission for certain activities, lobbying, being a discussion partner in trade-offs, and perhaps a restricted willingness to cooperate and support. Second, Beetham's concept has an important socio-historical component, which can easily go unquestioned as long as the concept is reflected on in relation to national governments. The rules to which an organization must conform, the shared beliefs on which these rules should rest, and the consent that must be given to the organization, will in every state and every society with its own culture and conventions easily take their own forms. These forms will not all be completely different from those in other countries and societies, but nevertheless major differences will appear. Of course, this is no problem as long as the scope of the concept is restricted to the context of one country or society. As soon as the scope surpasses the context of one country or society problems may arise, however, because of cultural and conventional differences. And of course, when the concept of legitimacy is applied to NGOs that operate in an international arena against the background of moral and cultural pluralism, the same kind of problems may occur. This should be kept in mind when we now turn to the positive part of applying Beetham's definition to NGOs.

Beetham's definition differs from the current and mostly implicit ways of thinking about the legitimacy of NGOs by its primarily procedural character. The current way of thinking about the legitimacy of NGOs mostly hinges on an appeal to substantial criteria. A justification using substantial criteria is a justification that refers to the degree to which an individual or an organization conforms to values and ideals. Here, one may think of arguments such as: this organization defends respect for human rights, animal well being, the protection of the environment, it helps the needy and the poor, etcetera. A procedural justification is a justification that refers to the formal aspects of the decision procedures of the individuals or the organizations involved. Does a decision that will initialize an activity rest on the consent of all people involved? Are the procedures for decisions and policies transparent and can they be checked? These are all procedural criteria. Beetham's first condition for legitimacy is clearly procedural, just as his third one is. Only the second condition indirectly uses a substantial criterion, i.e., the requirement that the rules to which the organization involved must conform rest on shared beliefs concerning values and ideals.

It may come as no surprise that procedural criteria do not as yet play such an important part in the traditional ways of thinking about the legitimization of NGOs. The procedural criteria to which Beetham refers mostly have an institutional basis in the community that must accept the government involved. No wonder then, that he refers to the rules to which a government should conform more often as legal rules than as legal *and* moral rules. And, naturally, "expressed" consent immediately reminds one of election-procedures and (implicit) societal and political mechanisms with the help of which one can express consent. The situation of internationally operating NGOs, of course, is best characterized as one in which institutional facilitation for legitimization through procedures often is absent. Nevertheless, international law has developed, and some commonly recognized legal principles could gradually come to function as institutional hinges in the international community for the application of a procedural criterion. Because of the lack of sufficient other common societal and cultural conventions and institutions on an international level which could provide the institutional bedding for the procedures, one could in addition introduce alternative procedural criteria that can be applied globally and against the background of a big cultural and moral pluralism. Starting points for this approach could perhaps be found in, for example, the procedures for accreditation of NGOs with international organizations such as the United Nations.[1] Here, the existence of an internationally recognized authority is used in order to vest the NGO with credibility. But of course the possibilities are not restricted to legal options. One can also think of options that are minimally dependent on specific cultural or institutional contexts. One relatively simple procedural way of improving the legitimacy and accountability would be increasing the degree of transparency of the organizational system and the decision procedures of the NGO, so that they can be checked against moral and, if available, legal criteria.

So there are some possibilities of applying procedural criteria in the case of internationally operating NGOs. But what about the substantial criteria? The degree to which the activities of an NGO conform to certain values and ideals can play a role in its legitimization. Requiring that these values and ideals rest on a certain commitment of all who are involved and affected, however, will be problematic for many a NGO, simply because, mostly, the values and ideals to which they connect are not supported by all the groups involved. In these cases there seem to be two ways out. The first is to back out, to leave substantial criteria for what they are, and to restrict oneself to procedural criteria. The second is to try to show that the values and ideals that one endorses ultimately derive from or are logically or conceptually connected to universal values. In the strategically strongest case, these happen to be universal values that have been laid down in international laws or legal principles. In the

---

[1] See http://www.un.org/esa/coordination/ngo (accessed on 27 May 2003).

strategically weakest case (which need not be the morally weakest case) the universal values involved would be values to which every rational person would commit herself on the grounds of a morally normative argument. By this I mean that every rational person would recognize it as an on principle defensible value, even if she herself would not commit herself to it.

It may, finally, also be helpful here to recall the distinction between the general legitimacy of NGOs with respect to their organizational system and their activities as a whole and the specific legitimacy of occasional activities of NGOs. Both the general and the specific forms of legitimacy can be a matter of procedural and/or substantial criteria. With regard to the legitimacy of specific actions, however, one can further differentiate. It would go much too far to spell out all possibilities, but it seems all but unreasonable that different requirements be applied to different kinds of activities. So, for instance, the mere participation in public debates or merely speaking up for a certain cause may be connected to fewer requirements than straightforward organization of boycotts. And maybe even the stringency of the requirements to be applied may be connected to the probability, extent and intensity of possible harm inflicted on the parties involved.

3 Internet NGOs: Opportunities and Risks

Bearing all this in mind, we must conclude that in the legitimization of internationally operating NGOs the emphasis must be on the satisfaction of procedural criteria (transparency of the organization, possibilities of checking decisional procedures, accreditation with international organizations) and the possible – i.e. primarily purely conceptual and normative – connection of the values and ideals of the NGOs involved with universal values (preferentially already incorporated in international law and legal principles). This brings me, finally, to the questions of accountability and legitimacy of Internet NGOs. New electronic information and communication technologies (ICT) open up new possibilities of organizing and operating. Besides any other uses to which they may put them (e.g. for *gathering* information about the regions and situation in which they are active), NGOs can profit from ICT with regard to their accountability and legitimacy. First, they can use electronic means (email, websites, discussion panels, intranet) in order to raise the transparency of the organization and to involve people in their ideals, mission and work. Second, ICT – especially all kinds of Internet applications – offers all kinds of possibilities of interactivity with regard to the processing of information and the creation of awareness, even to such a degree that supporting members or even people who are just interested, become active workers for the NGO involved. Here one may think of, for instance, people who gather information about certain social problems, and publish this information on the website of a relevant NGO, and of people who do all kinds of administrative jobs for an NGO by using the Internet. Interestingly, in the latter case the borderlines between the NGO as an organization and the field in which the organization operates, begin to fade away. From the vantage points of accountability and legitimacy, this may be good: It may be considered as an intense representation of members, interested people, supporters, etcetera. Sometimes, however, the lines between organizations and their field become so thin, that the organizations merely exist as "virtual" networks of activists who, for the most part, are only temporarily engaged with the NGO. When these NGOs are also exclusively active through the Internet (e.g., McSpotlight and Cokewatch),[2] requirements of legitimacy and accountability run the risk of being easily pushed aside. The account of legitimacy that I have developed in the preceding section – just as the account of accountability that is more or less implied in the conception of legitimacy – simply presupposes that the organization involved has some continuity and stability and ways of controlling and steering the work done by the NGO. Accountability an legitimacy are always based on the ability and willingness of the organization to take up retrospective responsibility for its past performance and prospective respondibility for its future activities. In the case of NGOs that consist largely of virtual networks, these requirements seem hard to meet. This, however, does not mean that it is impossible to do so. As I suggested earlier on, ICT offers splendid possibilities of promoting accountability and legitimacy. I would not be surprised, if, in addition to some adjustments to the organizational structures, solutions could perhaps be found by creating continuity and stability with electronic means.   An archive with past performance records and a database with plans for the future – both of them publicly accessible on the website of the NGO – would already be a big step in the right direction. Undoubtedly, however, more exciting options lie ahead.

References

1. Vedder, A. (ed.): The WTO and concerns regarding animals and nature. Wolf Legal Publishers, Nijmegen (2003) 1–6, 173–182.
2. Edwards, M.: Legitimacy and Values in NGOs and Voluntary Organizations: Some Sceptical Thoughts. In: D. Lewis (ed.): International perspectives on Voluntary Action: Reshaping the Third Sector. Earthscan, London (1999) p. 258–267.
3. Beetham, D.: The Legitimation of Power. MacMillan, London (1991)

[2] See: http://www.mcspotlight.org and http://www.cokewatch.org

Structuring Dialogue between the People and Their Representatives

Katie Greenwood, Trevor Bench-Capon, and Peter McBurney

Department of Computer Science
University of Liverpool
Liverpool, L69 7ZF, UK
{k.m.greenwood,tbc,p.j.mcburney}@csc.liv.ac.uk

Abstract. Conversations between citizens and their representatives may take a number of forms. In this paper, we consider one of these – letters between citizens and representatives – and explore the application of a well-known model of dialogue types to these. We provide a method to give these types a precise characterization in terms of the initial beliefs and desires of the participants, and then explore one type, persuasion dialogues. This work commences the formal modeling of citizen-representative interactions necessary for a fully electronic democracy.

1 Introduction

An important feature of a democracy is that those who rule should be accessible and accountable to those whom they rule. Citizens have the right to air their grievances and to seek justifications of policy from their Government, either by direct approach to the responsible Minister, or mediated through their elected representatives. Traditionally they exercise this right by writing letters. This correspondence is taken seriously and the Government organisation devotes considerable resource to replying to this correspondence. Can this process be made more effective by using electronic communication?

As with so many other aspects of Government, it is straightforward to offer some improvements by replicating the existing process in the context of currently available technology. Thus simply replacing the written letters by electronic mail will offer advantages of making access more direct and the exchange of views potentially faster. Additionally there is the potential for making the exchange of views more inclusive through mechanisms such as bulletin boards and discussion groups. Simply to replicate the current process, however, may fail to realise the potential advantages to the full. This lack of ambition can be seen in several areas addressed by e-government. Consider, for example, the use of forms. It is an easy matter to put the existing paper form onto the World Wide Web, giving ready access to the form and allowing immediate submission, while avoiding the problems associated with forms being out of stock, or outdated forms being issued. Thus there are clear gains. But many potential benefits are not realised by this approach. Forms create problems not only of availability, but also in their accurate completion. To take full advantage of the possibilities created by the new medium it is necessary to rethink the activity in the new context: what makes a good paper form, may

R. Traunmüller (Ed.): EGOV 2003, LNCS 2739, pp. 55–62, 2003.

not be what makes a good electronic form. As early as the late eighties Gilbert and his colleagues [3,4], looked seriously at the notion of a specifically electronic form, with the intention of exploring, though a detailed study of form filling behaviour, what support could be provided for the form filler, and conducted a thorough evaluation on a prototype system. Particular problems arose from two areas: people tend to ignore much of the information, instructions and notes on the form, and people often become disorientated and fail to progress through the form in the correct sequence. Both these aspects were able to be addressed in the electronic form by making the form dynamic: information was presented only as and when it was needed, so that it was recognised as relevant and heeded, and the route through the form could be tightly controlled. The evaluation clearly demonstrated benefits: both subjective, in that people felt it was easier to complete the form, and objective, in that the forms were complete with increased accuracy.

The work on electronic forms provides a clear example of how technology can give real gains through an analysis of the behaviour of those engaged in the activity so as to identify opportunities for providing real support for the activity not available in the paper system. Are there similar benefits to be realised for correspondence with Ministers? First, we can point to the range of topics which be found in such correspondence. Examples (couched in terms of welfare benefits) are:

1. Requests for information about available help given particular circumstances: (e.g., I am a lone parent,[1] with a part time job and two children under five: what support can I get?).
2. Requests for advice about particular circumstances: (e.g., I am in receipt of such and such benefits, and have been offered a part time job. Is it in my interests to accept it?).
3. Requests for information about available help for a class of people: (e.g., what support is available for lone parents?).
4. Complaints about particular decisions: (e.g., why was I refused benefit?).
5. Suggestions for policy change: (e.g., Better child care facilities should be provided for working mothers).
6. Demands for explanation of policies: (e.g., Why can I get financial help to pay for child care, when I receive nothing if I choose to care for my own children?).

There are, of course, other kinds of question, but these examples serve to show some of the variety. Also a single letter may in fact raise a number of different questions. This variety suggest that we may not wish to treat correspondence as a single homogenous whole, but to provide a range of tools to support these different kinds of exchange.

Second, we can pay attention to how the exchanges are structured and expressed. A letter, being written in natural language, has advantages of expressiveness and flexibility, and can be used to communicate whatever can be communicated. On the other hand, this very flexibility carries with in disadvantages of vagueness, ambiguity and lack of clarity. The reader must interpret the document to determine what question is being asked, and must work to extract the facts and arguments presented. This offers considerable scope for misunderstanding, both of the original inquiry and the reply. Expressing an argument clearly and understanding it correctly are not an easy tasks.

---

[1] A "lone parent" is a person with dependent children, not living with a partner.

Thus we see the role of an electronic tool as to facilitate communication and understanding both through clarifying the nature and intention of the exchange, and by assisting in the formulation and comprehension of the exchange. For this we draw on work aimed at supporting computer mediated dialogues. In section 2 we will recapitulate the work of Walton and Krabbe [11] on dialogue types, and present some additional analysis of our own which is intended to make these notions more precise and readily applicable. In section 3 we will focus on one particular dialogue type - persuasion - and present our work exploring the structure of persuasive dialogue. In the section 4 we will apply this work to the example of justifying a policy. Section 5 makes some concluding remarks.

2 Types of Dialogue

In [11], Walton and Krabbe have identified a number of distinct dialogue types used in human communication: Persuasion, Negotiation, Inquiry, Information-Seeking, Deliberation, and Eristic Dialogues. These types are characterised by their initial positions, main goal and the aims of the participants. They are summarised in Table 1.

Table 1. Types of Dialogue

Type	Initial Situation	Main Goal	Participants Aims
Persuasion	Conflicting points of view	Resolution of such conflicts by verbal means	Persuade the other(s)
Negotiation	Conflict of interests and need for cooperation	Making a deal	Get the best out of it for oneself
Inquiry	General ignorance	Growth of knowledge and agreement	Find a proof or destroy one
Info-seeking	Personal ignorance	Spreading knowledge and revealing positions	Gain, pass on, show or hide personal knowledge
Deliberation	Need for action	Reach a decision	Influence the outcome
Eristic Dialogue	Conflict and antagonism	Reaching an accommodation in a relationship	Strike the other party and win in the eyes of onlookers

We summarize the Walton and Krabbe descriptions as follows (in the order of [11]):

- A **Persuasion** dialogue involves an attempt by one participant to have another participant endorse some proposition or statement. The statement at issue may concern the beliefs of the participants or proposals for action, and the dialogue may or may not involve conflict between the participants. If the participants are guided only by the force of argument, then whichever participant has the more convincing argument, taking into account the burden of proof, should be able to persuade the other to endorse the statement at issue, or to give up the attempt.
- A **Negotiation** dialogue occurs when two or more parties attempt to jointly divide some resource (which may include the participants' own time or their respective capabilities to act), where the competing claims of the participants potentially cannot

all be satisfied simultaneously. Here, co-operation is required by both parties in order to engage in the negotiation dialogue, but, at the same time, each participant is assumed to be seeking to achieve the best possible deal for him or herself.

- An **Inquiry** dialogue occurs when two or more participants, each being ignorant of the answer to some question, and each believing the others to be ignorant also, jointly seek to determine the answer. These dialogues do not start from a position of conflict, as no participant has taken a particular position on the question at issue; they are trying to find out some knowledge, and no one need resile from their existing beliefs. Aircraft disaster investigations may be seen as examples of Inquiry dialogues.

- An **Information-seeking** dialogue occurs when one party does not know the answer to some question, and believes (perhaps erroneously) that another party does so. The first party seeks to elicit the answer from the second by means of the dialogue. Expert consultation is a common important subtype of this type of dialogue. When the information sought concerns an action or course of action, we call this type of dialogue, a **plan-seeking** dialogue.

- A **Deliberation** dialogue occurs when two or more parties attempt to agree on an action, or a course of action, in some situation. The action may be performed by one or more the parties in the dialogue or by others not present. Here the participants share a responsibility to decide the action(s) to be undertaken in the circumstances, or, at least, they share a willingness to discuss whether they have such a shared responsibility.

- An **Eristic** dialogue is one where the participants vent perceived grievances, as in a quarrel, and the dialogue may act as a substitute for physical fighting. We do not consider this dialogue type further in this paper as we see it being beyond rational discourse.

Most human dialogues are in fact mixtures or combinations of these ideal types. For example a debate may contain persuasion, information-seeking and antagonism all at once, each embedded in the larger interaction. Moreover a dialogue may shift between types as it proceeds. With the exception of eristic dialogues, we have taken the above dialogue types as a starting point, and given a more precise characterisation to them. This is done using the initial beliefs and aims of the participants and the ways in which these can change in the course of the dialogue. This allows us to identify any shifts in the dialogue type, and the changes which the parties can make to reach agreement.

Tables 2, 3 and 4 show our analysis for three typical situations. Table 2 shows the possibilities where two party discuss their beliefs regarding a single proposition. Table 3 shows the possibilities when two parties discuss whether a particular action should be performed or not. Table 4 shows the situation where two parties discuss the performance of either, both or neither of two actions, which may be performed.

These tables model the space of all possible dialogue types appropriate to these situations. Representing the dialogues in this way leads to a number of observations relating to reaching agreement:

    we can see the space of possible moves available to the participants;
    we can see how agreement can be reached;
    we can see how many changes are needed if agreement is to be reached;
    we can see which participant must change if agreement is to be reached.

Table 2. Model of a Discussion Over Beliefs

A/B	p	¬ p	p ∨ ¬ p
p	Agreement	Disagreement or Persuasion	B info seeks A
¬ p	Disagreement or Persuasion	Agreement	B info seeks A
p ∨ ¬ p	A info seeks B	A info seeks B	Inquiry

Table 3. Model of a Discussion Over Actions

A/B	B does p	B does ¬ p	B does p ∨ ¬ p
A does p	Agreement	Disagreement or Persuasion	B plan seeks A
A does ¬ p	Disagreement or Persuasion	Agreement	B plan seeks A
A does p ∨ ¬ p	A plan seeks B	A plan seeks B	Deliberation

Table 4. Model of a Discussion Over Multiple Actions

	A does $p \wedge q$	A does $p \wedge \neg q$	A does $q \wedge \neg p$	A does $\neg p \wedge \neg q$	no opinion
A does $p \wedge q$	Agreement	Conflict or Persuasion	Conflict or Persuasion	Conflict or Negotiation	Plan seeking
A does $p \wedge \neg q$	Conflict or Persuasion	Agreement	Conflict or Persuasion	Conflict or Persuasion	Plan seeking
A does $q \wedge \neg p$	Conflict or Persuasion	Conflict or Persuasion	Agreement	Conflict or Persuasion	Plan seeking
A does $\neg p \wedge \neg q$	Conflict or Negotiation	Conflict or Persuasion	Conflict or Persuasion	Agreement	Plan seeking
no opinion	Plan seeking	Plan seeking	Plan seeking	Plan seeking	Deliberation

We can use tables 2, 3 and 4 to classify the example queries 1–6 in the Introduction.

1. In (1), the inquirer (B) does not know a piece of information, and the recipient (A) does. Thus, we are at the top right of table 2 and have an info-seeking dialogue.
2. In (2), the inquirer(A) wishes to know whether or not to perform an action, and (B) will have the answer. This puts us in one of the first two cells at the bottom of table 3, as here we have plan seeking, a sub-type of info-seeking.
3. (3) is similar to (1), even though it is of a general nature.
4. In (4), the recipient (A) did p, but the inquirer (B) believes that ¬ p should have been done, giving rise to a situation of disagreement, requiring persuasion, as in Table 3.
5. In (5), we assume that the recipient's (A) policy is ¬ p and the inquirer (B) wants p to be done so again, this gives rise to persuasion, again as in Table 3.

6. Finally, in (6), the recipient (A) is currently performing an action p, where the inquirer (B) wishes for ¬ p to be performed instead so, we are in the third cell of the second row in table 4, again giving rise to a persuasion dialogue.

We believe that providing the information in the form of these matrices gives a more structured and precise characterisation of the dialogue types than the informal descriptions of [11]. When the participants have a clear understanding of the gaps between their positions the task of deciding what shifts in position they should try to induce, or may need to make, is facilitated. Of course, whether a party is willing to change their position will depend on their other beliefs, and the utility they ascribe to actions and the states resulting from action. The structures, however, do provide a basis for forming strategies and heuristics to inform the conduct of the various types of dialogue.

3   Persuasive Dialogue

We have previously offered an account of argument intended to persuade someone that an action is justified [6,7]. Here we summarise the important features of this account.

We see the key element in justifying an action as putting forward a position. This position comprises four elements: (a) The circumstances in which the action is performed; (b) The action itself; (c) The goal achieved by performing the action; and (d) The social values promoted by that goal. The position provides a justification, but in order to persuade it must be capable of being defended against attacks. There are a variety of ways in which a position can be attacked. We have identified fifteen different ways of attacking such a position [6], some of which have several variants. A persuasive dialogue is thus seen as a position being proposed, attacked and defended. In some cases persuasion may result, but often disagreement remains. In some cases the disagreement may result from a difference in factual belief: for example, the effects of a particular action may be disputed. In other cases the disagreement results from ethical choices: the disputants may differ as to the way in which they rate the social values promoted by an action. The key point is that conducting the dialogue in this way ensures that the argument is precisely stated, and that if disagreement remains, the exact points of difference can be located, so that what would be required for persuasion becomes clear, whether it is proof of some fact or causal mechanism, arguments designed to change the value order of the disputant, or even a new position which respects the opponent's ordering of values. A discussion can be found in [1,2] of how persuasion is possible even when there is no consensus as to which values are desirable.

By using computer mediated dialogue to structure the attempt at persuasion according to this model we minimise the need for interpretation and the scope for misunderstanding by ensuring that:

- The position is fully and explicitly stated;
- Attacks on the position are stated unambiguously and precisely;
- Where there is residual disagreement, appropriate means are taken to resolve it, or identify any irreconcilable points making persuasion impossible.

4   Policy Justification as an Example

To illustrate the foregoing, we present an example of policy justification. Suppose the Government had a policy of paying for child care for lone parents, in order to enable them to take paid employment. This might be objected to as taking biasing the choice of lone parents to care for their own children rather than take paid employment. Justification of the policy could take a number of forms, for example:

a1. lone parents wish to work;
a2. providing child care for such parents;
a3. would enable them to work;
a4. providing job satisfaction and increasing gross national product.

Or:

b1. lone parents are poor because child care prevents them working;
b2. providing child care for such parents;
b3. would enable them to work;
b4. taking them and their children out of poverty;

Or:

c1. providing an acceptable level of support for all lone parents is too expensive; however we could afford to pay for their child care;
c2. providing child care for such parents;
c3. would enable them to work at acceptable cost;
c4. taking them and their children out of poverty and increasing gross national product.

There are probably other justifications. Each of these justifications makes different assumptions about the choices and aspirations of lone parents, and expresses different views on their attitude to work: justification *a.* values work for its intrinsic benefits, justification *b.* sees work primarily as a source of income, while justification *c.* relies on perceived economic constraints. All the arguments assume that lone parents will have no difficulty in finding acceptably remunerated employment. None rate the values relating to choice or the benefits to parent and child of parental care as significant. In unstructured prose it might well be hard to tell which of these justification was being advanced, and responders might find it hard themselves faced with a moving target. Given a clear statement of the justification, it is possible to formulate a precise response; perhaps directed at the assumptions, either in lines 1 or 3, or at the values in lines 4.

5   Concluding Remarks

In this paper we have considered the prospects for improving the quality of communication between the people and their representatives through electronic dialogues. We have done this by exploring one of the many ways in which citizens exercise their right to communicate with their political representatives, namely, letter-writing. Our approach is complementary to recent proposals for argumentation-based information systems to support deliberative decision-making over public policy questions, as in [5,8,9]. We stress the point that the use of technology often requires a rethinking of the existing process if the full benefits are to be achieved. Drawing on the work of Walton and Krabbe [11], we have identified a number of different dialogue types, and we have provided a method to give them a precise characterisation in terms of the initial beliefs and desires of the participants. We have further explored one of these, persuasion dialogues, providing a detailed model of persuasion which can be used as the basis for a computer mediated dialogue, and illustrated this with an example. In future work, we hope to be able to complement this model with models of other dialogue types, so that dialogues which shift between, embed, and combine different types may be appropriately represented. General formal approaches for combining dialogues of different types have already been developed by, e.g., McBurney and Parsons [10], and such approaches could readily be instantiated with particular models. Experience will show whether it is possible to build a system which is sufficiently usable by the general public: even if it is not, however, such a system would increase the effectiveness of debate between organisations such as pressure groups and lobbyists and the Government. We believe that our discussion provides evidence for potential improvements in the important matter of communication between people and their Government.

References

1. T. J. M. Bench-Capon. Agreeing to differ: Modelling persuasive dialogue between parties without a consensus about values. *Informal Logic*, 2003. *In press*.
2. T. J. M. Bench-Capon. Persuasion in practical argument using value-based argumentation frameworks. *Journal of Logic and Computation*, 2003. *In press*.
3. N. Gilbert. The claimant advice systems. In T. J. M. Bench-Capon, editor, *Knowledge Based Systems and Legal Applications*, pages 115–128. Academic Press, London, 1991.
4. N. Gilbert. Support for members of the public. In T. J. M. Bench-Capon, editor, *Knowledge Based Systems and Legal Applications*, pages 183–198. Academic Press, London, 1991.
5. T. F. Gordon and G. Richter. Discourse support systems for deliberative democracy. In R. Traunmüller and K. Lenk, editors, *EGOV 2002*, LNCS 2456, pages 238–255. Springer, Berlin, 2002.
6. K. Greenwood, T. Bench-Capon, and P. McBurney. Argument over Proposals for Action. Report ULCS-03-003, Department of Computer Science, University of Liverpool, UK, 2003.
7. K. Greenwood, T. Bench-Capon, and P. McBurney. Towards an account of persuasion in law. In *Proc. 9th Intern. Conf. on AI and Law (ICAIL-2003)*, New York, 2003. ACM Press. *To appear*.
8. R. Luehrs, T. Malsch, and K. Voss. Internet, discourses, and democracy. In T. Terano *et al.*, editor, *New Frontiers in AI*, LNAI 2253, pages 67–74. Springer, Berlin, 2001.
9. P. McBurney and S. Parsons. Intelligent systems to support deliberative democracy in environmental regulation. *ICT Law*, 10(1):33–43, 2001.
10. P. McBurney and S. Parsons. Games that agents play: A formal framework for dialogues between autonomous agents. *J. Logic, Language and Information*, 11(3):315–334, 2002.
11. D. N. Walton and E. C. W. Krabbe. *Commitment in Dialogue: Basic Concepts of Interpersonal Reasoning*. SUNY Press, Albany, NY, USA, 1995.

Local Democracy Shaping E-Democracy

Zahid Parvez

University of Wolverhampton, UK
z.parvez@wlv.ac.uk

Abstract. This paper offers a fresh perspective to study the role and implications of information and communications technologies (ICT) in processes of local democracy. It moves away from earlier perspectives that have given privilege to information flows, information technology features or strategies employed by human actors in their accounts. The paper proposes a theoretical framework, derived from Giddens theory of Structuration. This framework suggests that the material technology cannot be understood in isolation from the way it is appropriated in social processes. It brings to the forefront technologically enabled social practices rather than the technology itself or the actions of human actors and thus avoids technological or social determinism. It highlights the importance of the interplay of the context, social structures and agency factors in the technologically enabled social practices. When applied to processes of local democracy, it brings forward a number of important insights for policy makers and ICT designers.

1 Introduction

Local governments in the UK are increasingly implementing and using ICT for improving their administration, coordination and local governance and democracy processes, as well as providing public services electronically to citizens. This paper has two broad aims. The first is to develop and propose a theoretical framework, derived from a structuration perspective, for studying technology in social processes. The second aim is to apply this framework to investigate the role and implications of ICT in processes of local democracy and to report the findings.

2 Structuration Perspective

Literature highlights numerous perspectives that have been advocated by different commentators to understand the role of technology in social processes. At one extreme, technology is viewed as an autonomous force or a key driver in shaping social processes. Perspectives at this end tend to emphasize the direct effects of technology on people and institutions. However, they underplay the influence of human actors and the role of social context in shaping and moderating the role of technology in institutions. At the other extreme, perspectives tend to place a greater focus on human and social factors in the technology process. Views from these perspectives tend to argue that human actors or social factors are the key determinants

R. Traunmüller (Ed.): EGOV 2003, LNCS 2739, pp. 63–68, 2003.

in social change. Technology is either assumed to be neutral or is believed that human actors and institutions can freely select them [1]. Thus, perspectives from this side emphasize the variable effects of technology on social processes, as the effects are perceived to be context dependent. However, when these opposing perspectives are applied to understand the role and implications of technologies in processes of democracy, conflicting scenarios emerge. These include the prediction of radical changes in democratic practices and the rise of new forms of governance and models of democracy. Views range along a continuum from utopian visions of Athenian style direct democracy to the other extreme of dystopian scenarios of Orwellian society [2]. However, as reported by numerous authors [1, 2, 3, 4] reality is far from these depictions.

There is no doubt that insights gained from the above perspectives have contributed much in developing current thinking on digital democracy. However, a broader perspective is lacking; one that would align theory more closely with empirical reality. It is argued that such a perspective need to give greater consideration to the interplay of technology, human agents and social processes. To move in this direction, the paper argues for employing the structuration perspective and believes that it could offer some deeper insights to explain the role and implications of technology in social processes.

The structuration perspective suggests that the material technology cannot be understood in isolation from the way it is appropriated in social processes. It therefore brings to the forefront technologically enabled social practices rather than the technology itself or the actions of human actors and thus avoids technological or social determinism. It highlights the importance of the interplay of the context, social structures and agency factors in the technologically enabled social practices. Technologies are employed to support social practices (e.g. for accessing information, on-line discussions, consultations, etc.). Human actors are enabled and constrained through the way these technologically enabled democratic political practices are structured in an institutional context. Orilkowski [5] draws on Giddens general theory of Structuration [6] to develop a model for understanding technology in social processes. She calls this model: the Structurational Model of Technology (SMT). This model emphasises the duality of technology - that is, 'technology is created and changed by human action, yet it is also used by humans to accomplish some action' [5, p405]. In other words, Orlikowski argues that social processes shape technology, but through the on-going use of technology, they are also shaped by it. Her model draws attention to the interplay of institutional properties, technology and human agents.

However, on a closer examination of the SMT as proposed by Orlikowski [5], it is felt that a number of issues require addressing in order to align it closer to Giddens general theory of structuration. First, Orlikowski focuses her model on the concept of the *duality of technology*. However, Giddens structuration theory emphasises upon the *duality of structure*. The SMT therefore, does not entirely conform to Giddens general theory of structuration. Second, the concept of 'institutional properties' in her model is vague and hence requires further development. Through addressing these issues, some adaptations have been made to the original SMT as proposed by Orlikowski [5]. The adapted SMT (or the ASMT) as a theoretical framework to analyse the role of ICTs in processes of local democracy is presented diagrammatically in Figure 1. This ASMT makes the following changes and elaborations to the original SMT that was proposed by Orlikowski [5].

1. Changes the focus from 'technology' and 'duality of technology' to the duality of structure of technologically enable social practices (TESP)
2. Elaborates on the concept of 'institutional properties' and argues for this concept to be equated with institutional 'context'. Also, using Pettigrew *et al* [7] developed notion of context, it differentiates 'context' into 'inner context' and 'outer context'.
3. Identifies the modalities (i.e. sources of structure) of TESP. These are located in both objective (i.e. codified) and virtual (i.e. subjective or exist as memory traces) sources. These modalities are enacted in the role of technology in TESP

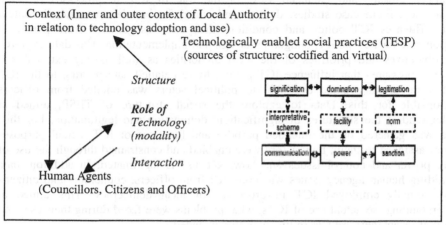

Fig. 1. Adapted Structurational Model of Technology (ASMT)

It is argued that these adaptations are more faithful to Giddens theory of structuration. The ASMT enables the examination of the inner and outer institutional context within which ICTs are shaped and employed, the role of human agency during interactions with TESP, and also how these practices are structured.

3 Empirical Work

The second aim of this paper is to report on the findings that have been gained from the application of the ASMT in processes of local democracy within the UK context. Employing this framework to analyse the role and implications of ICTs in processes of democratic political processes, the following research questions were addressed:
1. What TESP are being developed by local governments within the UK context?
2. To what extent does the context (inner and outer) influences the development of these TESP in local democracy?
3. To what extent does the structures of these TESP enable and constrain human actors in these practices?
4. Are there any implications of these TESP on the processes of democracy (i.e. are they influencing change in democratic processes and practices, and contributing to the formation of new models of democracy)?
The research strategy employed comprised of three strands: use of case studies; primary survey data to understand the general developments in TESP amongst the top

ten local authorities (i.e. the best case examples) that were awarded for their innovations in public electronic interaction during 2001 (by SPIN and SOCITM); and use of secondary survey data collected across local authorities in the UK on ICT in local governance and democracy. The methods employed included documentation analysis (e.g. documents on E-Government statements, ICT use policy, ICT strategy plans), observations, on-line questionnaires and semi-structured interviews from appropriate personnel in three local authorities in the UK.

The investigation aimed at eliciting data from different groups of actors in order to obtain a broader and balanced view of the role of ICT in processes of local democracy. From case studies, data to understand the broader institutional context that influences ICT policy and conditions their use was gathered from personnel responsible for ICT policy, budgeting, design and implementation. This data explored the objectives and priorities of the local authorities as well as any external and internal pressures that influence ICT policy. More detailed data relating to the ICT that were actually made available to political actors was elicited from officers responsible for this. Data to explore the social structure of TESP, aimed at understanding the structures of signification, domination and legitimation. For this, data was gathered on the intended purpose and functions of ICT, actual purposes actors assigned to them, how actors were enabled and constrained through the use of ICT, power and control issues and how ICT use is legitimated. In addition, data regarding human agency issues was collected from officers, councillors and citizens who actually employed ICT in processes of local democracy. This aimed at understanding the actual use of ICTs, what problems were faced during their use, and whether or not their use was in line with that intended.

4 Findings and Conclusions

Influence of Context: Findings indicate that the outer ICT context of local authorities plays an important part in driving the ICT agenda and subsequently influencing the shape and role of ICTs in local democracy. The three main drivers from the outer context include: consumerist and managerialist agenda, the theories of the information society (as these act as a source of ideas and concepts for the role of ICTs in society), and the information age models of democracy (as they influence thinking about democracy and how ICTs can be employed in improving and enhancing the processes of local democracy). The key drivers from the inner context of local authorities that influence the role of ICTs in local democracy includes: the vision policy-makers have for enhancing democracy, specific visions and agendas driving ICT strategies and budgets allocated for ICTs in local democracy. However, the strength of these drivers vary amongst local authorities and as a consequence there was some variations in the type of TESP in place in different local authorities. Thus, findings indicate that ICT, at the time of data collection, mainly served the managerialist, consumerist and e-government agenda and played little role in enhancing interactivity between political agents in local democracy.

TESP: ICT are being employed for providing local information and for speeding up or facilitating actors in performing their information related roles such as access to timely information and responding to communication. Communication flow structure was on the whole simply asynchronous and not interactive. In addition, officers are increasingly using ICT in the provision of services and are therefore able to capture citizens' preferences and choices at the point of service consumption (and this finding confirms what has been reported by Bellamy and Taylor [8]. Through this process, ICT are facilitating an 'informating' role for officers.

Agency issues: Actors primarily see ICTs in processes of local democracy as tools to support established processes and not as a means for bringing change to these processes. However, there was some evidence to suggest that some actors are beginning to employ ICT in different ways to that intended. For example, two councillors have attempted to set up an e-group for citizens in their constituencies. This is likely to increase through time, and hence would exert pressure for change. The use of the Internet in particular is empowering some of the elected Councillors who use this as a tool for enhancing their effectiveness. For example, it is enabling those who use this to access remote information directly – to become more aware of what other local authorities are doing as well as learn about the developments and research findings related to local authorities that are published by institutions on the Internet. This assists in enhancing their contribution to policy-making and improve their effectiveness in processes of local governance. However, this appears to be an example of 'unintended consequence' of ICT in processes of local democracy. An analysis of the data collected also suggests that there is a great deal of citizens' apathy and ICT has not helped to alleviate this to any great extent. Very few citizens actually appear to employ ICT for engaging in processes of local democracy. Thus, the provision of ICT to political actors on their own does not enhance political participation and engagement. Other factors such as the institutional context and the wider political culture also need to be addressed if citizens' engagement in democracy is to be increased.

Implications of ICTs: There was no evidence that ICT are leading to any radical change to the institutionalised models of democracy. However, evidence suggests that two sub-models of democracy are emerging under the dominant representative model, one on the policy-side (the Demo-elitist) and the other at the service delivery side (the Consumer democracy model). Evidence points to the existence of stronger interaction between officers and elected Councillors via ICT for policy issues than between Councillors and citizens. This suggests that there are signs of a Demo-elitist model of democracy emerging in local authorities, which has also been reported by Hoff et al [9]. In addition, at the service delivery side, evidence points to a greater interaction between citizens and officers than between citizens and elected Councillors. This suggests that a Consumer model of democracy is emerging at the point of service consumption. This again confirms the findings of Hoff et al [9].

In conclusion, on applying the adapted Structurational model of technology (ASMT) to investigate the role and implications of ICTs in processes of local democracy a number of insights were gained. Findings suggest that ICT in processes of local governance are in general being shaped by the institutional context and hence appear to be reinforcing the representative model of democracy. However, their continued and wider use could increasingly place local authority officers at the centre of power in local democracy, and thus introducing the possibility of strengthening the demo-elitist and consumer models of democracy. Moreover, as the elected Councillors begin to build their confidence with ICT, become more computer literate and acquire ICT skills, could use these to improving their role and effectiveness in the processes of local democracy.

Finally, for improving democratic participation and engagement, policy makers need to give due consideration not only to technological issues, but also to the existing institutional context, theories and models of democracy and the political culture, TESP, as well as the rules and resources that influence the development of these practices and conditions their use. Policies need to bring to surface the implicit social structures, which can enable or constrain human actors in TESP. Moreover, human agency issues such as citizens' access to ICT for political information and to participate in the decision-making processes, as well as issues such as computer literacy and training, user-friendly computer interfaces, and on-line costs that enable and constrain political agents in their interactions with ICT need consideration if democracy is to be enhanced. A consideration to these issues can guide policy-making in public administration in a more integrated way.

References

1. Hacker, K. L. and van Dijk, J. (eds.) (2000) Digital Democracy, Issues of Theory & Practice. Sage Publications: London
2. Donk, W.B.H.J.van de., Snellen, I.Th..M, and Tops, P.W. (eds) (1995) *Orwell in Athens: A Perspective on Informatization and Democracy.* Amsterdam: IOS Press
3. Heeks, R (ed) (2002) *Reinventing Government in the Information Age.* Routledge: London
4. Hudson, J. (1999) "Informatization and Public Administration: A Political Science Perspective". *Information, Communication & Society* 2 (3): 318–339
5. Orlikowski, W. J. (1992) *The Duality of Technology: Rethinking the Concept of Technology in Organisations.* Organisational Science 3 (3): 398–427
6. Giddens, A. (1984): *The Constitution of Society: Outline of the Theory of Structuration* Cambridge: Polity. Reed.
7. Pettigrew, A. (1990) Longitudinal field research on change: theory and practice. In *Organizational Science.* 1(3), pp 267–292
8. Bellamy, C. and Taylor, J.A. (1998) *Governing in the Information Age.* Buckingham: Open University Press
9. Hoff, J., Horrocks, I. And Tops, P. (2000) *Democratic Governance and New Technology, Technolgically mediated innovations in political practices in Western Europe.* Routledge: London

First Trials in Webocracy

Jan Paralic, Tomas Sabol, and Marian Mach

Technical University of Kosice
Letna 9, 042 00 Kosice, Slovakia
{Jan.Paralic,Tomas.Sabol,Marian.Mach}@tuke.sk

Abstract. The Webocracy project aims to empower citizens with innovative communication, access and polling system, supporting increased participation in democratic processes. One of the main project goals is to develop an open source web-based system called *Webocrat* as a multi-channel communication platform supporting e-government and e-democracy applications. Some of the *Webocrat* modules were tested in first trial of our two pilot applications, one of them running in Wolverhampton, UK and the other one in Kosice, Slovakia. Currently, whole integrated *Webocrat* system is being tested within the second trials.

1 Introduction

There are three roles in a political system: citizens, politicians, and government administrators. E-Government and e-democracy embrace transmission of political information and opinion among and within all the groups involved in politics. Proponents of e-government, in addition to advantages of improved communication - without constraints of place and time, point to an array of other new opportunities, such as electronic delivery of many public services to people's homes or multimedia kiosks, more access to a wider variety of public information, the creation of electronic forums, direct democratic participation through online voting and interactive polling (Dutton et al. 1999), electronic competitive public procurement etc.

At the first International Conference eGOV 2002 in Aix-en-Provence, 2002, proposed architecture and functionality of the *Webocrat* system, which is to be developed within the IST project Webocracy (IST-1999-20364 "Web Technologies Supporting Direct Participation in Democratic Processes") were presented (Paralic et al. 2002).

The Webocracy project aims to empower citizens with innovative communication, access and polling system, supporting increased participation in democratic processes. *Webocrat* system will support: communication and discussion, publication of documents (including notices for competitive tendering), browsing and navigation, polling, intelligent retrieval (access to requested documents), various types of reporting in order to provide evaluation and analysis tools. Moreover, personalised access to published resources as well as active delivery of new information within the system by means of alerting services will be offered (Paralic & Sabol 2002).

One of the novelties of our approach is the knowledge management part. Documents of all kinds produced by various modules (e.g. published documents,

R. Traunmüller (Ed.): EGOV 2003, LNCS 2739, pp. 69–74, 2003.

discussions or pollings) are linked to a shared ontology representing the domain of public administration (in this case local government). Such ontology serves as an index for structuring and organizing knowledge. The advantage of clear structuring is, first of all, a more powerful search and retrieval engine (Sarabjot 1995), and second, a more user-friendly content presentation (Dourish et al. 1999), as well as enhanced personalization support (Paralic & Sabol 2002).

In the Webocracy project special attention is being paid to the process of integrating the *Webocrat* tools into practical applications. Rather than separating phases of development followed by the deployment of pilot applications, the process of *Webocrat* tool and methodology development is intertwined with deployment from early beginning. Early deployment should provide important feedback and will drive their further development (Sabol et al. 1999).

2 Pilot Applications

Pilot applications are expected to provide the context for all implementation and evaluation activities within the project. All user partners conduct trials concurrently. WCC is responsible for the design, specification and evaluation of the trials in the UK. LATA and LAFU are responsible for pilot applications and trials in the Slovak Republic. During the pilot applications the *Webocrat* system is tested and users both working at the local authorities and citizens in the municipal areas are invited to participate. The goal of the pilot applications is to see how users react to the *Webocrat* system, whether the system (and its user interface) is appropriate to users' expectations and needs.

The aim of the first trials is to test those modules/functions, which are available at that phase of the project, namely Document publishing (WCM module), Support for discussions (DF module), Support for polling (OPR module), Support for formal and informal submissions (Communication module).

The second trials involve all functions to be implemented within the Webocracy project (including all features based knowledge modelling capabilities of the *Webocrat* system).

In order to learn from the trials it is necessary to evaluate them (and subsequently to compare obtained results with goals which the projects tries to achieve). Lessons learned from the trials can be used to enhance system's functionality, architecture of the system, and/or configuration of the project itself.

To fully understand results of the trials it is necessary to carry out a proper evaluation of these results. In order to track user behaviour when visiting a *Webocrat* site, a log file analysis can be used. The log files represent the easiest way how to track traffic on the pilot sites. Different statistics can be collected, for example how many different modules and sections were accessed, or how many people accessed the *Webocrat* pilot site. These statistics can be obtained by using a specialised software for web server log analysis.

Questionnaires can be used to receive answers from users on various questions about the system, which cannot be gained from log files. To get the correct results from a questionnaire, the design of the questionnaire is of great importance, as well as the process of interpreting results from the questionnaire.

3 First Trial

3.1 First Trial in Wolverhampton, UK

Running from mid-May to late August 2002, the first trail in Wolverhampton of the Webocracy software tested the OPR, DF and parts of the WCM module (http://www.wolforum.org) was thoroughly evaluated and appraised with comments, observations and changes being highlighted as part of the review process. Feedback and comments from WCC staff, citizens and partner agents were received on a number of broad aspects, these being:

– Citizen interaction and behaviour within the system and its subsequent use
– Administrator and Moderator system interaction
– Creation and management of content
– System and module functionality
– System integrity and reliability

Operation of the software, creation of content and administrations of the OPR and DF's was the responsibility of the Webocracy Project Officer at WCC where issues, e-mails and postings were dealt with as they arose on a daily basis. In undertaking the testing, there was a realisation that in no way could the process be exhaustive due to scale, physical resources and external factors to the project such as local elections, citizen inertia and familiarisation. The first trial was an opportunity to provide citizens with a 'taster' of modules and facilities and was therefore low-key in approach. Therefore a lengthy period of time was needed to establish the project within the public domain which has resulted in the forums and polling areas being continued outside the formal trial period.

Close co-operation between the Wolverhampton Life Long Learning Partnership and some 32 UK Online community Internet centres throughout the city enabled the project software to be available to several deprived communities including All Saints, Blakenhall and Pendeford Dovecotes. Centre co-ordinators provided support to citizens visiting the centres, giving encouragement and support to make postings in the DF's and distributing publicity material about the project.

Feedback and comments were received via a number or routes including postings via the Wolforum web site, anecdotal evidence from co-ordinators and citizens and WCC staff. These proved very useful in identifying areas of weakness or improvements required to software functionality.

In order to test the DF module, realistic content was used from previous consultation topics. These headings have been included: Local Environment, Law & Order, Leisure Opportunities, Built Environment, Road Safety, Transport & Environment, Future of Democracy, Entitlement & ID Cards.

The following topics were selected as suitable content for the OPR module: Future of Wolverhampton, Internet in Wolverhampton, Views about Wolforum, Road Safety in Wolverhampton.

A range of methods were employed to publicise the Wolforum web site. 2000 posters and flyers were printed and distributed around the city to community venues and information points where citizens could pick up information and read about how to access the site. WCC's Press Office ensured coverage in the pages of local newspapers and organises several radio interviews on local radio. A high presence on the WCC web site was established, linking both sites together with information and objectives about the project. UW publicised the First Trial by e-mailing staff within the University and encouraging them to contribute to postings or topics in whatever way they saw fit.

As a result of the First Trial, 72 DF postings were made and 92 votes cast in the OPR. Over the course of the period, traffic levels increased steadily, peaking in August with 3,330 site visitations. Although the trail ended in late August, the Wolforum site has remained open in order to build up a large user base for the Second Trial starting in March 2003.

The impact on the workings of the Council (which included Officers, Administrators and Elected Representatives) were minimal as the majority of activities were monitored and administered by the Project Officer, who ensured matters were dealt with effectively and content maintained in a timely manner. A number of functional and operational limitations were highlighted during the Trial Period and raised with the UW development team that when implemented should bring about a much more rounded and flexible series of software modules.

3.2 First Trial in Kosice, SK

The trial was distributed between two user partners – LATA and LAFU. The objective of LATA's part (http://www.tahanovce.sk/mutah) of the trial was to enhance the possibility of accessing documents via Internet. The first trial focused mainly on the following two general objectives.

1. Publication of all publicly available documents with respect to the Freedom of Information Act Nr. 211/2000 approved by the National Council of the Slovak Republic (testing the WCM module).

2. Providing citizens with new communication channel for expressing their opinions on selected issues (testing the OPR module).

Promotion of the first trial in the local ward has been done using multiple channels: informal communication with citizens, local TV channel broadcasting (Information text running on the screen, information provided within the regular news), newspaper articles (several articles in local newspaper), radio interviews.

The *Webocrat* publication system definitely simplified information flow from LA to citizens - it speeded up the process of publishing information. It should replace standing custom of asking for required information personally at the LA, which is time consuming and ineffective. The information can be available on the web at any time. Since the WCM module formed a new base of LATA's web site and new *Webocrat* modules integrated together will significantly extend the functionality offered, we decided to continue in Webocracy trial and evolve it into the second trial.

LAFU's objective was to provide simpler and more transparent communication of the Local Authority with citizens (to enable citizens to send their documents/mails to the LA in a more convenient way, and to enable them to monitor status of processing their documents/mails within the LA). In order to achieve this objective, mainly the Communication module, as a two-way communication channel between LA and citizens, has been tested (http://kosice-dh.sk).

Moreover, the OPR module as a one-way communication channel between citizens and LA has been tested as well. Three polls were published during the first trial period. The first one was about Internet access and use. The content of the second one has been based on topical issues in the city ward. The focus was on attempting to obtain such kind of information from citizens that could help public servants at LA to make more accurate decisions in current matters. The following topics were selected: Greenery situation at the city ward, Possibility to have an e-mail account at the LA server, Type of information to be published by LA, House pets problems, The possibility to submit property declaration electronically. The last poll was issued in order to get feedback about the *Webocrat* application itself.

Promotion of the first trial in the local ward has been done using multiple channels: informal interpersonal communication, presentation at various formal occasions (e.g. the mayor has conducted meetings with teachers, senior citizens, businessmen, and other social groups), radio interviews. Comprehensive information about the project has been published in the local newspaper of LA F-kurier (the average circulation of the F-kurier is 30,000 issues). A series of articles in the newspaper about the trials has been published.

As the electronic submissions needed to be handled in parallel with the traditional mail submissions and had to follow the internal regulations, the whole process represented a slight overhead in the work of user partner. In addition to it, in order to enable submissions of citizens' requests/complaints electronically and even tracking the processing status of submitted documents, some additional responsibilities were assigned.

The response from the public has been in general in accordance with expectations. We were not overly optimistic (since the penetration of Internet within the city ward is not too high) and the results we have achieved can be considered as satisfactory. Within 3 months of running the trial we received 16 messages with a request for information and in the 3 polls we conducted, we received 110 votes in the poll about Internet and 106 votes in the poll on issues in the Local Ward. From June 1 to August 31, the LA received and sent 1,614 mails. Of these, 84 were the sort of correspondence, which could have been submitted also electronically via the *Webocrat* (all these were of no legal binding and for that reason they did not require to be in a 'paper' form, nor did they require any written response). This means, 16 submissions via the *Webocrat* and 16 responses to them represent 27.6% of relevant correspondence carried out electronically.

4 Conclusions

Currently, the second trials are running. The whole, integrated version of the *Webocrat* system brings as a major technical innovation the use of ontology for better organisation of all *Webocrat* resources and intelligent retrieval support. However, more emphasis in the trials is still needed to evaluate its real impact on the users. Moreover, the organisational impact of deploying the *Webocrat* system from the process and personnel point of view needs to be elaborated as well.

Acknowledgements. This work is done within the Webocracy project, which is supported by European Commission DG INFSO under the IST program, contract No. IST-1999-20364 and within the VEGA project 1/8131/01 "Knowledge Technologies for Information Acquisition and Retrieval" of Scientific Grant Agency of Ministry of Education of the Slovak Republic. The content of this publication is the sole responsibility of the authors, and in no way represents the view of the European Commission or its services.

References

1. Bocock, R., Cizmarik, T., Novacek, E., Paralic, J. and Thomson, P. (2001) "Specification of pilot application and design of trials", *Webocracy* (IST-1999-20364) *Technical Report R12.1.*
2. Dourish, P., Edwards, W.K., LaMarca, A., and Salisbury, M. (1999) "Presto: an experimental architecture for fluid interactive document spaces", *ACM Trans. Comput.-Hum. Interact.*, Vol. 6, No. 2, pp. 133–161.
3. Dutton, W. H., Elberse, A., and Hale M. A. (1999) "Case Study of a Netizen's Guide to Elections", *Communications of the ACM*, Vol. 42, No. 12, pp. 49–53.
4. Paralic, J., Sabol, T. and Mach, M.: A System to support E-Democracy, In: Electronic Government, R. Traunmuller, K. Lenk (Eds.), Proc. of the First International Conference EGOV 2002, Aix-en-Provence, France, September, 2002, LNCS 2456, Springer, pp. 288–291.
5. Paralic, J., Paralic, M. and Mach, M. (2001): "Support of Knowledge Management in Distributed Environment", *Informatica*, Vol. 25, No. 3, pp. 319–328.
6. Paralic, J. and Sabol, T. (2002) "A System to support E-Democracy". Paper accepted for publication at the *Conference eGovenment* within DEXA2002, Aix-en-Provence, France, September, 2002.
7. Sabol, T. et al. (1999) *WEBOCRACY Annex 1 – "Description of Work"*, Proposal Nr. IST-1999-20364.
8. Sarabjot, S.A., Bell, D.A., and Hughes, J.G. (1995) "The role of domain knowledge in data mining" in *Proc. of the Int. Conf. on Information and Knowledge Management*, pp. 37–43.

Interlegis: Virtual Network of Communication and Information That Enlarges Brazil's Democracy and Citizenship

Adilson Luiz Tiecher[1], Hugo Cesar Hoeschl[2], and Patrícia Bonina Zimath[1]

[1] Program of Post-Graduation in Production Engineering
Federal University of Santa Catarina,
Trindade, Florianópolis-SC, CEP 88040-000, Brazil
adilson.tiecher@bol.com.br
patricia@ijuris.org
[2] Instituto Jurídico de Inteligência e Sistemas – IJURIS
Trindade, Florianópolis, Brazil 88036-003
Tel: +55 48 3025-6609
digesto@digesto.net

Abstract. This article aims to present the Interlegis program developed by the Brazil National Congress, in association with Interamerican Development Bank (IDB), which is about modernization and Integration of the Legislative command, in its federal, state and municipal levels and about promotion of the transparency and interaction of this command with society. The ways used are the new information technologies (internet, videoconferences and data transmission), that allow communication and exchange of experiences between the legislative houses and legislators and between the legislative and the public, seeking to raise the participation of the people on the legislative process.

Keywords: Electronic government, legislative, information, communication, Internet, democracy and citizenship.

1 Introduction

The Interlegis program is a virtual network of communication where circulates information that integrates the Federal Senate, Deputy Chamber, Account Tribunal of the Union, Legislative assemblies, Municipal chambers and the citizen.

Its strategic priority is to enlarge and solidify the modernization process of the Legislative command, in order to improve communication and the information flow between legislators and increase public's participation and representation on the legislative process.

Today, more than 1500 municipal chambers have already received computers and printers from the Interlegis program to process information, connect to the internet and put their own information at the disposition of the citizens. The Senate, the Chamber, the tribunal and the assemblies, count with extremely useful rooms and with special rooms that are prepared to the realization of events like videoconferences, where legislators and the community can debate live issues of society's interest. It is Brazil's democracy getting better and modernizing.

R. Traunmüller (Ed.): EGOV 2003, LNCS 2739, pp. 75–78, 2003.
© Springer-Verlag Berlin Heidelberg 2003

2   The Interlegis Program Enlarges Citizenship

The idea of creating a virtual community of the Legislative command emerged among the technicians from the Federal Senate Computing and Data Process Center - Prodasen, in 1997.

In the year 2000, the Interamerican Development Bank – (IDB) started to lead resources to the program, that had already been approved in the year before at a total of US$ 25 million, with a Brazilian counterpart of US$ 25 million, seeking the establishment of an unpublished pilot project of modernization and strengthening of the Legislative Command, that involves the Deputy Chamber.

By mediation of computers connected to the internet and videoconference rooms, Interlegis Program provides education at distance, creates a communication channel among legislators of all levels, promotes democracy on the access to necessary information of the Legislative process performance, develops computing technology to support the modernization of the Legislative Command and is a powerful mean of connection between legislators and society.

The Interlegis program searches the Legislative Command modernization, using information technology to the establishment of the Legislative Virtual Community. Four action areas form it: technology (necessary structure to the development of initiatives that raise the quantity and quality of the information), information (researches of specific content to availability community in general), communication (carrying information to these groups) and education (development of citizenship and the promotion of the Legislative Command frames of ongoing capacitance).

Making use of information technologies, the parliamentarians will be connected to a world in which information, fast and efficient, is a primordial instrument in the attending of needs of a new citizen and a new society.

3   The Interlegis Portal is the Legislatives Virtual Community Center

At the Interlegis Portal (www.interlegis.gov.br) the parliamentarian will have an e-mail, allowing communication with all legislators in the country, disclosing law speeches and projects, searching information through all internet, make on-line researches in public data banks and participating of virtual discussions.

"Community", "Press", "Education", "Legislative Research", "Inspection", "Citizenship", "2002 Elections", "Judicial", "Legislative", "Executive", and "Public Utility" are the main areas of the portal. Besides, everyone will be able to participate on the chats' debates and discussions, forums and discussion lists. To the Legislative Virtual Community, there will be a restricted area, as in all portals, so information can be insert and registered and the program's internal data can be accessed.

Interlegis Portal allows the constant renovation of its information, on a decentralized way, encouraging community members to participate on the elaboration of its content. The used programs are called "free softwares" (Conectiva Linux), that means they're not black boxes, they can be used by anybody, with no cost. Besides, it was designed a plan that allows all community members to propose an inclusion of documents, information, news... The sites will be updated for all the community. A local editor selects the content of each Legislative assembly and Municipal chamber and a national editor does the global selection of what is going to be at the portal. It is informatics approximating the legislative community members and connecting them to society. The system is open and democratic, like the legislative itself.

Fig. 1 Interlegis site

4 The Interlegis Program Priorizes Education in Promotion of Citizenship

Since the beginning, the Interlegis program has been working to offer new learnings, recycling and improvement to parliamentarians, assessors and Legislative's civil servants and also to citizenship sectors linked to the legislative activity. Education is one of the main aspects of the program; Education at distance is the main method used in the program, but many courses appeal, also, to an encounter between coach and learner. There are some foreseen post graduation and capacitating courses, conferences, debates and availability of study or reference material.

The activities of the Interlegis Education Center Nucleus, in Brasília, are oriented to help the community members and citizens in general to acquire capacities that are necessary to a productive life in modern society, guiding itself by the idea of doing education as a double road between educators and learners. Inside these capacities, we detach the critical thinking, making decisions and problem solution.

Technologies
The technologies used are the internet and the videoconference and phone or fax service systems. A variety of medias are applied, as the CD-ROM. When necessary, will be utilized, printed materials and audio and video tapes.

Courses
It has already been developed and are ready to be fulfilled the following courses: "Interlegis education at distance", "The alderman's role", "Introduction to public budget" and "The search for quality".

5 Conclusion

Supporting Brazil's Legislative modernization process, in its Federal, State and Municipal instances, the Interlegis program searches the improvement of communication and the information flood between legislators and society, raising legislative houses efficiency and competency. Promoting the citizen participation on legislative processes.

When providing conditions to new society participation on legislative processes, Interlegis program is making the parliament work in a more transparent way, displaying every event to society. By acting this way, it is giving the citizen the possibility of participating more actively in the political process.

Today, the Interlegis program is present in more than 1500 Municipal Chambers, in all Legislative Assemblies, on the Account tribunal of the Union (ATU), on the Deputy Chamber and on the Federal Senate. It is an immense network that connects parliamentarians, assessors, civil servants and society, promoting information democracy through Internet and the National Interlegis Network-NIT.

References

1. www.governoeletronico.gov.br
2. www.interlegis.gov.br
3. www.redegoverno.gov.br

How to Grow? Online Consultation about Growth in the City of Hamburg: Methods, Techniques, Success Factors

Rolf Lührs, Steffen Albrecht, Maren Lübcke, and Birgit Hohberg

Technical University of Hamburg-Harburg
Department of Technology Assessment
Schwarzenbergstr. 95
21071 Hamburg, Germany
{r.luehrs,steffen.albrecht,maren.luebcke,b.hohberg}
@tu-harburg.de

Abstract. This paper is concerned with the online public engagement 'Leitbild Metropolis Hamburg – Growing City' which has been conducted in the context of the EU project DEMOS (Delphi Mediation Online System). The result of DEMOS is an innovative Internet platform facilitating democratic discussions and participative public opinion formation. The test of the DEMOS approach and the software system during the online discussion in the City of Hamburg was one of the most successful projects in electronic democracy or participation ever conducted on a municipal level. The paper introduces the DEMOS approach and system, describes the political background of the discussed 'Leitbild Growing City' and the results. The authors try to identify success factors for online public engagement projects.

1 Introduction

As Coleman and Gøtze stated in their latest report about online public engagement in policy deliberation, "almost all cases one finds are frustrated by the same two problems: too few people knew about them (and) governments fail to integrate them into the policy process or respond to them effectively" ([3, p. 35]). A recently conducted experiment in the City of Hamburg (Germany) seems to be an encouraging exception. In co-operation with DEMOS[1], the local government initiated an online consultation, asking their citizens to discuss the 'Leitbild Growing City'. The discussion was accompanied by intensive advertising and resulted in condensed ideas which were then evaluated by an expert jury and recommended to Hamburg's First Mayor for implementation. In the following section, the background of the discussion and its results will be described (2). Chapter three is concerned with a general evaluation taking a closer look at participation issues and moderation strategies (3). Finally, success factors for e-participation will be discussed (4).

---

[1] DEMOS (Delphi Mediation Online System) is a RTD project under the 5th Framework Programme of the EU (IST) and is being developed by a research consortium of eight organisations from five different countries. For more information see the project website: http://www.demos-project.org

R. Traunmüller (Ed.): EGOV 2003, LNCS 2739, pp. 79–84, 2003.

2 Online Public Engagement with DEMOS in Hamburg

Faced by the changing geographical situation in Europe after the falling of the eastern borders, the local government of Hamburg developed a concept called 'Growing City' to cope with an increasing competition among European cities. It comprises the following goals: increasing the number of inhabitants, increasing economic growth, improving the traffic situation, increasing available apartment and industrial areas, increasing the international attractiveness and awareness of Hamburg.

DEMOS was chosen for an online public engagement to discuss the implementation of the new 'Leitbild' and to communicate its goals. The DEMOS approach aims to powerfully support the public debate online. It consists of two complementary parts, the participation methodology and the technical platform.[2]

The DEMOS *technical platform* provides tools for helping the participants to break up into sub-groups (user management), conducting surveys and collaborating on joint statements (discourse management). One of its most important components is the graphical user interface (GUI), as it communicates the underlying concept of DEMOS to the users. It has to visualize complex functions like forums, libraries, news section, process overview, personal bookmarks and mails. All functions are served by a powerful backend system, build upon only mature, well-supported, and widely used technology.[3]

The *participation methodology* integrates different sociological methods in the so-called 'DEMOS process', which provides support for three phases of discussions: broadening, deepening and consolidating the discussion. Ideally, this structured discussion process leads to political consensus. In practice, participants may continue to disagree, but the reasons for the disagreement will have been made clear and comprehensible. The participation methodology is also concerned with questions of motivation and how to relate the discourse to the political process, e.g. identification of suitable subjects, adaptable rule systems to encourage active participation, addressing problems of result implementation.

To integrate the results of the online discussion into the policy process and to democratically legitimate them, it seemed sensible to stage the discussion as a contest of ideas. All participants could mutually propose, elaborate and evaluate their particular ideas in a discursive process. The ideas would be evaluated and six of them recommended to the senate for implementation. Thus, the democratically elected local government still determines the city's policy and at the same time opens up a modern way to participate in the political process for its citizens.

The results surpassed expectations. During the four weeks of discussion, 265 out of almost 540 participants who had registered for the discussion wrote ca. 3900 individual contributions. The debate was characterised by a constructive and creative atmosphere, by highly engaged participants and by clearly focused contributions. For the 'Leitbild' of a growing city, the debate produced one of the most detailed elaborations, resulting in 57 ideas extensively elaborated by the participants. In the meantime, the debate helped to make the new political scenario widely known among the citizens of Hamburg.

---

[2] For more information on DEMOS, see [7], [6].

[3] The technical system used by DEMOS is based on the Zeno system [5], which has been further developed in the course of the project.

3   Evaluation

An introspection into actual user behaviour reveals some interesting aspects that we see as characteristic for the online debate:

Attractiveness: Due to the public and anonymous character, we can only estimate the number of people who were following the debate with or without registering. During the four weeks of debate, the web server was logging almost 1.4 million page views and 33.740 visits – a huge number, indicating that the number of people following the debate greatly exceeds the number of 538 registered users.

Virtuality: It was often said that the Internet as a medium lets people come together independently from constraints of time and space. Our experiences confirm this assumption. Participants did not only join the debate from the city of Hamburg and its suburbs, but also from other German cities and from abroad – two former residents of Hamburg were participating with a lot of engagement from the United States. Another specific feature was the asynchronous mode of debate. Participants were using almost all times of the day to read or write contributions.

Attracting new targets: The experience with the debate in Hamburg shows that the use of the Internet as a medium for political debate opens the way to reach new target groups, especially young people (16-30) who are typically bored by traditional politics. Politicians say they find it very difficult to reach this target, yet it was prominently represented in the online forum (15,7% of the participants were between 19 and 26 years old according to our user survey, which matches exactly with the Hamburg population). Obviously, discussing via a web-based platform is a form of political participation that is attractive even to young people. On the other hand, older people have not abstained from the debate (28,6% of the participants were older than 40).

Drawing participants in: Attracting citizens to participate is not all. The crucial point is to draw the visitors into the debate and to encourage them to return and engage in a mutual exchange. A look at the number of messages posted gives a good idea of what happened in the debate. In the first week, although the number of active participants was small, more than 1100 contributions were written. This seemed to be the critical mass of contributions needed to get the debate running. Among those who contributed, we can observe the evolution of a real community of users. Most users in DEMOS wrote two to five contributions (31,3%), and a relatively large number of users wrote more than 20 contributions (12,3%). This shows that DEMOS was able to foster sustained participation in contrast to the ad hoc manner of discussion that can be observed in most online (and perhaps even offline) debates.

Interactivity: A plausible reason for the community-building aspect is the interactivity of the debate [10]. Only 273 of all 799 new contributions (i.e., contributions that started a thread) received no reply at all. Almost 80% of all contributions were part of threads with more than three contributions, with an average length of 4,89 contributions per thread (max. 51 contributions). Thus, a participant could reasonably count on stimulating response when he started a new thread. The debate in most times was very lively. In average, a contribution received a reply after one and a half days (and almost half of the contributions received a reply after less than seven hours), so that participants were motivated to check for new contributions every day. Thus, the exchange of opinions was very fast. However, the participants also exploited the advantages of an asynchronous debate and did not ignore older contributions. The dual character of a highly dynamic, yet thorough discourse can be attributed to the task of moderation, that served to keep the large-scale (and thus dynamic) debate clearly structured, and that helped to involve participants more deeply by reacting to their questions in very short time, for instance.

User satisfaction: The participants' experiences with and reactions to the DEMOS forum were overwhelmingly positive, as the answers to a survey, conducted immediately after the trial, show.[4] Asked about their satisfaction with the debate, the majority of participants gives a positive vote. No respondent was in full opposition to the experiment, and a vast majority of 97% said they would likely be participating in future online debates. In comparison to other means of taking part in the political discussion in Hamburg, more than 75% of the respondents consider the DEMOS debate to be better.

Another unequivocal result of the survey was that many respondents were praising the effort of *moderation*[5], which had to be adapted to the case of an open online discourse with large numbers of potentially anonymous participants. The mediating of conflicts in this case was of minor importance.[6] The users appreciated that the debate was summarised regularly, that the moderators reacted promptly in cases of questions as well as conflicts, and simply that someone was there who took care. Thus, we can conclude that the constant attention of the moderation team was a key factor in fostering a serious and sustained debate.

Regarding the moderation, the trial exposed a remarkable trait: as if one only has to show a continuous supervision of mindful moderators, the participants in Hamburg did not misbehave seriously, but acted unexpectedly politely and respectfully, whereas in other forums, people tend to disturb the discussion in manifold ways. In correspondence to the strong community that evolved during the debate, the users showed a very high rate of self-criticism and self-regulation. Some of them never even gave up looking for more and more material (i.e. photographs, articles, scientific sources) to support their own suggestions or even the ideas of someone else. Accordingly, the moderators were mostly involved with helping and informing the participants instead of sanctioning them.[7] Though, most violations of rules the moderators had to deal with were done late at night when some participants became too heated, tried to overrun their opponents[8] or suggested ideas that were hardly acceptable. As it had to be expected, different interest groups used the discussion to foster their specific issues. Not all of them were interested in constructive debate. But as their attempts were too obviously selfish, the users ignored or even criticised them. Hence, moderators and users – co-operating tightly towards a goal-oriented debate – were able to stabilise the discourse.

---

[4] 70 participants answered to the survey. The answers are not representative in a strong statistical sense, however, they confirm the overall tendency observed by the moderators.

[5] The moderators were Hans Hagedorn, Birgit Hohberg, Oliver Märker and Matthias Trenél.

[6] Moderation is indispensable to stimulate the discussion and to keep it focused, to assure compliance with the rules, and to provide the participants with regular edited summaries, to mention just the most important aspects (cf. [8]). In contrast, mediation serves to resolve conflicts and to keep the debate from running into deadlocks. For more information, see [6].

[7] Just three times they showed a "yellow card". No user had to be excluded from the discussion platform.

[8] By using inadequate generalizations, overstatements or irony without making it unmistakable.

In general the moderators used two different ways to communicate with the users: messages in the forum (one-to-all-communication) and messages in the personal area or emails (one-to-one-communication). The strategy of the moderators was to intervene as early as possible. Nearly all messages concerning violations of rules were sent by email instead of posting them into the forum, in order to not disturb the constructive discussion. Almost all of the admonished participants acted insightfully and changed their behaviour after such an intervention.[9]

4 Success Factors for E-Participation: Marketing, Governmental Responsiveness, and Rewards

Finally, we want to take a closer look at the success factors for e-participation: First, the integration in the political context in Hamburg was crucial for the success: Hamburg's government took its responsibility serious and is about to implement the respective concepts.[10] The concept 'contest of best ideas' allowed to deal with a dilemma of direct participation in representative democracies: To assure a political impact for public engagement without questioning the political leadership of the democratically elected senate. Finally, PR and advertisement measurements including interviews of Hamburg's First Mayor with newspapers and local TV programs took place.[11]

From the experience within the DEMOS project we can further conclude that potential participants can be attracted and kept involved once they have visited the website, if the e-participation appears rewarding in at least three different regards:

1. The involvement in the debate must have a potential impact on the real life politics.
2. The software system and the GUI have to be rewarding in that the usage will lead to immediate and enjoyable results (instant reward).

3. The communication has to be interactively rewarding. There must be a considerable probability that the individual communication acts will be perceived and answered by other community members.

Compared with what has been achieved in Europe in the domain of online public engagement (e-democracy, e-participation) so far, the trial in Hamburg was successful and the DEMOS concept could be proved. But it also shows how much effort is required to get citizens to deliberate political issues on the Internet. People are still not used to this communication channel in the context of political engagement, nor are public administrations or local governments. Two years ago Coleman and Gøtze came to the conclusion that online participation is still in its infancy, after having reviewed all documented cases in Europe [3]. With respect to the trial described in this paper

---

[9] While some earlier experiments report that moderation is frequently experienced as censorship [4], this was hardly an issue in the DEMOS discussion. Just a few persons expressed their feeling of being misunderstood.

[10] For each concept, a responsible civil servant and a time frame have been indicated. Furthermore, responsible persons from different departments were engaged in the discussion.

[11] 25000 flyers and more than 1250 posters were exhibited all over Hamburg, complemented by online advertisements.

and to some recently conducted online discussions[12], especially in the U.S., we can say that online public engagement has in the meantime entered its adolescence.

References

1. Beierle, T.C.: Democracy On-line. An Evaluation of the National Dialogue on Public Involvement in EPA Decisions. RFF Report (2002). Available at www.rff.org
2. Blakeley, E., et al.: Listening to the City. Report of Proceedings. New York (2002). Available at www.weblab.org/ltc/LTC_Report.pdf
3. Coleman, S., Gøtze, J.: Bowling Together: Online Public Engagement in Policy Deliberation. The Hansard Society, London (2001)
4. Dutton, W.H.: Network Rules of Order: Regulating Speech in Public Electronic Fora. Media, Culture & Society 18 (1996) 269-290
5. Gordon, T.F., Richter, G.: Discourse Support Systems for Deliberative Democracy. In: Traunmüller, R., Lenk, K. (eds.): Electronic Government. Proc. EGOV 2002, Aix-en-Provence, France, September 2-5. Springer Verlag, Berlin, Heidelberg, New York (2002) 248–255
6. Hohberg, B., Luehrs, R.: Offline Online Inline. Zur Strukturierung Internetvermittelter Diskurse. In: Märker, O., Trenel, M. (eds.): Online-Mediation. Edition Sigma, Berlin (2003)
7. Luehrs, R., Malsch, T., Voss, K.: Internet, Discourses and Democracy. In: Terano, T. et al. (eds.): New Frontiers in Artificial Intelligence. Joint JSAI 2001 Workshop Post-Proceedings. Springer-Verlag, Berlin, Heidelberg, New York (2001) 67–74
8. Märker, O. et al.: Internet-Based Citizen Participation in the City of Esslingen. Relevance – Moderation – Software. In: Schrenk, M. (Ed.): Who Plans Europe's Future? CORP 2002. Technical University of Vienna (2002) 39–45
9. McKinsey: Hamburg Vision 2020. Vom nationalen Zentrum zur europäischen Metropole. Hamburg (2001)
10. Rafaeli, S.: Interactivity: From New Media to Communication. In: Hawkins, R.P., Wiemann, J.M., Pingree, S. (eds.): Advancing Communication Science: Merging Mass and Interpersonal Processes. Sage, Newbury Park (1988) 110–134

---

[12] See e.g. the National Dialogue on Public Involvement in EPA Decisions [0] or the online public engagement "Listening to the City" in New York [0].

Super Pilots, Subsidizing or Self-Organization: Stimulating E-Government Initiatives in Dutch Local Governments

Marcel Hoogwout

Department of Business, Public Administration and Technology (BBT)
University Twente
PO box 217, 7500 AE Enschede, The Netherlands
m.hoogwout@utwente.nl

Abstract. Like many other western countries, the Dutch central government has several programs to stimulate E-government development in local governments. The constitutional relations between central and local governments in The Netherlands, however, are such, that the development of online service delivery is part of the autonomy of the local authorities. Central government has little formal authority to command development efforts on a local level. Through a PR-offensive, subsidy programs and intervening as a market party, the central government tries to convince the local authorities to invest in the development of online service delivery. This paper describes three different approaches used by the Dutch central government to stimulate E-government initiatives in local governments. The central question is to what extent each approach contributes to the e-government aims of central government.

1 Introduction

In line with the e-Europe program of the European Commission (DGXII, Information Society) the Dutch central government also has formulated high aims to stimulate e-government (BZK 2000). These aims include to: get all local governments online by the end of 2002, have 75% of all services online in 2006, have 5 million citizens with electronic identity cards in 2006, decrease the administrative burden for companies with 25% in 2006, have online interactive policy development (E-democracy) commonly accepted in 2006 and increase productivity of public administrations with 10%. In the Dutch system, local governments account for approximately 70% of all government service transactions. It is therefore crucial to convince them to get their services online. The past years large sums of taxpayers' money have been allocated to realize the high aims. Example programs are Public Counter 2000 (OL2000), Electronic Government under Construction (ELO) and Knowledge Neighborhoods. The results of these programs are questionable. Even in 2003, only a few local governments offer limited online interactive services. The Netherlands is losing its position as a frontrunner in innovative and service oriented government. Even though much can be said about the soundness of the reports that compare the e-government positions of different countries, in the Netherlands it is generally accepted that the Dutch competitive advantage is changing for the worse. The pace in which Dutch governments can develop and adapt new internet technologies seems to have reached

R. Traunmüller (Ed.): EGOV 2003, LNCS 2739, pp. 85–90, 2003.

its limits. Three groups of causes can be distinguished to explain the limited progress in local government (Kraaijenbrink 2002): (1) Local governments are *not allowed* to deliver services through the internet. Legal constraints pertaining to, for example, online identification forbid them to accept online applications as legally binding. (2) Local governments are *not able* to do so. This is caused by a lack of budget, and/or knowledge. (3) Local governments are *not willing* to invest in e-government projects, even if they have the means. The local government system lacks the right incentives that are necessary to create a sense of urgency. Dutch central government tries to overcome these constraints in different ways. Three of them are discussed in this paper: The 'Super pilots' case is an example of straightforward subsidizing of some promising initiatives. In the super pilots project three city authorities have received considerable subsidies to build electronic counters for all transaction services. In a second approach, the central government developed an internet application, the 'VIND-catalogue' ('FIND'-catalogue), containing descriptions of all services local governments can offer. They offered the catalogue module free of charge to all 496 Dutch local governments. The third approach is the joint development of an internet interaction module by a group of cooperating local governments. This module enables citizens to track and trace the status of their building permit application online. In the next paragraphs these approaches will be described and analyzed. The primal focus will be on the effectiveness of each approach for the distribution of innovative E-Government solutions among local governments.

2 The Super Pilots

In March 2001, the Dutch Ministry of the Interior started a program that offered the cities of Enschede, The Hague and Eindhoven a sum of   2.8 mln. each to build functionally rich online electronic counters for local government services. In return for this financial support, these cities are obliged to publish the blueprints of their designs. The aim of this openness is to promote other local authorities to use these blueprints for designing and building their own electronic public counters. Also, commercial software developers can use the blueprints free of charge to develop their own standardized solutions to be sold to other local governments. The Ministry of the Interior hopes that the example set by the pilot cities and the free blueprints will stimulate the use of e-government solutions by local governments.

The main objection to this approach, typical for subsidizing pilot projects, is that the results are still very hard to copy by other governments. The solutions that are translated into blueprints, are tailored to the circumstances typical for only one local authority. Other local governments can only copy or take over a complete solution, if they are prepared to invest considerable amounts of efforts and resources into tailoring it to their situation. They still have to take the blueprints to their own software developer to build the plan. They still have to adjust the plan to their own processes and infrastructures. The reduction in development and implementation costs is very limited compared to the costs that still have to be made. As for the commercial software developers, who can use the blueprints for free, the risk of the development of their own commercial solution has diminished only slightly. Although the super pilot program is still not finished, the chances of a wide spread of the solutions developed by the three super pilot cities seem already very limited.

3   The VIND-Catalogue

One of the initiatives of the OL2000 Program Office, the Dutch government initiative to stimulate service oriented government, is a project called the 'VIND-Catalogue'. A project has been tendered to create a digital catalogue with information on all local government products and services. The catalogue is a product that can be incorporated in each local authority's website. It should be adjustable to the local offering of products and services. Citizens can consult the catalogue online for questions like, what services do I need, what procedure should be followed and which forms do I need to fill in. The catalogue is designed to determine which products and services are applicable to the citizen's specific situation. Because most local governments offer the same set of products and services (Leenes and Svensson 2002) the VIND-catalogue comes with a centralized content management solution. An editor, related to the association of local authorities, guarantees regular updates in return for a subscription fee. To introduce the VIND-catalogue in their local community, local governments could apply for a subsidy. This not only made the acquisition of the catalogue free of charge, but also generated direct financial benefits for them by acquiring it. This associated subsidy program contributed substantially to the success of the introduction of the catalogue in Dutch local governments.

The OL2000 Program Office, acting on behalf of the Ministry of Internal Affairs, has chosen to have the catalogue developed, instead of leaving the development, implementation and adoption to the market. By doing so, it purposely neglected the fact that several commercial software companies already offered a comparable product to local governments. There already was a market for this kind of product, although still immature. The Program Office even, for a while, negotiated with one of the suppliers to buy the rights of one of the existing products. However, since no acceptable price could be agreed upon, the Program Office decided to fund the development of a new catalogue.

The free of charge offering of the VIND-catalogue stirred up the discussion about the role of government in the marketplace. The investments in product development by the commercial software developers, who had already developed a catalogue solution, became instantly worthless. Something, that –obviously- did not amuse these developers. The question was raised if central government did not complicate matters by intervening in the market the way they did. The eagerness for software developers to invest in the development of e-government solutions for local governments could be extinguished for a long time. The chance that central government would repeat this kind of market intervention and, by doing so, destroy the initial investments could not be neglected anymore. A reluctant supply side in the market of e-government solutions increases the necessity for central government to intervene. This could provoke a negative spiral of events that could make the adoption of e-government applications in local government more difficult.

In 2000 the Nobel Price winner Joseph Stiglitz and his associates published a noteworthy report on this issue for the American based Computer & Communications Industry Association (CCIA) (Stiglitz, Orszag et al. 2000). Based on the current knowledge about market oriented economies, Stiglitz states three sets of principles for governments to determine if government intervention is opportune: green light principles (activities which governments should undertake with little concern), yellow light principles (activities which governments should undertake with caution) and red light principles (activities which governments generally should not undertake). The relevant principles in the VIND-catalogue case are: principle 1: providing public data and information is a proper governmental role (green light), principle 4: governments should exercise caution in adding specialized values to public data and information (yellow light) and principle 10: the governments should exercise substantial caution in entering markets in which private-sector firms are active (red light) The Dutch economy shares the basic neo liberal assumptions with the American economy. The Stiglitz principles could therefore be considered appropriate for the Dutch situation as well. Although the VIND-catalogue aims at providing public data and information (principle 1), the product adds value to this information by providing a complex search engine (principle 4), in a market where private firms are active with competitive products (principle 10). The VIND-catalogue approach conflicts with at least two of the principles. The VIND-catalogue, as a software product, does not fit one of the two critical properties for a public good. Although it can be considered as non-rivalrous, due to low reproduction cost, it is definitely excludable. So, also current economic theory suggests a less intervening role for central government in the VIND-catalogue approach.

4   The Track-and-Trace Module for Building Permits

A completely different approach was followed by a group of cooperating local government on the subject of building permit applications. This group is organized in a platform (Platform Bouw en Woningtoezicht Grote Gemeenten) and consists of the department heads of the 34 largest building permit departments in the Netherlands. This group was agitated by the fact that there are too few suppliers for innovative e-government solutions in the field of building permit service delivery. Together they developed a 'program of demands' for an internet module that should make it possible for citizens to track and trace the status of their building permit application online. The application for a (normal) building permit legally can take up to thirteen weeks in which the application has to pass several different tests. Each test can cause a change in the status of the application. The group used the program of demands to agree upon a protocol for information exchange between the two main suppliers of back office systems for building permits and developers of front office / internet modules. With this protocol in hand, and the guarantee that nine building permit departments would buy the product instantly, the two main suppliers each developed, for their own account and own risk, a version of a internet status information module. Now all departments can choose from at least three different products to disclose the information about application status in their back office systems. Central government subsidized the initiative with a small financial gesture at the end of the project to emphasize their appreciation of the approach and the cooperation between the building permit departments. The approach used by the building permit departments has several important advantages: (1) The development is demand driven instead of supply driven. It is fulfilling a need of the departments. (2) The dependency on the supplier that also has developed their back office system has been diminished. One can choose between several suppliers regardless of the brand of back office system that one is using. (3) The so called lock-in effect, the dependency on the one supplier that provided the main workflow systems, disappeared. (4) The approach was also interesting and profitable for the suppliers. The guarantee from a group of departments to buy the modules, was enough for them to invest in the development. The approach followed by the building permit departments also has disadvantages. Because of the cooperation construction and the multi party negotiations between several departments and suppliers, the process took a considerable amount of time. The lack of a central director reduced the incentives for the involved parties to deliver as soon as possible. The question whether this approach would work in other situations as well still stands.

5 Lessons Learned

The three different approaches towards e-government stimulation in local authorities, described in this article, are typical for a government that does not want to use hierarchical means to enforce the distribution of e-government innovations. The Dutch government did not -and still does not- want to interfere in the autonomy of the local authorities. Therefore a policy of facilitation and stimulation using only positive incentives is used to interest local authorities to invest in e-government solutions. The three approaches discussed in this chapter show this policy to be effective only in specific situations. What can we learn from this? The question how, and up to what extent, central governments should stimulate the use of innovations is a classical dilemma. In the case of the use of e-government solutions by local authorities we encounter two dominant dimensions that seem to determine the effectiveness of an approach.

First is the dimension of the stage of the innovation process. An approach can be effective in one stage while it seems to be useless in another. Stages that can be observed in the three Dutch cases are (1) the development of the new e-government technology, (2) the testing of the technology, (3) creating awareness for the new technology and (4) the distribution of the technology. The three cases in this article have been measured by their effectiveness in the last stage of the innovation process, the distribution of the technology over a large as possible group of local authorities. The super pilot approach is in this comparison the least attractive way to stimulate the distribution of e-government innovations by central government (i.e. the forth stage). The considerable costs of the approach only suits a very limited group of local governments and suppliers, while the chances of further adoption of the developed solutions are expected to be limited. The most important value of this approach is the awareness effect, the ability to interest other local governments in the possibilities of e-government (the third stage). Considering the costs of the super pilots the question can be raised if the same effects can be reached in a -for the tax payer- less expensive way. Both other approaches seem to build their success on the characteristics of the innovation at hand. They cannot be considered to be a first stage project. No existing primary processes had to be changed and no existing back office systems had to be replaced. The added value of both approaches towards e-government stimulation on a large scale is for that reason not certain.

The second dimension, that is highly relevant for the use and the effectiveness of the different approaches concerns the market characteristics. Are there enough local authorities that are willing to use the innovation? And, are there enough suppliers willing to take the risk to develop these solutions and to offer them to the local authorities for reasonable prices? If demand is evident but suppliers don't dare to take the risk of developing the right product, an approach as applied by the Dutch building permit departments, seems to be appropriate. If there are suppliers that only reach a small group of local authorities, further investigation of the demand side is desired: a subsidizing program, like the one that supported the VIND-catalogue, can be helpful if local authorities are willing to innovate, but have a financing problem, which prevents them from doing the right thing. Introducing an information standard or certification instrument can provide certainty if the risk of a dependency on one specific technology or supplier is too high. The building permit departments followed this approach. If the local authorities are unaware of the technology, pilot projects might offer a solution. If neither demand nor supply are interested in a specific e-government innovation, central government has a difficult choice. It may be wise to reconsider the need for the e-government innovation. The development of a local government e-government solution by central government - the way this is done in the case of the VIND-catalogue - is only worth considering in a situation where central government has ponderous arguments to thrive for the adoption of the innovation by a large group of local authorities. The Stiglitz principles for government intervention 'in a digital age' can be a useful tool to decide upon the type of innovation stimulation one should apply.

References

1. BZK (2000). Contract met de toekomst. Den Haag, Ministerie van Binnenlandse Zaken en Koninkrijksrelaties.
2. Kraaijenbrink, J. (2002). De lange weg: een onderzoek naar knelpunten bij interorganisationele samenwerking rond geïntegreerde loketten. Enschede, Univ. Twente.
3. Leenes, R.E., and J.S. Svensson. "Size matters – electronic service delivery by municipalities?" In Electronic government – first international conference, egov 2002, Aix-en-Provcence, France, ed. R. Traunmüller, K. Lenk, 150–156. Heidelberg: Springer, 2002.
4. Stiglitz, J.E., P.R. Orszag, et al. (2000). The role of government in a digital age, Computer & Communications Industry Association (CCIA).

Socio-technical Perspectives on E-Government Initiatives

Maddalena Sorrentino[1] and Francesco Virili[2]

[1] Dipartimento di Studi sociali e politici
Università degli Studi
Milano, Italy
maddalena.sorrentino@unimi.it
[2] Dipartimento Impresa e Lavoro
Università di Cassino
Italy
francesco.virili@eco.unicas.it

Abstract. ICTs are intended to be a powerful tool in support of government transition to the "Digital Age". The purpose of this paper is to emphasize the importance of integrating a socio-technical perspective into the body of eGovernment practices. The current realisation in Italy of an "Action plan for eGovernment" is a source of interesting preliminary evidence for our purpose.

1   Standard (Tool) Model vs. Socio-technical Model

In a highly relevant paper Kling and Lamb [5] observe that most IS projects are typically described in terms of what they refer to as the 'Standard (Tool) Model'.

In terms of this model, ICTs are often discussed as tools or simple appliances, even when they take the form of complex arrangements of varied equipment and rules/roles/resources [6]. Among other things, the Standard Model assumes that information systems are objective and rational, and thus, capable of being evaluated through the use of objective tools and techniques. Moreover, this model presupposes a one-shot implementation and assumes that an IT application has the same meaning and consequences for all users ("contexts are simple"). Finally, ICTs are expected to have direct and unambiguous effects.

As opposed to the Standard Model, the authors propose the adoption of the "Socio-Technical Model", in which IS projects outcomes are the result of a more complex interaction between technical and societal factors.

Is the Standard Model view still valid after thirty years of systematic, empirically grounded research on ICT and organisational change in business firms and public agencies? Kling and Lamb suggest not. It is widely acknowledged that ICTs and the social and organizational settings in which they are embedded are in a relationship of mutual shaping.

The Standard Model is simplistic and insufficient for adequately understanding the character of organisational change involving ICTs. In the opinion of Kling and Lamb, ICT-related innovation should be seen as an on-going social process that unfolds in the context of complex, negotiated relationships. A 'socially rich view' (i.e. based on socio-technical assumptions) seems to better conceptualise the role of ICT in the

R. Traunmüller (Ed.): EGOV 2003, LNCS 2739, pp. 91–94, 2003.

Table 1. Key differences between Standard (Tool) Model and Socio-technical Model ([5]).

Standard (Tool) Model	Socio-Technical Model
IT is a tool	IT is a socio-technical system
Business model is sufficient	Ecological view is needed
One-shot implementation	Implementation is an ongoing social process
Technological effects are direct and immediate	Technological effects are indirect and involve different time scales
Incentives to change are unproblematic	Incentives may require restructuring (and may be in conflict with other organizational actions)
Politics are bad or irrelevant	Politics are central and even enabling
IT infrastructure is fully supportive. Systems have become user-friendly, people have become 'computer literate' and these changes are accelerating with the "net generation"	Articulation work is often needed to make IT work. Socio-technical support is critical for effective IT use
Social relationships are easily reformed to take advantage of new conveniences, efficiencies and business value	Relationships are complex, negotiated and multivalent
Social effects of IT are big/extensive but isolated and benign	Potentially enormous social repercussions from IT
Contexts are simple (described by a few key terms or demographics)	Contexts are complex (matrices of businesses, services, people, technology history, location, etc.)
Knowledge and expertise are easily made explicit	Knowledge and expertise are inherently tacit/implicit
IT infrastructure is fully supportive	Articulation needed to make IT work

current e-business environment. The Socio-Technical Model takes into consideration important factors such as the social and organizational context of the technologies and the people who use them. Table 1 depicts some of the key characteristics of the two models.

2   Analysis and Conclusions: Adopting a Socio-technical Approach

In the context of public organisations "we cannot assume that any restructuring that may occur as a result of IT implementation is beneficial to performance"[4].

If we take into examination the Italian eGovernment Action Plan [3, 8], two questions may now arise: are we sure that the financial effort recently expended by the Italian government will lead to the expected outcomes? To what extent have socio-technical considerations been taken into account by the Ministry of Innovation?

In order to provide answers to these questions, we draw attention to the Italian Action Plan and its set of evaluation criteria adopted by the Government to select eGovernment projects for co-financing. Our aim is to understand what perspective, the Standard (Tool) or the Socio-technical Model, predominates in the plan. The criteria listed in Table 1 will be viewed in terms of the basic assumptions of the two models as outlined by Kling and Lamb; in our analysis we would take into account also aspects and issues typical of Public Management Information Systems as stated. For example, in [2].

Table 2. Evaluation criteria for eGov projects proposals (Italian eGovernment Action Plan, [8]).

Criteria	Score
1. Consistency with the objectives of local Territorial Plan	10
2. Quality of the proponent, in terms of: dimensions (internal staff and number of constituents); number of public bodies involved in the initiative; available IT and organizational resources; past experience and specific competencies in the field; financial commitment	35
3. Quality of the project, in terms of use of specific methods for project management and for analysis of user requirements	10
4. Overall quality of the proposed solution (compliance with specifications stated in Attachments; potential impact of on-line services to be developed; level of interactivity and accessibility; kind of technology tools employed; number and variety of delivery channels; long-term financial and administrative feasibility	35
5. Possibility of replicating the same experience in other contexts (portability and scalability of the project across public administration bodies)	10

1. *Consistency with the objectives of local Territorial Plan.* The scale and scope of the project should be consistent with the surrounding environment. This criterion does not imply the predominance of a particular view or belief.

2. *Quality of the proponent.* The fundamental factor is that the organisation in question should be in compliance with a series of "objective" parameters relating to staff, IT resources and operations, current application portfolio. Although it reveals an element of technological determinism, this criterion does not involve a recognition of the social, political and organizational dimensions of software projects. *Predominant view: Standard Model.*

3. *Quality of the project.* The gauge used to measure the quality of proposals is the extent to which appropriate methodologies are utilised in order to support the management of the project and to analyse user requirements. *Predominant view: Standard Model.*

4. *Overall quality of the proposed solution.* Again, the parameters adopted to measure quality involve merely formal methods of evaluation. It is assumed that the use of the "right" techniques (e.g. Web services) necessarily leads to "good" final solutions/outcomes. Users are considered as a sort of "variable" to be controlled; the involvement of them is confined to the post-implementation evaluation phase (the goal is to assess user satisfaction). Apart of deterministic considerations, it should be noted that "success or failure of development efforts cannot be attributed exclusively to the use, misuse or non-use of methodologies" ([1]). *Predominant view: Standard Model*

5. *Possibility of replicating the same experience in other contexts.* Here we may observe that (i) the level of portability of the proposed solution (i.e. the ability to transfer a particular application from one administration to another with minimal adjustments) is assessed only with reference to technical features, such as the use of open software and the utilization of standard components; and (ii) there is no recognition of the difficulty of transferring knowledge and expertise from one context to another. Both considerations lead us to suggest that this last criterion too is consistent with the Standard Model view, which implicitly assumes that an IT-

based solution is interchangeable, has the same meanings for all who use it and is expected to have similar consequences for all. *Predominant view: Standard Model.*

This brief review of the Italian Action Plan evaluation criteria reveals that they have been conceived almost wholly in terms of the Standard (Tool) Model. In such a conception a range of fundamental flows is dramatically evident. Perhaps the most important inadequacy is the about total failure to take into consideration the crucial social factors inherent to any form of technological development.

The failure of the evaluation criteria to envisage a serious process of feed-back stands as perhaps the clearest testimony to their neglect of the social factor. As [5] (pp. 19–20) put it: "a socially rich view (...) can help policy makers and practitioners anticipate some of the key organizational shifts that accompany introductions of new technologies".

In summary, the review has shown that project assessment has largely been based on an objective/rational grounding, very close to the Standard (Tool) Model of Kling and Lamb. We have tried to demonstrate that this view is incomplete and has called for additional efforts to systematically consider social factors as suggested in the Socio-technical Model.

Socio-technical principles provide an effective conceptual and theoretical framework for explaining why a lack of consideration of the possible effects of an IT initiative on the social system of an organisation might lead to sub-optimal IT investment evaluations.

The major limitation of our findings is that they have not been empirically tested. A longitudinal study designed to systematically analyse the 98 projects approved by the Italian government would provide a significant contribution to the further development of our research work.

References

1. Avison D. and Fitzgerald G., 2003, Where now for development methodologies?, Communication of the ACM, vol. 46, n. 1, January.
2. Bozeman B. and Bretschneider S., 1986, Public Management Information Systems: theory and prescription, Public Administration Review, n. 46, Special Issue.
3. EITO, 2002, European Information Technology Observatory 2002, Frankfurt am Main.
4. Heintze T. and Bretschneider S., 2000, IT and restructuring in public organizations: does adoption of IT affect organizational structures, communications. and decision making? Journal of Public Administration Research & Theory, vol. 10, Issue 4.
5. Kling R. and Lamb R., 1999, IT and Organizational change in digital economies: a socio-technical approach, Computer and Society, vol. 29, n. 3, September.
6. Kling R., 1999, What is Social informatics and why does it matter?, D-Lib Magazine, Vol. 5, n. 1.
7. Turban E. – McLean E. – Wetherbe J., 2002, Information Technology for management, Wiley, New York.
8. Virili, F., The Italian e-Government Action Plan: from Gaining Efficiency to Rethinking Goverment. Proceedings of DEXA 2001 International Workshop on e-Government, Munich 2001.

From Legacy to Modularity: A Roadmap Towards Modular Architectures Using Web Services Technology

Marijn Janssen and René Wagenaar

School of Technology, Policy and Management
Delft University of Technology
Jaffalaan 5, NL-2600 GA, Delft, The Netherlands
{MarijnJ,Renew}@tbm.tudelft.nl

Abstract. The principle of modularity is more and more applied in the engineering of information systems in e-government. Initiatives are confronted with a highly fragmented ICT-architecture that has been organized around departments and do not or hardly share functionality. A modular architecture can provide common functionality to all information systems and provide the flexibility to include functionality provided by legacy systems, which cannot be replaced easily and otherwise restrict further development. The goal of this paper is to explore the road towards a modular architecture. A case study is committed at the Ministry of Justice to illustrate and evaluate the first steps on this road. Based on this experience we identify the next steps towards market-based modular services architecture.

1 Introduction

A modular approach to information systems engineering has become more popular in recent years. The basic idea to break a system down into parts, designing the parts individually and constructing a new system using the single modules. The modular paradigm focuses on building information systems by discovering, matching and integrating pre-developed modules. A module can function independently of other components and communicate using well-defined, standardized interfaces. The manageability increases as large modules can thus be constructed from smaller components. In essence, a complex problem is split up into smaller problems, which can be solved independently. Openness and flexibility is created as new modules can be added and removed from the architecture and each single module can be replaced by another component without affecting the others. Modular architectures leverage investments in legacy systems running the enterprise's key business-critical applications [1]. Modularity should have three major advantages [4]. It increases the range of manageable complexity, allows different parts of a large system to be worked on concurrently and accommodates uncertainty. The principle of modularity can exist on several architecture levels, including business, process, functionality, application and technical infrastructure level. [2]

Modularity is often associated with the new paradigm of web-services. With web-services, functionality can be package up as web-services and assessed using a

R. Traunmüller (Ed.): EGOV 2003, LNCS 2739, pp. 95–100, 2003.

request-response protocol. The services-oriented paradigm offers many benefits to enterprises, and the creation of a class of enterprise services allows us to create services that are modular, accessible, well-described, implementation-independent and interoperable [6]. Modules can be found, described, discovered, and integrated using web-services technology. Service-based paradigms are becoming more important in today's design of information systems. Service oriented business integration enables the on demand composition of new business processes using already existing services possibly provided by other parties. In service-based applications, services are configured to meet a specific set of requirements at a certain point in time, executed and then disengaged. Services only 'exist' during execution, modules provide services.

For web services technology a few basic standards have been established like HTTP, XML, XSLT, XSL Schemas, SOAP, UDDI and WSDL. Although the basic protocols have been set and the concept of modularity has great promises, its application still stays far behind. Most organizations are relatively slow in adapting modular approaches as they lack sufficient insight into the pros and cons of such an approach and there is no supporting for decision-making about possible ways to implement a modular architecture [5].

The *goal* of this paper is to explore the road towards a modular architecture. In the following section a case study will be presented where some existing functionality of legacy systems has been replaced using a modular architecture. Based on the experiences gained in this case study shortcomings of the application of current technology are identified. In the following section a future scenario is discussed and in the last section conclusions on the road towards a modular architecture are drawn.

2 Case: Ministry of Justice

The Ministry of Justice in the Netherlands has more than 14000 employees working in the colleges of judges and public prosecutors. There are 19 County Courts, 5 Courts and 1 Supreme Court and three types of law: civil, public administration and criminal. Apart from standard office automation, each type of court and type of law are using different information systems. There are 22 heterogeneous types of information systems, having overlap in functionality and each having an own control and maintenance team. In total more than 250 FTE are involved in maintenance and control the systems.

Currently a large project called GPS is initiated to replace a large and complex legacy system (COMPASS) in the criminal law using innovative technologies. GPS consist of several projects, one is a pilot project aimed at verifying the concepts of modularity discussed in the preceding section and to explore the opportunities and limitations coming from the application of readily available technology. Document generation was taken as functionality to include in a module, as *all* existing information systems within the Ministry of Justice have to generate and print documents in some way or another.

Requirement elicitation of document generation was executed using interviews and analysis of existing applications. The current functionality of the information systems and the organizational characteristics were taking as a starting point for the requirement elicitation. The general requirements are summarized hereafter.

- Documents should be generated using a static and dynamic part. The static part is the body of the document containing the position of dynamic data, layout, logo's. Elements of the static part can be filled with dynamic data like name, address etc.;
- Dynamic data should be extracted from current and future databases;
- Documents like summons that seem to be similar on the first sight, are different for each court. As there are in total 25 courts (1 supreme court, 5 high courts and 19 courts), content managers in a court should be able to update the content of the static part of a document;
- Roughly speaking two types of documents should be created. The first type is incidentally created by users and is immediately needed. The other type of document is created automatically by the system based on the progress and status of cases. Often these documents are generated at night and include large volumes;
- Documents should be preserved, as they might be needed for evidence. It should also be possible to generate documents that can be changed by court employees before printing;
- There should be one single point where the document generator is developed, controlled and maintained in a technical sense;
- A prerequisite is the use of web-services technology.

The static part of a document was implemented as a template. Using a document editor in MS Word a template for a court can be created, edited and saved by the local content managers. For maintenance purposes, the templates are stored and retrieved at a central place and not local at a content manager's computer. The advantages of this construction are that a back-up can be automatically made after each change and that in case of conversion of document format all document templates can be converted. The document generator should be able to generate RTF, for use within a word processor, and PDF documents to ensure that content are not easily changed.

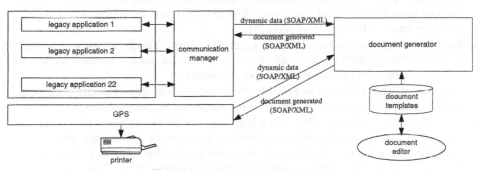

Fig. 1. Overview of the architecture

The architecture is schematically shown in figure 1. Communication between an existing legacy system to the document generation module will be intermediated by the communication manager, whereas the new system will communicate directly with the document generator. GPS and the communication manager communicate with the document generator using XML message over SOAP and HTTP. The Extended Markup Language is a language for describing hierarchical structured documents using tags. The simple object access protocol (SOAP) consists of an envelope/body structure and defines the way applications can request and deliver data using XML (extensible markup language). The HyperText Transfer Protocol (HTTP) is a simple request-respond protocol for communication between a client and server.

The legacy systems communicate with the document generator using the *communication manager*. The communication manager is a messaging application based on Oracle technology. The communication manager translates all incoming messages from legacy systems into XML format readable by the document generator. The document manager should also support the data exchange between legacy applications and the new GPS system and for accessing future modular functionality. This is a next step on the road, as legacy systems are viewed by the communication manager as a module providing certain functionality

3 Evaluation

In this section our experiences with developing a modular architecture are summarized.

1. Identifying functionality to transfer to a modular architecture: Document generation is an intuitive appealing functionality that is used by all applications, can easily be reused and does not need high-performance. Other functionality to put into a module will be more difficult to find;
2. Service levels control is not supported by web services technology: Communication and processing time can vary largely;
3. Asynchronous communication: When a large number of requests for document generation are submitted a none-response can occur and the request needs to be submitted again. Although HTTP is probably so commonly adopted due to it's simplicity, the web services model over HTTP fails as a time-out occurs if it takes more than several seconds to create a response. SOAP over HTTP should ideally support asynchronous communication. The re-submission of a request can already be easily handled by the SOAP protocol;
4. Security: the prototype has no secure communications. The prototype will be used by applications behind a firewall, however, need for secure communication to enable a more open market of services is necessary;
5. Integrity of transactions: functionality to generate a number of single documents and integrate them into one document is not supported by web services protocols;
6. Use of public registers. The following step would be to open the document generation functionality to other government agencies by making use of a public register. Open registry's actuality of information is often limited, contains many mistakes, and nobody wants to transact with an unknown party. This is due to the lack of clear responsibility of data and control and accountability mechanisms.

A number of problems can be dealt with by adding functionality to web services technology, however, this is a relative cumbersome way. Issues like guaranteed service levels, dealing with delays over HTTP, security, integrity of transactions seem to be typical functionality which should be handled by standardized web services technology. In our case study the middleware layer in the form of the communication manager had to deal with these shortcomings with, however, could lead to limited openness and flexibility in the future.

4 Outlook to the Future

The ideal of web-services would be to rent and deploy modules of functionality only when needed. Organizations can decide whether they make, buy or rent the services they require for their business processes. Our case study makes the case for a modular architecture using web services technology within a single organization. The use of an open modular architecture usable by independent companies needs mechanisms to pay for the use of functionality, security mechanisms in an open environment, support of complex business interactions and service levels controls. This demands high requirements on the infrastructures used to interact with organizations. According to a report of IDC will take at least 10 years before companies can actually build applications out of online components [7].

In the future software will be shaped by open, flexible, robust and living architectures consisting of active components. Modules will become intelligent and might even become mobile, i.e. moving over the communication network. Standard or dedicated modular services are procured off the shelf to select the best-of-breed software. The components are integrated with the rest of the systems, preferably automatically. Software suppliers can either assemble their modular services out of existing ones, or develop and evolve atomic components.

Organizations performing new roles will be necessary to support the next steps on the road. Trusted roles will be necessary to audit modular services offered by all kinds of organizations and for monitoring the use of modular services. When a business process consisting of modular services provided by different providers fails, the latter should be kept accountable for their performance. Trusted roles will have to provide transparency to find failures quickly without long-lasting discussions over whom is responsible. Payment roles are necessary for completing the deal based on a pay-per-use principle.

5 Conclusions

Rather than replacing legacy systems, modularity can help to leverage investments in legacy systems and incrementally remove functionality from legacy systems. With web services technology the life of legacy applications can be extended and a step-by-step migration towards a modular architecture is enabled. Although current technology can be used for a modular approach, current protocols have a number of shortcomings. SOAP over HTTP cannot offer guaranteed service levels, does not support asynchronous communication, has no security control and has no mechanisms for ensuring data integrity. In our case study, a middleware layer was introduced to overcome these shortcomings and to add the necessary functionality. As there are no standards available, the road towards an open modular architecture is still largely blocked. Moreover issues like trust, reliability and payment can possibly only be solved by organizations performing new roles.

Currently, integration of business processes and services is an arduous and time-consuming job. The real-time composition of a business process using services is still one step too far. The on demand buying or renting of services from external parties is even further away. This requires mechanisms that can deal with the characteristics of the required service, reliability, quality, granularity, transparency of processing, access and distribution of confidential information, and privacy policy and by the characteristics of the service provider trustworthiness, accountability, and performance. Government organization can make their applications read to function in a modular architecture, stimulate the development of standards and stimulate parties to perform new roles to shorten the road.

References

1. Arsanjani, A.: Developing and Integrating Enterprise Components and Services. Communications of the ACM **45** (2002) 31–34
2. F.J. Armour, S.H. Kaisler, and S.Y. Liu: A Big-Picture Look at Enterprise Architectures. IEEE IT Professional **1** (1999) 35–42
3. H. Chen: Digital Government: Technologies and Practices. Decision Support Systems, **34** (2002) 223–357
4. Baldwin, C.Y., K.B. Clark: Design Rules, The Power of Modularity. Cambridge, Massachusetts: The MIT Press (2000)
5. Fan, M. Stallaert, J. Whinston, A.B.: The Adoption and Design Methodologies of Component-based Enterprise Systems, European Journal of Information Systems **9** (2000) 25–35
6. Fremantle, P. Weerawarana, S., Khalaf, R.: Enterprise Services: Examine the Emerging Files of Web Services and How it is Integrated into Existing Enterprise Infrastructures. Communications of the ACM **45** (2002) 77–82
7. Tweney, D.: Still Waiting for the Web Services Miracle. Business 2.0 (2002)

Process-Controlling – An Instrument to Support the Sustainability of Process Improvements

Margrit Falck

University of Applied Sciences for public administration and legal affairs Berlin,
Alt-Friedrichsfelde 60
D-10315 Berlin, Germany
margrit.falck@fhv.verwalt-berlin.de

Abstract. Business processes in the e-Government are relatively complex, in particular which concerns the number of the persons and authorities involved. In addition business processes have the tendency to change with the time. The more complex the processes, the more largely is the danger, that they drift from and fail the goals of original process modeling within a short time. The process management requires therefore a process control, with which the constant actualisation of the process organization and a continuous adjustment at changed goals and basic conditions can be carried out. An organization concept is presented, with which the transition of a BPR project to a continuous improvement process is supported. It is reported on first experiences with this concept.

1 Theory and Practice

Phase concepts of the business process optimization usually prescribe a stepwise proceeding. The individual steps are very different in their temporal dimension. While the data collection and analysis of the present process as well as the development of a concept for a future improved process can take place into relatively short time, the conversion of the concept to the reality needs substantially more time. Of course concrete time conditions depend on the selected process, but the example of the city administration of Mannheim shows that it is possible to analyze and improve a process with 50-70 activities and 5-8 involved persons in 3,5 days. For the conversion against it are planned check intervals by 30 days and one year. Usually the catalog at conversion measures contains such, with those the change process can start immediately and such, which remain because of their complexity in a queue of planned projects. The longer the time up to the complete conversion, the more largely is the danger that the project runs out and that the remaining objectives and measures come into oblivion.

According to the method of process optimisation the new process organization is to be evaluated after the conversion of the concept, i.e. the achieved improvement goals are to be examined on the basis of the conceptual defaults. Time, duration as well as way of the examination are dependent on the conditions and requirements in individual cases. However, in each case the evaluation can take place only in an appropriate time interval after the implementation of new process organization,

R. Traunmüller (Ed.): EGOV 2003, LNCS 2739, pp. 101–104, 2003.
© Springer-Verlag Berlin Heidelberg 2003

because it must have become "lived" from the involved ones a certain time and have achieved a certain degree at routine, before sufficient data and experiences for a progress control are present.

Both the conversion and the progress control need time, so that it comes in practice to a temporal overlay of the two method steps.

Further it can turn out in the result of the progress control that optimisation goals were not or only partly achieved, that new problems developed or that basic conditions changed. Then influence is to be taken on the further process development, in order to still reach targets or react to changes. For it the goals are to be specified again and new measures are to derive.

In this way the different optimisation steps overlay each other. Therefore a stringent goal orientation and tracking is required.

Even without purposeful effort business processes have the tendency to change with the time. Carelessnesses develop or conditions change, on which involved persons ad hoc react. In this way it can happen that after some time of the originally conceived process organization nothing is more remaining.

It is therefore important to reach the sustainability of the process improvement beyond the first optimisation beginning.

2 The Role Concept of Process-Controlling

The suitable instrument is the process Controlling, whose most important element is **the process manager**. The process manager is responsible for the quality of the process and have the task to steer the further development of the process continuously on the basis of indicators and characteristic numbers. The main point of its work is the observation of the process. He/she collects information about the process and about problems during the process, evaluates the process quality, suggests measures for further improvement and reports regularly to the management. He/she is the "Coach" of the process or in context of e-government a "process-referred CIO".

The special at the function of process manager is the fact that its responsibility is integral i.e. transverse to the hierarchy and over organization borders away. This stands in contrast to the function-oriented responsibility of the line managers of the organizational units involved. The function of the process manager is a new role of e-Government.

The process manager is supported in his work by the participants of the process. Their co-operation consists in the following:

- they provide for the topicality of the documents and the information used during the process (e.g.. Telephone numbers, forms or templates),

- they supply or examine data for frequentnesses and characteristic numbers,

- they identify problems or weak points and

- they suggest after possibility measures for improvement.

They form the process circle (similarly quality circles), whose work is to be moderated of the process manager.

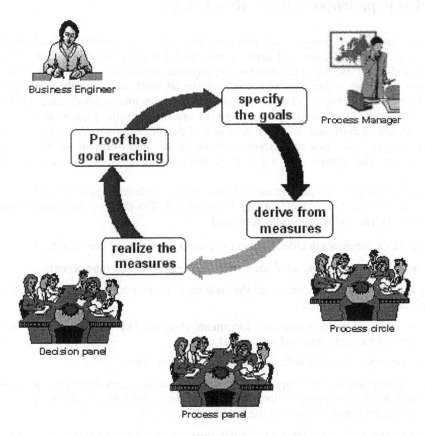

Fig. 1. The role concept of Process-Controlling

The common task of process manager and process circle is it to supply the process organization to a continuous improvement process that, beginning with the progress control the methodical steps: data acquisition, analysis and optimization go through regularly.

The conversion of the optimization is to be regarded in the connection to other processes, because changes in one process can lead quickly to unwanted side effects with other processes. This task has the process panel. It consists of the process managers of different processes, which coordinates the suggested measures for process improvement.

The final decision over the realization of the suggested measures for process improvement is task of the Decision panel. It consists of the line managers of the organizational units taken part in the process.

The business engineer supports the process manager in the process documentation. It knows GPM methodology and creates the connection to the information technology.

3 First Experiences with the Role Concept

In the context of a project for process optimisation of internal-official service processes 2002 was designated process managers for the first time in the citizens administration of Berlin. The process organization included a main case with 10 subprocesses. Two authorities with 7 organizational units and altogether 19 roles of co-workers were involved. To the assignment the principle applied: each business process has one responsible person, but to one responsible person also several processes can be entrusted. With the selection of the process manager we were guided by the slogan, who has the largest interest in an improvement of the process organization. The choice met on 3 participants of process, which was not line managers.

Process manager and participants of process was instructed into her tasks in the end of the project. Since that scarcely 1 year passed. The process circle met recently the first time. The following was determined:

- some of the measures decided during the project were not yet converted,

- some of the originally decided measures became obsolete by other events,

- some of co-workers changed and the new co-workers were not yet instructed into their process-referred role,

- informations in process-relevant documents changed, but the actualisation of the documents was only retarded introduced.

From these experiences the following conclusions were drawn:

- process manager and participants of process must understand themselves as a team beyond the primary optimisation project and must co-operate closely in the team in the continuous improvement of the process organization;

- process managers must be continuously possible to collect informations about the process organization. A support by automated procedures is desirable.

- for the process manager the requirements from communication with internal and external participants of the process are high. Communication does not only concern the information collection. It includes also elements of tuning, presentation and even from Mediation processes. The communication relations must be developed and maintained beyond the borders of the own organizational unit. A support by web-able instruments would be desirable.

- the actualisation of process documents requires the quick access by those, with which new contents develop. From this result requirements of content management.

Howto Hap Haring: Cross-Border Electronic Public Services in The Netherlands

Robbin te Velde

Zenc
Koninginnegracht 2514 AB
The Hague, The Netherlands
Robbin.tevelde@zenc.nl
http://www.zenc.nl

Abstract. Despite its perceived importance in Brussels, cross-border electronic public services are not a big thing yet in the Netherlands. There appears to be sufficient (yet rather partial) supply but insufficient demand. In the post dotcom era suppliers tend to look more critically at actual demand and balance their investments with perceived benefits. Decisions to invest in cross-border electronic services are based on the relative number of foreign customers. Due to the relative low number of foreign visitors public organizations put low priority to cross-border services, unless they have specific mandates.

1 Introduction

If there is one area where electronic service delivery could have significant impact it is the provision of cross-border services. It is often implicitly assumed that these services are of universal interest. When it comes to public services that assumption usually does not hold. Services from public authorities are often tied to a specific locality: a country, a region or a municipality. This kind of location-bound information is especially interesting for immigrants-to-be. This particular niche has considerable political weight in Brussels. In the grandiose scheme of a Europe without internal borders, one of the core objectives of the Commission is to boost mobility of people, services, goods and capital within its territory [1]. Great expectations exist about the use of ICT to stimulate the free movement for people [2]. The underlying thought is that the use of cross-border electronic services could increase and enhance (in terms of transparency) the supply of information, and that this in turn could boost mobility.

This paper is a first attempt to assess the actual demand and supply for cross-border electronic public services in one particular member state, the Netherlands. Although we should be careful to aggregate results to a European level we might derive some cautious and preliminary conclusions from this paper about the situation within the EU as a whole. Given the strong international orientation of The Netherlands it would be safe to assume that the degree of service delivery to non-national citizens and entrepreneurs would be relatively high. Reversing the argument, if the supply of cross-border electronic services is already limited in The Netherlands is would most likely be more limited in other EU countries that are less internationally oriented.

R. Traunmüller (Ed.): EGOV 2003, LNCS 2739, pp. 105–110, 2003.

2 Describing Supply

To our knowledge hardly any research has been done yet on the specific topic of cross-border electronic public services. As far as we know there are no studies at all to the (actual or perceived) demand for such services. At the supply side, one of the few studies available is IDA's exploratory case study [3]. It would have been nice to explore the terra incognito at the demand side. Alas, the mission of the research project on which this paper is based was to map the actual supply of cross-border public electronic services in The Netherlands. Hence the focus of this paper is also on the supply side. We do however have some anecdotical evidence on the demand side.

We were asked to cover the *entire* portfolio of public electronic services. If we would have followed the IDA method we would have ended up with describing a huge number of cases. Instead we decided to construct two sets (one for citizens, one for enterprises) of around ten basic component (themes) that could be used as building blocks for a great number of concrete mobility cases. We used Politi as a base for the classification [4]. The themes were broken up into subthemes which could be linked to concrete public services. For each of the subthemes the websites of all of the organisation involved were analysed. The scores of the individual organisations were then aggregated into subthemes and finally into themes again. The actual assessment of supply had to be done on the service level. The classification of themes is still far too broad to for that purpose hence the division into subthemes.

The most arduous task was to identify the organisations that were linked to a particular subtheme. We used the official overview of Dutch government at the central government portal www.overheid.nl. One major challenge was how to deal with the sizeable generic category of municipalities. The split between English and non-English home pages could (partly) be automated. This left us with a set of over 70 sites that were individually analysed (ENGBASIC, see next paragraph). Of this set 13 municipalities provided information in English on a service level (ENGPLUS). Subsequent analysis was based on this subset.

The web sites within one subtheme were measured along four dimensions: language (LAN: number of foreign languages used on website), technology (TEC: degree of advancement transaction), information (INF: completeness of information), and integration (INT: degree of cooperation between organizations). LAN and TEC are the average scores of all organization in a sub theme, INF and INT refer to the situation as a whole within a sub theme. All four scores were corrected for the number of organization. Generic categories (e.g., municipalities) were counted as one single organizations. Finally, the scores for the themes were calculated on the basis of the average scores of the sub themes.

The following general picture emerged. We found a nearly complete supply of information in English, that is, all themes were sufficiently covered. However, most of this information is rather general and lacks (practical) details. Private sites were exclusively in English – only some public organizations offered information in multiple foreign languages. In both cases the same organizations were responsible for the higher scores. At the citizen side there appears to be a trade-off between language and technology and integration. Thus, the more advanced the technology being used the higher the degree of integration but the lower the number of languages. In fact, with one exception (education) all cases of most advanced transactions were in Dutch only. In general, both for citizens and enterprises high scores on integration could be explained by the presence of a central (public) organization.

With regard to the split between public and private organizations there appears to be a marked difference between the supply of information (INF) to citizens and enterprises. At the citizen side, the supply of information by public and private organizations is more or less supplementary. At the business side, the supply is more or less complementary. In the latter case, private supply is clearly driven by commercial motives. Private organizations are highly active in the two domains were most money can be made (starting a company, finance & grants). They are, on the contrary, completely absent in the theme environment.

Looking across the themes we also find different structures at the citizens and the business side. At the citizen side, municipalities are by far the most important organizations. They are usually not associated with service delivery to non-national citizens but play a central role in the delivery of services to citizens – *including* residents from other countries. At the business side, (regional) development agencies and economic collaborations partly took over the role of municipalities. Overall, private organisations play a less important role than at the citizen side. This is because supply by big firms (either in-house or outsourced to one of the global consultancy firms) largely hides from public view. Secondly, overall supply of *electronic* services to firms is smaller than to citizens because service provision seems to be more centred around human intermediaries.

3 Enter into the Local Level

Both at the citizen and business side municipalities play a central role in the provision of electronic services. The fact that municipalities – as a generic category – are mentioned in about half of all subthemes (citizens) only signifies that *at least one* municipality offered services in that respective subtime. There are however large differences in levels of service provision within the group of municipalities.

Table 1. Levels of service provision by Dutch municipalities in a foreign language (February, 2003)

Number	%	Label	Description
420	84.8	ENGNONE	No information in a foreign language
75	15.2	ENGBASIC	At least minimum level of information in a foreign language
(13 out of 75)	(2.6)	ENGEXTRA	At least minimum level of information in a foreign language at service level
(5 out of 75)	(1.0)	ENGREAL	More detailed information in a foreign language at service level

At first glance, the population of ENGBASIC and ENGEXTRA are randomly dispersed across the country (fig. 1).

There are, however, significant differences in mean ranks between the two groups of ENGNONE and ENGBASIC with regard to technical advancement of the website (A: scores taken from official website benchmark [5]), size (B: number of inhabitants) and immigration (C: number of western immigrants).

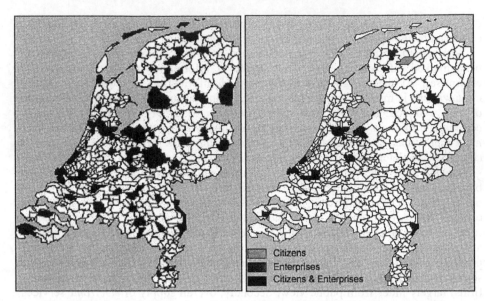

Fig. 1. Geographical distribution of ENGBASIC and ENGEXTRA (February, 2003)

Table 2. Mann-Whitney test for differences in means between ENGNONE and ENGBASIC on technical advancement, size, and immigration (grouped on ENGBASIC) and Pearson correlations between technical advancement, size, and inmmigration for three levels of service provision in a foreign language (n=495, one-tailed)

	A: E-Gov scores	B: Inhabitants	C: Immigration
Mann-Whitney U	9445,000	10927,000	6478,000
Asymp. Sig. (two-tailed)	0,000	0,000	0,000
	ENGBASIC n=75 (15.2%)	ENGEXTRA n=13 (2.6%)	ENGREAL n=5 (1.0%)
A: E-Gov scores	0,344**	0,328**	0,158**
B: Inhabitants	0,368**	0,576**	0,652**
C: Immigration	0,134**	0,183**	0,297**

** significant at 0.01 level (one-tailed)

Statistically significant but weak correlations where found for all three variables. A and C are both correlated to B and can partly be explained away[1]. Hence in both cases correlation to ENGx is exaggregated in the table. In summary, 15,2% of all municipalities provides some information in a foreign language. This group is slightly biased towards bigger (r^2=0,14) and more technical advanced (r^2=0,12) municipalities – the latter being partly explained by size. At higher levels of service provision, the explanatory power of size becomes stronger (ENGEXTRA: r^2=0,33; ENGREAL: r^2=0,43) with technical advancement remaining constant (ENGEXTRA) or even

---

[1] Pearson correlations between A-B and C-B are respectively 0,238 (0.01 significance) and 0,093 (0.05 significance).

getting less important[2]. Thus, when it comes to service provision which exceeds the levels of basic information, only the biggest municipalities remain – 1% of all municipalities.

4 Grasping Demand

The analysis in the previous paragraph showed that the actual supply of cross-border electronic services by a central actor in the overall supply at both the citizen and business side– municipalities – is very limited. One might assume that this is due to the fact that the supply of these specific services is still in its early stage. However, during the course of the research the number of municipalities that offered a minimum level of information in a foreign language actually *decreased*[3]. This might be witness to the fact that there was actually an overshoot of supply during the enfant stage, with its high expectations of e-things to come and ample financial space for pilots and other experiments. Somewhat ironically, we might conclude that there was sufficient supply of cross-border electronic public services but insufficient demand.

In the current situation of economic headwinds and post dotcom traumas, the rules of the 'old economy' (supply follows demand) seem to apply once again. Suppliers tend to look more critically at actual demand and balance their investments with perceived benefits. Next to this, having a sizeable number of (potential) foreign customers is not enough. One of the conclusions from the case studies was that the decision to invest in cross-border electronic services was based on the *relative* number of foreign customers. For example, in one of the few cases were there was a genuine demand for cross-border services (tax issues and social issues in border regions) the central actor decided not to put too much priority to these services because the number of foreign users (over 100.000) paled before the number of domestic users (over 6 million).

5 Conclusions

Despite its perceived importance in Brussels, cross-border electronic public services are not a big thing yet – at least not in the Netherlands – and it might remain a low priority for most national public organizations for many years to come. Demand for these services is a derivative from cross-border mobility. Current intra communitarian migration is still in its enfant stage. Furthermore, the contribution from information

---

[2] The high score for ENGREAL:Immigration is for the greater part caused by the fact that all municipalities in this group (Amsterdam, Maastricht, Rotterdam, The Hague, Wassenaar) have relatively large populations of western immigrants. Amsterdam, Rotterdam and The Hague are the three largest cities of the Netherlands with an adjoining cosmopolitan nature. Wassenaar is a fashionable suburb of the government centre The Hague and residence to many diplomats. Maastricht is strategically located in the border regions of Germany and Belgium.

[3] Three websites with information in English ceased to exist altogether. We were however not able to check whether some municipalities from the ENGNONE group had promoted to ENGBASIC or higher levels of ENGx.

services to increased mobility is only indirect, namely via an increase of transparency. The latter can also be achieved by traditional, non-electronic services. Due to the differences between the structures of demand, electronic services are more widely used at the citizen side than at the business side. There is a rather complete supply of information to foreign citizens and firms in The Netherlands. Leading themes are working, education/research and economic indicators/trade & import. However, overall supply is limited to general and static information. Real demand is for detailed and topical information. An increase of supply in terms of detail or frequency of updates requires significant investments. In the current situation of budgetary restraints, there is little space for such investments. Due to the relative low number of foreign visitors public organizations put low priority to cross-border services, unless they have specific mandates. There appears to be somewhat of a chicken-and-egg-problem: there is little demand for cross-border electronic services because the quality of information provided is too low, and public organizations do not want to increase quality because there is little demand. Just increasing supply would however not significantly boost demand. Public organizations should rather consider linking up with current supply from private organizations that have successfully managed to tap demand from expatriate communities.

References

1. Treaty Establishing the European Community as Amended by Subsequent Treaties. Rome, 25 March, 1957
2. Commission adopts New Strategy on building New European Labour Markets by 2005. http://europa.eu.int/comm/internal_market/en/update/general/01-276.htm, 28 February 2001
3. Donkersloot, M., Bredal, H.: Preliminary Study for the Implementation of a Portal for the EU Administration (version 1.1). IDA, Brussels (2001)
4. Politi, M.: A Digital Government for Development: Channels and Interfaces with Citizens and Business. UN conference on E-Government, Sicily (2002)
5. http://www.advies.overheid.nl

Affordances in E-Government

Reinhard Riedl

Department of Information Technology
Winterthurerstrasse 190
CH-8057 Zurich, Switzerland
riedl@ifi.unizh.ch
http://www.ifi.unizh.ch/egov

Abstract. If co-operating government agencies reside in different countries, they will differ in many respects: administrative ontologies and laws, political context, administrative culture, and computing infrastructure. Inter-organizational e-government services may provide technical interoperability, but do not necessarily solve the problem how to understand a foreign administration. In this paper, we shall discuss the difficulties of citizens in dealing with heterogeneous local e-government services.

1 Introduction

There have been very different approaches to standardization in e-government, such as e-Gif in UK and MOA in Austria, but we are still lacking practical, European-wide standards. This is partially due to national pride (and the ambition to teach the rest of Europe some lessons on e-government), but it also stems from the high heterogeneity within Europe. The successful employment of standards requires the acceptance by the majority of the users, who are mostly local civil servants and native citizens. As a consequence, standardization has to deal with contradictory requirements of local e-government solutions, and it has to resolve the contradictory needs between the majority of native users and the minority of foreign users. While the first is an administrative problem, the latter is a rather basic communication problem. Its failures usually manifest themselves in difficult-to-understand GUIs. Applying Don Norman's design theory (cp. [4]) drawn from Gibson's ecological psychology (cp. [3]), we may identify cultural conventions as the main source of problems. Indeed, it is hard to identify global cultural conventions for GUI design when the underlying cultures have lead to different administrative models.

Several documented research activities related to the FASME project on international e-government (cp. [5]) have confirmed the criticality of both the communication and the administrative problem, which is partially a communication problem, too. They have suggested that standards should be confined to inter-organizational communication, where they may help to separate the communication part of the administrative problem from the rest. In order to do that, apart from the syntactic standard, a semantic standard is needed, i.e. a virtual ontology. Such a virtual ontology does not fit exactly with the popular peer-to-peer paradigm, which would imply one-to-one mappings between countries, regions, or municipalities, but it

R. Traunmüller (Ed.): EGOV 2003, LNCS 2739, pp. 111–116, 2003.

provides much better scalability properties than true peer-to-peer administration, and its maintenance supports the convergence of administrative systems. The major drawback of the use of a virtual ontology is that it is not materialized in any existing administration. By its very nature, citizens lack practical experience with the virtual ontology. At home it creates an additional level of indirection them, remotely it does not solve their knowledge problem concerning the local administrative rules and culture. Even in case that the IT-architecture enables them to control the transfer of their personal data as digital documents, the content of these documents is no affordance for them. This renders the GUI design even a harder job than it used to be, because interoperability may have a negative impact on user-friendliness, and vice versa: On the one hand, the drawing up of a virtual ontology violates classical design principles as it destroys the perceivability of affordances. On the other hand, such ontologies are a necessity for scaling inter-organizational information exchange.

2 Dynamic Virtual Enterprises

Our discussion will be based on dynamic virtual enterprises as a generic, conceptual model for one-stop e-government (cp. [6]) in an inter-organizational setting. This eases the development of multi-disciplinary perspectives and it supports the integration of technical and organizational issues for design considerations. In general, a dynamic virtual enterprise is an organized and structured cooperation of otherwise independent business entities or knowledge workers, which is created for the only purpose to satisfy a particular customer need, which could otherwise not have been fulfilled. It ends once the customer need has been satisfied. From the perspective of European data-protection principles, this implies that its lifetime coincides with that of a lawful context for the storage and processing of personal data.

If several independent government agencies co-operate in the production of an instance of a one-stop e-government service, this may be viewed as a dynamic virtual enterprise, which takes care of the transfer of personal data between independent e-government application systems. Existing standards enhance its efficiency and may be understood as a contextual strategic co-operation for the enterprise. While in many industrial settings one partner usually dominates, in e-government all partners are equal, which has to be reflected by the design of the communication standards.

Standards must not be too flexible and should not try to control human-to-human negotiations in the rare cases that these are indeed necessary. Several examples in e-business, such as e.g. Covisint, have demonstrated that the digital implementation of co-operations in SW may dramatically fail if non-trivial human-to-human negotiations have to be modeled in SW. This imposes restrictions on the applicability of any model for inter-organizational workflow management, which equally hold for inter-organizational e-government. In particular, advanced forms of distributed, cross-organizational decision making should be rather avoided.

It is well known, that there are two basic approaches to deal with the challenges of inter-organizational work- and data-flows in e-government, namely variant-building based on agent models, and automatization plus manual exception handling. Both have been criticized in the literature, as both create significant problems, which cannot be solved satisfactorily so far. As there is no alternative, which is able to circumvent all problems, we shall adopt the second, more modest approach, which avoids some of the more serious data ownership problems. Note that automatization should be based on an optimistic algorithm: If data flows work smoothly (and the risk of misuse is estimated to be low), decisions in favor of the citizen are performed in a fully digitalized way, while if the automatic process halts, the request of the citizen is not automatically rejected, but a manual exception handling by a civil servant takes place.

Thus, we may design one-stop e-government as a dynamic virtual enterprise, based on a strategic co-operation, subject to possibly contradictory local laws and cultural conventions, defining a lawful data storage context and running an optimistic decision algorithm with human exception handling in case of failure. Information technology supports the execution of the dynamic virtual enterprise with the lots of standard Middleware services for distributed client/server systems, e.g. a naming service, an event service, a security service, and a transaction service. While most partners only have to provide interfaces and may remain independent otherwise, some local transactions may have to be coupled to the overall transaction of the dynamic virtual enterprise as nested sub-transactions. This will create some so far unknown consistency requirements for the distributed storage of personal data of a citizen as a price for better services – however in nearly all scenarios technical problems are low. In any case, the communication within the dynamic virtual enterprise ought to avoid the data consistency pitfall – i.e. it should not try to achieve full data consistency, where this is not a technical necessity. As the precondition will in general be a state with inconsistent personal data, there is little reason why the result should better. Therefore, the virtual enterprise should not deal globally with the management of personal data - instead, it should rely on a global information transfer based on digital documents containing data plus a description of the data context. This observation coincides with the major trend in information technology towards document-oriented interaction, which results from the success of XML technology.

From here on, building the IT architecture for one-stop e-government might seem to be a straightforward task. However, European data protection guidelines imply that the citizen owns her personal data, independent of their concrete form of storage. It has been demonstrated that the depicted approach to data-flow management is compatible with these principle (while these principles are hard to implement for agent-based workflow management, unless it is intra-organizational). For example, in the FASME architecture the citizen keeps full control on the transfer of her personal data. However, what has been deliberately ignored so far is the problem that the citizen will not be able to fully understand the information transfer process, which she controls unless she is able to understand the meaning and the relevance of the documents used for information transfer. Assuming that the documents refer to a virtual ontology, she would have to understand the virtual ontology. In fact, even if we did assume that a citizen does not want to control the use of her personal data, her non-understanding might nevertheless cause significant problems as it makes it hard for her to validate and confirm the correctness of the data in the documents or to add additional data where needed. Thus, we are back to the old problem, which now rephrases as: How can we enable the citizen to control the processing of her personal data within the dynamic virtual enterprise?

3 Design Theory

In the original scientific sense of the word, as Gibson introduced it, an "affordance" is an objectively existing subjective means to control the world in an ecological niche. This concept was later adapted by Don Norman to design theory, where an affordance is a perceptible property of an object, which enables the user to mentally simulate the handling of the object and thus to understand how it can be used and what it can be used for. Clearly such an affordance has to relate to and be consistent with the conceptual model and it should be complemented with physical or logical constraints. Cultural constraints might also help to improve the user-friendliness of the design, but they usually fail in a heterogeneous, international scenario. In his recent work, Don Norman has pointed out, that design should care about perceived affordances rather than on affordances themselves. This equally holds for e-government solutions: They may provide lots of affordances, including the generic affordance in the FASME architecture for a principal control of the transfer of personal data, but they may be hard to perceive and difficult to understand – both with respect to the selection of services and to the control of the processing of personal data.

Traditional personal documents are basically context-free certifications of personal attributes, and thus they lack perceivable affordances, unless the citizen knows the administrative affordances and (legal, cultural, etc.) constraints, which are valid in a particular administrative context. Although modern personal documents are designed for global use, their usability depends on non-global, local affordances, which may be perceived easily only if the cultural conventions are well known. The resulting problems are highlighted if we consider marriage certificates or certificates of living places, i.e. credentials for being married or credentials for living at a particular place. For the first, the meaning may differ strongly depending on the country of origin, while for the second the form may differ strongly depending on whether governmental agencies issue such a certificate or not. Taking this further, the estimate of the cultural heterogeneity with respect to the use of credentials indeed provides heuristic estimates for the implementability of an inter-organizational e-government solution. However, a detailed discussion of such estimates is beyond the scope of this paper. Therefore, let us consider the actual problems in the use of documents.

Consider first a civil servant dealing with a digital document provided by a citizen. If it is a document provided by another local, regional, or national agency, it will be more or less easy for him to deduce its meaning and relevance. If it was created by a foreign agency, that may be very difficult though. Letting the other agency create specific documents for foreign use does not really solve the problem as it only transfers it to a civil servant from the foreign agency. However, if there is a standard for inter-organizational information exchange, the foreign agency may create a transfer document from its local data-base and the local agency may translate the document into data which fit with its own data-base. In order to make this work, contents and trustworthiness must be separated and their definition must be separately included in the content specification for the document.

Consider now a citizen who owns a digital document and who wants to use it to gain access to some digital service. Again, the document may take different forms

1. Digitalized version of a traditional personal document (issues by a government agency, or an employer, etc.) from her home country

2. Digitalized version of a traditional personal document from the foreign country, whose cultural conventions she does not know well yet.

3. New personal document referring to a virtual ontology

In case 1, it may be hard for her to figure out what to do with such a document in a foreign country. A driving license may be good enough to rent a car, but neither the driving license nor the passport, nor both together may be good enough to rent a DVD, as we have observed in Sydney, Australia. In case 2, the situation is similar. Someone from Central Europe is unlikely to understand that a power bill could be used as a proof of living place in the UK. Finally, in case 3, the optimal one from the perspective of the civil servant, the situation is probably worst for the citizen. Unfortunately, we have no solution to deal with this dilemma, but only a few suggestions.

First of all, it is important that the underlying conceptual model is generic and that it applies to most services rather than being too much customized to a particular case. The FASME architecture is an example of a generic model for the control of personal data by the citizen. However, while the global use of only a few basic conceptual models will be critical for the success of e-government in the large, it may well be advisable to use different metaphors for their explanation.

Second, wherever possible, design should rather rely on perceived affordances than on cultural conventions. The real problems, which we face when dealing with a foreign culture and its user interfaces and documents, is the impossibility to mentally simulate implications of certain (inter-)actions, which are offered to us. This disables us to search for the way, how to fulfill our needs our duties. While a local citizen knows the affordance of a particular document or credential, in general the foreign citizen does not know. We may deliver lots of text to her explaining the what and why, but in general we will literally have to start with Adam and Eve. Moreover, since many citizens do have significant problems in understanding legal or administrative texts, this is not good enough anyhow.

We suggest that both techniques for the visualization of legal norms (compare [2]) and simulation techniques are exploited and jointly used to help the citizen to perceive local affordances and constraints. Control requires the possibility of cognitive or sub-cognitive simulation. Interoperability design addresses machines and administrative processes only and thus it has to be complemented with cognitive tools to perceive the affordances it provides. While simulation is sometimes used to enhance the quality of process or software implementations, it has been rarely used in authority-to-citizen (A2C) e-government so far. We believe that it is one of be the missing stones for global e-government buildings and needs further research. One possible approach would be to construct a "calculator" which tells the citizen, whether her documents suffice to obtain a service (and which suggests sufficient documents, which she could request from available services). An orthogonal approach would be to come back to the one-to-one concept and to provide separate cultural introductions to the administrative culture of a country for all other countries. Hereby, the introduction should focus on the communication of how basic concepts from a foreign country translate into basic local concepts.

Third, privacy has to be revisited again and the citizen's affordances to control her personal data ought to be further developed. The citizen should be able to simulate a priori, what the consequences will be if she delivers personal data to an agency. In particular, she should be enabled to simulate her traces in the system, which may result from consuming public or private services. The dynamic virtual enterprise should serve as her representative and advocate and not as a helpful civil servant!

In many cases, full digital identity is not needed for the implementation of secure service access, but trustworthy credentials suffice and the citizen may remain anonymous to agencies and commercial companies. That is, service access control may be based on access control lists, which consists of a set of rules defining the necessary (or admissible) attribute values and the necessary trustworthiness for each attribute value. The need to declare and certify the citizen's name may be one rule, but it need not be one in every case. Research is needed is how existing, advanced credential technology with untraceable anonymity may be used to implement anonymous digital identities consisting of a set of certified attribute values in practical settings. (Cp [1].) In particular, a dynamic virtual enterprise executing a service instance of a one-stop e-government broker should be able to handle privacy protection with anonymous digital identities for the citizen in a way, which is fully controlled by the citizen.

As a side-effect, viewing the dynamic virtual enterprises as citizen-owned agents (which is only a metaphor, of course, that refers to the transaction management as pars pro toto) rather than as digital civil servants, will make it easier to draw up financial business models for international e-government.

References

1. Auerbach, N.: Smart Card Support for Anonymous Citizen Services, In: Proceedings of e-Society 2003, Lisbon, Portugal (2003)
2. Brunschwig, C.: Legal Design and e-Government: Visualitions of Cost & Efficiency Accounting in the wif! E-Learning Evironment of the Canton of Zurich, In Traumüller, R., Lenk, K., Electronic Government, LNCS 2456 (2002), 430–437
3. Gibson, J.J.: The Ecological Approach to Visual Perception, Houghton Mufflin (1979)
4. Norman, D.: The Psychology of Everyday Things, New York: Basic Books (1990)
5. Riedl, R.: Interdisciplinary Engineering of Interstate E-Governmemnt Solutions, In: Beynon, M., Nehaniv, C.L., Dautenhahn, K.: Cognitive Technology: Instruments of Mind, Springer Lecture Notes in Artificial Intelligence, LNAI 2117 (2001) 405–420
6. M. Wimmer, Integrated Service Modeling for Online One-Stop Government, EM – Electronic Markets, Vol. 12, No. 3 (2002), 92–103.

Enhancing E-Governance through Scenario Approaches

Georg Aichholzer

Institute of Technology Assessment (ITA)
Austrian Academy of Sciences
Strohgasse 45, A-1030 Vienna, Austria
aich@oeaw.ac.at

Abstract. The paper conceives e-governance as the overall design and implementation of e-government strategies, structures and processes. It argues for paying greater attention to the sustainability of e-government strategies and examines the use of scenario methods for integrating a future-oriented perspective. Two major applications of scenario approaches in the field of e-government are analysed: a scenario project at regional level in the United Kingdom, and the pan-European project PRISMA, a research cooperation within the IST programme. With a focus on the latter, the contribution outlines scenario processes as well as outcomes and derives implications for strategy design. The scenarios suggest certain caveats for future-oriented design which can enhance e-governance. A number of design components which are robust across different scenarios are pointed out, e.g. target group and needs orientation, privacy enhancing measures, access to government-held information, one-stop service centred back-office reorganisation.

1 Introduction

Rational models of e-government postulate a sequence leading from vision, goals and action plans to an implementation of new structures and processes. Though such an ideal path is rarely the case in practice, the implementation of e-government is at least based on some implicit strategy. The overall design of e-government strategy, structures and processes by state agencies in co-action with the private sector and civil society can be grasped with the term 'e-governance'. This understanding of *e-governance* focuses on the state's function as a *strategic designer* of basic conditions for the use of ICT whereas the term *e-government* is used for the role of the *state as a user* of ICT.[1] It brings the general notion of 'governance' [3] together with the subject area of e-government. A major challenge for e-governance is designing e-government structures and processes which are not only short-lived but sustainable. Scenario approaches are an established instrument to improve strategic decisions in a context of change, uncertainty and complexity [4]. They can be employed to increase the

---

[1] A similar conception is held in [1] where e-governance is conceived as the way the state acts to create favourable basic conditions for the development of society and economy with the use of ICT, a function also called 'regulating e-government'. For a different conception see Perri 6 [2] who defines e-governance as digital support for the whole process of policy-making.

R. Traunmüller (Ed.): EGOV 2003, LNCS 2739, pp. 117–120, 2003.
© Springer-Verlag Berlin Heidelberg 2003

118   G. Aichholzer

capabilities of exploring and anticipating possible future developments which impact on e-government structures, and to adapt the design of e-government strategies accordingly. Scenario building can help to reduce uncertainties of strategic choice, improve capacities of coping with innovation risks and inform the design of more sustainable e-government strategies. The paper draws on two major cases of applying the scenario method in the field of e-government. Case 1 is a scenario project undertaken at regional level in the United Kingdom and case 2 is the European research project PRISMA (Providing innovative service delivery and assessment), carried out and financed within the European Commission's IST-Programme.

2 Applications of Scenario Methods

There is a great variety of scenario methods and application areas [5]; however, a common core is exploring possible development paths and plausible, alternative images of the future. Alternative portrays of future states are able to challenge accustomed lines of thought and assumptions. Opening up the view towards unexpected developments should draw the attention of decision-makers to critical factors and help taking decisions better prepared for an uncertain future. Individual scenarios can be used to assess the sustainability of a planned strategy. An ultimate goal is to promote the design of strategies which are more robust, i.e. which fit different future scenarios.

E-governance is faced with strategic choices to be made and uncertainties concerning socio-economic, political as well as technological developments which cannot be neglected in more long-term strategic planning. A demand for an increased awareness of the uncertainties involved in the change process and for designing more future-oriented strategies is clearly indicated by signs such as: ambitious e-government targets, resource intensive implementation programmes, experiences with failed projects [6] and warning signals of deficient service usage [7]. However, the potential of scenario methods as a tool to respond to these challenges has hardly ever been put to use in the field of e-government. Two such cases will be briefly examined with regard to their contributions to improving e-governance.

2.1 A Scenario Project at Regional Government Level

The first case is a scenario project at regional level in the UK. Northshire Council in cooperation with a telecommunications organisation employed a facilitated scenario approach described in detail in [4]. One goal was the "widening (of) perspectives on the future of technology and governance" (p.201). Four alternative scenarios of e-government with a time horizon towards 2006 were elaborated and labelled „Beyond the Kailyard" (this old Scottish term stands for a minimum level of subsistence), „Forward to the past", „Free enterprise" und „Technology serves". Outcomes and the resulting debate identified critical strategic requirements which then informed the e-government decisions and operational actions of regional government in Northshire in favour of a more viable, integrated and long-term perspective.

2.2   Scenarios for E-Government in Europe towards 2010

The second and major case, PRISMA (Providing innovative service delivery and assessment), is a pan-European research project in the field of e-government. The scenario process in PRISMA took place in 2002 and dealt – among others – with the future of e-government towards a time horizon of 2010 [8]. Like the former example, it used the STEEP approach [4] to analyse macro-environment of e-government in Europe in its societal, technological, economic, ecological and political dimensions. In a two-stage process, first the project team developed three macro-scenarios of Europe in 2010. In a second step, workshops with external experts scrutinised these macro-scenarios regarding their consequences for e-government services, with the aim to identify robust versus scenario-dependent elements of current strategies and good practice conceptions. In brief, the outcomes were as follows [9]:

Scenario 1, *"A prosperous and just Europe"*, represents in some sense a utopian scenario: The world is at peace and has experienced widespread economic and social progress as well as technological dynamic. In this environment e-government could fully unfold and progress in a balanced and generally accepted way. With investments on a grand scale and further technological progress, practically all services are fully available online, generally accessible, of high quality and trustful. Horizontal and vertical integration of back offices has significantly increased service quality for citizens and businesses. Internet portals integrate services according to relevant live events. Personalised services and multiple access channels provide individual choice. New human agents offer support to users of e-government services.

In *Scenario 2*, *"A turbulent world"*, economic volatility and conflicts predominate. E-government has progressed but in a socially very segmented way, increasing the digital divide. Efficiency pressure for public administrations impacts on the cost of user needs. Administrations have been modernised and downsized, but service quality is strictly limited by cost criteria. Trust in technical systems is given and security and privacy standards are a public concern. Fragmentation of societies penetrates all spheres of life; financial restrictions and skill deficits prevent large parts of the population from using other than simple e-government services, whereas a minority enjoys the benefits of personalised and premium services.

Scenario 3, *"Recession and reorientation"*, finally portrays a rebel against techno-logy, government and markets in favour of decentralisation and citizen empowerment, including a drastic demise of trust in e-services after scandals with misuses of personal data which largely undermines the prospects of more complex e-services. In this scenario many avoid using e-services. Especially advanced transaction and personalised services requiring authentication have lost attraction. Low value added of many simple information services adds to the decline of usage. Privacy and security are top issues; citizens rather trust in NGOs caring for these issues.

None of these scenarios might come true, but they might be possible and are internally plausible. Scenario building can improve e-governance and strategy development through widening perspectives, calling attention to critical assumptions, preparing for change and thus better coping with uncertainty. This is why the function of scenarios has been compared to the testing of a model aircraft in the wind tunnel: testing e-government strategies for the future (the model) in various scenarios (the conditions in the wind tunnel).

3 Conclusions

Different e-government scenarios suggest certain caveats for future-oriented strategies which can be used to inform the design of more robust policies. For instance, under specific scenarios highly personalised services or a generalised use of electronic signatures seem unrealistic whereas, e.g. user-centred design and multi-channel delivery fits all scenarios. PRISMA suggests a number of future-oriented strategic guidelines. In a nutshell, they include:

– strict target group and needs orientation in service design, pro-active services;
– trust and privacy enhancing measures (transparent processes, quality seals), use of privacy enhancing and calm technologies;
– multi-channel delivery and new human agents for flexible user support;
– systematic social inclusion measures (assisted public access points, design for all);
– high volume transaction services for businesses and professional mediators;
– back office reorganisation measures (intra- and intergovernmental) and one-stop service portals.

Practical roadmaps for today's actions include topics such as ratings of administrations to promote service ethic, quality controls and surveys of online services to increase user benefits, identification of service priorities and incentives for reaching critical mass for more complex (transaction) services, incentives for inter-governmental and trans-sector cooperation and integration, specific programmes for the elderly, and strategic alliances with private companies and community organisations.

References

1. Gisler, M.: Einführung in die Begriffswelt des eGovernment. In: Gisler, M., Spahni, D. (eds): eGovernment. Eine Standortbestimmung. Verlag Paul Haupt, Bern Stuttgart Vienna (2001) 14–18
2. Perri 6: E-governance. Do Digital Aids Make a Difference in Policy Making? In: Prins, J. E. J. (ed.): Designing E-Government. On the Crossroads of Technological Innovation and Institutional Change. Kluwer Law International, The Hague London Boston (2001) 7–27
3. Newman, J.: Modernising Governance. New Labour, Policy and Society. Sage, London (2001)
4. van der Heijden, K., Bradfield, R., Burt, G., Cairns, G., Wright, G.: The Sixth Sense. Accelerating Organizational Learning with Scenarios. John Wiley & Sons, Chichester (2002)
5. van Notten, P. W. F., Rotmans, J., van Asselt, M. B. A., Rothman, D. S.: An updated scenario typology. Futures 35 (2003) 423–443
6. The Economist: The health service's IT problem. October 19 (2002) 37–38
7. Tempest, M.: Official websites leave public cold. The Guardian, Monday, December 30 (2002)
8. Aichholzer, G., Winkler, R., PRISMA project partners: Report on pan-European scenario-building. Deliverable D4.1. Institute of Technology Assessment, Austrian Academy of Sciences, Vienna, February (2002) http://www.prisma-eu.net/deliverables/D4-1.PDF
9. PRISMA project partners: Pan-European best practice models. Deliverable D5.1. Institute of Technology Assessment, Austrian Academy of Sciences, Vienna, September (2002)

E-Procurement Adoption: Theory and Practice

Helle Zinner Henriksen and Kim Viborg Andersen

Department of Informatics
Copenhagen Business School
Howitzvej 60
2000 Frederiksberg
Denmark
{hzh.inf,andersen}@cbs.dk

Abstract. This paper addresses eProcurement adoption strategies in public sector institutions from four perspectives (capability, interactivity, value distribution, and orientation of the decisions). The paper analyzes eProcurement in the largest municipality (Copenhagen) in Denmark. Our analysis suggests that efficiency and effectiveness (capability), and improved coordination of private sector and public sector interaction (interactivity) are the drivers for the adoption strategy pursued by the municipality.

1 Introduction

It has been emphasized that an important part of eGovernment is to focus on the delivery of faster and cheaper services and information to citizens, business partners, employees, other agencies, and government entities (Layne and Lee, 2001). In this paper focus is on how the public sector manages its internal operations. Our focus is on the aspect of organizational management in eGovernment, which so far has received little research attention: eProcurement. eProcurement is here defined as the public sectors' potential improvement of operations through electronic means in the form of electronic purchase of goods and services.

eProcurement has been on the political agenda in EU for a while. At the Lisbon summit in 2000 it was decided that EU should pay special attention to eProcurement. It was emphasized that "The emergence of the new Information and Communication Technologies (ICTs) offer promising opportunities as regards the efficiency, transparency and opening-up of public procurement" (European Commision, 2000). However, European governments appear to have hesitated adopting the concept of eProcurement. One reason could be the burst of the dot.com bubble in the spring of 2000 and the concomitant reluctance to establish the underlying structures of electronic marketplaces. Another and maybe more likely explanation could be rooted in structural conditions in the public sector. In this paper we analyze the expectations to eProcurement and the consequently adoption strategy for eProcurement pursued by the largest municipality in Denmark.

R. Traunmüller (Ed.): EGOV 2003, LNCS 2739, pp. 121–124, 2003.

2 E-Procurement

As stated in the introduction eProcurement is referred to as "the public sectors' potential improvement of operations through electronic means in the form of electronic purchase of goods and services." Timmers (2000) suggested that the benefits derived from eProcurement include a wider choice of suppliers, lower cost, better quality, improved delivery, and reduced cost of procurement. This approach to organizational improvement of operations through electronic means is not significantly different from those ideas applied in the traditional strategy literature building on IT adoption and usage in private enterprises (e.g. Hammer, 1995; Porter, 1985). However, when it comes to procurement in the public sector most purchases in public sector institutions require a bureaucratic procedure to be followed due to different reasons. One reason is that the majority of items are bought on requisition. This means that enormous amounts of efforts are spent on sending forms back and forth in the system. Another reason for the bureaucratic procedures of public procurement is related to the tendering process. The public sector institutions in the European Union countries do, unlike private businesses, have to follow a highly regulated procurement process. In the EU it is thus illegal to favor domestic over foreign firms.

One consequence of these conditions is the increase of the complexity of the technical solution of a given eProcurement system for public sector institutions. However, another issue, which might play an even more important role, is that eProcurement adoption is a matter of change of organizational routines, which go beyond mere rationality.

3 Strategies for E-Procurement Adoption

Based on the particular characteristics of eProcurement we suggest a framework for eProcurement uptake, which embraces a number of different aspects related to the public sectors' internal operations. The framework is derived from a comprehensive study on impacts of IT on the public sector (Andersen & Danziger, 2001). The study found that IT had impacts in four areas: Capability, interaction, values, and orientation of the decision making process. In this context we apply the four areas for evaluating the adoption incentives of the municipality of Copenhagen.

The capability perspective suggest the motives for eProcurement adoption to be a matter of better access to valid information about products which could lead to improved quality of the information about eProcurement. The perspective also includes the expectation of more efficient routines and faster procurement processes inside the public sector institutions.

The interactivity perspective focuses on how digital procurement is corresponding with the patterns of power and control of the eProcurement process, communication among the units involed in eProcurement, and the coordination of the eProcurement tasks, people, and policies. It also considers the relations between the public and private sector such as enabling of shared eProcurement between the private and public sector and a different role of the suppliers.

Orientation of the decision-making processes is related to the impact of digital procurement on the unit's cognitive, affective and evaluative considerations. For example, we consider whether digital procurement makes actors structuring problems differently and whether the employees perceive that their discretion has been altered by digital procurement.

The perspective concerning value distributions is related to whether a public institution experiences a shift in values that is attributable to digital procurement. Specifically values associated with the well-being of employees (do they experience increased surveillance of their procurement behavior and do they disapprove this) as well as the job satisfaction and job (domain) enlargement of public employees (do they experience a more interesting job) are core attributes related to this perspective.

4 The Case of E-Procurement in the Municipality of Copenhagen

In the following an example of an eProcurement adoption strategy for a municipality is presented. The objective of the presentation is to illustrate how practitioners focus on the adoption of eProcurement. The case presented is related to the eProcurement strategy of the municipality of Copenhagen.

The municipality of Copenhagen is the largest municipality in Denmark. With its 60,000 employees the municipal supports 500,000 inhabitants with services related to schools, libraries, eldercare etc. The annual purchase in the municipality is around EURO 500 million. It is estimated that the 2,000 purchasing agents who perform the procurement in the institutions handle about one million invoices on an annual basis.

In 1999 when attention was first paid to the purchase behavior in the municipality of Copenhagen there was not an explicit purchase policy, purchase strategy, or any cross-functional activities. At that time it was demonstrated that there was none or little coordination of purchases between different units in the municipality, very few purchases were done jointly, and there was a limited use of collective framework agreements for procurement. Additionally, procurement was done through requisitions, which was a very resource demanding process. Given these conditions there was a limited overview of procurement behavior in the municipality. Based on these insights it was decided to pronounce an explicit strategy for the purchases for year 2001 and onwards. The official and articulated vision was that: "The procurement procedure in the municipality of Copenhagen is among the best in Denmark by the end of year 2003." Two means for achieving this vision were identified to be: 1) Improvement of IT usage and procedures and 2) Encouragement to better purchase behaviors.

Improvement of IT usage and procedures included to pursue an implementation of full electronic integration of all work-procedures from requisition to payment, gathering and use of management information, and finally full integration to the electronic procurement portal, which was planned to be launched by January 2002.

The strategy for achieving better purchase behaviors took an offset in a goal of using framework agreements in the procurement process. It was expected that framework agreements automatically would lead to higher volume, which again could lead to more information both with respect to purchase behavior and suppliers. Given these insights better framework agreements could be achieved, which again would lead to an increased use of framework agreements and so on, and so fourth. In 1999 the usage of collective framework agreements was about 20 percent of all purchases. The goal was to use collective framework agreements in 50 percent of all purchases by year 2003. One of the means for achieving commitment to collective framework agreements was according to the purchasing manager to use the public procurement portal.

5 Discussion and Conclusion

The case from the municipality of Copenhagen illustrates a mixed adoption strategy for eProcurement. Based on the information provided by the purchasing manager the adoption process appears to have been driven by rational choices related to improved efficiency and effectiveness. The two mentioned objectives for achieving savings relate to improvement of IT usage and procedures and encouragement to better purchase behaviors. The immediate categorization of the adoption strategy as outlined by the purchasing manager can therefore be classified as "capability" with respect to the improvement of IT usage. The objective of better purchasing behavior is related to a goal of improved control and coordination of processes and especially strengthened relations to suppliers. This lends support to that the "interactivity" perspective also played a role in the adoption strategy pursued in the municipality of Copenhagen. The softer approaches to eProcurement adoption ("value distribution" and "orientation of the decision-making process") on the other hand were not reported to have driven the adoption process from the purchasing managers' point of view. This could lead to the conclusion that adoption of IT-driven work practices such as eProcurement in public sector institutions is rather driven by rational concerns than aspects related to improvement of work environment and empowerment.

References

1. Andersen, K. V., & Danziger, J. N. (2001) Impacts of IT on Politics and the Public Sector: Methodological, Epistemological, and Substantive Evidence from the "Golden Age" of Transformation. *International Journal of Public Administration, 25(5)*.
2. European Commission (2000) Directive of the European Parliament and of the Council. On the coordination of procedures for the award of public supply contracts, public service contracts and public works contracts. In: *(COM(2000) 275)*.
3. Hammer, M. & Stanton, S. A. (1995) *The Reengineering Revolution: A Handbook.* New York: Harper Business Press.
4. Layne, K. & Lee, J. (2001) Developing Fully Functional E-government: A Four Stage Model. *Government Information Quarterly* 18, 122-136.
5. Porter, M. E. (1985) *Competitive Advantage: Creating and Sustaining Superior. Performance. New York:* The Free Press.
6. Timmers, P. (2000) *Electronic Commerce: Strategies and Models for Business-To-Business Trading.* Wiley and Sons, New York.

Delivering E-Government Services to Citizens and Businesses: The Government Gateway Concept

Jan Sebek

Microsoft Czech Republic
janseb@microsoft.com

1 Introduction

The aim of the Government Gateway is to provide better, customer-focused and more efficient public services.

Enabling citizens and businesses to transact electronically with government organisations and agencies is a key part of this strategy. The Internet is being used as the core delivery channel for enabling these improvements in service delivery. With its associated open standards and technologies, the Internet provides a major means of establishing electronic relationships between government organisations and their customers.

The Government Gateway concept as set up for UK government by Microsoft and its partners provides a consistent and secure interface to government departments and agencies for individuals and companies in the UK. This unified interface provides "functionality" for:

- registration (or *authentication*) of an individual or company to Government Gateway
- "enrolment" (or *authorisation*) to one or more selected government services available on the gateway and
- secure and reliable submission of documents (XML) in a format accepted by selected services
- integration of departmental applications and services including data translation as required

The gateway also allows citizens and businesses to seamlessly interact with government departments and bodies through a variety of diverse channels (including web and digital TV), services (whether the services are offered by the tax of health department) and third-party application software (including a business' pay-roll system).

On the opposite side it saves government departments a significant effort and investment these would have to spend if they were to build a secure and reliable application enabling electronic transactions with the government (therefore providing economy of scale).

The provision of this common infrastructure shared across national, regional and local public services:

R. Traunmüller (Ed.): EGOV 2003, LNCS 2739, pp. 125–128, 2003.

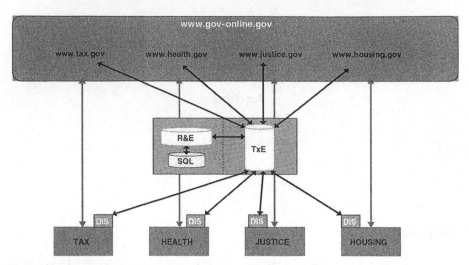

Fig. 1. Two possible options – vertical approach vs. the centralised approach as adopted by the Government Gateway

- avoids the duplication of the common facilities and services necessary to connect individual government organisations to each other and to customers over the internet
- delivers joined-up services by provisioning a common authentication service thereby enabling a user to interact with many government organisations in a single transaction using a single identity
- enables both the private and public sector to provide customer-driven applications that can interact with government in a consistent manner

2 Functions of the Government Gateway

Users interact with the Gateway, typically through a web browser and portal or through an application, for example an accounting package. Portals permit the completion of electronic forms interactively on the internet, while applications permit the completion of electronic forms locally on a PC. In both cases the internet and the Gateway provide the mechanism for the submission of completed forms to the appropriate department and the return of a corresponding receipt acknowledgement.

In fulfilling these scenarios, the Government Gateway provides the following functions:

- authentication and authorisation services – which ensure that users are who they claim to be and that they have the right to access a specific service or set of services
- a single sign-on facility and single-credentials that are supported across all government services, national, regional and local – so that users can have one user ID and password, or a digital certificate, for use with all online public services

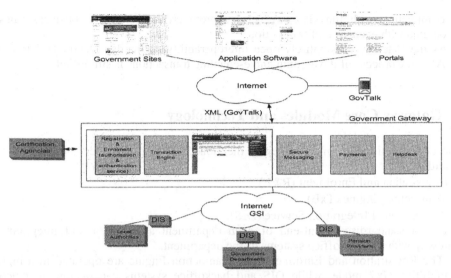

Fig. 2. The logical concept of the Government Gateway

- a common transaction and routing facility – which guarantees the reliable delivery of documents and messages. This includes both documents between business and citizens and government, as well as the routing of documents between government organisations
- a secure messaging facility – enabling secure communication between business, citizens and government organisations
- an integration tier – offering reliable delivery of standards-based information into the connecting organisation, including the option for customised local integration into existing systems and applications
- a payments facility – offering both unauthenticated and authenticated payments, ranging from credit and debit cards through to direct debit

The Gateway is part of the government's critical information infrastructure and provides a highly secure environment, a resilient "always on" service and a capacity to handle high volumes.

3 Gateway Services

The Gateway was designed to simplify and accelerate the UK e-Government programme. It achieves this by ensuring that the common building -block components of e-Government services are provided once, in a flexible, modular and scalable way.

A "service" is a set of tools and computer programs enabling registration of users for submission of a certain document and subsequent creation of the document, filling it with data and electronic submission through the Government Gateway.

It is the responsibility of government organisations to develop services compliant with the Gateway standards that can be accepted electronically by the Gateway and, in conjunction with the Gateway service provider, to devise the business rules associated with each type of transaction.

As the Gateway uses entirely open interoperability standards – XML, HTTP and SOAP – the process of developing and e-enabling transactions is simplified.

4 Gateway Core Modules and Technology

The core functionality of the gateway mentioned above is provided by three main modules:
- Registration and Enrolment (R&E)
- Transaction Engine (TxE)
- Departmental Integration Service (DIS).

DIS a standardised front-end of each department and also a tool integrating Gateway with the backoffice systems of the department.

The Registration and Enrolment and Transaction Engine are operated in a high availability 24x7 mode, while DIS and backoffice systems can operate in much "softer" mode.

The Gateway and DIS are built around a set of Microsoft products (Windows 2000 Advanced Server, BizTalk Server, Commerce Server, ISA Server, SQL Server 2000, MOM Operations Manager)

The mission-critical functionality is provided by Microsoft BizTalk Server.

5 Conclusion

The development of the Government Gateway and its first implementation was carried out by Microsoft in UK based on requirements of UK government, which is the owner of the intellectual property rights to the Gateway.

After 2 years of successful operations in UK one of the next replications is currently starting in the Czech Republic.

References

1. Microsoft internal documents
2. "What Is the Government Gateway" (© 2002 Crown Copyright, Office of the e-Envoy)

Conventional and Electronic Service Delivery within Public Authorities: The Issues and Lessons from the Private Sector

Nicholas J. Adams[1], Simon Haston[2], Nat Gillespie[2] and Ann Macintosh[1]

[1]International Teledemocracy Centre
Napier University
10 Colinton Road
Edinburgh, EH10 5DT, UK
Telephone: +44 (0) 131 455 2545
Fax: +44 (0) 131 455 2282
www.teledemocracy.org
[2]The City of Edinburgh Council
Wellington Court, 10 Waterloo Place
Edinburgh EH1 3EG, UK

Abstract. In this paper we compare and contrast the issues of providing conventional against electronic services within Public Authorities (PAs). We present a model suggesting the three dimensions to electronic service delivery are motivation, organisation, and technology (the MOT of service delivery). We observe that the motivations affecting service delivery differ greatly between PAs and commercial organisations, with PAs having certain obligations and responsibilities as to the services that they provide that do not constrain commercial companies. We argue that technologically many lessons learned by commercial organisations can be immensely valuable to PAs, and conclude that the key barrier to effective electronic service delivery within PAs is their culture and organisation.

1 Introduction

Provision of electronic services has grown rapidly, particularly within the past five years, to the extent that few organisations can afford not to have some web presence, and with many also now providing electronic transaction services. Much work has been done in the study of provision of electronic services in the commercial sector [1,3], but few have thought to contrast this with conventional service provision, and even less have considered the specific needs of PAs. (One of the few who have considered PAs is [4], but they consider only a specific example of the taxation system within the Greek Ministry of Finance.) For a recent survey on the status of electronic services of PAs within Europe consult [2], and [6] for OECD members.

This work has been undertaken as part of a two year collaborative European Union funded project under the Information Society Technologies (IST) programme called SmartGov (IST-2001-35399). Its aim is to develop a toolkit that will allow PAs to design, deploy and maintain online services with a minimum need of specialist IT

R. Traunmüller (Ed.): EGOV 2003, LNCS 2739, pp. 129–134, 2003.
© Springer-Verlag Berlin Heidelberg 2003

assistance [7]. It is comprised of 7 partners from across the European Union, including two Public Authorities, where pilot applications of the SmartGov Platform will be deployed and evaluated. The insights given in this paper have been gained through extensive dialogue with the participating PAs and will be encoded into the SmartGov knowledge-base to assist PAs in developing effective electronic services.

We start by introducing our model of factors behind service delivery in Section 2, consider each of the factors it highlights in the following Sections, before summarising and discussing their implications in Section 6.

2   The MOT of Service Delivery

Public Authorities by their nature are very different to commercial enterprises and as such pose an interesting challenge for developers of smart online services.   In providing e-commerce services, organisations are providing services to their specific customers whereas government services are for the public at large. A PA cannot choose its customers[1] but rather has a duty to ensure full access to all services by everyone. E-commerce services are typically focussed around single events, e.g. buying a car, where buyers and suppliers work in an environment that is open to competition. E-government services are much wider, encompassing a range of events, services and political processes that are by their nature open to contention.

Fig. 1. The MOT of Service Provision

The key issues relating to service provision (and therefore also applicable to electronic service provision) by a PA we shall argue can be broadly grouped into three orthogonal categories as shown in the Figure. These we have named the MOT of Service Provision. Motivation considers all aspects behind why an organisation may wish to deploy a service and includes things such as statutory requirements for PAs. Technology relates to items such as back-office equipment, and organisation things such as staff culture and business organisation. Each shall be considered in turn.

3   Motivation

Motivation for providing a service is probably the key thing that distinguishes a commercial organisation from a Public Authority. For a commercial organisation the driving force is undoubtedly financial, and companies usually have the luxury of choosing not to deploy a service (or product) if they deem it unviable. PAs on the

---

[1] For convenience we are using the term customer loosely to include citizens, businesses and any other organisation who may be required to interact with the PA.

other hand are driven by statutes, which dictate the services they have to implement and there is no element of choice. This can of course mean that many services a Public Authority might deploy may not be viable in a purely commercial sense.

Secondary, and closely related to this, is the customer base. Once again a commercial organisation can choose its customer base and if it has a particular product or speciality it can market it solely to its desired target group through whatever channels it believes they may prefer. However in its broadest sense a PA's customer base is by default all citizens and businesses, and neither it (and reciprocally they) are able to opt out. There are of course many services that will only apply to a distinct sub-set of these customers such as schools, but many services such as street lighting and refuse collection will impact on all citizens, and others which may not be important to a customer one day might become very significant the next - for example if a citizen loses his job and suddenly requires benefit. Given this, a PA is obliged to cater for all of its citizens and businesses, and it can't merely specialise in or solely take advantage of cost-effective channels favouring a particular group, such as online transaction services. Thus provision of electronic services cannot be considered in isolation to traditional means of delivery as these will still be required by a PA.

In an environment where funds are limited it is questionable that there is indeed a business case of cost saving for providing online services in many areas of the PA's activity where the customers are the poorest or neediest in society. Commercial organisations in the business of making profit would ordinarily choose not to target these people as they are unlikely to have money to spend. However these are the very people a PA exists to provide services for.

Also, while there are many similarities in the process of delivering a service and an e-service, one key difference is the assumption on how a customer will use the service. Non e-services assume that customers have access to the phone, mail or face-to-face service points, whilst e-service requires the users to have access to the Internet. In many cases, the user must acquire new skills, gain access to the infrastructure and hardware, and most importantly develop the confidence to use the e-service. Like any service, an e-service must address a need, and ensure that the potential user base has the access, culture and skills to utilise it. Only if it meets these objectives will it achieve a critical mass to justify the continuation of the e-service. Without encouragement from politicians – such as in the case of Britain a commitment from the government to make all services available online by 2005[2] – it is unlikely that many services would be made available online. Given this then, just because the technology exists it is important to ask firstly 'Is electronic delivery a suitable channel for provision of this service?'

4 Technology

IT infrastructure is obviously a very important consideration for electronic service delivery. In [5] Heim and Sinha present a framework for technologies and argue that the complexity of infrastructure is directly proportional to the number and variety of services an organisation may wish to provide. For a Public Authority it is safe to

---

[2] Stems from the eEurope initiative on e-government, which 'aims to ensure that citizens have easy access to essential public data, as well as promoting online interaction between citizens and government'. It was enforced by the Lisbon European Council, that called "Member States to provide generalised electronic access to main basic public services by 2003".

assume that they will sit at the high end of this scale as they provide many services across a very broad range. There will be a strong requirement for heavy integration of back-office systems, and during the course of a transaction, reference may need to be made to multiple databases. This may well cross organisational boundaries within a PA, and flags up another issue of the impact of administrative organisation of PAs on service delivery – which we shall discuss in the next Section.

Conventional service delivery within PAs is largely paper based with customers (or public service professionals acting on their behalf) filling out one or more forms requesting services. Over time databases have been built to assist in this work, but typically they provide only a supporting role with the majority of the service being largely paper-based. There are a number of reasons why this situation may have arisen. Firstly, is the need for signatory agreement or authorisation to supply/receive a service under a strict set of conditions governed by legislation, but it will also be historical in that before electronic media became widespread this was the only means available. For conventional service delivery this mechanism is long established and this is not an issue. However the need for signatures before delivery of many services can take place presents certain difficulties for electronic service provision within a PA. The issues are two-fold, technical and legal.

They are technical in that there needs to be an infallible means whereby a customer can be authenticated as being a particular person, and a secure channel opened up through which to pass confidential information. Given that one of the remits of a PA is to be as accessible as possible to the public it cannot be assumed that the customers who may wish to make use of electronic transaction services may have their own PC at home. Therefore the supplying of proprietary software by the PA to provide such a channel is a non-starter, and the use of cookies to coordinate secure transactions[3] could pose a security weakness – especially among naive computer users. Username and pin schemes are the only other option without requiring additional devices such as a smart card, and these too have their weaknesses.

The legal issue relates to having in place a means of digitally providing a signature that is deemed legally binding. Traditionally legislation has often been slow to keep pace with the changes in technology, and so it has been with digital signatures. To this end the UK government has published a framework document [9].

There is also the issue of processes behind electronic service delivery. Currently they are focused towards paper based methods as we have discussed, and a straight port from paper to electronic forms may not be the best approach. With the introduction of an electronic transaction service there exists the possibility for process re-engineering to make the experience of applying for a service more appealing or convenient from the user's perspective, and indeed the perceived wisdom of industry and most best practice guidelines (such as [8]) is that it is recommended as a first step. The challenge comes when this requires significant back-office re-engineering[4].

Most PAs will have a web presence, and probably also some databases to administer customer applications, however the link between the two is likely to be missing. Due to the longevity of PAs it is likely that many of their data repositories will be legacy systems that will not support the established gateways for communication, and thus be difficult to integrate.

---

[3] A common practice adopted by companies.

[4] This is generally the case with PAs, who, unlike many companies, cannot justify investing in necessary infrastructure until it has been both proven technically, and a business case made.

5 Organisation

Public Authorities are generally sub-divided into distinct departments. In the UK these divisions approximately reflect different work activities that the PA is required to perform, but their classification and the boundaries between them have largely arisen in an adhoc manner over time. Consequently there is frequent overlap and sometimes a customer applying for one service may also require another service that is actually handled by a different department or sub-department. This problem has been well recognised, and in an attempt to combat it the 'one-stop-shop' has been devised, and is currently very popular within PA circles. Generally this means a call-centre. This certainly is a step in the right direction, but may not be sufficient for a fully integrated electronic service delivery, as without a weakening of the departmental boundaries, it is likely to serve only as a channel through which customers are passed onto the appropriate back-office staff.

The current organisation of distinct autonomous departments has encouraged the emergence of a silo structure whereby each department holds and maintains its own silo of data pertinent to the services it offers. This can create inefficiencies both for the PA and the customer. It is inefficient for the PA because customers making use of multiple services from a PA will quickly lead to duplicate data about them being created in more than one silo. This clearly raises concerns about maintainability such as ensuring all records about the customer are updated when one of them is changed, such as if the customer moves house and informs only one department. It also raises questions of validation of the data. Under these circumstances which address for the customer is now the right one? It is also inefficient for customers in that a customer making use of more than one service may have to repeatedly duplicate a significant amount of personal information. Frequently this is seen on benefit application forms which always ask for name and address, etc.

What if there could be a way for a customer to uniquely identify themselves and thus the PA can then say 'I know this about you, but in order to provide you with this particular service I need the following extra information?' Here an electronic transaction service fed by a central repository could be extremely advantageous to the customer, by enabling just this kind of facility. Such a central repository would also aid fraud detection, and could also mean that the complicated set of checks and balances built into the conventional paper-based system could be relaxed, as a PA can now use existing information a customer has given it to verify a customer's eligibility. However it also raises questions of data protection, and centralised repositories are not without their own disadvantages. An alternative solution is highlighted by the connected silos of data model, adopted by the Kruispuntbank[5] (clearing house) in Belgium. In this, departments retain ownership of their own data, but there are connections between silos that enable data to be retrieved and deposited in a way that is seamless to the customer.

---

[5] See http://www.ksz.fgov.be for further information.

6 Discussion

We have sought to describe and discuss the issues associated with electronic service delivery in Public Authorities, comparing and contrasting it against existing conventional service delivery. We have also made reference to some of the lessons learned by the private sector where electronic service provision is already widely established. In doing so we have suggested that the aspects to e-service delivery within a PA can be categorised by the above framework of motivation, organisation and technology. The key elements of each of these are summarised in the table below.

Motivation	Organisation	Technology
Statutes	Silo architecture	Legacy systems
Can't choose customers	Culture	Processes
		Security

We have noted that the motivation behind PAs adds an important dynamic that clearly reveals a distinction between PAs and other organisations.

While it is important to sort out the infrastructure behind electronic service provision the majority of these problems have already been solved in industry, and through the extensive study already made in this area of the past couple of years, and we suggest that the key barrier to PAs providing effective electronic services are the organisational and cultural barriers. This is undoubtedly their biggest challenge.

References

1. Chan, E., and Swatman, P.M.C., Electronic Commerce: A Component Model, In Proceedings of 3rd Annual CollECTeR Conference on Electronic Commerce, Nov 1999.
2. European Commission, Web-Based Survey on Electronic Public Services: Results of the 2nd Measurement, Apr 2002. Available at http://europa.eu.int/information_society/eeurope/
3. Feinberg, R., and Kadam, R., E-CRM Web Service Attributes as Determinants of Customer Satisfaction With Retail Web Sites, In International Journal of Service Industry Management, Emerald, Toller Lane, Bradford, UK, 2002, 13(5), pp432–451.
4. Gouscos, D., Mentzas, G., and Georgiadis, P., Planning and Implementing e-Government Service Delivery: Achievements and Learnings from On-line Taxation in Greece, Workshop on e-Government at the 8th Panhellenic Conference on Informatics, Nov 8–10, 2001.
5. Heim, G.R., and Sinha, K.K., Design and Delivery of Electronic Services; In New Service Development, Creating Memorable Experiences, Sage, 1999, Chapter 8, pp152–178.
6. OECD, The e-Government Imperative: Main Findings (Policy Brief), Organisation for Economic Co-operation and Development, 2003. Available online at: http://www.oecd.org/
7. Georgiadis, P., et al, SmartGov: A Knowledge-Based Platform for Transactional Electronic Services. In Lecture Notes in Computer Science 2456, Springer, 2002, pp 362–369.
8. PRISMA, Pan-European Best Practice in Service Delivery, PRISMA Project (IST-1999-29088). Available online at http://www.prisma-eu.net/deliverables/D3-2.PDF
9. UK Office of the E-Envoy, E-government Strategy Framework Policy and Guidelines: Registration and Authentication, Sept 2002. Available online at http://www.e-envoy.gov.uk/

Conceiving and Implementing Pan-european Integrated Public Services

Otmar Adam, Dirk Werth, and Fabrice Zangl

Institute for Information Systems (IWi) at the
German Research Center for Artificial Intelligence (DFKI)
Postfach 15 11 50, 66041 Saarbrücken, Germany
{adam,werth,zangl}@iwi.uni.sb.de

Abstract. One of the main strategic goals of the European Union is a borderless Europe. In reality there are yet a lot of steps to achieve this ambitious goal. An impediment to this mobility is the lack of integration in pan-European administrative processes. To solve the problems these business processes have to be made transparent to the citizen and public services need to be integrated. To do so, public administrations have to interact seamlessly vertically (Europe, nation, region, municipality) as well as horizontally (between countries) with each other. This implies not only the use of standards for data exchange but also the interoperability of business processes. InfoCitizen is a "proof-of-concept" e-government project in the context of the EU IST Framework Program 5 with a budget of more than three million Euros. Within InfoCitizen a European Information Architecture dealing with the interoperability problem has been developed. Based on these blueprints a prototype has been implemented and currently user-partners are evaluating the concepts and the system in interacting local showcases. In this paper the results of the project are shown by summarising the project so far. Findings are used to map out future tasks.

1 E-Government: The Third Stage

In parallel to the e-business the area of e-government has arisen and established. E-government can be defined as the information technology based formation of processes for public services [1]. Using e-government offers new possibilities to public administrations (PA) to interconnect themselves with others electronically. New forms of decision making, service handling or simply communication can be executed via internet, intranet or extranet and thereby change the way in which the PAs act and how to interact with the PAs [2].

E-government can be used to finally overcome internal barriers in Europe but the degree of support strongly depends on the degree of realisation of e-government. A structured analysis concept is the stage-of-realisation model [3]. It describes the realisation using the three (resp. four) stages starting from "Information" via "Communication" to "Transaction" and "Participation" which is also named "Integration" (e.g. [4]).

Added value from e-government increases from stage one to four [5]. If the citizen is able to digitally invoke public services, then he can realise significant reductions in

R. Traunmüller (Ed.): EGOV 2003, LNCS 2739, pp. 135–138, 2003.

costs and time. The gain in cost and time is relatively small in the stages 'Information' and 'Communication' compared to the additional costs. The enabling of transactions within PAs is a technological and organisational challenge, as it demands at least the following requisites:

- *Double process front-end:* changes in process so that citizens can interact with the process via the PA employee and also via the new medium internet.
- *Identification and authentication:* citizen must be able to identify himself and the PA has to ensure the authentication of the citizen.
- *Digital signature:* substituting paper-based documents by electronic ones also implies to replace the personal signature by a digital mechanism.

2 Integrated Public Services

A simple, one-step transaction enabling only appears to generate benefit. Analysing this mechanism, it turned out to be only a new interaction channel between administration and citizen. Looking at the main advantages of this electronification, reveals that there is only small amelioration in time, cost and quality if the process structure is not changed at the same time. Observing the analogue development in businesses shows that only the change of procedures enabled by new electronic systems has truly lead to a significant improvement in business processes.

PAs are affected exceedingly by this effect since a single process (e.g. marriage) often initiates a set of other service executions (issuance of certificate of birth, etc.). Currently the interaction between PAs is mostly paper-based and uses either mail or the citizen himself as a carrier. Therefore the transmission of certain information is often delayed or deficient. Moreover a citizen-based messaging system provokes a number of inconveniences for the citizen.

The approach of integrated, transparent public services is to change the initiative of the process invocation in a way that the direct customer (citizen, enterprises, PAs) of a public service only invokes that direct service offer and all indirectly linked services will be invoked consecutively. This means that process steps of indirectly linked services will be executed transparently, hence there is no need for the customer to follow the process.

3 The InfoCitizen Approach

The project InfoCitizen [6], funded by the European Commission under the 5th Research Framework Program, aims to create a pan-European Information Architecture for European PAs as well as to develop specific information technology that supports this architecture and ensures a seamless information exchange between public administrations on a pan-European level. Moreover, with this solution the EPAs were enabled to provide transparent and integrated public services for their citizens as well as for external clients.

InfoCitizen started in September 2001 with a project volume of 3.3 million for a duration of 24 months. Eleven organisations within five different EU-countries

(Germany, Greece, Italy, Portugal, Spain) are working together to succeed in the challenge of pan-European interoperability.

The first major milestone was the development of a generic Interoperability Framework, the *InfoCitizen European Architecture*. It describes the relations and specifications of information exchange between EPAs. In order to create a long-living and stable result, we decomposed the European Architecture into three parts from a conceptual architecture over a technical architecture to the system architecture.

To successfully communicate the services must understand each other. For solving the Babylonian problem of data format mapping, the *Common Document Language*, similar to Dublin Core and eGIF, has been developed. This open and extensible specification describes the data to be exchanged within InfoCitizen. It relies on state-of-the-art XML technology and is based on existing standards. Through this solution it becomes possible to integrate public services in an interoperable manner without the need to harmonise, and thus without the need to standardise the processes of the EPAs.

The information-technological realisation of the concepts described uses agent-technology. This is most suitable for our purposes because it assists and facilitates the process of service search and discovery. Therefore the main component of the InfoCitizen platform is the interoperability agent. It plans, controls and executes the information exchange. Using the emerging agent-technology enables the platform to efficiently search for, retrieve and distribute documents in a seamless manner, hence to offer integrated public services. The knowledge about services, their provider and their location is handled by a Service Repository containing all the relevant data.

A problem in real scenarios is the heterogeneity of EPAs. Within the context of the electronic support of service transactions triggered from or targeted to external systems, the existing legacy systems of the EPAs have to communicate with the other systems and therefore have to be – at least indirectly - connected to them. This connection is realised through the Service Supply Component, which acts as adapter between the existing legacy or standard software application systems of EPAs and the InfoCitizen platform. The Service Supply Component Architecture is a source code framework that simplifies and fastens the implementation of specific Service Supply Components.

The front-end should satisfy user needs in usability and process support. Based on internet-technologies we are developing a multi-lingual, customisable information portal solution that interfaces between the user and the InfoCitizen Platform.

In order to prove our concepts and implementations we are setting up a pilot system, which includes a local pilot showcases and a generalised, pan-European InfoCitizen trial, which will reflect experiences and results in the international information exchange.

Even as this pilot is showing interoperability only between four different European public administrations, we not only evidence the conceptual and technical feasibility of integrating these four specific offices. Considering the conceptual ideas and the technical realisation, we can show that at least interoperability between any public administration within these four countries can be established using the InfoCitizen European Architecture and the InfoCitizen Platform.

The SSCs, the Interoperability Platform, the Service Repository, and the front-end are systems that can be used on multiple platforms. The SSCs have to be able to adapt to different legacy systems. The front-end runs on any workstation of a public administration. For widespread database systems pre-build SSCs are developed that can be directly installed for the end-user. When installed each SSC represents a Web-Service. Furthermore a standard SSC is provided, that can handle documents based on the above mentioned Common Document Language. The agents use a SOAP connection to access the Web-Services. The front-end is web-based as well and can be used with any current browser and can therefore easily be used by PA employees with little training.

4 The Future of E-Government: Participation through Integration

Even if the first level transaction support is not yet implemented, the InfoCitizen project already prepares the next step of full public administration integration. This is due to the concept of interoperable and integrated public administrations in the European InfoCitizen Architecture. Despite the heterogeneous environment an organisational compatibility and comparability can be achieved.

Although integrated and transparent public services are only a milestone on the participation level of e-government, it yet shows the potentials and possibilities that are related to it. The open and extensible possibilities proposed by the InfoCitizen project, to network public administrations on a pan-European level, will reduce administrative borders in Europe. It will therefore allow the European citizen to feel a little more integrated and less limited in his working location choices.

References

1. Schmidt, B.; Spoun, S.: Wege zum Electronic Government. IDT Working Paper No. 1, St. Gallen, 2001
2. Schedler, K.: eGovernment und neue Servicequalität der Verwaltung. In: Gisler, Michael; Spahni, Dieter (Hrsg.) eGovernment: eine Standortbestimmung, 2. aktualisierte Aufl. (Haupt) Bern et al., 2001, S. 13–30.
3. Gisler, M.; Spahni, D.: E-Government – eine Standortbestimmung. Haupt Verlag: Bern, 2001.
4. Seel, C., Güngöz; Ö.: E-Government : Strategien, Prozesse, Technologien, Studie und Marktübersicht (Oktober 2002). In: IDS Scheer AG (Hrsg.), IDS Scheer Studien, Saarbrücken, 2002.
5. Taylor Nelson Sofres: Government Online – an international perspective, Annual global report, London, 2002.
6. Fernandez A.: "Towards inter-operability amongst European Public Administration" in the Proceedings of EGOV 2002 (Aix-en-Provence) Springer (Eds. R. Traunmüller and K. Lenk) pp 105–110.

On the Evolution of E-Government: The User Imperative

Leif Skiftenes Flak, Carl Erik Moe, and Øystein Sæbø

Department of Information Systems
Agder University College
Service Box 422, 4604 Kristiansand
{leif.flak,carl.e.moe,oystein.sabo}@hia.no

Abstract. This paper focuses the need for more research on user involvement and the investigation of stakeholders in e-Government initiatives. An investigation of existing work revealed a lack of research on those topics. As e-Government evolves and users mature, the value of their input can increase. The paper discusses the need and potential benefits of this approach. Finally, we suggest that existing stakeholder theory is investigated for adaptation into e-Government settings in order to map the complex body of interrelated stakeholders.

1 Introduction

E-Government involves using information and communication technology to deliver public services through digital channels. The benefits are expected to come from increased efficiency, better and more available services and increased participation and democratization [1].

Throughout the world governments are realizing the potential of placing traditional government services online [2]. This shift is considered to be a major transformation, not only an introduction of new technology [3], [4]. Varying degree of complexity and success are reported from different parts of the world. State of the art examples include Canada, Singapore and USA [5]. Others show that e-Government initiatives can be chaotic and unmanageable [1] thus demonstrating that the transition can be difficult.

Until now, the need for increased efficiency in public sector and the potential in information technology seem to have been the primary drivers of e-Government [6]. Little user involvement is presented in literature on e-Government development. This may be justified at an early stage of implementing new services. However, as users mature, we argue that their input is increasingly valuable in terms of improving the services and perhaps suggesting new opportunities.

IS literature argues the critical importance of user involvement in information systems design and development in general [7]. This point of view has only partly been emphasized in recent E-Government research. To investigate users there is a need for knowledge on who the users are. Little emphasize has been put on the identification of stakeholders in e-Government. This paper argues the necessity of determining and characterizing potential stakeholders as a prerequisite for identifying users.

R. Traunmüller (Ed.): EGOV 2003, LNCS 2739, pp. 139–142, 2003.

2 Importance of User Involvement

User involvement is commonly accepted as an important element in information system design (see e.g. [8], [7]). Barki and Hartwick [9] stress the need to identify users and user needs before an information system is designed and implemented.

Recent research has questioned the general assumption that user involvement leads to success [8]. Uncertainties on the real usefulness of user involvement add further arguments to an increased research focus on these issues. Public sector employees have traditionally performed the paper work in public administration. By moving towards e-forms, e-democracy and e-administration the citizens and businesses may perform more of the work themselves [1]. These groups may become even more important in the development of more sophisticated e-Government systems. By investigating citizens and businesses and their sevice needs it may be possible to add knowledge on their impacts.

It seems difficult to suggest improved products and services without knowing what the users really want from an e-Government system. To address this issue and provide a comprehensive understanding of user needs in terms of e-Government, we suggest an increased research focus on user involvement in e-Government initiatives.

3 Stakeholders

Krenner [10] and Heinderyckx [11] mention three groups of stakeholders of e-Government; public administration, businesses and citizens. Others present a slightly different grouping of different private and public organizations, customers and suppliers [12], [13]. Researchers have also pointed at the importance of knowing who the stakeholders are and what expectations and requirements they have [14], [15].

There is a certain criticism on some of the current initiatives in e-Government for being too much top-down managed [16], [17]. There has only been minor focus on other stakeholder group, like businesses and citizens. This may reduce the possibility of addressing the diversity of stakeholder requirements.

Stakeholder theory (see e.g. [18]) has evolved over four decades and has proven useful in determining stakeholders and unveiling their different requirements and relative influence on organizations. Kotter and Heskett [19] proved the importance of addressing all groups of stakeholders in order to obtain success. By restricting stakeholders to different groups with uniform properties, research may fail to investigate distinct differences within the groups. Stakeholders in the same group can have different needs and requirements. Contextual dependencies can give stakeholders different roles and expectations at different times. Government employees are also citizens, and businesses consist of citizens. What are the consequences of this diversity? Is it possible to divide stakeholders into different groups? By identifying different stakeholders and their characteristics, research could add valuable knowledge on actual users of an e-Government system.

4 Discussion

A potential problem with investigating user involvement is eliciting the user needs. There is a methodological problem with asking users about their future needs. How do users know what they would like to have before the service is offered them? There is a strand of theory on user involvement which may be useful in this context. There are some methodological approaches that can be useful to investigate future needs. Interviews, focus group interviews, prototyping or lab-experiences can be possible methods to use in this respect.

Research on user involvement may be even more important when digital government services become more familiar and usage matures. Users may increase their expectations and their possibility to articulate requirements. Research should therefore focus on initiatives that have been running for some time. Investigating best-practice cases may be one opportunity. It is also important to add knowledge on user involvement in failure projects. This may reveal differences between user involvement in successes and failures.

Different E-Government areas may be more influenced by user involvement than others. E-democracy is one part of E-Government initiatives where user involvement should be of a primary concern. Increasing the democracy participation is not possible without direct involvement by citizens and politicians. E-democracy project should therefore be investigated as regards to user involvement.

This paper argues the need for further elaboration of the stakeholders. Stakeholder theory state the general importance of knowing who the stakeholders are as well as identifying their requirements. This may be especially important when entering a transition like e-Government. New digital services and communication channels towards government may alter the traditional clustering of stakeholders. Digital divide may split citizens and businesses into new clusters of stakeholders.

We therefore suggest that introducing and adapting elements from stakeholder theory is investigated. Especially the grouping of stakeholders on different levels, as well as the nature of accountability for the different stakeholder groups, should be further investigated. This, or similar approaches, may provide the necessary tools to form an essential basis for the evolution of e-Government.

References

1. Layne, K., Lee, J. (2001). *Developing fully functional E-Government: A four stage model.* Government information quarterly Vol 18, issue 2, p122 15p
2. Blakeley, Craig, J. and Matsuura, Jeffrey H. (2001). *"e-Government: An engine to power e-Commerce development."* Proceedings of the 2nd European Conference on e-Government, Dublin, Ireland, pp. 39–48
3. Roy J (2003). *E-Government – Introduction.* Social science computer review.
4. Ho ATK (2002). *Reinvening local governments and the e-Government initiative.* Public administration review
5. Doucet, Kristin, 2001. *Canada Ranks First in E-Government Services.* CMA Management, Vol. 75 Issue 4, p 8.
6. Muir, A. and Oppenheim, C. (2002). *National information policy developments worldwide: electronic government.* Journal of information science, Vol 28, Issue 3, pp 173–186

7. Ives B and Olson MH (1984). User *involvement and MIS success- a review of research.* Management of science 30 (5)
8. Gallivan MJ, Keil M (2003). *The user-developer communication process: a critical case study.* Information system journal (1)
9. Barki, H. and Hartwick, J. (1994). *Measuring user participation, user involvement and user attitude.* MIS quarterly, march 1994
10. Krenner, J. (2002). *Reflections on the requirements gathering in a one-stop government project.* Proceedings of Electronic Government, First international conference, EGOV, Aix-en-Provence, France, pp 124–128.
11. Heinderyckx, F. (2002). *Assessing e-Government implementation processes: A pan-European survey of administrations officials.* Proceedings of Electronic Government, First international conference, EGOV, Aix-en-Provence, France, pp 111–115
12. Christensen, T. and Egeberg, M. (1997). *Forvaltningskunnskap.* Tano Aschehoug
13. Beynon-Davis, P. and Williams, M. (2002). *Electronic local government in the UK.* Proceedings of the 2nd European Conference on E-Government, St Catherine's College, Oxford, UK, pp 79–89.
14. Klein G and Jiang JJ. (2001). *Seeking consonance in information systems.* Journal of System Software 56 (2): 195–202.
15. Vidgen R (1997). *Stakeholders, soft systems and technology: Separation and mediation in the analysis of information system requirements.* Information system journal 7 (1): 21–46
16. Leith, P. and Morison, J. (2002). *UK online: Forcing citizen involvement into a technically-oriented framework.* Proceedings of the 2nd European Conference on E-Government, St Catherine's College, Oxford, UK, pp 419–423.
17. Morris, R. (2002). *Electronic service delivery – More than just technology.* Proceedings of the 2nd European Conference on E-Government, St Catherine's College, Oxford, UK, pp 299–311.
18. Clarke, T. (1998). *The Stakeholder Corporation: A Business Philosophy for the Information Age*, Long Range Planning, Volume 31, Issue 2, pp 182–194
19. Kotter, J. P. and Heskett, J. L. (1992). *Corporate culture and performance.* The free press. New York.

Usage of E-Government Services in European Regions

Markus Lassnig and Mark Markus

Salzburg Research Forschungsgesellschaft
Jakob-Haringer-Strasse 5/III
5020 Salzburg, Austria
{Markus.Lassnig,Mark.Markus}@SalzburgResearch.at
http://www.salzburgresearch.at

Abstract. This paper presents some of the findings of an international research project entitled BISER (www.biser-eu.com) – "Benchmarking the Information Society in European Regions", namely in the field of e-government. Citizen-to-administration as well as business-to-administration demand is analyzed in 28 regions (from 14 EU Member States), e.g. Brittany, Friesland, Greater Manchester or Tuscany. The survey reveals significant differences between businesses' and citizens' usage of e-government services, as well as between different European regions. Furthermore, it discusses potential barriers.

1 From National Supply to Regional Usage

Existing benchmarking studies are based on surveys at the national level [4] and analyze mainly the supply side of e-government activities [1], [2], [5]. Even when the focus is put on demand and usage, this is done in a rather general sense, not specifying the type of service [3]. At the same time, the (possible and probable) variations between regions (at the sub-national level) remain unconsidered. Such a benchmarking approach is justified to some extent, as the supply of e-government services is largely determined at the national level. This is true especially for issues such as taxes and customs duties, or social contributions and benefits which usually fall under the competence of national governments. Yet, a nationally harmonized service offer (e.g. for online tax declarations) does not necessarily imply that this service is used homogeneously all over the country.

Therefore, the BISER project conducted two surveys on demand for and usage of e-government services in 28 European regions by means of computer assisted telephone interviews: A regional population survey (RPS)[1] targeted at a sample of more than 11,300 citizens (i.e. about 400 interviews per region) and a regional decision maker survey (RDMS) targeted at a representative sample of more than 8,500 executives in different establishments (i.e. about 300 interviews per region).

---

[1] All figures from the Regional Population Survey (RPS) are preliminary results, as not all calculations of the raw data gathered were finished at the time of writing this paper.

R. Traunmüller (Ed.): EGOV 2003, LNCS 2739, pp. 143–146, 2003.

2 Are There Any (Significant) Regional Disparities?

The answer to this question could be both, yes and no, depending on the point of view.

On the one hand, there are remarkable differences between the 28 analyzed regions in terms of overall usage of different public web-based administration services[2]. Three statistical groups of regions can be differentiated within the RDMS. Five leading regions from Greece (Central Macedonia with 69.1%), Denmark (Fyn with 49.7%), Finland (Central Finland with 46.7%), Austria (Salzburg with 38.6%) and Sweden (Smaland and islands with 34.3%) have an overall average of 47.7% of businesses which are using e-government services. With a significantly lower overall average of 24.0%, the midfield comprises fifteen regions from France (Languedoc-Roussillion 27.9%, Ile-de-France 27.0%, Nord/Pas-de-Calais 22.5% and Brittany 21.8%), Germany (Stuttgart 27.6%, Magdeburg 24.2%, Mecklenburg-Western Pomerania 23.9%, Darmstadt 23.1% and Braunschweig 20.5%), Spain (Catalonia 26.5% and Castile-Leon 22.1%), Portugal (Lisaboa e Vale do Tejo 26.4%), Belgium (Liege 24.0%), Ireland (Border, Midlands and Western 22.3%) and the Netherlands (Friesland 20.3%). Business' usage of e-government services is lowest in Italian regions (Sicily 15.9%, Lazio 12.5%, Lombardy 10.5% and Tuscany 9.5%) and, surprisingly, UK regions (Leicestershire, Rutland and Northants 14.1%, Berkshire, Bucks and Oxfordshire 11.8%, Tees Valley and Durham 10.6% and Greater Manchester 9.8%), making an overall average of 11.8% for this group.

On the other hand, national clustering is partly perceivable within the RDMS: French, German and Spanish regions can be found at the statistical center with about 24%, while Italian and UK regions represent the two national groups at the end of the ranking. Yet, despite national clustering tendencies, there are notable distinctions in the demand for e-government services between several regions from the same countries: For instance, between the two Italian regions Tuscany and Sicily there is a difference of 6.6% in business' usage of e-government services and between Braunschweig and Stuttgart in Germany the difference is 7.1%. Even stronger regional distinctions result from the RPS. Between the two UK regions Berkshire, Bucks and Oxfordshire (16.1%) and Tees Valley and Durham (8.7%) there is a difference of 7.4% in citizens' usage of e-government services. In contrast to the RDMS, the RPS revealed a less significant national clustering.

3 Low Usage of Different Services

According to the recent growth outlined in the Cap Gemini web-based survey on electronic public services [2], a rapid and sustainable rise of the supply side can be expected. This, however, illuminates only one side of the medal and presents a distorted image of e-government, as the intensity of usage remains mostly out of the focus. BISER complements this deficiency and focuses on the usage of specific public administration services at the regional level.

---

[2] RPS: Filing income tax returns, requesting any personal documents, registering a car or other vehicle; RDMS: Payment of social contributions for employees, submission of tax declarations, customs declarations, participation in public invitations to tender.

Generally, the population's usage of e-government services is very low. On average it does not even cross the 5% mark (in leading Friesland in the Netherlands 15.5% and 0.2 % in Border, Midlands and Western Ireland). With an average of 3.1% "filing the income tax return" via Internet seems to find the biggest interest among citizens of all regions, whereas "requesting personal documents" (1.3%) and "car registration services" (1%) find much less attention. To a high degree the ranking of these figures corresponds with the traditional (offline) interaction between population and public administration in the last 12 months: 37.1% of the population have "filed income tax returns", 18.9% "requested personal documents" and 13.5% "registered cars or other kinds of vehicles". This points to the fact that a big majority of citizens, for whatever reasons, still prefer the traditional way of government interaction – at least in respect of the services mentioned here.

On the whole, the usage of business-to-administration e-government services is slightly higher – again with significant differences between diverse types of services. On average, the transaction most often executed online is the "payment of social contributions for employees" with 15.2%. About 13.8% of all enterprises process "tax declarations, like corporation or value added tax" online, 6.6% "participate in public invitations to tender" via the Internet and about 3.7% "submit customs declarations" online.

Though still "immature", this indicator is nevertheless a reliable (because very precise) and valid indicator for measuring the demand for and the intensity of usage of e-government services. Therefore, it can be expected that it will gain importance, especially in future long-term data analyses.

4 Disparity between Population's and Business' Usage

The results of the two surveys reveal a remarkable imbalance in the usage of e-government services arising between the population (RPS) and businesses (RDMS). Though expected, this imbalance is still noticeable.

Generally, businesses do about twice as many interactions online as the population. While on average only about 12% of the population had "any e-government interaction" (with a regional distribution from 27.8% to 4.5%) in the last 12 months, there were about 25% of businesses involved with some kind of e-government services (ranging from 69.1% in Central Macedonia to 9.3% in Tuscany).

In the case of Central Macedonia, the discrepancy between the population's and business' usage of e-government services is most obvious, as this region has, simultaneously, the highest score of all regions in the RDMS and the lowest score in the RPS. Yet, this result appears to be an outlier, probably due to the high level of bureaucracy for businesses in Central Macedonia. About 85% of all Macedonian enterprises have to get in touch regularly with public authorities for the payment of social contributions for employees and about 87% for the purpose of tax declarations, which is nearly twice as high as in other European regions. This result points to a high complexity of (any) indicator for e-government usage and calls attention to a careful interpretation: In some cases, a strong usage of online transactions with the public administration may not primarily be explained by a high acceptance of e-government services, but more by an oversized bureaucracy in general – where e-government services are primarily a remedy for the vast red tape.

5 Barriers

Generally, there seems to be rising future demand for e-government services by both citizens and businesses. On average 41.9% of enterprises and 51.6% of the population (having used these services and the Internet in general in the last 12 months, but not having done this online) would like to use e-government services in the future. On the other hand, there is a high percentage of citizens (42.6%) and businesses (49.6%) who used these services (offline) in the last 12 months and have got access to the Internet, but still prefer to process these transactions in the traditional way. This nourishes the assumption that there are some barriers preventing citizens and businesses from the usage of e-government services.

Safety issues still constitute one of the biggest impediments for using e-government services, as both businesses (34.6%) and especially citizens (51.3%)[3] perceive public services on the Internet as less safe than using the traditional interaction with government bodies. Interestingly enough, businesses (30.4%) consider public services on the Internet just as difficult to use as citizens (30.9%). In comparison with other barriers, extra costs incurred by the Internet do not pose that substantial usage obstruction. Nevertheless, usage costs should not be neglected, as 19.7% of businesses and 34.4% of the population consider them as an obstacle.

According to the attitude of potential users towards e-government services and with regard to barriers perceived, it could be assumed that policies aimed at e.g. raising awareness of such services and improving (perceived) security and quality are likely to facilitate the demand for e-government services.

References

1. Accenture (2001). e-Government, the commitment continues. www.accenture.com
2. Cap Gemini Ernst & Young (2002). Webbasierte Untersuchung des elektronischen Service-Angebots der Öffentlichen Hand. www.de.cgey.com/servlet/PB/show/1005708/eEurope.pdf
3. EOS Gallup Europe (2001). Flash Eurobarometer 112. Internet and the Public at Large. http://europa.eu.int/comm/public_opinion/flash/fl112_en.pdf
4. SIBIS (2003). Statistical Indicators Benchmarking the Information Society. www.sibis-eu.org
5. World Market Research Centre (2001). Global e-Government Survey. www.worldmarketsanalysis.com/pdf/e-govreport.pdf

---

[3] Percentage of respondents who "agree somewhat" or "agree completely" to the statement that "public services on the Internet seem less safe than using the traditional way".

Processes in E-Government Focus: A Procedure Model for Process Oriented Reorganisation in Public Administrations on the Local Level

Jörg Becker, Lars Algermissen, and Björn Niehaves

University of Muenster
Dept. of Information Systems
Leonardo-Campus 3, 48149 Muenster, Germany
{becker,islaal,bjni}@wi.uni-muenster.de
http://www.wi.uni-muenster.de/is/

Abstract. Process oriented analysis and optimisation of administrative procedures are key prerequisites for the successful organisational and technical restructuring of municipal administration in the move to Electronic Government. The exploitation of the full potential of information and communications technology can only be achieved through structured processes. The complexity of process models requires both a systematic preparation, and a methodical approach to the implementation of process oriented E-Government projects. Therefore this article provides a procedure model for process oriented organisation design, underlined by a case study which describes an optimisation project of the building permission procedure in the German municipality of Emsdetten.

1 Introduction

Public administration has been confronted by a series of new demands on the one hand and has been forced to cost and staff cuttings on the other hand. For some years, the term 'E-Government' has been universally proposed as a way of closing the public administrations' modernisation and performance gap [1]. The core of E-Government is the execution of administrative processes [2], it entails the simplification and implementation of information, communication and transaction processes, in order to achieve, by means of information and communication technology, an administrative service, within and between authorities and, likewise, between authorities and private individuals or companies [3]. The exploitation of the full potential of E-Government modernisation efforts can only be achieved through structured processes. Therefore, this article presents a procedural model for the implementation of process modelling projects in public administrations. In section one we describe how modelling projects in the public administration should be prepared. In section two we show how the target environments for modelling projects can be identified. In section three we describe the current situation of the selected building permission procedure in the Emsdetten administration and the weaknesses that were identified. Based on this we derived improved optimized target processes which are described in section four.

R. Traunmüller (Ed.): EGOV 2003, LNCS 2739, pp. 147–150, 2003.

2 Preparation of Process Modelling

As a rule, comprehensive preparation is essential for process modelling, because, on the one hand, the model design is characterised by a high degree of process complexity and on the other hand, the information model is characterised by a high degree of object complexity. When considering the aim of the modelling ('why' modelling should be done, e. g. certification, selection of software, organisation design), it is necessary to determine both the object of modelling ('what' should be modelled, for example, a total model of the business vs. a partial model), and the modelling methods and tools ('how' modelling should be done).

The main *objectives of process modelling* are organisation and application system design [4]. Models for organisational design require a high degree of clarity, whereas models for application system design require a high degree of technical precision (for example, through prepared data models), because of their close relationship to the final implementation. The main purpose of process modelling by the Emsdetten administration was organisation design, in particular, the process oriented reorganisation of administration processes. An examination of application system design was only considered worthwhile on the basis of organisational process improvements [5].

The principal question to be answered in determining the *modelling object* is whether a total model or a partial model of an object system should be produced. Because the service portfolio of the Emsdetten city administration consists of more than a thousand individual products, selected key processes were focused.

The final preparatory step is the *selection of a suitable modelling method*. There are various and diverse model types for modelling (business) processes. Petri-nets [6], added-value chain diagrams [7], and event-driven process chains (EPC) [8], are amongst the best known. The choice of a model type to be used within the framework of process modelling is influenced mainly by the purpose of the application and the requirements of the model users. Application aims, such as simulation and workflow management, require model types which produce detailed, precise, formally itemised models. This excludes, for example, the use of added-value chain diagrams. Application objectives such as process oriented reorganisation, which underlay the case study, require less formal models. A detailed analysis of administrative processes' most salient characteristics and an analysis of the demands on a modelling method in E-Government can be found in [9]. Based on the requirements to a modelling method, in the case of the Emsdetten city administration, the event-driven process chain (EPC) was selected as a method, because of its high degree of clarity, and its potential for integrated evaluation. The high level of clarity was especially important in the interview phase as the results were documented in process models and had to be verified by the employees. Moreover the final presentation of target processes had to be easy understandable for a range of individuals with heterogeneous backgrounds (e.g. mayor, or information technology officer). The other advantage was that weaknesses in the processes could easily be identified by analyzing the models. Using this method the objectives were achieved and in hindsight, this choice proved to be valid.

3 Identification of Target Environments

Before the first modelling process, relevant problem areas should, first and foremost be identified, classified and then prioritised with respect to financial and personnel resource constraints. A pragmatic method of identifying target services for process improvements, hitherto used by many administrations in the context of the new public management concept, has until now centred around available product catalogues. The existing services are *classified by a matrix* which is based on two dimensions, the level of interaction (information, communication and transaction) and the degree of integration (media break, no media break, and automated). In order to select appropriate services on the basis of this classification scheme, a two-phase procedure comprising the successive application of the *portfolio method* and the *profile method* was applied. The main advantage is that, from phase to phase, the number of services considered and the level of precision of the investigation increase through using a rising number of decision making criteria.

The Emsdetten city administration followed this two step approach. After using the project profile method the council selected the building application process to be the object of further analysis and process modelling.

4 Modelling of Current Situation and Analysis of Weaknesses

In the process of modelling and analysing the current situation, the "state of play" is captured, analysed and evaluated according to the level of the attainment of the goals pursued. Thus, this modelling promotes administrative transparency and an understanding of specialist issues and problems. It forms a basis for identifying weak points and the interrelated potential improvements. In terms of the case study, the building consent procedure was analysed and documented in an interview phase that lasted several weeks.

The following weaknesses were discovered:
- Transferring from one employee to another
- Many offices participating
- Frequent media breaks

Additionally an information deficit is created amongst the service departments involved (unclear legal situation, forms that are difficult to understand etc.).

5 Target Modelling and Process Optimisation

To rectify weaknesses, a range of different measures was devised on the basis of target processes derived from the current processes and strategies recommended by the Civic Office Division for Administration Simplification.
- Introduction of building conferences
- Introduction of a process manager
- Utilisation of the workflow component of the building application
- Introduction of a Geographical Information System
- Enhancement of Information Quality.

6 Conclusions and Suggested Directions for Further Research

The procedural model that has been introduced and the proposed modelling technology have proven effective in achieving objectives and appropriate and correct for the case study. Despite some remaining developmental barriers, process management in an E-Government context, is a viable mechanism for advancing efforts to modernise an administration.

It is clear that there are considerable structural analogies amongst various administrative processes within a civic authority, and to a greater extent with similar processes between authorities. In moving towards an extensive process oriented and IT-supported modernisation of an administration, the development of a reference process model as a store of domain knowledge has the potential to significantly reduce the complexity of E-Government projects and to simplify their implementation by means of an orientation around reference processes.

References

1. Budäus, D., Schwiering, K.: Die Rolle der Informations- und Kommunikationstechnologien im Modernisierungsprozeß öffentlicher Verwaltungen. In: Scheer, A.-W. (ed.): Electronic Business und Knowledge Management, Heidelberg (1999) 143–165 [in German]
2. Langkabel, T.: e-Government – Der Weg ist das Ziel. In: V.O.P., Sonderheft 2 (2000) 6–8 [in German]
3. Becker, J., Algermissen, L., Niehaves, B.: E-Government – State of the art and development perspectives, Working Report No. 94 of the Department of Information Systems, University of Muenster. Muenster (2003)
4. Rosemann, M., Schwegmann, A.: Vorbereitung der Prozessmodellierung. In: Becker, J., Kugeler, M., Rosemann, M. (eds.): Prozessmanagement, 3rd Edition. Berlin et al. (2002) 48 [in German]
5. Raymond, L., Pare, G., Bergeron, F.: Matching Information Technology and Organisational Structure: An Empirical Study with Implications for Performance. In: European Journal of Information Systems, Vol 4 (1995) No 1, 3–16
6. Jensen, K.: An Introduction to High-Level Petri Nets, Int. Symposium on Circuits and Systems, Proceedings, Kyoto, Japan, Vol. 2. New York (1985) 723–726
7. Porter, M. E.: The Competitive Advantage of Nations. London (1999)
8. van der Aalst, W.: Formalization and Verification of Event-driven Process Chains. In: Information and Software Technology, Vol 41 (1999) No 10, 639–650
9. Becker, J., Algermissen, L., Niehaves, B.: Die Ereignisgesteuerte Verwaltungsprozesskette (EVPK) - Prozessmodellierung unter besonderer Berücksichtigung verwaltungsspezifischer Anforderungen. In: 2. Internationales Rechtsinformatik Symposium 2003 (Salzburg, Österreich) – Conference Proceedings [in German, in print]

Consumer-SC: An E-Gov Portal for Consumers Rights Protection in Brazil

Thais H. Bigliazzi Garcia[1], Irineu Theiss[1], Patrícia Zimath[1], Hugo Cesar Hoeschl[1], Fabrício Donatti[1], Gean Marques Loureiro[2], and Tânia Cristina D´Agostini Bueno[1]

[1] Juridical Institute of Intelligence and Systems
Lauro Linhares, 728, sala 212
CEP 88036-002, Florianópolis, Santa Catarina, Brazil
{thais,hugo,tania,irineu}@ijuris.org
patricia@quantico.com.br
[2] Municipal Chamber of Florianópolis
XV de Novembro, 214
CEP 88010-400, Florianópolis, Santa Catarina, Brazil
gean@cmf.gov.br

Abstract. Improving access to information and governmental assistance to citizens is nowadays considered as an important mechanism to enhance citizenship. As the number of web-enabled citizens increases, government is expected to deliver more effective on-line services, especially designed to meet the needs of the constituents. Since many citizens want to have the convenience of interacting with all levels of the government using information technology tools, the electronic government has consolidated its position as the best alternative to improve the interaction between government and citizen. It is described herein a Brazilian experience in developing an e-gov project for consumers rights protection. The project "Consumer-SC: Santa Catarina Consumer's Portal" applies Information Technology and Artificial Intelligence techniques to provide means of higher quality and efficiency on the field of consumer protection in Brazil.

1 Introduction

The Code for Consumer's Protection and Defense is a legislation enforced by the Brazilian government in the early 90's to update consumer's protection laws and regulation. Although this Code represents a huge progress in terms of consumer's protection in Brazil, the government policy is still inefficient.

The major problem faced by the government is that the consumers rights are unknown by the massive population. In the state of Santa Catarina, the problem is even worse: there is not enough information available to the citizens and the institutional support – from governmental and non-governmental organizations – is overloaded and rarely cost free.

With the aim of providing a solution to this problem, researchers from the Juridical Institute of Intelligence and Systems (IJURIS) and from the Federal University of Santa Catarina, joining forces with a number of governmental entities, especially the Consumers and Human Rights Commission of the Municipal Chamber of the city of

R. Traunmüller (Ed.): EGOV 2003, LNCS 2739, pp. 151–156, 2003.

Florianópolis and the State of Santa Catarina Consumers Rights Public Office, have developed "Consumer-SC – The Santa Catarina's Consumers Portal".

The Portal will assist consumer and community groups, government institutions and other interested groups and individuals in understanding and exerting their rights as consumers.

2 The Electronic Government and the Consumer's Rights Policies in Brazil

Since the introduction of the Consumers' Rights Protection and Defense Code, the legal shelter of the consumers is becoming more and more effective. The State acts positively, tutoring the consumer, in order to balance the power between the market forces.

However, the consumers rights remain unknown by the majority of the Brazilians. The weak performance of the state in protecting the consumers rights is attributable to the lack of information, people's unfamiliarity about their rights, and to the structural exhaustion of the consumer's protection institutions. Moreover, the intercommunication gap between federal, state and local consumer's protection agencies makes even harder to citizens the access to an adequate guidance and orientation.

The situation in the State of Santa Catarina does not look better: only 45 cities out of a total of 293 have a municipal consumer protection head office, the Consumer Protection and Defense Agency – PROCON. Currently, this agency provides a website where the citizen can just check the course of its administrative procedures, without any additional information.

Based on this diagnosis, there is no doubt that it is necessary to establish an entirely new policy to guide and protect the consumers, particularly in Santa Catarina. Electronic government is indicated as the best and the most efficient alternative to help the Brazilian government to promote and enforce consumer's protection. Based on e-gov services – and also by disseminating knowledge – the government can reorganize its consumer's protection policies.

With the objective of creating a model for the State of Santa Catarina, IJURIS researchers analyzed the most successful projects related to electronic government and consumers rights to develop the most appropriated strategy for the Brazilian consumers. To build a Portal came out as the best alternative to meet that objective.

2.1 Successful E-Gov Programs in the Consumer Protection and Best Practices over the World

In the scope of the consumer's rights, some successful initiatives use technological resources to develop projects with the purpose of improving electronic services offered to the public.

Among the categories of e-gov services applied to consumer protection offered nowadays two of them will be highlighted: informational services and virtual assistance.

Information services intend to provide awareness to consumers by turning available publications, guidelines, legislation; rankings of complaints and best price lists offered by consumer protection agencies and others. Spreading information helps to bring knowledge closer to the citizens. Being aware of their rights and duties as consumers, citizens will be able to co-operate with the government to have a more effective protection of the community interests.

Public services on the Internet providing information are basically made available through a Portal or a website. A Portal works as a true virtual counter of information and help desk for rendering services.

The informational services include also manuals with orientations; FAQs - Frequently Asked Questions, municipal and state legislation and sentences.

Another category of electronic service offered to consumers is the virtual assistance, which comprises basically the electronic complaint form and mail assistance.

The electronic forms assure a higher efficiency to the governmental performance in the protection of consumer rights, optimizing its agencies by eliminating the fulfillment and filing of papers. Some state agencies offer on-line claim forms, by which the citizen can file a complaint against any organization. The PROCON agency of the state of Minas Gerais, in Brazil, is distinguished by accomplishing this service, enabling the consumer to send a claim or any kind of request directly to the PROCON Decision Assembly.

3   Consumer-SC: Innovating in Electronic Services for the Consumers Rights Protection

After analyzing the e-gov services available to the consumers in Brazil, even though there were excellent services being offered to citizens, the social demand for free assistance about consumers rights in the State of Santa Catarina remains as a pending issue.

In the view of providing orientation to the consumers, IJURIS Institute and the Federal University of Santa Catarina joined efforts with the Santa Catarina State Government and with the Human Rights Commission of the Municipal Chamber of Florianópolis, also supported by the State of Santa Catarina Consumers Rights Public Office, in order to create a model of legal assistance on the consumers rights issue.

The project represents a pioneer initiative in terms of Information Technology (IT) and Artificial Intelligence (AI) techniques for e-gov implementation. Consumer-SC – The Santa Catarina's Consumers Portal, is intended to enlarge the consumers protection assistance and to spread related knowledge all over the country. The Portal should be a very important tool to strengthen consumer protection, therefore strengthening democracy and citizenship in Brazil.

Consumer-SC is the first Portal in the country to congregate scientific and academic researchers, e-gov services, the Aletheia software, and free virtual legal assistance for consumers rights protection.

The idea goes beyond delivering information; it is intended to promote innovative research related to consumer rights, in order to stimulate the discussion and enable new solutions to meet community needs. It will be an open space for discussion, for

154 T.H. Bigliazzi Garcia et al.

the exerting of citizenship, and for the promotion of awareness and social development.

Consumer–SC is intended to promote fairness in the marketplace and consumer protection in Brazil. By using intelligence systems and e-gov solutions, the Portal should promote the participation of citizens in public initiatives related to consumer rights; provide, virtually, free legal assistance on consumer rights, and stimulate the development of educational initiatives aiming at increasing the public awareness.

3.1 Aletheia: An Intelligent Software for the Consumers Rights Protection

Anywhere in the world, consumers become bewildering to know what to do or where to go when things go wrong. Intending to help the constituents, Aletheia is an intelligent guide for their rights and dues as consumers. Because of the general ignorance about the consumer's rights, Aletheia was developed as a system able to make the correspondence between the law and customary situations.

The software, by the way, does not require specific knowledge about consumer's rights and is a well-structured, easy tool to help citizens to understand the Brazilian consumer's laws. The domain is the Brazilian Consumers' Protection and Defense Code, which represents the consolidation of a huge amount of laws and regulations into a single act, with 119 articles.

The system allows the citizen to write a query in natural language - describing a customary situation - responding to the request with the legal solution to the case. Artificial Intelligence and Information Technology techniques were applied to solve consumers' major difficulty: the comprehension of the legal text and its correspondence with daily situations. The technology behind the intelligent system is mostly Case-Based Reasoning (CBR) [3] and Structured Contextualized Search (SCS) [4].

The above mentioned techniques reproduce the reasoning used by jurists when solving a problem [5], enabling Aletheia to be a "self-service" software, were the consumers can ask the system whether a daily situation – involving marketplace relationships – fits to any legal case described within the Code.

In Aletheia, the knowledge is represented in the form of cases, consisting of the original text of the law and a set of indexes in the form of six attribute-value pairs: *the Law Articles, Paragraphs, Legal Situation (Theme), Secondary Theme, Related Concepts* and *Daily Situations*. The indexes *legal situation* and *themes* are also part of a list presented by the interface, whereby the user can do direct search.

The indexes need to be determined from the viewpoint of the relevance in the domain in accordance with their importance for new situations. The objective of the system is to retrieve the most similar article from the Code in comparison a current situation described by the user. [6]

In order to achieve this goal, the system interface contains a search field, where the user describe a query and also two lists - organized by titles –, that contains the most asked queries and customary situations, classified by their Legal Solution.

The objective of the system is to retrieve the most similar article from the Code compared to a current situation described by the user. To achieve this goal, the system interface contains a search field where the user can write the query, and two lists containing the most frequently asked queries and customary situations classified by their *Legal Solution*.

Aletheia is a system for government-citizen transactions (G2C), as it enables citizens to become aware of their rights and duties as a consumer. The system is a strong enforcement mechanism of consumer's protection initiatives, designed to be available on the Internet, for free download from the Portal Consumer-SC.

Since the Portal was launched, in March, 2003, over 1.500 people have had contact with Aletheia. Reports shows that the software has being used in public offices, universities and comunity centers, in order to help citizens to comprehend theirs rights as a consumer.

4   Conclusion

Brazil has got to accomplish great performance in implementing e-gov initiatives, not limited to web sites providing information to citizens, but also a number of services with high interactivity and efficiency, as in the case of the annual income tax information, 90% of which is done on the Internet, and the *Comprasnet* Portal, which has already consolidated as an efficient purchasing tool for the government.

The Consumer's Portal (*consumer-SC*) is pioneering by presenting a new way of showing the consumers rights. Most of the sites about consumer defense have only text information about the citizen's rights and sometimes it contains a large number of pages using a difficult vocabulary. Aletheia software solves this problem, allowing the citizen to write a query in natural language, describing a customary situation, and responding with a legal solution to the case. The use of artificial intelligence techniques enables the system to make the correspondence between the law and customary situations presented by the user.

A strong point in the case of the *consumer-SC* Portal project is the integration of the entities involved: academic researchers, State and local government offices, and local legislative power. The result is a powerful tool to support the consumers rights protection initiatives, ultimately representing a contribution for citizens protection enhancement.

Acknowledgments. The authors would like to thank the support of the Juridical Institute of Intelligence and Systems – IJURIS, the Federal University of Santa Catarina, the Consumers Rights Research Institute and the Informática Jurídica Lab, the Municipal Chamber of the city of Florianópolis and the State of Santa Catarina Consumers Rights Public Office.

Special thanks to Prof Aires José Rover for the leadership in the project, Msc. André Bortolon and Msc. Eduardo Mattos for the implementation coordination.

References

1. Governments Using Technology to Serve the Citizen. Washington, DC. US Intergovernmental Advisory Board, 1999. 38p.
2. BITTENCOURT FILHO, J. C. M. The Public Services Provided by Brazilian Government over the Internet. Universidade Federal da Bahia - Escola de Administração - Núcleo de Pós-Graduação em Administração, 04/2000.

3. AMONDT A., Plaza, E. (1994). Case-Based Reasoning: Fundamental Issues, Methodological Variations, and System Approaches. AI Communications, 17(1), 1994.
4. HOESCHL, H. C., et all. Olimpo: Contextual structured search to improve the representation of UN Security Council resolutions with information extraction methods In: 8a. International conference on artificial intelligence and law, 2001, St. Louis.ICAIL 2001 Proceedings. New York: ACM SIGART, 2001. p.217–218.
5. BUENO, T. C. D., et all. JurisConsulto: Retrieval in jurisprudential text bases using juridical terminology In: The Seventh International Conference on Artificial Intelligence and Law, 1999, Oslo. Proceedings of the Conference. New York: ACM, 1999. v.1. p.147–155.
6. HOESCHL, H. C.; Bueno, T. C. D.; Mattos, E. S.; Bortolon, A.; Ribeiro, M. S.; Theiss, I.; Barcia, R. M.; Mattos, E. S. Structured Contextual Search for the UN Security Council In: ICEIS - 5th International Conference on Enterprise Information Systems, 2003, Angers Selected Papers Books: Enterprise Information Systems IV, Kluwer, 2003.
7. Consumer SC – Santa Catarina Consumer's Portal. <www.ijuris.org/consumidor.sc>
8. Juridical Institute of Intelligence and Systems – IJURIS. <www.ijuris.org>

Requirements for Using Agent-Based Automation in Distributed E-Government Applications

Jarmo Korhonen, Lasse Pajunen, and Juha Puustjärvi

Software Business and Engineering Institute
Helsinki University of Technology
P.O.Box 9600, 02015 HUT, Finland
{jarmo.korhonen,lasse.pajunen,juha.puustjarvi}@hut.fi

Abstract. This paper describes some requirements for using software agents to automate many tasks in eGovernment applications. First, the architecture must be able to support workflow engines, transparent reliability, and security. Second, data must be presented in a format that can be understood by any system component that uses the data. Third, it must be possible to define processes in terms of distributed workflows. These processes may be originated from laws, internal guidelines, or technical specifications. The definitions must in any case be unambiguous, finite, deterministic, and refer only to public data structures. Agents can then be used to run the defined long-term workflows. We also present a sample Web service –based eGovernment service, based on new Finnish law governing government processes.

1 Introduction

EGovernment applications often require combining several component software systems from same or different organizations into one distributed software system. To the end user, the whole system should be presented as a single service [1]. Most state-of-the-art eGovernment applications offer browser-based services to citizens, but do not have an interface for software system integration, such as Web services architecture. This makes it difficult for businesses to automate their government-related processes and it slows internal government systems integration.

We have developed a prototype system for Finnish Ministry of Finance that uses Web services, workflow specifications, and software agent technologies to implement a government process for petitioning an environmental permit. Our goal was to develop an architecture that can be used to automate the routine petition process. We present in this paper some requirements that we have noticed that can be used to make the systems more flexible for automating eGovernment applications.

2 Architecture

An eGovernment application requires combining component software systems into a combined architecture. The complete application consists of one or more government

R. Traunmüller (Ed.): EGOV 2003, LNCS 2739, pp. 157–160, 2003.

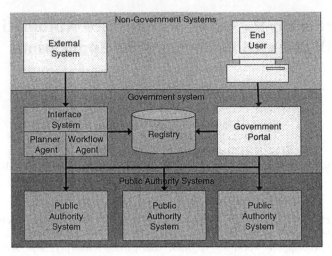

Fig. 1. Layers in System Architecture

internal systems. In addition, we have separated the interface component into a separate front-end layer and an application logic layer. This two-layer approach is similar to the One-Stop Government approach in [1] and the eGOV project [2].We also see a third layer consisting of component software systems in external organizations (e.g. companies) that may be needed to integrate to the eGovernment system. We present the whole three-layered architecture in Fig. 1.

The Interface System integrates separate public authority systems (PAS) into one automated eGovernment application. It provides automated Web service interface to external systems and makes self-management and self-configuration at integrated system level, as described in [5]. Government portal may use component systems (PAS) directly, or through the Interface System, to provide single user interface.

The Interface System consists of public interface, planner agent, and workflow agent. The public web service interface is the eGovernment application as seen from the outside. Planner Agent uses service calls, the registry, PAS service descriptions, system status information, and application-specific knowledge to construct a workflow for given service call. This workflow is given to workflow agent that is responsible for executing, monitoring and reporting the progress of the long-time workflow. As the execution may take long time, the workflow may also require re-planning. Planner agent is intended to make the workflows more flexible.

3 Prototype

We have developed an eGovernment application prototype for automating processes in petitioning of environmental permits. The process is specified in two Finnish laws: generic process law and a specific law for environmental protection. In addition, the participating organizations have their own practices. Developing the prototype has required co-operation from all parties. These organizations already work together so there were few difficulties in the co-operation. With new partners or partners at different levels of the hierarchy (e.g. integrating national systems with communal systems), more organizational problems may arise. There were no cultural problems, as all participants were from Finnish public sector.

The prototype includes three component software systems: from Kouvola town, South-Eastern Environmental Center, and Administration Court of Kouvola. There was no previous integration of their information systems. The system architecture also separates the front-end system from the internal systems of the organizations.

We designed the distributed workflow as UML diagrams based on the laws and practical processes. The BPEL4WS workflow specification was then defined based on the design documents. Communication with officials was non-technical.

Prototype was implemented using Java software tools for Web services, Apache Tomcat server, mySQL database and a workflow engine for BPEL4WS [3] language. We implemented a conceptual level interface system for each component system. For data transfer between systems, we used one moderately complex XML schema that is shared by all component systems. It consists of two parts: an application form section that remains constant during the whole workflow and processing information section that contains information and decisions added by different officials and stakeholders.

We perceived three main technical problems with this approach and current tools. First, the current distributed workflow model supports a centralized control. We were able to divide the workflows to the component systems, but there should also be a way to automate the composition and verify the overall workflow. Second, the backend systems are developed independently and have different architectures and development platforms. There should be recommended technologies and standard to integrate government systems; otherwise the integration mechanisms will also be incompatible with each other. Third, the integration mechanism is not flexible. Often a change in one component system requires changes in the workflows and interfaces of other component systems. With multiple concurrent distributed eGovernment applications, it is not feasible to restrict software evolution in this way.

4 Requirements and Conclusions

We have defined a set of requirements for automated distributed eGovernment applications to address the problems defined in previous section. The requirements are divided to process requirements, architecture requirements, and data requirements.

Processes may be defined in any methodology that suits the application. To be able to automate the eGovernment process, process must be unambiguous, deterministic, and finite. All activities and participants must have consistent and unique identifiers. All references must use those identifiers. This is needed to be able to re-use existing services in other applications. All conditions should be explicitly stated, except when a person is involved. Even then, all possible outcomes should be listed for routine decisions. The processes must also have clear starting and ending points to ensure the complete correct execution with transactions.

Architectural requirements include security, reliability, and flexibility requirements. EGovernment applications require high security and reliability to be legitimate and acceptable to citizens and businesses. Main requirement for automation is that the supported security and reliability features should be explicitly defined. Then it is possible to restrict automation based on supported features.

We divide the security infrastructure into three main areas: point-to-point security, registry-level security, and system-wide security. The point-to-point security concentrates on protecting the message content (e.g. SOAP message security [4]) and contains elements like authorization, encryption, signing, and non-repudiation. The registry-level security includes authentication and trust. The system-wide security contains elements like privacy, legal requirements, security policies, auditing, and monitoring.

There should be at least three levels of reliability in automated eGovernment applications. First, there must be web service message-level reliability infrastructure. Second, there should be support for very long-term transactions. We have recently implemented simple transactional workflow ontology [6] in DAML+OIL and a workflow engine for running those workflows. The proposed architecture includes a workflow agent that supports very long transactions by replanning the workflow if necessary. We are currently extending our workflow engine with planning features. Third, the legitimacy of process definitions is a key concern in eGovernment applications. All stakeholders and relevant officials must be provably informed and heard for the whole process to be legitimate.

Flexibility can be improved by using explicit descriptions of supported features instead of hardwired implementation. In practice, this means for example always using registry queries instead of fixed addresses. Data structures should also be defined explicitly by for example a public XML schemas or ontologies, to avoid hardwired integration at data level. The data structure definitions should be available online.

Processes, software platforms and data structures should all support automation as defined by these requirements. Then software agent and Semantic Web technologies can be used to increase automation of eGovernment applications and government productivity. Automation will also lead to more convenience to the citizens.

References

1. Traunmueller, R., Wimmer, M.: Directions in E-Government: Processes, Portals, Knowledge. Proceedings of the DEXA International Workshop "On the Way to Electronic Government", IEEE Computer Society Press, Los Alamitos, CA, 2001
2. EGOV – an Integrated Platform for Realising Online One-Stop Government. http://www.egov-project.org/
3. BPEL4WS – Business process execution language for web services, available online at http://www.ibm.com/developerworks/webservices/library/ws-bpel/
4. OASIS Web Services Security. Draft specification. http://www.oasis-open.org/committees/wss/
5. Jeffrey O. Kephart, David M. Chess. The Vision of Autonomic Computing. Computer, January 2003.
6. Jarmo Korhonen, Lasse Pajunen, Juha Puustjärvi. Using Transactional Workflow Ontology in Agent Cooperation. Agents in Information Management Workshop, EurAsian ICT conference, 2002.

The Role of Web Services in Digital Government*

Johann Gamper and Nikolaus Augsten

Free University of Bozen-Bolzano
39100 Bozen, Dominikanerplatz 3, Italy
{johann.gamper,nikolaus.augsten}@unibz.it

Abstract. Since a few years digital government is becoming an active research area with lots of promises to revolutionise government and its interaction with citizens and businesses. A crucial point for the success of e-government is the integration and sharing of services and information provided by different authorities. We argue that Web services are a promising technology to solve this problem.

1 Introduction

Since a few years digital government (or e-government) is becoming a very active and fast-moving research area with lots of promises to revolutionise government and its interaction with its customers including citizens, businesses, and other authorities. E-government can be defined as the use of information and communication technology (ICT) as a means to improve transparency, quality and efficiency of service delivery in the public administration. Thereby, a particular focus is on the use of the Internet as the most promising technology to change the traditional way of public administration.

From the operational point of view the integration of distributed services and information among different public authorities is one of the most pressing needs for e-government. We argue that Web services are a promising technology to solve the information integration problem for e-government.

The paper is organised as follows. In section 2 we motivate the need for information integration for e-government. Section 3 briefly sketches the basics of Web services. In section 4 we discuss the use of Web services in the context of e-government. Section 5 discusses related approaches and limitations of current Web service technologies.

2 The Need for Information Integration in E-Government

In this section we argue that one of the most pressing needs for e-government as envisioned today is the integration of the huge amount of information produced and the large number of services provided by the public administration.

One-stop government reflects the key trend within the current evolutions in e-government [4,8]. It refers to a single point of access, where the customers can access all public services and information. Delivery channels may vary from traditional offices to

* The work has been done in the framework of the "eBZ–Digital City" project, which is funded by the Municipality of Bozen-Bolzano.

R. Traunmüller (Ed.): EGOV 2003, LNCS 2739, pp. 161–166, 2003.
© Springer-Verlag Berlin Heidelberg 2003

self-service kiosks, call centres and, most importantly, Web portals with 24 hours access. Services and information on portals shall be organised in new ways, e.g. according to life events or business situations. One of the most basic prerequisites for this form of one-stop government is to interconnect the ICT systems of all public authorities [8].

Other problems are *data consistency* and *redundant data*. Once a citizen gets into contact with a specific department of the public administration, a new record is created which in addition to the specific information for this office stores general data such as address or job. In this way a lot of redundant data are created in a time-consuming process, and due to mistakes caused by the insertion of the same information at different authorities it is difficult to maintain the overall data consistent. Interconnecting all public administrations would considerably improve this situation which is crucial to increase efficiency and quality of service provision. For example, in a recent initiative the Ministry of the Interior in Italy proposed to establish a central database which contains name, registered residence and tax number of all citizens.

Some services require information from another department. In such cases the customer typically has to hand in a certificate about this piece of information in order to use the service. This kind of request for certificates is called a *false service*, since it provides no added value neither for the citizen nor for the public administration. False services could be avoided by enabling different department's systems to exchange and share data.

The *quality of services* as well as the provision of new services is a core objective of e-government. Combining existing services can lead to value-added services. For example, the WebDG infrastructure [5] composes distributed services of Indiana's Family and Social Services Administration and makes it easier or even possible to find the appropriate welfare programs for citizens. The possibility to integrate third parties value production activities could lead to new inter-organisational value configurations [7].

3 Web Services

Web services provide a new layer of abstraction above existing software systems, capable of bridging any operating system, hardware platform or programming language. While the Web is mainly for human users, Web services provide a framework for program-to-program communication. Web services are basically adapters between distributed applications, which allow to map messages into a canonical format and to send them across the Internet. Through the widespread adoption of this technology applications at various Internet locations can be directly interconnected as if they were part of a single, large information system.

XML (Extensible Markup Language) as a general portable data exchange format has been widely accepted the lingua franca for the future Web, which is flexible enough to accommodate any data type and structure and even to create new ones. Web services require the following XML-technologies [6]:

- *WSDL (Web Service Description Language)* is a language for describing Web services. WSDL elements include data and message types, interaction patterns, operations to be performed on that data and protocol mappings.

- *SOAP (Simple Object Access Protocol)* is a lightweight protocol for exchanging structured and typed information between peers in a decentralised, distributed environment. SOAP messages may be exchanged using a variety of underlying protocols including HTTP.
- *UDDI (Universal Description, Discovery, and Integration)* defines a standard for the registration and discovery of Web services. UDDI repositories are comparable to white, green and yellow pages for Web services.

The abstraction level of Web services allows different interaction styles between application. Current standards and technologies generally encompass two major interaction patterns: remote procedure call (RPC) and document-oriented interactions.

4   Web Services for E-Government

The size and complexity of the public administration, the inhomogeneous infrastructure, the different competences at the political level and the need for different services in different places require a powerful mechanism to interconnect different authorities at the application level. In this section we argue that Web services have the potential to solve the information integration problem of e-government.

4.1   A New Layer of Abstraction

Web services introduce a new layer which provides an integration mechanism at a higher level of abstraction as any other approach before. The core part upon which different Web services have to agree is the definition of a minimal communication interface between applications. There are no limitations on operating systems, hardware platforms or programming languages.

Government transcends all sectors in a society and by both its size and scope of activities represents the biggest single information content resource. As a consequence, the ICT infrastructure of the public administration, including servers, networks and applications, is necessarily *complex* and *inherently heterogeneous*: (1) government agencies have their responsibility on different political levels, such as national, regional or local level. Different regions have different competences and regulations. (2) Public administrations are split into numerous departments which are often dislocated in various places. This situation renders the establishment of a transparent ICT infrastructure difficult. (3) Even a single department deploys often various ICT solutions from different vendors. (4) For specific tasks out-sourcing is an efficient solution. Hence, public administrations charge semi-private or private organisations with carrying out public services. These organisations need to share data with the government [4].

For these and other reasons the ICT infrastructure of a typical public administration is a very complex conglomeration of isolated solutions using different platforms, programming languages and data formats. Therefore, the integration and sharing of data between applications is extremely difficult.

The reduction of common standards to a minimum such as Web services do is extremely important to facilitate data sharing and exchange in a large, heterogeneous infrastructure such as the public administration.

4.2 Wrappers Around Existing Applications

Web services bridge technology domains not by replacing existing technology, but by providing wrappers around existing applications. This allows application development to be continued in the preferred programming language and environment, and the many existing legacy applications need not to be replaced.

The public administration offers numerous services. For example, a typical Italian municipality has to deliver more than 200 core services to individual citizens and businesses. Due to different competences and autonomies, these services are not necessarily identical, and additional services have to be provided in various provinces. Some services are RPC-like, i.e. a request followed by an immediate answer. Other services are part of a more complex process, involving asynchronous negotiation with other authorities and citizens. The creation of new services with added-value requires the composition of basic services into more complex ones.

Due to this high variety of services a standardisation of the back-office applications is not realistic, except for the most basic services. Actually this is even not necessary. Only the flow of information is important, i.e. how a service is provided and seen from outside in terms of input and output. Web service technology works at this level in that it provides an easy way to glue all these services together by reusing the existing legacy applications and wrapping a Web service around them.

A department can then be seen as a single module with a clearly defined interface. How the services are provided, whether they are fully automated, require human interaction or are mapped to a traditional, paper-based and manual workflow is irrelevant.

4.3 Based on Standard Web Infrastructure

Web services are made for the Web and use the existing Web infrastructure: they are based on XML and can use HTTP as a transport protocol. This allows to bridge department and agency borders by exploiting the already available network infrastructure. Web services can be build in a bottom up process – the same way also the Web was built – and therefore the risk for failure is reduced by taking small steps a time.

Changing the infrastructure of the whole public administration is not feasible for many reasons, including technological and political reasons. Moreover, information and services of the public administration have to be accessible to *all* citizens and businesses. For these and other reasons it is important to base e-government on an already existing and widely used technology and infrastructure. Web service wrappers can be build in a bottom-up approach, which supports a smooth transition towards e-government.

4.4 Emerging Standards Accepted by Major Vendors

A number of Web service standards are currently under development in cooperation between leading companies and the academic world. Database vendors support Web service interfaces directly to database management systems. Enterprise resource planning and customer resource management packaged applications support Web services interfaces for integration with other packages and software products.

Depending on specific vendors is dangerous for public administration. Rather, an open standard which is accepted by major vendors forms a solid foundation for a new form of government which explores the full potential of new technologies.

5 Discussion

The size and complexity of the public administration, the inhomogeneous infrastructure, the different competences at the political level and the need for different services in different places require a flexible approach for a seamless integration of applications distributed among different authorities.

A centralized approach with standards released by the central government and central databases might partially solve the integration problem. While this might be a solution for a single department, we believe that it is not scalable to the whole public administration. A lot of organisational problems have to be solved, such as distribution, installation and maintenance of applications. Moreover, the integration with already existing legacy applications (possibly running on different platforms and architectures) and the acceptance of a centralized approach by the single authorities are crucial issues. Finally, as soon as third party solutions come into play the problem with integration re-arises and a decentralized approach is needed.

Traditional distributed computing technologies such as CORBA, Java/RMI or DCOM are all RPC based and tightly couple the service name to the program being invoked. They require too much agreement and shared context among communicating systems to be successful on a large scale. Issues related to architectural design and complexity, binary compatibility, requirements for homogeneous operating-environment, etc. kept them from being more broadly adopted for cross-platform peer-to-peer communication.

Web services provide a more loosely coupled integration which does not require or assume the existence of the same software system on both ends of a communication path. The same message type can be mapped to multiple applications. Web services are not limited to operating systems, hardware platforms, or programming languages. They can be compared to EAI (Enterprise Application Integration) for the Web on which all major vendors agree [6].

Although the core standards SOAP, WSDL and UDDI are sufficient for many purposes, complex and critical business applications require additional features and functions. Problems such as security, privacy, quality-of-service, reliability, transaction processing, performance and interoperability have to be addressed before critical tasks can be done via Web services. Another aspect which is still in its infants is the provision of semantics. While current standards focus on syntactic aspects, the explicit representation of semantic is important to explore the full potential of the Web for service delivery. The automatic composition of complex services from basic services as well as advanced program-to-program communication in general require the explicit representation of semantics.

Recently, some research work has been done on the use of Web services for information integration. Virili and Sorrentino [7] focus on the impact of Web services to the political value chain. Fernandez [1] proposes a framework, which is based on Web services and intelligent agents, to solve the interoperability problem amongst European public administration. Some experience in applying Web services in e-government for integration purpose has already been gained. Hu [3] reports about system re-engineering models for the Police Service in the United Kingdom and their convergence to XML/Web services based solutions. [5] uses Web services to integrate information sources across various agencies and focuses on privacy maintenance when querying these sources.

6 Conclusion

In this paper we argue that Web services are currently the most promising technology for the realization of modern e-government as envisioned today. The current trend in e-government is characterised by a one-stop government, which provides a single access point for all customers to the information and services produced by the public administration. This requires a transparent and efficient integration and sharing of information among all public authorities, which for several reasons is very difficult: heterogeneous ICT infrastructure, large size and scope of activities, decentralized organisation, etc. Web services provide a new level of abstraction for information integration, which is based on standard Web technology. Rather than replacing existing application, it forces the specification of a minimal interface to enable program-to-program communication. While this new technology is rather promising, a lot of issues have still to be investigated, e.g. the representation of semantics, composition of services, transactions or privacy issues.

References

1. A. Fernández. Towards interoperability amongst european public administrations. In R. Traunmüller and K. Lenk, editors, *Proceedings of EGOV 2002*, LNCS 2456, pp. 105–110, Aix-en-Provence, France, September 2002. Springer-Verlag.
2. D. Gouscos, G. Laskaridis, D. Lioulias, G. Mentzas, and P. Georgiadis. An approach to offering one-stop e-government services – available technologies and architectural issues. In R. Traunmüller and K. Lenk, editors, *Proceedings of EGOV 2002*, LNCS 2456, pp. 264–271, Aix-en-Provence, France, September 2002. Springer-Verlag.
3. M. J. Hu. System integration and re-engineering using XML/Web services. In *Proceedings of the 12th International World Wide Web Conference*, volume Alternate tracks, pp. 159–165, Budapest, Hungary, May 2003.
4. H. Kubicek and M. Hagen. One-stop-government in Europe: An overview. In *One-Stop-Government in Europe: Results from 11 national surveys*, pp. 1–38. Univ. of Bremen, 2000.
5. B. Medjahed, A. Rezgui, A. Bouguettaya, and M. Ouzzani. Infrastructure for e-government Web services. *IEEE Internet Computing*, 7(1):58–65, January 2003.
6. E. Newcomer. *Understandig Web Services: XML, WSDL, SOAP, and UDDI*. Addision-Wesley, 2002.
7. F. Virili and M. Sorrentino. Reconfiguring the political value chain: The potential role of web services. In R. Traunmüller and K. Lenk, editors, *Proceedings of EGOV 2002*, LNCS 2456, pp. 61–68, Aix-en-Provence, France, September 2002. Springer-Verlag.
8. M. A. Wimmer. European development towards online one-stop government: The "eGOV" project. In *Proceedings of the International Conference on Electronic Commerce (ICEC 2001)*, Vienna, Austria, 2001.

A Modular Open-Source Architecture for ICT Services in the Public Administration*

Marco Di Natale, Tommaso Cucinotta, and Shiva Kolachalam

Scuola Superiore S. Anna
Pisa, Italy
{marco,cucinotta}@sssup.it
shiva@gandalf.sssup.it

Abstract. This paper presents the efforts undertaken by the Scuola Sant'Anna in developing an open framework for document and workflow management within Public Administrations (PA). Goals of the project are engaging emerging and innovative technologies, interoperability standards and open architectures in the context of PA information systems, and providing a set of software components adhering to national laws. These tools constitute a basic lattice for providing advanced ICT services to the citizens and enterprises, and among PA themselves, making a step towards realization of e-Government principles. Further goals of the project are driving an experimentation of innovative open-source solutions within real case studies.

1 Introduction

Public services consist of a definite set of complex legally governed processes, wherein every single unit maintains its own set of data and information. Procurement/exchange of data from/among different units on a pre-agreed format is of outmost importance as it is a crucial key for realizing smooth integration of services. Further, for achieving e-Government goals, there should be capability for any agency to join with another electronically using known and agreed approaches and standards. The need for a better coordination of efforts and investments in the area of information systems for the public administration pushed the Italian Parliament in 1993 to create the Authority for Information Technology in the Public Administration (AIPA). The aim was promoting technological progress by defining criteria for planning, implementation, management and maintenance of information systems through their standardization, interconnection and integration. The main objectives were: better services, less cost, better communication, and a wider support to the decision process.

From inception, AIPA's objectives were mainly on the technical side (standards, rules and recommendations), but there was a firm understanding that ICT technologies are no silver bullet for solving all problems, but facing and solving organizational problems is key. This requires a careful analysis of the organization and its processes, modeling the processes and evaluating them by simulation or

---

* This work is partly supported by the EU ASWAD project and by the MIUR project Link

R. Traunmüller (Ed.): EGOV 2003, LNCS 2739, pp. 167–172, 2003.

prototyping of ICT solutions. Reuse of experiences (rather than just technology) was ultimately seen as one of the key factors for improving the quality of the processes of the PA.

Starting from 1990, the Italian Government issued new laws to regulate the procedures and the technologies to be adopted by the public administration for document management, electronic registry and digital signatures.

If exchange of experiences and solutions is the key factor for easing the adoption of new technologies, then open systems and their interaction by means of open standards are, from a technical standpoint, the enabling factors for such exchanges. In this view an open approach promises high levels of interoperability and availability of public data and information, allowing government agencies to operate more efficiently and cost-effectively. The adoption of open source software and open standards allows for an increased flexibility, as the source code of the software is available for customizations, maximizing reusability of software and being free from the vendor's lock-in of closed solutions. In fact, the EC has been focusing attention on the same issue for years, as witnessed by the document produced by the Working Group on Libre Software in April 2000 [1]. Scuola Sant'Anna and AIPA spent a significant effort in order to test a new approach to PA innovation through ICT based on the open source paradigm. The outcome is a very flexible system, entirely composed of open source components, cooperating by means of open standards.

This paper presents the result: an open framework for document and workflow management within Public Administrations (PA). The project follows an open and modular approach, where generic ICT components, interact with end-user applications in order to implement PA services, and exchange of data takes place by means of open standards. We adopted an Open source (OS) development paradigm that assures maximum software reusability and maximum freedom of customizing software.

There are many projects on open-source software for the PA and many others (not necessarily open-source) dealing with infrastructures for e-government [2, 3, 4, 5] or focusing on specific PA needs, like interoperability [6]. Some of these are cited in the referenced papers and many others possibly exist. Yet, as far as we know, no other project exists for a framework integrating modular open source components including document and workflow management and supporting PA processes.

2   The Electronic Registry System

Since 1993, AIPA has been studying various issues in adoption of ICTs within PA processes. Specific sets of these studies have focused on Electronic Registry Systems (ERS). Such systems allow to track the information flow that crosses PA boundaries, by means of recording the exact time at which a document arrives to or leaves from a PA, along with additional meta-information regarding, for example, the event, the sender or recipient of the document and the subject. This functionality was seen as a fundamental step for achieving the goal of making PA services transparent to the citizens, since the registry system is typically the interface between the PA and its customers. Furthermore, the unique registration number assigned to the documents upon registration can be used to track the document processing inside the workflow of the administration. In many PAs there was a trend to create a new registry office each time an information flow (or workflow) crossed the administration boundaries at some different physical point. The fragmentation of the registry offices became redundant as soon as the registry information was moved from paper to an electronic registry, which could be accessed from any location. PAs are now encouraged to merge the registry offices pertaining to a homogeneous organizational area (AOO).

AIPA soon realized that most public administrations exchange documents in paper format in spite of the ICT tools for ERS and document management they purchase. The use of an electronic format for interoperability had not been possible for at least two reasons: electronic documents and e-mail messages had no legal value, and there was no standard format for electronic interchange since most PA used proprietary software tools with little or no support for open standards. The legal issues were settled in 1997 by defining digital signatures compliant with the law [7] and by conceding them the same legal value that handwritten signatures have. The standardization issue was solved by enforcing the adoption of ERS systems within the year 2004 and by issuing a technical standard [8], which provides a specification for XML-based ERS interoperability messages.

3 Towards an Integrated Framework for One-Stop Government

The improvement and automation of registry offices operations by means of interoperable ERS systems is the starting point towards the goal of *one-stop e-government* [4], where other services beyond the registry are available to the users.

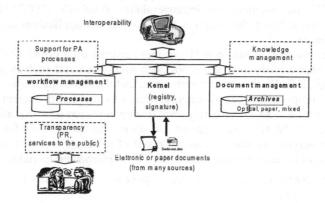

Fig. 1. Integration of ERS, WfMS and DMS systems.

Among those services, document management and workflow management should be deployed whenever allowed by the size and/or the organizational structure of the PA, allowing for greater efficiency, transparency and security of the processes.

As pointed out by several works [2, 3], process modeling and automation is recommended only when the process is stable, the complexity of the processes and the potential for improvement are significant (to justify the adoption of complex and costly technology) and a large number of instances exist for each process. Last two limitations can be ameliorated by the use of open standards and free software and by recent innovations in workflow management tools, which allow for a greater flexibility (even at run-time) in the definition and modification of the process models.

4 Reference Architecture Model and Development Framework

The AIPA reference architecture (implemented by our framework) aims at providing the best possible support for the technologies that enable a One Stop e-Government paradigm. This means providing standard functionality, such as: registry, workflow management, document management and digital signature in a modular fashion and also providing interoperability standards.

Services are subdivided into three classes [9]:

- *Base IT services*, like e-mail, DBMS, OS services and standard web services
- *Certification services*, like electronic registry and digital signature services
- *Vertical services,* which provide typical functionality to manage administration data and information, i.e. document warehouse.

Our architecture contains a large subset of the base services and applications. In particular, we aim at a system containing all the Base IT services, all certification services, and a transactional WF engine integrated with a document management system. Our reference implementation is based on a client-server, web-based, modular architecture and has the typical multi-tier structure of such systems, including: a database management system (DBMS); an application server, with its object Resource Broker (ORB) and support for interoperability standards (HTTP-HTTPS, CGI, SOAP/XML and others); the business logic part of the application and, finally, the presentation layer.

The implementation of the base IT services required little effort, since most of the components were already available from open source projects such as the Linux OS, the PostgreSQL DBMS, the Apache web server and the Zope application server.

The other components, (certification, vertical services and document management services) did not have an immediately available open source solution satisfying all the requisites for modularity and support of open standards. Therefore, they were developed on purpose or obtained as the result of joint projects with AIPA or local enterprises working on open-source projects. The implemented modules are:

- **Workflow Services**: provided by *OpenFlow*, an entity-based Workflow Management System;
- **Registry Services**: implemented by *PAFlow*: our Electronic Registry System;
- **Document Management Services**: obtained by extending the Content Management Framework (CMF) Zope product in our custom CMFGeDOC Document Management tool.
- **Digital Signature Services**: obtained by integrating a commercial smart-card based digital signature package with our Registry and Document Management systems. Integration required the development of an extended ActiveX control suitable for on-the-fly digital signatures, and the definition of reusable sub-workflows implementing the process of digitally signing documents.

Workflow Management System: Openflow

OpenFlow[1] has been developed according to the Workflow Reference Model by the Workflow Management Coalition (WfMC) [10]. The system consists of the following components:

- a *Workflow Process Definition* (WPD) tool, which allows defining all the activities which constitute a process and the transitions between them;

- a *Workflow engine*, which is responsible for generating instances of processes, creating and managing the user worklist, invoking the proper application for each activity, managing the workflow instances;

- a *Workflow monitor*, which allows to control the processes through their static structure and also allows to extract all the relevant statistics of the process; and

- a *Workflow API*, modeled on the WfMC interoperability standards [10].

OpenFlow features advanced functionality such as the support for the definition of subflows and the capability of dynamic reconfiguration of the processes.

Registry System: PAFlow

The PAFlow project[2] began as a test bed for experimenting the technical standards for the interoperability of ERS systems as issued by AIPA in 1999 and acted as a reference implementation to other PAs and software companies.

The ERS system has been developed as a python application running on the application server. The *ERS Server* consists of several components:

- *Registry Entries Management Module*, interfacing with the relational DB backend

- *Session Management Module*

- *Access Control Module*, handling role, user and permission information and the repository of the organization

- *User Interface Module*, responsible for the web-based interaction with the users

- *API Module*, exporting a set of methods towards external application programs.

- *Interoperability Module,* implementing the s-MIME and XML based standards for interoperability of ERS systems, and

- *Workflow interface module,* that allows routing the document to the selected assignment workflow activity after registration and classification.

Document Management: CMFGeDOC

A document management system or DMS is used to store documents in an electronic format allowing for a more efficient management (storage, searching and indexing) of document data. Furthermore, by allowing digital signature on electronic documents, a DMS system becomes the necessary condition for achieving a "paperless" administration.

We found that no available open source project could satisfy our requirements, but a neighboring family of products, the content management frameworks or CMF had very interesting representatives, offering a large subset of these functionality. Among those, we selected CMF-Zope, a general purpose content management framework.

---

[1] developed and currently being maintained by Icube s.r.l.
[2] The project's URL is: http://www.paflow.it

The CMF product offers document indexing and classification, extended access control and fast document storage/retrieval including full-text indexing for most formats. Furthermore, CMF also includes an entity-based workflow management system, which allows defining a workflow and applying it to a class of documents. However, it lacks support for some fundamental features, such as the capability of handling optical storage of documents, support for high-speed scanners and support for digital signatures. These requirements have been addressed in the design and development of our extensions in the Zope CMF-derived CMFGeDOC project.

5 Conclusions

The paper presents a project for an integrated infrastructure of IT services, developed in the context of national and European projects at the Scuola Superiore Sant'Anna, Pisa (Italy). The infrastructure is built around open source components cooperating by means of open standards. The project started from a cooperation with AIPA, a governmental agency dictating guidelines for ICT tools to be adopted by the PA agencies and offices. The overall open source framework is now completed and undergoing experimentation. It consists of the ERS system, a workflow engine (OpenFlow), and a document management system integrated with a law compliant, digital signature software.

We would like to thank AIPA, Luigi Palopoli, Antonio Massari and Icube s.r.l. for the roles they played in the context of the project.

References

1. Working group on Libre Software: "Free Software / Open Source Information Society Opportunities for Europe ?", April 2000.
2. M. Wimmer and J. Krenner, "An Integrated Online One-Stop Government Platform: The eGOV Project", In Hofer, Chroust, IDIMT-2001, 9th Interdisciplinary Information Management Talks Proceedings, Schriftenreihe Informatik, Universitätsverlag Trauner, Linz, pp. 329–337.
3. L.R. Jones, "Symposium on Public Management Reform and E-Government, International Public Management Review", Volume-2 Issue-1, 2001, pp. 01–27.
4. Thomas F. Gordon, "E-Government – Introduction", ERCIM News No.48, January 2002.
5. Lenk, K., Traunmüller R. 2000. Perspectives on Electronic Government. In Galindo, Quirchmayr (eds.). Advances in Electronic Government. Proceedings of the Working Conference of the IFIP WG 8.5 in Zaragoza.
6. Gagliardi R. and Fiorenzani P., Managing the Interaction between Citizens and Public Administrations: the One-Stop-Shop Model. ERCIM News No.48, January 2002
7. (Italian Law) Art.15, comma 2, Legge 15/03/1997, n. 59
8. Circolare AIPA n.CR/28/2000: "[...] Standard, modalità di trasmissione, formato e definizioni dei tipi di informazioni minime ed accessorie comunemente scambiate tra le pubbliche amministrazioni e associate ai documenti protocollati", May 7, 2001.
9. AIPA: "Linee guida alla realizzazione dei sistemi di protocollo informatico e gestione dei flussi documentali nelle pubbliche amministrazioni (GEDOC 2)", September 2000.
10. Workflow Management Coalition: Reference Model and Interoperability Abstract Specifications WFMC-TC-1012, May 2000, available at http://www.wfmc.org.

A Methodological Approach for Defining One-Stop E-Government Service Offerings

Dimitris Gouscos[1], Maria Lambrou[2], Gregoris Mentzas[3],
and Panagiotis Georgiadis[4]

[1] eGovernment Laboratory, University of Athens
Athens, Greece
d.gouscos@e-gov.gr
[2] National Technical University of Athens
Athens, Greece
marial@telecom.ntua.gr
[3] Institute of Communication and Computer Systems
National Technical University of Athens
Athens, Greece
gmentzas@softlab.ntua.gr
[4] eGovernment Laboratory, University of Athens
Athens, Greece
p.georgiadis@e-gov.gr

Abstract. This paper reports some methodological guidelines for categorizing administrative services on certain typological characteristics (informational vs. transactional content, acquaintance vs. operational usefulness, local vs. hyper-local value), defining one-stop service offerings and ranking their interest from an end-user as well as service integration perspective.

1 Elements of a Typology for Administrative Services

In order to establish true-one-stop e-Government service offerings [1], i.e. "integrated service packages" that can meet all the administrative service needs arising in the context of a given life or business event, it is necessary to model the events to be served as well as the essential characteristics of different services that justify their one-stop aggregation. A case worth particular emphasis in this last perspective is that of cross-border administrative services, offered by local or national administrations to foreign citizens or businesses, or demanding the interaction of administrations from different countries. This section presents a number of dimensions that can form the starting point for a typology of administrative services, the final objective of this approach being to facilitate identification of services that can be integrated into one-stop offerings on the basis of their typological characteristics.

Given that the most important aspect of a service is its content, administrative services can first of all be characterised on the level of content as

- informational services, for providing generic or personalised information, and
- transactional services, for handling (e.g. filing, cross-checking) administrative documents.

R. Traunmüller (Ed.): EGOV 2003, LNCS 2739, pp. 173–176, 2003.

These two generic classes of services have their counterparts in well-known e-service taxonomies, such as the ICDT model [2] as well as the eEurope 4-level framework for benchmarking the advancement of e-Government services [3]. Note, however, that this taxonomy is sometimes hard to apply: an essentially informational service may require filing an application form, in which case it could also be considered as a transactional service.

A more intuitive perspective for characterising administrative services is with reference to distinct phases of the transaction lifecycle, distinguishing between:

- "acquaintance" services that an end-user needs when totally unaware about the service context (one's rights and obligations, laws that apply, procedures to follow, service providers to contact etc.); by definition, these are informational services in essence, although they could be transactional in form

- "operational" services that end users need when they have learnt about the service context and wish to proceed and transact (e.g. make an inquiry, apply for a certificate, file a declaration etc.); these will typically be transactional services.

Finally, the value locality of a service is also important when looking for services useful across the borders; a distinction can be made between:

- "local value" services, meaningful only for end users residing within the provider's jurisdiction; e.g. a service to ask for a new telephone number, and

- "hyper-local value" services, useful for foreigners (and maybe locals alike); e.g. a service to find out business or employment opportunities.

Some services whose value locality is not so clear (e.g. a "change-of-address" service) can best be considered of hyper-local value.

2 Approaches to Composing One-Stop Service Offerings

Two approaches for composing one-stop service offerings can be considered:

- the "similarity approach": informational services from different providers about different subsets of the same domain can be combined into an one-stop offering that allows inquiries over the entire domain; employment services in different regions, for instance, can be combined with this approach

- the "complementarity approach": informational or transactional services from different providers about various aspects of the same user event can be combined into an one-stop service offering that covers this event in its entirety; consider, for instance, a student that learns (informational service) that in order to apply for a state subsidy (transactional service) it is necessary to have an income tax certificate (another transactional service).

Roughly speaking, the similarity approach to one-stop service composition can be thought of as taking the "union" of some individual services, whereas the complementarity approach would rather be to take their "concatenation". In either case, some intermediate workflow logic between the service providers is necessary to assure that the final service will be truly one-stop, i.e. offered through a single session with a single point of contact; this logic is more simple and standardized in similarity-based compositions, but it can have arbitrary and case-specific complexity in complementarity-based ones.

3   Interesting Cases of One-Stop Service Offerings

Of all one-stop service offerings that can be designed, the most useful ones will typically have hyper-local value, cover the full life-cycle of service provision (learn about the service and eventually transact) and meet the needs of a concrete user event. With a view to composing such interesting one-stop service offerings over a number of available administrative services, the following heuristic rules can apply as appropriate to help identify cases of interest and added value:

1. "more services": try to combine more services
2. "less locality": try for services of hyper-local value
3. "more providers": try to involve more providers
4. "more transactions": try to include the actual transactions
5. "full lifecycle" : try to complement transactions with service context information
6. "more collaboration": try to have providers interchange forms and information

The degree of collaboration between service providers for one-stop transactional services may vary from offerings including just one transactional service ("combined uni-transactional services"), to offerings including two or more transactional services that do not collaborate (i.e., they do not interchange documents or information, "combined multi-transactional services"), to offerings including some transactional services that do collaborate in the previous sense ("combined collaborative transactional services").

All the above rules should ideally be met by the "perfect" one-stop administrative service, which in practice may be difficult due to a number of reasons: service schemes are incompatible at a technology (e.g. platforms, channels), content (e.g. language, metadata) or policy (e.g. security, privacy, charging) level, whereas providers are reluctant to integrate their offerings, possibly due to legal restrictions, doubt about benefits or resistance to change. On the way to ideal one-stop services, however, a number of intermediate cases can be identified and ranked in order of interest according to the above heuristics. Table 1 presents such a list, together with associated styles of service provision.

Table 1. Types of one-stop service offerings and corresponding operational styles of service provision.

Category of services	Operational style
individual local-value informational services	
individual local-value transactional services	portal
individual hyperlocal-value informational services	
individual hyperlocal-value transactional services	
combined informational services	info-mediary
combined uni-transactional services	service-mediary
combined multi-transactional services	
combined collaborative transactional services	true-service-mediary

As can be noted from Table 1, portal schemes mainly provide a number of individual services, related with respect to content but not integrated at the level of delivery (which is left to the linked providers). Info-mediaries, on the other hand, mainly act as brokers to informational services. The systems that provide one-stop offerings over transactional services can be termed "service-mediaries" [4], whereas "true-service-mediaries" refers to direct interchange of documents and information between participating service providers, using some workflow logic to accomplish the "single session" property of the service provision scheme from the end users' perspective.

4   Conclusions

The guidelines presented in this paper can be employed to help design one-stop service offerings of increased interest and added value, especially in cases of addressing non-local clients who are not aware of the broader service context. A specific contribution of this paper are the elements of a typology for administrative services that have been introduced; it is considered as a direction of future work to incorporate such typological elements into metadata-based descriptions of e-Government services and investigate more formal ways for identifying service compositions.

Acknowledgements. A major part of this work (exemplar case and test application of the guidelines) has been performed within the CB-BUSINESS R&D project (IST-2001-33147, http://www.cb-business.com); the authors would like to thank the project team for comments and suggestions.

References

1. Hagen, M., and H. Kubicek, *One-Stop Government in Europe – Results from 11 National Surveys*, COST Project Action A14 – Government and Democracy in the Information Age – Working Group "ICT in Public Administration", University of Bremen, 2000.
2. Anghern, A., *Designing mature Internet business strategies: the ICDT model*, European Management Journal, 15(4), August 1997, pp.361–368.
3. Commission of the European Communities, *eEurope 2002 Impact and Priorities*, Communication to the Spring European Council in Stockholm, 23-24 March 2001, Brussels, COM(2001)140 Final.
4. D. Gouscos, G. Mentzas & P. Georgiadis, *PASSPORT : A Novel Architectural Model for the Provision of Seamless Cross-Border e-Government Services*, 12th International Conference on Database and Expert Systems Applications (DEXA 2001), Munich, September 2001, IEEE Computer Society Press, pp. 318–322.

Supporting Voting Decisions: Two Municipal Referendum Websites

Arthur Edwards

Erasmus University Rotterdam
Department of Public Administration
Postbox 1738, 3000 DR Rotterdam, The Netherlands
Edwards@fsw.eur.nl

Abstract. Two Dutch municipal referendum websites were evaluated with regard to their potential for supporting voting decisions. The websites embodied different approaches to information provision. Both approaches showed disadvantages. In particular, the websites fell short on 'argumentative empowerment', in the one case by not providing any argumentative frames within which information could be evaluated, in the other by providing information solely within the argumentative frame of the municipality.

1 Introduction: The Institutional Context

The relation between referendums, democracy and citizenship can be constructed in different ways [1]. In this paper, we look at referendums that function as a complement to representative democracy. Two variants of the referendum will be examined. Firstly, before taking a decision, a parliament may submit a proposal to the public in a *consultative* referendum. By consulting the public, the initiating politicians aim to strengthen the legitimacy of a certain policy choice. Secondly, a *corrective* referendum allows for intervention by citizens in a parliamentary decision that they strongly oppose. The corrective referendum can be taken as a means for exercising 'monitorial citizenship' [2]. In this study, we will consider both a consultative and a corrective local referendum. The research question is how municipal referendum websites function as a support for voters' decisions.

2 Theoretical Framework: Empirical and Evaluative Premisses

We see the impact of government websites on voting decisions as being mediated by two factors. Firstly, the functions and contents of the referendum website can be 'read' as embodying a certain *approach to information provision*. Secondly, the use of the website by citizens will be influenced by their *information strategies*.

With regard to the municipal information provision in Dutch local referendums, there are two approaches to be distinguished. One approach is to aim for information to be objective and strictly informative. In no case the municipality (as an 'organization') should assume a campaigning role. The task of campaigning is left to

R. Traunmüller (Ed.): EGOV 2003, LNCS 2739, pp. 177–180, 2003.
© Springer-Verlag Berlin Heidelberg 2003

social organizations and political parties. The other approach derives from the idea that the municipality is entitled to pursue a campaigning role and may therefore provide persuasive information.

From empirical research on voting decisions, we know that citizens use various simplifying strategies to reduce information costs and, thereby, make political choices in a fairly rational manner [3]. As an alternative to the costly acquisition of 'encyclopaedic' information on policy platforms and referendum propositions, voters may choose to use information short-cuts. For instance, voters may consider the points of view of political parties and interest groups, and use these as 'signals' for their own voting decisions. Lupia [4] shows that access to such information short-cuts allows badly informed voters to 'emulate' the behavior of well-informed voters. Contrary to the proposition that one should educate the people about policies, Lupia suggests that directing efforts towards the provision of credible and widely accessible 'signals' may be a more effective and cost-efficient way to ensure the responsiveness of electoral outcomes to voters' preferences. The importance of information short-cuts indicates that expectations with regard to the Internet's potential for increasing the voters' 'encyclopaedic mastery' of political issues may be ill-founded. Nevertheless, in view of the Internet's possibilities to provide information from various sources, structure it in efficient formats, and tailor it to individual needs, the Internet has the potential for changing the cost structure of gathering information. This may lead to voters becoming better informed on the issues at hand. Furthermore, the Internet can give access to relevant 'signals' from intermediaries.

In order to establish which effects a certain approach to information provision has on the functionality of a website, I constructed a framework on the basis of standards of "maximal assistance to the voters' judgmental process". Standards 1-5 are democratic norms; standards 6-8 connect the referendum to other democratic arrangements within the polity.

1. *Information and argumentative empowerment.* The communicative intention of the information should be clearly recognizable. In particular, persuasive information should be distinguishable from factual information. The information should be relevant and complete enough to enable the citizen to form an opinion about a proposition. Argumentative empowerment means that voters are stimulated to judge the proposition and the information from different perspectives.

2. *Equal opportunities for advocates and opponents.* Arguments in favor and against the proposition should be given an equal place. At the minimum, the website ought to provide links to the sites of all organizations that have taken up a position for or against the proposition [5] .

3. *Openness to citizens' input.* There should be room for questions and remarks. In addition to this, citizens should be offered the opportunity to forward information.

4. *Discursiveness.* The website has a discussion facility.

5. *Transparency.* The website discloses the sponsors of the campaign and of campaign finances [5]. It provides warrants for the authenticity of information, disclaimers and so forth.

6. *Connection with representative democracy.* The website provides access to all documents that refer to the discussion in the representative bodies, and it informs the visitor on the points of view of the different political parties.

7. *Connection with deliberative democracy.* The website provides access to the public discussion on the proposition. This may include an archive of newspaper articles or links to media sites.

8. *Connection with pluralist democracy.* Links are provided to the websites of the organizations that have formulated a point of view on the proposition concerned. An overview is given of the points of view of all organizations that have formulated such 'signals'.

3 An Analysis of Two Municipal Websites

In Utrecht, a provincial capital of about 200,000 inhabitants, a *consultative* referendum was held on the reconstruction of the area around the central railway station. Two propositions were submitted, Plan 1 ('Compact City Centre') and Plan A ('Extended City Centre'). The city administration did not express a preference for either of these plans. The referendum turnout was 65 %. Plan A won with 59.1 % of the vote, Plan 1 received 24.5 % of the vote, and 16.4 % of the voters turned in a blank ballot. This rather high percentage of abstentions was due to the campaign of the Committee *'Utrecht Stemt Blanco'* (Utrecht Abstains from Voting). According to the committee, neither plans offered a real choice, and both had important drawbacks.

The referendum site provided clear information on the differences between the two plans. However, the site provided little assistance as to the possible argumentative frames within which this information could be evaluated. While the site met the standard of information empowerment, it met the standard of argumentative empowerment to a far lesser degree. Almost no points of view were provided by the political parties and social organizations in the city. No confrontation on the site between advocates and opponents of the two plans was attemped. Moreover, there was no link available to the website of the committee that campaigned for abstention.

With its *Suggestion Box*, the site did meet, to some degree, the standard of openness. However, it barely met the standard of discursiveness, as the feature *Your Opinion* did not function as a discussion facility. The standard of transparency was met with regard to authenticity. There was no information available, however, on discussions in the municipal council about the two plans. Points of view of social organisations were virtually lacking. On the other hand, the site did provide a connection with deliberative democracy. Documentation was available on the public discussion about the two plans, including an archive of newspaper articles.

On the same day, May 15 2002, a corrective referendum was held in Amsterdam on the council decision to privatize the city transport company (GVB). The referendum was first initiated by a committee that opposed the decision, after which the city administration decided to campaign in favor. The turnout was 61 %; the privatization decision was defeated by two-third of the vote.

The municipal website provided information on several aspects of the privatization decision. The site contributed to information empowerment, yet the information was solely provided within the argumentative framework of the municipality. The arguments of the opponents were not voiced on the site, although there was a link available to their website. As the site provided an opportunity to ask questions, it met, to some degree, the standard of openness. In view of the discussion that developed on the section *Have a Say?*, the website met the standard of discursiveness. This was the only section on the website where the site-visitors could take cognizance of other points of view. Apart from some official documents, there was no information available on the discussion that had taken place in the municipal council. And, disregarding the link to the opponents' committee, there were no references to points of view of political parties and social organizations. Finally, the public discussion in the press was only made known, insofar as it gave support to the position of the municipality.

4 Conclusion

We considered two local referendums that contrasted on two points, (1) the institutional form of the referendum (consultative or corrective) and (2) the approach taken by the municipality to information provision. In the consultative Utrecht referendum, the voters were offered two alternatives, for either of which the city administration did not express a preference. In the corrective Amsterdam referendum, the voters had to decide for or against a decision; the municipality pursued an active campaign in favour. It can be concluded that both approaches taken had some drawbacks. The Utrecht website provided the voters with balanced information on the two plans, yet it did not give any argumentative support to evaluate the alternatives. Because of this, the referendum could function as a (more or less binding) opinion poll, but not as an opportunity for public discussion of different views on the city. On the Amsterdam website, the city administration did provide reasons to support the privatization decision; however, it did not engage into an open discussion with the opponents. The website fell short on argumentative empowerment as well.

References

1. Budge, I.: The New Challenge of Direct Democracy. Polity Press, London, New York (1996)
2. Schudson, M.: The Good Citizen. A History of American Civic Life. The Free Press, New York (1998)
3. Lupia, A., .McCubbins, M.D.: The Democratic Dilemma. Can Citizens Learn What They Need to Know? Cambridge University Press, Cambridge (1998)
4. Lupia, A. Shortcuts Versus Encyclopedias. Information and Voting Behavior in California Insurance Reform Elections. American Political Science Review, 88 (10) (1994) 63–76
5. Schevits, J.A.: The Fourth Branch of Government. An analysis of the initiative and referendum process and how the Internet might improve it. Initiative and Referendum Institute (2000). www.iandrinstitute.org (retrieved May 30, 2003)

Computer Supported Collaboration in the Public Sector: The ICTE-PAN Project

Euripidis Loukis and Spyros Kokolakis

University of the Aegean
Dept. of Information & Communication Systems Engineering
Karlovassi GR-83200, Samos, Greece.
{eloukis,sak}@aegean.gr

Abstract. Electronic Government today focuses mainly on offering citizens-enterprises the capability to perform electronically their transactions with the Public Administration (PA). However, the huge potential of ICT has only to a small extent been exploited in the most critical higher level functions of PA, such as the development, monitoring and evaluation of public policies and programmes, etc. This paper is dealing with the exploitation of the technologies of Computer Supported Collaborative Work (CSCW) in PA. A general architecture of a flexible Government to Government (G2G) collaborative environment is described, for supporting the higher level functions of PA, which has been designed as part of the ICTE-PAN Project.

1 Introduction

Most of the current research in the area of e-Government is focused on offering citizens and enterprises the capability to perform electronically their transactions with the Public Administration (PA) and also on the electronic delivery of the currently existing public services over the Internet [6]. The ICT-enabled innovation in this area is limited mainly to the development of 'virtual public agencies' or 'one-stop e-Government', i.e. of single points of access (e.g. portals) to many related electronic transactions and services [2], [8].

However, the innovation potential of ICTs concerning the reform and modernisation of PA is much larger and has only to a small extent been exploited [4], [6]. Therefore, the concept of e-Government should be broadened and enriched, in order to exploit to a much larger extent the huge innovation potential of ICTs. e-Government should be directed not only to electronic transactions and services, but also to the critical higher level functions of PA [5], [6], such as:
- the development, monitoring and evaluation of public policies and programmes;
- higher decision-making, concerning difficult and complex social problems.
These higher level functions are of critical importance for the PA and the society, and at the same time highly difficult and complex; they usually require close collaboration among many Public Organizations (POs) and very often participation of citizens, enterprises and their associations, as well.

In particular, the development of effective public policies and programmes for complex problems requires close collaboration among many POs from many regions

R. Traunmüller (Ed.): EGOV 2003, LNCS 2739, pp. 181–186, 2003.

or countries. Each of these POs possesses one small, but valuable, piece of information, knowledge and competence about the problem. Very often, there are differences among their values and interests. Therefore, it is necessary to organize properly the synthesis of these valuable 'pieces of information, experience, knowledge and competence', and also of their different values, interests and expectations, though close and effective collaboration among these POs. However, geographical distance and time & budget limitations do not allow this collaboration to be close enough, resulting in ineffective public policies and programmes, developed without the required wide participation of all competent and knowledgeable parties.

Therefore, it is of critical importance to exploit the capabilities of modern ICTs for supporting and facilitating the required wide participation and collaboration for the aforementioned higher level functions of PA.

This paper is dealing with the exploitation of the methodologies and technologies of Computer Supported Collaborative Work (CSCW) for this purpose. In Section 2 initially the objectives of ICTE-PAN (Methodologies and Tools for Building Intelligent Collaboration and Transaction Environments in Public Administration Networks) Project are described. Then is presented the architecture of a Government to Government (G2G) collaborative environment for supporting the critical higher level functions of PA. Section 3 is dealing with the use of modelling techniques and ontologies for configuring and customizing such an environment. Finally, in Section 4 the conclusions are presented, together with directions for further research.

2   The ICTE-PAN Project – G2G Collaborative Environments

The ICTE-PAN Project, which is implemented in the context of the European Union IST Programme, has been initiated to address the G2G collaboration needs of POs. The main objectives of this project are:

i) to develop a methodology for modelling collaboration among POs, and also for redesigning it based on the state-of-the-art ICTs,

ii) to develop a complete electronic platform with all the required meta-tools for creating high quality G2G collaborative environments,

iii) to elaborate sustainable measurement methods for evaluating such environments.

The project is implemented by a well-balanced consortium of technology providers and users: European Dynamics (Greece), University of the Aegean (Greece), TXT Solutions (Italy), National Environment Research Institute (Denmark), Ministry of Environment of Lower Saxony (Germany) and Province of Genoa (Italy).

2.1   Functional Architecture

From the analysis of the collaboration processes of the user POs in the project consortium, and in general of the PAs of the four participating countries (Greece, Italy, Denmark and Germany), it was concluded that an electronic environment for supporting effectively G2G collaboration should have a functional architecture of an 'Extended Workflow Management System', which can manage workflows:

- crossing more than one POs, i.e. workflows with some Activities executed by one PO, some other Activities executed by another PO, etc.;
- and consisting of both 'Single Person Activities' and 'Collaborative Activities'.

An Activity is characterized as a 'Single Person Activity' (SPA), if for each particular case this Activity is executed by only one person. On the contrary, an Activity is characterized as a 'Collaborative Activity' (CA), if for each case a number of individuals have to be involved, contribute, collaborate and interact for executing this Activity. The development of public policies and programmes usually includes a sequence of CAs, in which representatives of several POs (and in some cases also citizens and enterprises) collaborate for understanding the corresponding problems and situations, generating and discussing alternatives, designing public policies, etc.

Therefore the classical Workflow Model and Wide Area Workflow Model [7], which includes only SPAs, should be extended, in order to include both SPAs and CAs. For each case, an appropriate electronic environment should be created for each CA, in order to support the corresponding argumentative discourse, interaction and in general collaboration among remote participants. This collaborative environment should give to each participant the capability to contribute various 'elements', e.g. issues, alternatives, positive or negative arguments, etc.; each of the other participants should be given the capability to read them immediately, and possibly add positive or negative arguments on them, or add new issues or alternatives, etc.

From the analysis of the collaboration processes and requirements of the PA, it was concluded that for the development, monitoring and evaluation of public policies and programmes, and for the decision-making for complex social problems, or for granting licenses with high social impact, a big variety of CA types are required. These numerous CA types differ in the kinds of elements contributed by the participants, and the kinds of associations allowed among them. However, we can distinguish eight basic types of CAs, which are the most usual ones in the PA practices:

- *Problem/Goal Understanding*: understanding better a social problem, or a particular situation, by collaboratively elucidating its main dimensions.
- *Strategic Analysis*: conducting collaboratively a Strategic SWOT (Strengths, Weakness, Opportunities and Threats) Analysis.
- *Alternatives Generation and Unstructured Evaluation*: collaborative generation of alternatives for an issue, and also first-level elaboration and unstructured evaluation of them, in order to elucidate their advantages and disadvantages.
- *Evaluation Criteria Generation*: collaborative generation of evaluation criteria for evaluating alternatives, which have been proposed for a problem or issue.
- *Structured Multicriteria Evaluation of Alternatives*: collaborative structured multicriteria evaluation of alternatives, which have been proposed for an issue.
- *Design of Public Policies and Programmes*: for each of the selected alternatives, collaborative design of public policies and programmes for implementing it, in the required analysis level, e.g. up to sub-programmes, measures, etc.
- *Design of Projects*: for each of the above lower level programmes, collaborative design of projects for implementing it, and for each of these projects design of its internal structure, e.g. tasks, subtasks, deliverables, etc.
- *Project Monitoring and Evaluation*: collaboratively monitoring and evaluation of these public projects.

2.2 Technological Architecture

In order to support this large variety of collaborative processes and CAs morphologies in PA, the most appropriate technological solution is to develop a generic electronic platform, consisting of general purpose units of functionality (meta-tools). The main units of functionality of the ICTE-PAN platform are:

- **Environment design:** This functionality is supported by the Designer Center module, which provides users with all necessary tools for creating, maintaining and expanding user-friendly electronic environments for supporting collaboration.
- **'Extended' Workflow Management System:** It will consist of a visual tool for designing 'extended' workflows and rules, and an engine for executing them.
- **Collaboration:** It supports the management and maintenance of virtual teams operation, consisting of remote participants (members) from several POs.
- **Decision Module:** An application co-operating with the workflow module, which will support collaborative decision-making processes.
- **Storage:** Repositories for storing structured and unstructured data for easier access and faster response of the system.
- **Information extraction:** Tools and methods for extracting, tagging and storing information out of unstructured data in XML.
- **Intelligent agents:** A personal assistant and a search support agent are included.
- **Security:** Providing to the system, its users and the administrators a secure environment to operate and store information.

3 Modelling Techniques and Ontology for G2G Collaboration

In order to support the development of Collaborative Environments for PA, based on the meta-tools of the ICTE-PAN platform, a methodology for modelling collaborative operations/processes in PA, named PA-OMIM (PA Operation Modelling Integrated Methodology), was developed. In particular the objective of PA-OMIM is to support:

- Describing and understanding PA collaborative processes, in which several POs are involved, via building their "AS-IS" models.
- Redesigning PA processes, so as to become more efficient and effective, based on ICTE-PAN Platform, via building from their "AS-IS" models their "TO-BE" ones.
- Specifying the requirements for customisation of the ICTE-PAN platform, in order to support specific PA collaborative processes, based on their "TO-BE" models.

The methodology consists of two components: the PA-OMIM Redesign Method and the PA-OMIM Modelling Language. The PA-OMIM Redesign Method includes the following basic seven stages: (1) Definition, (2) Project Initiation, (3) Diagnosis, (4) Redesign, (5) Requirements Specification/Environment Design, (6) Implementation, (7) Evaluation, but it can also take any iterative form. In this context the PA-OMIM Modelling Language has been developed to be used in the above stages 3, 4 and 5 with two objectives : to model and redesign collaborative processes in PA (consisting of both SPAs and CAs), and to support the configuration and customization of the

ICTE-PAN platform for supporting them. The PA-OMIM Modelling Language is a graph-structured language and constitutes an extension of the XML Process Definition Language (XPDL) [10], which can support both SPAs and CAs. It has an intuitive format, that enables model building by non-experts, and a simple, nevertheless powerful, notation that allows the modelling of the most complex PA collaborative processes. A multi-view approach has been adopted, to model all relevant aspects of PA operation. The PA-OMIM views are: (1) Environment View, (2) Process View, (3) Organisation View, (4) Resource View, (5) Information View.

3.1 Ontology

As mentioned above, there is a big variety of CA types in the PA, which differ in the kinds of 'elements' contributed by the participants, and the kinds of 'associations' allowed among them. For this reason, it is necessary during the definition of the activities of a collaborative process in the Process View, for each CA to modell this aspect of it as well; therefore it is necessary to define the kinds of elements (e.g. issues, alternatives, arguments, programmes, projects, tasks, etc.) which can be contributed by the participants in this CA, and also the kinds of associations which are allowed to be made among these elements (e.g. an alternative can be associated with an issue). Based on these definitions, the ICTE-PAN Platform for each case will create the appropriate electronic environment for the execution of this CA.

In order to support the above definitions, an Ontology is required for the domains of PA policies and programmes development, monitoring and evaluation, and also PA higher decision-making, consisting of the main kinds of concepts-elements used in these domains and of their associations. Such an Ontology was developed, based on the relevant research literature in this area [1], [3], on the analysis of the pilots of ICTE-PAN and the collaborative processes of the PAs of the four participating countries, and on the experience of the members of the project team in these domains.

Using this Ontology we can easily define the nature of each CA, by selecting a small subset of the kinds of elements and associations of the Ontology. In this way, a high level of flexibility and adaptability to particular collaborative process requirements can be achieved, and a large variety of CA types can be supported. Also eight CA 'templates' have been defined, corresponding to the aforementioned eight basic CA types. Each of them corresponds to a specific subset of the kinds of elements and the associations of the above Ontology. We can use these templates as typical examples of CAs in PA, and also for the quick definition of new CAs.

4 Conclusions and Further Research Directions

In the previous sections a general functional and technological architecture of a flexible G2G collaborative environment for supporting higher level functions of Public Administration has been described. It is based on an extension of the classical Workflow Model, supporting both 'Single Person Activities' and 'Collaborative Activities'. In order to achieve a high level of flexibility and adaptability, modelling techniques and ontologies are used. The first comments on this architecture from the Administrations of the four participating countries (Greece, Italy, Denmark and

Germany) were quite encouraging. Further research is required in the direction of implementing and evaluating this architecture, in order to determine its strengths and weaknesses, and also possible needs for modification, elaboration, or extension of the architecture. We plan to proceed in this direction with four pilot implementations in the user POs of the ICTE-PAN Project consortium.

References

1. Conclin, J., Begeman M. L. gIBIS: A Hypertext Tool for Exploratory Policy Discussion. *ACM Transactions of Office Information Systems*. Vol. 6 (1988) 303–331.
2. Gouscos, D., Laskaridis, G., Lioulias, D., Mentzas, G., Georgiadis, P.: An Approach to Offering One-Stop e-Government Services, In: Traunmüller, R., Lenk. K. (eds) Electronic Government – 1st Intl Conference EGOV2002, Aix-en-Provence, France, (2002).
3. Karacapilidis, N., Papadias, D.: Hermes: Supporting Argumentative Discourse in multi-Agent Decision Making. In Proc. of the AAAI-98 Conference, MIT Press, (1998) 827–832.
4. Lenk, K.: Reform Opportunities Missed: Will the innovative potential of information systems in public administration remain dormant forever? *Information, Communication & Society*, Vol. 1, (1998) 163–181.
5. Lenk, K., Traunmüller, R.: Broadening the Concept of Electronic Government. In: J.E.J. Prins (ed.) Designing e-Government, Amsterdam, Kluwer (2001) 63–74.
6. Lenk., K., Traunmüller, R.: Electronic Government : Where Are We Heading? In: Traunmüller, R., Lenk. K. (eds) Electronic Government – 1st Intl Conference EGOV2002, Aix-en-Provence, France, (2002) 1–9.
7. Riempp, G. (ed.): Wide Area Workflow Management, Springer-Verlag, (1998).
8. Wimmer, M.: A European perspective towards online one-stop government: the Egov project. *Electronic Commerce Research and Applications*, Vol. 1 (2002) 92–103.
9. Workflow Management Coalition: Workflow Interoperability – Abstract Specifications, Document TC-1012 V.2 (1999).
10. Workflow Management Coalition: Workflow Process Definition Interface – XML Process Definition Language, Document WFMC-TC-1025 (2002).

E-Government in the European Commission

Erich Schweighofer*

University of Vienna
Center for Legal Informatics
Department for International Law
Universitätsstraße 2
A-1090 Vienna, Austria
http://www.univie.ac.at/RI/erich.html

Abstract. The European Commission's working plan for the e-Commission is very ambitious and provides for a comprehensive redesign of information and communication technologies according to the *leitbild* (leading motive) of the reformed Commission. The already existing IT infrastructure of the e-Commission and gained practise with previous applications provide a good start for the next steps to an efficient e-government. Many existing IT systems must be adapted and integrated into the e-Commission that will take some time. After finishing this phase, the next step will be transaction services as well as the use of electronic signatures.

1 Introduction

The initiative e-Commission has to be seen in the context of the initiative e-Europe as well as the administrative reform of the European Commission. The European Commission has started the initiative eEurope in 1999 [2] leading to two action plans so far. The comprehensive introduction of e-Government with modern public online services is one of the main aims of the action plans.

The European Commission pursues as part of its administrative reform [3] the goal "to become an 'e-Commission' leading the field in the use of information technologies, and a shining example of an efficient, modern and accountable administration" [10].

2 Aims of the E-Commission

The communication of the Commission "Towards the e-Commission: Implementation Strategy 2001-2005" of June 2001 [1] contains the implementation of the measures 7, 8 and 9 of the Reform White Paper: The e-Commission should ensure the optimum use of the information and communication technologies (ICT) and communications

---

* Professor at the University of Vienna (on leave), at present working for the European Commission, Directorate-General for Agriculture, unit competition. The expressed views are those of the author and do not represent those of the European Commission.

R. Traunmüller (Ed.): EGOV 2003, LNCS 2739, pp. 187–190, 2003.
© Springer-Verlag Berlin Heidelberg 2003

networks. This modernisation should lead to more efficiency with same expenditure. Communication with external partners is to be organised more efficiently (feedback, interactive policy design, Europe web-site). For citizens and companies better civil service shall be offered. The electronic procurement is an important step in this direction (cf. for further information: [4, 5, 6, 9]).

The Commission is thus only one of many public administrations, who see in the use of ICT an important instrument of reform (cf. for administrations [8, p. 1] and the other conference contributions). A substantial difference exists in the challenges of a multilingual and multicultural administration.

The project e-Commission concerns the change in organisational structure and procedures using IT. The role of IT is subject to the needs of the organisation and its users. Management and staff have to cope with the organisational change. A simplification of the procedures is a requirement for success [12, p. 19 et seq.], when procedures and practices are *digitised*.

The timetable for the implementation of the e-Commission is set for the period of 2001-2005. The implementation requires higher IT budgets, which are mostly used for the development of software as well as for further training. Details on the various projects can be found in [11].

3 Steps to the E-Commission

The already existing basis of the e-Commission is the quite sophisticated existing ICT and the remarkable acceptance of electronic working environments (e.g. document writing, communication by e-mail, information by Internet portals). The e-Commission will focus on strengthening this basis and improving and integrating major IT applications.

The demand for the necessary management information is supplied by the System of Integrated Resources Management System (IRMS) that is the basis of the Activity-Based Management (ABM).

The comprehensive introduction of electronic documents facilitates the creation, forwarding, archiving and searching and is thereby a substantial improvement of the document management. The challenges are not only limited to the simplification of documents, the improvement of the document flow within the Commission and the archiving of documents, but also cover the access to documents [7]. The *OPTIMAIL* project deals with organisational, functional and technical end user needs of e-mail. *Legiswrite* is a Word *add-on* application with provides over one hundred text templates for a multiplicity of COM/C and SEC-documents. *Adonis* is the office information system for the registration of mail in paper, fax or e-mail that was introduced in the 1990ies.

For the horizontal procedures special document management systems are in use: *CIS-Net* (management of the quantitatively very extensive consultations between the Directorates-General), *QP/Basil* (questions of the European Parliament), CIRCA (co-operative working place), *Greffe2000* (decision-making processes of the Commission), *Infractions et ASMODEE* (actions for infringement of the Treaty as well as the national transformation acts of directives), *POETRY* (translations) and *SINCOM2* (budget). Since November 1999 *Greffe2000* is obligatory for the registration of non-confidential non-legislative and legislative COM and SEC-documents, which are sent to other institutions.

The internal as well as external access to the different document management systems is to be improved and facilitated by portals. The first examples of internal information are *SG-Vista* (internal distribution of the documents of the *Greffe*), *GINA* (administration information), *IRMS, SINCOM* etc. For the public, access to documents is granted by the EUR-Lex portal of the Office for Publications as well as the public register of Commission documents (http://europa.eu.int/comm/ secretariat_general/regdoc/).

For finance management, a bundle of ICT systems is in use. Reform aims at the integration of the systems, the improvement of the real-time information concerning the state of transactions for the responsible persons as well as the internal control and the inclusion of the ABM in the finance management.

Similar to the finance management, many applications are used for personnel administration. As a central personnel information system, *SYSPER2* has been introduced and is now improved constantly. Most important applications are: job descriptions, objectives, career development evaluations, vocational training plans, promotion plans, vacant posts, mobility and recruitment, assigning of resources and job management, individual rights, time management and information about the job holder.

The digital technologies have enabled considerably more efficient communication. The next step to transaction services requires a development of harmonised technology standards and software tools, which ensure an interoperability of systems. The communications network TESTA is increasingly used. Some Directorates-General have already good experience with communication networks (e.g. Taxation and Customs Union).

The web-site EUROPE (internally named as EUROPE 2) was presented in 2002 after perennial revision. One of the most visited sites has been adapted in design and technical functions. It corresponds to the highest standards for electronic authority news services.

Teleworking has been tested in pilot projects.

4 Evaluation

E-Commission is still *work in progress*. Existing network PCs and servers form the basis for this ambitious undertaking. The link between organisational and technical reform is remarkable. Only if the organisational questions are clarified, then the subsequent steps are taken with ICT.

At present many ICT applications are evaluated and re-designed for the new task in the e-Commission framework. The required integration of many systems is very difficult and time-consuming and will take some years.

Even a more efficient ICT support for administration is an important success for such a huge organisation like the European Commission. This goal has been already achieved. The electronic working environment is highly accepted. The laborious, but necessary improvement of the ICT systems will bring users considerable advantages. With an integrated system, filing, forwarding and archiving becomes much easier allowing also data recycling and data sharing.

Like with all applications of e-government, the step from information services to interactive transactions is the *crucial point* of the long-term success. This implies to a large extent abandoning of paper transactions and paper files. Here the goal is pursued also consistently, but carefully. At present, the use of electronic signatures as well as XML standards remains insufficient. Certainly applications such as *CIS-Net* will internally open the way to intensified use. Externally the Commission depends on the readiness of the Member States and citizens for advanced electronic communication using electronic signatures.

5 Conclusions

The working plan of the European Commission to e-Commission is very ambitious and provides for a comprehensive redesign of the ICT according to the needs of the reformed Commission. The further development is supported by good practice with present e-Government applications and the efficient link between organisational reform and enhanced use of ICT. Many IT systems must be adapted and integrated into the e-Commission. If these laborious tasks are finished, the further expansion to transaction services as well as the use of electronic signatures will be implemented in practise.

References

1. European Commission: Towards the e-Commission: Implementation Strategy 2001–2005 (actions 7, 8 and 9 of the Reform White Paper). Communication, 8.6.2001, SEC (2001) 924,
    http://europa.eu.int/comm/di/pubs/e-comm/sec_2001_0924_en.pdf, 2001
2. European Commission: eEurope web-site.
    http://europa.eu.int/information_society/ eeurope
3. European Commission: Reforming the Commission – A White Paper. April 2000, COM (2000) 200 final. Brussels (2000)
4. European Commission: e-Commission website. (only accessible on the Intranet)
5. European Commission: Implementing the e-Commission, Proceedings Informatics Directorate Symposium 2001.
    http://europa.eu.int/comm/di/symposium2001/ index_en.htm (2001)
6. European Commission: Making the e-Commission Work, Proceedings Informatics Directorate Symposium 2002.
    http://europa.eu.int/comm/di/symposium2002/ proceedings_en.htm (2002)
7. European Commission: Simplification and modernisation of the management of the Commission's documents. Communication, 23.1.2002, C(2002) 99 final. Brussels (2002)
8. Lenk, K. and Traunmüller, R.: Electronic Government: Where are we Heading. In: Traunmüller, R. and Lenk, K. (Eds.): Electronic Government, Proceedings First International Conference EGOV 2002. Springer, Berlin (2002)
9. Moran, F. G.: Towards the e-Commission.
    http://europa.eu.int/comm/di/pubs/e-comm/e-commission_en.pdf (2001)
10. Prodi, R., President of the European Commission: The Commission's contribution to the Lisbon special European Council on employment, economic reforms and social cohesion-towards a Europe based on innovation and knowledge (23–24 March 2000). SPEECH/00/81, http://europa.eu.int/rapid/start/cgi/guesten.ksh (2000)
11. Schweighofer, E.: E-Government in der Europäischen Kommission. In: Wimmer, M. A. (Ed.): Quo Vadis e-Government: State-of-the-art 2003, Tagungsband zum zweiten eIGOV Day 2003 des Forums eIGov.at. OCG, Wien (2003)
12. Wimmer, M. A. and Traunmüller, R.: Geschäftsprozessmodellierung im Bereich E-Government: Eine Zwischenbilanz. In: Schweighofer, E. et al. (Hrsg.), IT in Recht und Staat, Aktuelle Fragen der Rechtsinformatik 2002. Verlag Österreich, Wien (2002)

Framing E-Gov: e=mc3

Åke Grönlund

Örebro University
701 82 Örebro, Sweden
ake.gronlund@esi.oru.se

Abstract. There is a need for discussing the role of IT use in government and governance beyond the information processing aspects, but theories are badly lacking. The literature on various aspects of government tends to underestimate the role of IT while IT studies tend to overestimate it. IT and information systems are not much studied in political science. While some thirty years of studies of information systems have produced many theories concerning IT use in organisations, e-government studies require going beyond the border of the organization as government/nance cannot be reduced to individual organizations, not even if interorganisational cooperation is included. This paper proposes a model that considers governance as a system rather than in terms of its individual organizational units and processes, and views information systems from that perspective.

1 Introduction

While there are many theories of government, there is a lack of theory in the field of what has been called electronic government and (broader) electronic governance ("eGov" is here used to cover both: how government, administration and citizens interact, and how IT is involved). Such a theory would be useful as there is a need for discussing the role of IT use, more informatively termed "informatization" (Snellen, 1995), in government and governance beyond the information processing aspects. It appears that the literature on various aspects of government tends to underestimate the role of IT while IT studies tend to overestimate it. This seems to be by design rather than by analysis. IT and information systems are not much studied in political science. In IT-related fields of study, on the other hand, there are hosts of speculations, usually extrapolating extensively from limited studies of IT use, about how government will change as IT use becomes the norm not only in internal operations but also in inter-organizational and client-organizational relations.

While some thirty years of studies of information systems have produced many theories concerning IT use in organizations, eGov studies require going beyond the border of the organization as government/nance cannot be reduced to individual organizations, not even if interorganisational cooperation is included. Hence, this paper proposes a theory that considers governance as a system rather than in terms of its individual organizational units and processes, and views information systems from that perspective.

R. Traunmüller (Ed.): EGOV 2003, LNCS 2739, pp. 191–198, 2003.

The theory draws on both theories of government and theories of IT in organizations, and proposes the following:

1. Governance is for this purpose best described in terms of a system consisting of three interrelated societal spheres: the political sphere, the administrative sphere, and civil society (including individuals, organizations, media and the public sphere).
2. These spheres have different nature in terms of their motivation, interests, focus unit, and mode of operation.
3. The successful eGov information systems will be those who best and most constructively integrate interests and modes of operation of all three spheres.

This paper briefly outlines these three points.

2 A General Governance Model

To discuss electronic governance or electronic government theoretically, there is a need for a model of government that goes beyond the individual organization. Most e-government discussions and systems so far do not do that. They focus on the operations of one single organization - e g job office e-services (Wiberg, 2002) or car license renewal (http://www.servicearizona.com) – or one or a few processes that stretch over two or more organizations but without changing the rationale of any of the organizations (e. g. one-stop shops). Also, as some authors have noted, eGov projects typically apply an information processing view of government activities and do not consider other aspects of government (Zouridis & Thaens, 2002). In a systems perspective such narrow approaches mean a risk for suboptimisation in two respects, technically (information processing regarded too narrowly in terms of coverage of the whole government) and functionally (a too narrow view of what government is all about). As an example of the latter, Zouridis & Thaens (2002) argue that this approach to eGov will lead to solidification of a certain distribution of power, transformation of citizenship into consumership, and rationalization of legal and policy processes into administrative-technical ones (ibid, p 127-128).

To create a framework for eGov studies that avoids falling into such traps we will here consider government as a system, just like organizational sciences consider organizations as more than individual departments or processes.

Unlike businesses and individual government organizations, government as a whole (as opposed to individual politicians and parties) does not have a clearly defined goal in terms of where to go. It does have a goal, however, in terms of maintaining a balance among different interests in society so as to maintain general interests such as peace, individual freedom and privacy, a viable economic system and so on. Hence, government is an infrastructure guarantor.

Discussing eGov stringently requires defining the context in which it appears in terms of a public sector model. In simple terms, drawing on a textbook in political science, and at a general level where national differences do not matter, a democratic[1]

---

[1] This is a restriction, but one without which eGov risks losing all credibility as information systems cannot be reduced to technical systems only.

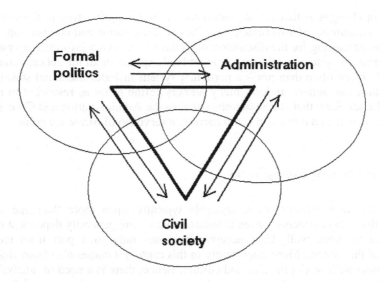

Fig. 1. Basic spheres and relations in a democratic government system. Arrows indicate influence, and circles indicate domains of control. Intersections indicate "transaction zones" where control is negotiated by e g lobbyists and media on the left-hand side, intermediary service deliverers on the right-hand side and professional interaction in government boards and committees on the top side. (Adapted from Molin et al, 1975;16)

government can be described as shown in Figure 1. It consists of three interrelated spheres, the political sphere, the administrative one, and the civil society one. Each sphere contains individuals, organizations, technical systems, social relations, and value systems.

Often, an overly simplified view of a democratic system is propagated, where the relationships of the model are presented as straightforward; citizens elect officials, which then go to work in a formal political system containing certain institutions and rules. Their work produces results in the form of directives to the administration, which with blind obedience – without any influence on the political decisions – executes the decisions.

In practice, the system is of course much more complex. The political impact administrations can exert by having the expertise necessary to prepare decisions in complicated matters is often acknowledged (Snellen, 2001; Watson et al, 1999). Citizens act in many other ways than by casting votes, for example they organize in many ways, and they lobby. This is not the place for enumerating and analysing all aspects of this, neither to discuss different variations of democratic systems. For now, let us just observe that there are *a number of relations*, and that each node in the system influences both the others by a number of relationships: *all nodes are interrelated*. The details of these relations are always under discussion and borders are changing slightly over time. Currently, however, they are in a process of profound change in many countries, for several reasons including globalisation, economic constraints, changing demographics, declining appreciation for the political system (as measured by declining turnout in elections) and the availability of IT. One example of changes is that private enterprise is increasingly acting in the system by means of outsourcing of government activities or deregulation and competition.

What is interesting for the discussion of (a theory for) eGov information systems is that information systems under the eGov umbrella appear in all the spheres, and often – arguably more often than not – a particular system includes users and stakeholders in more than one sphere. Indeed, many authors define eGov as restricted to include only public services, that is transactions between the Administration and Civil Society spheres. While such a definition is too narrow, it serves to illustrate the point.

3   The Nature of the Spheres

eGov information systems often, arguably typically, span more than one societal sphere. Information systems – even mandatory ones – are generally dependent on user acceptance to work well. User acceptance comes only to a part from technical qualities of the system. More importantly in this context it comes also from alignment of the system with work practices and culture. Hence, there is a need for analysing the nature of the spheres – if there are differences among them on any of the above criteria, there is likely a complication for implementation of information systems.

The below table summarizes some salient features that distinguish the three above-mentioned major spheres of a governance system. These spheres have different nature in terms of their motivation, interests, focus unit, and mode of operation; variables that are individually, and certainly together, important for the implementation and operation of any information system. Therefore they can be seen as "modalities", or as "superinstitutions", clusters of institutions operating under the same general conditions. They each set the scene for the actors that operate within them, not just formally but also culturally.

Table 1. Modes of operation of eGov spheres

	Political sphere	*Administrative sphere*	*Civil society*
Motivation	- Representation - Balancing interests - Incompatibility management	- Economic and legal rationality - Equality - Inspectability	Individual or community welfare and emancipation
Focus unit	Groups (representation)	Individual as social unit	Individual or group (as humans with interest)
Interest	Room to manoeuvre	- Complete data - Universal/compre-hensive models - Value-freeness	- Privacy - Expression
Mode of operation	- Value (policy)-based rhetoric - Negotiation	Engineering	Ad hoc, situational or issue-based (e g social movements)

As space does not allow a thorough discussion of the categories, let us just make a brief illustration in terms of the ongoing development.

3.1 An Illustration

In the development of democracy there is generally an ongoing struggle between two perspectives, both beneficial for democracy but neither sufficient (Goldkuhl and Röstlinger, 2001). The *top-down perspective* is about implementing political decisions in activities directed towards the citizens; *politics as design*. The *bottom-up perspective*, sometimes called user democracy or consumer democracy (Bellamy & Taylor, 1998), is about interaction between users and suppliers leading to user influence over service design and content; *politics as evolution*. Real user influence over services means real influence over politics.

In Figure 1, the top-down perspective can be seen as a command chain going clockwise starting in the politics sphere and ending with reactions on decisions picked up by that same sphere. The bottom-up perspective starts on the right-hand side in "service dialogues" involving the administration and civil society spheres and leaves the political sphere somewhat outside of the decision-making process as administrative processes implemented in routines and computerized systems make changes cumbersome.

A brief look at the current development of information systems relevant to eGov shows that different forces are stretching the spheres of influence of the political system, the administrative one, and the civil society respectively (Fig. 2).

1. The increasing use of IT in administrative processes – a more comprehensive electronic information infrastructure – restricts the action space of the political sphere as this infrastructure becomes increasingly hard to change (and indeed understand). This means the influence of the administrative system is increased at the expense of the political one (Arrow 1 in Figure 3). Zouridis & Thaens (2002) provide some evidence to suggest this.

2. The civil society cultures, in the electronic world for instance manifested in virtual communities of different kinds, contain strong social elements but less of the characteristics of formal politics ("citizen" and "member" are not synonyms, for instance). To the extent that electronic tools and techniques from such cultures become used in formal politics it will become less formal and thus more open to the influence of active minorities (Arrow 2).

3. The official e-democracy initiatives, as indeed municipal practice, generally endorse information rather than participation (Anttiroikko, 2001). "Participation" typically means "everybody should know about...." rather than something that involves citizen influence. These efforts can be seen as a means to reinforce the current procedures of formal politics by complementing them with increased direct communication with citizens (Arrow 3).

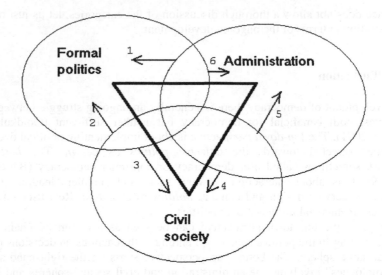

Fig. 2. The government model under change – different actors affect the development in the transaction zones

1. Often local e-democracy projects are in practice controlled by the civil servants rather than politicians due to their control of the IT systems. In a study of four Swedish local e-democracy projects, Grönlund (2002b) found that sometimes politicians did not control the development, but had to adjust to the development at a later stage when important components of the information infrastructure were already implemented. This means the action space of the political system has been reduced and that of the administration has been increased (Arrow 1).

2. Increasing IT use in the civil society includes efforts to affect services in practice by individuals, by using electronic communication to influence individual administrative decision makers or simply by acquiring a better understanding of how the administration works by using the electronic information and tools provided as a necessary precondition for implementing self-service systems. This includes new pressures on the administration, which can no longer hide behind an information monopoly, and hence increases the influence of civil society at the administration's expense (Arrow 5).

3. Initiatives like the eEurope electronic government strives for more administrative control over, and efficiency within and among, the many activities of the public sector by formalizing them to the point of being implementable in electronic tools. To the extent that this succeeds it means not only that the action space of civil society actors diminishes as their interactions with government are more formalized (Arrow 4), it also means that the political system's control over the administration is strengthened as political initiatives are more directly expressed in computer code and hence can be more easily inspected and evaluated (Arrow 6).

From this brief review we can see that there is no single development in terms of the relative strengths of the "influence" arrows in Figure 4. But as we clearly cannot just assume that everything will eventually add up to a balance quite similar to what we have today, it is important to try to assess the development more in detail. Which arrows are strongest, most likely to prevail? And what will the resulting balance become? This is the area for our theory, which we now turn to.

4 The Theory

Considering the discussion above we now suggest a theory of eGov IS (elaborated and discussed in Grönlund & Ilshammar, 2003). The theory proposes that eGov information systems will only succeed when they sufficiently well implement interests and modes of operation of all three spheres of a governance system as of above. This is not a suggestion of an either-or situation. Rather, different proposals for information systems will exist, and the more successful ones will be, the theory predicts, those who score better in these respects. More formally the theory states that the viability of an eGov information system, by which is meant not just a software system but also the organizational arrangements in which it is embedded, can be expressed as $e = mc3$, with the variables defined as follows:

e = energy (viability, sustainability of an information system).

m = mass (the magnitude of the problem it solves).

c (1) = compatibility (of interests among the relevant actors).

c (2) = communication (of a common understanding across spheres: benefits to all by shared motivation. While c2 is dependent on the existence of some amount of c1 (there cannot be c2 if c1=0), it rather refers to the ability of a particular system to unleash some of the potential given by c1. C1, thus, is potential while c2 is trigger).

c (3) = clarity (user understanding of some application, system, procedure, concept, etc. For software applications, usability can be a rough indicator).

5 Conclusions

In this paper we have presented a model of governance derived from a general model of society. The purpose was to provide a general framework within which to assess the development towards electronic government. Based on this, we have suggested a theory for eGov IS. We have identified factors at a general level. Certainly other factors, such as technical issues and cost are also important for the development, but these are considered as being at a lower level of analysis. They can be integrated in studies using this model – a cost calculation, for instance, will appear quite different depending on which sphere perspective is applied.

198   Å. Grönlund

References

1. Anttiroiko, A-V. (2001) Toward the European Information Society. *Communications of the ACM*, January 2001.
2. Goldkuhl, G. & Röstlinger, A. (2001). IT som möjliggörare och hinder – i samspel mellan politik och verksamhet i kommuner (IT as enabler and obstacle). In Åke Grönlund & Agenta Ranerup (red) *Elektronisk förvaltning, elektronisk demokrati (Electronic government, electronic democracy)*. Studentlitteratur, 2001.
3. Grönlund, Å. (2002) *Electronic government – Design, Applications, and Management*. Idea Group Publishing.
4. Grönlund, Å. (2002b). Emerging Infrastructures for E-democracy – in Search of Strong Inscriptions. *eService Journal*, Vol 2, No 4 (2002).
5. Grönlund, Å. & Ilshammar, L. (2003) e=mc3. A theory of electronic governance information systems. Forthcoming in proceedings of IRIS 2003.
6. Heeks, R. (2002) *eGovernment for Development. Causes of eGovernment Success and Failure: Factor Model* (http://www.egov4dev.org/causefactor.htm#model, visited Dec 1, 2002).
7. Molin, B., Månsson, L., Strömberg, L. (1975) *Offentlig förvaltning (Public Administration)*. Bonniers.
8. Snellen, I.Th.M.. (1995) Channeling Democratic Influences Through Bureaucracies. In W.B.H.J. van de Donk, I.Th.M. Snellen, & P.W. Tops (eds) *Orwell in Athens – A Perspective on Informatization and Democracy*. (pp 51–60). IOS Press.
9. Zouridis, S., Thaens, M. (2002) *eGovernment: Towards a Public Administration Approach*. In Proceedeings of Global e-Policy eGov Forum (pp 119–133), Seoul, Korea, Nov 6–7, 2002. Seoul: SungKyunKwan University, Global e-Policy eGovernment Institute.
10. Watson, R., Akselsen, S., Evjemo, B., Aasaether, N. (1999) Teledemocracy in Local Government. *Communications of the ACM*, December 1999; 58–63.
11. Wiberg, M (2002). e-Government in Sweden: Centralization, Self-Service and Competition. In Å Grönlund (ed) *Electronic Government – Design, Applications and Management*. Idea Group Publishing, Hershey, PA, USA.
12. World Bank (2002) *A Definition of E*Government* http://www1.worldbank.org/publicsector/egov/definition.htm (visited Nov 13, 2002)

Methodology for Analysing the Relationship between the Reorganisation of the Back Office and Better Electronic Public Services

Herbert Kubicek[1], Jeremy Millard[2], and Hilmar Westholm[1]

[1] Institut für Informationsmanagement GmbH
Universität Bremen
Am Fallturm 1
D-28359 Bremen, Germany
Tel.: +49 421 218 2211
Fax: +49 421 218 4894
{kubicek,westholm}@ifib.de
[2] Danish Technological Institute
Kongsvang Allé 29
8000 Aarhus C, Denmark
Tel: +45 72 20 14 17
Fax: +45 72 20 14 14
jeremy.millard@teknologisk.dk

Abstract. This paper reports on a methodology for analysing the relationship between the reorganisation of government back offices, which contributes to the full realisation of eGovernment, and efficient electronic public services. It derives from research currently being carried out for the European Commission in which about 400 cases from around Europe are being subject to preliminary survey, from which a selection of between 20 and 30 of the most advanced 'good practice' cases will be studied in depth. Preliminary results are expected in September 2003 and full results in October 2003.

1 Introduction

The purpose of this paper is to:

- present a methodology for analysing the relationship between the reorganisation of government back offices, which contributes to the full realisation of eGovernment, and efficient electronic public services. The framework for this includes the various forms of integration developed as an analytical framework at the Brussels eGovernment conference in November 2001.

- show how this methodology can investigate the link between the back office reorganisation and the quality of the delivery of the service at the front office.

The paper is based on research currently being carried out for the European Commission by the Danish Technological Institute and IfIB, the Institut für Informationsmanagement GmbH, based at Bremen University, Germany. About 400 cases from around Europe are being subject to preliminary survey, from which a selection of between 20 and 30 of the most advanced 'good practice' cases will be

R. Traunmüller (Ed.): EGOV 2003, LNCS 2739, pp. 199–206, 2003.

studied in depth. Preliminary results are expected in September 2003 and full results in October 2003.

2 Understanding Back Office Reorganisation

The Ministerial Conference "eGovernment – From Policy to Practice", held in November 2001 in Brussels, clearly demonstrated what key note speakers had called a generational change from a shop window of isolated examples to a second generation characterised by integration. The quality of service delivered to the customer/citizen decisively depends on the degree of such integration. The same is the case with respect to increases in efficiency which administrations can, and must, achieve by putting services online. The 2001 Ministerial Conference suggested different types (or dimensions) of integration, including the integration of services and their integration with back offices, in particular with existing so-called legacy or ERP applications which are often up to 20 years old and which form the basis of existing workflows. In order to achieve progress it is necessary to better understand the complexity of back office integration and reorganisation and of the different dimensions creating this complexity. Because e-government services themselves are very heterogeneous there is not one general model of back office integration. On the other hand it would not be very helpful to insist that each case is unique and that no generalisation is possible. This paper suggests a conceptual framework with four models of different levels of complexity which are able to grasp the diversity of the cases and still allows for generalisations and comparability.

2.1 Definition of 'Back Office Reorganisation'

Back office is a term relative to the front office which in this context is a user interface to an online service. The back office receives and processes the information which the user of a service enters in order to produce and deliver the desired service. This may be done completely manually, fully automated or by any combination of both. In some cases such a service is produced by one unit or back office (BO), in other cases several BOs of the same organisation or of different organisations, at the same government level or at different levels may be involved. In order to recognise the complexity involved and to achieve comparability of different cases a common terminology is needed. We suggest the concept of a government agency, which contains one or more BOs. An agency is defined as a formal organisation with a separate legal standing and which has one or more formal purposes (e.g. a public administration, a hospital, a passport agency, a school, a railway authority, a tax authority, etc.). The difference between an agency and a BO is that the latter, although it may or may not be a formal organisation, does not have a separate legal standing. A BO may be located at the same or a different physical address as other BOs within the agency, and is normally distinguished within the agency from other BOs by having one or more formal functions and normally by its own organisational structure and management, although these are joined at the higher levels within the agency.

The term reorganisation refers to changes in workflows (process reorganisation or re-engineering) or changes in the structure of one or more agencies involved, i.e. the distribution of authority, which occur when making services available online. The interest in reorganisation is based on long experience of applying information technology to government, i.e. that the greatest benefits do not come from replicating paper based processes directly on a computer, but rather from using the potential of the technology to re-engineer the process, to check whether each step is still necessary, whether steps might be merged, etc. In terms of the quality of service experienced by the customer, this might include a change in the way service delivery is initiated. Recently some agencies have changed from reacting to requests to the proactive delivery of the service based on information (such as dates) available to the system.

2.2 Two Basic Dimensions: Stages and Services

In order to estimate and categorise the complexity of the whole process of service production and delivery, it is necessary to examine the relationships between the BOs involved arising from the division of labour and of authority between them. There are two basic dimensions which combined lead to four models, as described in section 3.

In industrial analysis, the concept of the supply chain helps to distinguish different stages of the production and delivery of a product. If the division of labour in the overall governmental organisation results in the production and delivery of a service being divided into two or more stages assigned to different agencies, a need for coordination arises which increases complexity.

It is useful to distinguish between one stage and multi stage services. A one stage service is, for example, the request and delivery of a birth certificate from the local government. An example of a multi-stage-service is the request for a passport made at the local government which has to be forwarded to a national agency. In more general terms, a stage is defined as a task performed by a BO which is necessary for producing and delivering a service. Of course, complexity increases with the number of stages and the number of BOs involved. From a technical point of view, the ideal case is where the technical systems of different offices are integrated in such a way that incoming data are processed automatically and the result is forwarded to the office in the next stage, until the service is delivered online to the customer. However, for reasons of equitable judgement or of security, human intervention may still be necessary, thus interrupting the electronic process.

Different overall divisions of labour and distributions of authority, and thus different degrees of complexity, result from different organisational principles applied at each stage. In the passport example, several BOs at the local level need to forward applications to one central second stage BO. In the German context, citizens registering a new address need to de-register their former address, which means forwarding the de-registration to one of 14,000 local governments. In such cases, it is useful to build an index of supply chain complexity which takes account both of the number of stages and the number of potential BOs being addressed in each stage.

In order to increase benefits or convenience for the customer, as well as reduce the cost of processing data, the integration of two or more services is promising. But this also calls for coordination and thus increases complexity. A service is defined as a public eService experienced by the user (whether citizen or business) which directly serves an ultimate user objective. For the purposes of the present study, these are eEurope's 20 benchmarking services[1]. Other specific services can also be considered. All services may be offered to the user either singly or integrated into bundles, such as built around citizen life events or in other user-centred formats. Integration, from the user perspective, means more than listing different services in one menu. It is better understood, for example, as the automatic re-use of a user's data input made into one service by other services. These 'primary' services are distinguished from 'secondary' (or 'auxiliary') services which do not directly serve an ultimate user objective themselves but which may be used to support the attainment of such objectives. In the context of the present study there are two main types of auxiliary service: on-line payment and digital signature.

2.3   Institutional Configuration

The challenge of achieving the necessary coordination depends to some extent on the kind of agencies involved and their organisational affiliation. Because of its common decision making authority, it is easier to coordinate two BOs within the same agency than two BOs at two different levels of government, or governmental agencies with private companies. In order to capture such institutional configuration we distinguish:
- horizontal relations, i.e. interaction between public agencies at the same level of government, whether local, regional, national or European
- vertical relations, i.e. interaction between public agencies at two or more levels of government, e.g. between local, regional, national, European level.
In addition, agencies can be distinguished by ownership, funding and/or purpose:
- public agency, i.e. financed mainly or wholly by public expenditure for non-profit purposes
- private agency, i.e. businesses operating within a market context, designed to make a profit, and privately owned by one or more legal entities
- third sector agency, i.e. community, voluntary, charitable or other non-profit and non-public agency.
For the purposes of the present study we are only interested in public eServices (i.e. involving at least one public agency) offered to non-public agency users (i.e. individual citizens, third sector agencies or private agencies). We are interested in PPPs (public-private partnerships), as long as they include at least one public agency.

3   Four Models of Back Office Integration

The two dimensions of service and stage result in four models of back office reorganisation differentiated according to their degree of digitisation.

Model A: One Service, One Stage
Most of today's eGovernment applications in Europe can be assigned to Model A in which only one service is involved and interaction is only between the user and the

---

[1] European Commission, 2000, eEurope -- an information society for all, 23-24 March 2000, Lisbon: http://europa.eu.int/comm/information_society/eeuropa/pdf/com081299_en.pdf

BO. The following three steps show increasing automation, and thus represent a framework for evaluation and analysis of the degree of BO process digitisation:
1. Human interface break in both data input and data output – the interaction between the user and the BO is only partially digitised so that the process of both user data input and data output response by the system are still mediated by a human agent, e.g. by an employee who reads e-mail or pdf-forms from the user, checks the data, then keys them into the BO application, and where the data response also needs a human interface break.
2. Automatic input but human interface break in output response – the interaction between the user and the BO is subject to more digitisation so that no keying-in by human mediation is necessary, but checking and response initiation still need to be undertaken by an employee, so there is no automatic data response but one which requires a human interface break.
3. Full automation – the interaction between the user and the BO is now fully digitised and the only need for human intervention is in exceptional circumstances, i.e. there is full automatic data input, checking and response.
Additional process digitisation can be provided by the integration of secondary services, such as electronic payment or digital signature.

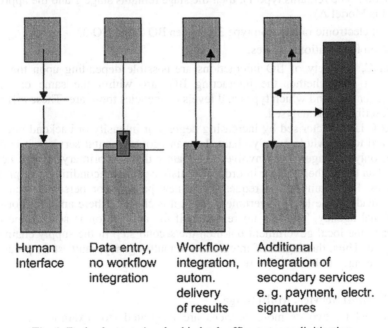

| Human Interface | Data entry, no workflow integration | Workflow integration, autom. delivery of results | Additional integration of secondary services e. g. payment, electr. signatures |

Fig. 1. Basic elements involved in back office process digitisation.

Model B: Multi Service, One Stage

In Model B, two or more services are integrated (for example in citizen or business life events) but interaction is still only between the user and the BO. Integration here means more than just a list of links between services but rather the integration of data, i.e. some of the data entered for one service in the bundle are at least used by one other service as well. The three steps of BO process digitisation and additional process digitisation are as in Model A. Further, the total number of services integrated can also be taken as a measure of the sophistication of process digitisation.

The quality and ease of use of services for the customer and the efficiency for the administration at this level depend upon what has been described during the Ministerial Conference in 2001 as the integration of data, in particular whether there is single filing or redundancy free data entry, and whether open standards for Electronic Data Interchange (EDI) are applied. These standards refer to the syntax, such as XML as well as to the semantics of different messages such as EDIFACT, HBCI or OSCI and to protocols for secondary services.

Model C: One Service, Multi Stage
In Model C, only one service is involved but there are two or more types of electronic interaction, including between the user and the BO and between BOs. The three steps of BO process digitisation and additional process digitisation are as in Model A. Further, the increasing progress of BO process digitisation can be analysed as follows:

- Stage 2: electronic interaction type 2 between BO 1 and BO 2 (note: if more than one BO is involved but the interaction type is the same with each one (e.g. interaction type remains type 1), then the stage remains stage 1 and the appropriate model is Model A)
- Stage 3: electronic interaction type 3 between BO 2 and BO 3
- and so on for additional stages.

In Model C, a variety of BO interactions are possible depending upon the agency involvement and whether the interacting BOs are within the same or between different agencies, and which types and levels of agencies these are. These differences can be described and analysed.

Model C is characterised by increasing degrees or intensity of backend integration with regard to the whole supply chain. In many governmental services it is not the case that only one agency is involved, but rather that the primary agency needs to forward data to another agency in order to satisfy certain preconditions for providing its services. For example, the request for a new passport or personal document is normally made at the local government level, it is checked there and then forwarded to a national agency. There is no real gain if the application is sent online by the customer to the local government but then the second step in the supply chain is still paper-based. Thus, the degree of integration in multi-agency, multi-stage processes is of great relevance to back-office reorganisation.

Model D: Multi Service, Multi Stage
- In Model D, two or more services are integrated (for example in citizen or business life events), and there are two or more types of electronic interaction, including between the user and the BO and between BOs. Integration here means more than just a list of links between services but rather the integration of data, i.e. that some of the data entered for one service in the bundle are at least used by one other service as well. The three steps of BO process digitisation and additional process digitisation are as in Model A. Further, the total number of services integrated can also be taken as a measure of the sophistication of process digitisation. Finally, the increasing progress of BO process digitisation can be analysed as in Model C.

In Model D, a variety of BO interactions are possible depending upon the agency involvement and whether the interacting BOs are within the same or between different agencies, and which types and levels of agencies these are. These differences can be described and analysed.

The quality of integration at this highest level can be evaluated by:

- the completeness of the service according to usability (e.g. through availability of transactions, data re-use) and the degree of fulfilment (i.e. how much the service fulfils user need)
- the integration of auxiliary services like payment or authentication by electronic signature according to open standards (syntax such as XML, including semantics such as EDIFACT, HBCI / OSCI messages)
- the completeness of integration of sub-processes in all stages of the supply chain (i.e. technical interoperability within and between government agencies and other involved actors)
- the intensity of integration – electronic data exchange only, or integration of workflows, with the highest level also enabling monitoring/tracking by the customer, or re-organisation of BO interaction e.g. through platform and project-oriented work
- the application of open standards in the whole supply chain (syntax such as XMLor semantics such as EDIFACT, OSCI messages).

4 Preliminary Findings and Perspectives

The methodology presented here has been applied to an EU-wide analysis carried out by 16 experts covering the 15 Member Status together with Norway and Iceland. The preliminary findings of this study, as well as an analysis of the contributions for the European Commission's eGovernment Awards, show that there still are very few cases which have reached the level of model D, and that the more advanced cases of models B and C are not evenly distributed over services or countries. As the overall organisation of the production and delivery of similar services varies greatly across Member States, the preconditions for back office reorganisation are also very different. For example, Member States with a federal structure, such as Germany and Austria, have one additional level of government without a higher level decision making unit, which makes coordination much more difficult. And there are many other reasons why the provision of services is organised differently. There are two consequences following from this.

The present study can not be used to quantitatively benchmark or rank national progress in eGovernment. Where there has already been a high degree of BO integration with legacy systems, it is relatively easy to put a virtual front office in place and achieve full integration. But where there has been no re-organisation so far, it will be a long and complicated process to achieve at least some BO integration because the structure for managing the coordination process has to be established before or during such a process.

The diversity of preconditions and technical solutions instead offers two types of benefit. Where preconditions are comparable, innovative technical solutions and changes of work flows may immediately be adopted. On the other hand, where preconditions, in particular the overall organisation of a service including its legal provisions, are different, the need to achieve enhanced quality of service or efficiency of service delivery could be taken as an occasion to rethink the present situation and to consider a basic reorganisation of the whole supply chain.

To date, government organisation within Member States has tended to leave established structures and procedures in place. In contrast to the private sector, including telecommunications, public utilities and broadcasting, the European Commission has not been given any competency with regard to regulating governmental services. The authors are not proposing this, but are suggesting that national and regional governments, more so than in the past, should take the opportunity to learn from their peers how to improve service delivery, even accepting the need to retain different institutional, cultural and political structures according to democratic need. And the Commission could support this process. To restrict this support to technical issues only will not be sufficient, given that the real benefits stem from reorganisation. The analysis of 20-30 good practice cases of back office reorganisation by this study will provide important input to this process.

References

1. PRISMA (2002) *Pan-European best practice in service delivery*, deliverable D3.2 of Prisma, a research action supported by the Information Society Technologies Programme of the European Union, 2000-2003: http://www.prisma-eu.net
2. eGovernment 'back-office survey' (2003), final report on the 'relationship between the reorganisation of the back office and better electronic public services' a survey for the Information Society Technologies Programme of the European Union, 2000-2003, contact jeremy.millard@teknologisk.dk.

Six Actions to Initiate PPR

Kim Viborg Andersen

Department of Informatics
Copenhagen Business School
Howitzvej 60
DK – 2000 Frederiksberg, Denmark
Phone: +45-3815-2400
Fax: +45-3815-2401.
http://www.cbs.dk/~andersen
andersen@cbs.dk

Abstract. The main focus of the Public Sector Process Rebuilding (PPR) method is to orient information systems (IS) towards the end-user of the public services. This paper presents six actions implementing the PPR-concept: (1) bring order in the digital tool box; (2) argue which processes can not be 100% digitalized; (3) explain what the IS-benefits are for citizens, decision-making and prioritizing; (4) distribute new IS leaving 10% for intra departmental solution and 20% on other inter/intra governmental communication; (5) access the formal IT capability; and (6) identify the radical IS implementation.

1 Introduction

During the 1990s, rigid institutional practices and embedded practices were addressed by several writers on re-engineering the public sector (Heeks 1999; Osborne & Gaebler 1992; Thaens, Bekkers, & Van Duivenboden 1995). The IS-research community was rather segmented by application development area with only a small community studying the overarching issues of IS in government. At the start of the new millennium, research on IS in government – often labeled e-government or digital government - has gained new research momentum and with less ideological disagreements.

One of the strongest pieces of evidence of this change is the shift from the Hammer and Champy book on Reengineering the Corporation (1993) to the Champy book on X-engineering. (2002) where the management-led, closed company and share-holder approach is replaced by participation, cross-organizational processes and customer centric approach. One reason for this change to reengineering is the critique on the BPR–method that evolved during the 1990s (Galliers 1997). More important reason for this change is the nature of IS-application and business operations have changed during the past ten years. In this paper we continue where we stopped at last years DEXA conference on EGOV by providing six actions each grounded in the PPR-concept.

R. Traunmüller (Ed.): EGOV 2003, LNCS 2739, pp. 207–212, 2003.

2 Research Arguments for Studying IS in Government

Despite the many years of research on IS in government – with highlights as the Reinforcement Hypothesis (Danziger et al. 1982), the study on Fiscal Impact Budgeting Systems (Dutton & Kraemer 1985), the reinventing government study (Osborne & Gaebler 1992) and the book on Public Administration in the Information Age (Snellen & Donk 1998) – the field is still lacking coherent views on the need for and the approach to theory construction (Weick 1989; Whetten 1989). The PPR method presented in this paper is targeted primary action research (Argyris, Puttma, & Smith 1995; Baskerville 1999). Yet, we welcome studies that document impacts and experiences with the PPR-method and discuss the ontological, epistemological, methodological, and axiological dimensions (Fitzgerald & Howcroft 1998).

Beyond the need for helping building a more coherent research community, there are three overall arguments for doing research on IS in government. First of all there is a high level of *policy saliency* of applications in areas as health care and development of new generations of vertical and horizontal infrastructure.

Second, there are solid *scale* arguments for doing research on government. Government might be decentralized and segmented in silos, but at the application level most applications are identical or even shared applications across departments. With the diversified user environment this provides unique opportunities to study variance in the implementation of applications.

A third argument for researching IS in government is that researchers' *access to quantitative and qualitative data* sources might be less challenging as compared to research in the private sector. Although issues on privacy, confidentiality, etc. are equal research concerns, the public sector might be more keen to open the gates for researchers. In the next section, we will summarize the overall PPR-concept and then proceed to outline the action oriented elements.

3 Re-capping the PPR-Concept

The overall purpose of the PPR-method is to glean for some useful parts of BPR and process innovation ideas while giving ear to criticisms of the concept's application in the public sector. At the one hand PPR is founded in the normative statement that governments should be as small as possible and contract out tasks as much as possible. Yet, PPR acknowledge that political processes set the overall goals for the public sector.

Equally important to setting specific goals, is the rebuilding of the structures to support these goals along with implementing the new IS. This requires that we know the work processes. Although this is the case in a large part of the public sector, the flow of information, the share of information, and the manipulation of the information are just some of the items where our knowledge is in fact quite limited. However, without such knowledge prior to rebuilding the structures, the outcome will depend more on luck than professional responsibility, commitment, and involvement.

Also, the keywords "measurement" and "expectations" should be considered carefully. Within the public sector, it is difficult, but not impossible, to measure the processes. Likewise, the expectations from the "stakeholders" must be identified and tied to the performance management. This is naturally complicated by the often rigid systems for the users/ citizens to impose their influence on the content of the public service. Nevertheless, our message here is that rebuilding public organization is not successful if the only thing accomplished is increased satisfaction for the employees, or information systems that has a better user interface.

4 Six Bullets to Start the Process of Rebuilding

PPR is concerned with information systems in non-trivial settings and when it is likely to face major implementation challenges. As part of a EU Asia ICT project we were asked to help specify an IS that could help the government to better analyze and prioritize their resources. After various rounds of data gathering on the data flow, system architecture, etc., we found the true implementation hurdle: "If the system makes anybody unhappy, you will have to redesign the system…people will not support the system if it makes anybody unhappy. It needs to make people happy". The PPR approach advocated here will not be likely to succeed with such restrictions! The generation of IS implemented in government now is not going to be less challenging and laborious. The cross-departmental, multi-functionality, and constant upgrading with ntegration modules is likely also to make people unhappy from times-to-times. We have formulated six elements in the PPR concept.

Action I: Bring order in the digital toolbox

Manifold routines could in theory be digitalized. Yet, reality is that most routine processes are not digitalized. One of the reasons that this mismatch occur is similar to that of the handyman that needs yet another tool before fixing the house. Yet, if back tracking the record, one indeed would be skeptical if it is the tools only that holds the Lion's share of fault in the lopsided homemade garage.

In most public offices the digital toolbox is to a large degree already full. The problem is more that the toolbox owner has disorder in the toolbox that he is not able to find the tools when he has to use them. Onwards, he might not know which tool to pick or how to use them. Finally, when he finds the right tools they might be rusty because it is day and year since they have last been used and no attempt has been taken to secure and maintain the tools.

Action II: Describe and/ or model your work related actions and processes. Argue which of these cannot be digitalized

"All I need is time to concentrate – I do not need more distractions" "Videoconferencing – no, we need face-to-face meetings to solve things out. The internet is not really suitable for that" These quotes from public employees shape a picture of the public sector as a unity of workers that will use any mean to prevent direct digital contact with their citizens, users & business partners. Clearly there are plenty of (policy) reports that argue for more computers and web-services in the public administration, but the main challenge is the perception that certain type of public services cannot be digitalized.

Using process-description techniques, the processes could get visible and decompressed. The process modeling literature has plentiful examples on the challenge on how to model the most critical processes. Yet, the challenge is to focus on the parts and the whole. For example, few would argue that public supported childcare or eldercare can be digitalized. Yet, in a Danish municipality videoconferencing is enabling contact between parents, children, and the personnel.

The second benefit from action II is to get the public servant/ sector to start arguing which processes can not be digitalized. Most often the public sector gets the advantage of selecting the processes that can be digitalized. The disadvantage to that approach is that institutional forces and inertia gets the pole position.

Action III: Terminate all new IS application that do not bring benefits for the enduser, political decision-making and prioritizing

Geographical information systems, legislative systems etc. form another important body of IS that might play a role in actual policy processes but could also "live their own life". In the third action bullet, we enforce the focus the analysis on the enduser. Asked to address the benefits of IS, employees, consultants and analysts would start arguing on impacts of IS on areas as internal administrative efficiency and effectiveness and improvement of information access and quality. Indeed there have been important positive impacts of IS on these areas (Andersen & Danziger 2001).

The main challenge in action III is to address the benefits of the new IS for the enduser. The enduser is not the public employee that uses the new application. Rather it is the *citizen/* user. Also, IS has a legitimate role as input to decision-making, prioritizing, and implementation of policies by the means of economic models, various business intelligence systems. The residual from the action bullet three is what you do not want to keep. As long as there are benefits for the citizens/ user of the public services and/ or the policy processes only, no further action is needed. Otherwise, the IS need to be terminated.

Action IV: Distribute the list of existing IT-applications in three target groups: 1) direct citizen/ user contact, 2) inter/intra governmental organizations, and 3) your own department/ office

In action IV, we ask you to distribute the existing IS in three target groups: 1) direct citizen/ user contact, 2) inter/intra governmental organizations, and 3) your own department/ office. Our hypothesis is that you will find a distribution of 10% of the IS oriented towards citizens/ user contact, 20% towards intragovernmental or intergovernmental communications, and 70% are oriented towards internal communication.

You will need to change this, making the citizen orientation 70% and the internal communication 10%. This action will be meet by strong reactions as: "Do you want us to drop existing, well-functioning application just for the mere sake of re-orienting the applications?" Not so. We will ask you to seek the redistribution over time for new IS.

Action V: Make a mini-survey about when and possible which IT-tool oriented courses your colleagues have attended

In action V we address the update cycle of the IS-capability by asking your colleagues, including the managers, the following question: "when did you last participate in a formal IT-course?" You will be met by total salience broken by one that claim the general public managers and servants do not need hands-on courses in IT – that's what is meant for the IT-professionals. Managers are not meant to program, but to manage and decide. From the rest of the crowd they will argue that they have learnt it by themselves, with help from colleagues when they need specific assistance. The last time they attended a formal IT-course was when DOS and programs as WordPerfect and Lotus Symphony/ 1-2-3 were introduced.

We test this by asking one of your colleagues to mail you a random word document of 10 pages or more. After receiving this document, please access whether any style sheet functions or any post-electronic typewriter functionalities have been used – beyond digital storage and retrieval of the data.

Clearly a few had training transforming to the Windows platform but the majority learned it by doing. Our hypothesis is that most did this in a fashion where the fundamentals of the programs were never acquired. The consequence is that the potential of the program are not exploited to even partly full extend and that in most cases any thinking of the technology networked organization of the activities would be very costly due to inadequate and wrong use of the IS.

Action VI: Please distribute the newly proposed IS in two groups: 1) functionalities that already are covered of existing IS and 2) IS that radical challenges the distribution of tasks and implementation of tasks

In the sixth action, we ask you to identify the radical IS-challenges. Important concepts as the virtual organization (Hedberg et al. 1998), knotworked organizing (Engeström, Engeström, & Vähäaho 1999), and X-engineering (Champy 2002) call for radical changes and for a more open information and communication infrastructure. Establishment of home offices, process improvement across organizational boundaries, and implementation of open source are examples that most likely would radical challenge the existing organization of work. There is a need for ongoing updates of the existing applications and the infrastructure. Yet, simple software updates and hardware replacements are examples of initiatives that most likely will not radical challenge the organization of work. E-procurement, new accounting software package, and a new Intranet platform are examples of initiatives that could fall in both categories.

5 Conclusions

In this paper we have presented six actions each grounded in the PPR-concept. PPR holds its strength in its simplicity. Of the same reason, the PPR and the six action points is an obvious target for critique. First, the action points need to be supplemented by more fundamental methodologies and techniques. The action point is more a list of diagnostics principles rather than a tool-kit for the actual process rebuilding. In particular input from the IS public administration is welcome to give them a more active role rather than just an analytical/ impact assessment role.

Second, the actions can be criticized for being extremely actor biased and leaves little room for the more structural oriented approaches. Third, most processes are cross-departmental and would therefore be challenging to identify the processes and process owner as well as identifying the ones willing to change.

Despite these reservations, we use them in training of public managers and found the combination of the six actions as a stimulating tool for triggering focus of on the role of IS in their work settings. We recognize that there is much more research to be done to test the solidity of each of actions and welcome research that put attention on one of more the actions.

References

1. Andersen, K. V. & Danziger, J. N. 2001. IT Transformation of the Political World. *International Journal of Public Administration*.
2. Argyris, C., Putnam, R. & Smith, D. 1985. *Action Science*. San Francisco, CA: Jossey-Bass.
3. Baskerville, R. K. 1999. Investigating Information Systems With Action Research. *CAIS, 2*.
4. Champy, J. 2002. *X-Engineering the Corporation*. London: Hodder & Stroughton.
6. Danziger, J. N. et al. 1982. *Computers and Politics*. Colombia University Press.
7. Dutton, W. H. & Kraemer, K. L. 1985. *Modeling as Negotiating*. Ablex.
8. Engeström, Y., Engeström, R., & Vähäaho,T. 1999. When the Center Does Not Hold: The Importance of Knotworking. Chailkin, M. Hedegaard, & U. Juul Jensen (eds.), *Activity theory and social practice: Cultural-historical approaches*. Aarhus University Press.
9. Fitzgerald, B. & Howcroft, D. 1998. Towards Dissolution of the IS Research Debate: From Polarisation to Polarity. *Special issue of JIT on research methods*.
10. Galliers, R. D. 1997. Business Re-Engineering: The Fad That Forgot People. In *The Dynamics of Strategy*, Sems, University of Surrey, pp. 1–13.
11. Hammer, M. & Champy, J. 1993. *Reengineering the Corporation*. HarperCollins Publishers.
12. Hedberg, B. et al. 1998. *Virtual Organizations and Beyond*. New York: Wiley.
13. Heeks, R. 1999. *Reinventing Government in the Information Age: International Practice in IT-enabled Public Sector Reform*. London: Routledge.
14. Osborne, D. & Gaebler, T. 1992. *Reinventing government*. New York: The Penguin Group.
15. Snellen, Ig. Th. M., & Donk, W. B. H. J. van de. 1998. *Public Administration in an Information Age*. Amsterdam: IOS Press.
16. Thaens, Bekkers, & Van Duivenboden. 1995. BPR in the public administration. *Conference for the European Group of Public Administration* (EGPA). Budapest, Hungary.
17. Weick, K. E. 1989. Theory Construction as Disciplined Imagination. *Academy of Management Review*, 516–531.
18. Whetten, D. A. 1989. What Constitutes a Theoretical Contribution? *Academy of Management Review*, 490–495.

Processes in E-Government – A Holistic Framework for Modelling Electronic Public Services

Silke Palkovits[1] and Maria A. Wimmer[2]

[1] BOC GmbH
Baeckerstrasse 5/3, A-1010 Vienna,
silke.palkovits@boc-eu.com
[2] Institute of Applied Computer Science
University of Linz
A-4040 Linz, Altenbergerstr. 69
mw@ifs.uni-linz.ac.at

Abstract. Recently, process modelling and process reorganisation have been recognised as being of utmost importance for making e-government implementations success. Due to the high complexity of governmental processes and organisational structures, appropriate modelling methodologies and tools are, however, not really available yet. In our contribution, we describe the needs for a comprehensive Business Process Management methodology and toolkit targeted for the public sector. We present a solution to support public administrations in the reorganisation and re-engineering of administrative processes towards online service provision.

1 Introduction

The internet and applications based on internet technologies present more and more diverse possibilities to users like organisations, public authorities or private persons, to interact with each other and to realise business activities or services through the internet. In the public sector, e-government is the catchword to express the huge immersion of internet technologies in governmental activities and to shift towards online public service provision.

E-government applications are known as being rather complex as a number of actors (citizens, clerks, authorities, etc.), different business processes and heterogeneous technologies have to be integrated [9]. Following this fact and due to a currently running modernisation issue of public administrations, an urgent need for a model-based transformation of traditional public services towards web-supported service provision rises.

Current modelling of organisations and business processes is based on fixed metamodels. With fast changing business conditions and the requirements of the public sector for an appropriate tool for the depiction of e-government processes the complexity to find an appropriate solution for each application area rises tremendously. To be able to cope this complexity the use of tools offering flexible methodologies proved successful. This fact leads us to the challenge to develop a tailor-made modelling tool specifically targeted for the public sector.

R. Traunmüller (Ed.): EGOV 2003, LNCS 2739, pp. 213–219, 2003.

In this paper a holistic framework for the modelling and the management of applications in e-government is introduced. This framework integrates knowledge-oriented as well as teaching aspects on a process basis and redresses deficits of traditional modelling frameworks (cf. section 2). Section 3 investigates the characteristics of e-government processes and the specific requirements for the holistic framework. Section 4 introduces the solution in terms of methodological framework and first design issues for the implementation.

2 Business Process Management

Business Process Management (BPM) comprises a number of different tasks concerning the organisational processes. BPM is often used as generic term for Business Process Reengineering (BPR), Quality Management or Implementation of Workflow Management Systems [10]. Important parts of the Business Process Management are the acquisition of relevant data and the illustration of models of the organisation, the products and processes as well as the usage of resources like for example information technology. The analysis and simulation of the models deliver advice for the strategic optimisation and quality assurance.

The state-of-the-art in the area of modelling of organisations is based on fixed metamodels [5]. A meta-model is the formalism the modelling bases on. Product models are created by using product modelling environments, process models are created in business process modelling tools and organisational models are realised in personnel management tools. Additionally, business architectures highly depend on the branches under consideration. In the public administration for example knowledge management aspects, training and learning management, document management, but also the depiction of web-based applications have to be integrated.

Further requirements for a modelling platform are flexibility, adaptability and openness to integrate models based on different modelling paradigms such as decision support models, descriptive models or predictive models. These requirements have to be fulfilled by environments providing flexible metamodelling capabilities [5]. The main characteristic of such environments is that the formalism of modelling – the metamodel – can be freely defined. Platforms based on metamodelling concepts should support the following topics:

- Engineering the business models and their web services

- Designing and realising the corresponding information technology

- Evaluating the used corporation resources and assets.

3 Requirements for the Modelling in E-Government

A number of different definitions of business processes can be found in the literature. A fitting one for the public administration could be: "A business process is a bundle of activities, where one or more different inputs are needed and that produces a valuable result for the customer" [4]. Central components of business processes are therefore: A *bundle of activities* – one single task is not a business process - and a business process must produce a *valuable result*, for the *customer* as well as for an *organisation* to reach their goals.

The aim of e-government is to get aware of and structure governmental and administrational tasks and make them executable via electronic media. Business, administration and legal relations must be worked out in an integrated way [12]. The provision of services in the public administrations via online transactions requires continuous process restructuring - starting from the reallocation of activities to topics like data security, digital signature or online payment. Some processes are no longer executed by the authority alone but are partially done by the citizen with the help of an online portal.

In a current research and development project called ADOamt[1], the approach is to develop a modelling tool which realises the most important requirements to support the implementation of e-government solution from a business process management (BPM) and integrated service modelling perspective. Some of these requirements are the identification of actors and their roles, the definition of possible communication channels, the transparency of the flows, the standardisation of terminologies for an efficient and transparent communication, the integrated modelling from the portal to the back office and the integration of the citizen and company clerk as service consumer.

With this BPM tool developed within the ADOamt project, the problems occurring due to the characteristics of e-government should be solved. With the integration of organisational and technical perspectives as well as internal and external perspectives, the consideration of the unique characteristics of administrative processes and of strategic thoughts of the governmental development to face the informatised economy, a holistic realisation of process modelling in e-government is guaranteed. In the following, a methodology is introduced that helps developing and realising this modelling tool for the public administration.

4 A Holistic BPM Framework and Comprehensive Tool

4.1 The E-BPMS Paradigm

In the course of a number of projects, BOC has developed a framework called E-BPMS which integrates business-oriented modelling approaches and approaches for the modelling of information systems (IS) and IT infrastructures [2].

For the depiction of a model a certain modelling language is used. A modelling language consists of modelling elements and rules describing how to use these modelling elements. A web modelling language has modelling elements and rules where web applications can be described [9]. A number of web modelling languages do exist that would be applicable for the use in e-government. These can be languages resulting from university research or approaches coming from industrial developments of web applications (OOHDM, WebMS, UML WAE, etc.)

---

[1] www.adoamt.com, national (Austrian) co-funded FFF project of BOC GmbH Vienna together with University of Linz, A-Sit Graz and Fachhochschule für Verwaltungswissenschaften Berlin.

The E-PBMS Paradigm [1] focuses on the requirements definition and the technical modelling of web application. Basis for this framework is the modelling on four levels to get control over the complexity of web applications. On the strategic level the business model is depicted. Additionally decisions about objectives, the common organisational structure and the core business processes are made. On the business level the business processes as well as the working environment are modelled and on the implementation level the organisational and technical realisation is executed. The aspects of runtime environment and the IT infrastructure are considered on the execution level.

In the course of a study different modelling languages for web applications were compared and classified [9]. The evaluation based on seven classification criteria (roles and authorisations, navigation, operations and logical usage, business processes and workflows, size of the application, application architecture and procedure model) showed a consistently positive assessment of the E-BPMS Paradigm. Roles and authorizations are depicted in the working environment, the business processes and the interaction processes in a detailed way. The representation of navigational structures of a web application can be found in different model types. In the E-BPMS Framework the logical usage is described with the specification of business processes and workflows on one side and with references to elements in information system models on the other side. With the help of different abstraction levels starting from the business model to the IT infrastructure the paradigm is useful for big applications. These abstraction levels are separated with data, logical usage, navigation and presentation using different model types. As the E-BPMS is derived from the BPMS-Paradigm [6], it contains a generic procedure model for the development of web applications. Based on this generic procedure model concrete procedure models can be developed.

4.2 Procedure Model for the Realisation

When modelling business processes in e-government two different steps are identified [5]. The first step is the design and the optimisation of the process models of the public administration. The focus is laid on the development of a tailor-made modelling methodology within a business process management tool. In the second step the addressed business type (business to business, business to administration, business to customer, administration to customer, etc.) has to be defined. With the use of information technology, new business models should be introduced to be able to realise the tight integration of the authorities with the citizen. The next few paragraphs mainly focus on the first part of the realisation.

In projects of BOC in the public administration the standard methodology of the metamodelling tool ADONIS® was used for the modelling of business processes. As described above it is necessary to find or develop the most appropriate modelling methodology to realise a successful project. The aim of BOC is to define and realise such a tailor-made modelling methodology for the public sector together with its project team. Basis for this tool is the metamodelling platform of BOC.

Starting from the E-BPMS paradigm different modelling types are defined according to the concept of life events [13] (see figure 1).

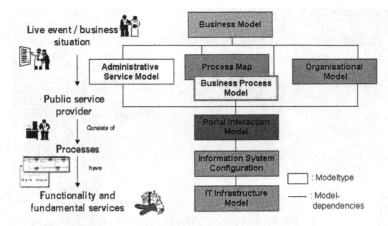

Fig. 1. Holistic Process Modelling Framework

On the strategic level questions like "Which processes and products/services should be realised?", "Who are my participants and partners in e-government?" and "Do the strategies of the participants and partners match with each other?" can be answered within a business model. The Strategy-/Planning Model gives a detailed overview of products and services provided by the public administration. The modeller can decide whether to follow the life event concept, where the products/services are depicted concerning life events and business situations, or to use the alternative Business Model.

The business level contains a number of different model types. The Process Map should give an overview of the different processes. To structure the working environment within an authority, a ministry or a city, two different model types are used in ADOamt. In the Organigram, the rough organisational structure is modelled to give an overview over the organisational units servicing the citizen. The Working Environment Model is part of the standard methodology of ADONIS and was changed according to the requirements of the public administration. The performers, roles and organisational units in this process-related model type are connected to the activities of a process. The skill profiles of the employees should be depicted here to guarantee the best management of each individual's knowledge.

Business process models are the main point within the modelling in the public administration. With the help of a number of workshops with public administrations, a requirement profile for the development of an appropriate methodology for the modelling of business processes was created. Some of the most important points are the determination of deadlines, the possibility to depict legal and security aspects or references to external documents and data.

Last but not least, the IT level is described with the help of different model types like an interaction model depicting the process flow directly on the platform level or the IT-architecture model for the organisation of the IT landscape of an authority. Security aspects like the digital signature can be modelled here.

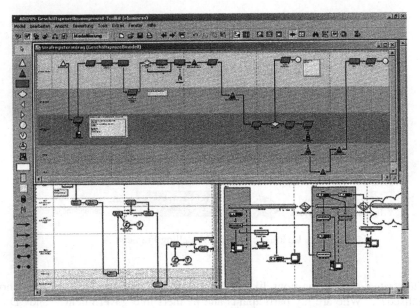

Fig. 2. Sample Processes for Web Applications

Figure 2 shows a sample model used in an e-business project. The business process, modelled in "swimlanes" (one for each process participant), is supported by an interaction model that describes the same process on the portal level, and an IT architecture model. The representation of the models can be taken as anchor for the methodology for e-government that is currently under development.

5   Conclusions

Process modelling in e-government is a big challenge in connection with its characteristics and specifics that have to be considered. With the approach introduced in this paper integrated Business Process Management in the public administration should be guaranteed. Our aim is to provide a holistic reference methodology and modelling functionalities within in a tailor-made metamodelling tool for the public sector.

References

1.   BAYER, F., JUNGINGER, S., KÜHN, H.: A Business Process-Oriented Methodology for Developing E-Business Applications, in: Baake, U. F., Zobel, R. N.; Al-Akaidi, M. (Eds.): Proceedings of the 7th European Concurrent Engineering Conference 2000 (ECEC'2000), Leicester, Society for Computer Simulation, 2000, pp. 32–40

2. BAYER, F., JUNGINGER, S., KÜHN, H., PETZMANN, A.: E-BPMS: Ein Modellierungs-Framework für E-Business-Anwendungen, in: K. Bauknecht, W. Brauer, Th. Mück (Hrsg.), Informatik 2001 – Wirtschaft und Wissenschaft in der Network Economy – Visionen und Wirklichkeit. Austrian Computer Society, book series # 157, Vienna, pp. 922–927

3. FALCK, M.: Business Process Management – As a Method of Governance, in: Traunmüller, R., Lenk, K., Electronic Government, First International Conference EGOV 2002, Springer LNCS # 2456, Heidelberg et al, 2002, p. 137–141

4. HAMMER, M.; CHAMPY, J., Business Reengineering: die Radikalkur für das Unternehmen, 2nd edition, Campus, Frankfurt, 1994

5. KARAGIANNIS, D., KÜHN, H.: Metamodelling Platforms, in: Bauknecht, K., Min Tjoa, A., Quirchmayer, G. (Eds.): Proceedings of the Third International Conference EC-Web 2002 – Dexa 2002, LNCS # 2455, Springer, Berlin, Heidelberg, 2002, p. 182

6. KARAGIANNIS, D., JUNGINGER, S., STROBL, R.: Introduction to Business Process Management Systems Concepts, University of Vienna, The BPMS-Group, 1996

7. KARAGIANNIS, D., PALKOVITS, S., Prozessmodellierung in der öffentlichen Verwaltung – Ein ganzheitliches Rahmenwerk für E-Government, in: Wimmer, M. (Ed.): Quo vadis e-Government? State-of-the-art 2003, Austrian Computer Society, Book series # 165, Vienna, 2003, pp. 271–280

8. KLISCHEWSKI, R., LENK, K., Understanding and Modelling Flexibility in Administrative Processes, in: Traunmüller, R., Lenk, K., Electronic Government, First International Conference EGOV 2002, Springer LNCS # 2456, Heidelberg et al, 2002, p. 129–136

9. KÜHN, H., Modellierungssprachen für Web-Anwendungen: Klassifikation und Vergleich, erschienen in: P. Horster (Hrsg.): Elektronische Geschäftsprozesse - Grundlagen, Sicherheitsaspekte, Realisierungen und Anwendungen. it Verlag, Klagenfurt, 2001, S. 379–390

10. POOK, K., STARKLOFF, P.: Geschäftsprozesse und Wissensmanagement – vom Umgang mit erfolgskritischem Fachwissen, in: Praxis Wissensmanagement 4/01, p. 2

11. PROBST, G., RAUB, S., ROMHARDT, K. (Hrsg.): Wissen managen: Wie Unternehmen ihre wertvollste Ressource optimal nutzen. 3. Auflage Frankfurt am Main 1999

12. WIMMER, M., TRAUNMÜLLER, R.: Geschäftsprozessmodellierung im Bereich E-Government: Eine Zwischenbilanz, in: Schweighofer, E., Menzel, Th., Kreuzbauer, G. (Eds.): IT in Recht und Staat. Aktuelle Fragen der Rechtsinformatik 2002. Schriftenreihe Rechtsinformatik # 6, Verlag Österreich, Vienna, S. 19–27

13. WIMMER, M.: Integrated service modelling for online one-stop Government, in: EM – Electronic Markets, special issue on e-Government, vol. 12(3):2002, pp. 1–8

Electronic Government: Make or Buy?

Hans J. Scholl

University of Washington
Seattle, WA, 98195-2840, USA
jscholl@u.washington.edu

Abstract. The information systems-related sourcing literature has recently largely emphasized a portfolio approach in which homegrown, hybrid, and outsourced systems are combined. In electronic government, similar approaches are found in practice. Since electronic government is predicted to have a major impact on government business processes, an increased understanding regarding the optimal sourcing mix of e-Gov systems is needed in order to direct the scarce resources into strategically relevant areas. In the absence of a developed sourcing theory, an exploratory approach has been employed for this research undertaking. Elements of a sourcing theory are proposed for testing.

1 Introduction

During the high tides of outsourcing and reengineering in the 1990s, information technology (IT) infrastructures, information systems (IS), IT-related skills, and information organization-related expertise became primary targets for reassessing sourcing decisions in many organizations. Firms went as far as outsourcing their entire IT departments and operations with the arguments of dramatic cost savings and strategic refocusing on core competencies rather than non-core activities. IT and IS were seen as commodity-type goods and services comparable to relatively easily reversible investment decisions. As the tides began to ebb, a more cautious and perhaps more considerate approach has been observed in this first decade of the 21st century regarding both reengineering and outsourcing. Many reengineering projects have failed miserably (Hammer 1996), so have quite a few outsourcing efforts (cf., for example, (Lacity, Willcocks et al. 1996). Due to its different drivers and its lower agility (Mohan and Holstein 1990), the public sector has seen less numerous failures in both regards, even though some were quite spectacular along the lines of cost and schedule overruns, content deficiencies, and stakeholder dissatisfaction. A growing body of literature suggests that the frameworks for make-or-buy decisions, which inevitably have an impact on an organization's business processes, need to be revisited and potentially revised. In this paper the IT- and IS-related, mostly private-sector oriented literature regarding make-or-buy is reviewed. The tenets of this sourcing literature are then compared with the results from an exploratory, interview-based study in which senior state government officials were asked about their sourcing decisions and experiences with electronic government projects. The results show a non-uniform approach in electronic government sourcing policies, resulting in an accidental rather than well-grounded portfolio approach. Finally, elements of an e-Gov sourcing theory are proposed for testing.

R. Traunmüller (Ed.): EGOV 2003, LNCS 2739, pp. 220–227, 2003.

2 Buying versus Making in the Literature

Sourcing discussions have traditionally started from and revolved around the concepts of transaction cost (TC) theory (Coase 1937; Williamson 1975). The boundary of the firm according to Coase's argument can be defined by a transaction cost advantage that the firm enjoys through lower-cost internal integration and coordination over contracting the same goods and services in an exchange economy. At some point internal coordination ceases to be advantageous. Williamson argues that in cases of low asset specificity suppliers enjoy economies of scale over buyers. However, as asset specificity increases transaction cost theory favors making over buying rather early (Williamson 1981).   Nam et al., though, are unable to demonstrate any significant influence of even asset specificity in IT- and IS-related sourcing decisions (Nam, Rajagopalan et al. 1996). As predicted by TC theory, high competition among suppliers decreases opportunism in contracting, so that outsourcing decisions are supported (Walker and Weber 1984). Walker and Weber also obtain evidence for supplier production advantages influencing make-or-buy decisions in favor of buying but summarize that over all only mixed support for transaction cost-based explanations of make-or-buy decisions is found in their research (ibid.). Those relatively weak results notwithstanding, outsourcing decisions traditionally seem to be driven by the cost argument (also in the form of projected efficiency gains and redistributing cash-flows), even though the promise of significant savings generated by outsourcing remains questionable (Lacity and Hirschheim 1993). Comparisons demonstrate that internal IT departments using cost-reduction strategies as used by outsourcing bidders were capable of achieving similar savings without external assistance. Kogut and Zander observe that once survival pressures mount, organizations tend to buy rather than make (Kogut and Zander 1992). Beside the main focus on cost cutting, Le Blanc finds that other motives for outsourcing comprise those of intended knowledge transfer, increased flexibility, or new technology adaptation (Le Blanc 1993). With growing experience in the subject matter, strategic intent with respect to business impact, the potential for commercialization, or the capacity to improve information systems in use may drive outsourcing decisions (DiRomualdo and Gurbaxani 1998). Some authors present rules for outsourcing. Buying is recommended, for example, in cases where the IT activity in relation to the business operations though being useful is just a commodity in regard to positioning the business (Lacity, Willcocks et al. 1996). Also, if the in-house IT activities have only sub-critical mass from an economies-of-scale perspective and managerial practices are lagging at the same time, outsourcing is proposed (ibid.). Or, if the significance of IT for the organization's competitive advantage is low, then purchasing appears as best choice (Le Blanc 1993). To actively develop vendors is proposed for situations, in which there is future high competitive significance of an IT in growth or already in maturity, but the organization's expertise in this area is weak compared with competitors' (ibid). Generally, the outsourcing of technically mature activities is seen as of lower risk (Lacity, Willcocks et al. 1996). Lacity and colleagues also point out that, while commodity IS may be candidates for outsourcing as opposed to strategic IS, the distinction between the two can become difficult (ibid.). In a prescriptive checklist, Lacity and Hirschheim summarize lessons learned from unsatisfactory outsourcing experiences, for example, to hire outsourcing experts, to avoid standard or incomplete contracts, to include in contracts termination and change of character clauses, to establish baselines for measurement, and to take care of stakeholders (Lacity and Hirschheim 1993).

In recent years, the application service provider (ASP) model has been discussed as a further variant of outsourcing. Beyond a reemphasis of the cost argument for outsourcing, particularly, for applications with low asset specificity, the ASP model is heralded for its scalability and accessibility, for the capability of pooling IT expertise, and the implicit coverage of upgrade and maintenance needs (Patnayakuni and Seth 2001). From a TC theory vantage point, making has to be favored over buying the higher the organization's IT/IS-related asset specificity. Beyond this, Hirschheim and Lacity emphasize that internal IS departments can employ the same cost reduction tactics as the outside bidders, for example, data center coordination, unit cost charge back systems, and standardizing software (Hirschheim and Lacity 2000) arriving at similar cost as those (Lacity and Hirschheim 1993). However, as the authors point out, cost reductions under whatever sourcing regime come at the expense of service quality. A high impact of an IT/IS on an organization's core business is generally seen as an indicator in favor of insourcing. For instance, if IT/IS provides a major differentiator in the organization's business positioning and if it is highly critical to business operations, the case for making is made (Lacity, Willcocks et al. 1996). Also, if the IT/IS-related managerial practices provide the organization with an edge, while at the same time in-house economies of scale have critical mass, making has to be favored (ibid.). Further, if IT/IS is emerging or growing and competitively significant at the same time, making would be the choice (Le Blanc 1993). Finally, strategic impact, the frequency of change to IS and business processes along with the high availability of skilled IT personnel signal the case for making (Scholl 2003). Along these lines Nam et al. highlight the close relationship between in-house IT/IS and in-house experts' tacit knowledge in those technologies and systems (Nam, Rajagopalan et al. 1996; Scholl 2003) which cannot be substituted by external bidders. Last not least, a growing record of failures and the fading of myths lead to a re-examination of outsourcing decisions (Lacity and Hirschheim 1993). Senior managers' growing appreciation of both role and importance of IT in the organization also foster insourcing decisions (Hirschheim and Lacity 2000). In the public sector, homegrown systems may also be mandated by law, statute, or regulation (Scholl 2003).

In summary, organizations increasingly seem to rely on a portfolio approach in their sourcing decisions (Lacity, Willcocks et al. 1996) which combine in- and outsourced IT/IS along various dimensions among which supplier stability and service offerings play a role as well as the organization's own IT and learning capabilities, and also the extent to which those capabilities are scalable to serve as platforms into new areas of engagement (Kogut and Zander 1992). IT managers seem to play an increasing role in designing IT sourcing portfolios (Hirschheim and Lacity 2000).

3   Research Question and Study Design

Electronic government-related sourcing has been little studied so far. Little is known what sourcing policies and practices are used in electronic government projects. The purpose of this research is to help uncover those policies and practices, that is, this study is exploratory in nature. The project reported here is part of a larger research undertaking focusing on the relationship of electronic government with business process change in government (cf., (Scholl 2003)). In a series of fifteen semi-structured interviews, twenty-three senior-level government managers who had been personally involved in and responsible for e-Gov projects from thirteen New York State agencies were asked to comment on a set of statements derived from the business process change literature. Interviews were conducted with single individuals, with groups of two, and in one case with a group of three individuals. The interviews were conducted in person and over the telephone. Statements were read to the interviewees, one at a time. Interviewees were then asked to comment on those statements from their own experience and involvement in e-Gov projects. The interviews were audio taped and transcribed for analysis. Two statements were particularly directed toward sourcing. Those statements read:

1. Commercial off-the-shelf e-Gov systems are inadequate if they do not support all existing organizational and process knowledge
2. Areas of strengths and core competencies predispose an agency to make rather than buy its electronic government systems.

The conjectural phrasing of the two statements was used to induce ample comments from interviewees reflecting on their experience and practice in the sphere of their responsibility.

4 Results

The detailed comments from interviewees indicated that most agencies indeed employ a portfolio approach in their IT/IS sourcing, albeit not in a strategically planned fashion. Depending on the stage the agencies were in along the lines of the Layne and Lee model (Layne and Lee 2001), and also subject to the area of predominant focus in the e-Gov projects, the split between in- and outsourced IT/IS varied. Interestingly, 46.6 percent of interviewees rejected the conjecture in the first statement, that is, they found commercial off-the-shelf systems (COTS) quite adequate even if not all organizational and process knowledge could be maintained when using those systems, while 33.3 percent confirmed it, and 20 percent would neither accept nor reject it. The conjecture in the second statement was accepted by 53.3 percent of interviewees, that is, areas of strength and core competencies were seen as predispositions for an agency to make its e-Gov systems rather than buying them, whereas 13.3 percent rejected it, and 26.6 percent found arguments both in favor and against. However, due to the exploratory nature of the research aiming at surfacing and describing policies and practices used in electronic government sourcing decisions, these figures just roughly illustrate overall distributions of bias in regard to electronic Government-related sourcing decisions as laid out in the following sections.

Unsurprisingly, the cost argument played a central role in making the case for *buying e-Gov systems*. E-Gov COTS were perceived as becoming ever more inexpensive, and, hence, good alternatives to costly in-house development. Also, making its own e-Gov systems appeared to some agencies no longer affordable as making was seen as prohibitively expensive and resource consuming in budget-constrained times. However, another major argument rested on the need for government to offer services quickly, that is, the governmental analog to "time to market" was invoked to justify the deployment of e-Gov COTS. Fast deployment was explicitly favored over service completeness, system perfection, and system elegance. A third line of reasoning focused on the assumption that e-Gov COTS would embody best practices. Since these systems were widely used, it was concluded that they represented the state-of-the-art in practices and processes. Agencies, hence, had at least a point of reference through these commercial systems enabling them to assess their own practices and redesign those if found necessary. E-Gov COTS were also seen as more stable, better tested, and more predictable than homegrown systems. Some interviewees argued that agency processes and practices should be shaped along the lines of COTS with little or no customization, whereas others maintained that COTS were viable alternatives to homegrown systems if they could be modified to address specific agency needs. A number of interviewees held that customization while necessary should be kept to a bare minimum. If not, the benefits of future revisions of the system might not be easily obtainable, or the system, if not upgraded, could even fall out of vendor support. Moreover, such systems, if unaltered, could more easily be phased in and out. With an accelerated rate of technology changes and new generations of systems every three years, investing into one generation too heavily could be counter-productive. Others, however, argued that while commercial systems provided a starting platform, sometimes even extensive customization might be necessary and also viable. COTS would provide a basis, to which incremental, also homegrown subsystems could be connected via application program interfaces (API). Once commercial systems meet a critical few requirements, they might be acceptable candidates for a platform system, as long as modifiability and API access were provided. In this context, vendors were summoned to better respond to government-specific automation needs in their packages. The curtailing of government over the last decade was also cited as major motive for buying e-Gov COTS. Due to massive loss of IT/IS expertise to the private sector and long periods of underinvestment in IT/IS, agencies seemed to be forced to make rather than buy in many instances. Buying e-Gov systems it was hoped could help to replace outdated systems. In the absence of qualified staff and recent technology, making was not seen as an option, particularly, since any longer-term projects were hard to pursue under the constraints of annual budgetary cycles. Finally, proponents of outsourcing cited failures of insourcing projects and argued that homegrown systems were challenging to maintain through loss of key personnel, defective documentation, and unnecessary uniqueness.

Unsurprisingly again, the cost argument was also advanced for *making e-Gov systems*. Some interviewees pointed at cost blunders of outsourced and customized systems maintaining that in-house systems compared favorably to very favorably with those systems. In one case, the cited customization costs for a commercial package were four times higher than its initial purchase price, by which it had beaten the insourcing bid. Customization, it was also said, could not be greatly avoided, as outsourcing advocates propose, since the commercial packages are too strongly geared towards private-sector requirements, for example, in areas like procurement. Further, since a core of systems tended to remain in operation for twenty to twenty-five years, that is, much longer than their initial life-cycle projections, homegrown and home-maintained systems could have enormous cost advantages in the costly late years of operation. Making systems, it was further argued, could not be eliminated, since there were business processes and procedures, for which no commercial package existed. Because many of those unsupported processes were unique and could not be eliminated for various reasons (including legal, statutory, or regulatory requirements) to fit commercial packages, agencies had to maintain application system development proficiency in-house anyway. Critical knowledge in both the IT/IS and the business side could not be outsourced either, it was argued, since otherwise the management of these processes and practices would no longer be possible. In other words, even if keeping current and maintaining homegrown systems over time might pose certain challenges, core compound knowledge of systems and business processes must not be lost. The more resourceful and skillful an agency in this regard, the more should it maintain its proficiency and the critical mass for building critical components of its e-Gov systems. Almost naturally, areas of competency and strength were those where systems had been homegrown, albeit the danger of overinvestment in these insourced systems was clearly seen also by proponents of making. Areas in which skills and expertise were lacking should, in these interviewees' perspective, not necessarily trigger a buy decision, but rather lead to building the skill base in critical areas of knowledge, which might have strategic impact on the agency's business. Internal expertise, it was maintained, was more trustworthy than relying on external sources.

Even strong proponents of making conceded that making should focus on core areas only. However, even in non-core areas customization could become difficult, if the commercial systems were either too simplistic in terms of functionality, or too complex, in terms of configurability and maintainability. A major concern, not only with respect to cost, existed regarding too high a frequency of system revisions by vendors rendering the agency either without support or with unplanned and unwanted updating in exchange for minor improvements. While some proponents of making redefined the building process as "customizing, configuring, and designing database queries," others emphasized the use of API to link outsourced commodity systems and homegrown core systems. Vendor viability and stability was among the major concerns even for outsourced commodity systems. The size of a vendor or her large market share was not necessarily seen as an insurance against sudden lack of support and supply calling for only limited dependency on any vendor. So, the mix between made and bought systems should be carefully monitored. Finally, agency users as well as internal IT/IS staff, it was argued, would have more identification and commitment to in-house rather than outsourced systems. Case examples were given, in which outsourced systems were imposed on users and IT/IS staff resulting in total system failure. Insourcing provided a more inclusive approach addressing constituents' needs via ongoing involvement and feedback.

5 Discussion and Conclusion

In the private sector, a trend towards a portfolio approach to IT/IS-related sourcing decisions has been observed (Hirschheim and Lacity 2000). Our research confirms this trend also for the public sector. Similar arguments for in- or outsourcing are found in both the private and public sector. Similar experiences seem to derive from an overemphasis of either sourcing approach. As Hirschheim and Lacity suggest, particularly the make option must be better researched (ibid.). There is no tested theory regarding an optimal composition of such an IT/IS sourcing portfolio. However, as in the private sector, there is a certain core-related bundle of system and process knowledge, which is indispensable to maintain and grow internally for any organization regardless whether private or public. In the words of Nam and colleagues, that knowledge is inalienable (Nam, Rajagopalan et al. 1996), and, hence, not outsourceable. Agency management must understand what and where precisely this inalienable knowledge is, and also which systems must be homegrown. Underinvestment in those critical areas could come at a very high cost to the taxpayer. This may call for revisiting governmental IT infrastructure investment and IT staff compensation schemes. Underpaying IT staff may backlash over time leading to dangerous dependencies and depriving the public sector of essential strategic options. One way of identifying the optimal mix between make and buy in electronic government may lie in relating these findings to the Layne and Lee framework of e-Gov development. The two authors predict electronic government (e-Gov) to advance through four stages of (1) catalogue/presentation, (2) transaction, (3) vertical integration, and (4) horizontal integration, the latter two of which would lead to major change in government operations and processes (Layne and Lee 2001). Applying the portfolio approach to e-Gov sourcing, leads to the following two propositions:

1. E-Gov IT/IS with strategic impact in the area of application AND with the potential for a high frequency of change in operations and processes AND with a high degree of combined tacit IT/organizational process knowledge are predominantly candidates for making;
2. E-Gov IT/IS with low or no strategic impact in the area of application AND with the potential for a low frequency of change in operations and processes AND with a low degree of combined tacit IT/organizational process knowledge are predominantly candidates for buying.

The two propositions determine the extremes of a three-dimensional continuum, which demarcates the portfolio space for the purpose of this discussion. The catalogue and presentation stage of the Layne/Lee framework, for example, suggests a relatively high number of outsourced e-Gov systems, while the latter two stages comprise a relatively high number of insourced e-Gov systems. Future research will more deeply develop and test these propositions also comparing total benefits of ownership (TBO) over total cost of ownership (TCO) as an important part of the equation.

References

1. Coase, R. H. (1937). "The nature of the firm." Economica(4): 386-403.
2. DiRomualdo, A. and V. Gurbaxani (1998). "Strategic intent for IT outsourcing." Sloan Management Review(Summer): 67–80.
3. Hammer, M. (1996). Beyond reengineering : how the process-centered organization is changing our work and our lives. New York, HarperBusiness.
4. Hirschheim, R. and M. Lacity (2000). "The myths and realities of information technology insourcing." Communications of the ACM 43(2): 99–107.
5. Kogut, B. and U. Zander (1992). "Knowledge of the firm, combinative capabilities, and the replication of technology." Organization Science 3(3): 383–397.
6. Lacity, M. and R. Hirschheim (1993). "The information systems outsourcing bandwagon." Sloan Management Review(Fall): 73–86.
7. Lacity, M., L. P. Willcocks, et al. (1996). "The value of selective IT sourcing." Sloan Management Review(Spring): 13–25.
8. Layne, K. and J. Lee (2001). "Developing fully functional E-government: A four stage model." Government Information Quarterly 18(2): 122–136.

9. Le Blanc, L. A. (1993). Strategic sourcing for information processing functions. ACM/SIGAPP symposium on applied computing: States of the art and practice, Inidianapolis, IN, ACM Press, New York, NY.
10. Mohan, L. and W. K. Holstein (1990). "EIS: It can work in the public sector." MIS Quarterly **14**(4): 434–448.
11. Nam, K., S. Rajagopalan, et al. (1996). "A two-level investigation of information systems outsourcing." Commuications of the ACM **39**(7): 36–44.
12. Patnayakuni, R. and N. Seth (2001). Why licencse when you can rent? Risks and rewards of the application service provider model. SIGCPR : ACM Special Interest Group on Computer Personnel Research, San Diego, CA, ACM Press, New York
13. Scholl, H. J. J. (2003). E-Government: A special case of buisness process change. 37th Hawaiian International Conference on System Sciences (HICSS37), Waikoloa, HI, IEEE.
14. Walker, G. and D. Weber (1984). "A transaction cost approach to make-or-buy decisions." Administrative Science Quarterly **29**(3): 373–391.
15. Williamson, O. E. (1975). Markets and hierarchies, analysis and antitrust implications : a study in the economics of internal organization. New York, Free Press.
16. Williamson, O. E. (1981). "The economics of organization: The transaction cost approach." American Journal of Sociology **87**: 548–577.

Problematisation and Obfuscation in E-Government

Peter Kawalek[1], David Wastell[2], and Mike Newman[1]

[1] University of Manchester
Oxford Road, Manchester, UK
0161 275 6518, fax 0161 275 7134
pkawalek@mbs.man.ac.uk
[2] Information Systems Institute
Salford University
Manchester, UK
0161 295 5102, fax 0161 745 8169
D.Wastell@salford.ac.uk

Abstract. This paper is concerned with e-government implementation at the local level. It proposes that effective realization of the radical change promised by e-government depends upon a sense of crisis, a problematisation, which motivates the organisation to respond with urgency and vigour. The paper reports a study of one leading local authority based upon interviews of its senior managers. It finds no sense of crisis, and instead obfuscation and psychological distancing, as the potential of e-government is marginalized, and the status quo is reinforced.

1 The Rhetoric and Reality of IT-Enabled Change

'E-government' refers to IT-enabled change in governmental institutions at all levels from national to regional to local. In the UK, the Labour government in its first term of office (1997-2001) put considerable emphasis on the need to modernise local and national government, with IT seen as an important key to the realization of this policy [1]. This commitment to public service reform and e-government in particular, has been boldly restated in the government's second term (2001-present) [2]. Given the radical nature of e-government, how will governmental institutions, considered in the popular imagination to be cumbersome self-serving bureaucracies, respond to the formidable challenges (technical, organisational, cultural) posed by such a reforming agenda? Considerable resistance might well be expected.

The general question of IT-enabled change has been the subject of a very wide literature over recent years. In general, the literature addresses the all too common failure of such change efforts to achieve hoped-for performance gains despite the much-bruited potential of IT to bring about organisational transformation [3], [4]. This potential is most clearly articulated in the discourse of business process reengineering (BPR) which explicitly champions the potential of IT to effect revolutionary change in organisational structures and processes. Davenport [5] speaks of "process innovation" in order to highlight the radical, transformational potency of IT. Yet despite this rhetoric, much IT-enabled change results in failure [3], [6].

R. Traunmüller (Ed.): EGOV 2003, LNCS 2739, pp. 228–233, 2003.

In this paper, we will be concerned with e-government implementation at the local government level. We will report an interview-based case study in one local authority that has attracted national recognition for its apparent progress in this area, focusing on the preparedness of the organization for e-government as revealed through the attitudes and perceptions of the senior management team. Regarding the change process, we will adopt a broadly Lewinian view [7] which sees change as a three phase movement, proceeding from an initial phase of "unfreezing" in which the old order is "let go", followed by a transitional phase leading to the "refreezing" of the new "steady state". We contend that failed change efforts often reflect a failure to "unfreeze", to abandon the old institutional order. Extant structures and processes provide organisational members with a sense of identity and security; their reassuring certainties a refuge against existential and task-specific anxiety [8], [9]. Such psychological fortifications will not readily be given up and need to be confronted through cognitive and motivational challenge [10]. Failure to do so results in obfuscation of a change project's aims, a distancing from its true ramifications, and a paradoxical perpetuation or strengthening of the *status quo* [11].

2 Methodology

The field partner in this research will be referred to as Erewhon City Council (ECC), a recognized leader in the UK's e-government programme. Nine internal e-government projects were underway at the time of the study. Most were apparently progressing satisfactorily, although there was slippage on some. The study reported here was commissioned by the senior management team of ECC, in response to prompting by the manager of the IT department who was concerned that, despite some successes, there was a lack of genuine "buy-in" and commitment on the "user" side. Not all projects were being actively led by users, and several had not moved beyond design work into implementation. The practical remit of the study was to explore "e-government awareness" at a senior level in the authority, to assess "preparedness" for implementation and to propose interventions that would facilitate progress.

The study was interview-based, with all heads of service (directors) being interviewed (Housing, Social Services, Corporate Services, Environment, Education, Planning, Development Services, Partnerships and Regeneration) as well as the Chief Executive. This entailed a total of 10 interviews, each with a single manager. Interviews were all face-to-face and took around one hour. They were not tape-recorded; instead detailed notes were taken, including direct quotations where these were felt to be pithy or particularly revealing. Prior to the study, a focus group session was held involving representatives of the IT department in order to generate a list of indicative questions to be put to the directors. These questions were used to compile a semi-structured interview schedule, which was circulated in advance to the interviewees.

The questions revolved around three broad areas:

- The meaning of e-government: What does e-government mean to you? Can you think of specific examples of e-government projects relevant to your directorate? What level of awareness exists amongst your staff with respect to e-government?

- Planning and management: What are the main features of your plans for service improvement and what role does ICT play in this? Does your directorate have specific e-government plans? Do you have a senior person leading your e-government activity? What personal involvement will you have?
- Capacity and implementation: Do you feel you have sufficient internal capacity to address the e-government agenda? What shortcomings do you face and how might these be met? What are the main obstacles to e-government being a success? How many of your transactions will be electronically enabled by 2002/2005?

3   Results

3.1   The Meaning of E-Government

The directors gave a variety of specific interpretations of e-government: new channels of service access; joined-up services across and within directorates; cost saving; quicker, streamlined services; more effective communications, internally and externally; freeing resources to concentrate on core service aims; flexibility and responsiveness of service provision. In general, these broad views manifested a strong service orientation, very little mention was made of either the democratic or policy making role of local government. The following quotes are typical:

"For me e-government means rapid access to joined up services. I'm very committed to this... People expect a 24 hour a day service. It's all about the standard of service... we need to be as good as the private sector providers. We need to be in a position where receptionists can directly commission work even though resources are in the directorates".

"E-government is about a new means of delivering service using computers, a 24-7 culture that's customer led."

When prompted to provide e-government exemplars, the illustrations given were almost exclusively centred around service improvement within individual departments. Examples included: on-line job applications; E-learning initiatives such as induction training and renewal of qualifications, Web advertisement of planning applications; Housing repairs and estate agency functions to be put on the Web. No applications involving cross departmental collaboration were cited and only one example was given of external partnering, namely the provision of a joint occupational health service with other LAs. Several directors questioned whether e-government was fundamentally new, identifying the long history of IT use in their departments. One commented: "E-government is nothing new... we do it anyway"

3.2   Planning and Management

Only two of the directorates had specific e-government plans or were in the process of creating these plans. The others reported different ways of planning for e-government, including progressing it through a series of different initiatives or through the normal business planning process. Some saw e-government as being a corporate concern, largely addressed in current plans to set up a call-centre.

"We have no separate e-government plan, but we need to fit within the corporate plan, we want to be part and parcel of this and work within it"

"We need to rationalize and fit in with the corporate approach, to take advantage of the call centre somehow. Our existing systems are disparate. We need an integrated system, this will make a vast difference to the service"

Although all directors acknowledged that e-government was a priority, with the overwhelming majority indicating that they expected to play a personal role, there was general lack of clarity as to what this would entail beyond being "facilitative". The gap between espoused commitment and actual engagement is starkly shown in the following quote:

"E-government is about real communication, internally and externally, regarding what the Council is really about.... I don't know though how many of my staff use email... perhaps this is a weakness of mine that I don't know..."

3.3 Capacity and Implementation

Five directors identified resource issues as presenting a key obstacle to e-government. They described difficulty with capital investment and pressures from alternative priorities and needs. Other obstacles included: change resistance, lack of awareness/appreciation, legacy systems, problems of delivering complex IT solutions on time and to budget. All directors reported that there were issues with capacity. Two commented directly on the need to strengthen their IT teams. There were some positive comments on the lines that "awareness creates capacity" and that many problems could be put down to poor planning and lack of preparedness. Despite these prevalent concerns, five directors were bullish that the 2005 e-government targets would be met.

"There's no alternative... we just have to do it. By 2002, we'll have done a lot... by 2005 everything"

"Capacity is constantly a problem with the Council but we have to manage... if we use capacity as an excuse we'll never achieve anything...can't accept NO as an answer"

Others were more sober. One took something of an extreme position regarding the real commitment to achieving the 2005 targets:

"I haven't really thought about this... I would be fibbing if I said I had!"

4 Discussion

Disquiet voiced above regarding the readiness of local authorities in the UK to embrace fully the e-government agenda is substantiated by the findings of this case study. Local government generically has three conventional functions [12]: to provide the mechanisms of local democracy, to be the focus for public policy-making, and as the provider a range of services. E-government has the potential to enhance all three: local democracy (provision of information, voting etc.), policy-making (assessing local needs, facilitating multi-agency cooperation) and service delivery (e.g. 24/7 service access). Yet the most prominent feature emerging from the interviews was the preoccupation with internal service improvement, rather than integration with other directorates (or external partners) or other potential aspects of the e-government agenda (policy-making, e-democracy). There is little sense that e-government is really seen as anything new or radical; it has seemingly, for the moment at least, been translated into old and familiar issues, namely the ongoing need for professional providers, operating largely within their own prerogative and perception of the world, to review and enhance service delivery. This serves to obfuscate the more radical potential of e-government and reveals a "psychological distancing" that comes over in other ways: the dearth of departmental e-government planning, the view that e-government was largely a corporate issue, the paucity of joint ventures despite the rhetoric of "joining-up", the lack of real personal engagement, the plaintive comments regarding resources. In short, there is the danger that the reforming nature of e-government will be neutralised and absorbed by the status quo. There is little evidence of unfreezing and genuine mobilisation for change.

The case clearly demonstrates the importance of problematisation to the change process. Only if a problem is perceived will there be motivation to change. We are exploring this in greater depth through the notion of "organisational crisis" [13], [14], defined as "a situation that threatens the high priority goals of the organisation and surprises organisational decision-makers by its occurrence" [14]. Such crises can arise from several possible sources, both internal and external. These may be structural (e.g. decentralized organisation when centralized is more appropriate); financial (budget deficits, losses); technological (e.g. Y2K, IT failures), legislative (e.g. the e-governmental imperative); and competitive (e.g. new market entrants, market pressures). The degree to which the crisis is recognised by key stakeholders, and the innovation seen as the key to its resolution, is critical. Where recognition is pervasive, the motivation to change will be strong and the prospects auspicious for "unfreezing". Thus, a stark "problematisation" of the situation, embracing cognitive and motivational strategies, pushes an organization towards the "tipping point" described in [10].

To these ideas, we would add a further factor, perceived readiness for change [15]. The importance of this has been demonstrated in recent work in [16]. The concept embraces staff perceptions of such factors as trust, participative management style, flexible policies, and the presence of appropriate logistics and systems support. Where perceived readiness is high, the likelihood of successful execution of the change effort is also high; where it is low, resistance leading to miscarriage is the more probable outcome. Organisational change thus depends on the conjunction of three key factors: the existence of a perceived threat to the organisation, the degree to which the threat is internally acknowledged, and the degree of perceived self-efficacy to implement the change.

Applying these embryonic ideas to ECC, we have an external stimulus for change, namely the legislative injunctions to modernise local government. These are accompanied by weak financial incentives and, perhaps, relatively distant sanctions (the 2005 target). The sense of genuine crisis is limited to a small group of stakeholders (primarily the IT department) in a low-prestige area of the organisation. Efforts to mobilise other more important decision-makers have been largely ineffective and there is a general impression of low readiness for change. As a result little unfreezing or innovation has occurred, reflected in many quarters in a general sense of lip service to e-government. Things will undoubtedly change should external imperatives to improve services and to limit public expenditure become more forceful, underpinned by effective sanctions and accountability mechanisms. To drive forward the change agenda once recognised as an organisational priority, a new organisational entity, powerful and autonomous, could be a key mechanism. But for now the change has been assimilated and has, if anything, reinforced the status quo. The departmental empires in ECC are as strong as ever.

References

1. Silcock, R. (2001). What is e-government? *Parliamentary affairs*, 54, 88–101.
2. Public Service Review (2001) Foreword by the Prime Minister, Public Service Review, Autumn 2001, Public Sector Communications Agency, www.publicservice.co.uk
3. Cooper, R.B. (2000) Information technology development creativity: a case study of attempted radical change. MIS Quarterly, 24, 245–276.
4. Westrup, C. (1996). Transforming organisations through systems analysis: deploying new techniques for organizational analysis in IS development. In: Orlikowski, W. et al. (Eds.) *Information technology and changes in organisational work*, Chapman and Hall, London, pp. 157–176.
5. Davenport, T. (1993). *Process innovation: reengineering work through information technology*. Harvard Business School Press.
6. Tissan, T, Heikkilä, J (2001). Successful Re-engineering-Learning by Doing. *International Journal of Logistics: Research and Applications*, 4, 329.
7. Dent, E.B. (1999) Challenging resistance to change. *Journal of Applied Behavioural Science*, 35, 25–41.
8. Hirschhorn, L. (1988). The workplace within: the psychodynamics of organisational life. MIT Press: Boston.
9. Wastell, D.G. (1999). Learning dysfunctions in information systems development: overcoming the social defences with transitional objects. MIS Quarterly, 23, 581–600.
10. Kim, W.C., Mauborgne, R., (2003) Tipping Point Leadership, *Harvard Business Review*, April 2003.
11. Molinsky, A.L. (1999). Sanding down the edges: paradoxical impediments to organizational change. *Journal of Applied Behavioural Science*, 35, 8–24.
12. Pratchett, L. (1999). New technologies and the modernisation of local government. *Public administration*, 77, 731–750.
13. Guth, D.W. (1995). Organizational crisis experience and public relations roles. *Public Relations Review*, 21, 123–129.
14. Edwards, J.C. (2001). Self-fulfilling prophecy and escalating commitment. *Journal of Applied Behavioural Science*, 37, 343–360.
19. Clark, C.E., Cavanaugh, N.C., Brown, C. and Sambamurthy, V. (1997). Building change-readiness capabilities in the IS organisation: insights from the Bell Atlantic experience. *MIS Quarterly*, 21, 425–455.
16. Eby L.T., Adams, D.M., Russell, J.E.A. and Gaby, S.H. (2000) Perceptions of organizational readiness for change: factors related to empoyees' reactions to the implementation of team-based selling. *Human Relations*, 53, 419–442.

Deploying Electronic Democracy for Public Corporations

Alexander Prosser, Robert Kofler, and Robert Krimmer*

Department Production Management
Vienna University of Economics and Business Administration
Pappenheimgasse 35/5
A-1200 Vienna, Austria
Phone +43 (1) 31336 – 5615
{alexander.prosser,robert.kofler,robert.krimmer}
@wu-wien.ac.at

Abstract. The term electronic voting is often used as a method to stop sinking voter turnout or to enhance the accessibility of the election. Before conducting an election using electronic voting, technical standards and legal issues have to be solved.

In Austria the "social partnership" model is built upon numerous public corporations, such as the chamber of Commerce or the Student Union. These corporations suffer in contrast to elections to the national parliament from a low voter turnout. As e-voting is seen as one measure to raise voter participation, the Austrian national parliament passed the Student Union bill on 1st of February 2001 that allows e-voting in the context of the bi-annual student elections.

In this paper the authors present e-voting in the Student Union in a three-fold way. First the legal situation is addressed, then the acceptance of e-voting by voters and finally the technical solution of a two phased method that is used for a test election during the 2003 Student Union elections. It is based on a Kerberos-style algorithm designed to guarantee the separation of the identification process and the registration process as well as to prevent a malicious server administration from generating fake votes.

1 Introduction

Austria as a country of the European Union has been in the last decades a place with a very stable political, social and economic development after the Second World War. This development is attributed to the so called social partnership (Sozialpartnerschaft) [1], that is a structure of public corporations, that represent interests of persons with the same "personal attributes, properties or the same economical, cultural and political aims" [2]. Special attributes of those corporations are compulsory membership, elected political representatives and routine elections every two to five years. One example for those corporations is the Student Union whose members only participate in low numbers in the elections [3].

---

* The work of Kofler and Krimmer was supported by the City of Vienna under grant number JUB0109.

R. Traunmüller (Ed.): EGOV 2003, LNCS 2739, pp. 234–239, 2003.
© Springer-Verlag Berlin Heidelberg 2003

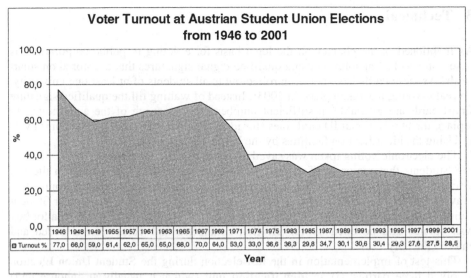

	1946	1948	1949	1955	1957	1961	1963	1965	1967	1969	1971	1974	1975	1983	1985	1987	1989	1991	1993	1995	1997	1999	2001
▢ Turnout %	77,0	66,0	59,0	61,4	62,0	65,0	65,0	68,0	70,0	64,0	53,0	33,0	36,6	36,3	29,8	34,7	30,1	30,6	30,4	29,3	27,6	27,5	28,5

Fig. 1. Turnout at Austrian Student Union Elections from 1946 to 2001 [4]

The low voter turnout of below one third during the last elections is argued by the Student Union that (i) before 2001 no tuition fee was levied and some students were only nominal members and (ii) many students were working part-time and have only attended the university for exams and it is time consuming for them to come to the university separately for the Student Union Elections.

2 Legal

The constitutional court ruled in 1985, that postal voting is not constitutional. Due to this ruling e-voting is currently not possible for national elections like the Nationalratswahlen to the national parliament [5]. For public corporations another ruling in 1989 that lowered the level of requirements of the principles of general, immediate, equal, personal, secret and free voting [6]. Upon the effort of the Student Union the national parliament passed the Student Union bill on 1st of February 2001 that allowed e-voting under the following conditions [7]:
1. Identification of the voter using qualified digital signatures complying with the Austrian Signature Law
2. Check upon vulnerabilities of the deployed e-voting system through a third party certification by the Austrian A-SIT
3. The data protection commission, established in the chancellery, has to approve the e-voting System.
Another corporation where the legal basis for e-voting has been provided for, is the chamber of commerce.

3 Technical

As mentioned in the chapter on the legal basis for e-voting in public corporations is based on a technical solution using qualified digital signatures that are stored on smart cards. As these cards have not been rolled out to all students of at least one university, no real e-voting has taken place in 2003[1]. Instead of waiting till the qualified signature smart cards are available in sufficient numbers; the approach of the authors was to replace the two National ID card roles (for identification and as storage medium) by
1. Using the identification facilities by the WU computer center.
2. The electronic voting token was saved on a non-specific medium.
978 students that major in IT related studies were eligible to participate in the test election. The application for the voting/validation token could be signed from 1st of May to 19th of May 2003, the vote casting itself took place during the regular Student Union voting days, from $20^{th} - 22^{nd}$ of May. On 22nd of May at 3 pm the ballot box was opened and decoded by the election committee and votes were decoded and entered the tally.

This test of implementation in the test-election during the Student Union Election involved three parties: (i) an **identification unit** (which is usually an inhouse unit) which supplies the list of persons, entitled to vote, (ii) an **external registration unit** which supplies the registration tokens (iii) an **external ballot-box unit** which collects the submitted ballot "sheets" and the registration tokens.

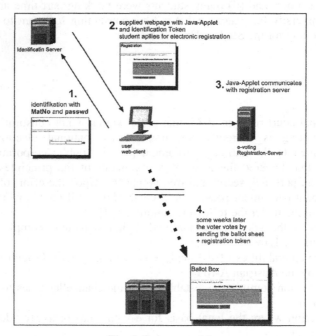

Fig. 2. Process model

---

[1] For a further explanation on smart card based e-voting protocols see [8]

Step 1: In contrast to the original algorithm [9] the student does not use her student ID card with the digital signature but applies for an electronic voting token. This is done at a webpage of an in-house identification system by entering the student identification number (the MatNo) and their password.

Step 2: This system identifies the students and sends them a different web page which is secured by SSL and contains
1. The unique identification token and the
2. The Registration Applet

This unique identification token is used to pass on the identification information from the service provider (in this case the university's IT department) which makes it not necessary for the organization conducting the election to pass on individual data to service provider of the voting process. To do so this unique identification token consists out of several components:

- (e,d) .... RSA keypair of identification unit
- MatNo......... Student's identification number
- S................... secret number, only known to the identification unit
- tokentime ... is a Unix timestamp

The unique token is generated by adding the secret number S to the unique student information number MatNo and hashing this information using the SHA1 algorithm, then adding a timestamp and finally signing the data with the private key of the identification unit. This includes the following properties: (i) this identification token can only be created by the identification unit, as it is signed with its private and secret RSA-key (d) so nobody else can calculate it, (ii) the combination of SHA1-encryption and (MatNo+S) guarantees a unique primary key in the registration database which cannot be decrypted and finally (iii) the timestamp is used to prevent resend-attacks by somebody who breaks the SSLv3/TLS-Protocol – therefore the identification unit and the registration unit must synchronize their system time. Timeout is calculated between the tokentime and the system time of the registration server. Useful values are between 30 and 60 seconds to prevent resend attacks. It is then passed on the registration unit.

Step 3: The registration server decrypts the token with the public-RSA key (e) of the identification unit and calculates the validity of the tokentime. If the tokentime is valid the registration server compares the "SHA1(MatNo+S)" of the token with its registration database and when TRUE it returns the constituency specific public key, so that the Applet can process its numbers for the blind signature according to [10], and the electronic voting token can be stored on a medium of choice of the student.

Step 4: This voting token can then be used as described in the original algorithm for exchanging it with the ballot sheet with the ballot-box unit and vote up to several weeks later.

When the eligible voter casts the vote on Election Day then the authentication is done using the electronic voting token. This step is completely anonymous.

The election committee known from conventional voting is emulated, it serves as measure to prevent manipulation by the administration of the election servers. Its members are nominated by the candidating parties. Each member creates an asynchronous key pair, and the ballot sheet is encoded with each separate public key of the committee members. The secret (private) key is kept secret.

The votes are submitted encoded; they can only be read after the members of the election committee have entered their private keys in the system. After the end of the election the encoded results will be published in the Internet. The committee members can then provide their private keys for the results to be decoded and counted.

All key pairs of the election committee members are also published so that everybody can reconstruct the final result. Further cryptographic protocol parts prevent the administration from inserting votes or from deleting encoded votes before the end of the election.

4 Resume

This paper gives a short overview how one public corporation – the Student Union – implemented electronic voting from three points: (i) first from the legal point of view, (ii) from the acceptance of the voters and (iii) how to implement a test-election to keep the voters aware of the future possibility of e-voting and to gain experience with the new technology.

All components of the system – registration, vote casting and the opening/counting of the ballot box worked perfectly well. For the support of the user a helpdesk was available where hardly any user request had to be solved. Rather more students called to ask why this vote was not valid for the regular Student Union election. It was also shown that persons that can use a web browser can also use an e-voting system.

Using National ID cards will facilitate the use of the e-voting system even further, as all read and store operations will be done automatically by the card readers – the respective file dialogues which are necessary in the current prototype will be eliminated.

For the results of the Internet election, the authors defined two hypotheses:

H1:   E-voting raises the voter turn out

H2:   E-voting results in the same results in the digital voting process as in the paper based voting process.

The voter turnout for the test election was 36%; the real paper-based Student Union election could attract 26%, hence the turn-out in the electronic election was 40% higher than in the conventional, paper-based system.[2] The allocation of the votes in the test election corresponded to the result in the real election.

---

[2] This result was indicated in a study conducted right after the last Student Union Elections in June 2001 were two issues were under concern: (i) whether or not the students want to elect their representatives over the Internet and if (ii) e-voting will replace traditional voting in the near future. In the study with 1033 participating students 83,6 % answered that they would prefer e-voting over Booth voting and 71 % are of the opinion that e-voting will replace traditional forms of voting. [11]

References

1. F. Karlhofer, "Interessensverbände im Umbruch," in Materialpaket Politische Bildung, Forum Politische Bildung, Ed. Wien, 2001.
2. F. Koja and W. Antoniolli, Allgemeines Verwaltungsrecht, Lehr- und Handbuch für Studium und Praxis, 3 ed. Wien: Manz, 1996.
3. F. Karlhofer and E. Tálos, "Sozialpartnerschaft unter Druck," in Die Zukunft der österreichischen Demokratie. Trends, Prognosen und Szenarien, vol. 22, Schriftenreihe des Zentrums für Angewandte Politikforschung, A. Pelinka, F. Plasser, and W. Meixner, Eds. Wien: Signum-Verlag, 2000, pp. 381–402.
4. Österreichische Hochschülerschaft (ÖH), Wien 2001.
5. "VfGH-Erkenntnis G18/85," Verfassungsgerichtshof, 1985.
6. "VfGH-Erkenntnis G218/88," Verfassungsgerichtshof, 1989.
7. Bundesgesetzblatt 18/2001, "Änderung des Hochschülerschaftsgesetzes", http://bgbl.wzo.at/pdf/2001a018.pdf accessed on 2002-08-15.
8. R. Kofler, R. Krimmer, and A. Prosser, "Electronic Voting - Algorithmic and Implementation Issues," presented at HICSS-36, Hawaii, 2003.
9. A. Prosser and R. Müller-Török, "Electronic Voting via the Internet," presented at International Conference on Enterprise Information Systems ICEIS2001, Setùbal, 2001.
10. D. Chaum, "Blind Signatures for Untraceable Payments," presented at Advances in Cryptology, 1982.
11. R. Krimmer, "e-Voting.at - Elektronische Demokratie am Beispiel der österreichischen Hochschülerschaftswahlen," thesis at WU Vienna, Vienna, 2002.

E-Voting: Powerful Symbol of E-Democracy

Ella Smith and Ann Macintosh

International Teledemocracy Centre
Napier University
10 Colinton Road
Edinburgh, EH10 5DT
{e.smith,a.macintosh}@napier.ac.uk
http://www.teledemocracy.org

Abstract. This paper focuses on an Internet-enabled remote voting system for a young people's parliament in the Highland region of Scotland. The parliament was established to increase young people's participation in local government. Two elections have been held to constitute the parliament. For both elections, the International Teledemocracy Centre (ITC) provided e-voting systems. The second system is part of a larger participatory design project, to develop an e-democracy website that serves the parliament and increases participation in a variety of ways[1]. This paper investigates our motives for including e-voting, especially in relation to modernisation. We then evaluate the project and appraise the results according to these motives. While acknowledging the differences between this election and a statutory one, we then look at the relationship between modernisation and e-voting, in the light of our results.

1 Introduction

The most potent symbol of a democracy is the involvement of the citizens in the free and fair election of representatives to govern them. Those identifying a 'crisis in democracy' use decreasing election turnout as their central premise. While lack of other forms of participation may be the cause of decreasing turnout, or certainly a cause for concern, voting is seen as the act that currently defines the relationships between citizens, government and democracy. As such e-voting takes on a powerful symbolic role in e-democracy.

A modern e-enabled system of democratic governance seems to require some sort of modernisation of the voting process, whether through electronic counting methods or remote voting over the Internet. However, the process is fraught with secrecy, security and access issues.

This paper asks whether modernising the voting system is a reason for introducing e-voting or whether it can be seen as an umbrella term, offering citizens a range of advantages and potentially increasing turnout. To do this we recount our experience of developing and evaluating an e-voting system, for use by young people to elect representatives to a youth parliament: Highland Youth Voice.

---

[1] http://www.highlandyouthvoice.org/

R. Traunmüller (Ed.): EGOV 2003, LNCS 2739, pp. 240–245, 2003.

2 Project Outline

Highland Youth Voice is a democratically elected youth parliament: a way to involve young people in local government. Every secondary school in the region has 2 or 3 representatives. Each school chooses a voting method: paper ballot or online election. The first members were elected in 2000, through paper ballots or an Internet enabled e-voting system, designed by the International Teledemocracy Centre and BT Scotland. Evaluation of this led to a specification for an e-democracy website, to be developed with Youth Voice members. In October 2002, the second elections took place, with e-voting enabled through a revised system, housed in the *Elections* section[2] of the new website. The *Elections* section also contains comprehensive information, including candidates' manifestos, turnout, results and help pages.

Each student is allotted a unique user-ID, a password and a 5-digit personal identification number (PIN). The e-voting system consists of 3 consecutive screens. The first contains a login form, where the voter enters user-ID, password and PIN. The system checks that the details are correct: the voter has not voted, their school is voting online and the election is contested. If these all point to a valid e-vote, the system checks the number of votes available to the student and shows a 'ballot' form. This lists the candidates for that school, each accompanied by a checkbox. The 'submit' button is labelled *Vote*. The final screen gives a personalised confirmation message. The vote is stored against the PIN, rather than with the student's details, fulfilling secrecy obligations, but enabling controlled rollback if necessary.

2.1 Motives for Incorporating E-Voting

The aim of Youth Voice is to give young people in the region input on issues that affect them. There is also a tangential motive of learning about democracy through a participatory experience [1]. In terms of symbolism, the election and youth parliament show that young people's opinions are respected and valued by the local council.

Increase turnout. It was hoped that there would be a good turnout, turnout would increase from one election to the next and turnout for schools voting online would be higher than for those using a paper ballot.

Modernisation to Increase Enthusiasm. The e-voting option was initially a way to capitalise on young people's perceived enthusiasm for new technology and give a contemporary edge: helping to promote the elections and parliament as modern and exciting. Further, there is some evidence that use of technologies can have a positive impact on learning attainment [2, 3]. This could add to the efficacy of the experience.

Modernisation to Increase Convenience. It was hoped that e-voting would make the elections more convenient for everyone, especially teaching staff. Remote e-voting enables students, with access, to vote from outside school. This also symbolically affirms young people's value as individuals, rather than parts of a school 'group'.

---

[2] http://www.highlandyouthvoice.org/elections

Provide Information. The website structure enabled provision of comprehensive election information, including candidates' manifestos. The Electoral Commission (UK) suggest that *"More pilots aimed at increasing the information available to voters about candidates would be welcome, both stand alone and linked to electronic voting"* [4]. In October 2002, the website gave a full picture of the parliament, including a thriving content management system with news and 'case studies'.

Increase Participation and Interest in Politics. Lupia and Philpot suggest that when visitors to a political website feel that it provides information effectively, they are likely *"to report increased interest and desire to participate in politics"* [5]. Publicity generated through the elections was a strong symbol that the council valued young people's views. The website includes an online policy debating forum. The third debate, on health and exercise, was running during the election. All young people in the region, provided with login information, could contribute to the debate.

2.2 Outline of Evaluation Methods

This paper is based on one quantitative evaluation method and one qualitative method. The quantitative method was based on turnout figures for the elections in 2000 and 2002. Comparisons were also made across electoral methods. The qualitative evaluation took place in focus groups of elected members. These were partly inspired by Henderson et al [6]. The groups gave insights into the success of the system and the differing contexts of use. A good impression of the universality of experience was gained, compared to interviews conducted individually [7]. However, there was presumably some bias created by the representatives' electoral success.

3 Results

3.1 Results Based on Figures

About a third of schools (out of 30) used the e-voting system; a third held a paper ballot and in a third the election was uncontested. Two sets of figures were calculated. The *turnout* formula produced the number of students who voted as a percentage of those registered in that school. In 2002, this figure was only available from 3 schools out of those holding ballot box elections. The *percentage of votes cast* formula produced the number of votes cast as a percentage of possible votes for that school (with figures calculable from all schools).

The figures for 2000 show a slightly higher turnout in schools holding a paper ballot, but a greater percentage of votes cast in schools voting online. In both cases the turnout was good. There was a drop in turnout from 2000 to 2002 and figures for 2002 show a higher turnout in schools using a paper ballot (See Table 1).

For schools voting online, the teachers' main task was distribution of login information. In 2002, this was distributed up to 6 weeks before voting began[3], by

---

[3] In 2002, the log-in information was distributed earlier to enable students to use the discussion forum on the website, which requires a valid user-ID and password.

which time many students had lost the information. In schools where e-voting was supervised, teachers had to organise students' sequential access to computers. It seems that an overestimation of convenience had a negative effect and the distribution of login details will always be a problem.

Table 1. summary of figures (* figure based on results from 3 schools only)

2000				2002			
Turnout		Percentage of Votes Cast		Turnout		Percentage of Votes Cast	
e-voting	Ballot box	e-voting	Ballot box	e-voting	Ballot box*	e-voting	Ballot box
71 %	73 %	67 %	60 %	52 %	70 % *	48 %	66 %

3.2 Results Based on Focus Groups

No major usability problems were reported. The Youth Voice members, who composed the focus groups, were enthusiastic about the e-voting system, calling it *"simple"* and *"fun"*.

Convenience. Members liked being able to vote from home. Asked to decide on the best and worst aspects of the website, this was on the 'best' list. However, they felt that each student, rather than each school, should decide whether to vote using paper or online. This would mean integration between the two voting methods, resulting in a 2-stage ballot or in teachers checking an online register of who had voted, before distributing ballot papers. This would slow the paper ballot process down.

Provide Information. Another popular aspect of the website was the quality of information: *"interesting and useful"*. Most people had seen the website, whether their school voted online or not. In this case, the election itself, rather than the e-voting option, prompted students to visit and explore the Youth Voice website. Server log reports indicate that unique visits increased by a factor of 10 during the election.

Increase Participation and Interest in Politics. Many students used the website's Guest Book[4]. They said that the website had a *"cool voting system"*; was *"full of useful info"* and *"great web page really enjoyed voting great way to learn about voting and parliament"*.

Secrecy, Security and Privacy. The e-voting system was designed to achieve levels of secrecy and security at least as high as for a paper ballot. In terms of security, no votes or results were disputed and no one claimed to have 'hacked' the system[5]. In terms of privacy: in some computer labs screens could be overlooked.

---

[4] http://www.highlandyouthvoice.org/GuestBook02.asp
[5] Although a significant number of students did attempt to vote more than once, either by resubmitting the 'ballot' form or trying again at a later time or date.

4 Conclusions

If modernisation had been our aim, the results indicate that e-voting was unsuccessful. It was not more convenient. Novelty and innovation may have had a positive effect in 2000, but this seems to have worn off by 2002. The e-voting format did, however, increase opportunities for informed voting. It also gave Youth Voice the ability to control information centrally[6]. The elections drew people to the website, raising the profile of the parliament in the area. The election also increased participation among young people: many of those who visited the website joined in the online debate.

5 Discussion

It is perhaps disingenuous to separate the provision of information from modernisation, especially information provided over the Internet. However, research into voting patterns indicates that people feel they lack the information to confidently cast their vote. In terms of local government this applies to both issues and candidates [8]. Research undertaken with younger voters indicates that this extends to most of electoral practice. They feel that they do not know *how* to vote [9] and ask for information covering process, as well as issues [10].

The ability to vote from home proved popular. For those who have difficulties accessing polling stations, this would be a great advantage [11]. However, the current pattern of access to technology causes some concern. We should be cautious about making voting more convenient for one section of the population than another.

The fall in turnout between the 2000 and 2002 Youth Voice elections may indicate that increase in turnout as a result of novelty or convenience may not be sustainable.

The problem of secrecy is significant for remote voting in statutory elections. The UK is bound by international protocols to ensure that votes can be cast in secret [12]. When voting is unsupervised, the voter must guarantee this. There will be occasions where, for some, this is not possible.

Our e-voting system had provisions to deal with system failure or disputed votes. These could be used as part of a controlled rollback. In a national election, there would be a greater incentive to attack the system and rollback could have a detrimental effect. An allegation that an attack had taken place could potentially do as much damage as an actual attack. Fairweather and Rogerson [13] suggest we assume *"100% probability that hackers/publicity seekers would see a UK general election conducted largely by electronic means as a target."* What provisions would be in place to deal with an attack or to restore confidence, if an attack was alleged? As developers, we had more to lose than gain by influencing the results. This may not be the case in a statutory election.

Our evaluation indicates problems with the distribution of login information, rather than problems with entering it into the form. Usability problems will arise with longer PIN numbers [12] and problems with confidential distribution of login information may increase opportunities for personation.

---

[6] For example, by providing a question-oriented template for manifestos, each candidate had to give a good account of why they were standing.

The e-voting system proved a useful way to give relevant information about elections and the Highland Youth Voice parliament. People found the system easy and fun to use and appreciated its advantages. The election demonstrated that the local government valued young people as citizens and wanted to hear their ideas. Hopefully, this experience will encourage increased participation in government.

References

1. Macintosh, A., Robson, E., Smith, E., Whyte, A. (2002); Electronic Democracy and Young People *Social Science Computer Review*; Spring 2003, **21** (1); pp43–54
2. Becta (2002); The impact of information and communication technologies on pupil learning and attainment; Nottinghamshire: DfES Publications; p45
3. Druin, A. (1999); The Role of Children in the Design of New Technology in *Behaviour and Information Technology (BIT)*, 2002, 21 (1), pp1–25.
4. Electoral Commission (2002); Modernising elections: a strategic evaluation of the 2002 electoral pilot schemes; London: Electoral Commission;
5. Lupia, A. and Philpot, T.; (2002) *More Than Kids Stuff: Can News and Information Web Sites Mobilize Young Adults?*;   Paper delivered at the 2002 Annual Meeting of the American Political Science Association, Boston, August 29-September 1, 2002
6. Henderson, R.D., Smith, M.C., Podd, J. and Varela-Alvarez, H. (1995); A comparison of the four prominent user-based methods for evaluating the usability of computer software; *Ergonomics* **38** (10), pp2030–44
7. Shneiderman, B. (1997); *Strategies for effective human-computer interaction* (3rd edition) Addison Wesley Longman: Harlow, UK
8. Electoral Commission (2002); *Public opinion and the 2002 local elections: findings*; London: Electoral Commission; p2
9. Bentley et al (1999); The Real Deal – What young people really think about government, politics and social exclusion; DEMOS: London
10. Children and Young People's Unit (2002); *Young People and politics: A Report on the YVote? /YNot? Project*; pp15-16; CYPU: London
11. Morris, G.; Scott, R. and Woodward, A. (2002); Polls apart: a future for accessible democracy: An evaluation of the accessibility of the May 2002 electoral pilot voting schemes; report produced by Scope for the Electoral Commission.
12. Pratchett, L.; Birch, S.; Candy, S.; Fairweather, N.; Rogerson, S.; Stone, V.; Watt, B. and Wingfield, M. (2002); *The implementation of electronic voting in the UK*; Chameleon Press Ltd: London. This is also known as the De Montfort Report
13. Fairweather, N. and Rogerson, S. (2002); *Implementation of Electronic Voting in the UK Technical Options Report;* Office of the Deputy Prime Minister

Secure E-Voting for Preferential Elections*

Riza Aditya, Colin Boyd, Ed Dawson, and Kapali Viswanathan

Information Security Research Centre,
Queensland University of Technology,
GPO BOX 2434, Brisbane, QLD 4001, Australia
{r.aditya,c.boyd,e.dawson,k.viswanathan}@qut.edu.au

Abstract. Electronic voting (e-voting) systems can greatly enhance the efficiency, and potentially, the transparency of national elections. However, the security of such systems is an area of on-going research. The literature for secure e-voting is predominantly concerned with 1-out-of-m voting strategies, where m is the number of candidates running for the elections. This paper presents a case study of cryptologic protocols for secure e-voting systems that use preferential voting strategies.

1 Introduction

Many types of voting strategies are employed around the world. Although there has been extensive research for cryptologic protocols for binary voting strategies (yes or no votes), the attention to preferential voting systems [2] is minimal. In such voting systems, each voter is required to rank, provide an order of preference for, the candidates. If no candidate receives a majority, more than half of first preference votes, the candidate with the lowest first preference vote is eliminated. Votes of the eliminated candidate are redistributed to the remaining candidates depending on the second preference. Repeatedly, more candidates are eliminated until one reaches a majority.

A notion of security for e-voting systems can be summarised as the confidentiality service for individual voter-vote relationships. This can be formalised as $Conf(ID, Vote)$, where $Conf(\cdots)$ is a confidentiality service, ID is a voter's identity, and $Vote$ is the vote of that voter. Such a security is achieved using one of two techniques, namely $(ID, Conf(Vote))$ or $(Conf(ID), Vote)$. The vote either remains confidential or anonymous even after the end of the elections. This paper will adapt a proposal from each of these two techniques to preferential voting systems and study the resulting efficiency.

2 Preferential Voting Using Homomorphic Encryption

This section will discuss the use of homomorphic encryption in secure e-voting systems, which uses the $(ID, Conf(Vote))$ technique, to accommodate a preferential voting strategy.

---

* Project funded by ARC Discovery 2002, Grant No: DP0211390

R. Traunmüller (Ed.): EGOV 2003, LNCS 2739, pp. 246–249, 2003.

2.1   Homomorphic Encryption

Assume that $E^k(v)$ is a public encryption function, where k is a random value chosen by the voter and v is a vote, and $D(\cdots)$ is the corresponding private decryption function known only to the election officials, such that they form a public-key encryption system. The encryption function is said to be homomorphic when $E^{k_1}(v_1) \odot E^{k_2}(v_2) = E^{k_3}(v_1 \oplus v_2)$, where $\odot$ and $\oplus$ are some binary operators. In the LHS of the previous equation, the ciphertexts of individual votes can be *combined* using a binary operator, $\odot$. The RHS of the equation suggests that such a combining operation will result in another ciphertext, the decryption of which will result in an *accumulation* of the individual votes, $v_1 \oplus v_2$. Thus, it will be possible to compute the accumulation of the individual votes without having to retrieve the individual votes.

The Paillier cryptosystem [5] contains a homomorphic encryption function, used for voting, which operates on the congruence class   mod N^2, where $N = pq$, and p and q are large prime integers such that the factorisation problem is intractable. The next section will use the above cryptosystem.

2.2   Preferential Voting and Paillier Cryptosystem

Baudron *et al.* [3] proposed a novel technique for the design of 1-out-of-m electronic voting systems using Paillier cryptosystem. The vote is structured in a special form to be combined using homomorphic encryption.

We propose the following *simple* adaptation of the message structure to design an electronic preferential voting system. In this system, the voter is expected to vote for a particular sequence of candidates rather than to vote for the candidates themselves, as was proposed in the original scheme.

Preferential vote: A system constant $M = 2^{\lceil \log_2 l \rceil}$ is chosen, where l is the maximum number of voters in a constituency. The officials assign a unique number, $i \in \{0, \cdots, m!\}$, to every possible sequence (permutation) of m candidates, and accommodate for empty votes. The voter must provide a rank for every candidate or submit an empty vote. The size of the vote in this cryptosystem is $\log_2 M^{m!}$ bits. That is each sequence is represented by a counter that can count up to M. The voter encrypts the vote, M^i, using a homomorphic encryption scheme for the election officials. Equation 1 presents a pictorial representation of the vote (M^i), which chooses the first sequence of candidates, namely, $i = 0$.

$$
\overbrace{\underbrace{|00\cdots00|}_{i=m!}^{\lceil \log_2 l \rceil}\underbrace{00\cdots00|}_{i=m!-1}^{\lceil \log_2 l \rceil}\cdots|\underbrace{00\cdots00|}_{i=2}^{\lceil \log_2 l \rceil}\underbrace{00\cdots01|}_{i=1}^{\lceil \log_2 l \rceil}\underbrace{00\cdots00|}_{i=0}^{\lceil \log_2 l \rceil}}^{M^i} \tag{1}
$$

The public key for a Paillier cryptosystem must be generated such that the modulus $M^{m!} < N^2$ so that the entire vote can be encrypted in one block.

When $m = 20$ and $l = 1000$, the size of the modulus is: $|N| = 10 \times 20!$ bits. Clearly, such a size for a modulus is impractical as numerous exponentiation operations are required.

3   Preferential Voting Using Mix-Networks

This section will discuss the use of mix-networks in secure e-voting system. It presents an implementation, using the $(Conf(ID), Vote)$ technique, of a robust mix-network for a simple and relatively secure preferential e-voting system.

3.1   Mix-Networks

Let D be a decryption algorithm computable only by the mix-network. Let $\phi : \mathbb{Z}_n \to \mathbb{Z}_n$ be a randomly chosen secret permutation function. The operation of the mix-network can be described by the following operation: $m_{\phi(i)} = D(c_i)$, where $i \in \mathbb{Z}_n$. The LHS of the previous equation is a random sorted set of plaintexts, $m_{\phi(i)}$, corresponding to the RHS, decryption, D, of a set of input ciphertexts, c_i.

The input to the mix-network could be of the form $(ID, Conf(Vote))$, and the output would be of the form $(Conf(ID), Vote)$. Thus, a mix-network can be viewed as a confidentiality translation service translating the confidentiality service from the vote (or data) to the identity.

Abe [1] proposed a mix-network using ElGamal encryption algorithm in re-encrypting the set of input messages, $I_v = \{c_i | i \in \mathbb{Z}_n\}$, to produce a randomly permuted set of output messages, $O_v = \{m_{\phi(i)} | i \in \mathbb{Z}_n\}$. The next section will use the mix-network by Abe.

3.2   Preferential Voting and Mix-Networks

The mix-network by Abe can be used to construct electronic secret ballot voting schemes. In such schemes, the vote need not be in a special form as the tabulation phase is conducted using the plaintext vote anonymised. In contrast to schemes based upon homomorphic encryption, the size of input messages does not directly affect the efficiency of the mix-network.

In electronic preferential voting employing mix-network, the vote can be of the form an integer ranging from 1 to $m!$, where m is the number of candidates running for the election. Thus, the message size is $\lceil \log_2(m!) \rceil = 62$ bits, where $m = 20$. Let $j \in \mathbb{Z}_l$ be an index into a list of voters, so that l is the number of voters.

We propose a generic e-voting scheme utilising the above mix-network as follows:

Set-up: The election officials publish the parameters for a threshold decryption cryptosystem [4], (E, D), such that $E^k(\cdots)$ is the public encryption function, where k is a random value chosen by the voter, and $D(\cdots)$ is a t-out-of-n decryption function.

Vote submission: Each voter j:
1. selects a sequence, $i_j \in \{1, \cdots, m!\}$, to represent his/her preference;
2. encrypts the selection, e.g: $E^{k_j}(i_j)$;
3. identifies itself to the vote collecting official to establish its identity, ID; and,
4. communicates the encrypted vote, $E(i_j)$, to the vote collecting official.
The voting official verifies the identity of every voter and forwards the set of votes from valid voters, $U = \{E^{k_j}(i_j)\}$, to the mix-network.

Vote mixing: The mix-network permutes and decrypts the objects from the set U and outputs a set of plaintext votes V, such that the correspondence between the objects in U and the objects in V are a secret.

Vote tabulation: The election official electronically processes the plaintext vote in V by using a program for counting the preferences and calculating the elected candidate.

The processing cost is mainly contributed by the mixing operation. The mix-network is composed of a number of gates, and the computational cost for each gate is 23.6 modular exponentiations [1]. Each voter generates exactly one input message to the mix-network. Providing $2 \log_2 l - 1$ delay [1] per input, where $l = 1000$ is the number of inputs to the mix-network, total computational cost of the mix-network is $23.6(2 \log_2 l - 1)t = 448400$ modular exponentiations.

4   Conclusion

The size of the electronic vote for a preferential voting system is inherently larger than a 1-out-of-m voting system, when the number of candidates, m, increases. In preferential voting system, the size of the vote is at least $\log_2(m!)$ bits. Therefore the voting systems using some form of homomorphic encryption [3] tend to be inefficient or impractical.

Voting systems that employ mix-networks, on the other hand, do not require a special form for the electronic vote. The computational complexity is not adversely affected by the number of candidates. Therefore, mix-network based voting systems are ideally suited for preferential voting systems. Future research will be directed towards the design of more efficient robust mix-networks.

References

1. Masayuki Abe. Mix-networks on permutations networks. In *Advances in Cryptology–ASIACRYPT 99*, pages 258–273, 1999.
2. Australian Electoral Commission. *Australian Electoral Commission*, 2002. Available from http://www.aec.gov.au, last accessed 17 February 2003.
3. Olivier Baudron, Pierre-Alain Fouque, David Pointcheval, Jacques Stern, and Guillaume Poupard. Practical multi-candidate election system. In *ACM symposium on Principles of distributed computing*, pages 274–283, 2001.
4. Yvo Desmedt and Yair Frankel. Threshold cryptosystems. In *Advances in Cryptology–CRYPTO 89*, pages 307–315, 1989.
5. Pascal Paillier. Public key cryptosystems based on composite degree residuosity classes. In *Advances in Cryptology–EUROCRYPT 99*, pages 223–238, 1999.

OSCI
A Common Communications Standard for E-Government

Frank Steimke and Martin Hagen

OSCI Co-ordination office
Bremen, Germany

OSCI is the name of a two-layered protocol for the secure exchange of messages in the E-Government context. It has been developed within the German MEDIA@Komm project [4], and now it became an important part of the German E-Government infrastructure. It will, for example, be a major part of the secure technical infrastructure for Bund Online 2005, which is the E-Government program of the German federal government. The security layer of OSCI, called OSCI-Transport, is a mandatory standard in the federal governments IT - architecture program SAGA [1]. It is part of the European IDA program, too.

With OSCI, governments and municipal institutions are able to use the internet for a secure, confidential and reliable communication. OSCI is based on international standards, especially XML, and is well suited for offering common government services over the Internet in a secure way. It supports asynchronous (E-mail like) message exchange as well as request - response scenarios. The application-layer of the OSCI protocol is used for the standardized representation of content data. Together with the underlying secure transport layer, this allows highly automated transactions, which are especially useful in the government-to-government scenarios.

OSCI is up and running. In the city of Bremen, Germany, there are more than 100 applications online which are based on OSCI. They are available at http://www.bremer-online-service.de. Federal laws are in preparation, which will lay down the use of OSCI for the G2G communication between all the civil registration offices in Germany. This will be mandatory from 2005, and is expected to save more than 3 Mio Euro each year.

There are two distinct layers in OSCI:

- OSCI-Transport is the application independent part of OSCI. All of the cryptographic functions are defined in OSCI-Transport, which is used for the secure, reliable and traceable transport of content data of any kind.
- The real advantages of electronic transactions will come to effect in highly automated processes. To achieve this, the content data has to be structured in a standardized way. This allows legacy systems to read and process the customers data.

  In OSCI, this standardization of content data takes place at the application layer. There are several projects dealing with content data from different applications. The most popular is called OSCI-XMeld. It its used in processes for the registration of citizens.

R. Traunmüller (Ed.): EGOV 2003, LNCS 2739, pp. 250–255, 2003.

The development of both levels of OSCI is co-ordinated by the OSCI Co-Ordination office. It is part of the government of the German city Bremen. The OSCI co-ordination office offers its services to other governments and municipal institutions in Germany.

The office is funded by the federal government of Germany, by the state government of Bremen, and by private sector parties. The standardization process itself is an open process, involving public sector institutions from all levels of government as well as private sector companies.

OSCI-Transport

OSCI Transport 1.2 describes the *data exchange format* through an automated interface for the secure transfer of messages using digital signatures via the Internet or other comparable communication media. OSCI is used for the secure transfer (according to the German Digital Signature Act) of business transaction data between two communication partners. This communication is supported by an *intermediary* that besides transferring the messages offers additional services via OSCI.

The design principles and goals of OSCI-Transport are:

Interoperability. It can be used for any kind of business process. The cryptographic functions are clearly defined in terms of XML Schema definitions.

Application Independent. OSCI-Transport allows secure exchange of any kind of data, generated by any application.

Scalable. It supports all the different levels of signature which are defined in the German and European signature laws. It is compliant with the German *Digital Signature Act.*

It is also possible to use OSCI with no signature at all. This will often make sense for *some* of the messages which are sent in a whole business transaction. In practice, we often see the pattern of *Identification and Authorisation* (electronic signature is needed), then messages for *information exchange and data validation* (without signature but encrypted), and – as the last step – a message which is *finally signed* by the customer.

Open User Group. OSCI has no explicit user administration, but works with an open user group.

Users of the application don't have to be explicitly registered as online users first. This is especially useful in G2C scenarios. But because internal addressing in OSCI is accomplished using encryption certificates, the possession of such a certificate is required to take full advantage of the services provided by OSCI-Transport. The recipient in particular must possess an encryption certificate.

Platform Independent. OSCI uses XML technology and is operating system independent.

Complete platform-independence has a strong influence on the security concept of OSCI. This is related to the objective of implementing security primarily on the OSCI level, as independent as possible of the security standards used in other components, e.g. the carrier network and the operating system and browser being used.

These requirements are described in full detail in [2].

OSCI-Transport allows *economical* solutions for the government, because expensive equipment can be shared by different offices within the same government without loss of confidentiality.

OSCI-Transport [3] is completely based on international standards like XML, XML encryption, XML digital signatures and *SOAP with attachements*. These standards are used in a way which is compliant to the German Digital Signature Act. Technically, the w3c Schemas for *XML encryption* and *XML digital* signature are redefined, so that only those key-lenghts and algorithms are allowed, which are considered to be secure enough for E-Government. The "German Federal Office for secure information technologies" has checked OSCI-Transport against ITSEC with a positive result.

The security objectives, which are supported by OSCI-Transport, are:

Confidentiality. The content data is end-to-end encrypted with the mechanisms of XML-encryption.

Integrity and Authenticity. Content data and messages can by digital signed with the techniques of XML digital signature to provide integrity. The authenticity relies on an external public key infrastructure.

The connection between the OSCI Transport infrastructure and the external PKI is defined in terms of ISIS-MTT compatibility. This means, for example, that the certificates for the users of OSCI-Transport have to be in X509v3 Format. The PKI service providers are accessed the ways defined by the ISIS MTT standard [7].

Non-repudiation and Traceability. There are different levels of non - repudiation, including non - repudiation of authorship and of the whole communication process. All of these are supported by OSCI-Transport.

OSCI takes into account both communication of public administration with customers (the general public and companies) by offering and handling administrative services on the Internet and also internal communication between different public administration offices and departments.

Because there are so many possible scenarios in such an environment there are many functional and security-related requirements that result in a very specific communication role model for OSCI-Transport. There is a clear distinction between *authors* and *readers*, and the *sender* and the *receiver*.

The basis for all digital communication is the transfer of data from a sender to a recipient. It's important to remember that in general several people are responsible for the content of messages by working on it together or by giving approval or consent, while only one person actually sends a message. There are different sets of responsibilities for each of these two roles. Responsibility for content lies with the authors, while the sender is responsible for sending the message to the correct recipient at the correct time. On the recipient side there is a similar difference between the recipient who receives the message and the readers of the message who work with the actual content.

The existence of a central message exchange point, the *intermediary,* who can provide added value services without endangering the confidentiality of the content data, is typical for OSCI communication and is partly founded on the need for asynchronous communication. An OSCI message can be delivered to a communication partner without sender and recipient being online at the same time. This is because many E-Government processes are provided that are initiated by a customer message, but are not completely machine processable. Modifications must frequently be made by hand by a clerk on the public administration side. When doing so the reverse flow from administration to public must also be taken into account. In this case it cannot be a requirement for message recipients to always be available online. OSCI therefore supports not only the synchronous (or *blocking*), but also the asynchronous (or *non-blocking*) exchange of messages.

To enable asynchronous communication the intermediary administers *mailboxes* for potential recipients. OSCI messages are temporarily stored in these mailboxes. Accessing the mailbox to pick up messages requires prior authentication as part of the mail fetch request. When authentication is successfully completed, a delivery request is initiated via synchronous communication between the intermediary and authorised recipients. The possession of a mailbox does not require prior registration with the pubic administration department, but is tied to the possession of an X.509v3 certificate and the mailbox is automatically created when the first message is received. Linking mailboxes to the certificate guarantees clear and unambiguous authentication for authorised recipients.

The other reason for the intermediary is an economic one. Subdivisions in local Governments can share expensive Equipment without loss of privacy. That means, that the different offices in a local government are able to share one intermediary. It acts as the single access point to the external public key infrastructure. While the connection is end-to-end encrypted, the intermediary can provide all the information from the PKI that is needed by the recipients and readers to validate the certificates and signatures.

OSCI-XMeld

OSCI-XMeld is the name for standardized messages in the transactions and processes for the registration of citizens in Germany.

The organization of the citizen registration is decentralized. There are more than 6.000 registration offices. Every time when someone is moving from one city to another, there has to be a message exchange between the two offices involved. Up to now, most of these messages are sent in form of conventional letters with the traditional post service. There are millions of these letters every year. The estimated cost for each of these messages within the overall process is about 2.50 Euro each. There are three main reasons, which prevented the electronic message exchange up to now:

1. there are many different legacy systems for the citizens registration process from different vendors. There was no common data exchange format on the application level between these systems.
2. There was no reliable and secure transport network.
3. Because of the potentially security risks, the electronic message exchange was allowed only in very limited ways. The use of the Internet was not allowed at all. This changes with the upcoming techniques of electronic signatures.

In 2002, the federal law has changed. The processes around the registration of citizens process are provided to become one of the first big E-Government applications in Germay. The amandmented law forces the use of electronic data exchange with the goal of speeding up the processes, and to reduce the costs. There are different scenarios, including

- Government to citizen: People are allowed to registrate themselves via Internet. A qualified electronic Signature is required by law, that means that Smart Cards and Card terminals have to be used by the citizens.
- Government to Business: Private parties are allowed to get Information about peoples addresses over the Internet.
  Most of the traffic for this messagtype is done by *power users:* big companies try to find out the adresses of their customers, who have moved within Germany.
  There is no signature and no encryption mechanism required by law for these messages. But because the information is sold by the registration offices, they are interested in a secure way for the authentification of their customers. The use of advanced electronic signatures is one solution for this authentification.
- Government to Government: The new law allows not more than three days for the delivery of messages between registration offices. It encourages the use of electronic message exchange over the Internet. Advanced electronic signatures are used for the authentification of these offices.

With the two-layered OSCI Protocol, there is a technical solution for the challenges of this E-Government application. While OSCI-Transport gives the secure and reliable transport layer, OSCI-XMeld defines and standardizes the content of the messages in an vendor- and product - independent way. The messages are described in terms of XML Schema files. These are composed from building blocks like names, addresses and so on. They are defining the syntax and the semantic of all messages in a formal way. See [5] for a more detailled description.

The development of the standardized messages in done in an open process, which is described in [6]. The XMeld community consists of people from all over Germany. Most of them are from the local, regional or federal governments, but the legacy systems vendors are represented, too. The next version of XMeld, XMeld 1.1, will be ready in June 2003.

In December 2002, the German states' Ministers for internal affairs decided to use OSCI-XMeld together with OSCI-Transport for all cross-country message exchanges for citizens registration processes. Of course, this is quite a challenge, because all the different legacy systems have to be interconnected. There will be a secure and reliable network based on OSCI-Transport between all the registry offices in Germany in 2005.

Products

While OSCI-Transport and OSCI-XMeld are free available and open specifications, there are implementing products, too.

The company *"bremen online services"*, founded within the MEDIA@Komm Project, has developed a commercial product called *Governikus*. It consists of modules, built around a *kernel* which implements OSCI-Transport. This product is an implementation of the OSCI intermediary. This is where the PKI connection takes place and where the "user mailboxes" are located. It is designed as a centralized ressource which can be used, for example, by many villages and their local governments. There are other implementation expected from other companies, which will probably be commercial products, too.

But there is, of course, also need for the client components, which have to be implemented in client application at the customers side, as well as in the legacy systems used by the government. To enable all these systems to 'speak' OSCI Transport, an *OSCI-Transport library* has to be developed. Up to now, these libraries are available only as parts of commercial products like *Governikus*.

But in order to enable and push the use of OSCI-Transport within the Government in Germany in a reasonable time, it should be very easy and cheap to get and use this library. That is why a new version of this library is under development. It will be paid for by the federal government, and it will be given to the local governments for free. It will be implemented in Java and in Microsoft's .net technology and will be available at the end of 2003.

References

1. Germany Federal Minister of the Interior. Standards and architectures for egovernment applications 1.1. www.kbst.bund.de/saga, February 2003.
2. OSCI Leitstelle. Osci transport 1.2 - principles, security objectives and mechanisms. http://www.osci.de, June 2002.
3. OSCI Leitstelle. Osci transport 1.2 -specification-. http://www.osci.de, June 2002.
4. Federal Ministry of Economics and Labour. Media@komm - focus project of the federal republic of germany for the implementation of virtual town halls and market places. http://www.mediakomm.net/documents/halbzeitbilanz_en.pdf, August 2001.
5. Frank Steimke. Buergerfreundliches e-government: Das projekt osci-xmeld. In *Handbuch IT-Sicherheit*. Addison-Wesley, 2003.
6. Frank Steimke. Osci: Sicherheit und performanz im e-government. In Matthias Fluhr, editor, *Die Chipkarte: Fester Bestandteil unseres Alltags*, pages 180–192. Omnicard, January 2003.
7. T7 and TELETRUST. Common isis-mtt specification for interoperability and test systems. http://www.isis-mtt.org, July 2002.

Trust in E-Government: Digital Signatures without Time Stamping?

Mitja Dečman

University of Ljubljana
School of Public Administration
Slovenia
mitja.decman@vus.uni-lj.si

Abstract. The successful delivery of electronic services is a primary objective of modern e-government and their successful introduction depends on the users trusting these services and the privacy of their personal data. Digital signatures are one of the security elements that make these services possible, but they feature some weaknesses – weaknesses that can be surmounted by the use of a digital time stamp. These do not only add a certified time to the data but also make many of other methods that increase security and trust possible. Since digital certificates are widely used in today's information society, digital signatures should be easy to implement. However, implementation must be studied carefully because abuse can have critical repercussions. Without 100 percent trust from its users, e-government and its services will be unsustainable. Slovenian e-government is in this situation, stranded with good infrastructure and legal bases, but services that are not trusted.

1 Introduction

Today's government is one of many social structures that must keep up with modernisation in society and keep pace with the latest technological developments. Perhaps it is not so that it must, but given the benefits to be seen in the private sector, it should. Even the previous DEXA declaration [8] on e-government stated theses promoting e-government. With regard to service provision, DEXA claims that only if citizens have the capability and self-confidence to perform e-transactions and trust that the e-government will protect their personal data, will the services be successful.

In the case of trust and security, we speak about authentication, integrity, non-repudiation, confidentiality and authorisation. As we move into the information society, data on paper is merging with electronic forms. Normal means of communication are switching to computer networks, intranets and the internet. A written signature is giving way to an electronic signature. Processes in the private and public sectors are coming face to face with new technologies and new ways of work.

Most countries have put forward strategies and action plans, while the politicians promise that life will improve in the information society. Users that have heard and understood this message are making preparations. If the services provided by e-government satisfy their needs, the end-users – citizens or employees in private and public sector – will use them. If not, the efforts will be lost and wasted. The services

R. Traunmüller (Ed.): EGOV 2003, LNCS 2739, pp. 256–259, 2003.

must therefore be effective, fast, easy to use and safe. The users must trust the security mechanisms supporting the services. E-governments must study and implement the most advanced security technologies to gain confidence and succeed.

2 Digital Signature, Digital Certificate, and Digital Time Stamp

In an electronic world, data exists in electronic form, and just as we need a mechanism for signing data on the paper, we need the same for electronic forms of data. As with physical paper-and-pen signatures, electronic signatures are required to demonstrate the intent of the signer at the time of signing. Digital signature, as a special form of electronic signature, uses in this case asymmetric cryptography.

When making the digital signature, the signer encrypts the hash of the signed data [1] with a private key thus making a digital signature. The person verifying the signature uses the signer's public key. The problem is how the verifier knows that the public key belongs to the signer. The answer is by obtaining it in the form of digital certificate, which is a form of data including a public key and some personal identification data from the certificate owner, digitally signed by a trusted third party called the Certification Authority (CA). Every digital certificate has a time limitation, i.e. expiring date (even a CA certificate), or can be revoked. After the expiry date, no signatures made and verified by a public key from within this digital certificate are valid and none of the existing digital signatures as well. A similar situation occurs when a user or CA revokes its certificate because of a compromised (stolen) private key [5]. Sometimes revocation is made intentionally.

Given all the above, time is an extremely important issue. Moreover, every official paper document has a time mark on it stating when a document existed. The same requirement exists for electronic forms of data. We therefore need a secure and trusted time certification attached to signed electronic data, stating that data existed in this form before or at that stated time. We can do that by using a time stamp. A time stamp is an addition to electronic data, providing an answer to the question of "when". A time stamp is therefore a set of digitally signed data by a trusted third party known as the Time Stamping Authority (TSA) that includes a valid time and thumbprint (hash) of user's data (e.g. hash of a text document or a digital signature itself). Since only the hash is sent to TSA, data privacy is assured. Of course, the signer and verifier must trust the TSA and since digital signatures are used, integrity and authentication are assured. The signer can check the time stamp to prevent communication errors, the time stated, to make sure the right time has been stated and the hash in the time stamp to make sure the hash from his or her document was time-stamped. Using time stamps also guarantees authentication of digital signatures in the past. Without time stamping, all digital signatures are invalid when the digital certificate expires. But if they were time stamped, the verifier can check if they were signed before expiration, i.e. when digital certificate was still valid. Using a time-stamp enables non-repudiation.

The problem that remains is the trust in the TSA. Let us imagine the user is a crooked politician living in a corrupt world. He bribes a TSA and time-stamps a document of a now unwanted political agreement he signed with a union before the revocation of his digital certificate with a time after the revocation. Now he can claim that he himself did not sign this agreement since some opponent politician has stolen his private key and signed it in his name after the revocation. To solve this problem linking time-stamps schemas were introduced. There exist many different linking schemes [4, 6] but one thing is common to all. They enable non-repudiated determination of temporal order of time-stamped data and assure that TSA is accountable. Linking schemes rely on the fact that it is impossible to know the future sequence of time stamp requests and the hash values they include. If a specific time stamp includes parts of data from previous time stamps then we can assure that this time stamping happened after the time stamping of the time stamps which are included in this manner [3]. This solution also solves the problem of time limitation in other direction. But it has to include a mechanism that allows a verifier to check this linking chain. Each time stamp should therefore include all data from previous time stamps made in one time period that form a final checksum that can be compared to publicly, generally accessed, non-changeable data. This final checksum should be published in a newspaper that is widely distributed and stored in different archives, libraries, etc. In the case of e-government, this could be an official gazette.

3   Aspects of Time Stamping Implementation in E-Government

Considering the legal basis, a large number of countries have already passed a range of electronic signature acts. These have primarily focused on two basic principles, which are also defined in the EU directive accepted and implemented by EU member states and many of the candidate countries [7]. In addition, acts on electronic or digital signatures in different countries in the world generally include articles on time stamping and time stamps. Most of them provide a basic definition and do not give adequate attention to the issue, e.g. the Slovenian Electronic Commerce and Electronic Signature Act [2]. Others, for example the Estonian Digital Signature Act [9], thoroughly define time stamping services and time stamping service providers. Since time stamping is not yet recognised as a necessary part of PKI, the lack of legal support will have to be resolved in the future. The setting up IT infrastructure is also an important basic phase that supports services built upon it. E-government should take care of the supply and demand side by providing enough web servers, firewalls, intranets, databases on one hand and internet service providers, public access to internet and cheap broadband internet access on the other. PKI should be set up to enable digital signatures and time stamping. One or more CAs should be set up or public CAs should be recognized as authorized to issue digital certificates for use in e-government services. A TSA should also be established to enable time stamping. A secure source of accurate time has to be provided with an additional TSA mechanism that allows users of e-government services to time stamp their digitally signed data. Once the appropriate infrastructure is in place, secure and trusted services should be built upon it. Knowledge is an important issue within the provision of trusted e-governments services. It is important to educate users to use IT and at the same time explain the basic security issues and build their trust in the services offered. People will not use a gas oven if they are afraid of using gas. Nor will they digitally sign and send data if they fear the data could be stolen or forged.

4   The Case of Slovenia

Slovenia is a transitional county trying to advance to the information society as fast as possible. Slovenia's legal bases for secure e-government services were laid out in 2000, when the Electronic Commerce and Electronic Signature Act was passed by parliament, in accordance with the EU directive. Other regulations had to be changed because of this law. The situation is still confusing in some legal areas and more work needs to be done. Time stamping is only defined in outline and no special articles in the law or additional decrees accurately specify a time stamping service or time stamping authority. With the law's adoption, a PKI was established. Two root CAs were set up in the Government Centre of Informatics: a CA issuing digital certificates for public administration employees and another issuing digital certificates for end users, citizens and private companies. Smart cards were introduced for employees in public administration while end users have to solve this problem by themselves. No time stamping authority was established yet. There is an accurate and safe time source established in the Government Centre of Informatics and Entrust technology, used by CAs, supports time stamping as well. A government portal was set up and offered the first basic services using digital certificates. The services enable end users to obtain birth, death and marriage certificates using their digital certificate to authenticate or identify themselves. There is no service using digital signatures or time stamping yet.

References

1. Adams, C., Lloyd, S.: Understanding Public-Key Infrastructure. Macmillan Technical Publishing, Indiana ZDA (1999).
2. Electronic Commerce and Electronic Signature Act, Official Gazette of Republic of Slovenia, 57/2000 (2000).
3. Bayer, D., Haber, S., Stornetta, W.S.: Improving the Efficiency and Reliability of Digital Time-Stamping. Sequences II: Methods in Communication, Security, and Computer Science. Springer-Verlag, Berlin Heidelberg New York (1993) 329–334.
4. Buldas, A., Laud, P., Lipmaa, H., Villemson, J.: Time stamping with binary linking schemes. Advances in Cryptology – CRYPTO'98, LNCS 1462. Springer-Verlag, Berlin Heidelberg New York (1998) 486–501.
5. Maniatis, P., Baker, M.: Enabling the archival storage of signed documents, Computer Science Department, Stanford University, 24th July 2001
6. Benaloh, J., de Mare, M.: Efficient Broadcast time-stamping. Technical report 1, Clarkson University Department of Mathematics and Computer Science (1991).
7. European Community: A European Initiative on Electronic Commerce. COM(97) 157 (1997).
8. Traunmüller, R., Lenk K. (Eds.): First International Conference, EGOV 2002, Aix-en-Provence, France, September 2–5, 2002. Proceedings. LNCS 2456. Springer-Verlag, Berlin Heidelberg New York (2002).
9. Tõlge inglise keeled: Eesti Õigustõlke Keskus, Estonian Digital Signatures Act, (RT I 2000, 26, 150), Estonian Legal Translation Centre (2000).
   URL="http://www.riik.ee/riso/digiallkiri/digsignact.rtf".

E-Signatures for Delivery in E-Government

Peter Reichstädter

Federal Chancellery of the Austrian Republic
Staff Unit for ICT-Strategy
Ballhausplatz 2, A-1014 Wien
peter.reichstaedter@cio.gv.at

Abstract. Delivery of documents is an elementary process in public administrations. For e- Government, electronic delivery is a central process, complementary to the electronic input process of form data. In the following article, the Austrian model is introduced, the characteristics of which are openness, security and simplicity. Electronic delivery takes place in the form of a deposit and is accompanied by a notification. By using electronic signatures we can solve the problems of signing the deliverables, receiver authentication and confirmation of delivery.

1 Introduction and Basics

For public administration the delivery of documents is a central and resource - intensive interface with customers. For example, the Ministry of Finance and Ministry of Justice in Austria invest over 50 million Euros annually for postage (the costs for paper and for press are not included in this amount). Electronic delivery is therefore an essential component of a future oriented electronic administration. The model described in the following paper offers on the one hand service and comfort for customers (citizens), and on the other hand essential simplification, synergies, and savings potential for public administrations.

1.1 What Is Needed?

Qualitative identification and authentication of the receiver is required throughout the delivery process. These needs can be fulfilled by using electronic signatures. The signature law also forms a solid basis for e-Government [5], [16]. The law also offers the possibility to use the identification, which must be carried out in the framework of the registration process of the qualified certificates, in further administrative procedures, because the once evaluated and reconfirmed identity of a person during registration does not change.

Absolutely necessary for a successful delivery is the confirmation of the receipt of the document. Electronic signatures may also be used in this case. In the legal sense [4,1], documents are not delivered directly (e.g. e-mail), but will be put in an electronic storage facility (inbox) of the individual. In e-Government, the individual inbox is a server in the internet which informs the person of the deposit on suitable manner (e.g. e-Mail, SMS, ...).

R. Traunmüller (Ed.): EGOV 2003, LNCS 2739, pp. 260–265, 2003.

1.2 Demands on the Delivery Process

Focusing on data protection and security a few points should be kept in mind:
- Delivery through open networks (internet) generally has to take place encoded. Moreover documents should be transmitted to the delivery service already in a receiver-related encoded form.
- Documents to be delivered should be electronically signed on behalf of the issuing authority. With this additional security it will be possible to check the authentication of the document [13].
- In case electronic delivery is not possible, the delivery must either be initiated in paper form and/or feedback must be given to the authority.

2 Model of the Delivery Process Itself

The model is based upon the following principles: the public authority delivers the document at a suitable delivery service and after that neither the document nor the document's Meta information may be kept within the government applications. The following figure gives an overview of the necessary steps within the electronic delivery process:

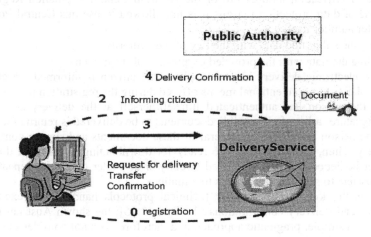

Fig. 1. Sample Model for Electronic delivery

The person registers himself/herself with the delivery service and enters the necessary data for identification and encryption ({0} in the figure above). This can happen at different delivery services; how the public authority chooses one electronic delivery service is described in the next section.

The public authority prepares the data for electronic delivery (could be judgements, notifications, simple letters, ... either in XML-format or also as .pdf documents, ...) and sends payload and identification-data to a module {1}, which is responsible for the further delivery process. Within this module the following steps are taken:

- Querying of 'responsible' delivery service for the citizen in a central LDAP scheme and returning which delivery service to choose, the Crypto-key of the citizen, possible absence times, ...; should more than one possible delivery service be returned, the public authority will choose the one with best cost-value ratio.

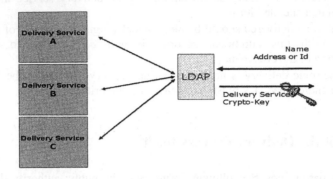

Fig. 2. Central Directory Service for getting necessary delivery service metadata

- Generating [8,9] the identification number of the delivery process further on based on the identification number out of the Austrian Central Population Register [6]; because of data protection reasons it is not allowed to use this Central Population Register number itself.
- Signing the submitted data with the key of the authority
- Encoding the data with the provided crypto-key of the citizen

When the electronic delivery has taken place, the citizen is informed via electronic (SMS, e-Mail, ..) or conventional means offered during the registration process ({2}).

After the person has authenticated himself/herself at the delivery service by a unique signature, a list of all possible documents to be delivered is returned to him/her ({3}). The person selects one or several of these documents and signs a confirmation of delivery. Then, the documents are ready for downloading. Confirmed documents can either be decoded and downloaded directly or at a later time (also repeatedly). It is also possible to send the documents to a mailbox.

There is the knowledge of other technical protocols handling the exchange of documents and delivery-confirmations [2,3,7,11,12,15]; the shown Austrian model is based upon a simple, pragmatic approach and therefore does not consider the delivery possibilities via third parties.

The signed delivery-confirmation ({4}) is finally transmitted to the public authority and included in the workflow of the application, which initiated the e-Delivery process.

The delivery confirmation contains only the metadata about the document being delivered electronically. For security reasons (against or for third parties), no indication of the document's contents is given in the delivery confirmation.

Data within the delivery confirmation can therefore be described as:

- Data concerning the sender: name and address of authority
- Data concerning the receiver: name and data for identification (address, calculated hash function out of the Central Population Register number [8,9], ...)

- Unique description of the document (e.g. file-number) or an artificial number (sequence, ...)
- Timestamp data for delivery at the delivery service and for acceptance of delivery by the user

In case of failures within the delivery process, the delivery service provides this information to the public authority and/or a conventional postal-delivery can begin.

The input of the keys for document encoding and signing is essential. Because according to Austrian law, individuals must explicitly agree to electronic delivery, the registration process may also include this approval.

The described model is premised upon the fact that neither the delivery service nor any other third party can view the document. This also offers the possibility to outsource the delivery service to business because businesses cannot gain access 'inside' the documents, but can perform the delivery.

3 Interfaces and Formats

The model contains three interfaces: public authority – delivery service, the notification and person – delivery service. As already mentioned, notification may be achieved through different techniques and is therefore not described in this paper.

3.1 Person – Delivery Service

In the frame of the Austrian e-Government model the person requires only the following tools: a capable computer and the possibility of creating an unique electronic signature.

- The communication must take place over web-interfaces.
- The signature takes place via the Security-Layer interface of the Austrian citizen cards concept [10].

3.2 Public Authority – Delivery Service

The interface between public authority and delivery service is carried out as an online service (that means XML and SOAP). The functions being performed on this interface are:

- Querying of a crypto-key for encoding of a certain individual
- Transmission (depositing) of a document for an individual
- Transmission of delivery confirmation
- Feedback transmission of a corresponding negative message of electronic delivery

3.3 Formats

The central document format in the Austrian e-Government strategy is XML. XML offers a wide application basis (also Open Source), is easy to structure, offers standards for using signatures and encoding and can be represented by use of Stylesheets. The XML is constructed as an onion structure. The external part of the generic XML structure is a container holding the data of the issuer and the receiver [14]. For each document type, like the reply, there are increasingly more specialized structures. This onion structure fosters a homogenous data structure, which leads to desirable synergy effects, like the use of generic application modules. Moreover, attention is focused on the fact that that these documents can serve as input data of other administration processes. A reconstruction of the electronic document (including-public authority signatures) out of a hard copy is also an important design criteria.

4 Future Aspects

The specification of the described Interfaces is already being performed; a prototype of the delivery service is being developed. Different companies have shown interest in developing and providing a delivery service and/or beginning implementation. Some legal external factors have to be discussed. The described model offers advantages for all participants: for the authority, there are synergy and savings, not only through the electronic delivery itself, but rather because the total delivery process can be separated from the application itself. e-Government procedures are now possible without changing the media and therefore the reply can again become input data for other processes; this produces a new dimension and new qualities for e-Government. Citizens benefit from simple and uncomplicated personal delivery without having to go to the post office. The operators of the delivery services benefit from the open draft which allows delivery to include other parts of the economy and market with large volume. Moreover, the delivery services can be used by the private economy for invoices and other documents. Whether the confirmation of delivery should be of the same quality as the conventional delivery confirmation at this point depends on the application itself.

References

1. Allgemeines Verwaltungsverfahrensgesetz 1991, BGBl.Nr. 51/1991, i.d.F. BGBl. I Nr. 137/2001
2. Asokan, N.: "Fairness in electronic commerce". Ph. D. thesis, University of Waterloo, 1998
3. Asokan, N., Shoup, V., Waidner, M.: "Asynchronous protocols for optimistic fair exchange", Research Report RZ 2976 (#93022), IBM Research, November 1997
4. Bundesgesetz vom 1. April 1982 über die Zustellung behördlicher Schriftstücke (Zustellgesetz) StF: BGBl. Nr. 200/1982, i.d.F. BGBl. I Nr. 65/2002
5. Bundesgesetz über elektronische Signaturen (Signaturgesetz – SigG), BGBl. I Nr. 190/1999, BGBl. I Nr. 137/2000, BGBl. I Nr. 32/2001.
6. Central Population Register (http://www.bmi.gv.at/zmr)
7. Gartner, F. C., Pagnia, H., Vogt, H.: "Approaching a formal definition of fairness in electronic commerce", in Proceedings of the International Workshop on Electronic Commerce (WELCOM'99), Lausanne, Switzerland, October 1999

8. Hollosi, A.: Sicherheit der Verfahrenskennung, November 2001.
9. Hollosi, A.: Algorithmus zur Berechnung der verfahrensspezifischen Personenkennzeichnung, Februar 2002.
10. Hollosi, A., Karlinger, G., Posch, R.: Security-Layer zur Bürgerkarte, November 2001.
11. Liu, P., Ning, P., Jajodia, S.: "Avoiding Loss of Fairness Owing to Process Crashes in Fair Data Exchange Protocols", Decision Support Systems, Vol. 31, No. 3, 2001, pages 337–350.
12. Pagnia, H., Gärtner, F.C.: "On the impossibility of fair exchange without a trusted third party", Technical Report, TUD-BS-1999-02, Darmstadt, Germany, 1999
13. Posch, R. et al: Weißbuch Bürgerkarte, Stand Mai 2002.
14. Reichstädter, P., Hollosi, A.: XML-Spezifikation der Personendaten-Struktur, Version 1.0.1, April 2002
15 Shmatikov, V., Mitchell, J.: "Analysis of abuse-free contract signing", in Financial Cryptography '00, Anguilla, 2000
16. Verordnung des Bundeskanzlers über elektronische Signaturen (Signaturverordnung – SigV), StF: BGBl. II Nr. 30/2000.

Security Aspects within E-Government

Sonja Hof

Institute of Applied Computer Science
Division: Business, Administration and Society
University of Linz
Austria
`sonja.hof@freesurf.ch`

Abstract. The aim of e-Government projects is bringing the appropriate services within an authority as close to the citizens as possible. Due to interdisciplinary cooperation the formerly ambitious project "e-Government" has become a fairly well introduced platform. This paper focuses on the security aspects and the different views within e-Government projects towards their relations. The first part presents an overview of the security fields and refines them into their different aspects, while trying to cover the whole range of security within a holistic view. Because of the complexity of security, as it contains diverse aspects that all have to be considered, the second part focuses on the single security area "data protection", which with its weaknesses and its strengths serves as an example. Data protection regards such diverse issues such as encryption, access rights as well as the corresponding security awareness of the employees handling the data. This also involves the corresponding backup and recovery strategies, as well as the data storage itself.

1 Introduction

Quite a few different research projects started to develop security based measures to prevent security incidents. The main part of such investigations focused on a special area within security [7][8][9][16]. Some of them also combine different aspects and tried to figure out feasible ways to put security into practise [11][12][15][3] focus on a generic security solution, an architecture that integrated already a wide range of general security means like auditing, encryption and protocols. On the other hand, detailed security solutions based on requirements engineering in combination with process reengineering are published [4]. The targeted strategy of this work is to transform e-governmental services into a secure process by introducing well defined rules that simplify the necessary IT security strategies inherent to the implemented processes. The aim is a wide and holistic view like in [1][2], in combination with organisational as well as technical approaches. The strategy of [5][6] is to restrict the scope by focusing on a well defined issue.

This paper tries to join the different security aspects as well as to incorporate their relations to each other. To outline the different areas in which security is important, it tries to divide them into logical branches and gives some proposals how security can be improved. However, it does not focus on one specific area and underlines the necessity of practising security as much as possible.

R. Traunmüller (Ed.): EGOV 2003, LNCS 2739, pp. 266–271, 2003.

All businesses require – to some degree – a secure environment to work according to their requirements. In some areas, they are quite detailed [13][14] and clear but the whole range of security issues isn't easily overlooked. From the security side, there are only few differences between an e-business transaction and an e-Government process. Depending on what the citizen/user wants to do, the process has to be better more or less secured. The different approaches concerning security are that wide and diverse, that the first question, which is typically discussed first, is the relevant security area(s) itself: Social security, like relevant privacy concerns in combination with the wide range of trust issues, or, on the other hand, technical security issues, legal issues or questions about person to person interactions. A classification of the different areas and sub-issues within its complex structure seams to be the feasible way to handle this complex area.

A classification of the different security assets, introduces a structure into the actual project that helps to make it manageable and eases the project's implementation audit. Different security assets have to be split into smaller security means and these results may have to be refined again recursively. This subdivision also enables the security engineer to find appearing security issues more easily and to hint into a direction for a solution. Additionally, it also offers a feasible way to approach the arising issues. To be able to analyse such processes, as well as to find out where the main areas are a structured matrix is helpful and can also enable people not trained in security issues to find weaknesses.

This paper proposes a structured customisable matrix for a stepwise refinement process to a process's security issues. This enables a structured analysis. The matrix is customisable and it is meant to be further developed and to be adapted to the circumstances of the handled project as well as to the handled assets. This "living" matrix is meant to support both non-technical or not security trained staff, as well as security trained technical staff, e.g. some system administrators, to build up an expandable list of security issues and to improve their processes by locating weaknesses and to transform their processes towards solutions with improved security. The matrix manages a major part of security relevant aspects and points out their minimal requirements.

2 The Security Matrix

The matrix's first level consists of 6 areas:
- Network security. It includes all concerns regarding the network on the actual hardware level as well as firewall configurations and low level hardware specific wire rules, e.g. routing.
- Functional security is a combination of development rules with some interdisciplinary regulations, e.g. versioning or controlling mechanisms.
- Data protection is probably the most sensitive area any security sensitive system has to cope with. This is especially valid for e-Government systems, as even loosing the users confidence in the system largely diminishes its acceptance, which may even turn the system completely obsolete. Additionally, data protection is also mandatory for most systems from a legal point of view due to several laws concerning privacy issues. These laws clearly state the necessity that, depending on its classification, data has to be protected with suitable measures [10].

- Organisational security concentrates on the non-technical issues that require support and regulations of the underlying organisation. As part of this area one has to define such issues as who is responsible for a given set of information, whose duty it is to check the audit logs created by the system, or who is responsible to define and recheck the necessary security policies.
- Social security is concerned about the social aspects of a system, e.g. the user's trust in its security or the "sensed" degree of privacy.
- The final area contains miscellaneous aspects that do not fit into one of the above security areas. This includes such diverse issues as insurance questions, physical security (access to buildings) or emergency scenarios as , e.g. loss of power.

2.1 Security Areas

Describing all six areas would be too much for the scope of this paper. Therefore, it mainly focuses on the field of network security and data protection. It explains the usage of the security matrix with the help of the network security area. Afterwards, the paper goes into some details in the area of data protection to further clarify the intentions behind the proposed security matrix.

Network Security			
	Internal	Pubic	..
		Internal	..
		Secret	..
		Top Secret	..
	External	Rent Wires	..
		Other Wires	..
		Virtual Networks	..
	Firewalls	Internal User	..
		External User	..

Fig. 1. Sample network security area within the security matrix

2.1.1 Network Security
The matrix's horizontal separation denote - starting on the left – more and more detailed security concerns and solutions (see Figure 1). The first column denotes the currently examined security area (in this case network security). The following column splits this area into a finer grained view on the different aspects of this security area. In this example, the second column divides the network security area into three sub-sections. They denote three different aspects of network security that can be handled separately. Of course, one could imagine other separations of the network security area that are – in some context - also "correct". The most suitable separation depends on the actually examined system as well as the goal of the executed security analysis. The splitting continues until one actually reaches such a fine grained view that one has readily available technologies and/or solutions. The number of refinement steps actually depends on the examined area and is not given by

a constant number. Figure 1 shows a possible refinement of the previous step, by showing an extract of the possible sub-sections. The example table also does not show that newly introduced sub-sections may – of course – occur multiple times, e.g. the data classification scheme shown in the section on internal networks may, depending on the actual set-up of the examined system, also show up in the section on external networks. The matrix itself does not define an order for the columns. Depending on the current situation it may either be suitable to first make the distinction on the type of external wire and to examine the type of transmitted data only afterwards, or to do it vice-versa.

Data Protection	Data Security	Data-Protection	Authorisation	
			Authentication	Password Token/ SC PKI
			Access Control	ACL
			Protection	
		Information Management	Encryption	AES IDEA
			Classification	
	Data Safety	Authorisation	Redundant Systems	RAID
		Data/ Information Exchange	Transaction	ACID Database System
			Backup/Archives	Backup Media and Procedure
		Internet Access : :	Disaster & Recovery Plan	
	Data Integrity		Protection/ Journals	Transaction Logs Tech. Logs
			Digital Signature	RSA Elliptic Curve
			Access Control	ACL
			Handling	Security Policy
			Data Exchange	Disconnection
			...	...

Fig. 2. Data protection area within the security matrix

2.1.2 Data Protection
If one has to take a closer look on the area of data protection (see Figure 2). In order to show this as a detailed example on how to read and deploy a security matrix. We start on the left-side of the table to the first row marked "data protection". In the adjacent column we see a distinction into three different aspects: security, safety and integrity. Each of these aspects covers – within the area of data protection – a completely different set of problems and requirements.

- Data security covers the wide range of "securing" your data/information against third parties. It makes sure that your data remains secret outside of its designated group of users, i.e. giving its members access to the clear-text data. Even if an outsider succeeds to steal some data files, data security still guarantees that the data is in a non-usable form.

- Data Safety: The necessity of choosing the right backup media and how to cover all ranges of a data recovery in combination with or without a possible disaster recovery.

- Data Integrity deals with the modification of data. It defines how the integrity of data is guaranteed and which requirements, e.g. encryption or digital signatures, are necessary to satisfy the system's requirements..

The next column (see Figure 2) merges the three sections shown in column two. This is actually an abbreviation for shortness' sake that denotes that the mentioned issues are valid for all of the three aspects, i.e. the merging is just part of the notation. The aspects are actually still separated because, dependent of the handled aspect, the solution to one and the same issue may be completely different. In the above example, this column handles the data protection issue depending on the actual action executed on it, i.e. is the data transmitted or is it stored on a permanent memory. E.g. if data is stored on a disk, data security may demand its encryption, while data safety may require a backup and data integrity may require a digital signature of the data to guarantee detection of unauthorized tampering.

The following column again divides the different aspects. It describes existing theoretical concepts that may be used to guarantee the necessary properties defined in the previous column. E.g. the "transaction" concept in a database system can be used both as a means for data safety as well as data integrity. Its actual technical implementation is described in the final column that describes actually existing technologies as, e.g., the database system deployed in the system's environment or a RAID system ensuring a higher percentage of successfully completed transactions.

Unfortunately, creating a security matrix that covers a complete project is non-trivial. The intention is to offer a set of predefined partitioning sets that serve as a pool of decision helpers. These sets can either be applied directly or can be slightly adapted to suit the current situation. As an example for such a predefined set, we can look at data classification.

Another possible aspects that may be used to further distinguish different requirements is, especially in the area of e-Government systems, the strict separation (seen from a system side) between different government agencies. Often, it has to be ensured that data does not travel from one agency to another. This is the case for read accesses (privacy) as well as for write accesses to the data. In the later case, it is also necessary to guarantee a tamper-proof audit trail that ensures a complete coverage on who changed what and when.

3 Conclusions

The advantage of the proposed matrix is the combination of a ordered step by step process towards security in combination with the flexibility introduced with predefined separations that serve as a guideline for further possible refinement steps.

Depending on the complexity of an aspect, one can refine the result further until a satisfying granularity is reached. At this point, it is often possible to come up with a proposition on how to solve the issue. Of course, due to its flexible nature, the result of such a refinement may lead to a result that does not offer a direct solution, but may require a combination of existing and possibly even new security methods. This again shows that the scheme of a security matrix not a static construct, but is rather part of a dynamic process that – in time – requires modifications. On the other hand, a well completed security matrix with a extensive set of predefined separation criteria is a substantial simplification for all security relevant structures and processes within every organization.

References

1. M.Wimmer, B.von Bredow; Ein ganzheitliches Sicherheitskonzept für den Bereich von eGovernment; in Enterprise Security; Hrsg. Partick Horster, IT Verlag; 2002
2. P.Kunz; IT Sicherheitsmanagement als Grundlage für erfolgreiches e-Business; in Elektronische Geschäftsprozesse; Hrsg. Partick Horster, IT Verlag; 2001
3. M.Hübner; Sicherheitsarchitekturen für elektronische Geschäftsprozesse; in Elektronische Geschäftsprozesse; Hrsg. Partick Horster, IT Verlag; 2001
4. M. Rohde; IT- Sicherheit als Motor im e-Government; in Elektronische Geschäftsprozesse; Hrsg. Partick Horster, IT Verlag; 2001
5. S.Wapper; Whyless.com Ein neues Sicherheitskonzept; in Enterprise Security; Hrsg. Partick Horster, IT Verlag; 2002
6. P. Wohlmacher; Digitale Signaturen und Sicherheitsinfrstrukturen; IT Verlag; 2001
7. K. Fuhrberger, Dirk Häger, Stefan Wolf; Internetsicherheit, Browser, Firewalls und Verschlüsselung, Hanser Verlag 2001, ISBN 3-446-21725-8
8. R. L. Scheier Firewalls still lack multivendor management, 2002, searchSecurity.com
9. C.Schulzki-Haddouti; Automatisch gesichert; Zentral Firmen-E-Mails verschlüsseln und Datenflüsse steuern c't 25/2003
10. A.Saarenpää et al; Data Security and Law; perspectives on the Legal Regulation of Data Security; www.urova.fi/home/oiffi/julkaisut/datasec.htm
11. Pharow Peter, Blobel Bernd, Wohlmacher Petra. 1998. Chipkarten als Sicherheitswerkzeug in einem regionalen klinischen Tumorregister. In Patrik Horster (Hrsg) Chipkarten – Grundlagen, Realisierungen, Sicherheitsaspekte, Anwendungen, pp45–58, Vieweg Verlag
12. P. Zängerle; Sicherheit ist konstruierbar; IT-Security-Spezial 1/2002
13. Remote Access VPN und IPSec; Höchste Datensicherheit; IT Security 1_02.2002
14. M.Mazzucca; Email Security; SC 8/2001 p24–30
15. M. Jak, DigiNotar, e-Government Business Case Study Dual Gate, proc. of ISSE 2002
16. R. Schild, Sichere Firmenzugänge über öffentliche Netze durch VPN und PKI- Technologien, in Sicherheit in Informationssystemen, in proc. SIS 2002, Hrsg. D. Karagiannis

Secure Online Internet Reservation of E-Government Service (ORGS) Using Java Card Applications Toolkit (J-CAT)

Shinyoung Lim[1] and Youjin Song[2]

[1]Electronics and Telecommunications Research Institute
Kajong-dong, Yousung-gu, Daejeon, 305-350, Korea
limsy@etri.re.kr
[2]Dongguk University
707 Seokjang-dong, Kyoungju, Kyoungbuk, 780-714, Korea
song@mail.dongguk.ac.kr

Abstract. e-Government service will be beneficial to citizen for its efficiency and security. From the citizen's point of view, although the e-Government service brings citizens online service, citizens need to visit at least one of the governmental offices for receiving specific service such as job interview, ID card issuing, or attending social events. These kinds of service often accompany with payments for the service charge. It means that the citizen has to do three things: request for reservation, payment for the service, and visit at least one of the governmental offices. In this paper, the Online Internet Reservation of e-Government Service(ORGS), one of the smart card based models for online Internet reservation accompanying with payment, is proposed for its efficiency and security of these kinds of service. Java card security functions are part of the building components of the Java Card Applications Toolkit(J-CAT). The J-CAT is designed to provide developers with security, easiness and efficiency in developing Java card applications. In this paper, the proposed ORGS implemented by the J-CAT provides users, developers, and managers with security, easiness, and efficiency.

1 Introduction

e-Government service provides citizens with diversified and immense governmental information service efficiently, but the citizen must visit one of the governmental offices for receiving specific service. For instances, job interview, ID card issuing, or attending social events are the simple examples of online Internet request of service that accompanies with paying for the service charge and visiting. In this service, the citizens need to reserve the time and place for the specific e-Government service with his or her payment. The technical approach for solving this kind of issue is proposing a common model for the online reservation and payment of e-Government service. In this paper, the Secure Online Internet Reservation of e-Government(ORGS) model is proposed for this purpose. The smart card system is recognized as one of the solutions of information security attacks as well as service implementation flexibility[3,5,6,10]. In this paper, the technical issues are discussed for applying citizen's use case of

R. Traunmüller (Ed.): EGOV 2003, LNCS 2739, pp. 272–277, 2003.

online reservation accompanying payment for the service charge and visiting one of the governmental offices. For these technical issues, secure Java card applications toolkit(J-CAT) is proposed. Specifically speaking, the issue of difficulty in development can be solved by applying defined APIs in the J-CAT. The recommended APIs is composed of two parts: on-card toolkit API and off-card toolkit API. With these APIs, software developers are able to develop their own Java card applications more easily than those of hard coded developments. And the issue of inefficiency in operation can also be solved by applying concept of the distributed application service provider(ASP) to the ORGS model.

2   Proposed Java Card Applications Toolkit (J-CAT)

The purposes of using Java chip that is on the Java card are the integrating different functions of smart cards into one smart card and the diverse applications on the single Java processor[2,4]. Due to these purposes, the effect of platform independence of Java card provides flexibility and scalability when upgrade and change of the user computing environments[8,10,11]. Smart card applications can be programmed with a variety of computer programming languages depending on the areas of applications service such as an ATM system that recognizes and chooses an appropriate program for the cardholder[1,5,6,7,12].

2.1   Architecture of J-CAT

The proposed architecture of Java card applications library and its service system is shown in figure 1. It is a web-based secure smart card application system based on public cryptographic key infrastructure(PKI) and its digital signature. As shown in the figure 1, this architecture provides Java card application developers with fast and easy way of developing the variety of Java card applets as well as integrating Java card applications on to service systems using Java APIs[13].

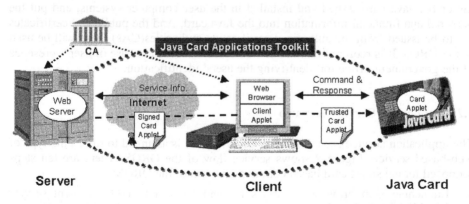

Fig. 1. The Conceptual diagram of Java Card Applications

2.2 Java Card Applications Programming Interfaces (APIs) in J-CAT

The recommended APIs is composed of two parts: on-card toolkit API and off-card toolkit API. The on-card API of Java card API provides upper level API for developing Java card application applets. The off-card API of Java card API provides APIs for developing Java card terminal applications and backend applications for user interface those are implemented on user computer systems. Each API is provided in the form of Java package and its classes[14,15]. The Cardlet class is a subclass of *javacard.framework.Applet* providing various methods for basic framework of Java card applet. CardletLoader class is a core module of Java card APIs performing the download of digitally signed Cardlet package from Internet, verifying digital signature, uploading it on the Java card, and implementing it.

3 Proposed Online Internet Reservation of E-Government Service (ORGS) Model

In this chapter, the proposed ORGS model is presented. The ORGS model presents smart card based common platform for online Internet reservation of e-Government service. Joining paid social events and receiving tailor-made health care service are good examples of fulfilling three continuous tasks: reservation, payment, and visit. The ORGS model, one of the common models for online reservation service, is proposed for solving these kinds of service issues. The contents of this chapter are prerequisites for the ORGS and service scenario of the ORGS.

3.1 Prerequisites for the ORGS Model

There are some prerequisites for applying the ORGS model. The handling processes of Java card applications service are implemented in all the service providing systems of the ORGS model. The card reader and Java card applet loading program must be installed on every system in the ORGS model. The user of the ORGS needs to have his or her Java card issued and installed in the user computer systems, and put the personal and financial information into the Java card. And the public key certificates are to be issued from the authorized certification authorities(CAs) those will be used in the ORGS. It is required that the new Java card is issued in case of user's presence of the government office for identifying the users' identification.

3.2 Application Service Scenario

The application service scenario of the ORGS model is assumed to run as the type of web-based service. Figure 2 shows service flow of the ORGS. There are ten steps proposed for the smart card based common platform of the ORGS:

— Launching web browser on user's PC and connect to e-Government service provider's web site;

— Submitting user registration form to the provider and download e-Government client runtime module on user's PC;
— Downloading CA's and other service systems' public key certificates, and install them on user's PC;
— Inserting user's Java Card into card reader connected to PC;
— e-Government card applet is downloaded from service provider's server and its digital signature is verified;
— If the signature is valid, e-Government card applet is uploaded and installed into the card, if invalid, display warning messages;
— Put user's service request information(name, social security number) into the card;
— Connect to reservation service provider of e-Government's web site and choose one or more service, and download reservation information into the card;
— Resource availability check is processed in Reservation Service Provider of e-Government and Resource Manager, and all service request information transferred between user's PC and resource manager is encrypted and digitally signed;
— After verifying the identification of the requester, the user gets confirm message of his/her request of service reservation from the Resource Manager. At the e-Government Service Organizations, sub systems of Resource Manager, the user gets his or her reserved service of e-Government by inserting his or her card into the card reader in front of the organizations.

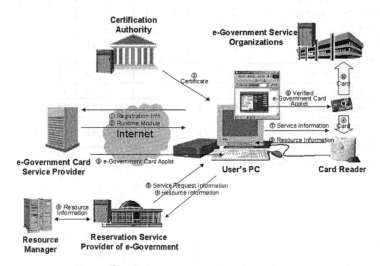

Fig. 2. Service flow of the ORGS

And the payment for the service charge will be billed to the user's bank account or credit card after the use of the service. Whether the service is off-line or on-line, the user is able to get timely reserved service at the e-Government service organizations. The development and running environments of the ORGS are as follows: computer operating system is Microsoft Windows NT(2000); Pentium III CPU; the Java platforms of JDK 1.2.2. and Java Card 2.1; and the Java card and its terminal environments are the versions of GemXpresso 211 and Gemplus GCR410.

4 Analysis

In this chapter, the analysis of the proposed ORGS application with its efficiency and security is discussed.

4.1 Efficiency

Applying the APIs of the J-CAT to the ORGS model solves the issue of the difficulty in development of the ORGS application. With this APIs, the Java card applications program developers are able to decrease from 50% to 70% of size of the non-API, namely hard coded, source code. In case of inefficiency in operation of e-Government service can be solved by applying the concept of ASP in the ORGS. The e-Government Service Organizations are able to serve their service to the citizens when the Reservation Service Provider of e-Government sends the request message after verifying the availability of service resource of their organizations by way of the Resource Manager that manages the available resources of the registered e-Government Service Organizations.

Table 1. Security relationships of the ORGS model

Security functions \ Steps in Scenario	1	2	3	4	5	6	7	8	9	10
Long term Key Generations	-	O	-	-	-	-	O	-	-	-
Encryption	-	O	-	-	-	-	O	O	O	O
Digital Signature	-	O	-	-	-	-	O	O	O	O
Authentications	-	O	O	-	O	O	O	O	O	O
Secure Message Transmission	-	O	O	-	O	-	O	O	O	O

Legends: O: Applied, -: Not applied

4.2 Security

As the PKI is one of the prerequisites of the J-CAT, the ORGS users are required to request and install their own private and public keys before using the ORGS. Therefore, e-Government Card Service Provider and the authorized certification authority are also serving the security of e-Government clients, citizens, by the J-CAT security functions. There are two major areas applying security service to the applications made by the J-CAT: Between Java card and card reader; and between Java cad client system and Java card ASPs. The table 1 depicts relationships of security functions applied such as long term key generation, encryption, digital signature, user and message authentications, and secure message transmission in the ORGS model.

5 Conclusions

In this paper, the secure J-CAT based ORGS is proposed for solving online Internet reservation accompanying with payment and on-line/off-line visit of e-Government service. The issues of e-Government service are discussed and the technical solutions for these issues are presented. Although the secure J-CAT is developed and evaluated, more research is still going on for the remaining part of the issues related to the J-CAT. And there will be more research on queue management of reservation requests between the Reservation Service Provider and the Resource Manager in ORGS model because the relevant algorithms are required for the behavior of request calls which are characterized as unexpected and random. For the further studies in this field include developing applications of the ORGS and performance test with the large-scaled service transactions. The smart card based common platform of the ORGS is regarded as current solution to be used in many kinds of online reservation of e-Government service because it provides real world technical methodologies for the development, operation, and security issues of e-Government service.

References

[1]   Zhiqun Chen, "JavaCard Technology for Smart Cards", Addison-Wesley, 2000.
[2]   Dongjin Choi, "Multi Smart Card using Java Chip", Korea Patent-1999-038700, 1999.
[3]   Jorge Ferrari, et. al, "Smart Cards: A Case Study", IBM, 2000.
[4]   Michel Frenkiel, Paul Grison, and Philippe Laluyaux, "Clip Card: Smart Card Based Traffic Tickets", pp. 313-319, EGOV 2002, LNCS 2456, 2002.
[5]   Joseph C. Kawan, et.al, "Method and System for Using an Application Programmable Smart Card for Financial Transactions in Multiple Countries" US Patent-5844218, 1998.
[6]   Yong Kim, et. al, "Study on the multiple authentication method for smart card based online electronic payment service", Vol. 16, No. 2, pp. 76–88, Journal of Information & Communications Research, 2002.
[7]   Korean Information Security Agency(KISA), "A Guide on Smart Card Products Security Evaluation Criteria", 2000.
[8]   Philip S. Lee, "System for Securely Exchanging Data with Smart Cards", US Patent-5923759, 1999.
[9]   Gary McGraw, Edward W. Falten, "Securing Java", Wiley Computer Publishing, 1999.
[10] Thomas Menzel and Peter Reichstädter, "The Role of Citizen Cards in e-Government", pp. 446–456, EGOV 2002, LNCS 2456, 2002.
[11] Reinhard Riedl and Nico Maibaum, "FASME. From Smartcards to Holistic IT-Architectures for Interstate e-Government", pp. 173–179, EGOV 2002, LNCS 2456, 2002.
[12] http://www.smartcardbasics.com/overview.html, "Smart Cards and Security Overview".
[13] http://www.smartcardcentral.com/technical, "Smart Card Technical Information".
[14] SUN Microsystems, "JavaCard 2.1 Specification", 1999.
[15] SUN Microsystems, "JavaCard Developer's Guide", 1999.

Co-operative Software Development for Secure Online Services – Experiences and Results within the MEDIA@Komm-Project of Nuremberg

Uwe Schmalfeld

Curiavant Internet GmbH
Nuremberg
Uwe.schmalfeld@curiavant.de

Abstract: With their joint concept for a digital town hall the cities Nuremberg, Furth, Erlangen, Schwabach and Bayreuth were among the prizewinners in the national competition MEDIA@Komm. The five municipalities are in the process of creating an innovative and networked administration. In addition to more service, better availability and a higher transparency of administrative transactions for citizens and business companies, the municipalities implement many improvements within their administration. Curiavant Internet GmbH was founded as a project company. It develops e-government solutions for the region and implements them together with partners. The technical basis consists of the e-government infrastructure CuriaWORLD™.

1 The MEDIA@Komm-Project of Nuremberg – Background

The MEDIA@Komm- Project of Nuremberg municipal association involves the cities of Nuremberg, Furth, Erlangen, Schwabach, Bayreuth. It has been set up for participation in the municipal competition MEDIA@Komm. The challenge is to develop a range of software modules to support online services in all five municipalities. These online services include public-private partnership projects to address information and service needs of citizens, other public service organisations and the private sector. The product is being delivered by a company wholly owned by the participating municipalities, including staff seconded from the municipalities for the duration of the project.

The goal of the project "MEDIA@Komm in the Nuremberg region", is to offer legally binding multimedia services with digital signatures in a municipal association. A regional communication platform is to be created, which will support secure communications and offer citizens various communal and private services. The Nuremberg municipal association consists of five municipalities of different size in the region, namely Nuremberg, Erlangen, Bayreuth, Furth and Schwabach. The special challenge here is to develop online services and products which are equally fitting for all municipalities.

On the basis of past experience and the difficulties in transferring pilot projects for the individual municipalities, it was decided to develop a series of software modules (eg for signature, payment etc) that can then be used for the implementation of the respective individual online services.

R. Traunmüller (Ed.): EGOV 2003, LNCS 2739, pp. 278–281, 2003.

2 The Target Groups of the Nuremberg Project Are Various

1. Local communities, as providers of public services for citizens and private business companies
2. Local communities, as users of the electronic signature in internal business processes
3. Citizens, as user of public services
4. Citizens, as user of the services of private companies (e-commerce)
5. Private companies and chambers of trade, as users of public services
6. Private companies and chambers of trade, as providers of their own services and users of digital signatures.

3 In Nuremberg, There Are Three Pillars within the Project, but They Are Addressed Differently

1. Infrastructure projects include the e-government platform, security concept, electronic signatures, payment function, document management, user interface, and proposals for standards for administrative procedures (geographical information systems). They provide important services for all communal and public-private-partnership-projects.
2. Communal projects are the essential municipal services made available to customers via the Internet: education services, parking permits for residents, electronic support for the council, electronic house construction file, geographical information, residential register (entries, changes and deletions), information from the residential register, information from the trade supervision register, business registration, changes and closure, vanity vehicle numbers, online libraries, invitations for tender, award of public contracts and public participation in communal construction planning processes.
3. Public-private-partnership-projects include applications for the medical intranet, online judicial practice, company identity cards and secure webshops. Work is also being carried out to facilitate access to the Internet not only via a PC but also via digital TV and mobile appliances (cellular phones, hand-held devices, etc).

4 Leadership Momentum

The development and technical implementation of specific online application for citizens and businesses in all five municipalities is being undertaken in collaboration with a single project sponsor, Curiavant Internet GmbH. A wholly-owned subsidiary of the participating municipalities, Curiavant is responsible for the overall project management, including the technical implementation of all sub-projects. The committee of shareholders, in which all five municipalities are represented by heads of department, is responsible for project control and questions of finance. Local community core teams formulate the various content and technical requirements of the municipalities and pass them on to the Curiavant project managers.

Strategic and financial decisions concerning the MEDIA@Komm project are made by the committee of shareholders. On questions of content, the committee takes advice from the project management. By appointing a project office with responsibility for financial control, quality management, communication and marketing and creating municipal core teams to link Curiavant more closely to the municipalities, it is hoped that communication will be assured.

A measure to improve internal and external communication is the creation of a MEDIA@Komm domain for the region that will contain internal information in a protected area and information for external project partners and anyone else who is interested. For the staff and project partners, this will help to ensure that every person involved in the project can obtain information about the goals, activities and the current progress of the project. (www.digital-ins-rathaus.de)

The creation of e-government offices and centres in the individual municipalities is a first step towards creating a general plan of activities for the implementation of the e-government goals. Information on the necessary infrastructure, planning and deployment of personnel, financial resources required, definitions of projects and milestones etc is already collected in many sub-projects, but a co-ordinated strategy will only be possible when it has been combined in an e-government office. These offices or centres have a "high" organisational status. In Erlangen, the centre is a co-ordinating department assigned to the lord mayor, in Nuremberg the office is assigned to the head of department for personnel and administration.

5 Management Skill Set

The MEDIA@Komm project is concerned with research, testing and development of the use of electronic signatures, multimedia and the Internet in local communities, so a failure of individual projects is fundamentally possible. The restructuring of individual projects in the municipal association for technical reasons or due to generally unsatisfactory conditions (diffusion, legal framework, acceptance by the citizens) has shown that this project does not just involve designing applications and developing a technical platform to run them.

Experience must be gained in devising implementation strategies and measures to increase acceptance, and steps must be taken to ensure that this experience can be transferred to other local communities.

In the initial phase of the project, there were deficiencies in project management. Up to the end of 2001, for example, the communication between the municipalities and the project organisers was not organised successfully enough to enable them to develop coherent goals for the activities and time schedules in subprojects. This conflict was overcome by a change of management and by the creation of committee to ensure and organise the exchange of information.

The co-operation with private partners is time-consuming and it has not always led to marketable result. The subject of the digital signature is relatively new and is influenced by many factors, including the decision-making processes within companies. Some companies are still in the process of finding out about the use and possibilities of digital signatures and do not (yet) want to commit themselves. Cupertino with business companies has so far been characterised by a large number of contacts and discussions with regional and local businesses, but these have not always been carried through to specific projects.

6 Infrastructure

The entire MEDIA@Komm project is subsidised by the national government up to 2003. The Nuremberg municipal association is currently considering how the operation of the newly-developed online services can be continued after the subsidies end and who will be responsible for the organisational and technical supervision. The deliberations are tending towards a solution in which the largest municipality in the association, Nuremberg, would operate the technical platform and handle the online services that are offered. The existing expertise and equipment will continue to be used in any case and, if possible, it will be extended further. A number of municipal employees currently work for Curiavant; they were delegated there for the duration of the project and have a right to return to the administration. Participation in the MEDIA@Komm project is also regarded as a qualification in the area of e-government and it thus offers good prospects of subsequent, continued employment in the individual municipalities.

Personnel continuity is important for the municipalities in the continuation of their sub-projects. The municipalities appreciate established teams and familiarity with specific local problems and situations. The development of a platform to handle online services between the administration, citizens and businesses can be regarded as a key technology in Nuremberg municipal association. The platform has been developed with a partner (the company 100world) as a modular system. It forms the basis for all online applications in the virtual town halls of the five participating municipalities. It is the foundation on which numerous administrative processes can be handled electronically, irrespective of the heterogeneous systems that already exist in the administrations.

In the final stage of development, the individual modules are to have the following functions: user of electronic signatures (processing of incoming and outgoing signatures), integration of payment transactions and booking of payments, administration of user data and authorisations, form administration, integration of the back-end systems by linking work flows and document management systems.

The development of the platform CuriaWORLD™, the knowledge of local community requirements and the implementation of solutions in the municipal associations are regarded as good qualifications to survive as a service provider in the market place after subsidies end. There are other innovative developments, especially in the area of alternative methods of access. For example, projects are in progress which explore alternatives to the PC as the access medium to the virtual town hall (eg access via TV, mobile phones, signatures with PDAs and access to government via voice communication).

Privacy Enhancing Technologies: A Review

John Argyrakis, Stefanos Gritzalis and Chris Kioulafas

Department of Information and Communications Systems Engineering
University of the Aegean, Samos, GR 832 00, GREECE
{cs98004,cs98020}@icsd.aegean.gr
sgritz@aegean.gr

Abstract. The spread and development of e-Government services caused significant interest in maintaining security, trust and privacy. This paper presents a state-of-the-art review of the widely accepted Privacy Enhancing Technologies (PETs). A strict classification of several parameters is performed in order to conduct a comparative analysis among *Anonymizer, Crowds, Onion Routing, TRUSTe, P3P, LPWA, Hordes* and *Freedom*. The selection of the comparison criteria is relevant to Security Threats, Technological Issues and User Demands.

1 Introduction

E-Government focuses on relatively simple transactions between identifiable customers and a multitude of government organisations in charge of Web activities. The nature of these Web-transactions endangers anonymity [2]. Moreover, certain malicious tactics may be used to decline privacy over e-Government services [1], [5], [8]. These technologies focus not only on achieving trust and security among users and Web sites, but they also apply to e-Government transactions, such as voting procedures.

The current section presents relations between PETs and e-Government needs and provides a description of several PETs. A comparative analysis is presented in the second section. The final section refers to concluding remarks about PETs.

2 Privacy Enhancing Technologies Description

Although there are several PETs, we choose to describe only the most important for e-Government users. *Anonymizer* is a proxy-based service that submits HTTP requests to Web sites on behalf of its users [1]. *Crowds* is an agent based on the idea that people can be anonymous when they blend into a crowd [3]. *Onion Routing* provides anonymous connections using different layers of encryption [2], [5]. *TRUSTe* is a non-profit, privacy seal program for web sites [4], [5]. *P3P* is a framework for informed online interactions [7]. *LPWA* is a software system designed to allow users browse the Web using aliases and other LPWA features [5]. *Hordes* employs multiple proxies to anonymously route a packet towards the responder and uses multicast for replying to the initiator [2]. *Freedom* intends to protect the privacy of users sending e-mail, browsing the web, posting to newsgroups and participating in Internet chat [6].

R. Traunmüller (Ed.): EGOV 2003, LNCS 2739, pp. 282–287, 2003.

3 Privacy Enhancing Technologies Comparison

3.1 Confronted Security Threats

3.1.1 Trace Back Attack

An attacker may start from a known responder and trace the path back to the initiator along the forward path or the reverse path [2]. *Anonymizer* and *LPWA* do not protect from this attack since there is no data processing. Although *Crowds* protects the forward paths, several jondos could be exploited to obtain routing information. *Onion Routing* protects forward paths with different layers of symmetric cryptography, but *Crowds* drawback applies in the reverse path. *Crowds* and *Onion Routing's* static paths decrease protection. *TRUSTe* and *P3P* do not protect from these attacks. *Crowds'* unicast techniques are also applied to *Hordes* although the connections are not static. *Hordes'* IP multicast protects the reverse path. *Freedom's* asymmetric cryptography and dynamic paths protects only forward paths [6].

3.1.2 Malicious Collaborators

A group of collaborators are malicious if they try to discover the identity of the initiator [2]. *Anonymizer, TRUSTe, P3P, LPWA* and *Freedom* architecture is based on a single proxy. The criterion is not applicable since legitimate actions could be carried out against it. *Crowds'* and *Onion Routing's* users may choose the jondos at the establishment of the protocol and the random creation of the path increases the provided protection. *Onion Routing* uses different layers or encryption. The use of IP multicast through the backward routing protects *Hordes'* users from malicious collaborators.

3.1.3 Eavesdroppers

Attackers are able to monitor all communications of one participant in order to find either the initiator or the receiver. Connections among users, *Anonymizer* and *LPWA* could be easily compromised. *Crowds* protects against eavesdroppers due encryption of emitted data. The strong cryptography used by *Onion Routing* protects from eavesdroppers. *TRUSTe* and *P3P* focus on presenting and negotiating security policies among different Web sites. *Hordes'* packets are encrypted and its members use shared multicast groups so that they receive and discard unnecessary traffic. *Freedom* uses a symmetric encryption algorithm that prevents eavesdropping attacks.

3.1.4 Message Attacks

A global observer is able to associate a communication relation and trace messages, if their coding is not changed during transmission. *Anonymizer* and *LPWA* do not protect from these attacks, although data could not be correlated with their initiator. *Crowds* protects from message attacks triggered outside the crowd. *Onion's Routing* different layers of encryption protects against these attacks. *TRUSTe* and *P3P* are not focused on protecting from these attacks. *Hordes* uses pair-wise keys between two jondos and multiple routing to prevent deciphering of data. *Freedom's* asymmetric cryptography (Key Query Server) prevents data decryption [6].

3.1.5   Timing Attacks
Packets that are transmitted periodically could be analyzed due to timing correlations. Any host outside a secure group is vulnerable to timing attacks. *Crowds, Onion Routing, Hordes* and *Freedom* are able to prevent timing attacks against internal proxies.

3.1.6   Flooding Attacks
If a router supports n users an attacker may send n-1 packets to trace the original one back to its source. User's authentication counter attacks flooding. Thus, *Crowds, Onion Routing Hordes* and *Freedom* provide means of authentication.

3.1.7   Connection Periods Attacks
Most users establish a limited number of connections and have a fixed type of Web behavior. These activities could be analyzed and dramatically decrease the size of anonymous users in a specific group of *Crowds, Onion Routing,* and *Hordes.*

3.1.8   Cookies
They threat users' privacy since personal data may be processed by various Web entities. *Anonymizer* does not allow the use of Cookies. *Crowds, Onion Routing, Hordes, and Freedom* do not protect against this threat [6]. *TRUSTe* may take measures against untrustworthy partners in case the mentioned policies have been compromised. *P3P* is more flexible than *TRUSTe* since it can also modify policies that refer to Cookies [7]. The pseudonyms that are provided by *LPWA* replace Cookies.

3.1.9   Personalized Services
There is always the threat of revealing personal information during registration procedure. *Anonymizer* could not exchange any real credentials of the user with those services and no registration could be submitted. *Crowds, Hordes* and *Onion Routing* do not use any pseudonyms and personal data could not be concealed. *TRUSTe* uses trust marks to ensure the proper management of personal information. *P3P* users have the right to know and negotiate the policies followed by a Web site and then entrust personal data. *LPWA* proxy supports the creation and storage of different pseudonyms for each Web site. *Freedom's* multiple nyms ensures the secure use of these services [6].

3.2   Applied Technological Issues

3.2.1   Reliability
This criterion refers to the trustworthiness of PET entities. *Anonymizer, TRUSTe, P3P, LPWA, and Freedom* authorized proxies are trusted, since in case of a deliberate information disclosure the users know whom to blame. *Crowds'* users have to trust several participants by revealing their true identity. *Onion Routing* is reliable due to multi-layer cryptography and the capability to select the connection path. The use of pair-wise cryptography keys protects personal data against any member of the horde or other entities. Moreover, the increase of *Hordes* members protects users' anonymity, as it is more difficult to compromise their identities.

3.2.2 Installation Complexity

PETs' installation procedure is an important issue. *Anonymizer, TRUSTe* and *P3P* are Web services so there is no installation need. *Crowds'* and *Hordes'* installation demands source code's download and compilation. Although *Onion Routing's* next version has not been available yet, the previous one requires a lot of effort to be installed [2]. *LPWA* requires the submission of users' personal information and some changes in browser's settings. *Freedom* provides help through installation procedure.

3.2.3 Performance

The performance of PETs is judged by the link utilization of each connection. *Anonymizer's* and *LPWA's* communication line is separated into two connections and this causes no-detectable latencies. *Crowds'* and *Onion Routing's* communication path is separated into several TCP connections among different jondos so the performance is not optimized. *TRUSTe* and *P3P* provide the best performance since they do not interfere with TCP connections or add any traffic to existing links. *Hordes* uses UDP packets to transfer data between jondos and therefore re-transmission of packets is prevented. *Freedom* performance depends on the use of asymmetric cryptography and the continuous queries for the public keys and nyms [6].

3.2.4 Overhead Latencies

The protection of privacy may cause overhead latencies to browser Web activities. *Anonymizer, TRUSTe, P3P, LPWA,* and *Freedom* demand no further actions during Web browsing since the relevant proxies perform all necessary actions. *Hordes'* members do not perform any complex activity during the backward routing procedure and the initiator has no capability to choose the path. *Crowds* is better than *Onion Routing* as it does not support complex cryptography techniques [2].

3.3 Satisfied Users Demands

3.3.1 Anonymity

Anonymity can be applied to separate aspects such as data anonymity, connection anonymity, and personalization [1], [2]. *Anonymizer* provides poor connection anonymity since there is only one proxy. It also provides average data anonymity as each exchanged Web page is secured by hiding the users requests. Finally, it does not provide any kind of personalization. *Crowds, Onion Routing* and *Hordes* provide high-level connection anonymity because of jondos. Although *Crowds* and *Hordes* achieve medium level of data anonymity, *Onion Routing* provides a higher level because it uses stronger cryptography techniques. However, none of these systems supports personalization. *P3P* and *TRUSTe* do not provide any kind of connection anonymity. They support data anonymity and personalization, though the degree of success depends on the users' decisions. *LPWA's* connection anonymity is low since there is only one HTTP proxy. It achieves average data anonymity as well as high personalization due to pseudonyms. *Freedom* supports connection anonymity due to asymmetric cryptography. It also achieves data anonymity and personalization because of pseudonyms and cryptography.

3.3.2 Low Cost

Nowadays Web users insist on buying tools of low cost and average quality. Most of PETs, except Anonymizer and *Freedom*, are freely provided through Internet. There is also a development cost concerning application based on *Crowds*, *P3P* and *Hordes*.

3.3.3 Usability

Easy to use applications are preferred. *Anonymizer* and *LPWA* are very usable, as only a few fields should be completed with usual or special characters. *Crowds* and *Onion Routing* are demanding protocols due to selection of companions and multi-layer cryptography. *TRUSTe* is the most convenient PET because the user should only read a comprehensible document. *P3P* provides average usability since the user should be familiar with privacy policies to make the appropriate decisions. *Hordes'* forward routing and the cryptographic techniques being used specify its usability. *Freedom* provides average usability since the user has to create an asymmetric pair of keys.

3.3.4 Services

The majority of the examined tools or protocols do not directly support Internet services. On the other hand *LPWA* and *Freedom* use anti-spamming e-mail filters.

3.4 Comparison Results

The following comparison table summarizes the deductions from the above sub-sections according to three categories of comparison criteria.

Table 1. Comparative Analysis of PETs (High, Medium, Low, x ≡ Not applied)

Criteria / Technologies	Trace back attack (active)	Trace back attack (passive)	Malicious Collaborators	Eavesdroppers	Message Attacks	Timing Attacks	Flooding Attacks	Connection Period Attacks	Cookies	Personalized Service	Reliability	Installation Complexity	Performance	Overhead Latencies	Connection Anonymity	Data Anonymity	Personalization	Low Cost	Usability	Services
	Confronted Security Threats								Applied Techn. Issues						Satisfied User Demands					
Anonymizer	–	–	x	–	–	–	–	–	–	–	H	L	H	L	L	M	x	L	H	L
Crowds	+	–	+	+	+	–	–	–	–	–	L	H	L	H	H	M	x	M	L	L
Onion Routing	+	–	+	+	+	–	–	–	–	–	L	H	L	H	H	H	x	H	L	M
TRUSTe	x	x	x	–	–	–	–	–	+	+	H	L	H	L	x	x	x	H	H	L
P3P	x	x	x	–	–	–	–	–	+	+	H	L	H	L	x	x	x	M	M	L
LPWA	–	–	x	–	–	–	–	–	+	+	H	M	H	L	L	M	H	H	M	H
Hordes	+	–	+	+	+	–	–	–	–	–	M	H	M	H	H	M	x	M	L	L
Freedom	–	+	x	+	+	–	–	–	+	+	H	M	M	L	H	H	H	L	M	H

4 Conclusions

The weakest and strongest points of each system differ since their design is not focused on identical parameters. Indeed, technologies that are based on single HTTP proxies such as *Anonymizer*, and *LPWA* could be easily used to achieve anonymous browsing while *Crowds*, *Onion Routing* and *Hordes* succeeds in data protection and attackers' confrontation. On the other hand, *TRUSTe* and *P3P* have great performance and guarantee the presentation and negotiation of security policies provided from e-Government services. Although *Freedom* provides average protection from security threats its high cost downsides these advantages. Moreover, *Onion Routing* could be used as a basis over which other protocols would be established in order to achieve higher level of protection. Furthermore, *TRUSTe* and *P3P* negotiation techniques may be used as a trusted third party so as to ensure that e-Government sites do not violate legitimate security policies or diffuse privacy data.

References

1. Carlos A. Osorio: A new framework for the analysis of solutions for privacy – enhanced Internet commerce. eJeta-PRIVACY (2001)
2. Brain Neil Levine, Clay Shields: A Protocol for Anonymous Communication Over the Internet. Conference on Computer and Communications Security, Proceedings of the 7th ACM conference on Computer and communications security Athens, Greece (2000)
3. Reiter M., Rubin A., *"Crowds*: Anonymity for Web transactions", in *ACM Transactions on Information and System Security*, Vol. 1, (1998)
4. McCullagh A., "The establishment of trust in the electronic commerce environment", in the *Proc. of the Information Industry Outlook Conference*, Australia, (1998)
5. Goldberg I, Wagner D. Brewer E., "Privacy-enhancing technologies for the Internet", in *Proc. of IEEE COMPCON '97 Conference*, (1997)
6. Philippe Boucher, Adam Shostack, Ian Goldberg: *Freedom* System 2.0 Architecture. Zero-Knowledge Systems, Inc. (2000)
7. *The Platform for Privacy Preferences 1.0 Spec*, W3C Candidate Recommendation 15, (2000)
8. Cranor L., "Internet privacy", in *Com. of the ACM*, Vol. 42, No. 2, pg. 29-66, (1999)

Semantic Web for E-Government

Ralf Klischewski

Hamburg University
Informatics Department
Vogt-Kölln-Strasse 30
D-22527 Hamburg
klischewski@informatik.uni-hamburg.de

Abstract. As the e-government domain is about to become a field of application for Semantic Web technologies, the actors involved still lack reasoning to decide on critical issues such as organisational cost/benefit, „user" involvement, technical integration, and implementation strategy. Firstly, the paper seeks to identify "semantic problems" in e-government as prerequisite for discussing the requirements for the application of Semantic Web technologies. Secondly, experiences from an ongoing project are discussed to identify critical issues from the systems development perspective. Thirdly, taking into account the problems identified and the case findings, a research agenda is laid out aiming to guide and support the application of Semantic Web technologies in e-government.

1 Introduction

The World Wide Web Consortium (W3C) defines the Semantic Web as "the representation of data on the World Wide Web" (www.w3.org/2001/sw). The vision of the next-generation internet (a "Web for machines"), posted by Tim Berners-Lee and others (e.g. Berners-Lee et al. 2001), has inspired many to work on technologies and standards such as RDF (Resource Description Framework), DAML+OIL (a semantic markup language for Web resources), OWL (Ontology Web Language) etc. (see www.w3.org for details). The promises of Semantic Web technologies are manifold. Most of the envisioned applications are based on anticipated advances in knowledge representation, intelligent retrieval (interference) and facilitation of communication (or a combination of those), mostly based on the use of ontologies (formally specified shared conceptualisations; Gruninger & Lee 2002).

Meanwhile Semantic Web technologies and related development environments, although far from being stabilised, have matured far enough to provide a basis for application system development (e.g. ERCIM 2002). However, developing applications for certain domains on the basis of Semantic Web technologies is still at the beginning, and for the development of semantic-based systems many questions concerning technical and organisational issues still need to be resolved, and answers may differ significantly depending on the domain and the kind of applications.

This paper intends to look for some preliminary answers in the domain of e-government. This application domain is unique because of its enormous challenge to achieve interoperability given the manifold semantic differences of interpretation of e.g. law, regulations, citizen services, administrative processes, best-practices, and,

R. Traunmüller (Ed.): EGOV 2003, LNCS 2739, pp. 288–295, 2003.

not the least, many different languages to be respected within and across regions, nations and continents. These semantic differences are related to a great variety of IT solutions (on local, regional, inter-/national level) which will have to be networked (despite any effort of standardisation).

However, the term e-government is used here in a rather technical sense: the integration and application of internet technologies to the area of public administrations. In section 1, the paper starts out from the literature to identify "semantic problems" in e-government from the application point of view as prerequisite for discussing the requirements for the application of Semantic Web technologies. In section 2, experiences from an ongoing project are discussed to identify critical issues from a systems development perspective. In section 3, taking into account the problems identified as well as the case findings, a research agenda is laid out concerning the application of Semantic Web technologies in e-government.

2 Semantic Problems in E-government

Semantic Web is about representing data, but this is done with the expectation of processes operating across borders of systems and organisations to integrate available data in applications. The semantic markup and semantic links are to "allow machines to follow links and facilitate the integration of data from many different sources" (Berners-Lee & Miller 2002). Therefore the Semantic Web initiative seeks to alleviate interoperability problems from the data perspective (just as the idea of Web Services is an effort rooted in the process perspective).

In the following, "semantic problems" are those kind of barriers in which the lack of interpretation of the meaning of the data objects and interfaces in focus is the key obstacle for networked computer applications in administrative processes and services. Technically, those problems are referring to semantic mismatch or "interoperability clashes, caused by differences in the conceptual schemas of two applications attempting to cooperate" (Missikoff 2002, p. 33). These clashes can be classified (e.g. in "lossy" and "lossless"), typical problems are the use of different names, structures or scales for the same kind of information, as well as information represented at different levels of granularity, refinement, or precision (l.c.).

The "semantic problems" in focus here are not of the same kind as the ones being addressed in the area of knowledge management in e-government (e.g. Wimmer 2003). The point of departure in Semantic Web applications is to enable machines to find their way around in a world of meaningful objects. On the contrary, knowledge management is concerned primarily to enable humans to find their way in world of knowledge – with the help of machines. However, it is foreseeable that both areas will be closely interlinked (if not merged) within the next couple of years, and some EC-funded projects are already paving the way (see, e.g., Kavadias & Tambouris 2003 on a markup language for describing public services; Fraser et al. 2003 on the use of taxonomies based on e-government service ontology).

Semantic Web has started out with a document oriented approach; the basic idea was to annotate Web pages with semantic markup. This has been challenged by requirements from knowledge management, suggesting focusing on knowledge items which might be structured and codified in much more detail (cf. Staab et al. 2001). Therefore, one of the challenges in identifying semantic problems is to identify the objects which will need semantic markup, the other one is to understand the processes which will use those semantic markups.

Objects or, more generally speaking, informational resources on e-government websites (accessible through public internet or secured intranet) can comprise a variety of electronic "things": information elements (possibly multimedia content), files (for downloads, e.g. documents, forms, client applications), transactions (processed by backend applications), links (to other sites and their resources), services (e.g. authentification), user related objects (e.g. user profiles) etc. All of these are meaningful for site users, all of these are searched for and being used – thus all of these are candidates for semantic markup. In the visions of Semantic Web, humans as Web users are accompanied by machine actors searching for "meaningful" resources and seeking to use/compose seamless services:

1. **end users**, such as individual citizens or employees of some organisation, using an internet browser
2. **electronic agents** on behalf of a third party (end user, organisation)
3. interoperability components of **e-government sites** (e.g. searching for additional resources on other sites to reply to a primary user or agent request)

All of these actors could search for and/or use (a) **public resources** (which are of the same kind for every potential requestor) or (b) **"private" resources**, i.e. parts of or the whole assembly of the resources are related to a specific user case (i.e. incorporating/drawing on specific information about the user, usually concealed from the public). It is state-of-the-art to use ontologies to structure and guide the markup process, i.e. to codify information, as well as to support semantic interoperability (e.g. Kim 2002). Table 1 gives some examples of how those actors and resources might be involved in search and use processes:

Table 1. Examples of processes which are likely to encounter semantic problems

Examples of search and use processes	public resources	"private" resources
end users	Searching an e-gov site for information on work permit	Applying for an individual work permit
electronic agents	Comparing information on premises of work permit on different e-gov sites	Monitoring an application for an individual work permit
e-government sites	Checking for legal updates (e.g. terms related to country of origin)	Searching in a legal data base based on the applicant's profile

These kinds of applications involve a variety of semantic objects (and the data representing them) which corresponds with the multitude of dimensions which have to be taken into account when setting up seamless e-government services (Lenk & Traunmüller 2002). Some important areas of semantic problems in providing e-government services and other governmental functions have already been identified:

- *Unsatisfying user experience:* presentation of information not guided by unified structure, style, principles (Kavadias & Tambouris 2003)
- *Lack of interoperability:* semantic mismatches (see above) of data to be exchanged have a vertical and horizontal dimension on the technical level (front-/back-end and back-to-back interoperability) as well as on the organisational level: "For a smooth online one-stop government, all public authorities need to be inter-connected horizontally (e.g., municipality and provincial authority) as well as vertically (e.g., local municipalities)" (Wimmer & Traunmüller 2002).

- *Poor document management:* physical resources (e.g. paper-based records) are no longer and electronic resources are not (yet) complete and well organized; there is no distinct interface to archive processes, and even the administration itself lacks an overview on how to (possibly) find relevant information (cf. Klischewski 2003).
- *Barriers in information retrieval:* standardisation of metadata is prerequisite for a national (or international) information management: the currently most advanced initiative in the UK (Office of the e-Envoy 2003) has already provided metadata components including a content management metadata definition, content management metadata elements, a government category list and data definitions.

Meanwhile, there are some efforts to adapt and apply Semantic Web technologies in those areas in which the primary concerns are data representation and information management; and all of them are also related to e-government interoperability.

3 Semantic Web Technologies for a Citizen Information Service

In October 2002 an explorative project started at Hamburg University (in cooperation with city state administration and the provider of www.hamburg.de) which focused on the application of Semantic Web technologies to enable the "contextualisation" of DiBIS, i.e. Hamburg's citizen web information service (www.dibis.de). The overall strategy has been to obtain knowledge about the users' context, make it computer readable and use it for enhancing the service quality.

Within this project, contextualisation (not to be confused with personalisation) was defined as striving for (1) display of information relevant (only) for the context of the user, (2) context-sensitive control of the user dialog, and (3) use of available context-relevant data. For prototyping purposes, it is assumed that knowledge about the users' context may be obtained through interpretation of user navigation and of user input (e.g. in forms) as well as through reuse of data from recent sessions. As this strategy must raise serious concerns about privacy, the overall premise was from the beginning that all (!) information obtained is to be displayed to the user and to give him the complete control over what to do with this data.

For requirement analysis, the project focussed on the scenario of a citizen using the web information service to support his/her move to, from or within Hamburg as one example of a life event. During analysis we found all the complexity of semantic problems in e-government interoperability, such as:

- Citizens need to match their own understanding of the domain issue (here: the life event moving home) with the understanding underlying the website services.
- Citizens may (have to) use other websites which are likely to incorporate different understandings and ways of expressing the domain issue (e.g. life event moving home), leading to a variety of "corporate" life events, different in each portal.
- Offering life event services (e.g. for moving home) requires a variety of public and private resources which need to be interrelated.
- Offering life event services (e.g. for moving home) requires service integration and process management across organisations and IT systems (e.g. integration of back end applications and services of other providers) – both of theses need to share an "understanding" on how to "interpret" the data exchanged.

- The semantic problems do not only occur within one life event, but may relate to services crossing borders between any topic specified in advance. For example, a citizen's (or a company's) move may well be connected with (multiple cases of) work permit application (see example section 1).

The main question for research and development was how to construct objects which represent the context of the individual user which would be machine readable for any component within or outside the server environment providing the site. The following strategy was chosen to solve the problem (see also figure 1):

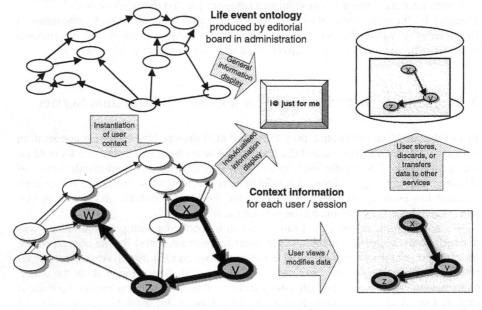

Fig. 1. Citizen information service employing ontology-based context information

1. An administrative editorial board produces an ontology (e.g. for the life event 'moving home') which represents the semantic structure of all resources incorporated in the Web-based information service (topics, key words, information elements, transactions, downloads, relations/links, services, etc.).

2. This ontology serves as a schema for creating a representation of the individual life event including specific user context. Through this all elements of these instances are machine readable, marked up and semantically interrelated.

3. Presentation of public resources through the web site follows the structure of the life-event ontology. If "private" (case-based) resources need to be displayed, the individual life event instance is taken into account.

4. The data representing the individual user context within the life event instance is visualised so that the user can view/explore all information elements and their interrelations which the website has stored about him/her at the time of viewing.

5. The user is given complete control over his individual user context instance, e.g. he/she can decide about deletion or storing all or part of the information, or about passing on all or part of the information to other web site services.

The first prototype (presented to city representatives in January 2003) has basically provided the functionality to support the strategy as described above. It is based on a standard 4-tier Web architecture in which the interaction layer (i.e. the server side production and delivery of browser content) is provided by a commercial content management system supplemented by a visualisation component developed within the project. The application logic layer is based on the "Jena Semantic Web toolkit" (a Java-based framework provided by Hewlett-Packard; www.hpl.hp.com/semweb), relying on persistent data in RDF format according to the DAML-OIL specification.

Besides mastering the new Semantic Web technologies and tools, the main challenge within the development process was how to obtain an ontology for the life event services on the conceptual level and to determine the needs for processing semantics (which also influences the choice of Semantic Web technologies). While modelling the life event, it happened many times that the scope and granularity of concepts to be included (e.g. "person", "family member", "address") and the (changing) relations between them turned out to be very difficult issues to elucidate.

At first, it seemed that the project would imperatively need an on-site domain expert from the Hamburg administration. But discussions with those in charge of information management for the web information service revealed that production of this kind of ontologies is a difficult task for which the administrative staff is not prepared.

The presentation of prototype to city representatives raised interest in the continuation of the project. However, from the service provider perspective a number of unresolved issues remain for systems development, among the most pressing are:

- taking care of privacy, data protection and authentification

- selecting and structuring domain information and related resources in relation to life event ontologies

- supporting the editorial process for ontology production

- control of user dialog based on ontology interpretation

- integration of external services

At the time of writing the exploratory project continues research and development aiming to support an editorial process for ontology creation and maintenance as well as to provide a web service interface for (requesting or responding from other websites). Issues concerning privacy, data protection and authentification are expected to be solved on a general basis since the city is preparing a single sign-on gateway for all kinds of e-government services employing private informational resources.

Given the tight budget restrictions, the city state government does not plan investments to reach for possible service quality improvements related to Semantic Web. However, it currently seeks to streamline its information management for citizen services through creating centralised information pools and establishing integrated editorial processes for information provision through several channels (Web, call centre, print on demand). In the search for increased effectiveness in service provision there is an increasing awareness of the need for information and knowledge management across the borders of systems and governmental bodies which calls also for technical solutions being able to incorporate the semantics of information services for the citizens (and other clients).

4 Research Agenda for Application of Semantic Web Technologies

It is still a long way for e-government to exploit the potentials of the Semantic Web. But it is reasonable to start preparing for it now and making use of the new technologies. This section seeks to lay out a research agenda to support these endeavours within administrations. As argued above, strategies for representation of data for the Web are related to ideas for cross-organisational processes (and to interoperability requirements/barriers). Therefore, research and development should concentrate on the two main steps encountering semantic problems which are related to production and use of semantic expressions and which need appropriate IT support:

1. *Markup of informational resources:* Each provider of e-government websites needs his own strategy to markup all informational resources accessible through e-government applications. For example, an ontology for the life event services 'moving home' can provide a frame for semantically marking up and interrelating all resources (public and private!) relevant for servicing the citizen (or other clients) in their specific context. To some extent markup can be supported through shared and standardised ontologies and metadata.

2. *Infrastructure for semantic interoperability:* The variety of terms and semantic concepts is a great challenge especially in e-government, and there will always be individual implementation and markup strategies. No standardisation will avoid semantic mismatches or interoperability clashes. But if the individual semantics can be encapsulated in distinct objects (i.e. specific ontologies) and it is known how those objects are constructed – then there is hope for machine interpretation and paving a common ground for true seamless services.

The individual markup and the common infrastructure are both prerequisite for exploiting the potentials of Semantic Web, i.e. to enable applications which explicitly process semantic expressions. However, to make administrations *successful* in their Semantic Web projects (or even to get them started) applied research needs to address some more issues within the next years:

- **Organisational cost/benefit:** To create semantic based systems on a professional basis requires time and effort (in particular to create or contribute to those virtual knowledge spaces which are intended to be exploited through the future application) – how can administrations evaluate and justify their investment? The finding in our case (which is strongly supported by Kim 2002) is that in the first phase of Semantic Web technologies are likely to be adopted if the administration benefits from application irrespectively of sharing the data with external partners.

- **„User" involvement:** New semantic-based applications can only deliver enhanced value when the domain experts are actively involved in creating new services – who are the experts? How can they be supported? What are the prerequisites that the primary information providers and consumers (administrative staff or clients who are not the technology or ontology experts) may work effectively with or on top of the new technologies? The critical issue is mainly the production of semantic expressions: it needs understanding and reference models of editorial processes and tools for the domain experts.

- **Technical integration:** What is the centre of gravity for integrating Semantic Web technologies – front-end, middleware or back-end? How do new tools for ontology construction and knowledge representation relate to given IT environments? It needs shared or standardised ontologies and metadata suggesting the basic elements, relations and structures to be embodied in application specific ontology production (e.g. through anchoring of application ontologies in upper and lower domain ontologies; cf. Missikoff 2002). It needs middleware components and/or services (shareware, open source) to support local activities as well as interoperability (mapping of / translating between ontologies, resolution of semantic conflicts).

- **Implementation strategy:** What are the best practices and methods for implementing semantic based systems? What are the success factors? We surely need more empirical research and project evaluation to provide guidelines for administrations.

To sum up: research must acknowledge that the roll-out and application of IT in public administration will continue to be based on individual organisational and technical strategies: organisational units (or even individuals) decide on the application of standards (if available) and how existing and new meaningful "business" objects are represented by data structures and processed by computerised applications. This semantic variety and related interoperability problems and inefficiency will even increase with the complexity of applications and data structures.

References

1. Berners-Lee, T., Hendler, J., Lassila, O. (2001). The Semantic Web. Scientific American, May 2001
2. Berners-Lee, T., Miller, E. (2002). The Semantic Web lifts off. Special issue of ERCIM News, No. 51, October 2002, pp. 9–11
3. ERCIM European Research Consortium for Informatics and Mathematics (ed.): Semantic Web. Special issue of ERCIM News, No. 51, October 2002
4. Fraser, J., Adams, N., Macintosh, A., McKay-Hubbard, A., Lobo, T.P., Pardo, P.F., Martínez, R. C., Vallecillo, C.S. (2003). Knowledge Management Applied to e-Government Service: The Use of an Ontology. In: Wimmer 2003
5. Gruninger, M., Lee, J. (2002). Ontology Applications and Design. CACM 45 (2): 39–41
6. Kavadias, G., Tambouris, E. (2003). GovML: A Markup Language for Describing Public Services and Life Events. In: Wimmer 2003
7. Kim, H. (2002). Predicting How Ontologies for the Semantic Web Will Evolve. CACM 45 (2): 48–54
8. Klischewski, R. (2003). Towards an Ontology for e-Document Management in Public Administration – the Case of Schleswig-Holstein. Proceedings HICSS-36, IEEE
9. Lenk, K. Traunmüller, R. (2002). Electronic Government: Where Are We Heading. In: Proceedings Electronic Government.EGOV 2002. Springer, Berlin
10. Missikoff, M.: Harmonise – an ontology-based approach for semantic interoperability. ERCIM News, No. 51, October 2002, pp. 33–34
11. Office of the e-Envoy (2003). e-Government Interoperability Framework. (Version 5.0, April 2003). London, UK
12. Staab, S., Studer, R., Schnurr, H-P., Sure, Y. (2001). Knowledge processes and ontologies. Intelligent Systems 16 (1): 26–34
13. Wimmer, M. (ed.) (2003). Knowledge Management in e-Government. Proceedings KMGov 2003. Springer Lecture Notes #2645
14. Wimmer, M., Traunmüller, R. (2002). Towards an Integrated Platform for Online One-Stop Government. ERCIM News, No. 48, January 2002, pp. 14–15

Intelligent Agent-Based Expert Interactions in a Knowledge Management Portal*

Witold Staniszkis and Eliza Staniszkis

Rodan Systems S.A.
Poland
{Witold.Staniszkis,Eliza.Staniszkis}@rodan.pl

Abstract. The goal of the Structural Fund Project Knowledge Portal is to support organizations and individuals involved in the SF project proposal development processes to achieve the highest possible number of high quality eligible project proposals meeting the stringent EC criteria. Interactions among experts playing different roles within a project definition case, are an important element of all Knowledge Services that include manual (i.e. expert) interventions. Therefore we present a typical expert interaction workflow exploiting the negotiating capabilities of the ICONS intelligent agent environment that will typically appear in a knowledge portal.

1 Introduction

The Structural Fund projects represent a vital opportunity for the new Member States to join the European Community in May 2004 to close the social and economic gap between these countries and the European Community. The challenge recognized by all new Member State Governments is to create conditions for best possible use of the funds made available to them by the EC. The goal of the Structural Fund Project Knowledge Portal is to support organizations and individuals involved in the SF project proposal development processes to achieve the highest possible number of high quality eligible project proposals meeting the stringent EC criteria.

The secondary goal, consistent with the ICONS knowledge management paradigm, is to provide access to the structural funds benchmarking data to be used in the project proposal development processes to support the planning and cost estimation, as well as the cost-benefit and the risk analyses. The feedback loop ranging the project proposal development and the project execution phases represents the Knowledge Management Life-cycle underlying the ICONS knowledge management architecture [1]. An important characteristic of the SFP KP system is integration of Communities of Practice involved in the SF project proposal ecosystem. Support and partial automation of expert interactions as well as facilities for documenting, verifying and dissemination of knowledge generated by these processes provides for continuous improvement of the system knowledge services. A schematic view of the system architecture is presented in figure 1.

---

* This work has been supported by the European Commission Project ICONS IST-2001-32429.

R. Traunmüller (Ed.): EGOV 2003, LNCS 2739, pp. 296–299, 2003.

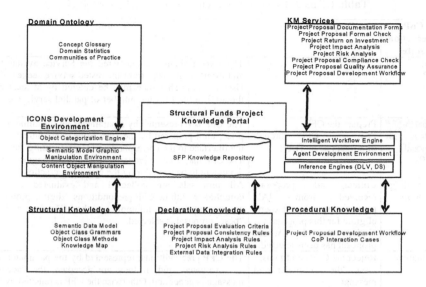

Fig. 1. The SF Project Knowledge Portal architecture.

2 Expert Interactions in the CoPs Interaction Processes

Interactions among experts of distinct Communities of Practice, or rather playing different roles within a SF project definition case, are an important element of all Knowledge Services that include manual (i.e. expert) interventions. Therefore we present a typical expert interaction workflow exploiting the negotiating capabilities of the ICONS intelligent agent environment [2] that will usually appear. Ontology of CoP interactions based on the negotiating intelligent agents is presented in Table 1. The negotiating agent environment is compliant with the FIPA Contract Net Interaction Protocol [3]. State graph of the Expert agents are shown in Figure 2.

The agent interaction protocol is to be implemented by an automatic process allowing the Initiator (the User proxy) agent to send a Call for Proposal (CFP) to a set of Responders, evaluate their proposals and then accept the preferred one. The Initiator solicits proposals from other agents by sending a CFP message that specifies the action to be performed and, conditions upon its execution. The Responders may then reply by sending a PROPOSE message including the pre-conditions that they set out for the action, for instance the service price or the service execution time. Alternatively Responders may send REFUSE message to refuse the proposal or, eventually, a NOT-UNDERSTOOD message to signal communication problems. The Initiator can then evaluate all received proposals and choose agent proposal to be accepted. The accepted Responders, who receive an ACCEPT-PROPOSAL message, will enter the manual contracting protocol via an appropriate channel (e.g. e-mail).

Table 1. The CoPs intelligent agent-based interaction ontology.

CoP interaction state	Output (Protocol)	Meaning
Wait for CFP		The Expert agent has registered the Service availability and awaits a message from interested service seekers (i.e. User agents). This state may be entered by at least one thread, if a limit for the number of parallel services is not exceeded for an Expert.
Preparing a Call for Proposals (CFP)	Prepare the CFP. Post the CFP through intelligent agent (IA)	The CFP is represented by a parameter set (deadline, max. price, etc.) prepared by the User to be communicated via the interface to the corresponding IA representing the user. The CFP may also be prepared as a complete requirements document to be used during the manual interactions.
Assembling Proposals	Collect all proposals received from IA's representing the Experts eligible for this proposal. Notify the IA whose proposal has been selected.	All proposals are collected and evaluated for the compliance with he CFP preconditions. Eligible proposals are evaluated by an inferential method (Datalog) and the "best" proposal is selected.
Evaluate CFP	Reject the CFP conditions. Issue the not-understood message. Accept the CFP conditions.	The CFP preconditions, represented by the parameter set, are evaluated, and, if they are accepted, the "accept" message is generated. Otherwise the CFP is rejected by the agent.
Contracting Service	Prepare a contract document defined in the manual interaction process.	Contracting Service is the manual interaction of negotiations between the contracting parties. Negotiations are expected to stay within bound of the automatically selected proposal's preconditions.
Executing Service	Service results are transmitted via the system or rendered manually.	The manual process of execution of the contracted service. The corresponding thread of the intelligent agent is waiting on the Service completion message.
Wait for Service Result	Confirmation of Service completed.	The User Agent thread corresponding to this particular Service is blocked until a notification arrives (manual or automatic) that the service results have arrived and have been accepted.

Note: Interactions that entail manual actions (i.e. human agent interaction) are indicated by the grey background.

Note, that Contracting Service and Wait for Service Results states suspend the agent in a WAIT generic state on messages that inform about the respective outcomes of the manual actions. The scope of agent decisions based on CFP and the corresponding proposal contents depends on the contents of received messages as well as the properties of the corresponding content objects (i.e. the Service Case) as defined the structural knowledge schema. Thus, the agent code implemented as a Java Class has access to all content object procedural and inferential methods. Definition of these methods, in particular execution of the inferential methods, supports intelligent agent behaviours. Since agents may be migrated to different execution platform, an appropriate connectivity structure must be put in place to provide support for the RMI protocol executions between agents and the ICONS content object methods. For each Service Case an independent thread of the User or the Expert agent is to be invoked, hence care must be taken in entering the generic WAIT state in order not to block the entire agent rather then the current thread. Appropriate programming techniques and the FIPA agent ontology are presented in [2 ,3 ,4].

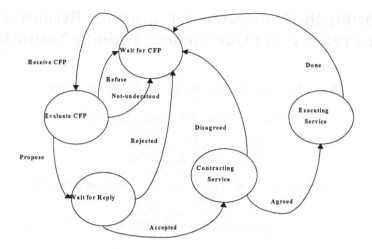

Fig. 2. The Expert Agent FSM states.

The contracting protocol is performed entirely manually, although appropriate communication services of the SFP KP system may be used, so are the ensuing services that have been negotiated for. In most cases results of services, such as for example a project proposal review report, will be stored in the knowledge repository and the state of the corresponding role agent may be changed. This will normally be accomplished by sending an INFORM message to signal the successful completion of a service or the FAILURE message if the expected results have not been reached.

3 Conclusions

Presented solutions are currently implemented within the IST ICONS project to demonstrate the ICONS platform knowledge management features as well as to propose a feasible knowledge management application. The partial results already obtained are encouraging and it seems that the proposed knowledge portal architecture may be used in different application domains that require tapping expert's tacit knowledge and to organize expert interaction processes.

References

1. The IST-2001-32429 ICONS Consortium, Intelligent Content Management System. Project Presentation, www.icons.rodan.pl, April 2002
2. The IST-2001-32429 ICONS Consortium, Specification of the ICONS architecture, www.icons.rodan.pl, February 2003
3. FIPA Abstract Architecture Specification, 2002, www.fipa.org
4. JADE Programmer's Guide, CSELT S.p. A., http://sharon.cselt.it/projects/jade, Italy, 2002

Supporting the Management of Learning Resources for the French Local Government Training Network

Michel R. Klein[1], Jacques Dang[2], and Dominique Roux[3]

[1] Information and Decision Science Department
[2] Technology Department
HEC School of Management
78350 Jouy-en-Josas France
{Kleinm,DangJ}@hec.fr
[3] Ecole Nationale d'Application des Cadres Territoriaux (ENACT)
Rue du Nid de Pie
49016 Angers cedex , France
dominique.roux@CNFPT.fr

Abstract. We examine the possibility of using the software developed during the UNIVERSAL project to help improve the service provided by the CNFPT. We present briefly the main design ideas and characteristics of the software as well as the way we plan to integrate to the system the latest version of a Decision Support System (DSS) for training in the financial planning of towns.

1 Problems and Challenges for the CNFPT

The CNFPT is the main organisation in charge of training the 1.2 million local government French civil servants. The reader interested to understand the structure of the French Local Administration and of the CNFPT and the educational challenges facing these organisations is referred to Klein (2000, 2003a). A first challenge is to constitute a nucleus of good quality seminars for training local governments personnel. The second is to update the portfolio of seminars to mirror the needs of local governments. The CNFPT being a decentralised organisation, seminars on a similar topic are offered by different instructors in 40 educational centers (EC). These seminars rely on a great variety of learning resources (LR) in their content, form and quality. The manager of an educational centre does not have an easy access to the LR used in other EC and cannot compare easily the evaluation of the LR and instructors, carried out by participants. Another challenge is to attract experts to teach. These experts are very reluctant to provide the LR they use in their seminars. The reason for this reluctance is that they are afraid that their LR will be copied and used without due reference to the authors and without receiving financial compensation. In other words the protection of the Intellectual Property Rights (IPR) of the authors is a key issue.

R. Traunmüller (Ed.): EGOV 2003, LNCS 2739, pp. 300–304, 2003.

2 Design Decisions and Functions Provided by UNIVERSAL

The primary goal of the UNIVERSAL Brokerage Platform (UBP) is to provide a service for exchanging digitalised learning resources and for sharing learning activities.

The UBP was designed to support the needs of *faculties, teachers and content creators* as well as the managers of educational institutions (public and private) in their task of creating courses and seminars from *elementary* Learning Resources (LR) and to provide support to organisations looking for quality LR to train their employees. In contrast to an other European project like CUBER which uses standardised *description of courses* to provide user guidance in the search of on line or blended courses offered by various European universities, the UBP concentrates on providing a way to describe LR , search and access them. It must be pointed out that the UBP is *not* designed to *provide an e-learning service* to learners as is the case with Learning Management System (LMS). It is not geared to supply access to on-line self study materials through the Internet even if such materials form part of the LR described in the system and if the UBP can inter-operate with LMS. The UBP aims at *supporting* instructors and faculty in their task of creating courses and learning experiments and *does not try to replace* them.

An important aspect of the UBP is that it makes a distinction between a Learning Resource (a static concept) and a learning activity (a dynamic concept) such as a live lecture. Digitalised LR already exist in large numbers in higher education institutions and companies and are already stored in a wide variety of software environments. These environments are PCs of faculties and instructors, course web sites and Learning Management Systems (LMS) or Learning Content Management System (LCMS). Also specialised LR such as business case studies have been stored and traded by specialised organisations such as the "Centrale des Cas" of the Paris Chamber of Commerce or Cranfield Case Study Centre in the UK. The consequences of this observation are that the desire to create a central repository of LR for a large number of Educational Institutions is somewhat illusory. A better strategy is to provide the possibility of describing existing LRs and/or transfer the description from existing LCMS and making these descriptions easily accessible through the Internet. This improves the awareness of their existence among the teaching staff and increase their ability to search for the LR they need and easily import *them provided they have agreed to the conditions of use*. The idea is thus to constitute an exchange system or *electronic market for LR*, even if many exchanges are made without cost. (for example between members of the same institution or between members of institutions belonging to the same alliance). Another consequence of this observation is that in order to be able to provide (upload) and deliver (download) through the internet a LR stored in a number of heterogeneous environment (operating system, LMS, LCMS,...), a *distributed delivery system* has to be designed to interface with the local PC and various LMS. A second observation is that the descriptions of LR vary widely according to their nature and the institutions developing or trading them. The definition of standards to describe LR is essential to provide inter-operability between LCMS. This standard must take into account, as far as possible, what is already existing in terms of international standards to facilitate the exchange of LR descriptions in an automatic way. A final observation is that the faculty is often very keen to protect its intellectual property rights on LR because it is a basis for their professional evaluation and publications as well as a source of additional revenues when used in continuous education or consulting. As a consequence it is important to provide a versatile way of controlling the *access* to a LR and to be able to do it at the LR level. The UBP is also designed to support the exchange of LR themselves (and not just their description). Access to LR without the possibility to interact with the author or other experienced users is not be very useful. Also it is important to provide access to *learning activities such as live lectures or project work*. To fulfill this need the UBP provides access to ISABEL a video based CSCW tool which supports video communication between teachers involved in network teaching and/or students collaborating through the Internet. For examples of use of such collaborative tool in teaching and research in management see Klein (1998, 2003). The UBP functions were briefly described in Klein, Dang (2002). The reader is invited to find out more about these functions by visiting the EducaNext website (www.Educanext.com.)

3   Structure of UNIVERSAL Brokerage Platform (UBP)

The EducaNext exchange service uses the Universal Brokerage Platform (UBP) and a number of delivery systems (DS) installed on a machine located in each educational centre. The fig. 1 shows the structure of the system. For more details on the architecture see Brantner (2001). The web application written in java Servlets interacts with the data base server via JDBC API and provides for data base-independent connectivity between java and the DBMS. The formal presentation of the characteristics of LR was modelled using the Resource Description Framework (RDF) which is then encoded in records using the Extensible Markup Language (XML). The UBP is then ready for semantic web development.

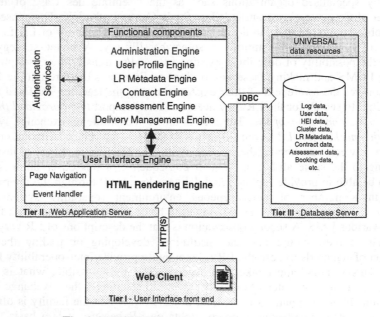

Fig. 1. UNIVERSAL architecture (Brantner 2001)

4   Integration of a Knowledge Based DSS with the UBP and Its Use to Support Learning Activities

With respect to the possible impact of the UBP in an organisation such as the CNFPT we refer the reader to Klein (2003). Simulation and knowledge based systems are important applications not only because they support decision making but also because they can play a central role in speeding up the learning process of users (Klein, 1995). A DSS for supporting financial diagnosis and planning in French towns was described in Klein (1993, 2000) and was also used in educational seminars for local authorities. The application provides the participants with access to historical accounting data on towns as well as statistical results concerning key fiscal and financial criteria and   standard presentations of town   financial information. The application then provides the possibility for a given horizon to input hypotheses such as trends in tax basis, central government financing , to input decisions concerning tax rates, investment,... and finally compute cash position through a use and source of funds equation. These kinds of   applications are costly to develop but are very effective LR which deserve to be shared between users connected to the UBP. We would like to give here some ideas concerning the work currently being carried out which could facilitate the sharing of this kind simulation between users during seminars at the CNFPT and also at the place of work.

4.1   Use of the Simulation

The seminar is run in five main phases. During the first phase there is a face to face lecture on the concepts and methodology of financial historical analysis. A case study is then used to teach the participants how to use the DSS application. In a third phase the participants returning to their work place can apply the methodology and the DSS to the data of their own town. They can access all documents and the DSS through the UBP. In a fourth phase during a face to face meeting at the CNFPT they present their analysis of their own town's financial situation and planned investments. They also receive a series of lectures on financial planning and practice using the simulation part of the application. In the next phase the participants apply what they have learnt to their own town. In a last phase during a presentation session at the CNFPT they present the various scenarios with the recommended financing policy for their town.

4.2   Structure of the Application

The structure of the application is best explained by fig 2. The dynamic html pages are used to capture historical accounting data of the town and generate a file on the web server. The application reads the file of historical data. The application computes the results which are stored in a file. These results are displayed to the appropriate user using dynamic html page. The user then interact with the planning module. A series of html pages are used to input the hypotheses, which are stored in another file of the same directory on the server. The simulation computes the forecasted values corresponding to these hypotheses. The user can then select the various reports to read the results and can change his hypotheses if he so desires.

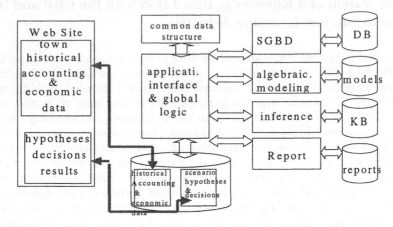

Fig. 2. Structure of the simulation application accessible through internet

5 References

1. Brantner Stefan et als, UBP Platform description, UNIVERSAL internal doc, 2001
2. Brantner , Enzi., Guth, Neumann., Simon , UNIVERSAL, Design and Implementation of a Highly Flexible E-market Place of Learning Resources, in Proceedings of the IEEE International Conference on advanced Learning Technologies, IEEE, Press 2001.
3. Klein Michel, Borgman Hans, PC based video as a tool for supporting collaborative work in teaching and research in Management, Procceedings, 3 rd Academic CEMS Conference, Louvain-la-Neuve, May 1998.
4. Klein Michel, Supporting Financial Strategy Development in French Towns using a Financial DSS, in Proceedings Symposium on Information Systems in Public Administration, Quirchmayr , et al (Eds) Osterreichische Computer Gesellschaft, 2000.
5. Klein Michel, Methlie Leif, Knowledge based DSS, John Wiley 1995.
6. Klein Michel, Dang Jacques, E-Learning for E-Government, in proceedings EGOV 2002, Traumüller Roland. , Lenk Klaus (Eds), Springer Verlag, LNCS 2456, 2002
7. Klein Michel, Supporting the Management of Learning Ressources for the French Local Government Training Network, Research paper , HEC 2003
8. Klein Michel, Web based Support for Collaborative teaching between Universities Faculties, in Proceedings International Society for DSS, Sroka, Stanek (eds), University of Economics, Katowice, Poland, 2003

Models of Trust for Knowledge-Based Government Services

Andy McKay-Hubbard and Ann Macintosh

International Teledemocracy Centre
Napier University
10 Colinton Road
Edinburgh, EH10 5DT, Scotland
{a.mckay-hubbard,a.macintosh}@napier.ac.uk

Abstract. This paper draws on current research and from it isolates a framework of trust definitions. From these definitions models of the trust relationships specific to the implementation of knowledge management within a governmental organisation are developed. As a foundation for the paper we address the nature of knowledge, adhering to current accepted definitions of tacit and explicit knowledge, while introducing a third knowledge type – obscured explicit knowledge. We argue that this third type is a subtype of explicit knowledge, and has been misidentified as tacit knowledge. We also argue that this third type is fundamental to the models. We argue that social acceptance of knowledge management is fundamentally based on trust and subsequently develop the models that describe the complex trust relationships involved in this acceptance.

1 Introduction

As governments across Europe progress to e-government, and e-transaction services become the norm, managing the knowledge within these services becomes critical. However, knowledge management in government cannot be equated straightforwardly to knowledge management in manufacturing and engineering industries. Although many of the issues associated with industry-related knowledge management are also associated with government knowledge services, and consequently research and development undertaken in one area supports the other, there is a major difference and this is *'trust'*. People dealing with government agencies expect integrity and confidentiality and importantly trust in the service being provided. This social need for trust in order to accept knowledge-based government services is the motivation for our work presented in this paper.

We use the following as our definition of the concept of knowledge management:

"the identification and analysis of available and required knowledge assets and knowledge asset related processes, and the subsequent planning and control of actions to develop both the assets and the processes so as to fulfill organizational objectives." [1]

Kingston and Macintosh [2] argue that the above definition implies that it is necessary for organizations:

R. Traunmüller (Ed.): EGOV 2003, LNCS 2739, pp. 305–312, 2003.
© Springer-Verlag Berlin Heidelberg 2003

- to be able to capture and represent their knowledge assets;
- to share and re-use their knowledge for differing applications and differing users; this implies making knowledge available where it is needed within the organization;
- to create a culture that encourages knowledge sharing and re-use.

In this paper we focus on the last of these 3 issues and investigate the social issues of knowledge management. We use existing models of trust and knowledge to develop models describing the trust relationships that occur within a government agency implementing a knowledge management system.

The nature of knowledge has been discussed at length within the knowledge management literature, and so an extensive re-examination of it is not given here. However, we briefly outline a working framework of this as a foundation for the exploration of trust. Alongside existing definitions of Tacit and Explicit knowledge, we introduce a subtype of explicit knowledge; *obscured explicit* knowledge. We argue that this is often mistakenly labeled tacit knowledge. This knowledge is explicit, in that it can be expressed, formalised and codified, however it is deeply buried in the procedures and understanding of the individual or group concerned. We argue that the elicitation of obscured explicit knowledge is deeply reliant on a particular aspect of the Domain expert/ Knowledge engineer trust model. That is the process whereby the nature of trust between the two entities progresses from largely institutional in its basis to more personal trust.

Our research forms part of the SmartGov[1] project. The aim of SmartGov is to specify, develop, deploy and evaluate a knowledge-based platform to assist public sector employees to generate online transaction services by simplifying their development, maintenance and integration with already installed IT systems. The project has been previously described by Georgiadis, et al. [3] and Fraser, et al. [4].

We argue that, for an e-transaction service to be accurately developed and successfully deployed, various models need to be represented and a framework for e-government services needs to be developed. We are developing such a framework under the SmartGov project. A key component of this framework is concerned with the issues of trust and social acceptance of e-services.

In section 2 of this paper the social acceptance of knowledge management within a government agency is detailed. We argue that this is fundamentally based on trust and, in section 3, subsequently develop the models that describe the complex trust relationships involved in this acceptance. In our conclusions, section 4, we return to the SmartGov project and provide implications for the successful development and deployment of the system.

2   Models of Trust

We argue that the foundation of social acceptance of knowledge management within a government agency is trust. We begin by examining current descriptions of trust within the field. From these descriptions we develop models of trust to describe the

[1] Project partially funded by the European Community under the "Information Society Technologies" Programme (1998-2002) (Project Number IST-2001-35399).

relationships between the various agents during the events that form the knowledge management implementation/acceptance process.

It is generally agreed that trust is fundamentally important to knowledge management [5], however little discussion is devoted to how trust functions in this context and which agents are involved. We draw on previous work, defining various types and bases of trust that are useful to our overall model of the trust system. For Smartgov to be of any value to the organisation employing it, it has to be accepted by the people who make up that organisation, including domain experts. This is essential not only to ensure that the system will be used and relied upon by the users, but also so that the Smartgov system is trusted such that people are willing to submit knowledge to it. There needs to be trust between the various agents involved.

There are several events, which form the implementation process and each event is associated with a system of trust relationships. Current literature has tended to focus on the knowledge-sharing event in any studies of trust in this respect. However, this ignores the trust relationships involved in knowledge use, reliance and the investment of time and money in knowledge managment as a whole. We deconstruct the complex trust system into its constituent parts and develop models of these.

The very essence of any description of trust begins with a definition of what it is to trust. Philosophers have defined trust as the placing of one's self in a position of vulnerability in some form, in relation to another entity in the belief that that entity will not take advantage of this imbalance. Trust is thus a relationship between two entities (people or groups) involving and imbalance of power. There is a reliance, on the part of the powerless component, on the empowered component to act in the former's interest.

Self trust is a concept that is a necessary part of our trust model. Given that the trust relationship is essentially a dichotomy of power, self trust would require the conscious to be two entities, with a disparity of power between them. However, the dichotomy could exist between the conscious and the unconscious, in that a person could have distrust of their unconscious reasoning (i.e. one may distrust one's initial, instinctive judgment of a situation, or one may distrust ones senses). Thus it is in our reliance on our subconscious reasoning that trust becomes a factor. By this token, in terms of knowledge management, there is a trust relationship between one's tacit knowledge and one's conscious self, and by extension the decisions and explicit knowledge that we base on this tacit knowledge.

The construct that is trust varies with its target, basis and the nature of the trusting relationship [5]. Ford [5] identifies nine bases for trust existing in literature on the subject. We briefly outline those relevant to this paper.

Deterrence based trust [6] exists where the trustor and trustee are aware of sanctions that will be brought to bear on the trustee if there is a breach of trust. *Knowledge* based trust [6] exists where the trustor has knowledge of the trustee such that he/she is able to predict their likely behaviour, and trust accordingly. *Identification* based knowledge [6] exists between two persons where an empathy exists, i.e. one is able to identify with the other. *Institutional* trust [7], is a form of deterrence based trust, where the trust is in the institution providing laws and rules to protect the trustor, where the trustee is subject to those rules.

We examine proposed trust types such as definitions of personal and impersonal trust [8], or interpersonal and organisational trust [9]. From these one can see that, trust may be placed by one person in another person based on that person's personal traits/behaviour. Conversely, trust may be placed in a person based on their role/position/office, not the actual person. These distinctions are used in developing the models. The target of trust varies being, personal or organisational, i.e. aimed at a specific individual, or at an organisation. This is represented in the dichotomous relationships that form the structural elements of the models.

3 The Models

We propose two models to adequately describe the complexity of trust relationships present in the acceptance of a knowledge management initiative, such as Smartgov, within an organisation. These are the micro level model from the "domain expert - knowledge user" perspective, and the macro level, holistic model of the organisation as a trust relationship system.

From the perspective of the domain expert/knowledge user, there are two roles which he/she plays in the trust model; knowledge contributor and knowledge consumer. Current literature agrees that, in order for knowledge to be shared, there must be trust and that the sharing of knowledge is fundamental to the success of knowledge management. However, the second role, that of knowledge consumer/user, is no less fundamental and is perhaps the greater indicator of acceptance of knowledge management. The Smartgov system would be of little use if people did not trust it sufficiently to rely on its knowledge in their service development processes. Thus the model from this perspective must accommodate these two roles. Within this model, various forms of trust apply. The User, in the role of domain expert with knowledge to share, has to trust the organisation to accept his/her knowledge and to use it for the purpose stated and not in some other detrimental manner (this could be a combination of organisational, interpersonal and institutional trust). There will be an immediate interpersonal trust relationship between the domain expert and the knowledge engineer within the process of knowledge elicitation. The trust here is likely to be based largely on institutional trust. Some trust in this relationship may be based on personal traits of the knowledge engineer. This could be based on several trust foundations, as discussed by [6], this personal trust is also likely to be dynamic in nature, changing as the elicitation process develops. Thus the proportional basis of trust in this relationship may vary from initially being largely reliant on institutional trust to increasingly relying on personal trust.

This user/domain expert, needs to trust the Smartgov system, in order to be comfortable submitting knowledge to it and to be able to rely on its knowledge. Much of this trust is likely to be institutional in nature and directed at the organisation, however the knowledge engineer may be viewed as representative of the Smartgov system, and thus an element of personal trust may be involved. Also, through trusting the organisation, the user is trusting the other sources of knowledge, and is thus able to rely on that knowledge. The domain expert needs also to be able to trust his/her own knowledge. This is the self trust described above, where the domain expert is trusting their tacit knowledge. Distrust in ones own knowledge may present a barrier to sharing that knowledge.

There is a trust relationship between the user/domain expert and the organisation where the former trusts the latter's motivation for implementing knowledge managment and commitment to it. This relationship also forms part of the basis for any institutional based trust relationships in the model.

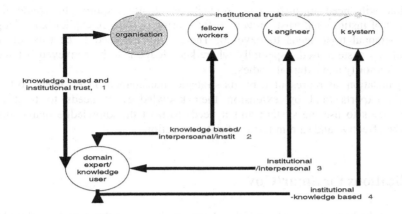

Fig. 1. Topography of trust

In trust relationship 1 the nature of the trust is likely to be a composite of institutional and knowledge based trust . The target is the organisation encompassing both the will of the strategic management body, and the structure of the organisation as a whole. There may be a variance over time of the proportional significance of either trust component.

In trust relationship 2, the trust is institutional, knowledge based and both interpersonal and organisational in its target. Here the domain expert/knoweledge user cannot know every other knowledge user/contributor, and so must trust them as part of the organisation, however those with whom he/she has personal interaction, could be trusted on knowledge based or even empathetic terms. Again the proportions of trust that exist are dynamic.

In trust relationship 3 the trust is initially based upon institutional trust, however there may develop an interpersonal trust relationship based on increasing knowledge or empathy. In fact, we argue it is essential for the nature of the trust involved to undergo this evolution in order to elicit *obscured explicit* knowledge.

In the final trust relationship 4 the trustor is "trusting" a system not a sentient entity, thus he/she trusts the entity responsible for the system. In this case the trustor may have no contact with or knowledge of said entity, but may mediate their trust through institutional trust of the organisation. The knowledge engineer may also be a target of trust in this instance depending on their relationship with the system.

The second model is an overall, macro level, description of the organisation as a system of trust relationships. It can be regarded as constructed of instances of the first model within a strategic trust framework. Government agencies can be said to differ from commercial organisations in their highly compartmentalised structure, which often extends to external bodies such as health services and police services. This presents a complexity of interconnecting trust relationships when examining the acceptance of the knowledge management initiative. SmartGov is a platform to support the development of electronic service delivery and these services will typically involve several departments of government, if not external bodies. For the knowledge management component of Smartgov to be accepted, there needs to be trust across these boundaries. Interdepartmental collaboration and communication are vital components and require trust. This will largely be institutional trust and so the organisation will need to have such regulations as are required to create this environment of institutional trust. However, for sharing of obscure explicit knowledge to occur, personal trust needs to develop. There will also need to be trust of the integrity of any system used, especially where knowledge is to be conveyed between the Public Authority and external bodies.

The organisation, as represented by its strategic management layer, needs to trust the domain experts (and by extension their knowledge), it needs to trust the knowledge users to use the system and it needs to trust the knowledge managment system to be effective and safe in terms of data protection.

4 Implications for SmartGov

The Smartgov framework includes the development and use of the models explored in this paper. These models provide an understanding of the mechanisms involved in the social acceptance of a knowledge management system within a government agency. They can be used to assist government personnel in the implementation of the knowledge management element of the SmartGov platform. These models of trust should allow the organization to modify processes and address issues of internal co-operation in a targeted, trust focused manner. This would facilitate a reasonably smooth transition to an e-service environment supported by the Smartgov platform. The models also have implications for the design of the software element of the SmartGov platform.

The models show a complex system of mutually dependant trust relationships. These trust relationships have varying targets and bases, and thus have specific antecedents. It is therefore useful to examine these antecedents with a view to developing methods that promote them. These methods would then be applied to existing process models and models of co-operative work in an attempt to create an environment conducive to trust.

Many of the trust relationships are based initially on institutional trust. An antecedent to this type of trust is the existence of protective sanctions. In this sense the governmental institution is essentially providing an environment that encourages openness and communication. The model also shows instances of trust developing from an institutional base to a more person centred base such as knowledge or empathy. Such a transition is not possible without adequate communication and co-operation between individuals and groups or departments as agents in the system. Thus the government agency should consider methods to reduce departmental isolation and encourage communication at an interpersonal level and at an interdepartmental level.

Trust of the knowledge management system by the knowledge contributor and by the knowledge user, also has to be motivated. Communication of the motivations for, and nature of the knowledge management system will be essential, as will communication of the existence of the antecedents to institutional trust in this specific relationship.

Trust of the knowledge engineer responsible for the elicitation process initially relies heavily on the institutional trust environment, but is likely to, and will need to, develop toward personal based trust for the full depth of knowledge elicitation to occur. This development is a function of the individuals concerned and the environment in which it occurs. The former cannot adequately be prescribed, but the latter could be accommodated through the use of specific elicitation techniques and the effective communication of the motivations for the elicitation process.

The SmartGov knowledge repository may initially be populated by knowledge engineers through a process of elicitation of knowledge from the governmental domain experts. As the model suggests, trust is essential here. This will initially be based on institutionally protected trust. As the elicitation process proceeds to examine obscured explicit knowledge, this trust element will be required to develop too [10]. This is were a transition from trust based on institutional rules and sanctions to one based on interpersonal elements such as empathy and increasing knowledge will occur. Wooten and Rowley 's work on the use of anthropological elicitation methods provides an approach to this issue.

Where users themselves populate the repository, trust relationships contain a strong interpersonal element, and a greater element of self-trust. Hence a reliance on effective communication between staff, particularly across departments, will become apparent.

Design of the SmartGov software element will have implications for the social acceptance of the knowledge management system based on the models. To facilitate a wider trust base, the SmartGov software could be designed to include author information for each knowledge unit, thus allowing personal trust based on knowledge of the author, to develop from the initial base of institutional sanctions. The design of the HCI element of the knowledge management component must be capable of accurate, reliable presentation of, and access to the knowledge in an intuitive manner. This is essential if the knowledge based trust in the Smartgov is to develop. In this sense the knowledge base should be founded on a logical knowledge map. In Smartgov this Kmap has been developed from an ontology of government service provision [11,12]. It is this trust, based on positive experience of the Smartgov that allows a stronger trust relationship to develop.

References

1. Macintosh, A., I. Filby and J. Kingston, Knowledge Management Techniques: Teaching & Dissemination Concepts. International Journal of Human Computer Studies (Special Issue on Organizational Memories & Knowledge Management), vol. 51, no. 3, Academic Press, September 1999.
2. Kingston, J. and Macintosh, A.; Knowledge Management through Multi-Perspective Modelling: Representing and Distributing Organisational Memory; Knowledge Based Systems Journal, Vol. 13 (2-3), pp. 121-131, Elsevier Science, ISSN 0950-7051; 2000.
3. Georgiadis, P., Lepouras, G., Vassilakis, C., Boukis, G., Tambouris, T., Gorilas, S., Davenport, E., Macintosh, A., Fraser, J., Lochhead D.; SmartGov: a knowledge-based platform for electronic transactional services; In: R.Traunmuller and K.Lenk (Eds); Electronic Government, First International Conference; proceedings / EGOVS 2002, Aix-en-Provence, France, September 2002. Springer (Lecture Notes in Computer Science; Vol. 2456). pp362-370.
4. Fraser, J., Adams, N., Macintosh, A., McKay-Hubbard, A., Lobo, T.P., Pardo, P.F., Martínez, R. C. and Vallecillo, C.S. (2003); 'Knowledge Management Applied to e-Government Services: the Use of an Ontology'; KMGov2003, the 4th working conference on Knowledge Management in Electronic Government; Rhodes, Greece, May, 2003

5. Ford, D.P. (2002, in press). "Trust and Knowledge Management: The Seeds of Success". In Holsapple, C. Handbook on Knowledge Management, Springer-Verlag.
6. Shapiro, D., Sheppard, B. & Cheraskin, L. (1992). Business on a handshake. Negotiation Journal, 8, 365–377.
7. Zucker, L. (1986). Production of trust: Institutional sources of economic structure, 1840-1920. In Straw, B. & Cummings, L. (Eds.) Research in Organizational Behavior, vol.8. JAI Press, Greenwich, CT, 53–111.
8. Morris, J. & Moberg, D. (1994). Work organizations as contexts for trust and betrayal. In Sarbin, T., Carney, R. & Eoyang, C. (Eds.) Citizen Espionage: Studies in Trust and Betrayal. Praeger, Westport, CT, 163–187.
9. Gilbert, J. & Li-Ping Tang, T. (1998). An examination of organizational trust antecedents. Public Personnel Management, 27(3), 321–338
10. Wooten, T. & Rowley, T. (1995) Using Anthropological Interview Strategies to Enhance Knowledge Acquisition. Expert Systems with Applications 9,4, 469–482.
11. Adams, N., Fraser, J., and Macintosh, A.; Towards an Ontology for Electronic Transaction Services; presented at "AI in Business Workshop" at ES2002 the 22nd International Conference of the BCS Specialist Group on Knowledge-Based Systems and Applied Artificial Intelligence; Cambridge, December, 2002.
12. Adams, N., Fraser, J., and Macintosh, A., McKay-Hubbard, A.; Towards an Ontology for Electronic Transaction Services. Special Issue International Journal of Intelligent Systems in Accounting Finance and Management D. E. O'Leary and A. Preece 11 (2002) 173–181

Cooperating Strategies in E-Government

Francesco Bolici[1], Franca Cantoni[2], Maddalena Sorrentino[3], and Francesco Virili[4]

[1]CeRSI –Centro di Ricerca sui Sistemi Informativi-
Università LUISS Guido Carli
Roma, Italy
fbolici@luiss.it
[2]Università Cattolica del Sacro Cuore
Piacenza, Italy
franca.cantoni@pc.uicatt.it
[3]Dipartimento di Studi sociali e politici
Università degli Studi
Milano, Italy
maddalena.sorrentino@unimi.it
[4]Dipartimento Impresa e Lavoro
Università di Cassino
Cassino, Italy
francesco.virili@eco.unicas.it

Abstract. Public administration (PA) has significantly shifted its interests to reach the innovative Information and Communication Technologies (ICTs), as a result of e-Government projects. The new challenge for public administrations is based on the exploitation of their knowledge resources in order to improve their processes and to offer better services to the users. The aim of this contribution is to investigate the spreading of cooperating strategies in public administrations in order to better understand why and how these organizational behaviors could assure advantages for PA and citizens.

1 Introduction

In each industrialized country, public administration (PA) has significantly shifted its interests to reach the innovative Information and Communication Technologies (ICTs), undergoing important Business Processes Reengineering (BPR) as a result of e-Government projects. The new challenge for public administrations is based on the exploitation of their knowledge resources in order to improve their processes and to offer more effective and efficient services to the users. Knowledge has to be managed as a valuable asset and a key resource. Organizations will gain a consistent and durable competitive advantage improving their internal knowledge and enhancing the knowledge creation process (Nonaka and Takeuchi, 1995; Davenport and Prusak, 1998). A plentiful access to remote information and knowledge resources is needed in order to facilitate the deliverance of citizens' oriented services, it is required to generate a more proficient and successful communication and cooperation between administrations, and it is necessary to support the complex administrative decision processes.

R. Traunmüller (Ed.): EGOV 2003, LNCS 2739, pp. 313–318, 2003.

The aim of this contribution is to investigate the spreading of cooperative strategies in public administrations in order to better understand why and how these organizational behaviors could assure advantages for PA and citizens. First, we will analyze from a theoretical perspective (*prisoner's dilemma*) the advantages of a collaborative strategy based on the transfer and the share of knowledge among different administrations. Second, we will propose network as the most suitable organizational form to implement a knowledge management (KM) strategy. Third, we will analyze the *web services* technological standard as a mean to facilitate the organizational adjustment towards a public administration focalized on the management of knowledge in the network.

2   Why the Cooperative Strategy Could Be Considered Advantageous

The objective of this paragraph is thus to investigate whether the Prisoner's Dilemma (Axelrod, 1984) - which is a non-zero-sum game usually analyzed in game theory to explain cooperation mechanisms - is a good framework to explain the knowledge transfer and sharing mechanism among PAs.

The two players (in our analyses two PAs) in the game can choose between two moves, either "cooperate" or "defect". The idea is that each player gains when both cooperate, but if only one of them cooperates, the other one, who defects, will gain more. If both defect, both lose (or gain very little) but not as much as the "cheated" co-operator whose cooperation is not returned.

Let us see it in detail: Two players (administrations, departments or offices), A and B, have to decide whether to transfer mutually their knowledge or not (cooperate or not). Fundamental Assumptions: 1) we have two players: A and B; 2) payoffs are so expressed: T>R>P>S; 3) the players are composed of people acting rationally, aimed at obtaining the s maximization of payoff.

Each A and B is offered by the Chief Knowledge Officer (CKO) a bargain (Tab. 1):

- if A and B decide not to transfer their own knowledge everyone will possess their own and the transferring cycle does not start at all (strategy 4);
- if A refuses to cooperate and B decides to transfer knowledge, B would lose his own knowledge which is absorbed by A (or vice versa) (strategies 2 and 3);
- if they both decide to cooperate, each would spend/lose some time in absorbing knowledge, but a learning circle is created (strategy 1).

Table 1. The prisoner's dilemma applied to the knowledge transfer case.

		Player A	
		Transfer	Don't Transfer
Player B	Transfer	R, R(1)	S, T (2)
	Don't Transfer	T, S (3)	P, P (4)

Summarizing: A's choices (A's hypothesis on B's behavior): 1) if B's strategy is to transfer, it is better if A does not transfer (T>R); 2) if B's strategy is not to transfer, it is better for A not to transfer (P>S). So whatever B's choice is, for A it is better not to transfer (dominant strategy), and symmetrically also for B it is better not to transfer.

Therefore each player (administration) chooses his optional strategy, taken as given the other player's one. The combination of the decision of the two players leads to the Nash-equilibrium (4) where neither has an incentive to unilaterally change his strategy. But this equilibrium, which is stable, is not Pareto-efficient, because there is another one (1) where both are better off without anyone being worse than in (4) (i.e. for each player R>P). So if they were able to cooperate and decide to mutually transfer their knowledge they would be better off, but there is no opportunity to make any formal agreement, they just have to act making hypotheses on each other's strategy. If this game is played just once (one-shot game), or a finite number of times, the final equilibrium is the Nash one. But it is almost unreal: in an organization, business units will interact an infinite number of times. So it is reasonable to assume that this game is not played one shot, but an infinite number of times: in this situation it is optimal for both players trying to cooperate (even without formal agreement) and play (1). This is because each of their "payoffs" are maximized in the partnership, causing each to believe the relationship won't be unilaterally ended.

3 Network as Cooperating Relationships

In the previous part, we conceptualized the Prisoner's dilemma in a public environment, proposing and supporting the idea for which cooperation among different actors is a valid strategy in the long term perspective. Following this observation, we propose the network model as the most suitable organizational form for a renovated and dynamic public administration.

Planning the innovative e-services, the PA must avoid the mistake that consists in imitating the traditional services and processes, just striving to reproduce them better. Instead, exploiting the new opportunities offered by technology, PA should manage the practice of re-thinking its services as a radical change that might add dynamism and flexibility to its structure and activities. To achieve these aims, the new e-Government paradigm should become founded on some shared points (Friis, 2002): 1) services focused on the citizens' requirements and needs; 2) integrated structure that could assure a strong link among different administrations, their activities, processes and services; 3) a real and radical BPR (Business Process Reengineering) in order to change not only the technological aspects, but also the organizational processes inside PA. It is easy to observe the tendency to facilitate communication between administrations, to reduce the waiting time citizens spent, to delocalize services, to increment integration among the different parts of the PA, and also to share knowledge, information and best practices. The new public organization needs ample access to remote information and knowledge resources in order to facilitate the delivery of citizens' oriented services, a more efficient and effective communication and cooperation among administrations, and a support for complex administrative decision-making. Naturally, to develop these transformations, the PA must re-think not only its processes and its services, but also its structure.

Our idea is that, at the same time as in many cases in the business sector, the network model could assure the organizational characteristics required to satisfy the change of citizens' needs, furthermore it can guarantee them in a public context focused on a knowledge perspective. Huge support for our suggestion on the importance of this kind of structure can be found in the work of Carlsson (2001) and in a large number of empirical studies here described: "KM has to become network-focused if knowledge intensive firms are to gain and sustain competitive advantage from KM". Moreover Kogut (1998) suggests that, in a network, the membership generates value for the organization not only assuring the access to information, but constituting in itself capabilities to support coordination and learning among different members. Following this concept, the PA could increase the value of its services adopting a network form, since it improves and increases the connection among different parts of administration.

Network, as an intermediate model between market and firm, respects specialization (as in an individual organization), promoting contemporary variety through the relation among the different nodes (as in the market) guaranteeing a balanced combination of specialization, delocalization and integrated processes as required by the new PA paradigm proposed above. Following this perspective, the next section will introduce the Web Services. This kind of technology is a clear example of the opportunities generated by adopting a network cooperative structure.

4   Web Services: A Solution for Knowledge Sharing through Software Reuse

Common network infrastructures (like Internet/Intranet) have greatly facilitated cooperation and knowledge sharing, but one of the most troublesome and complex issues to solve when collaborating and sharing knowledge (Markus 2001) is inter-administration business process integration, and, consequently, system integration (Markus 2000). Even when using common platform, sharing different software applications poses enormous technical and organizational challenges.

One of the ways to facilitate system integration and knowledge sharing would be through enhanced software reusability: for example a well-working application developed by a local administration should be easily adapted to the needing of other administrations and integrated into their local information systems.

Software reuse and system integration would be greatly facilitated by having a central repository for standard software components, open to any authorized user with standard access channels, rules and documentation. Web services technology was designed to make it possible. Web services are self-contained, modular business process applications that Web users or Web-connected programs can access over a network via a standardized XML-based interface, in a platform-independent and language-neutral way (Kreger, 2001; Hagel and Brown 2001).

In practice, a Web service is a software reusable component (i.e. a small functionality, a little 'piece' of an application) that can be written by anybody (for example a software vendor), and published to be later retrieved and dynamically used within an existing application by anyone (for example an IS developer). Adopting this framework, companies in the future will be able to buy their information technologies as services provided over the Internet, rather than owning and maintaining all their hardware and software (Hagel and Brown 2001). The functionalities that can be implemented by Web services have virtually no limits, ranging from major services as storage management and customer relationship management (CRM) down to much more limited services such as the furnishing of a stock quote and the checking of bids for an auction item. They provide a means for different organizations to connect their applications with one another to conduct dynamic e-business across a network, no matter what their application, design or run-time environment.

So the revolutionary aspect of using Web services is that they are self-integrating with other similar applications. Until now, using traditional software tools to make two e-business technologies work together required lots of work and planning, to agree on the standards to pass data, the protocols, the platforms, etc. Thanks to Web services, applications will be able to automatically integrate with each other wherever they originate, with no additional work.

5 The Role of Web Services in the Italian E-Gov Action Plan Actuation

Given the early stage of maturity of the Web Services technology, we cannot yet observe significant applications in the PA at an advanced stage of adoption. Nevertheless, the Italian ongoing experience with the actuation of the "Action plan for eGovernment" is already a source of interesting preliminary evidence for our purposes. Recently, with the Decree (DPCM) 14 February 2002, a first advance of 120 million Euro was directed to the financing of eGovernment projects presented for evaluation by the PA organisms. A system of "co-financing" was provided, where eGov public funds could cover only a part of the total amount of the projects, up to 50%. The rest of the expenses should be financed directly by the project proponents.

The "heaviest" criteria are the quality of the proponent (criterion 2, weight 35%) and quality of the proposed solution (criterion 4, weight 35%). The remaining 3 criteria (alignment with territorial objectives, project quality, possibility of reuse) were assigned a 10% weight each. Analyzing in detail the criterion 4 (refer to the "Avviso per la presentazione dei progetti", http://www.pianoegov.it/avvisi/, in Italian) we could conclude that the eGovernment projects, to be positively evaluated for financing, should make use of the Web Services architecture.

Why this prescription? In such a complex and fragmented context of hundreds or thousands of territorial administration offices using their own hardware and software in each region, knowledge-sharing is strictly connected to infrastructures, software integration and reuse. We examined three of those projects: AIDA, a service portal to enterprises presented by the municipality of Livorno, SIRA-Net, an environmental services portal by Toscana Regional Government, SITAD, a Geographical Information System by Piemonte Regional Government. What we found is that the adoption of the Web Services technology is mentioned in the projects only incidentally, by a generic adherence to the technical specifications emanated by the Government, but the potential use of the Web Services architecture to enact reusability is not leveraged in any way in non of the three projects.

Moreover, the risks and uncertainties connected with the adoption of this architecture (i.e. security and performance) are not considered in any way neither in the projects nor in the Government action plan actuation guidelines.

6 Conclusion

We have conceptualized the Prisoner's dilemma in a public environment, proposing the idea for which cooperation among different actors is a valid strategy in the long-term perspective. Following this observation, we have suggested the network model as the most suitable organizational form for a renovated and dynamic PA.

Network structure allows the management of inputs from different origins and the possibility to combine them in an effective way. Following this perspective, we have introduced Web Services. This kind of technology is a clear example of the opportunities generated by adopting a network structure. The main idea is to answer to the PA's need that consists in having a common solution, shared with all the administrations, where different added modules could satisfy the different and individual requirements of each single administration.

In our work, we underline that public administrations have to improve their efforts to cooperate in an intra-organizational way, by the use of network structure and web services in order to access to multiple sources of information and knowledge, but this requires a more substantial effort than those made in the development of the Italian eGovernment Plan. The Italian Government embraced the new technology simply by putting the Web Service standards in a list of technical specification required for e-Government project financing. On the other side, the projects presented by the PAs had just declared a generic adherence to the technical specifications. Clearly, additional efforts are required to better understand Web Services knowledge sharing potentials and issues and to develop practical guidelines for its implementation.

References

1. Axelrod, R.M. (ed.) :The Evolution of Cooperation, Basic Books, NY (1984)
2. Carlsson, S.A.: Knowledge Management in Network Contexts. In Proceedings of the 9th European Conference on Information Systems (ECIS-2001), Slovenia (2001) 616–627
3. Davenport, T. and Prusak L. (eds): Working Knowledge: How Organisations Manage What They Know. Harvard Business School Press, Boston (1997)
4. Friis, C.: Knowledge in Public Administration. In Proceedings of the Workshop on Knowledge Management in e-Government '02 (KMeGov'02). Copenhagen (2002)
5. Hagel III, J. and Brown J.S.: Your Next IT Strategy. In Harvard Business Review. October, (2001) 106–113.
6. Kogut, B.: The Network as Knowledge. Wharton School Working Paper (1998)
7. Kreger, H.: Web Services Conceptual Architecture, white paper, IBM Group, (2001)
8. Markus, M.L.: Toward a Theory of Knowledge Reuse: Types of Knowledge Reuse Situations and Factors in Reuse Success. Journal of MIS, 18(1), (2001) 57–93.
9. Markus, M.L.: Paradigm Shifts: e-Business and Business/Systems Integration. Communications of AIS, vol. 4, November (2000), art. 10, 1–44.
10. Nonaka, I. and Takeuchi H. (eds.): The Knowledge Creating Company. How Japanese Companies Create the Dynamics of Innovation. Oxford: Oxford Unity Press (1995).

The four authors wrote this paper in collaboration: in particular Francesco Bolici worked on sections 1, 3 and 6; section 2 is written by Franca Cantoni; Francesco Virili focussed his attention on section 4; finally in section 5 the empirical evidence is presented by Maddalena Sorrentino.

A Knowledge Perspective on E-Democracy

Jan Aidemark

School of Management and Economics
Växjö University
SE-35195, Växjö, Sweden
Jan.aidemark@ehv.vxu.se

Abstract. This paper takes an information systems development perspective on e-democracy. A case study in the area of e-democracy, a number of different types of information systems applications, is presented. These are discussed from three perspectives on knowledge, (cognitive, social, and critical), using an analytical framework that is based on some general direction in the area of knowledge management. The lesson of the case study is that full support from all these perspectives are needed to make IS an effective support to democratic processes. The analysis shows that it is not a technical problem, most types of support are readily available and in use. There is an insight in the area that success rests on a match between IS, understanding democratic processes, and peoples' expectations. The trouble, it seems, is to convert this into a system development perspective. Here findings from knowledge management could provide support.

1 Introduction

The area of knowledge management (KM) is a perspective on the use of information systems (c.f. [1]). Within the KM field, a need for a focus on people issues has become apparent, e.g. how people learn and use what they know and how IS can support these processes.

Knowledge can be viewed from a number of perspectives depending on how the concept of knowledge is understood (see for example [2]). In this paper three perspectives are used, a cognitive (e.g. [3]), a social (e.g. [4]), and a critical (e.g. [5]), (also discussed in [6]). All three go on all the time, human perception goes on in a social discourse that is controlled by a set of powers. Knowledge is what we see, what we talk about and a way of limiting what we may think of. An information system directly contributes to the cognitive perspective, but operates in a field of social interactions and power struggles.

E-democracy (the use of IT in the democratic process) can be seen as a knowledge project, in the sense that it seeks to educate and engage the public in democratic processes and issues. Barber [7] calls for a knowledge perspective in the use of e-democracy. The problem is not a lack of information, but how to support the creation of knowledge. Barber sees IT as essentially being the opposite of what a "strong" democratic process really needs, providing, speed, fragmentation, distance and so on. The development of KM within the IS field, focusing more on context and people related issues, should provide important lessons for e-democracy.

R. Traunmüller (Ed.): EGOV 2003, LNCS 2739, pp. 319–324, 2003.

The question for this research is how we can understand e-democracy as a knowledge process. The research approach is a literature study of case descriptions of e-democracy projects. The focus is on the IS/IT system that been used and what they seem to contribute to e-democracy processes. These findings are then analyzed regarding the different aspects of knowledge.

2 E-Democracy Case Studies

This study builds on a number of reports of studies of e-democracy. In these case studies a number of applications of IT systems used for e-democracy initiatives are accounted for.

- Discussion forums, generally these had a dual direction, both to put questions to the public, to inform the public and to give politicians feedback on issues. Rosén [8] reports that forums are used in initiating processes like drafting and defining political issues, as well as following up on decisions in order to ensure the quality of decision implementation. Both positive and negative aspects on this were reported. Carlsson et al [9] report good results in some cities together with reports of the forum becoming a "wailing wall" in some cities. A need to moderate was expressed, a problem with the possibility of posting offensive or even unlawful messages was clear. But, many forums were unmoderated. The general view of coordinators of the forums is that the forums should contribute to a feeling of "being listened to" and "being a part of" by the public. For the whole of Sweden just 19 % of the municipalities have forums, [10]. But among these most of them allowed people to freely choose what topics that should be discussed. Ranerup [11] examined these more closely and concludes that these systems are not used very much. Low traffic on the forums might be explained by how they are introduced to potential users and their real role in the political decision making process.
- Dialogue systems are discussed by Rosén [12]. Here citizens are invited to submit suggestions to issues. This provides a possibility for people to submit their views and contribution, organized as a homepage where the comments are posted.
- Citizen's suggestions, i e an open invitation to submit a suggestion to the municipal board can be found in 44 municipalities (http://www.kommunaktuellt.com/). This was made possible by a change in the law, taking away the privilege of political parties to submit suggestions.
- Examples of referendums that have been supported by IT have been reported. On-line voting was tried in two cities [9], but none of them bound the decision makers to the outcome (something which is not possible in Sweden). The experience was mixed, the applications created a great deal of interest, but when the outcome was ignored the result was a general air of resentment among the public. The questionnaires are often a way of collecting facts about the opinions of the public. The results of such that have been tried are mixed. For example The Association of Democracy and Self-government [13] reports a participation of between 9-14 % in 3 on-line voting cases. One of these examples [14] was a trial vote conducted by the student union at Umeå University, here the low figure of 9 % was reached. The aim of engaging more participants in student elections was not achieved. That is, the turn out was about the same as usual. But of the people that voted, 62 % did use

the internet. On the other hand, the city of Kalix (www.kalix.se), presents us with another view. In 2000, the municipal sought advice from the public on the issue of remodelling the town center. Some 1200 individuals or 8 % took part, giving their view what should happen. This is in contrast to less than a hundred responses that had been more common. The possibility to use a paper formula was also given, but 86 % used the internet alternative.

- A chat system is often cited as a possible technique (Rosén, 2001). The technique is used by some, for example in Kalix and more generally in the region of Norrbotten (http://www.norrbotten.se/vagval2002/).

- E-mail is the most widespread support tool. Carlsson et. al. (2002) report that the general experience of e-mail was positive, creating good contact between the public and politicians. Among politicians the asynchronous nature of E-mail was appreciated, to be able to answer each mail when time permitted. The factor of causing stress or information overload was also noticed by one coordinator, who saw the need for additional support to handle an increasing amount of e-mail. Rosén [12] notes that it is largely the most established politicians that get mail, the majority do not get any. Some 37 % of all municipal homepages have contact information for local politicians, [10].

- E-lobbying is reported [14] as a special use of e-mail. This refers to organized campaigns of sending e-mail to decision-makers. Grönlund [14] cites a comment from the Social Democrat party that 25 % of all mails (about 500 mails a day) belong to this category.

- Homepages are used to provide the public with current facts about ongoing affairs. This is generally considered as a simple and effective way of publishing large quantities of written material for easy access for citizens when they need it. Carlsson et. al. [9] reports that coordinators saw a possibility to express the views of the city that politicians wanted to display. One perspective on this was that a different view than expressed in local media could be given to the public. Rosén [12] also notes the same view. Looking at the content, SKTF [10] reports the following types of information are provided on municipal homepages: protocols (73 %), addresses (74 %), information about political parties (57 %), Calendars (75 %), decision processes (36 %), official records (1 %), documentation for current issues (2 %).

- Web-TV, on-line transmissions of meetings on the internet, was tried in four of the seven cities in a study [9]. In three of them it was also possible to put questions and get answers. Again, the technology was deemed to increase the interest of the public in the affairs of local political processes.

- A citizen's or people's panel is conducted by appointing a panel against which new proposals are tested. According to [10] 1 % of the investigated sites had this function. One example is in Älvsjö (http ://195.178.172.193/mpanelen/panel.asp), where three panels were appointed during 2002/2003, with the ambition of up to 6 panels a year. Here the opinions of 500 selected citizens are sampled.

- Community networks or electronically mediated networks, created and controlled by citizens for their own purposes, are another method. These provide space for discussion on social and political issues and a possibility for individuals to come together on common and often local issues. Grönlund [14] reports that this not a large movement, but examples are to be found.

- On-line questionnaires, structured requests for opinions, are used by some cities. In general 25 % of the municipal homepages invite the public to contribute with opinions [10]. Rosén [8] reports on two cases. In both, anyone could give their view. But the project leaders seemed satisfied, the opinions were a help in the process, although questions about who really took part were raised.
- An internet party is one exceptional use of the internet. An example is Demoex (http://www.demoex.net/index2.htm), a local party in the city of Vallentuna. It promotes a mix democracy, something in between direct and representative democracy. In the last elections in 2002 they got a seat on the municipal council. A member was elected to take the seat and today there is a process among members to decide how that person should vote. The process consists of a number of steps, suggestions, debates, screenings, meetings, and voting. Anyone can make a suggestion and then pros and cons are brought forward in a debate. The screening is made by people ranking the importance of the issue from 1 to 5, if the issues are rated below 3, no vote will be cast at the council meeting. If rated over 3 a voting procedure is conducted and the representative will vote in this way

3   Analysis of the Cases

The ambitions of the e-democracy initiatives have as aims to make information more available, citizens more involved in local democratic processes, and provide a them with a possibility to affect the these processes. From a knowledge and learning point of view this implies a number of different and sometimes contradicting processes and problems.

3.1   Knowledge as Cognitive Process

From a cognitive perspective the assumptions are that easier access and faster feedback will increase the involvement and interest. On a personal level, support for cognition processes points towards *homepage*. Knowledge is personal and homepages make facts available when a person feels the need for it, not only when a sender judges relevant. From a group perspective, *e-mail* lists and *discussion forums* distribute information to many individuals in an effective and fast manner. The politicians have an opportunity to get a quick overview of how the public perceives current issues, using dialogue, panels or questionnaire systems.

3.2   Knowledge as a Social Process

The knowledge perspective includes the socialization process, to create a context for understanding and discussion, creating a base for future action and opinion. On a personal level this is about creating an identity as a being a part of these democratic processes. Identity is built on personal interaction with other people, traditionally this is done by face to face interaction with others. Direct contact with individual politicians, using *e-mail* or *chat* applications, provides an environment where personal contact and trust can be developed. *Web-TV* could be a component, watching politicians in action, expressing themselves in interaction with others, gives a more personal connection to them. From a group perspective, it is a clear ambition of the projects including *discussion forums* to create a group feeling. To create communities on the Internet is a successful way of rallying people around a cause. The problem here is that, as pointed out in the case, if the ideas and discussions do not lead to a feeling of belonging and reaching out to the politicians, the community idea will fail.

3.3 A Critical Perspective on Knowledge

The support systems should empower the individual to develop personal knowledge and provide a possibility to change the current situation. Different types of web *referenda* provide the natural support system for this. But just as important is the possibility to set agendas. There is a political dimension to how the world is categorized in different information types [15]. Here the initiative with *citizen's suggestions* is an important step. Fair and free communication between people is a precondition for a critical debate. *Discussion forums* can be a good place for free communication. Many forums seem to be uncontrolled and that could stimulate a critical debate. But this opens up just as much for dishonest people who might be able to spread lies unhindered. But most important is that the discussion itself matters. Transparency of how decision processes work is important for an effective participation in the processes. Here it is about the information content. Homepages often contain process descriptions together with, key actors, background material, schedules, search systems and so on. The difficulty is that this constitutes a massive bulk of information, which does not necessarily contribute to personal knowledge and the ability to act. People are informed but not necessarily empowered by IS/IT systems. The *internet-party* shows the complexity of a number of technical solutions, processes of knowledge creation, social interaction and the ability to make a difference to make the internet into a powerful force in a democratic process.

4 Discussion

The important lesson is that there is no simple connection between the problems of democracy and the IT based systems that are supposed to be supportive. It is the intention and strategies behind the democratic processes that are important. Depending on how the knowledge process is understood, the use of IS will be different even though the technology involved is the same. The focus was on the distribution of information and on collecting opinions and suggestions from citizens. But for this to work there must be a feeling of being involved. According to [7] the use of IT might support such a situation but it will not produce it. The interest to be a part of a process is determined by the ability to make a difference. In this sense, the three knowledge processes are connected. The critical processes are a condition for the social dimension and these, in turn, for the cognitive. This can be compared to the ideas of Toumi [15], who argues that these knowledge processes should be understood as building on a reversed process. KM often assumes that people are informed, forming knowledge for action, and developing a wisdom dimension. Toumi argues the opposite, people develop knowledge within their current beliefs about the world and in turn information is understood in this context. The argument here is that it is not the direction, but the interaction between concurrent and interdependent processes. IS support must be planned for each aspect and the total impact must be taken into account, to avoid conflicting effects for the large set of systems needed for democratic purposes.

References

1. Alavi, M and D. E. Leidner, Knowledge management and knowledge management systems: conceptual foundations and research issues, MIS Quarterly, vol. 25, no. 1, March, (2001).
2. Schultze, U. and Cox, E. L., Investigating the Contradictions in Knowledge Management. Proceedings of IFIP Working groups 8.2 and 8.6 joint Working Conference on Information Systems: Current Issues and Future Changes Helsinki, Finland, December 10–13, (1998).
3. Piaget, J. The Psychology of Intelligence, Ruthledge, London, (2001).
4. Berger, P. L. and T. Luckmann, The Social Construction of Reality, New York, (1966).
5. Foucault, M, Discipline and Punishment, Harmondsworth: Penguin, (1977).
6. Aidemark, J., Cognitive, Social and Critical Perspectives on Planning a Knowledge Support Portfolio, Accepted for publication, DEXA, Workshop, Theory and Application of Knowledge Management, (2003).
7. Barber, B.R., En Plats för Kommers eller en Plats för Oss?, In: IT i Demokratins Tjänst, Barber et. al., Demokratiutredningen Forskarvolym 7, Sou 1999:117, (1999).
8. Rosén, T., Med Orat mot Bredbandet, kan E-demokrati Stärka Medborgaredialogen, www.lf.svekom.se/demos/medborgarinflytande/e-demokrati/med_orat_mot_bredbandet.pdf, (2000).
9. Carlsson, L., A. Sandberg and M. Waxelius, E-demokratins påverkan på den demokratiska processen. Working paper in Information science, Dept. of Management and Economics, Växjö Universisty, (2002).
10. SKTF, A report about democracy and influence on the net, (In swedish: En rapport on demokrati och inflytande på nätet), http://www.sktf.se/media/pressm/2002/020703.asp, (2002).
11. Ranerup, A., Elektroniska dialoger för kommunal debatt, In Electronsik förvaltning, elektronisk demokrati,: Grönlund, Å. and Ranerup (ed.), Studentlitteratur, (2001).
12. Rosén, T, E-democracy in practice, Swedish experiences of a new tool, http://www.svekom.se/skvad/E-democracy-en.pdf., (2001)
13. Democracy and Self-government, In swedish: Demokrati och Självstyrelse, http://www.publicist.lf.se/demos/medborgarinflytande/e-demokrati/index.asp, (2002).
14. Grönlund, Å., IT, Demokrati och Medborgarnas Deltagande, Vinnova Report: VR2001:26 and Teldok report 142, http://www.vinnova.se/publ/pdf/vr-01-26.pdf, (2001).
15. Suchman, L., Do categories have politics? The language/action perspective reconsidered. Computer supported co-operative work, 2, pp. 177–190, (1994).
16. Toumi, I., Data is more than knowledge: Implications of the reversed knowledge hierarchy for knowledge management and organizational memory, Proceedings of the 32nd Hawaii international conference on system sciences, (1999).

Process Reengineering on Base of Law – The New Austrian States Budgeting and Bookkeeping System

Josef Makolm

Austrian Ministry of Finance
Austrian Computer Society
josef.makolm@bmf.gv.at

Abstract. E-Government brings a shift of paradigms. New speedy, smart and simple processes are imperative. Existing processes should stay unnoticed, when these new processes are modeled. The development of the new Austrian state budgeting and bookkeeping system has followed these new paradigms and has brought impressive rationalisation effects.

1 Process Reengineering as Base for E-Government

1.1 A New E-Government Paradigm

E-Government brings a shift of paradigms. The mere functioning of an authority's processes and structures is no longer adequate. Customer service is now in the focus of interest; regardless whether customers act in the role of citizens (in case of G2C-applications) or in the role of company employees (in case of G2B) or even as civil servants just using e-Government applications of other authorities (in case of G2G-cooperations). Speediness, smartness and simplicity for the users are necessary conditions to provide these expected new services. Last but not least attention to cost efficiency and economy has to be paid.

1.2 New E-Government Processes

This new e-Government paradigm generates great demands for new governmental processes. Existing paper driven processes often include lots of auxiliary steps, just coming from the paper world. These auxiliary steps are partly carried out by divisions responsible for the main duty, partly by specific auxiliary support divisions. Therefore these old paper driven processes are not a good basis for creating new e-Government processes. All these paper steps have the effect of big blinkers, which obstruct the view to the real and basic needs of organisation and users. Therefore existing processes and structures of organisations should stay unnoticed first!

R. Traunmüller (Ed.): EGOV 2003, LNCS 2739, pp. 325–328, 2003.

326   J. Makolm

1.3   A Roadmap to New E-Government Processes

To create these speedy, smart and simple processes, it is necessary to go back to the legal roots. And even legal directives should be scrutinised, whether these directives just organise the former paper world or whether they really constitute functional instructions. The most important questions are: What are the basic needs of citizens and authorities? And how can the actual potentialities of information technology be used to transform these needs into e-Government Processes.

To find the answers to these two questions, it is necessary to involve experts:

- Legal experts will have to define the basic requirements needed for the new processes. And they will have to deal with change requests coming from the other experts and affecting this legal basis.
- Governmental experts responsible at a high level for these specific e-Government processes will have to define the precise governmental needs concerning the new organisational structure.
- Experts in process engineering should give their know-how in designing effective application flows.
- Last but not least it is the duty of experts in standard business software and workflow tools to face the requirements of the aforementioned specialists and to adjust them to the potentialities of the software world.

People dealing daily with the "old" process should not be involved until a prototype of the new system can be presented to them. If these people are involved too early, the risk of including steps and procedures of the old processes – just for themselves – is very high. In the same way the risk of not seeing new opportunities would be high, because the mere knowledge of the old system could have the effect of blinkers, and therefore only allows a very restricted view. It is the job of these "experts in practice" to test the proposed processes and organisations, and to check their practicability.

On the other hand the above mentioned four types of experts should not have the authority just to implement their developed new processes and to order their use. It is their task to convince the users of the advantages of the new work flow or - in other words - it is the job of these experts to sell the system to the users.

The above described method of debarring users from the creative design step, but letting them participate in a second step of evaluation and fine design, guarantees full creativity for the design step and full usability for the result. Speedy, smart and simple processes for the users become possible.

2   The New Austrian State Budgeting and Bookkeeping System

2.1   The Starting Situation

The starting situation was characterised by an online budgeting and bookkeeping system designed in the sixties, which has been repeatedly renewed. The system was designed for bookkeeping specialists and was exclusively operated by the accounts departments. The workflow between the organisations and their accounts departments was characterised by a lot of paper forms and printouts of accounts and statistics.

For the new millennium a complete new design was essential. Two main goals were identified:

- Use of standard software with appropriate user interfaces.
- Complete redesign of the bookkeeping processes as an integral part of the organisational workflow and reduction of the accounts departments to their core capabilities.

As a result of the selection process within a public tender SAP/R3 was chosen as an appropriate system to meet the above mentioned first goal. But information technology, hardware as well as software systems, is just one means to reach the target. To realise the main goal a process reengineering project was started.

2.2 Defining New Processes

What was the situation like before the beginning of the reorganisation project? All twelve Austrian ministries used the same bookkeeping software system as described above. But in every ministry a lot of processes were used that differed in a highly sophisticated way. It was nearly impossible and without any sense to count or register these wide field of variations. In addition these processes were designed to be operated within a paper driven workflow and to co-operate with the specific bookkeeping system.

So the decision not to start from this position was easy. It actually seemed to be better to go back to the legal roots and see, which were the requests constituted by the law. No legal reason could be found for the phenomenon of the different processes within different ministries. These differences were just the result of different evolutions driven by different organisational cultures, but not really necessary for doing the job.

On the legal basis fourteen main processes could be identified as being necessary to do all governmental bookkeeping, from the budgeting process to the ordering process and finally the paying process. Special attention was directed to keep these processes slim, speedy and simple. The new processes support the whole organisation and break up the information monopoly of the accounts department.

Furthermore it has been possible - from the legal point of view - to reduce the number of dual control steps. In return enhanced documentation features and audit processes were designed. At least some legal changes were necessary so that several legal orders could be adapted to the new requirements.

2.3 Used Tools

The Aris Toolset was used to model the above named fourteen processes. Just for documentation of the improvement, one of the so far used old processes was modelled too.

As mentioned before, SAP/R3 was installed as bookkeeping software. To bring information about the new system and the new processes to the users, an e-learning platform was installed on the intranet. Last but not least an extensive help system was built to support users doing their job.

2.4 The Rollout

The Ministry of Finance is only responsible for the organisation of the accounts departments and the accounting IT-solution, but it is not competent for the organisation of the other ministries. Therefore a special rollout team has been set up for each ministry to roll out the new system separately for each ministry. Each of these rollout teams consists of members of the concerned ministry, responsible for the ministerial organisation, and of technicians from the federal computing centre. Last but not least specialists responsible for the new processes and IT-systems from the Ministry of Finance are involved.

As mentioned before, the Ministry of Finance does not have the authority to install the new system out of the box in another ministry. It is the job of the rollout team to implement the new processes in the concerned ministerial organisation. And it is the job of the staff of the Ministry of Finance to convince the colleagues from other ministries. The result is a good combination of the generalised creative process for solution finding and of fine designing a system, which can be fully used in the special environment of the concerned ministry.

Nine ministries have completed their rollout and the new system is already on duty there. The rollout for the rest of three ministries is planned to be completed in the third quarter of 2004.

2.5 Organisational and Commercial Effects

The new system leads to the following effects:
- Activities are transferred from the accounts departments to the other departments. Nevertheless staff reduction is planned for these departments. This should be possible due to better software support and higher efficiency of the new processes.
- The accounts department's staff will be reduced by 40%. First reductions have already taken place. The reduction process is planned to be finished after a transitional period of 18 months.
- Topical controlling and audit information is available immediately after booking.

3 Outlook

It is a phenomenon of bureaucratic systems: Once optimal designed processes tend to develop themselves backwards to former sophisticated processes, they tend to grow or to "get fat" in some way. To be effective against this phenomenon, a reverse business engineering tool has been planned to be installed within the SAP-System to measure the new processes and to track their development. With this tool it will be possible to save the achieved rationalisations further on.

Ontologies, Web Services, and Intelligent Agents: Ideas for Further Development of Life-Event Portals

Boštjan Berčič and Mirko Vintar

University of Ljubljana,
School of Public Administration,
Gosarjeva 5, 1000 Ljubljana, Slovenia
{bostjan.bercic,mirko.vintar}@vus.uni-lj.si

Abstract. This paper present possible further development of intelligent life-event based portals. Introduction of 'deep' knowledge (semantics) in the shape of ontologies, distributed components in the shape of web services and intelligent agents are three main topics of probable future architecture of e-gov. This paper relates to the developed prototype of life-event based portal and its possible future architectural refinement.

1 Introduction

After a few years of intensive research into the area of e-government in EU and accessing countries, it became apparent, that one of the main obstacles for quicker further development of e-government is a lack of common conceptual and methodological framework, which would allow a unified approach to the development of e-services.

Building an ontology of public administration would provide a common semantics for development and representation of life-events. Life-events (in e-government) share a number of common characteristics (viz. data objects), such as institutions that provide administrative services to citizens, administrative procedures needed for different services etc., but basically all relying on general administrative procedure, coded in a statute, and rights and duties that these procedures confer to or impose on citizens. It would therefore be of great help if a standard vocabulary of objects from administrative procedures would exist, describing, say, agents, documents, roles, activities, rights and duties that exist in these life-events. They should be general enough to encompass any particular legislation (preferably based on EU statutes and directives), but specific enough to confer modeler with enough building elements to be able to construct specific life-events, tied to specific legal and other contexts of each country.

On the other hand, ontology would not only help make existing life-events models more precise, it would in our opinion also considerably broaden the subject of life-event modelling. Existing approaches to life-event modelling almost all rely on process mapping of life-events. These means that life-event is deemed

R. Traunmüller (Ed.): EGOV 2003, LNCS 2739, pp. 329–334, 2003.

to be identical with some (decision) process. While this may be so in many respects, there is a context knowledge (e.g. substantive law vs. procedural law) surrounding pure process models.

Ontologies and life-events are not an end in themselves. Having constructed public administration ontology and appropriate set of life-events on top of it, one is faced with the need to develop information systems which would use this explicit knowledge. Such information systems, would be based either on decision support or expert systems technology or both. They could have distributed architecture with knowledge base of life-events on one machine and intelligent processing algorithms (agents) locally on clients' machines. One of the most promising distributed architectures, web services, drafted by W3C, which also bear close relationship to other web technologies (XML, semantic web etc) will be examined in this paper.

2   Ideas for the Further Development of Life-Event Based Portals

Research projects in the field of e-government should have as an ultimate goal formalization of knowledge in public administration viz. public sector (legal, economic, business and organizational) and the integration of such knowledge in intelligent components which would help end-users to interact more efficiently with government [5]. We sketch some of these ideas in the next sections and relate them to the prototype of intelligent life-event based portal that we have built [3].

2.1   Ontology Building

Some building blocks of public administration ontology already exist (such as specific domain ontologies, existing (ER,OO,XML) data models, informal knowledge from the field etc.) and many will have to be developed from scratch.

We consider the best approach to ontology building to be a bi-directional approach:

- a deductive one, involving the creation of ontology,which is based on pre-existing general (upper) ontologies and specialized ontologies (microtheories), with the assistance of field experts, and
- an inductive one, involving text mining, automatic knowledge extraction from corpora and semi-automatic creation and/or refinement of ontology.

Manual creation of ontology would be entrusted to field experts which would be assisted by ontology building experts.

On the other hand, corpora of texts would be compiled which relate to e-government and public administration on general (e.g. legal texts such as statutes, decree,decisions as well as strategic and action plans such as white books, guidelines etc.). This corpora would be linguistically and semantically

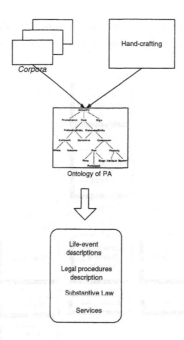

Fig. 1. Creation of PA Ontology and its use

annotated with the use of existing general (such as Wordnet) and domain ontologies and would, at the end of this process, serve as an input for (semi-)
automatic ontology refinement, which would be performed by machine learning
technologies in relation to natural language processing. As a result, important
terms would be extracted and checked for their existence and position in existing domain ontology. In case the results of this automatic process would differ
significantly from the existing ontology, certain terms would either have to be
introduced to ontology or withdrawn form it. Some terms in ontology would
possibly have to change their position to better reflect their relation to other
terms as observed in corpora.

2.2   Contents of PA Ontology

Public administration ontology would consist of many terms which could broadly
be classified according to classic views of public administration: legal view, organizational view, business view, IT view and end-user view. Legal view would encompass the totality of legal rules relating to public administration (general administrative procedure, substantive laws related to public administration such as
laws relating urban and environmental issues etc). Organizational aspect would
cover organizational rules, business processes, institutions, agents and their hierarchy. IT aspect would cover data in public administration and its collection
and processing. It aspect would also include documents, electronic forms, web
portals etc. User aspects would cover services for citizens and businesses, en-

try points for citizens to connect to e-government etc. Possible elements of such general public administration ontology are depicted in figure 2

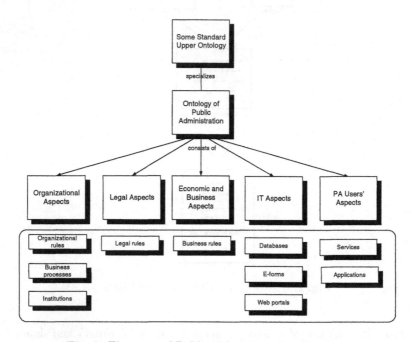

Fig. 2. Elements of Public Administration Ontology

2.3 Life-Events, Administrative Procedures, and Services Modelling

Formal description of public administration related terms would serve as building blocks for the description of various higher-level data models in public administration, such as life-event, legal procedures and services provided to citizens. These data models were developed in our prototype of life-event portal ([2]).

Aim of this prototype was the development of a formal framework for intelligent life-event portals with a special focus on processes, data models, decision elements, business rules and normative contents underlying life-events in the area of public administration. Methodology for life-event mapping is based on eEPCs and complemented with additional elements (most notably the decision element and several container elements, comprising complete administrative procedures or sub life-events). It encompasses three levels: the level of life-events , the level of administrative procedures and the level of services (life-events can branch to sub life-events and ultimately to the level of administrative procedures, defined by the appropriate statutes, which can in turn contain several services. Comparatively, our methodology resembles most ([1].

Thus, a general ontology of public administration, depicted in figure 1 would serve as a building block for life-events modelling, administrative procedures description and substantive law modelling. Substantive law (regulating when one is entitled to some right or duty), alongside with user interface, represents contents of different services.

2.4   Distributed Architecture and Intelligent Components

Creation of public administration ontology is of course not an end in itself, neither are life-events. Final goal is to build user-friendly interfaces which would seamlessly provide a wealth of e-services to citizens. One way of doing this is to build intelligent life-event portals with lists of life-events which would guide citizens through different procedures and services. Alternatively, one can introduce intelligent agents to browse for him through lists of life-events, choose appropriate procedures and services and carry out the required steps on his behalf.

Architecture of web services ([4]) has been taken as a reference architecture because it is being widely popularized by W3C and because it presents a relevant and growing in importance alternative to other distributed architecture models such as COM and CORBA. Also, it is a more or less open standard based on web technologies, which could play a major role if ontology itself was created with the use of semantic web technologies, such as XML, RDF, RDFS, OWL and others. Example architecture is taken from ([4]). Web service provider, basically a supplier of services which reside on his server, publishes his services to Service Description Agency (using WSDL- Web services description language). Service requestor first connects to this Agency in search of appropriate services. Here, all services that have been previously published are available in service registry, along with URLs of respective providers. When appropriate service is found, URL of provider of that service is sent to the requestor, which then connects directly to (is bind to) the provider of that service. In our framework, Service Description agency does not only relegate specific services to specific providers but provides a higher level mapping of life-events (consisting of administrative procedures which themselves consist of services) to services that they ultimately consist of. This mapping is normally a task of an intelligent life-events portal. In the framework of web services, this portal also needs a functionality of providing web addresses of specific services. Thus, in this framework, life-events portal becomes Life-event description & Service Discovery Portal.

Service requestor (end-user, citizen or business) can connect to this life-events portal, browse through list of life-events, see description of specific life-event (with administrative procedures and services contained in it) and then connect to servers running these services. If one employs intelligent agents technology, one need no more search through lists of life-events and services contained in them himself, but lets his personal (intelligent) agent do this. In a sense, 'intelligence' moves from intelligent life-events portal to (end-user run) intelligent agent, residing on end-user machine. User runs his agent, inputs what life-event he is interested in and the rest is done by the agent. Agent connects to life-events description & service discovery portal, retrieves from the knowledge base the appropriate life-event, dissects it to the level of services needed to be performed and eventually, with explicit or tacit permission of user, begins connecting to servers with different services and requesting, on behalf of the user, that this services be performed. He can also furnish user's data without having to trouble him with continual input of the same data, but he also has to operate in conformity with some privacy policy that has been installed in him.

3 Conclusion

We presented some of the possible futures of architectures of e-gov related information systems, above all life-event based portals. Final cause of supply-side oriented e-gov systems is a quicker, better and more efficient satisfaction of end-users needs related to public administration, vested in form of (e-) services such as applications for permissions, issuance of documents etc. This can be achieved with better integration of existing IT systems in public administration and introduction of new technologies. Most promising ones have been described in this paper as a potential architectural extension of the developed prototype of life-event based public administration portal. The are:

- ontologies which would formally define semantics of various e-gov and public administration related terms
- distributed web components architecture which obeys the paradigm of ubiquitous (or environmental) computing and divides tasks in the service supply chain to many machines and
- intelligent agents which act as a proxy for their owners and help them interact with government.

Other technologies in connection with this paradigms have also been investigated, such as techniques for natural language processing and machine learning from texts, which result in automatic ontology refinement. Only future will tell which of these technologies and how quick they will be implemented to yield value-added to the interaction of e-gov service requestors (citizens) and service e-gov service suppliers (government).

References

1. LEAP Life-Events Access Project, available at www.leap.gov.uk
2. Vintar, M., et al.: Report on the project: Development of a public web portal (in Slovene). University of Ljubljana, School of Public Administration, Ljubljana,(2001)
3. Vintar, M.,Leben A.: The concepts of an Active Life-Event Public Portal. Proceedings of the First International Conference,EGOV 2002, Aix-En-Provence, France (2002) 383–390.
4. W3C: Web Services Architecture W3C Working Draft 14 November 2002 [URL:http://www.w3.org/TR/ws-arch/]
5. M. Wimmer ,J. Krenner (2001) An Integrated Online One-Stop Government Platform: The eGOV Project *Proceedings of 9th Interdisciplinary Information Management Talks*, Schriftenreihe Informatik, Universitätsverlag Trauner, Linz, pp. 329–337 (ISBN 3-85487-272-0)

Spatial Data Warehouse – A Prototype

Lionel Savary and Karine Zeitouni

Computer Science Department
Versailles Saint-Quentin University
PRiSM laboratory
45 avenue des Etats-Unis
78035 Versailles, France
{Lionel.Savary,Karine.Zeitouni}@prism.uvsq.fr

Abstract. Nowadays, there are an emergence of spatial or geographic data stored in several and heterogeneous databases, mostly in Geographic Information Systems (GIS). The diversity of GIS and the increasing accumulation of non-spatial (simple attributes) and spatial (geometric shapes) data make it difficult to apply conventional OLAP and data mining tools. Thus, the need to build a spatial data warehouse over heterogeneous GIS is becoming necessary in many fields. Our architecture is a central type architecture based on GML (for spatial data representation) and more generally on XML (for all data). In this paper we will focus on the study of data integration into a data warehouse, and data representation. We will show how the specificities of our architecture contribute to manage spatial and non-spatial data.

1 Introduction

Designing a data warehouse implies to face up problems like scattering information in different sources (Geographic Information Systems) and the ability of these sources to answer a particular query. One of the major problems encountered in the design of a data warehouse is the schema and data integration. In this case, the data warehouse designer must take into account the heterogeneity of data formats stored in a specific Geographic Information System (GIS). A common solution to overcome this problem is to convert all heterogeneous data into a single standard data model, once schema conflicts have been resolved.

This paper is organised in four sections. The second section enumerates the schema integration process and emphasises the problems encountered in schema and data integration for *non-spatial* and *spatial* data. In the third section, we will review and discuss about existing architectures and especially spatial data warehouse architectures. The fourth section details our prototype and highlights its specificity. Finally, we will conclude by giving the major contributions of our proposition.

R. Traunmüller (Ed.): EGOV 2003, LNCS 2739, pp. 335–340, 2003.
© Springer-Verlag Berlin Heidelberg 2003

2 Schema and Data Integration

The integration task refers to the problem of integrating the data from two ore more different data sources. Integration is often required between applications or databases witch differ in the way data are stored, the semantic of the data and the way it is organized. Two types of heterogeneity are distinguished: schema and data heterogeneity.

2.1 Schema Heterogeneity

Since database systems are generally developed independently, integrating different database schemas becomes difficult because of different structures, terminologies and focuses [2] used by each database designer. Moreover, in GIS case, managing heterogeneity among data is much more complex, because it must take into account *non-spatial* and *spatial* data [3]. Conflicts associated to spatial database include previous conflicts and specific conflicts due to [4]: different scales in spatial representations, different spatial referential, different geometry types depending on the specific point of view in a given GIS application.

2.2 Data Heterogeneity

Conflicts encountered at this level result usually from [1]: different data formats for the same field in semantic, abbreviation data encoding, missing values, duplicated information.

To face the problems of database and more specifically GIS interpretabilities, some methodologies have been defined and are commonly known as *integration process*. But *integration process* is difficult because conflicts at both structural and semantic level must be addressed. One can consider two integration levels: *schema* and *data integration*.

2.3 Schema and Data Integration

Before integrating data, one must first consider the *schema integration*. This phase consists in combining database schema into a coherent and global view. This operation is divided into four steps [1]: pre-integration, schema comparison, schema conformity, and finally schemas fusion and reorganization.

After this phase, *data integration* phase could start. Before the data being integrated into the data warehouse, they pass by the *preparation* phase. This phase is divided into three steps [1]: data extraction, data storage, and data cleaning. Data cleaning is one of the most important step in the *preparation* phase, and includes four principal functionalities: conversion and normalization of target data, field dependant cleaning, and rule based cleaning.

For integrating *spatial* and *non-spatial* data, specific components must be introduced into common data warehouse architecture, in order to manage these types of data. In this field, only few works have been done and they only focus on managing *spatial* and *non-spatial* data.

3 Review of Existing Architectures

Existing approaches for managing *spatial* and *non-spatial* data are based on Geography Markup Language (GML) and more generally, in XML. The reasons of using XML as the common protocol for geo-referenced information exchange are as follows [7]:

- Text-based information exchange protocol ensures platform independence and easy implementation.
- XML may describe any data format of produced datasets or any GIS.
- The generated XML document is application independent, which can be used in any application as long as the application can parse XML documents.
- Storing and transferring Geo-Referenced Information (GRI) in XML could be more compact because usually there are many attributes in a whole dataset but few attributes are associated with each object.

Some works carried out by Gupta et al. [5] propose a three tier architecture composed of database wrappers, two levels of mediators and clients. The first level are composed of mediators appropriate to the specificities of the different sources (i.e. spatial mediator for GIS and another for image databases sources). The second level is composed of the main mediator witch receives the client query, applies a set of rules to identify the spatial and non-spatial part of the query witch are cut into sub-queries. These sub-queries are then routed to the specific mediator. The returned results are then gathered into a single document using the XMAS [6] language witch allows the fusion of objects like pictures and maps into a new XML composite object.

Other works done by J.Zhang et al. [7], propose a prototype for wrapping and visualizing geo-referenced data in a distributed environment using XML technology. In this prototype, XML is used as a communication protocol between distributed web sites that provide GRI and the mediator, and between the mediator and clients. Java Servlets implement data translation into XML documents. Data in distributed websites can be stored in a flat file, relational database, object-oriented database or object relational database. A Java Servlet in the mediator server retrieves data from related distributed websites in an XML format upon a request from the client side, parses the retrieved XML documents, performs merge or other operations on the retrieved XML documents to build a new XML document and sends it to the client side. When the client side gets the requested data from the mediator server, it parses the returned XML document and draws it inside the browser window by using a Java applet.

In these two works [5], [7], the author suppose that spatial queries are processed by the sources and the wrappers, before being integrated in a common XML document with other data types. So, they do not implement any spatial query engine in the mediator itself. This limits the system by not allowing queries that combine different sources. To overcome this problem, we propose a new prototype also based on XML language offering more capabilities at the mediator level.

4 Our Prototype

Our prototype is a three tier architecture based on XML and GML. The communications between clients and mediator, mediator and wrappers are based on the Simple Object Access Protocol (SOAP). This protocol allows exchanging information over distributed environment. It is based on XML and can be generalized beyond HTTP. It can be implemented over CORBA/IIOP, COM, TCP/IP or SMTP and it is independent of any platform. SOAP can be used as a Remote Call Procedure (RPC) to send a message query and retrieve responses.

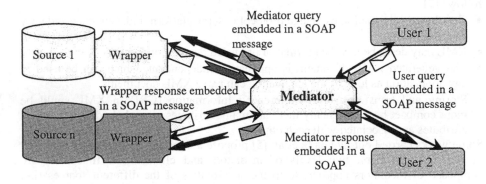

Fig. 1. Three tier architecture based on SOAP protocol

The three main components of the architecture in figure 1 are composed of sources and wrappers (the first tier), mediator and the mediator database (the second tier), users (the third tier).

4.1 Source and Wrapper Level

At this level, each data source is composed of a GIS like ArcView or a database like Oracle and a wrapper. The wrapper transforms data stored in an original format (such as ArcView or Oracle formats) into XML/GML format. Because ArcView data are stored in flat files, they could be accessed in any programming language without on-line access to the GIS. Whereas in Oracle, a connection to the database is required. *Non spatial* data are coded into XML format and *spatial* data into GML. These two types of data are embedded in a SOAP message and are sent to the mediator. If the capabilities of the sources are limited, for queries that can not be processed by the source, the wrapper should provide all capabilities of XQuery and spatial queries. It returns all the data in XML/GML format to the mediator. Otherwise, if the source allows handling XML data, but not spatial queries and operators, the non-spatial part of the query could be easily wrapped in the specific language of the source (such as DBMS_XMLQuery for Oracle), whereas the spatial part necessitates the implementation of spatial engine within the wrapper, generating a GML result.

4.2 Mediator Level

4.2.1 Mediator Components

The purpose of our work is to propose an architecture based on standard components that allow to plug in any other component without any modification of the whole or a part of the architecture. To achieve this goal, the mediator is based on standard components like Java Topology Suite (JTS) and XQuery. JTS [8] is an open source conform to the Open GIS Consortium features specifications. It implements spatial predicates and functions for managing two dimensional data stored in GML format. Thus, we are using JTS to deal with *spatial* data, and XQuery for *non-spatial* data. The advantage of these components is the allow the support any type of databases at this level since all operations are computed by specific components. Oracle has been chosen for the mediator database, for the moment, because it holds the management of XML database (XML_DB) and should optimise data retrieval using specific indexes. The figure below summarises this prototype architecture.

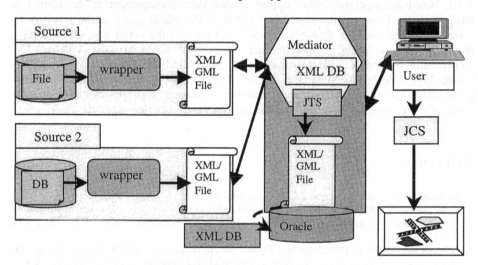

Fig. 2. Prototype architecture

4.2.2 Query Processing

Once the SOAP message containing one user query is received by the mediator, the XML documents is extracted. Then the mediator first queries the Oracle database. If this mediator database can not answer the user query, the query is then split into sub-queries and sent to the distributed servers concerned by these sub-queries. The returned results from the distributed servers are then processed by the mediator. If no more treatment is required, the results are gathered into a single XML/GML document, stored in the XML_DB and rooted to the user. If any treatment is required, the mediator computes the required operations before merging the result into a single XML/GML document.

4.3   Client Level

The message received by the user is then extracted and displayed using Java Conflation Suite (JCS). JCS is an open source conform to the Open GIS Consortium features specifications. It allows a graphical visualization of geographic data and supports GML and operations on graphical display such as zoom-in, zoom-out, etc.

5   Conclusion

This article has pointed out the problems encountered during *non-spatial* and *spatial* data integration into a data warehouse. *Spatial* data are more complex and more difficult to be integrated and require specific architecture. In the review section, it has shown existing architectures for *non-spatial* and some for *spatial* data. But these XML-based architectures only support *spatial* data management at the source or wrapper level. One solution could be to process the whole query at the level of the warehouse database (for example Oracle), and convert the result into GML format. However, this solution is not optimal because of the data flow volume. Our architecture overcomes this problem by using XML SQL Utility, Java Topology Suite, Java Conflation Suite and SOAP. Using these technologies, the mediator capabilities and performances are enhanced in answering a *spatial* query and the client allow the users a powerful graphic interface and map viewing tool.

References

1. Fundamentals of data warehouses, Springer edition, 2000
2. P.Johannesson, M.Jamil.: Semantic interoperability context, issues, and research directions. In: Second International Conference on Cooperating Information System, Eds. , 192–199. 1984
3. schema integration methodology and Toolkit for Heterogeneous and Distributed Geographic Databases. In: Journal of the Korea Industrial Information Systems Society, V6, 3 (September 2001), 51–64
4. *Data* and Metadata: Two-Dimensional Integration of Heterogeneous Spatial Databases .In: Spatial Data Handling 98 Conference Proceedings, Vancouver, BC, Canada, July 1998, 172–179
5. A.Gupta, R.Marciano, J.Zaslaviska, G.Baru: Integrating GIS and Imagery through XML-based Information Mediation. In: Digital Images and GIS, Lectures Notes In Computer Science, 1999, Vol.1787
6. C.Baru,   A.Gupta,   B.Ludäscher,   R.Marciano,   Y.Papakonstantinous,   P.Velikhov, A.Yannakopulos: XML-based Information Mediation with MIX. In: proceeding of the SIGMOD, 1999
7. J.Zhang, M.Javed, A.Shaheen, L.Gruenwald: Prototype for Wrapping and Visualizing Geo-Referenced Data in a Distributed Environment Using XML Technology. In: Eighth International Symposium of ACMOS, McLean, Virginia, November 2000
8. http://www.vividsolutions.com/jts/jtshome.htm

SINUP: Using GIS to Support *E-Democracy*

Alexandre Carvalho, Artur Rocha, and Marco Amaro Oliveira

INESC-Porto,
Rua Dr. Roberto Frias, N° 378 4200-465
Porto, Portugal
{alexandre.carvalho,ajrocha,mao}@inescporto.pt,
http://www.inescporto.pt

Abstract. SINUP consists of a geographical information system whose purpose is to store, in a coherent manner, data resulting from key activities of Oporto local authority, allowing to better structure the knowledge about the urban reality. In the possession of such knowledge, and with the revision of Oporto's Municipal Master Plan taking place soon, the municipality is making an effort to develop an electronic citizen service that will allow a large number of citizens to consult it, and more important, participate in its public discussion prior to approval thus creating a major instrument of *e-democracy* in Oporto's municipality.

1 SINUP

SINUP is the foundation of an e-LocalGovernment solutions for the Oporto's municipality and consists, generally, of a geographical information system (GIS) whose purpose is to store data resulting from key activities of Oporto's local authority, mainly related to land use, either in a planning, management, assessment or decision support perspective. Started from a joint effort, involving the local authority (Câmara Municipal do Porto), Sociedade Porto 2001 and INESC Porto, SINUP's main goal was, at that time, to assist the activities of urban transformation and requalification in the context of the cultural event "Oporto, European capital of culture 2001"[AC2001]. Another reason for the existence of SINUP is to better structure the knowledge about the urban reality, by allowing to store, in a coherent manner, every urban activity, independently of being a requalification process or a land management activity.

SINUP's philosophy relies on the concept of geographical information (GI) share and reuse: every data producer in the local authority, from the cartography department to the urban projects department, accesses and updates the same pool of data. This institutional policy eliminates the fact of existing several instances of the same data, which often leads to inaccurate or incoherent GI. It also contributes for a serious reduction of investment in data acquisition.[AC2001]

By allowing such an operative system, SINUP performs the important role of supporting collective information. In other words, every group of data belongs to a specific department, which is responsible for maintaining it accurate and up to date, but that is also available to everybody inside the local authority. Being

R. Traunmüller (Ed.): EGOV 2003, LNCS 2739, pp. 341–344, 2003.

able to access, at the same time, multidisciplinary data, the local authority has now the possibility to elaborate new sorts of studies.

The Architecture. In order to better manage the computational means and infrastructures, in an optimized perspective of the cost/benefit relationship, the SINUP system has adopted, from the beginning, a client-server paradigm, based on a multi-technological (commercial and non-commercial) platform. This allowed better levels of integration and data share, multi-user environment with several levels of access to informational resources.

In a functional perspective, SINUP's architecture is the result of integrating three components, the store of urban data, the viewing and editing of such data, and the internal and external broadcast of data.

Storage Component: The storage component has for main purpose to allow the persistence of data that is of interest to more than one department and results of the local authority activity. The confluence of such data in one repository has several advantages: To increase the universe of available data for everyone inside the local authority; the elimination of undesirable redundancy; people know that data coming from this storage is accurate and up to date; by using data produced by others, each department must be aware of the definitions used to represent it. This leads to the fact that definitions and concepts about the urban reality can be standardized all over the organization.

Application Component: The second main component of SINUP gathers a group of back-office client applications that work inside the intranet and support activities like viewing, printing or updating data. Such applications are aimed to both GI consumed by most people, and to specific department data.

e-*Services Component:* The last component of SINUP is related to the broadcast of data to the public through the web portal. Nowadays, there are already available a group of non-payed electronic citizen services like latest city information, for example local traffic, and an interactive map of the city. Nevertheless, much is to be done in this functional component like, for example, allowing the citizens to request permits or official documentation online (some of these e-services should be payed).

2   Supporting *E-Democracy*

The Municipal Master Plan is defined in [DL380/99] and represents the model of the spacial structure of the municipal territory in accordance to its soil classification and qualification, as well as defined planning and managing operative units, it must also identify all the restrictions and servitudes of public utility that may constitute a limitation or impediment to any specific form of exploitation.

Among other major activities taking place, nowadays, in Oporto, one of great importance is the revision of the Municipal Master Plan (PDM). Such task takes place every ten years, according to the current legislation.

The revision process of the PDM has a sequence of several steps that are to be executed: The process starts with the debate, by specialists, about how the urban space should be used. The decisions taken by these specialists, are based in several diagnostics and prospective studies previously elaborated; a public discussion of what has been previously decided takes place. This action is of democratic importance since it allows every citizen to tell its opinion about the revision of the PDM; after the public discussion results being analyzed, a final revision of the PDM is proposed for approval.

With such an event taking place soon, the local authority is making an effort to develop an electronic citizen service that will reach more citizens and, the most important feature, by removing physical and time restrictions allows citizens to participate, electronically, in the city main decisions, thus creating a major instrument of *e-democracy*[SC2003] in Oporto.

As identified in [HW2002] *e-democracy* can improve deliberations by enabling asynchronous communications, a more rational than emotional flow of the discussions, flexibility related to time and location can improve public participation, planning can be visualized more easily, communications can work on a qualitatively higher level due to the ability of previous preparation by accessing the planning via Internet, the anonymity empowers people to participate who normally would not do that and enables discussion among citizens who usually don't have contact.

3   Municipal Master Plan Public Discussion

The right to information (to consult and obtain copies and informations) mainly through informatic means, and the right to participation (suggestion formulation, elucidation request, and intervention) is well defined in Portuguese Legislation in [DL380/99]. It is asserted the duty of pondering all the proposals made by the citizens as well as the duty to clear every doubt or information request. To allow citizens to public discuss about the PDM is to allow them to give their opinion about a feature, area or the plan as a whole.

Therefore to express it's opinion, each citizen must be able to specify a location or a feature in the master plan map. Therefore, the system must be aware of such specification and record the citizen opinion. By collecting not only text input but also GI, the citizens, as well as the local authority must be able to make questions like "Until now, what is the public opinion about this specific area, or geographical location?"

For the citizen to specify a location or feature, the system must be able to display the master plan map, as well as other layers of information, allow user navigation and to collect user input from it. Every layer of information is provided by SINUP storage component or, for security reasons, by a replicated database. The system must also allow everyone to easily (one click on the map) consult the legislation associated to a specific feature, location or land area.

Besides the fact of welcoming the greatest number of contributions possible, there are, however, aspects of security that should not be neglected. For instance, if surveys about what to do in a certain place are to be made, the system must not allow one citizen to vote more than once in that specific survey. Another security detail is that in order to avoid a minority of citizens to jeopardize the whole process by making "rude comments", instead of constructive ones, each citizen should be responsible by its contribution. This means that anonymity is out of the question and that people should be identified if not to other citizens when online, at least by the system and, consequently, by the local authority. Like in other on-line services, for example, bank account management or tax management in state web servers, people must identify themselves.

Although people can consult this e-service anonymously, there must be a registration process prior to their first active participation, this process is made simple by an semi-automated process that associates a citizen with an email and its home address.

The local municipality is responsible for guaranteing the availability of a group of resources: Human resources must be available for administrative tasks such as mail addressing and manage information requests; there must be an appointed technician, in each department that will be responsible for answering to question made by the citizens during the entire process; info-exclusion must not be used as an argument for citizens not to participate in this process, so, as a consequence, the local municipality should provide free technological access to this electronic citizen service.

One critical advantage of the public discussion of the PDM being on-line is that the evaluation of results can be more accurate, the universe of questions that can be made is wider, like "What are the critical areas of public interest?". Finally, since citizens take an active part of the process they also are more willingly to know the results.

References

[DL380/99]   Decreto-Lei 380/99 de 22 de Setembro In: Diário da Républica I Série-A nr.222, Imprensa Nacional-Casa da Moeda, 1999

[AC2001]   Carvalho, Alexandre et all., SINUP - Sistema de Informação Urbana do Porto In: Proceedings of the VI Encontro de Utilizadores de Informação Geográfica, 28-30 November, 2001, Oeiras, Portugal.

[KL2002]   Lenk, K., Traunmüller, R., Electronic Government: Where Are We Heading? In: Proceedings of the 1st International Conference EGOV2002, 2–6 September, 2002, Aix-en-Provence, France, Springer pp.1–9.

[HW2002]   Westholm, H., e-Democracy Goes Ahead. The Internet as a Tool for Improving Deliberative Policies In: Proceedings of the 1st International Conference EGOV2002, 2–6 September, 2002, Aix-en-Provence, France, Springer pp.240–247.

[SC2003]   Clift, S., e-Democracy Resource Links, http://www.publicus.net/articles/edemresources.html, Visited 12 May, 2003.

An Interoperable GIS Solution for the Public Administration

Artur Rocha, João Correia Lopes, Luís Bártolo, and Rui Chilro

INESC-Porto,
Rua Dr. Roberto Frias, Nº 378 4200-465,
Porto, Portugal
{ajrocha,jlopes,lbartolo,rchilro}@inescporto.pt
http://www.inescporto.pt

Abstract. Geographical information is of strategic importance, when comes to land use management decision-making and GIS are essential resources for the production of land use management instruments, commonly known as plans (e.g. master plans).

To build them, local authorities require multi-disciplinary teams with different competences and responsibilities. Many of these teams are external to the municipality and in the position of sub-contractors. With so many actors involved, the result is often a complex mesh of incoherent spatial data. Overcoming this problem often leads to huge overheads for the public administration.

This paper addresses a possible technical solution for this issue, based on international standards (e.g. OpenGIS) and profiting from the current state of technological development.

1 Introduction

Local authorities are responsible for innumerable decisions related to land use management. Some of these decisions must be taken in accordance with metropolitan/regional authorities and central government, and involve a set of complex tasks with a large volume of data of different nature and origin. Undoubtedly, geographical information (GI) is of strategic importance, when comes to land use management decision-making. Geographical information systems (GIS) are essential resources for the production of land use management instruments, commonly known as plans (e.g. master plans).

A report elaborated by the Portuguese National Institute for Statistics (INE)[1] refers that 63% of all plans executed by the local government are done by external companies. Some information must be transferred to these companies in a friendly way. Likewise, both external and internal access to this data must be granted according to specific profile definitions, suggesting the need for distributed access.

Project teams, often external and in the position of sub-contractors, encounter the same sort of problems during their intervention, despite of the plan

---

[1] *Instituto Nacional de Estatística (INE).*

R. Traunmüller (Ed.): EGOV 2003, LNCS 2739, pp. 345–350, 2003.

they are working or the granularity of GI data. Most of these problems are related to the lack of a common spatial infrastructure and lead to serious accuracy and coherence issues. Overcoming these issues often leads to huge overheads for the public administration.

The delays in the development of a common Spatial Data Infrastructure (SDI) at the European level contribute to the chaos installed. Even if such infrastructure were in place there would be a long way to go until it fits the regional or local level of detail.

This is the context in which municipalities, metropolitan and regional authorities have to keep producing their plans to support their daily land use decisions. As such, a spatially-enabled distributed work environment seems a natural solution to reduce the aforementioned overhead, creating the assets for a SDI at the local level.

This paper addresses a possible technical solution for this issue, based on international standards and profiting from the current state of technological development.

2   Characterisation of the Actual Situation

Local authorities land management decisions are based on heterogeneous data – from several sources, in different scales, projections and formats. Thus the decision-making process relies on data produced by several organisational units which frequently use different and incompatible systems, often resulting in poor integration and lack of data sharing. Desirably, teams should be able to use their own data and be able to access data produced by others, in a constructive and cooperative way: in other words, a distributed shared environment where everyone can benefit from the combination of multiple information sources. The resulting environment is an information sharing network, where the most important feature is interoperability.

Being the creation of data sources the most expensive part of any GIS effort, reusing spatial data seems a natural solution. However, there are institutional impediments in making data accessible (e.g. intellectual property rights), difficulties in finding and assessing the appropriate data sources (metadata is scarce or often inexistent) and technical problems in data transfer and conversion [Cot03].

This paper describes an architecture which addresses these problems *via* distributed access to data and the provision of a catalogue service.

3   Goal

The strategic goal of this framework proposal is to improve access to geographical information resources for decision-makers as well as other parties involved in the plan making process.

It will address the problem of finding and assessing data by means of a catalog service and the institutional constraints issue by proposing services to access remotely to data that is stored at the systems of their rightfull owner. Having means to cross-access data residing on the systems of the institutions that have the duty to maintain them, also contributes to clearly define responsibilities and help solve incoherence and accuracy issues.

4   Reference Architecture

4.1   Framework Architecture

The proposed architecture implements a typical n-tier, basing its structure on the distributed model suggested by the OpenGIS and TC211 standards. This arrangement provides a high degree of flexibility in a distributed environment. By cleanly separating each layer, and using Geography Markup Language (GML) for data transport, encoding and request formats, many individual participants can contribute to the network without the overhead of negotiating these agreements on a case-by-case basis. This is one of the advantages of the architecture. The global view of any data flow in this architecture comprehends a client requesting the map, data or service; a service that receives, processes and execute the request; and a tier that permits distributed access all over the system to transfer and integrate both ends. This tier may be an Object Request Broker (ORB) or be based on Web Services.

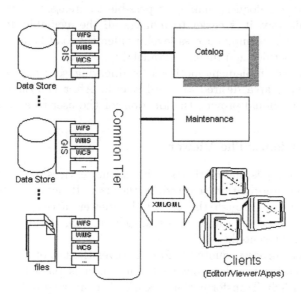

Fig. 1. Framework architecture

A detailed view of each component from this architecture follows.

4.2   The Common Tier

For a correct data transfer, over a distributed and shared environment, there should be a common tier responsible for transportation of all data and requests, even in heterogeneous environments.

This is by far the most important tier, since all the components need its support. It is responsible to interconnect all services and, transfer requests and responses between them. The data needs to be delivered making all the necessary adjustments between environments.

Additionally it must be able to connect to other nodes geographically distributed, using any arbitrary available Local Area Network (LAN), in a way that is transparent to the user. All he must know is that there is a service that shows him all the available geographical data.

If there are any performance or security issues to satisfy, this layer should be able to compress and/or encrypt the data passed.

4.3   The Catalogue

The catalogue service acts as the *yellow pages* of this system, a queriable list of all available data.

After each service is started and initialised with the common tier, it must register itself in the *catalogue* so that all its services be widely available.

As suggested by the OpenGIS consortium, the catalogue can derive is information from other catalogues, making it possible to create a hierarchy tree of catalogues. In this way, it is easier to manage all the available data and give access to data by, for example, access level, implement load balancing, fail-safe and/or redundant service and increase availability.

This service must implement methods for querying/searching geographical data based on type, area desired or word search. After choosing the desired data, the catalogue should provide the location for the user to access them.

4.4   A Simple Client: The Viewer

The interactive viewer is one of the possible client services and is responsible for showing all the information selected by the user. It acts as a front-end to the system. The user, through the use of the viewer, accesses the catalogue and chooses the desired data and, in a transparent way, the data is extracted transformed and represented.

The transparent process, quoted before, involves the use of the common tier to request and receive the data involved. This data is passed in GML[2] and through the use of XSL Transformations (XSLT) is converted to Scalable Vector Graphics (SVG), the format chosen for visualisation of Geographical data. The decision behind SVG was based on open source render formats without loss of detail and quality, flexibility and adaptability to almost any situation. With this

---

[2] The possible use of GML 3.0, approved in 06-Feb-2003 by OpenGIS is in review.

front-end is possible to save the data onto the desired device (remotely through one of services or in local disk), access geographical information by selecting any feature on the map, add red-layers and in future geographical objects.

4.5   The Data Providers

The data is accessed through any of the services described next. These services provide data on a standard way (OpenGIS) allowing flexibility and ease for future developments and integration with other systems.

Any developed component may implement more than one service or even all, providing that all the services are registered individually in the catalogue. These services implement OpenGIS standards so, a simple front-end, with one-to-one method wrap over all services, may provide the information available on each of the wrapped service, in OpenGIS standard to the web (i.e. a *servlet*).

The WMS Service. The simplest service of all, is described in the specification of OpenGIS and TC211 under the name of Web Map Server (WMS), and is intended to deliver an image map, customised by the client request, in this particular case, *via* the common tier.

The client can decide on the output image format requested from a list of formats defined in the standard (`image/gif`, `image/jpg`, `image/tiff`, `image/geotiff`, `image/png`, `image/ppm` and `image/wbmp`). The metadata with the map and services available can be queried at any time from the catalogue and the subsequent response is sent in XML format.

The WFS Service. Web Feature Servers are designed to provide access to (and interaction with) non-image data collections. OGC has followed one of the main axioms of Extensible Markup Language (XML) in its Web services architecture — the separation of structure, style and content. Web Feature Services, specified by this consortium, enable sophisticated, Web-based geoprocessing. Yet it doesn't necessarily mean the user must deal with anything more complex than the interface in basic WMS applications. Generally, WFS operations support `INSERT`, `UPDATE`, `DELETE`, `QUERY` and `DISCOVERY` of geographic features and the solicited data is passed in standard `text/xml` format.

The WCS Service. This is a very recent service[3] and is intended to *simple coverages* (defined on some regular, rectangular or tessellation grid of space) and anticipates other coverage types defined in the OpenGIS Abstract Specification. The specification document explains how *"WCS serves to describe, request, and deliver multi-dimensional coverage data over the World Wide Web"*[Con02e].

This service is based on this specification and receive requests and delivers coverage data. Web Coverage Service provides access to intact (unrendered — as needed for client-side rendering) geospatial information, multi-valued coverages, and input into scientific models for advanced rendering and visualisation clients.

---

[3] RFC for technologies and needed interfaces launched in 24-Dec-2002.

4.6   Maintenance

Anyone responsible for the management of all system needs some tools to maintain and audit the system. This component tries to respond to this need. It is able to start and stop any service or interrupt any damaged or malicious access.

In future developments, this component may be enhanced to take statistics of the system and help on pro-active maintenance, load balancing, service replication, security, profiling, etc.

5   Conclusions and Future Work

This paper aims to conclude on the adequability of the proposed architecture to help solving the issues initially proposed.

A prototype driven approach is being used to assess the framework and identify problems on an early development stage, resulting in a evolving architecture that starts to prove its strengths — interoperable and distributed access to several GI collections (currently only for browsing), through a catalogue.

So far, the preliminary tests have served to provide a proof of concept for the implemented services, even if on an embrionary development stage.

At this point we believe that this framework implementation will contribute to resolve the issues initially proposed, seeming that there is almost no practical limit to scaling or extending this framework architecture to take advantage of additional data resources, services or applications.

References

[Con02a] Open GIS Consortium. OpenGIS Abstract Specification.
          http://www.opengis.org/techno/abstract.htm, September 2002.
[Con02b] Open GIS Consortium. OpenGIS Catalog Services Implementation Specification v1.1.1.
          http://www.opengis.org/techno/specs/02-087r3.pdf, February 2002.
[Con02c] Open GIS Consortium. OpenGIS Web Feature Service Implementation Specification v1.0.0.
          http://www.opengis.org/techno/specs/02-058.pdf, September 2002.
[Con02d] Open GIS Consortium. OpenGIS Web Map Service Interfaces Implementation Specification v1.1.1.
          http://www.opengis.org/techno/specs/01-068r3.pdf, January 2002.
[Con02e] Open GIS Consortium. Request for Comment – OpenGIS Web Coverage Service.
          http://www.opengis.org/techno/02-024r1.pdf, December 2002.
[Con03]   Open GIS Consortium. OpenGIS Geography Markup Language (GML) Implementation Specification c3.0.
          http://www.opengis.org/techno/documents/02-023r4.pdf, January 2003.
[Cot03]   Paul Cote. The Future of Spatial Data Sharing.
          http://www.sdvc.uwyo.edu/metadata/cote.html, May 2003.
[Gro02]   Object Management Group. Catalog of OMG Specifications.
          http://www.omg.org/technology/documents/spec_catalog.htm, November 2002.
[New02]   Eric Newcomer. *Understanding Web Services*. Addison-Wesley, 2002.

ISP (Information Strategy Planning) for 4S-Based Integration of Spatial Information Systems as Korean Nationwide Project

In-Hak Joo[1], Ki-Won Lee[2], Min-Soo Kim[1], and Jong-Hun Lee[1]

[1] Electronics and Telecommunications Research Institute
Daejeon, Korea
[2] Dept. of Information System, Hansung University
Seoul, Korea

Abstract. This paper presents goals and contents of ISP for a nationwide project in Korea called "Development of 4S-based Integration Technologies." Results of this ISP can be utilized for establishing nationwide 4S architecture, strategy, business model, and plan for related current and future projects. 4S project is a government-supported program for the purpose of development of core technologies and integration methods for four systems that are commonly related to spatial information. Application items of 4S such as projects of local governments are also defined and developed in this task. However, there were few systematic approaches about derivation of application items, propulsion strategies and policies, relationships between technical components, and future plans, till now. In this research, by establishing a comprehensive ISP for the 4S project, we form a foundation of nationwide 4S industry and promote integration and utilization of 4S technologies. This ISP is also used for a master plan or guideline prior to system design and implementation for nationwide projects or business items related to spatial information.

1 Introduction

As the demands for value-added spatial information are increasing, a lot of attention is being focused on spatial information system and related technologies. Spatial data is regarded as profitable investment resource and very important digital information that can satisfy various public needs. At present, most developed countries have established long-term strategy planning and are now making lots of investment in concerned technology development and database building. From the view of e-government, many government-supported or public projects are related to spatial data. Furthermore, the spatial data is closely related with daily life of human being, and thus can be served as useful e-government contents. Most of technologies and contents related to spatial data can be used as national and public SOC (Social Overhead Capital) or infrastructure.

Along with the importance and social needs of spatial data, a nationwide project named 4S project has been being carried out in Korea. In the first stage, ISP for 4S project is established to present strategy and future plan for 4S project and related technologies, business item, and application projects. In this paper, we present the goals, contents, and expected effects of the ISP for 4S project.

R. Traunmüller (Ed.): EGOV 2003, LNCS 2739, pp. 351–354, 2003.

2 4S Project: Overview

In Korea, a national-level GIS (Geographic Information System) program named NGIS (National GIS) has been being carried out since the mid-1990s. NGIS program is participated with many domestic companies, universities, and research organizations, as well as supported by some government departments. Since 2001, a new project named as "Development of 4S-based Integration Technology" (4S project) was followed by NGIS program and has been being executed with the goal of nationwide integration of spatial data and information [1]. The 4S project has been performed by ETRI (Electronics and Telecommunications Research Institute), a leading research organization in Korea, and several cooperative companies. It is also supported by Ministry of Information and Communications in Korea.

4S can be defined as core technologies and integration methods for four systems dealing with spatial information: GIS, GNSS (Global Navigation Satellite System), SIIS (Spatial Imagery Information System), and ITS (Intelligent Transport System). In general, the systems have been developed separately without any integration until now, which causes redundancy and inefficiency. The main goals of 4S technology are to integrate the four systems and to reduce redundant time, effort, and investment of developing each system separately, which brings in synergy effect to each system.

The main item of the 4S project is development of "4S core components" that implement core functions for 4S linkage. With open and standardized interfaces adopted, the components increase interoperability and reusability of already constructed spatial databases and systems. Other items are non-technical researches about formation of 4S foundation, international cooperative program, development of collaborative utilization system for 4S data, development of 4S-Mobile technology, and development of a mobile mapping system called 4S-Van.

4S technology is of great value for it can be broadly applied to many actual application fields. It is expected to activate 4S industries and application businesses. After the first-phase of 4S project is completed at the end of 2003, a following project will be launched in the near future, where 4S technologies will be naturally extended to mobile environment, web service, and LBS (Location-Based Service), with other technologies such as wireless communication merged.

3 4S ISP (Information Strategy Planning)

Background and Goals of 4S ISP. Till now, 4S-related business and projects have been developed and performed separately and without any systematic development strategy and plan, which results in insufficient outcome, lack of inter-project relationships, limited utilization of spatial data, and national-level duplicated investment. To solve the problem and get successful outcome of 4S project, it requires that strategy and vision for nationwide introduction and expanding of 4S should be presented. For this reason, we first establish an Information Strategy Planning for 4S project (4S ISP) to present strategy and future plan for 4S project, related technologies, business item, and application projects [2].

Main goal of 4S ISP is to establish nationwide foundation of 4S technology. It also presents inter-organization integration and process plan for successful projects. The strategy planning should minimize trial-and-error and make the projects to settle down effectively. In other words, 4S ISP aims at publishing documents that can be used as guideline for planning, propulsion strategy, and development of 4S-related technologies and business items.

Development of 4S ISP

Considering the particularity of the 4S project, modified establishment process is applied for the 4S ISP in case of need. The distinctive characteristics are 1) domain area that 4S covers is very wide, both public and private sectors; 2) technical elements that comprise 4S are very complicated; and 3) information providers and consumers cannot be completely predefined.

The draft version of 4S ISP was developed in the early 2001, by staffs of ETRI and several experts in the 4S domain. Now it is approved and referred by Ministry of Information and Communications in Korea. 4S-related technologies are being developed with a short-term cycle, and each 4S-related business item in the progress dynamically changes its strategy and plan. Therefore, the initial version of 4S ISP has been continuously reviewed, updated, and complemented to reflect rapidly changing requirements and related circumstances.

Contents of 4S ISP

4S ISP covers all 4S technology, business items, and projects. It consists of five parts whose detailed contents are as below. *4S Strategy Establishment* includes goals, vision, and overview of 4S project; list of possible 4S-related projects; goals and strategies of 4S ISP establishment; and short-term and long-term propulsion plan. *4S Circumstances Analysis* includes recent domestic and international trends and technological policies; problems, issues, and future direction of information technologies; and current status of 4S industries. *4S Business Analysis* includes definitions of 4S applications; analyses of elementary technologies and their relationships; and requirement analyses and definitions for business applications. *4S Technology Structure* includes technological architecture; data model and logical design; and technical roadmap and component matrix. *4S Business Planning* includes current and future business models; roadmap of future business items; relationships and priorities of business items; and overview and detailed plan of each business item.

Expected Influences and Effects of 4S ISP

By specifying whole and detailed structure of 4S technology, 4S ISP supports fast, efficient, and non-duplicated technology development and its efficient utilization. 4S ISP is expected to present a guideline for various projects and business items related to spatial information, to lead the 4S project successful results, and to greatly develop related industry. All future government projects and civil business items that are related to spatial information will refer the 4S ISP as a guidebook when they are planned and launched. Expected influences and effects of 4S ISP are establishment of all elements for basis of the 4S project; consistent propulsion of the 4S project; early settlement of outcome of 4S technology; formation of foundation of 4S technology and infrastructure; and reduction of development cost of 4S technology and applications.

Application Projects Based on 4S ISP

According to 4S business planning part of 4S ISP, some pilot projects are planned and actually operated at local governments. An example of current projects is "urban facility management system based on 4S technology," at the Daejeon city, Korea. In this project, a mobile mapping system called 4S-Van is utilized for semi-automated surveying of facilities such as road, traffic sign, and building. 4S-Van and its application are developed by integrating and linking 4S technologies in distributed or wireless environment. Location determination technology (GNSS) is used to locate spatial objects, and the objects are constructed and managed by GIS technology. For the processing of spatial data, developed 4S core components are used. Further, the collected data from 4S-Van will be used together with ITS data. In this project, it is expected that high-quality spatial data can be constructed with 4S technology utilized.

Other current application project is "119 emergency control center" at fire department of the Daegu city, Korea, where 4S core components are used to manage spatial data and 4S technology is implemented in mobile environment. With these projects actually operated at local governments, 4S technology contributes to development of e-government field related to spatial information. There are also some application projects that use 4S technology in civil areas.

4 Conclusion

In this paper, we present a nationwide project of Korea named "Development of 4S-Based Integration Technologies" and its strategy planning. 4S project is currently being executed with the goal of nationwide integration of spatial data and spatial information systems. To provide foundation of 4S project and to support strategy and plan for 4S technology and applications, 4S ISP is established and used as a master plan or guideline of national 4S businesses and projects.

The 4S ISP is expected to bring many effects on national 4S industry. First, it enables consistent propulsion of future 4S-related projects. Second, it prevents duplicated investment and reduces the costs for technology development. Finally, various future projects that related to 4S will refer the 4S ISP and thereby make their establishment of strategies and planning easier. The 4S ISP is going to be publicized to whoever in need, and will be utilized as basic data that determines direction and strategy of future development of 4S technologies and applications.

References

1. ETRI: Annual Report on Development of 4S-Based Integration Technologies. (2001)
2. ETRI: Reports on Establishment of 4S ISP. (2001)

Spatial Data Infrastructure and E-Government: A Case Study of the UK

Pauline Pollard

Faculty of Computing, Engineering and Mathematical Studies
University of the West of England
Bristol BS16 1QY, England
pauline.pollard@uwe.ac.uk

Abstract. This paper considers the effectiveness of the UK's geographic information network in developing a Spatial Data Infrastructure (SDI). It argues that despite domain expertise and considerable consensus the network has failed to establish a vision for an SDI at the heart of the UK's e-government strategy, a failure that may be impacting on that strategy. The paper concludes that European organisations may become significant actors in the network.

1 Introduction

The underlying context for any discussion on Spatial Data Infrastructure (SDI) is the pursuit of 'information age government'. In 2000 the UK government issued a strategic framework paper as part of its modernising government programme that focused on 'better services for citizens and businesses and more effective use of the Government's information resources'. It challenged 'the centre of government to provide the common infrastructure which is needed to achieve these goals' [1]. The spatial dimension of this information resource in the form of an SDI was not recognised in the framework paper. An SDI being generally understood to be a national framework of policies, institutional arrangements, technologies, data, and people that enable sharing and effective use of geographic information for good decision-making in public policy (in for example, protecting the environment, disaster planning, crime reduction) although the components and success of an SDI may vary significantly between countries [2].

This paper examines the success of the UK's SDI initiative utilising a governance approach to developing structures of public management. This perspective recognises that a top-down, hierarchical approach is not likely to be effective because knowledge about problems and solutions is dispersed over many interactive organisational actors. It recognises that attention needs to be given to the role of these actors and the nature of the relationships between organisations in the development of policy and action agendas [3]. However, it also focuses specific attention on the co-ordinating, network building role of governments because they often occupy a unique position that can not be filled by other actors [4]. This governance approach is enhanced by an understanding of the implications for inter-organisational relations of sharing information systems across organisational boundaries, in particular, the openness of

R. Traunmüller (Ed.): EGOV 2003, LNCS 2739, pp. 355–358, 2003.

the network to information-mediated changes which can radically alter organisations [5]. The method adopted in this paper draws from process research [6] and is based on data gathered over a period from 1995.

2 The UK Geographic Information Network

Since the 1970s a self-organising geographic information network has had an action agenda aimed at facilitating inter-organisational sharing of spatially referenced data sets. In 1987 the government had an early opportunity to take a network building role when a seminal report recommended establishing a Centre for Geographic Information to develop national policy [7]. But the government preferred voluntary arrangements between existing organisations. As a result, an independent association, the AGI (Association for Geographical Information) was set up comprising of members from key government agencies and departments, Geographic Information Systems organisations, local authorities, academics, etc. Organisational actors worked together on joint projects to develop data sets, inter-organisational information services, metadata services, standards, etc. However, the lack of an overall co-ordinating structure was identifiable as a barrier to the development of the geographic information agenda [8].

In 1995 the mapping agency (Ordnance Survey Great Britain) proposed the setting up of a conceptual geospatial 'one stop shop' managed by data providers to develop such a co-ordinating structure. It was launched as the NGDF (National Geospatial Data Framework) and was described by the management board as the UK's SDI. The board identified that key to its success was the recognition by the whole geographic information community of itself as an authoritative 'effective body' [9]. Some headway was made and a web-based metadata service established, now run under the auspices of the AGI. However, whilst this service could become a key part of Britain's SDI, the NGDF itself has lost impetus.

The limits of the NGDF concept were discernable from the outset. The then chief executive of the mapping agency acknowledged that, although it was like an SDI, the NGDF critically had 'less political support and less central funding' [10]. It was also acknowledged that, because of the autonomy of UK government organisations and the 'unremitting pressure' of cost recovery targets, conditions were less favourable than in the United States where the SDI concept originated. However, perhaps the most significant problem identified by a key member of the AGI was the inability to win a clear 'mandate'. In 2000 the AGI lobbied for the NGDF to be included in the strategic framework for information age government, it failed. Responsible for setting its own strategic direction the NGDF lacked legitimacy.

There is evidence that the UK's e-government strategy, like the NGDF, has lost some momentum particularly in the provision of mature e-government services. A recent management consultancy survey warned that the UK has lost ground to countries in a similar stage of development concluding that despite a 'promising start' the UK government appeared to have 'stalled somewhat of late' [11]. Several causal factors have been identified: the lack of strategic leadership, poor lines of accountability (the e-envoy responsible for the strategy is answerable to three ministers), strong individual departments each with their own agenda, the vertical structure of UK government which makes joined up thinking difficult, entrenched civil service attitudes, technical problems with database integration and usability, slow progress on data protection and privacy legislation, and the failure to be customer focused [11].

This paper argues that another factor, in danger of being overlooked outside the geographic information community, is the failure to develop and integrate an SDI into the e-government strategy. In 2000 the AGI warned this failure may lead to a failure in the e-government strategy itself and to costly rebuilding. There is a strongly held view amongst many members of the AGI that a new strategic initiative is now required to develop a UK SDI that provides: clear vision and leadership, a coherent geographic information policy, an adequate legal framework (to resolve cost recovery and privacy issues), and sustained funding. A Geographic Commission with a clear mandate has been suggested. This can only be achieved if the UK government recognises the strategic role of geographic information within the e-government agenda.

The UK geographic information community is increasingly looking to Europe. In 2001 two potentially competitive European initiatives were launched, GINIE (the Geographic Information Network in Europe) and INSPIRE (Infrastructure for Spatial Information in Europe). GINIE's remit was to develop a cohesive geographic information strategy at the European level, and address the organisational, institutional and political challenges crucial to the development of a European SDI. INSPIRE focuses on environmental policy but it is also intended to activate the creation of a European SDI. Both initiatives had strong claims for legitimacy. INSPIRE because it has been developed by the European Commission inter-service group on geographic information and GINIE because it has developed from the pan-European network of national associations. Although this could have led to competition between the two initiatives, the pan-European network of national associations adopted a non-competitive stance publicising the INSPIRE initiative, requesting representation on its working groups and offering its network so that INSPIRE could reach a wider audience. As a result complementary roles may develop. The European Parliament and the European Commission may emerge as network builders capable of providing the vision, legal framework and resources necessary to build a harmonised, distributed European SDI that is, of necessity, based on a network of national SDIs. National organisational actors, both governmental and non-governmental, will be influenced by developments in Europe, and will also feed into European decision-making thereby impacting on progress.

3 Conclusion

The UK geographic information policy network is an effective self-organising network of domain experts with a clear consensus to promote the use of geographic information. Although the network is self-organising, government does have a crucial role to play in the network and the government is failing in this role. This failure has caused the NGDF to lose impetus whilst SDI initiatives in other countries (e.g. USA, Australia and Canada) are moving ahead. There is also some evidence that the UK's plan to build e-government services may be losing momentum and this paper suggests that, if this is the case, one of the potentially overlooked causes may be the failure to develop an effective SDI. The paper concludes by suggesting that European organisational actors may increasingly play a network building role in developing SDIs, not just in the UK, but in other member states and candidate member states too.

References

1. Central IT Unit (2000) [online] *e-government a strategic framework for public services in the information age* Available from www.e-envoy.gov.uk Accessed 20th March 2003
2. Annoni, A. Craglia, M. Smit, P. (2002) [online] *Comparative Analysis of NSDI 8th EC-GI & GIS Workshop ESDI – A Work in Progress* Dublin, Ireland July 3–5, 2002 Available from http://www.eurogi.org/index_800.html Accessed on 30th April 2003
3. Kickert, W., Klijn.E-H., and Koppenjan, J. (1997) *Managing Complex Networks: Strategies for the Public Sector*, London: Sage
4. Kooiman, J. (Ed) 1993 *Modern Governance*, London: Sage
5. Bellamy, C. (1998). ICTs and Governance: Beyond Policy Networks? The Case of the Criminal Justice System. In: Snellen, I.Th.M., W.B.H.J. van de Donk. *Public Administration in an Information Age.* Amsterdam: IOS Press. Pp. 293–306.
6. Pettigrew A.M. (1997) *What is a Processual Analysis* Scandinavian Journal of Management Volume 13 No. 4 pp337–348
7. Chorley, Lord (1987), *Handling geographic information: report to the secretary of state for the environment of the committee of enquiry into the handling of geographic information* HMSO
8. Pollard, P. (2000) *Geographical Information Services: A UK Perspective on the Development of Interorganisational Information Services'* Information Infrastructure and Policy 6 (2000) 185-195 IOS Press
9. National Geospatial Data Framework Board (1998) *Establishing the UK National Geospatial Data Framework Strategic Plan - 2000* Available from http://www.ngdf.org.uk Accessed on 2nd November 2000
10. Rhind, D.W. (1997) [online] *Overview of the National Geospatial Data Framework* Presented at the AGI-GIS conference NGDF Available from www.ngdf.org.uk Accessed on 12th March 2000
11. Hill, S. (2003) *System error: why UK online failed* The Independent Review 30th April p11
12. www.agi.org.uk
13. www.ec-gis.org/inspire
14. www.e-envoy.gov.uk
15. www.eurogi.org
16. www.gigateway.org.uk
17. www.gsdi.org
18. wwwlmu.jrc.it/ginie/home.html

URN:Technology – A Building Block of the Swiss E-Government Platform

Dieter Spahni

University of Applied Sciences Berne
Institute for Business and Administration IWV
Eigerplatz 5, Postfach
3000 Bern 14, Switzerland
Dieter.Spahni@iwv.ch

Abstract. In the year 2003 the administration portal for Switzerland, the Virtual Desk www.ch.ch, went live. This portal is based on a powerful meta-database of all available resources and services of the federation, the cantons and the districts and allocates a unique name, the URN (Uniform Resource Name), to every resource. The URN:Technology, adapted to the requirements of www.ch.ch, became an open standard and a building block of the Swiss e-government platform. This article highlights the URN:Technology and shows how portals in powerful and established federal structures benefit from this innovation. URN:Technology represents nowadays a key factor in the success of building and operating large portals with split responsibility for the content and interlinking. The present meta-database of URN:Technology, already similar to UDDI, can be developed with the help of web services into a registry with UDDI conformity.

1 Introduction

In January 2003 the Virtual Desk Switzerland (VDS), was opened to the public. The information presented, analyzed by subject, leads the visitor finally to the relevant place in each instance, be this in the federation, the district or its canton. The portal is to be understood primarily as a guide. The number of links needed is enormous. Thus, for instance, each of the 2,880 districts responsible has to maintain links at the local level to all relevant subjects provided by the portal.

The Swiss Federal Chancellery, as the project leader with its Virtual Desk Switzerland, decided to implement the URN:Technology developed by the author to solve the problem of interlinking with the aid of a central database in which all portal partners (here federation, cantons and districts) independently maintain the description of the resources they offer on the relevant subjects, in particular providing the current valid address (URL) of the resources. On this point, resources can be both simple information provision, forms and also web applications and web services. Resources also keep a unique name (URN) that serves to identify them. The URN:Technology is particularly suited for networking in complex federally structured portals with decentralized responsibility for the content and interlinking but is in no way limited to e-government in its application.

R. Traunmüller (Ed.): EGOV 2003, LNCS 2739, pp. 359–362, 2003.

2 URN:Technology

The URN:Technology[1] describes the access to resources on the worldwide web by means of unique global and persistent names, URN. For access to resources available via the Internet, various partly overlapping approaches exist under the title Uniform Resource Identifier (URI[2]). A distinction is made between Uniform Resource Locator (URL) and Uniform Resource Name (URN). URL designates an addressing scheme for finding resources on the Internet. URLs represent the most familiar approach because of their use in the worldwide web.

URN:Technology is based by contrast on the concept of the URN, whose aim is the allocation of a unique global and permanent name to resources. The referencing of such resources thus becomes independent of the place of storage. In addition, opportunities arise for the preparation of different data formats (e.g. HTML, PDF, RTF) and language versions of a resource.

Resources can be described by numerous attributes. Some of these attributes are particularly suited for referencing resources. The URN:Technology of the VDS uses the four attributes language, portal partner, subject and data format for referencing and identification by URN. For the VDS all permissible values of the identifying attributes were coded[3]. Open standards were used in this as far as possible.

In order to access resources via URN on the worldwide web, the portal partners must put each URL into the description of the resources stored in the central meta-database. Portal users can then access resources by URN with the widespread technology of the worldwide web, hence with almost any browser, just by embedding the URN into an URL addressing the URN resolver www.ch.ch in case of the VDS:

```
http://www.ch.ch/urn:ch:de:ch.be.6509:ch.01.01.02.01:01
```

The prefixed urn:ch indicates the URN's namespace name[4]. The language is determined by de (German). Then follow the hierarchical code ch.be.6509 to indicate the district of Schönbühl-Urtenen in the canton of Berne BE and the subject "Pass" ("passport"), accessible via the subjects "Privatleben", "Ausweise" and "Identitätskarte und Pass"[5]. The closing 01 represents the data format HTML. The individual attributes are separated by ":". The URN resolver finds the corresponding URL at run time (see figure 1):

```
http://www.urtenen-schoenbuehl.ch/ve/sa/vesa001.htm
```

---

[1] URN:Technology: http://www.urn.ch
  URN Syntax: RFC 2141: http://www.ietf.org/rfc/rfc2141.txt
[2] URI in general: RFC 2396: http://www.ietf.org/rfc/rfc2396.txt,
  http://www.w3.org/Addressing/URL/Overview.html
[3] http://www.admin.ch/ch/d/egov/gv/themen/urn/urn.html
[4] Namespace names are globally maintained by IANA: http://www.iana.org.
[5] "private life", "proof of identity" and "ID card and passport"

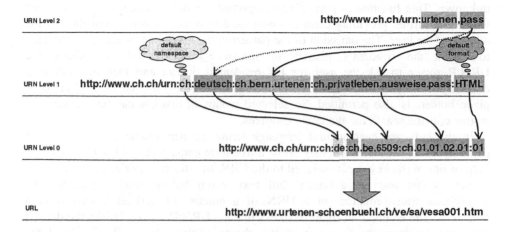

Fig. 1. Three levels of abstractions for valid and resolvable URN: A free-form enquiry (URN Level 2) is transformed by the URN resolver into a descriptive form (URN Level 1) and then translated into an URN Level 0 before assigning the appropriate URL.

3   URN Resolver

The URN:Resolver has the task of turning a URN into a URL. A unique assignment can then only take place if the correct URL was assigned to the URN in the database by a portal partner.

As shown in figure 1, only the address of the URN:Resolver is prefixed to the URN. The client passes a URN embedded in a URL (hence as a URI) to the URN:Resolver in the form of an HTTP request. It extracts the URN from the URI and searches for the URL that corresponds to a URN in its database. It sends an HTTP response (content: "Redirect") back to the client's browser. The client then directs a request to the URL supplied and so accesses the desired resource.

The URN:Technology tries to ensure that the most appropriate resource is actually transmitted to the user even if:

1. no resource at all was recorded by the relevant portal partner for the URN sought,
2. the supplied URN proves to be not unique or
3. instead of a URN, natural language search terms are used.

In the first case, that is when absolutely no resource was recorded by the desired portal partner for the URN sought, the URN:Resolver searches with a complex procedure for the most suitable resources on the basis of the descriptions recorded in the central meta-database. Thus for instance it checks whether appropriate resources are available in other languages or on lower or higher level subjects instead of on the subject sought. In this the URN:Resolver follows the hierarchical structures of both the subjects and the partners and thus leads the user to an appropriate target.

In the second case, the use of URN which are not unique is only permissible and logical if the expression for an attribute e.g. the language or the portal partner, is unknown. This function is particularly important for the direction to resources, for which the partner providing them can only be determined after determination of the district of the user. The omission of the partner in the URN (e.g. when being directed to check the resident's district in urn:ch:de:ch.01.01.02.01:01) allows the URN:Resolver to ask the user for his residential district and then to guide him correctly. Alongside the omission of individual attributes, the use of wild cards or place holders is also permitted. So selected groups of districts can be scanned, for instance, in the search for available resources.

In the last case even natural language terms are permissible instead of coded expressions for attributes and they allow a free-form enquiry (URN level 2). With the help of one of the keywords assigned to the URN, free-form enquiries can be made. It is not in this instance a typical full text search but an intelligent-as-possible algorithmic transformation on a URN of a number of defined keywords in a thesaurus. The example in figure 1 shows that the URN:Resolver derives the desired language de from the language of the chosen subject "Pass". The code of the appropriate district is determined from the district identifier "Urtenen". Further assumptions relate to the domain ch and the data format 01 (HTML) which are provided as default by the Virtual Desk Switzerland.

4 The Way Forward

With the VDS, Switzerland is the first country to have not only a comprehensive guide covering about 600 subjects but also a standardised national resource registry of public administration with already far more than 100.000 entries from about 4.000 partners after a six month period since its implementation. The portal guides users through navigation structures and supports them by explanatory texts until they obtain the information.

Interestingly, the VDS has already shown itself in its structure to be a registry conforming to UDDI[6] in its approach. All the partners are listed in it (white pages) and their resources described (green pages) if these fall within the portal's subject structure (yellow pages). However, further research is necessary in order to make a complete UDDI registry out of the URN:Technology. With the present operational infrastructure the further development into the UDDI registry with help from web services succeeds in fulfilling the special requirements in the public sector for public registries. Based on the central meta-database, a set of tools supports web masters and offers new ways of controlling and improving the quality of the managed resources.

In addition to technical aspects, further research will focus for instance on interconnecting name spaces from different registries, providing group- or user-specific subject structures spanning multiple registries or on separating navigational structures from content by the application of a central meta-databases.

---

[6] http://www.uddi.org/

Towards a Process Model for Efficient Advertised Bidding in the Field of Software Projects

Peter Regner, Thomas Wiesinger, Josef Küng, and Roland Wagner

Institute For Applied Knowledge Processing (FAW)
University of Linz
Austria
{pregner,twiesinger,jkueng,rrwagner}@faw.uni-linz.ac.at

Abstract. The award procedure has a great deal of influence on the software process. Therefore the choice of a qualified type of award procedure is of particular importance for the success of a software development project in the public sector, as well as electronic government projects. The condition for the use of the open procedure or the restricted procedure is a complete and detailed requirements specification, to enable the comparison of the tenders. From a software development point of view, the application of one of these types means using the waterfall model. The disadvantages of the waterfall model are well known. The approach presented in this paper uses the negotiated procedure to support the advantages of an iterative, risk mitigating software process.

Keywords: award procedure, electronic government, negotiated procedure, software process model

1 Motivation

The appearance of electronic government has a wide influence on existing information systems so on core information systems. Core information systems in the governmental field are often legacy systems and mostly older then one decade if not much older. Due to changing requirements, these systems where changed and extended over the time [11]. The implementation of changes and extensions to the legacy systems are often no longer cost-effective and from a technical point of view simply impossible. These systems often fail in supporting all aspects of electronic government processes. The introduction of electronic government could be seen as a chance to replace these old information systems [7]. The replacement of a large software system, often responsible for core business work, is very risky, so there is the need for a risk mitigating software process [2][3][8].

The passage above describes one common reason for large software projects in the public sector, driven by the appearance of electronic government and therefore changing business processes and requirements. The development of electronic government software systems or the introduction and customization of enterprise resource planning systems are other software projects in the public sector. This paper describes an approach for the award of large software projects in the public sector with simultaneous consideration of the public award procedure constraints.

R. Traunmüller (Ed.): EGOV 2003, LNCS 2739, pp. 363–368, 2003.

The choice of a qualified type of award procedure has a great deal of influence on the software process and therefore on the quality of the result. Not enough that the software process itself is complex and therefore risky [10], the award procedure is a supplementary source of complexity and risk. And so, the award procedure is one more source that can make a government project fail. Comparing public customers to private ones, contracting authorities have additional requirements in the form of laws with large-scale consequences on the process.

Underpinning the public procurement rules are the four principles "Equal Treatment", "Transparency", "Proportionality" and "Mutual Recognition". The principle of "Transparency" for example, requires that information regarding forthcoming contracts and the rules to be applied should be readily available to all interested candidates [5].

2 Types of Award Procedures Determine the Software Process

Open procedures are those award procedures whereby all interested service providers may submit a tender. There is no possibility to negotiate about the incoming tenders. In Practice, the open procedure could be seen as the common award procedure. It is mostly applied in the building sector and it is the core field of activity for lawyers [1].

Restricted procedures shall mean those procedures whereby only those service providers invited by the authority may submit a tender. As in the open procedure, negotiations about the content of the incoming tenders are not allowed. The restricted procedure is divided into two parts, the goal of the first part is to select a limited number of service providers. This limited number of service provider submits their tenders [1].

Negotiated procedures, a special form of the restricted procedure, are those award procedures whereby authorities consult service providers of their choice and negotiate the terms of the contract with one or more of them [1]. The negotiated procedure is described more detailed in chapter 3.

The general opinion is, that a complete and precise requirements specification is the basis for the calculation of a tender. This assumes, that the specification of the requirements, the functional and the non functional ones, is as complete as it is necessary to evaluate the service to be provided. In this case the comparability of the tenders is an expected precondition.

There are basically two possibilities to specify services, constructive ore functional, both have to be complete, explicit and neutral [12]. A constructive specification of services means the definition of a detailed specification for tenders. In this case, the comparison is very easy because it is a description of the "what" and the "how", but there is no degree of freedom for the service provider, for example the choice of a software architecture, and it is necessary to solve all risks in advance. The functional specification of services is the specification of the objectives. The functional specification should contain the purpose of the service and the functional, non functional and economical requirements. The functional specification describes the objective and not the process to reach the expected service. This means that the service provider can specify the methods and techniques he intends to use to reach the goal.

Both, the constructive and the functional service description can be used with the open or restricted procedure. The functional description however, is the basis for the applicability of the negotiated procedure. The criterion for the use of the negotiated procedure is the fact that it is impossible to create a complete service description at one time and the fact that the tenders based on the service description could not be compared.

From a software development point of view the application of the open or restricted procedure with constructive or functional service description means using the waterfall model. The disadvantages of the waterfall model are well known. A primary source of difficulty with the waterfall model has been its emphasis on fully elaborated documents as completion criteria for early requirements and design phases [2]. For some classes of software this is the most effective way to proceed, however it does not work well for many classes of software, particularly interactive end-user applications, the type of software we consider in the context of this paper.

The problems with the waterfall model are mitigated by iterative software process models [2][3][8][11][13]. The negotiated procedure is the only award procedure that allows an iterative approach in a reasonable way. In iterative software processes the requirements are captured and detailed over the time, in consideration of an architecture and the project risks. The requirements prosper with the product.

3 Integration through Milestones

We present a solution based on the negotiated procedure with prior publication and an iterative software process based on two main concepts, the integration of the award procedure and the software process and the application of milestones from both processes.

The integration of the award procedure and an iterative software process enables a continuous process. From the beginning of the process, the elements (activities, artifacts and roles) of both, the award procedure and the software process, are considered. This leads to more efficiency in the process work.

Milestones are a common way to anchor the phases of a process model. Milestones make the application of the waterfall model clear, therefore it is still used, and were introduced to iterative process models by Barry Boehm[2][3] as anchor points to guide through a more complex process. The milestones of the award procedure should not be seen as a necessary bureaucratic evil, but to improve the quality of the software process.

For example, the Prior Publication Milestone of the award procedure can be used to gather valuable information in the inception phase of the software process. Figure 2 shows the integrated process and the milestones. According to the Rational Unified Process [8][13], the Inception Phase is the phase from the beginning of the process to the Life Cycle Objectives Milestone and the Elaboration Phase is the phase from the Life Cycle Objectives Milestone to the Life Cycle Architecture Milestone.

Table 1. Award procedure milestones and software process milestones

Software Process Phases	Milestones	Award Procedure	Software Procedure
Inception Phase	Prior Publication Milestone	X	
	Life Cycle Objectives Milestone		X
Elaboration Phase	Award Milestone	X	
	Life Cycle Architecture Milestone		X

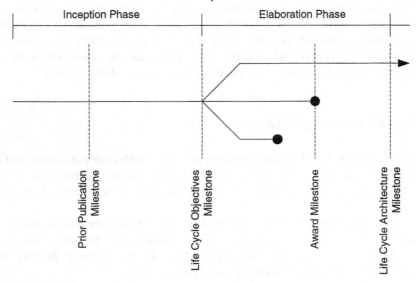

Fig. 1. Integration via milestones

The award procedure starts during the inception phase of the software process. This is not the first public information about the planned project. The possibly interested parties are already informed by a publication in the Official Journal of the European Communities that is announced at the beginning of the year, but from a juristic point of view the award procedure starts with the prior publication. The reason for the prior publication is to inform potential candidates about the planned project so that they can decide if they are qualified and capable. The essential information necessary are the criterions for the **Prior Publication Milestone**. The goal of this phase is to shortlist the most eligible candidates. Based on the prior publication the candidates send in a request for participation together with a realisation concept based on the information in the prior publication.

The quality of the content of the prior publication affects the quality of the request for participation and the realisation concept. One important part of the prior publication is the definition of the project's scope and boundary conditions, including an operational vision, acceptance criteria and what is intended to be in the product and what is not. It is maybe necessary to include constraints about the candidate hardware and software architecture but the chosen approach allows to ignore this in the first part of the award procedure and to focus on the functional requirements only. The prior publication should also contain information about the chosen process, its activities, artefacts and roles to inform the service provider.

The essential criterions in the inception phase for the **Life Cycle Objectives Milestone** are the identification and reduction of the risks critical to the system's viability, the movement from a key subset of requirements into a candidate architecture, the making and initial estimation within broad limits, of cost, effort schedule and product quality, the initiation of the business case that the project appears to be economically worth doing, again within broad limits [8].

As the title says, a very important part of the selected award procedure is the negotiation of the requirements based on the realisation concept. Negotiation partners of the contracting authority are the service providers left over. In groups, the requirements are detailed under consideration of a concrete architecture and concrete risks. During the negotiation process unqualified service provider drop out, not because of the application of skin deep criterions, but on the basis of detailed negotiations to find the best project partner for the given problem. The **Award Milestone** constitutes the selection of one service provider and the end of the award procedure.

In the elaboration phase, the essential criterions are the identification and reduction of the risks significantly affecting system construction, the specification of the requirements to be developed, the extension of the candidate architecture, the preparation of the project plan, the making of an estimate within limits narrow enough to justify a business bid and the finalization of the business case [8]. These are the criterions of **the Life Cycle Architecture Milestone**.

At the end of the award procedure after passing the Award Milestone the service provider, now the project partner of the public authority, has all necessary artefacts to continue the work with the software process.

4 Conclusion

The execution of a large governmental software project is without any doubt a challenging plan. It is very important to choose the right software process to face the problems and risks. The choice of such a problem and risk mitigating process is strongly influenced by the award procedure. The negotiated procedure is the only type of award procedure that enables an iterative software process. Our approach is to integrate the negotiated procedure into the software process and to use the requirements of the milestones of this procedure to improve the results, necessary to fulfill the requirements of the software process in an efficient way.

Further research is required on following topics:
* activities – detailing and adjusting the activities of both, the award procedure and the software process
* artifacts – detailing and adjusting the artifacts of both processes
* roles – among other things, to support the integrated process, the installation of a third, a coordinating project instance is necessary

References

1. Council Directive 92/50/EEC of 18 June 1992 relating to the coordination of procedures for the award of public service contracts, Official Journal L 209 , 24/07/1992 P. 0001 – 0024
2. Boehm, B. W.: A Spiral Model of Software Development and Enhancement, Computer, May 1998, pp. 61 – 72
3. Boehm, B. W.: Anchoring the Software Process, IEEE Software, July 1996, pp. 73 – 82
4. Bundesgesetz über die Vergabe von Aufträgen, Bundesgesetz 2002 – BVerG, BGB1. I Nr. 99/2002
5. Guide to Tendering for Public Sector Contracts, produced by Enterprise Ireland in co-operation with The Forum on Public Procurement in Ireland
6. Heinrich, L. J.: Management von Informatik-Projekten, Oldenbourg, München/Wien 1997
7. Heinrich, L. J.: Informationsmanagement, 6. Aufl., Oldenbourg, München/Wien 1999
8. Jacobson, I., Booch, G., Rumbaugh, J.: Unified Software Development Process, Addison-Wesley, February 1999
9. König, W., Reichel-Hozer, C., Bundesvergabegesetz 2002, Kurzkommentar und Leifaden für die Praxis, Linde, Wien; 2002
10. OECD PUMA Public Policy Brief No. 8, March 2001, The Hidden threat to E-Government. Avoiding large government IT failures
11. Sommervill, I.: Software Engineering, Addison-Wesley, 2001
12. Sturm, O.: Die funktionale Ausschreibung nach dem BVergG 2002, ZVB 2002/121
13. Versteegen, G.: Projektmanagement mit dem Rational Unified Process, Springer, 2000

Interoperability Issues of Shared Infrastructures for E-Government

Inmaculada Cava[1] and Luis Guijarro[2]

[1] Generalitat Valenciana (Regional Government of Valencia),
Valencia, Spain
icava@gva.es
http://www.gva.es
[2] Communications Department,
Polytechnic University of Valencia,
Valencia, Spain
lguijar@dcom.upv.es
http://www.dcom.upv.es

Abstract. This communication describes the activities carried out by the Shared Infrastructures Working Group of the E-Forum Association and its early results. This group is devoted to study the interoperability issues of e-Government shared infrastructures. Firstly, the initial task of analysis of existing initiatives is described and some concluding remarks are given. Secondly, an Interoperability Framework is proposed as a methodological approach to analyze interoperability issues of e-Government. The paper ends up with some ideas for further work.

1 Introduction

This paper deals with the early results of the Shared Infrastructures Working Group (SI-WG) of the E-Forum Association[1]. This group is chaired by the Regional Government of Valencia (Spain) and its members come from different sectors both public and private, as well as some academic institutions such as the Technical University of Valencia.

The SI-WG was created by decision of the Directors Board of E-Forum to study the interoperability issues of the shared infrastructures that support the delivery of public services by electronic means (e-Government). The first period of the SI-WG activity will end with the celebration of the First Public Event of E-Forum Association[2] where the first results will be publicly presented.

Certainly, Interoperability is regarded as a major issue to be addressed by all e-Government agencies. In fact, during late 90s, most Administrations in OECD countries have released their e-government strategies. Each e-government strategy is supported by its own framework policies and one of such policies is the interoperability framework.

---

[1] Further information on E-Forum can be found at http://www.eu-forum.org.
[2] This event is scheduled for the 15th and 16th of September 2003 in Valencia (Spain). Further information at http://www.eu-forum.org

R. Traunmüller (Ed.): EGOV 2003, LNCS 2739, pp. 369–372, 2003.

Interoperability is usually understood as the ability to ensure seamless flow of information both between citizens or businesses and government as well as between different agencies or government layers (local, regional, national or international). Interoperability is also regarded as a means to provide services to the citizen and to the business in an integrated way, regardless the specific agency that provides the requested service or the type of access device. Besides this, interoperability is a means to achieve the re-usability of e-government modules by fixing comparable procedures for services providing and for the definition of data models.

This document deals with the description of the SI-WG activities and the results obtained so far. In Section 2 the analysis of existing public initiatives phase is detailed and some concluding remarks are given. In Section 3, a proposal of an Interoperability Framework as a methodological approach is presented. Finally in Section 4, we end up this paper with some ideas for further work.

2   Analysis of Existing Public Initiatives

In order to analyze the existing public initiatives two stages have been carried out: (1) collection and general classification and (2) deeper analysis through Zachman Framework.

The first task of the SI-WG consisted of gathering information about existing public initiatives and make a preliminary study. This would, in principle yield a general classification of adopted initiatives. Accordingly, the SI-WG members gathered information about the following public initiatives carried out by e-government agencies in the interoperability arena: e-SDF and e-GIF [1], FEAF [2], REACH [3], SAGA [4], IDA [5] and the initiative of ADAE [6].

After the initial analysis of these public initiatives, it came up that two stages could be distinguished in most of them: implementing interoperability and leveraging interoperability.

In the first stage, implementing interoperability is regarded as an issue at the application level, that is, interoperability is agreed to be understood as the "ability to exchange functionality and interpretable data between software entities" [7]. If so, the approaches of the e-Government agencies agree on mandating a full set of standards, which addresses those areas that are relevant to the interoperability, according to the definition above.

The second stage, leveraging interoperability, deals with the building of an enterprise architecture for e-Government. Enterprise architecture is defined as a logical structure for classifying and organizing the descriptive representations (i.e. models) of all the key elements and relationships that make up an organization. Among the public initiatives considered by the SI-WG, only the e-SDF of UK, the FEAF of USA and SAGA of Germany, have used an enterprise architecture to define the models and standards of e-Government.

For the second task of the SI-WG many different approaches to describe the elements of an enterprise architecture can be adopted. Nevertheless, in the last few years the framework developed by John Zachman in 1987 [8] has grown popularity. Table 1 makes use of this framework to analyze the interoperability initiatives.

Table 1. Analysis of public initiatives according to Zachman Framework

	DATA	FUNCTION	NETWORK
BUSINESS MODEL (conceptual) Owner	[e-SDF] Government Data Standards Catalogue (GDSC)	[e-SDF] Government Common Information Model (GCIM) [FEAF] Business Reference Model. [SAGA] Tools and procedure models.	[e-SDF] Government Message Reference Model (GMRM)
SYSTEM MODEL (logical) Designer	[SAGA] Data model	[FEAF] Conceptual/Process Model. [FEAF] Interoperability Model.	[FEAF] Technical Reference Model. [SAGA] Distribute systems architecture.
TECHNOLOGY MODEL (physical) Outsourcing	[e-SDF] e-GIF [FEAF] Voluntary industry standards. [SAGA] Basic Components and mandatory and recommended standards.	[e-SDF] e-GIF [FEAF] Voluntary industry standards. [SAGA] Basic Components and mandatory and recommended standards.	[e-SDF] e-GIF [FEAF] Voluntary industry standards. [SAGA] Mandatory and recommended standards.

From our point of view, the first stage is essential for e-government implementation success and it would enable the seamless information flow between institutions. However, it may not be enough to enable the sort of interoperability required for a true seamless service delivery to citizens and business, which is the goal of the e-government strategies.

Not all the agencies under study addressed the stage of building an enterprise architecture, and when they did it, their achievement degree was not homogeneous. Some agencies have only identified that business requirement are an issue to be addressed, whereas others have already succeeded in providing the models and tools for the description of the enterprise, and in founding the technical architecture in this description.

3 Proposed Methodology

After the analysis step, the SI-WG followed to address the interoperability problem of shared infrastructures in e-Government. This task consisted of defining an Interoperability Framework as a comprehensive, logical structure for descriptive representations (i.e. models) of any e-Government initiative. The utility of this approach is twofold. Firstly, it allows defining a comprehensive set of interoperability models to cover all the range of aspects regarding e-Government, from the conceptual to the physical ones. And secondly, it allows to focus on selected aspects without losing a sense of the contextual perspective.

The Interoperability Framework is based on the Zachman Framework and sketches the interoperability models or standards that constitute the intersection between the rows or different interoperability levels, from the more concrete issues to the more abstract ones, and the columns or the types of objects to the interoperability model or standard.

As regards of the columns, the terminology could be:

- **Data interoperability**, which includes both the data interpretation, by means of XML schemes, and the knowledge representation and exploitation, by means of ontologies and agents.
- **Function interoperability**, which deals with business process modelling inside the organizations and among partner organizations. It also deals with methodologies and tools for aligning the organization goals with the technical architecture which support e-Government initiatives.
- **Network interoperability**, which deals with communication issues. It includes, both aspects at the telecommunication network level (access and interconection) and at the distributed application level (remote method invocation mechanisms and the public interface exportation or binding).

For each interoperability category, the rows would represent the level of abstraction which are, from low to high level of concretion, the conceptual level (Business Model), the logical level (System Model) and the physical level (Technology Model). With the Interoperability Framework it is possible to build a complete description of the models and standards to guarantee the interoperability of shared infrastructures involved in e-Government.

4 Further Steps

Regarding the future, the second period of the SI-WG activities are devoted to use the proposed Interoperability Framework to define the standards and the models that the public agencies should define to build their own interoperability program. This contribution would constitute a useful and long-term recommendation for any decision-maker in the field of e-Government.

References

[1] Office of the e-Envoy. UK On-line. e-Government Interoperability Framework. Available at: http://www.govtalk.gov.uk, April 2002.
[2] FEA Working Group. E-Gov enterprise architecture Guidance (Common Reference Model) [on-line]. Available at: http://www.fwapmo.gov, July 2002.
[3] REACH Agency. Irish Government. Public Services Broker Phase 1 - Requirements Statement. Available at: http://www.reachservices.ie, July 2002.
[4] Bundesministerium des Innern. Germany Federal Government. Standards and Architectures for e-Government Applications (SAGA). Version 1.1. [on-line]. Available at: http://www.kbst.bund.de/saga,http://www.e-government-handbuch.de, February 2003.
[5] Enterprise DG.European Commission, IDA. Architecture Guidelines For Trans-European Telematics Networks for Administrations. Version 6.1. [on-line]. Available at: http://www.europa.eu.int/ispo/ida, June 2002.
[6] Agence pour le Développement de l'Administration Électronique(ADAE). Le cadre commun d'interopérabilité des systèmes d'information publics [on line]. Available at: http://www.atica.pm.gouv.fr, February 2003.
[7] R. Zahavi. The Essential CORBA: Systems Integration Using Distributed Objects, August 1995.
[8] J. A. Zachman. Concepts of the Framework for Enterprise Architecture. Background, Description and Utility. Available at: http://www.zifa.com.

Integration of E-Government and E-Commerce with Web Services

Alexander Elsas

Institute for Information Systems
Goethe-University Frankfurt, Germany
elsas@wiwi.uni-frankfurt.de

Abstract. E-Commerce and E-Government applications are traditionally seperatly developed and come from different backgrounds. As the applications become more and more sophisticated and citizen-centric, the need for communication and integration between those two paradigms arises. Web services, as the emerging standard for the implementation of distributed applications, support this on both a technological and a process level.

1 Introduction

The overwhelming success of the Internet technology as the foundation for E-Commerce and E-Business applications has caused considerable pressure on the public sector to modernize administrative processes and implement interaction with the citizens via the World Wide Web. The so-called E-Government applications range from information-offering static web sites to sophisticated transaction-oriented applications, supporting the administrative processes and interaction with the citizens. A typical representative of this kind of application is the One-Stop-Government-Portals concept.

However, the development of E-Government applications is driven by a paradigm that is not identical with the E-Commerce paradigm: A different cultural background for the dealing with administrative processes and more restricting legal regulations differentiate the E-Government world from the E-Commerce.

With the introduction of the One-Stop-Government-Portals the need for collaboration with the E-Commerce world arises. An example can be found in the E-Government process of registering a car in Germany: from a citizens point of view it would be most convenient to integrate the licence plate producer into the process Car Registration. The need for communication and thus integration between E-Commerce and E-Government applications is evident.

From a scientific point of view there are two levels of integration which have to be supported: the *technological* level (to allow communication between distributed applications) and the *process* level (to support the modeling of the processes).

During the last years, the *Web Services Framework* has developed as a standard for the implementation of distributed applications. It addresses both the technological and process level of integration and is therefore presented here as a solution to the above described integration problem.

R. Traunmüller (Ed.): EGOV 2003, LNCS 2739, pp. 373–376, 2003.

2 Web Services

2.1 Service Orientation

In contrast to traditional IT systems, which can be characterized as tightly coupled systems, Web services implement a loosely coupled approach.[4] A Web services framework is consisting of three basic services:

- Communication,
- Service description and
- Service discovery.

These basic functionalities are implemented by protocols, the three basic standards within the Web services framework for these protocols are SOAP, WSDL and UDDI, all based on the common XML meta language.[2] Figure 1 shows a graphical overview over the interaction concept of these protocols, in the notation of an *UML component diagram.*

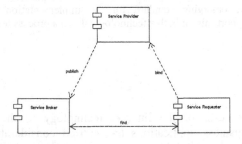

Fig. 1. Service Orientation

This architecture is often referred to as a *Service Oriented Architecture* (SOA), in the case of Web services, this SOA-approach is implemented with the before mentioned protocols:[7]

- A specific Web service announces its WSDL definition to a UDDI registry (*publish*), realized with WSDL.
- A client searches the registry for a service's definition (*find*), realized via UDDI.
- The client sends messages or requests directly to the service via SOAP, based on the information of the WSDL definition from the directory (*bind*), realized with SOAP.

2.2 Core Protocols

SOAP
The *Simple Object Access Protocol* (SOAP) [5] is a joint development of Microsoft and IBM and a few other companies, whose further development is in the hands of the W3C.[1] It is a XML based protocol for messaging and remote procedure calls (RPCs), the execution of programs or program fragments (procedures) on remote computers. SOAP defines how distributed applications can communicate in a message-oriented way.[2]

WSDL

The *Web Services Description Language* (WSDL) describes Web services as a collection of end-points for communication that can exchange messages. A complete service description consists of two parts of information:[2, 8]

UDDI

The *Universal Description, Discovery, and Integration* (UDDI) can be seen as an online, automated "phone" directory of Web services. An UDDI registry holds three types of information about Web services:[2]

- Names and contact details (*white pages*),
- A categorization of business and service types (*yellow pages*),
- Technical details (*green pages*).

2.3 Process Modeling

SOAP, WSDL and UDDI are the *core protocols* of the Web services framework, or the "base standards of the Web services technology stack",[3] they implement the technological level of integration, by ensuring the communication between distributed applications.

To implement advanced processes (like the *Car Registration* process), discrete Web services have to be orchestrated into complex services, supporting complex transactions and workflows. To support this configuration of Web services, additional Web service protocols like the *Web Services Flow Language* (WSFL) or the *Business Process Execution Language for Web Services* (BPEL4WS) are in various states of development. Table 1 gives an overview over those languages.

Table 1. Web Services Business Process Languages

Acronym	Name	Developer	URL
WSFL	Web Services Flow Language	IBM	http://www-4.ibm.com/software/solutions/webservices/pdf/WSFL.pdf
XLANG		Microsoft	http://www.gotdotnet.com/team/xml_wsspecs/xlang-c/default.htm
BPEL4WS	Business Process Execution Language for Web Services	IBM, Microsoft BEA	http://www-106.ibm.com/developerworks/webservices/library/ws-bpel/
BPML	Business Process Modeling Language	BPMI.org	http://www.bpmi.org/bpml-spec.esp

The state of development of those *Business Process Modeling Languages for Web Services* is not as mature as the core protocols are, "this technology is immature and further research needs to be done in this area."[6] But it certainly has the advantage of being independent from the underlying E-Commerce or E-Government paradigm, it implements the process level of integration.

3 Conclusion

The most important advantage of the Web services concept is the integrative aspect: discrete components, exposed as services can be orchestrated into complex services and flows. Whether those components come from an E-Commerce or E-Government background does not matter. So the integration of E-Government applications and E-Commerce applications into a joint process can be achieved.

References

1. Box, Don: A Brief History of SOAP; 2001;
   URL: http://www.xml.com/pub/a/2001/04/04/soap.html (6.8.2002)
2. Curbera, Francisco; Duftler, Matthew; Khalaf, Rania; Nagy, William; Mukhi, Nirmal, Weerawarana, Sanjiva: Unraveling the Web Services Web – An Introduction to SOAP, WSDL, and UDDI; in: IEEE Internet Computing, March / April 2002, p. 86–93
3. Fremantle, Paul; Weerawarana, Sanjiva; Khalf, Rania: Enterprise Services; in: Communications of the ACM, October 2002, p. 77–82
4. Kleijnen, Stans; Raju, Srikanth: An Open Web Services Architecture; in: acm queue, March 2003, p. 38–46
5. Mitra, Nilo (Eds.): SOAP Version 1.2 Part 0: Primer; 2002, URL: http://www.w3.org/TR/soap12-part0/ (26.8.2002)
6. Stal, Michael: Web Services: Beyond Component-Based Computing; in: Communications of the ACM, October 2002, p. 71–76
7. W3schools (Eds.): XML Schema Tutorial; URL: http://www.w3schools.com/schema (7.8.2002)
8. Weerawarana, Sanjiva; Chinnici, Roberto; Gudgin, Martin; Moreau, Jean-Jacques (Eds.): Web Services Description Language (WSDL) Version 1.2 – W3C Working Draft 9 July 2002; URL: http://www.w3.org/TR/wsdl12 (6.8.2002)

A Legal Framework for *E*-Government

Ahti Saarenpää

Institute for Law and Informatics, Faculty of Law,
University of Lapland, Box 122 Rovaniemi 10, Finland
asaarenp@urova.fi

Abstract. The transformation of our society into a network society is proceeding at a startling pace. One often hears the term legal framework in this context, but few details of that framework are forthcoming. What this framework is or should be like has generally not been adequately discussed. If we are content to watch it take shape guided by directives formulated on varying bases and their equally varied implementations, there is serious risk that the legal order will become fragmented. A clear frame of reference can easily became chaos, which, will pose a threat to our basic rights. The point of departure in this article is the assessment of e-government as a complex of information processes. These are evaluated in the light of the requirements of the modern constitutional state. The aim is to determine the relationship between the requirements for good government and the new digital operating environment. Such an analysis is a rarity, although different countries have set out to develop electronic services in government on the strength of advances in information technology.

1 Government as Information Process

What is government? This question is a difficult one indeed. Government comprises so very many different elements: actions, people, legal provisions, decision-making, openness, secrecy orders, service, communication. Above all, it is an *information process*. It has always been one, of course, but the electronic, digital environment urges us to look at it afresh as an information process.

This point of departure is a simple one to observe. The moment we interact with government, a legally regulated information process is and must be set in motion. And it continues until our file - the documents and descriptions of our case - is archived. There are numerous legal challenges along the long path that this information takes. A good example is that in modern Nordic law a document has already had to be defined as a message attached to a particular platform. This definition in turn means that a *cookie* is to be considered a document. This is something which was hardly noticed when information systems were being designed.[1]

---

[1] Section 5 of the Finnish Act on Openness in Government Activities, reads as follows: For the purposes of this Act, a document is defined as a written or visual presentation, and also as a message relating to a given topic or subject matter and consisting of signs which, by virtue of the use to which they are put, are meant to be taken as a whole, but are decipherable only by means of a computer, an audio or video recorder or some other technical device.

R. Traunmüller (Ed.): EGOV 2003, LNCS 2739, pp. 377–384, 2003.
© Springer-Verlag Berlin Heidelberg 2003

A. Saarenpää

2 The Legal Framework

As an information process, government, especially the new *e-government*, is also a challenge to the quality of legal regulation. We speak of the *legal framework of government*.[2] It was comparatively difficult to build even at the time of traditional spoken and written work. Regulation is substantially more difficult in the case of e-government. That government is hard to manage using traditional legal provisions and approaches, for information takes on a variety of forms in its life span. The acceptable legal framework must be able to follow this path all the time. This is one remarkable part of the new *juridification* we are or at least we should be witnessing in *e*-Europe.

Since the *Bangemann* report, if not already before, we in Europe have become accustomed to thinking that the *information society* requires a proper legal framework to govern its various activities. At the time, what we meant was largely a legal framework for the *information market*.[3] And, in that spirit, we have witnessed a veritable flood of directives from personal data protection to the digital signature and from copyright of computer programs to consumer protection in e-commerce.

There is no shortage of directives in or for the information society. Here we can speak of quantitative *juridification*. The number of provisions is increasing significantly.[4] And this is no longer a question of what in a technical sense is essential in telecommunications legislation. We are witnessing the regulation of the *convergence* of information technology and of the various ways in which that technology is utilized. Diverse operations and markets are becoming regulated in new ways.

Most new directives have until now been directives for markets and citizens. Government has been a bystander of sorts.[5] However, *data protection* in particular should have been taken seriously by government as well, seeing that it is a large-scale processor of personal data. But it is precisely government that has been a principal source of trouble for data commissioners in different countries. The *bureaucracy* has had great difficulties in accepting protection of personal data. Ubiquitous computing is an enticement to bureaucratic efficiency at the expense of citizens' privacy.[6]

When planning the new e-government, the *legal framework* takes on importance in a new way. It has gradually become an essential pillar of e-government. Today, more than ever, it is the practice to enact laws dealing with government, but we do not have

---

[2] We should also speak of the legal framework of governance. Governance is a broader concept than government. In this paper I limit my point of view mainly to e-government.

[3] The establishment as early as in 1985 of the Legal Advisory Board (LAB) can be taken as recognition of the need for a more uniform legal framework. Unfortunately, the LAB has largely ceased operating during the last years; precisely when it would be needed most .

[4] Juridification has often been linked to the increase in the number of statutes and provisions. It is much more than this. We see juridifcation for example when new legal safety requirements are introduced and when legislation is passed to limit the discretion of the authorities.

[5] I sidestep the issue of telecommunications. It has had a strong administrative background but this has been forgotten fast with the liberalization of the telecommunications markets. The UMT auctions were even a clear move against citizens' rights. Network communication was made expensive, with the right to communicate jeopardized in the process.

[6] There is also resistance to change in various fields. In Finland the healthcare sector has long been one that has kept the Data Protection Ombudsman's office particularly busy.

a terribly detailed picture of the legal framework of e-government. We live like in a jungle of provisions that have been drafted in different ways, have been conceived at different times, and serve different ends. [7] One of the principal reasons for this lack is our *conceptual uncertainty* where e-government is concerned.

E-government is still a comparatively diffuse, novel concept. We are well on our way towards e-government, but we do not know enough about what the actual content of that government is. We have a great deal of legislation dealing with government but we lack the big picture. In this situation we should analyze the concept and the whole governmental process from the legal point of view.

In examining e-government from a legal perspective, I opt to proceed from the concept of *the constitutional state* [1, 2]. Electronic government, too, must comply with the legislative and procedural framework of the constitutional state.

In the *constitutional state* it is essential that recognition of our rights take place earlier in all activities that affect us, both in government and the market. This would ensure that our rights are realized more effectively, and we would be entitled to expect better quality service from different institutions in legal terms as well. For this reason too, the legal perspective is a cornerstone of the *planning of government* and *governmental information systems*. At the same time, the responsibility of those who influence our rights grows. We speak of the principle of *confidence*[3]. Citizens must be able to rely on the information provided by government. And they should be fully confident that the information systems work properly.

3 Different Levels of Analysis

The simplest way to assess the legal framework of e-government is to ask whether there are gaps in that framework? In other words, do we need more legislation in addition to what we already have? It is however essential to point out that we cannot address the opportunities and problems of the development of e-government using a single-dimension legal framework. Not all legal issues are of the same order; not at all. *Juridification is a multifaceted phenomenon.*

Here, I am not talking only about the different levels of legislation from constitutions to different kind of guidelines. This is extremely important in *the constitutional state*. Indeed, one of the characteristics of the modern constitutional state is the requirement that citizens rights and any restrictions on those rights be set out in the law.[8] But the depth of sources alone will not help us enough in assessing information processes. We still need to analyze the structures and activities of government on several different levels. We should at least distinguish *meta-level issues*, *decisions involving legal principles*, and *decisions at the system level*.

---

[7] One of the legal ramifications of technical convergence in many countries, especially Finland, has been a shift in the focus of drafting from some ministries to others. In a short time, the Finnish Ministry of Transport and Communication has become a far more significant an actor than it had been before. This in turn necessarily has implications for how laws are drafted. Different ministries have different legislative traditions.

[8] This is one of the crucial distinctions between what was known as the administrative state and the new constitutional state. Regulations and guidelines on a level lower that that of a law must have a firm legislative basis.

380   A. Saarenpää

Meta-level issues fall into at least three main categories. These are the *information infrastructure*, *data security* [4] and the *identity of the individual in networks* [5]. Each is a fundamental legal question; and each has been addressed in different ways in different countries, often without due consideration of the issues.

For example the *data security* of open information networks is primarily the outcome of something other than the development of e-government. The new information infrastructure as an *information superhighway* is not carefully planned for modern government; for citizens and their rights. If we set out to design electronic government such that from the outset information systems are constructed to serve the needs of administration as well, we cannot, in my estimation, even begin to consider using open information networks such as we have today in government. We should look for a *data-secure information infrastructure* and ask how our identity is protected when we deal with the government. Today, data security receives precious little attention although it is duly mentioned in the E -Europe 2005 program. The recognition of a need for data security is quite a way from appropriate implementation, however.

The level of information processes in e-government below the meta-level is the level of principles. It reveals a typical confrontation between *law and technology* [6]. This level of analysis that is essential in the constitutional state. We are looking for a *positive voluntaristic* solution to the question of how technology can be utilized. One good example is the *electronic signature*. Where and when do we need such a "signature"?[9] Far too often in recent years we have read or heard as a given of sorts that the successful function of e-government requires a digital *signature*.

It does not and it cannot. In the European tradition, we have the *right to anonymity* when dealing with administration. Openness gives us the right to obtain information on authorities, their work and the information systems without having to reveal our identity in any form. This is an essential basic right. The right to anonymity cannot be circumvented or its exercise hampered by using a digital signature. It is only when the exercise of our rights or duties expressly requires identification can the electronic signature be applied. If e-government is designed primarily to work using a digital signature, an essential aspect of our rights will have been disregarded.

A second, opposite example can be found in Finnish legislation. *Act on Electronic Services in the Administration* came into force in February 2003. It regulates the conditions for electronic services provided by government and the responsibilities of the respective parties but leaves questions of substance, e.g., the need for strong identification, to be decided on a case-by-case basis. What we are dealing with here is the external infrastructure of e-government. The law obligates the authorities to set up information systems that can be accessed 24 hours a day so that citizens may conduct their affairs electronically. It obligates an authority to acknowledge the receipt of a message; it requires compatible software solutions and all electronic messages falling within the scope of the authority's work, with the exception of telephone calls.[10] But it

---

[9] It is unfortunate that the term "signature" has been adopted here. After all than electronic signature is a system – and a complex one – which seeks to provide reliable identification when the desire for such is expressed.

[10] The concept of an electronic data transmission is defined as follows: electronic data transmission means telefaxes and teleservice, such as electronic forms, e-mail or access rights to electronic information systems, and other methods based on electronics, where data is being transferred either wirelessly or via cable, with the exception of telephone calls;

does not require the use of the digital signature. The legislator has given our basic rights due consideration.

At the lowest level - the system level - of our analysis we should seek for answers in appropriate methods and technologies. Here we are face to face with the workings of *good government* on the everyday level in the building and utilization of public information systems. Let us take a closer look at the concept of *good administrative practice*, which still as a legal concept – not only political - may be new to many.[11]

4 Good Government

The new *Charter of the European Union*, which is still being debated, mentions the right to *good administration*. It has been accepted as a legal concept in too Europe. However the Charter seems to give a simplified picture of good administration. To an extent, what we see represents an old-fashioned notion of government:

1. Every person has the right to have his or her affairs handled impartially, fairly and within a reasonable time by the institutions and bodies of the Union.
2. This right includes:
   the right of every person to be heard, before any individual measure which would affect him or her adversely is taken;
   the right of every person to have access to his or her file, while respecting the legitimate interests of confidentiality and of professional and business secrecy; the obligation of the administration to give reasons for its decisions.
3. Every person has the right to have the Community make good any damage caused by its institutions or by its servants in the performance of their duties, in accordance with the general principles common to the laws of the Member States.
4. Every person may write to the institutions of the Union in one of the languages of the Treaties and must have an answer in the same language.

The Charter merely lists the *minimum requirement* for the constitutional state, and no more. In reading them, the notion of good administration seems to fade away almost entirely. A reader of the Charter gets a different picture of good administrative practice than a reader of the more recent literature on European administrative law.

We can see a different approach in new Finnish legislation. In Finland, which is considered as one of the forerunners in the area of good administration, the idea of good administration has already found its way into the present *Constitution*. It is – a little bit misleading however - under the section 21 entitled *protection under the law*:

"Everyone has the right to have his or her case dealt with appropriately and without undue delay by a legally competent court of law or other authority, as well as to have a decision pertaining to his or her rights or obligations reviewed by a court of law or other independent organ for the administration of justice.

Provisions concerning the publicity of proceedings, the right to be heard, the right to receive a reasoned decision and the right of appeal, as well as the other guarantees of a fair trial and *good governance* shall be laid down by an Act. "

---

[11] For example, the *Eurovoc, multilinqual thesaurus* of 1987 makes no mention of the term. The novelty of the concept can be seen in the fact that it was not highlighted by professor *Olli Mäenpää* when presenting Finnish administrative law to an international readership in an extensive piece of scholarship in 1993 [7].

As we can see, good administration, which here is translated with the somewhat misleading term *good governance,* is already *a constitutional concept* in Finland .[12] But what all can be considered *good administration* from the conceptual, legal point of view? I think this question can be broached in a least two different ways.

First, as a basic concept, *good administration* or *good government,* is indisputably related to other *good practices.* These exist and are increasing in number. Indeed, the Finnish Act on Openness in Government Activities adopted the concept of *good information management practices* when the law was enacted in 1999. Information systems are to be planned in keeping with good information management practices.[13]

Good practice is a legally complicated concept. In particular, the implications of observing good practice are disputed. For present purposes, however, it is important to note the central feature of good practice: It is a code of sorts which comprises a number of different components that change over time. The concept is always *an open one* but its core content at any given time is known. This applies in equal measure to the concept of good administrative practice. It is largely the task of the sciences to write accounts of good administration. And – I would like to point this out here already - e-government is now changing some or even many of those accounts.

Second, good administration as a statutory requirement is a matter which links government to the realization of citizens' rights, above all fundamental rights, in the constitutional state. Administration can in no way be an area detached from citizens' rights. Administration is for citizens, not the other way around. We can speak of a bond between government and fundamental rights. Good government at least in Finland is something more important, than conventional good practices or good practices that are provided for in some other way in the law. When we assess the operation of the information systems used in administration, in light of section 21 of the Constitution cited earlier, we can justifiably say that the appropriate functioning of the system, as part of good practice, is a basic right of every Finnish citizen. We have the right to demand a working information system. It is not merely a technical tool.

This approach allows us to elaborate and assess *the main principles of good government.* These are necessarily linked to the older principles based in administrative law, which in the Finnish context have been the following [8]:

1. Lawfulness of government, 2.Observance and safeguarding of fundamental rights
2. The principle of a government of civil servants, i.e., organizing government primarily through a civil service, 4. General principles of administrative law, and 5.The principle of right of access to government documents.

This list is interesting in terms of *legal theory*. It demonstrates how research in administrative law – or in *legal informatics,* which studies administration from the perspective of information processes – plays a crucial role in describing good administrative practice. What we see here is the formation of a concept in which the legislator has a part, Law as an academic discipline another, and legal practice, naturally, a third. In this triangle it is important the background of good

---

[12] This translation is the one produced and published by the Finnish Ministry of Justice, but it is unofficial. Only the Finnish, Swedish and Saami translations of the Constitution are official.

[13] Section 18, which provides for good administrative practice, is long and detailed. However, its first paragraph describes the underlying idea of the legislation rather well:: In order to create and realise good practice on information management, the authorities shall see to the appropriate availability, usability, protection, integrity and other matters of quality pertaining to documents and information management systems and, for this purpose, especially:........

administration, rooted in the constitutional state, remain visible. Otherwise, we run the risk that the guarantees of good administration which are listed in legislation will be seen as an exhaustive list that can be interpreted in a *bureaucratic* manner.[14]

It is not self-evident that we can go on with the same principles of good government as we make the transition from conventional government to e-government. The principles of good administrative practice date from the era when citizens conducting their affairs with the government manually using paper documents. Most likely we will need something more. Nor is it a given that old principles will be applicable as is to the new electronic environment [9].

Let us examine an example crucial to information systems. Often we meet the distinction *front office/back office*. It is generally considered that this is adequate for purposes of planning e-government. The *front office* opens up to the customer; the *back office* is for internal administrative use. This idea is essentially a sound one, but in the era of electronic activities, it is no longer sufficient. Openness, publicity, privacy and anonymity have different implications in different phases of dealing with the government electronically. This is not merely a question of citizens' rights but also one of the position of the media as a user of public documents. Moreover, we must ask whether openness should include information on how data is processed on the systems.[15] Here, we must broach the question whether the software used in the public sector should be based on open code and, if we decide that other than open-code software may be used, we must go on to ask how comprehensive the information ought to be that citizens receive in keeping with the requirements of openness.

5 What Should We Do?

Good government and the legal framework it entails are essential but, at the same time, dangerous concepts. They easily become detached from their contexts. The terms make for facile slogans. They can be readily bandied about in discussing societal and organizational issues. Indeed, they have already begun to lose their power to discriminate as search words on the networks. In our new e-government we should, however, take both more seriously. We are discussing not only slogans but our constitutional basic rights. In this discussion the multi-level analysis of the new legal framework is one of the key elements. E-government is challenging the legislators and system designers too.

Only when we have worked through the different components of government and situations responsibility from the perspective of information processes can we hope to progress with confidence to building e-government in the constitutional state and the legal framework e-government requires.

---

[14] The Finnish Act on Administration which is to come into force in 2004 will also have a chapter on good administrative practice whose sections to some extent cover matters similar those in the European Charter mentioned above. In the context of the Constitution and in general terms they do not increase the risks associated with enumerating of characteristics.

[15] We should recall that the European Personal Data Directive required descriptions of how software worked where this was used to assess persons. We would do well to extend this same idea in a more general form to cover all the software used in public administration.

The issue involves more than just information systems. If we look at the transformation of good government into e-government analytically, we are compelled to discuss in all seriousness how the requisite education can be provided for government personnel too. The user of every information system in e-government is at the same time a new *gatekeeper for the constitutional state,* and in this capacity is required to have sufficient legal skills. This, too, is part of the early appearance of law in the governmental process in the constitutional state. Proper use of public information systems requires that there be proper users.[9]

In closing, I would like to return the question of what new principles of good administrative practice the network society requires. Here, there is one answer that stands out above the rest: we need a principle of the *legal assessment of the information systems* used in e-government. As soon as we start thinking of how data is attached to a particular information technology platform, we must ask what impact and *risks* the implementation we choose might have on our rights [10]. And this question is not only for lawyers. It does belong to all of us.

References

1. Tuori, K.;The "Rechtsstaat" in the Conceptual. Field– Adversaries, Allies and Neutrals. Associations (2002) pp 201
2. Saarenpää, A.; Oikeusvaltio ja verkkoyhteiskunta (Constitutional State and Network Society), in Aarnio – Uusitupa (Eds.) Oikeusvaltio. Kauppakaari,Vantaa(2001)
3. Kuusikko, K.; Advice, Good Administration and Legitimate Expectations: Some Comparative Aspects. European Public Law, Volume 7, Issue 3. September 2001
4. Saarenpää, A.; Data Security: A Fundamental Right in the e-Society? in Traunmüller – Lenk (Eds.) Electronic Government. Springer Verlag (2002) pp 424-429
5. Saarenpää, A.; The Constitutional State and Digital Identity, Madrid 2002, http://www.ieid.org/congreso/ponencia_i.htm.
6. Benno, ,J.; Why the Use of ICT Engenders Legal Problems – in Search of a common Denominator . Law and Information Technology. Swedish Views. Swedish Government Official Reports, SOU 2002:112 44 pp
7. Mäenpää, O.; Administrative Law in Pöyhönen (ed) An Introduction to Finnish Law pp 295-343. Finnish Lawyers Publishing, Helsinki (1993)
8. Mäenpää, O.; Hyvän hallinnon perusteet. Forum Iuris, Helsinki (2002).
9. Saarenpää A.; E-Government – Good Government – An impossible equation? in Galindo – Traunmüller (eds.) E-Government: Legal, technical, and Pedagogical Aspects (2003)
10. Wahlgren, P.; Juridisk Riskanalys.Jure, Stockholm (2003).

Legal Aspects of One-Stop Government: The Case of Applying for a Building Permission

Michael Sonntag[1] and Maria Wimmer[2]

[1] Institute for Information Processing and Microprocessor Technology
University Linz
sonntag@fim.uni-linz.ac.at
[2] Institute for Applied Computer Science
University Linz
mw@ifs.uni-linz.ac.at

Abstract. Online one-stop government is a current development of public administrations for offering services and information through a single point of access in cyberspace. Current developments implement initial information and download of forms as well as delivery service and associated payments. Since the legal frame is the basis for governmental activity, legal regulations have to be thoroughly studied for online service delivery. In this paper, we investigate the Austrian laws for the case of online one-stop government service provision in general, especially in the area of electronic service of official documents (when allowed, how, what remedies are available in case of errors, etc.). We detail the legal aspects with the official proceeding of a building permission.

Keywords: one-stop government, e-government, electronic proceedings, building permissions

1 Motivation

Online one-stop government is a current development of public administrations for offering their services and information through a central point of access in cyberspace. Starting from existing and successful projects (see e.g. [6]) offering static information, extensions are under development to introduce more stages of contact with administration to these portals (e. g. the eGOV project [4], [3]). Not only information and download of forms, but also delivery of forms to administration (officially handing them in), and answers to the citizens or companies (official delivery of notifications), as well as associated payments (taxes and fees) shall be possible through a unified and logically[1] central portal. All these actions shall be fully legally valid and not just a substitute which might be accepted or not, or only possible in addition to conventional forms (=on paper).

When introducing e-government, it is important to focus on those areas, where advantages are clear to see. This results in a shift of attention from consumers to businesses, as frequency of contacts is much higher[2]. Also the costs involved (both for companies and administrations) are higher. Because of the number of contacts,

---

[1] One webserver and a single view on the content; produced by several distributed divisions.
[2] At least once a month for registering the VAT pre-registration, but usually much more often.

R. Traunmüller (Ed.): EGOV 2003, LNCS 2739, pp. 385–392, 2003.
© Springer-Verlag Berlin Heidelberg 2003

reductions in work or improvements in quality/response time are more important, resulting in stronger motivation to actually use it.

In this paper we discuss aspects of the electronic realization of one particular type of proceedings through a portal: Applying for a building permission. In Austria this consists of two parts: permission for erecting the building and permission for using certain machines and procedures within it (environmental protection against noise, waste, ...)[3]. Only the latter (company facilities permission) is focused on here from both a theoretical/legal and practical (implementation in the eGOV project [4]) view.

2   Legal Aspects in One-Stop Government

One-stop government possesses many legal implications. Previously communication between companies/citizens and administration went through the department responsible for the decision. Only in rare cases (e.g. in appeals) another instance receives it and is responsible for passing it on. However, then the receiving unit usually is or was also involved in the proceeding. One-stop government does not touch material jurisdiction and therefore no problem in this area arises. Still difficult situations can be imagined: E. g. the company timely sent the response to the one-stop unit, but this delays it unduly so it reaches the final recipient (the one legally prescribed) too late.

Another issue is who is responsible for checking e.g. applications. Obviously the deciding unit has to do this. But is the initial receiving unit also obliged to do some (and to which extent) checking? Is it a difference whether this is a private company or a branch of administration? As a service for customers this checking should take place as early and quickly as possible. However, a portal would probably try to avoid obligations of verification (usually included in general terms) because of liability.

Serving official documents is another problem. Since the postal service (in Austria in this respect) is seen as a part of public administration, serving then happens "officially" and by public servants. In the Internet this is not possible. Also evidence for serving (often required) is difficult because of many, and not always predictable, intermediaries like ISP's or network operators[4]. In Austria therefore new laws have been passed for managing (at least some of) these issues.

3   The E-GOV Project

For a smooth online one-stop government, all public authorities need to be interconnected vertically (e.g. municipality and provincial authority) as well as

---

[3] The material legal rules are found in the trade regulations (Gewerbeordnung) in § 353-359c. In the following the legal parts are discussed according to (this and other) Austrian law, for which this type of electronic proceeding is developed.

[4] These might also be foreigners, introducing different legal rules to a single (and relatively simple) serving. Also, serving in another country is usually not allowed (but see the European Convention on the Service Abroad of Documents relating to Administrative Matters; BGBl. Nr. 167/1983).

horizontally (e.g. several local municipalities). To provide online public services through one single entry point, an integrated platform is needed that connects the authorities and that provides a single entry point to the customers. The main objective of the eGOV project[5] [3] is the provision of an open, extensible and scalable platform for realizing online one-stop government. This platform is deployed and evaluated in three European countries, namely Austria, Greece and Switzerland.

The eGOV platform enables the public sector to provide citizens, businesses and other public authorities with information and public services that will be structured around life events and business situations, thus increasing public authorities' effectiveness, efficiency and quality of service. The technical components consist of:

- the next-generation online one-stop government portal and the according network architecture. The portal acts as the front-office and global entrance point to the electronic public services. It features a number of advanced functions such as personalisation, customisation, multilinguality, support of push services, digital signatures and access from different devices including mobile devices.
- one national and many local service repositories (SR). In addition to supplying online data and information relating to public services, the SR also provides a transactional service structure. Furthermore it provides the interfaces to local legacy systems already utilised by public administrations.
- the service creation environment (SCE). The SCE is a collection of tools that serves as the front-end to the SR. It allows the public services available in the Service Repositories to be maintained and updated.

In the eGOV project, nine public services have been modelled and will be implemented employing the platform. Among them, the building permission was chosen as a use-case.

4 Applying for a Company Facilities Permission: Procedure and Electronic Model

In Austria, the company facilities permission is based on the law Gewerbeordnung §§74 ff[6].

In the traditional manner, the applicant has to physically hand in four copies of the company description, of the plans, of a directory of machines and other operating equipment, of the waste management concept and one copy of the technical documents as well as a list of the names and addresses of the site owner and the neighbors. Depending on the circumstances, further documents may be required.

Whether the permission is granted or not depends on the experts' reports, the hearing of the involved parties and/or the inspection on sight.

When the result is determined, an official notification is sent to the applicant. The invoice is included in this official letter, no matter whether the decision is positive or negative. The payment is therefore done after the notification has been issued.

The notification comes into effect as soon as the appellation period is over.

---

[5] An EC-co-funded project under IST FP 5, IST-28471, http://www.egov-project.org/
[6] BGBl. Nr. 194/1994

This procedure has been re-engineered in the eGOV one-stop portal. The applicant can retrieve all information s/he needs on the procedures and conditions online. Having logged in to the platform, s/he can hand in the application form online together with all requested documents. The procedure of this handing in is implemented in a way to guide users to completing the service invocation successfully.

The platform then routes the application directly to the responsible authority and provides feedback to the application about its receipt.

In the respective authority, an automatic check of completeness of online forms and documents is performed first, and then the application is handed through to the servant responsible for verifying and processing it. If s/he encounters some missing parts, s/he sends a message to the applicant (online, email, SMS or other means) with the request for the additional material. When the application is complete and verified, the act is sent to the experts for approval. A date for on-site inspection is set and all neighbors and the applicant are invited (either online or by ordinary mail).

After positive inspection and approval by the experts, the official notification is written and sent to the applicant through the platform. The fee is also paid online.

If nobody appeals within the next three weeks after the information on the positive decision, the final archiving of the record is performed by the servant.[7]

5   Important Elements of Electronic Proceedings in One-Stop Portals

Considering electronic applications and orders, legal requirements must be met equally as if all were done on paper. However, differences not accounted for by changes in law exist.

5.1   General Procedural Aspects

Time: For technical delivery of communication to administration § 13 para 5 AVG states that the time of actually "entering" it is important, regardless of office hours[8]. If a third party manages a web portal, it is the citizen's agent and therefore the risk of transmission from it to administration is on the citizen. If it is conversely managed by administration and provided as a service to citizens, it serves as a mailbox for accepting communication from them. Therefore sending information to it (i. e. clicking on the final button) is the relevant point in time. This is also according to the theory of spheres: When employing an agent the responsibility for it is on the person using it.

Determining the recipients address: Before thinking about the time information is received by administration, it must be decided whether this is allowed at all and which protocols and addresses may be used. Technical abilities alone are insufficient. Official publication of fact and circumstances are needed (comparable to unlisted fax

---

[7] Due to space restrictions, no model is shown here. It is available on request, though.

[8] This was included because of differences in decisions between VfGH (e. g. 26.6.2000, B460/00) and VwGH (e. g. 5.8.1999, 99/03/0311).

numbers). If it is known, documents can be sent there, but other than on publicly announced line/address, delays can happen and no guarantee for availability exists. Therefore only published addresses and officially accepted protocols and formats may be used. However, administration is under obligation to try interpreting all communication. Misdirected letters must be sent to the correct recipient on the sender's risk (§ 6 para 1 AVG). This also applies to el. communication received not at official endpoints. No extensive research is required: most errors in forwarding are on the original sender and the time required counts against time set for responding. If content is not understood, administration must try finding out the senders' intention for determining actions[9]: El. analogs are unknown formats. Citizens must be asked for re-sending in another format. If el. communication does not work (no right for this exists), paper must be used and the risk of passing a deadline[10] is on the citizen.

Incorrect addressing: What happens if a wrong address (e. g. E-Mail address on a letter, wrong username or incorrect method of delivery in a portal) is published by administration? According to the UVS Vorarlberg[11] this is similar to incorrect instructions on where remedies must be sent. This would mean that the legal *and* the stated addresses are both valid. The UVS Steiermark[12] contrarily decided that this is the citizen's risk, as the authority the remedy should have been sent to was still the same (only the address was wrong). It seems more appropriate that the address on a letter is irrelevant: law is concerned only with the administrative unit, but not its location[13]. Information on a letter is just a hint: wrongly addressed communication must be sent by the recipient to the correct unit (see above). It is therefore on the citizen to look up the correct address for a certain type of communication he/she wants to use[14]. A portal used for delivering communication to administration should therefore provide reliable notification whether a document was successfully delivered (and when) or not.

Large proceedings: For very large proceedings[15] (expected number of interested parties > 100) administration can use a publication of the application instead of individual communication with every (prospective) party. This requires publication in two large newspapers and the federal gazette[16]. The Internet can be used additionally, but does not count as one of the newspapers. Web portals can be of factual, although not legal, utility here. With less cost the most interested part of the population[17] can be reached more actively (using personalization), resulting in stronger participation.

---

[9] VwGH 3.4.79, Zl 2651/78.

[10] Deadlines differ for paper (beginning of office-hours) and electronic submissions (midnight)! At 23 o'Clock data can be sent electronically and arrive timely, but no longer physically.

[11] UVS Vorarlberg 1-0232/00 from 13.6.2000

[12] UVS Steiermark 30.12-95/2000 from 8.11.2000

[13] Wrong addresses are never mentioned in the rules for wrong information on remedies, and addresses are never contained therein. They are therefore "unimportant" and only the administrative unit is relevant.

[14] Reinstatement is the proper remedy in cases of wrong addressing because of incorrect information by administration. This is an unexpected event and there is no fault by the citizen: contact details on official documents are usually reliable.

[15] Common for this type of proceeding of applying for a building permission.

[16] Which must also be available in the Internet (§ 2a VerlautbarungsG).

[17] Actually a (currently probably rather small) subset: Only those employing the portal.

5.2 Specifics When Applying for a Building Permission

Some elements are specialties of the proceeding of applying for a building permission. One of those is the usually rather large and occasionally even huge number of parties, which poses communication problems. The notification that such a proceeding was started and an oral hearing will be held must be posted as notices in each surrounding building. If suitable, an individual invitation can (and must) be sent. Instead of sending a letter this can be fulfilled through a portal. Because of its one-stop function, it will be visited rather often[18], compared to dedicated portals for individual proceedings/administrative units. Also, participating in such a portal requires a valid E-Mail address, which could also be used for actively sending this information. This even enhances the transparency of a proceeding, as the application, plans, etc. can be presented electronically and are therefore always easily accessible[19].

Another (but not so rare) specialty of this proceeding is payment of fees. According to § 356d these can also be paid by money transfer[20]. This special rule can be seen as intention to support distance communication. Therefore this proceeding is a prime target for introducing electronic forms of payment. This ties in with the promise of the Austrian banking sector to provide electronic (=el. signed data) proofs of payment (instead of currently only proofs of issuing a direction to the bank). These could then be used beside credit cards or other payment methods.

5.3 Electronic Signatures/Encryption

Signatures are no longer required for written requests to the administration (§ 13 Abs 4 AVG), therefore obviating the need for secure el. signatures. This especially eases the use of a portal, as document can now be created on the server (signatures would have to be created on the citizen's computer). If in doubt about the sender of the request, administration can always request a full signature (which can be on paper or electronically). For both, download of the text of the request as a file must be offered. The citizen can then print, sign, and send it per post, or affix an electronic signature and send it per E-Mail.

A technically complicated issue are e. g. signatures for building plans. These often exist in rather uncommon electronic formats and must be signed by several persons.

Electronic signatures are difficult in this case, as appropriate software is rather rare[21]. Also, software for viewing or manipulating these plans is usually not equipped for this, requiring extraction of the raw document as an additional step. Electronic

---

[18] As we focus on companies. For private persons this assumption would not hold because of rather infrequent visits.

[19] Otherwise plans etc. can usually be inspected only at special locations (mostly the local authority) during office hours.

[20] Which is now available for all proceedings (cash and money transfer). El. forms of payment are available only according to techn. and organizational support by the administrative unit.

[21] Current software (see e. g. http://www.a-trust.at/docs/verfahren/a-sign-premium/) supports html, xml, text and bitmaps. This is unsuitable for large plans with very fine details as huge files would be the result. Allowing another (probably some kind of vector graphic) , perhaps extensively checked, file format would be a solution here.

signatures might still be useful in this area, as passing plans from one person to another just for signing is even more cumbersome and time-consuming. Also, these (then digital) plans are much easier and cheaper copied than when existing only on paper.

5.4 Serving Documents

(Nearly) Everyone can be expected to have an address or at least be found. However, most citizens cannot be expected to be able to accept electronic delivery. It is therefore permissible (§ 18 para 3 AVG) to use only in the following cases:

- If the party expressly (implied consent insufficient) agreed to this delivery method.
- If the party has sent some communication to the administrative body in this way and has not explicitly prohibited administration using this method for serving. According to the wording this is regardless of the proceeding, i. e. if once an E-Mail was sent, any administrative unit can forever use this address/method of delivery. Keeping track of this fact could be an additional service of a webportal.

Electronic serving is only possible if "serving without evidence" is done (set under this heading). Technical delivery is therefore equal only to a normal letter, but not a registered one. This restrictive and careful approach is common with new technology, as electronic delivery in the form required by law will with respect to security in most cases be equal to serving with simple evidence (RSb).

Another issue is when exactly the risk moves. Conventional mail is the recipient's risk when put into his mailbox or handed to him personally. Electronic delivery in contrast requires several steps: First the document is stored on a server, then a notice is sent to the recipient that a certain document awaits retrieval, and later the person actually fetches this document. The document has already been legally served when it is ready for download (§ 17a para 1 ZustellG). This must be interpreted, however, that the notice of this act (second part of the procedure outlined above) has actually reached the recipient (§ 26a ZustellG; but who need not have read it!). When sending this notice, risk passes to the recipient upon arrival at his e-mail server. Administration must therefore ensure that the notification has actually reached the final server[22] and that the document can be retrieved from its own server[23]. The risk for the transmission over the Internet (modifications, loss ...) is on the administration, while checking for notifications and actual retrieval of documents on the citizen. Of special importance is here the reference in § 17a para 1 last sentence, referencing § 17 para 4: If the notification of deposition is destroyed or removed, this is the risk of the recipient. Applied to electronic delivery this means that the notification E-Mail must have reached the destination safely. Only subsequent problems (e. g. accidental deletion by the user or the ISP) do not touch delivery. If the mail however never reached the recipients sphere, delivery has not taken place.

If the user changes (not merely not checking for new messages) his/her E-Mail address during a proceeding, she/he must notify administration (§ 8 ZustellG). In case

---

[22] Intermediate E-Mail servers ("relaying") are the risk of the administration, unless they are from the users ISP: It is the user's agent and therefore his area of control. Administration: Own servers + general Internet; Companies/Citizens: Own server + their ISP.
[23] In the manner described it should be and that it is readable/viewable with the published software. This also includes the administrations own network.

a company forgets this, serving might be done by simply depositing the document (i. e. putting it on the server) and sending the informational E-Mail. However, this will usually not be successful because of § 17a ZustellG prohibiting electronic serving if the administration received notification that the user is not reachable under the electronic address. This is primarily meant for temporary absence (e. g. automatic vacation replies), but also applies to the termination of an account. In this case E-Mail "bounces" and is returned as undeliverable. This is notice enough that the company is no longer reachable under this address: conventional serving must then take place. This also applies if a portal is used for serving: Any error message that an account no longer exists or is temporarily offline must results in the same consequence.

6 Conclusions

Additional legal rules for e-government were created, but their result is not always obvious (see the example of the notification E-Mail) and they must be looked at in detail. In one-stop government through a portal as seen here another issue is the legal position of this portal. Whether it is operated by a private company or part of administration need not be clearly visible for users just from its look and the circumstances. However, this has large ramifications on legal result, e. g. when risk passes. A clear description and information of users in simple language is therefore needed.

Implementing an individual and more complex type of proceedings is a good test for an online portal, as it is a test of its flexibility. Each actual proceeding is at least slightly different and the portal must cope with this. Seen in this light, a portal is not a static product, but rather a kind of framework allowing to implement types of proceedings in an easy way and by experts in the topic, as well as performing them on individual cases with small modifications done by non-experts.

References

1. HENGSTSCHLÄGER, J.: Verwaltungsverfahrensrecht. Wien: WUV 2002
2. WALTER, R., MAYER, H.: Grundriß des österreichischen Verwaltungsverfahrensrechts[6]. Wien: Manz 1995
3. TAMBOURIS, E.: An Integrated Platform for Realising Online One-Stop Government: The eGOV Project, in: Proceedings der DEXA Internationalen Workshops, IEEE Computer Society Press, Los Alamitos, CA, 2001, 359–363
4. eGOV (An integrated Platform for realising online one-stop Government, IST-2000-28471), http://www.egov-project.org/
5. SONNTAG, M., WIMMER, M.: Datenschutzaspekte von e-Government mit besonderem Bezug auf das eGOV-Projekt. In: Schubert, S., Reusch, B., Jesse, N. (Eds.): Informatik bewegt. Informatik 2002 - 32. Jahrestagung der Gesellschaft für Informatik e.V. (GI). Bonn: Gesellschaft für Informatik 2002
6. @mtshelfer online: Austrians online information and consultation system for citizens, businesses and people with special needs, http://www.help.gv.at/

A Taxonomy of Legal Accountabilities in the UK E-Voting Pilots

Alexandros Xenakis and Ann Macintosh

International Teledemocracy Centre
Napier University
10, Colinton Rd., Edinburgh, EH10 5DT
{a.xenakis,a.macintosh}@napier.ac.uk

Abstract. In this paper, a process approach to the investigation of e-voting is adopted defining the process stages and the agents involved in each stage. The technologies used in the delivery of electronic voting, the locations related to the different stages of the process and the main legal issues involved have been identified in the existing literature. These five elements, namely agents, legal issues, process stages, technologies used and locations involved, form the framework of this taxonomy. The aim of the taxonomy is to provide an insight into the legal issues emerging according to the different combined relationships between these five elements, and provide a tool for the identification of legal accountabilities amongst the different agents involved.

1 Introduction

The first e-voting pilots in the UK took place in May 2000 [1], with 16 more in May 2002 [2]. These concerned elections for local councils, and 18 more are to follow in May 2003 according to the procurement of the Office of the Deputy Prime Minister[3]. According to the same source similar pilots are to be operated on local elections level until May 2005. These pilot schemes reflect the government's intention to develop "the capacity of holding an e-enabled general election some time after 2006" as quoted in the Electoral Commission's strategic evaluation report[4]. The taxonomy of legal accountabilities provided hereafter forms part of a doctoral research programme exploring the use of business process re-engineering (BPR) methodologies to provide management, modelling and analysis methods for electronic voting. This taxonomy is based on five basic concepts: the agents involved in the e-voting process, the related locations, the technologies used to deliver e-voting services, the process stages identified and the relevant legal issues.

2 Agents

In their technical option report, Fairweather and Rogerson [5], suggest a set of stakeholders involved in the deployment of electronic elections. They name seven different stakeholders: central government, local government, those seeking election,

R. Traunmüller (Ed.): EGOV 2003, LNCS 2739, pp. 393–400, 2003.
© Springer-Verlag Berlin Heidelberg 2003

minority groups, citizens as voters, suppliers of technological elements and systems developers. In our taxonomy we propose five agents who are actively involved in one or more of the e-voting pilots process stages. Central Government is one of them as the pilots are organised by the Office of the Deputy Prime Minister[6]. Local Government are another as they are the local authorities conducting the pilots in their local council elections. Those seeking election in the taxonomy are defined as candidates. As this is a local election context the notion of political parties is included in the candidate concept. Citizens as voters are referred to as "voter", and suppliers of technological elements are defined as "vendors" which is also the term used by Fairweather and Rogerson [5] to define the suppliers' role. That leaves out minority groups and system developers. For the purposes of this research we consider that minority groups to be voters who are covered under the legal issue for accessible[7] elections, free to all[8]. System developers on the other hand are considered to be part of the vendor concept as they are not contracted as independent agents in the case of the UK e-voting pilots. That provides us with the first set of concepts of this taxonomy, the agents: **Central Government, Local Authorities, Candidates, Voters** and **Vendors.**

3 Locations

Fearweather and Rogerson [5], in their electronic voting options taxonomy suggest four locations related to the conduct of e-voting, namely home, work, polling station and public space. To these we add the concept of the count location as our process stages include a count stage as part of the e-voting process. Past experience has proved that some technologies of electronic voting involve separate count locations. This was the case in Stratford[9] and Bolton[10] in the May 2002 pilots. The specific voting kiosk used involved a detachable module containing cast e-ballots which was physically transported to a separate counting location. Similarly in Swindon[11] landline telephone votes once cast were stored in the vendor's premises. We therefore introduce the second set of concepts of this taxonomy, locations: **Home, Work, Polling Station, Public Place** and **Count Location.**

4 Technologies Used in the E-Voting Process

In the May 2002 e-voting pilots many different technologies were used as stated in the Electoral Commission's strategic evaluation report [4]. On-line voting, landline telephone, SMS text messaging from mobile phones, direct recording e-voting kiosks, kiosks providing a paper audit (-although it did not produce a paper proof for each vote, as suggested by Mercurri [12] and the Caltech-MIT Voting Technology Project [13]), e-counting machines of paper ballots, and standard PC with suitable software. Digital television will be used for the first time in the UK pilots in May 2003. Finally one should refer to the use of the internet for voter registration offered in US [14]. In this taxonomy we provide nine technologies in the service of the agents within the e-voting process: **Internet** (internet based applications, services other than on-line voting), **On-line voting, DTV** (Digital television), **Landline telephone** (used as a channel for e-voting through an interactive voice response system), **PC + software** (standard pc for the non on-line activities with specialised software), **Kiosk DRE** (direct recording e-voting machines), **Kiosk Paper-Proof** (providing paper proof for each vote cast), **E-count** (either of paper ballot papers or e-ballots) and **SMS/Mobile** (text message voting).

Within the concept of on-line voting we include all internet based application which would allow a voter to access a relevant internet interface, be authenticated, cast his vote, and the vote then to be archived, all in real time. We differentiate that from the concept of internet, as we consider the internet to be more than a tool to cast an e-ballot. In the context of this taxonomy the concept of internet is related to web based applications which enable the electronic servicing of the electoral process, related to campaigning, procurement, registration, and declaration of results.

In their e-voting options taxonomy Fairweather and Rogerson [5] suggest the use of WAP enabled and third generation mobile phones. In our taxonomy these are included in the concept of on-line voting and the concept of internet, as WAP voting would in practice be on-line voting through a different- WAP developed- interface and the same applies regarding the internet offered services related to voting . They also propose the use of ATM and the National Lottery networks. These last two options are excluded from our taxonomy as there is no immediate plan regarding their deployment in the forthcoming pilots nor have we encountered the use of such VNP technologies (Virtual Private Network) for legally binding elections other than in the case of a very small scale pilot run by the US Department of Defense in the 2000 US presidential election [15].

5 Process Stages

In the presented taxonomy we propose eleven process stages for the e-voting process. These are mostly in line with those presented by OASIS[16]. However, looking at the general UK election legislation framework we have also come across election campaign law[17] and therefore included an election campaign stage. We have also included a pilot procurement stage; this process stage was encountered in the May 2002 and 2003 pilot schemes. The stages which are hereon presented are not consecutive as some stages may run in parallel to each other. We therefore propose the following e-voting process stages: **Election Campaign, Procurement** (In this case it is in the notion of the e-voting pilot procurement), **Registration** (voter registration), **Nomination** (of candidates), **General Administration, Authentication** (of voter), **Casting the vote, Verification** (either verification of correct casting of the vote or numerical audit of voters per votes cast), **Counting** (of paper or e-ballots), **Tabulation** (of result), **Declaration** (of result).

One must bare in mind that these are high level stages which can in turn be analysed into more detailed processes.

6 Legal Issues

In the Watt [8] report we identified fourteen legal issues which we included in our taxonomy. Another two were included from additional literature. However in the context of the UK local authority pilots, for which this taxonomy is intended, the Watt report[8] provided the main guidance, as it did for the development of questionnaires, given to local authorities and vendors by the Office of the Deputy Prime Minister, to assist in the production of statutory orders. The legal issues addressed in this taxonomy are:

Commercial contract disputes: Since vendors are contracted by the central government to provide products or services in the conduct of election one can envisage the possibility any kind of commercial contract disputes. However the only relevant issue up to now identified is the case of St Albans pilot in 2002 [19].

Accessibility issues: The Representation of the People Act 2000 and The Representation of the People Act 1983 set out a wide range of limits to local authorities to ensure disenfranchised voters' participation. These have been the basis for the access standards applied to the 2003 pilots [7].

Vote trading: Vote trading itself, as in selling of votes, is a corrupt practice[1].However the case of tactical voting over the internet has been encountered both at the US where it was considered illegal [17], as well as in the UK where no action was taken. Watt in his report relates the case of paper proof of cast e-ballots to the possibility of it being used for vote selling.

Identification: The issue of identification is closely related to the issue of personation. Identification of the voter is necessary in order to avoid personation. Fairweather and Rogerson [5], include five options for the provision of identification: CD Rom, Polling Official, Biometrics, Password/PIN, Smart card. Out of these, the 2002 pilots have used the password/pin, smart card and polling official identification methods [4].

Eligibility: Although the constraint of voter eligibility is related primarily to the formation of the electoral register, the right to elect and be elected, as mentioned in the OSCE legal framework for elections report[20], relates this issue to candidates as well. In some cases there are restrictions as to who may exercise this right, becoming of age being a simple example. There are however circumstances in which one's right to elect and be elected may be revoked. If the registration of voters and the nomination of candidates is done electronically then these principles should be kept in mind when developing an e-voting system.

One ballot per vote: This is an issue mainly related to the simultaneous use of multiple channels of voting. Referenced in the Watt [8] report as the possibility of double voting both in person and by post, the same issue was encountered in the 2002 pilots is Liverpool [21] and Sheffield[22]. The solution was an on-line register, common for all voting channels.

Free to cast a ballot: This issue, also mentioned by Watt [8], relates to the issue of undue influence inflicted on the voters options, but also to accessibility issues earlier

---

[1] The Representation of the People Act 1983, s.113

mentioned. In the May 2002 pilots none of the e-voting systems used offered the option to cast a spoilt ballot [4]. One could argue that this was a way the voters' right to a free choice was limited as one of the options available in traditional voting was excluded from the e-voting options.

Unlawful influence: This is an issue related to remote, unsupervised voting. When voting is done at home, there is no way to establish that the vote was cast without any kind of influence from family members. Watt [8] refers to it as 'family voting' and relates it to voting channels such as the internet and digital television. In the same report it is suggested that undue influence can be imposed upon by landlords or employers. In the 2002 pilots in the case of Swindon [11], workplace internet voting did take place although no effort to influence employees on their choice was reported.

Secrecy: The secrecy of the vote is secured under RPA 19832. In it the actual process of voting is described in order to maintain secrecy. The aim of the secrecy rule is to safeguard voter privacy and anonymity, privacy against others present during the casting of the vote and anonymity towards the state [8]. Privacy issues are probable in unsupervised locations voting such as home, work and public space. According to the NOP survey[23], 71% of voters and 61% of non-voters found the new methods piloted in the 2002 UK pilots provided privacy for the voter.

Tampering with election material and data: Tampering with ballot papers, nomination papers and election material is an offence3. In the case of e-voting tampering with voting data should also be one [8]. Hacking of e-voting systems is primarily addressed by the Computing Misuse Act 1990, where issues of unauthorized entry and tampering are covered.

Personation: According to Watt [8]"Pretending to be another person for the purposes of voting is described as personation". According to RPA 1983 [18] personation is a corrupt practice4. Watt in his report refers to 'offences akin to personation', such as voting while suffering from legal incapacity, related to the eligibility issue and voting in more than one way, related to the one ballot per vote issue.

Verifiable count: Counting the votes can be verifiable when the a recount produces the same result. In the case of e-voting verification of the count can be achieved by the storage of voting data in parallel ways. In the UK pilots in 2002, in Stratford [9] and Bolton [10], election data were stored in three different ways (kiosk hard disc, detachable module and printed version. Watt [8] recommends each e-vote being down loaded onto paper and counted as paper votes. However the technical requirements[24] for the 2003 pilots although requiring double server hosting do not demand the Watt recommendation.

Transparency: The OSCE report [21] considers transparency as a main issue during the counting process, imposing it through the presence of observers from political parties, candidates and the media. Watt [8] refers to it as the principle of the transparent count. Most e-counting of paper ballots done in the 2002 UK pilots provided the opportunity for adjudication of disputed ballots [4]. Transparency

---

2 Representation of the People Act 1983, r37, s1.
3 Representation of the People Act 1983, s66.
4 Representation of the People Act 1983, s60

nevertheless should be considered as an important issue of e-voting connected to all of its stages.

Openness to audit: The OSCE report [20] points out the need for 'procedures for audit'. Although in the report it is related to the counting process, one could argue that publication of results is also a form of audit and an effort to avoid fraud. In the context of this taxonomy we consider the audit concept to be a form of controlling and monitoring the e-voting process as a whole.

Accuracy: The need for accuracy is underpinned in Watt's [8] report. However in the case of e-voting, the voting process is serviced by technology which according to the technical requirements for the 2003 pilots [24] must deliver 100% accuracy of count and 100% accountability for all ballots entering the system. The issue of accuracy is greatly related to the integrity of the supplier

Campaign Law: According to Ballinger and Coleman[17], there are several issues such as campaign expenses, making use of state resources for the re-election of already elected politicians, and the use of web casting. The sale of an updated electoral register indicating those who have already voted when the voting is run over a prolonged period of time is an issue closely related to the campaign, which could lead to heavily targeted campaigning efforts, as happened in the Chorley 2002 pilot[25].

7 Developing Relations between Concepts

The static relationships between the concepts of the taxonomy were the first to be developed. Locations were related to the technologies used in e-voting on the basis of where these technologies have been or could be used from. These were depicted in a table (Table 1- not presented due to space restrictions). Technologies used were then related to the different election stages on the basis of which technology has or can be used in each stage. These were depicted in a second table (Table 2). Twenty three relations were produced from Table 1 and 42 relations from Table 2. The combination of Tables 1 and 2 provided in turn inherited relations between locations and process stages. A total of 109 inherited relations were produced showing the connection between locations-technologies-process stages.

In developing dynamic relationships, for every one of the five agents a matrix was produced showing the relations between the legal issues and the different stages of the process concerning each agent. Agents were related to legal issues according to examined literature either because they were legally accountable or protected by the law on each of the issues, and legal issues were related to each of the process stages on the basis of the same literature. Thus inherited relations were created between agents and process stages. To verify the inherited agent-stage relations, process stages were then related to agents directly on the basis of the 2002 e-voting pilot descriptions. The 5 tables depicting the issue-stage relationships for each of the agents, although developed, are not shown in this paper because of limitations of space in this space. Taking into account the inherited static relations for each of the process stages, 1425 possible relations were calculated relating location-technologies-process stages- legal issues-agents. In specific 452 were related to vendors, 174 were related to candidates, 67 were related to central government, 272 to voters and 455 to local authorities.

8 Using the Taxonomy

The final, five concept relations, resulting from the inherited relations produced from the combination of tables 1 and 2, and the legal issue per agent tables, can be put in words in a sequence of five terms (each term resulting from one of the taxonomy basic concepts): **Agent _ Location _ Technology _ Process stage _ Legal issue.**
The agent term identifies the agent concerned, the location term indicates where the issue arises, the technology term informs us of the technology involved, the process stage term indicates which stage of the electoral process we examine and the legal issue term indicates the legal issue involved. An example would be :
"voter _ home _ on-line voting _ casting the vote _ personation"
   The above sequence of terms describes the case of the voter (agent), voting from home (location), using an on-line voting system (technology), to cast one's vote (process stage) and relates this case to the offence of personation (legal issue). In simple terms, the combination of circumstances described by the first four basic concepts of the taxonomy, create a suitable environment for a certain legal issue to occur which is described by the fifth and final concept of the taxonomy.
   Abstraction can be achieved by excluding technologies if not used or locations; that would limit the multiplicity of cases that have to be considered. The different authentication technologies related to the authentication stage, as suggested in the Fairwheather and Rogerson [5] taxonomy, have deliberately been omitted to avoid further multiplicity.

9 Benefits

The taxonomy of legal accountabilities in the UK e-voting context presented in this paper, provides a mapping of the different legal cases which could arise and the legal points that have to be covered by the legislation put in place in order to introduce e-voting. It indicates legal accountabilities per agent, a feature which may prove especially useful considering the multiplicity of agents involved in the delivery of e-voting services and e-enabled elections. It relates procedural responsibility to legal accountability, therefore indicating cases where one is legally accountable without actually being responsible for the action which is not done according to the existing legal restrictions. Finally, it identifies all the possible combination of circumstances which could foster the creation of a legal issue or offence. Therefore it could be used as a tool for prediction of these cases so that appropriate measures are taken to prevent legal problems and contested election results. Accordingly, it could be used to create a set of possible cases to be covered in commercial contracts between suppliers of e-voting services and equipment, and government organizations.

References

1. Coleman, S. *et* Independent Commission on Alternative Voting Methods *Elections on the 21ᵗ Century: from paper ballot to e-voting* Electoral Reform Society, 2002
2. Pratchett, L. " The implementation of electronic voting in the UK " LGA Publications, the Local Government Association, 2002
3. http://www.odpm.gov.uk/
4. Electoral Commission Modernising Elections, A strategic evaluation of the 2002 electoral pilot schemes, August 2002 available on-line at http://www.electoralcommission.gov.uk/
5. Fairweather, B. and Rogerson, S. , Technical Options Report, De Montfort University, Leicester, 2002
6. Office of the Deputy Prime Minister, The Electoral Commission and the Local Government Association Modernising Elections Prospectus for electoral pilots - local elections 2003 available at http://www.local-regions.odpm.gov.uk/elections/index.htm
7. Disability Access Standards for the Electoral Modernisation Pilot Projects Access standards for e-voting and e-counting technology, SCOPE, 2002.
8. Watt, B. Implementing Electronic Voting, A report addressing the legal issues by the implementation of electronic voting, University of Essex, 2002
9. The Electoral Commission, pilot scheme evaluation Stratford on Avon District Council 2 May 2002, 2002
10. The Electoral Commission, pilot scheme evaluation Bolton Metropolitan Borough 2 May 2002, 2002
11. The Electoral Commission, pilot scheme evaluation Swindon Borough Council 2 May 2002, 2002
12. Mercurri, R. Rebecca Mercuri's Statement on Electronic Voting, available on-line at http://www.notablesoftware.com/RMstatement.html
13. www.vote.caltech.edu
14. www.election.com
15. E-voting security study, The Crown, 2002
16. OASIS Election and Voter Services Technical Committee, Election Mark-up Language (EML): e-voting process and data requirements.
17. Ballinger, C. and Coleman, S. Electoral and the Internet, Some Issues Considered, Hansard Society, 2001
18. Representation of the People Act 1983
19. The Electoral Commission, pilot scheme evaluation St Albans City and District Council 2 May 2002, 2002
20. Office for Democratic Institutions and Human Rights, Guidelines for reviewing a legal framework for elections, Warsaw, 2001
21. The Electoral Commission, pilot scheme evaluation Liverpool City Council 2 May 2002, 2002
22. The Electoral Commission, pilot scheme evaluation Sheffield City Council 2 May 2002, 2002
23. NOP World, Public Opinion in the Pilots, A report summarising the aggregate findings from surveys carried out by NOP Research in May 2002 in 13 electoral pilot scheme areas, 2002
24. Electoral Modernisation Pilots, Statement of requirements, ODPM, 2002
25. The Electoral Commission, pilot scheme evaluation Chorley Borough Council 2 May 2002, 2002

Anti-corruption Information Systems and E-Government in Transforming Countries. A Point of View

Nicolae Costake

Consultant (CMC)
ncke@starnets.ro

Abstract. Corruption is important, in particular for transforming countries. Anti-corruption approaches are briefly examined. The conclusion is reached that more attention should be given to the aspect of the necessary support by information systems. A case study was selected. A simple model of corruption is proposed. It is used for formulating general informational requirements to support anti-corruption actions. These requirements suggest that effective anti-corruption actions imply the infrastructure of e-Government.

1 Statement of the Problem

A representative theoretical paper by Ceobanu [1]. suggests corruption as an inter-action between social actors who act to achieve profits using bribery, nepotism and illegal appropriation of public resources. Di Pietro [2] said "democracy and liberal economy...contain a virus: the corruption" (quote in [3]) Transparency International (TI- e.g.[4]) and others. produce reports including the "National Integrity System" for anti- corruption (AC) proposed by Pope [5]. Other studies (e.g.[6], [7]). link corruption and governance. However, the possible support of information technology (IT) received little consideration. One of the few explicit references to both AC and e-Government (eG) is found in [8], the author remaining sceptical on effectiveness. In Transitional countries (TCs), move from the communist-type socio-economic system (SES) to an advanced capitalist one. Corruption can change it towards a quasi-primitive capitalist SES (e.g..[9]). The necessary high governance's performance, practically implies eG. (Described by Lenk and Traunmuller.[10]): However, the topic of AC information systems (ACIS) is not found in most strategies for the information society, though AC is mentioned in the Estonian one [11]. The present paper selects a case study. A number of corruption cases are briefly analysed and a simple model is sketched. Existing and promoted AC activities are briefly discussed. Informational requirements are deduced. Many are common with eG's ones [12].

R. Traunmüller (Ed.): EGOV 2003, LNCS 2739, pp. 401–406, 2003.

2 Selection of a Case Study. Possible Corruption Processes

Romania was selected as a case study because: a) it has a high corruption rank in the tables produced by TI; b) corruption is mentioned in the yearly regular EC Reports (e.g.[13]); c) AC measures were taken (creation of the AC Prosecutor's Office and a recent AC law [14]). d) the press is active, providing quasi- factual information. Newspaper reports are not necessarily true, nor scientific evidence, but can suggest possible mechanisms. Tips are offered / asked / received by civil servants to perform their normal jobs. (possible systemic corruption in the TI's sense [5]). At a press conference of the Minister of Justice [6] following facts were stated: a) turning child adoption procedures into business; b) doubtful privatization (e.g. prices much less than some offers, poor terms of reference, etc.); c) incorrect VAT refunds and high tax evasion in the business with alcoholic drinks; d) ineffective AC institutional measures. In an interview, the President of the Court of Audits declared, among others [15] a) before 2002 the Court had no access to privatisation transactions; b) legislation is insufficiently precise; c) one mechanism is to successively approve postponements of the payment of taxes till the prescription term is reached A newspaper [16] reported how a supermarket was financed by a mayoralty before its Council's official decision and public works were contracted without public tendering Another article [17] reports about how the prefect of a county created a network of companies which he acquired in very favourable terms and permitted to control a category of supplies to the mining companies in that county. Another example [18] refers to a local ruling party leader, now under arrest, who apparently sponsored the party, obtaining influence to create a number of companies involved in using false payment documents. The initial frauds were reported but no action followed. There are many more examples (e.g.: approving. bank loans without a credible guarantee or the mechanism to buy at a low price a company offered to be privatised, then getting an important bank loan guaranteed with the market price of the acquired company and not repaying the loan etc. The examples suggest influence factors such as: a) Primary e.g: (i) incomplete or insufficiently precise legislation;. (ii) influences on the Judiciary; etc.. b) Systemic, e.g. (i) Poor remuneration of public persons => need to accept tips (to perform *or* delay *or* deny a service which is a normal obligation) *or* commissions (to influence the selection of a certain supplier *or* customer) *or* bribes (to influence a decision *or* a service beyond the scope of the law);..(ii) intoxication with power of public persons, creating a positive feedback for accumulating wealth, using imperfections of the law *or* modifying the law *or* disposing beyond the law. On the other hand, legislative or judicial measures are insufficient to cope with a mass of information, without any effective means to filter, select and prioritise which implies the use of IT. The quoted recent law [14] covers a broad area: a) transparency of the due financial obligations to public institutions and of the public information and services, b) prevention and combating of information crimes; c) definition of conflict of interests regarding public persons; d) transparency of preventive and corrective AC actions: e) transparency and stability of the business environment etc.

3 A Simplified Model of the Corruption Process

Corruption generates great losses. (e.g. A Pricewaterhouse report [19] estimated that in 2001 only 1/3 of the normal foreign investments arrived to Romania, due to the image of corruption. See also [20]). It certainly represents a major contribution to the high transition cost, which accumulated in Romania the equivalent of min. 40 mild USD (1989) in the interval 1990...2001 [9]. This also suggests the need for a model.
Definitions of public person (PuP), powerful person (PoP), week person (WP), interested person (IP), related person (RP) are given in the annex. Corruption appears as an underground transaction between (i) an IP (corruptor- Crr) and a PuP (corruptee- Cee)- accepting to perform the IP's demand (corruption service -CS), in exchange of an underground gain («coruption fee»-CF). for the PuP and a benefit («corruption gain»-CG) for the IP (and, possibly for a RP). A corruption transaction (CT) can be intermediated, if between the corruptor and the corruptee one or more intermediate agents, possibly.gaining part of the corruption fee ("corruption vectors"), are interposed. A model is presented in fig.1 . It illustrates the potential of building

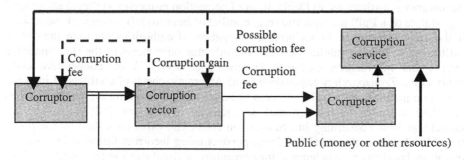

Fig. 1. The model of the corruption process

a positive feedback. The weak point of corruption is the underground character, making it vulnerable to transparency. Some relevant particular cases are exemplified as follows: a)*«petty corruption»*: IP=WP; Crr=IP or RP, Cee=PuP *and* WP; CS= normal job; CF=tip; CG ~0. *If* the remuneration of PuP is below a decent limit *then* the corruption can become systemic. b) *public procurement, low values*: IP=supplier; Crr=IP or RP Cee=PuP; CS=preferntial contract allocation; CF=tip, CG=contract with high price to quality ratio (pqr). c) *public procurement, high values*: IP=supplier *and* PoP; Crr=IP or RP Cee=PuP *and* PoP; CS=preferential contract allocation; CF=commission; CG= high pqr contract. Cooperation between PoPs may create a systemic corruption. d) *hiring or acquisition of public resources, low va-lues* : IP = PoP; Crr=IP or RP; Cee=PuP *and* WP; CS= preferential contract; CF = bribe; CG = small price for a good value; e) *hiring or acquisition of public re-sources, high value*: IP = PoP; Crr=IP or RP; Cee=PuP *and* PoP; CS= preferential contract; CF= commission; CG = small price for a good value. Cooperation between PoPs may create a systemic corruption. f) *privatization:* IP=PoP; Crr=IP *or* RP; Cee=PuP *and* PoP; CS= preferential contract; CF= commission; CG = small price for a good value. Cooperation between PoPs may create a systemic corruption. g) *judiciary, small goals*: IP=defendant; Crr=IP or RP; Cee=PuP *and* WP; CS= delaying or loosing documents; CF=bribe; CG= gain of time.h) *judiciary, high goals*: IP=defen-dant; Crr=IP or RP ; Cee= PuP *or* RP; CS = pustponmrnt or minimal punishment; CF = bribe; CG = continuation of an illegal activity. i) *legislation*: IP = PoP; Crr = PoP (if neded) ; Cee=PoP (if needed); CS = regulation in IP's interest; CG = strong posi-tion against competitors; CF = bribe *or* commission. Cooperation between PoPs may create a systemic corruption. "Political investments" can be particular cases.

4   AC Informational Requirements in Transforming Economies

Relevant examples of specific AC informational requirements, are presented below; .they are proposed to complement the requirements proposed by TI [2]. *General requirements*: a) Coherence of the information content of the three Authorities of the State *) => mandatory use of standardised nomenclatures and concepts;b) Unique identification of basic entities (natural persons, organizations etc) *) => centrally updated computerized registers => mandatory use in the relations with state, banking and insurance institutions ;c) Declaration of corruption processes as illegal => general (e.g. statute of a PuP) and specific (e.g. conflict of interests):d) Sinergy of the actions of the state institutions *) => precise delegation of authorities between the public institutions e) Interoperability between the information systems of the state (national level) and information exchange (international level) *) => cooperative eGIS architecture. *Transparency requirements*: a) Automatic check of conflicts of interests at the nominations of PuPs; b) . Access to information concerning the wealth of PuPs and their closed relatives, granted for judicial actions => PuP's database ;c) Knowledge base concerning information on corruption cases published by the press; d) Public database of natural and legal persons using incorrect financial instruments **or** not paying debts **or** condemned for corruption or fiscal evasion (by–product of the integration of judicial, executive and banking information systems);e) Public database of effective owners of businesses *); f) Integrated statistical information system acting also as a distributor of nationally shared metadata and a converter of sectoral and local specific data into a coherent public statistical database / data warehouse *) *Requirements specific to the Legislative Authority: a*) Standardisation of the structure of the content of the normative documents and of the process of proposal, approval and quality assurance; b) Quality management of the legislation => computer-aided control of drafts and use of feedback from the judicial activity *) *Requirements specific to the Judicial Authority* a) Definition, computation and publication of the judicial performance => informatisation of the judicial processes *); b) Judicial quality management => dimensional and cluster analysis of a case data warehouse*); c) Powerful interrogation and analysis of specific information from existing data bases and warehouses by AC Prosecutor's Offices. *.Requirements specific to the Executive Authority a*) Operational cost control => integrated financial management system for the state's treasury and its organizational users, including electronic archiving of primary documents *); b) Investment cost control => mandatory use of project management technology and centralised public e-procurement with feedback concerning the actual contract and cost of possession versus tender specification *);c) Integrated taxation information system (including for custom taxes) => registers of obligations, taxpayers, payments and debts => optimisation of taxation *).

5 Sketch of a Possible Strategy of an AC Information System

One can notice that many requirements for ACIS coincide with those for an eG.information system (eGIS – they were marked with *)) This suggests the need to consider eGIS as a necessary infrastructure for ACIS, as suggested in fig.2.

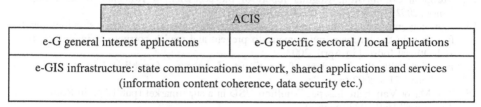

Fig. 2. The position of ACIS within eGIS

6 Conclusions

Following conclusions are proposed:
1. Corruption can be a great danger for the transfoming countries.
2. AC actions, in particular the «National Integrity System» proposed by Transparency International need the support of a performant ACIS, having in mind the large volumes of information implied and the limited specialized AC resources; at least parts of the corruption identification process should be computer aided
3. In transitional SESs, a performant ACIS implies the infrastructure of an eGIS, in order to assure the trajectory towards the advanced society.

References

1. Ceobanu, A.: When socialism meets. Capitalism. Corrupt practices and post- communist transition. A comparative analysis. Thesis University of Nebraska, 1998. http://www.google.com
2. Di Pietro, A. : Statement ao the Forum organizaed by the Romanian Parliament (summarized in Romanian in "Ziua " 30.11.2002 page 3)
3. Press Conference of the Minister of Justice (published in Romanian by "Curierul National, 30.11.2002 page 2)
4. Transparency International Global Corruption Report 2001 http:// www. transparency. org
5. Pope, J.: The TI Source Book 1999: National Integrity System Transparency International Berlin, 1999 /2000 http:// www. transparency. org
6. World Bank Development Report: The state in a changing world Oxford University Press Oxford, 1997
7. Governance and Anti-corruption World Bank Institute Washington DC, 2002 http://www.worldbank.org/wbi
8. Bhatnagar, S.: E- government and access to information *in: Transparency International: Global Report 2003 pp 24–32. http:// www. transparency. org*
9. Costake, N.: Sketch of a pragmatic theory of e-Government for transforming countries *in: Wimmer, M (ed): Quo Vadis e-Government: State-of-the-art 2003 Oesterreichische Computer Gesellschaft Wien, 2003*

10. Lenk, K., Traunmueller, R.: Electronic Government Where Are We Going? Electronic Government Springer Berlin, pp 1–9
11. Principles of the Estonian Information policy http:// www.eik.ee/english/policyprincip.htm
12. Costake, N., Jensen, F.H.: Towards an Architectural network framework of e-government information System *in: Wimmer, M. (ed.): Knowledge Management in e- Government KMGov-2002 Trauner Linz, 2002 pp 87–95*
13. European Commission: Regular report of the accession of Romania to the European Union, 2002 http:// www. infoeuropa. org
14. Law concerning some measures to ensure transparency exerting public dignities, public functions in the businee environment, to prevent and punish corruption (in Romania) no 161 Official Journal in April, 2003
15. Interview with the President of the Court of Accounts (published in Romanian by "National" 21.9.2002 (page 3)
16. The Mayor Vanghelie has put 7 million USD in a supermarket (published in Romanianby "Adevarul" 16.9.2002 (page 1)
17. The Nabob of the Jiu Valley (published in Romanian by "Ziua" 20.9.2002 page 9)
18. The baron from Arad. The increase and decrease of Mehedintu's empire (published in Romanian by "Jurnalul National" 24.2.2003 (page 7)
19. Pricewaterhouse: Report presented at the Workshop on Problems of Corruption Bucharest, April 2002
20. Kaufman, D., Kray, A: Governance and growth in the very long run: updated indicators, new results. *In: Transparency International: Global Report 2003 Research pp 41–44* . *http://www.transparency.org*

Annex

Some definitions

Public person (PuP) ::= person employed in a (state **or** public interest) institution: **or** member of the Parliament. He / she can be elected **or** politically nominated **or** magistrate **or** other (civil **or** public) servant who is empowered with an authority.

Powerful person (PoP)::= person possessing a high financial wealth **or** personal influence power (e.g. due to interpersonal links with PuPs).

Weak person (WP)::= person without financial wealth and / or personal influence power.

Interested person (IP)::= person ready to pay for obtaining (a right to which the access is arbitrarily (denied **or** made difficult) **or** an advantage beyond the law).

Related person (RP) ::=relative (e.g. degree 1..4) **or** closed friend of another similar person.

E-Governance: Two Views on Legal Environment

Mindaugas Kiškis and Rimantas Petrauskas

Law university of Lithuania
Ateities 20, LT-2057 Vilnius, Lithuania
mk@is.lt
rpetraus@ltu.lt

Abstract. Legal reform aimed at creating of favorable legal environment is important part of e-government development. E-government legal solutions need to be legally binding and sound in order to succeed. Legal framework initiatives for e-Governance so far have followed two concurrent approaches. First one infers development of separate regulations covering individual questions pertaining to e-Government, under umbrella of special programs-plans. Second one, is a holistic framework, which could identify and address legal principles of e-Government in a single regulation. This approach may especially be applicable to cross-border issues and challenges common within any e-government environment. The article provides comparative review of these views on e-Governance regulation and their suggested benefits and flaws.

Keywords: e-governance, legal environment of e-government

1 Introduction

The multiplicity of e-Government issues formulate the need to identify key areas to be addressed for successful implementation thereof. Legal framework may be identified as a priority area. Legal reform aimed at creating of favorable legal environment is very important part of development of e-government, since governmental activities are regulated and driven by legal framework including national constitutions, laws and other regulations. Also, e-Government solutions need to be legally binding and sound, and shall address major issues impacting e-Government development – among them – different user groups with diverging service needs and interaction requirements, distinct government processes, internal and external transformation of governance, legal and processes reform, etc. Additionally the formalities of e-government have to be addressed including to e-signatures and e-documentation, communication among governmental agencies and citizens, data protection and security, access to public information, public networking and databases, among other legal issues of e-government.

Legal framework initiatives for e-Governance so far has followed several different paths, which may be merged into two concurrent approaches:

First one, which currently dominates the legislation worldwide, is to develop separate laws and regulations covering individual questions pertaining to e-Government, and in most cases unified under umbrella of special programmes-plans, which also assist with the practical implementation thereof. Issues addressed within

R. Traunmüller (Ed.): EGOV 2003, LNCS 2739, pp. 407–412, 2003.

such separate regulations include different user groups with diverging service needs and interaction requirements, distinct government processes, internal and external transformation of governance, legal and processes reform, etc.

Second one, which is presently acquiring stronger theoretical following, is a holistic framework, which could identify and address all relevant issues impacting e-Government development under a single principal law or regulation. Such holistic framework may be somewhat similar to or maybe even imply the need for the relevant supra-national legislation. This approach may especially be applicable to cross-border issues and challenges common within any e-government implementation environment.

During the last years the European Union has introduced important new legislation in this area and a high number of new regulatory texts are still in the stage of preparation. Because the initiatives in this area are so numerous and divergent, it is not always easy to see clearly the overall policy behind all this activity, hence national laws enacted by the European Union members and accession countries are rather incoherent and sporadic [1], and create the evidence for identification of the above suggested theoretical differences in two concurrent approaches to legalities of e-governance, which both are comparatively analyzed below.

2 Features and Failures of Fragmented E-Governance Regulation

At the moment, large number of the European countries, in particular most of Eastern and Central European Countries, e.g. Latvia, Lithuania, Poland, Slovakia, does not have any special law, which would regulate the development of e-government and its processes. Nevertheless, some laws contain provisions, which refer to the e-government or the regulation of it development: these may be laws on Telecommunications, laws on Electronic Signature, laws on Provision of Information to the Public, laws on Legal Protection of Personal Data, laws on Consumer Protection and similar. In most cases certain by-law regulations in the form of Governmental regulations exist to address the e-government issues on a need-to-regulate-now basis [2]. This state of legal system in addressing the regulation of e-government, clearly suggest the existence of the above described first approach.

However, this way suffers from the common disadvantages of the fragmentary regulation of the development of e-government [3]. Likewise the fragmentary regulation, which in many cases has been drafted not in accordance with uniform principles, it covers only separate aspects (for instance, utilisation of electronic signature, main problems of data protection and data security, the fundamentals of regulation of telecommunications sector, etc.), thus missing the global picture and coherence of the subject.

This approach also emphasizes high technological centralization and standardization. It somewhat continues the soviet regime principles which where implemented in such programmes as State automated control system or State automated scientific technical information system. E-government is understood as specialized activity or even a business sphere, which is governed by departmental principle. Centralized orientation is reflected in such projects as Single Governance Internet Portal, State Administrative Information System, infrastructure for electronic signature, integration of state registers and other similar projects, which present e-government as a cohesive normative system, hierarchically and functionally covering all the state ruling and public administration. Thus, separate legal, or even technical i issues of e-government are in the regulatory focus, according to this approach. Unfortunately, this approach fails to acknowledge the emergence of knowledge society and knowledge economy. It does not emphasize the inherent knowledge society values of diversity, decentralization, pluralism, personalization and oneness. Cultural and social priorities are more important than bureaucratic and normative centralization.

Regardless of the above shortcomings the advantages of this approach include rather simple and hasty introduction of legal framework for beginnings of e-governance in a particular society. It shall be especially noted that it does not need any substantial pre-regulatory research and need-identification efforts, and allow addressing e-government issues on a need-to-regulate-now basis. This may e perceived as an advantage in societies having no long standing traditions of market economy and democracy. Additionally, this approach prevent possible failures of a inadequately justified holistic approach, which may fail to address certain key issues of e-governance, which at the time seemed not important for the regulator.

The above arguments on advantages are supported by the fact that this approach is historically preceding any holistic regulation of the e-government, especially in emergent societies such as Lithuania or Poland, thus allowing the authors to suggest that in the newly emerging knowledge societies this approach is the natural evolutionary step into coherent regulation of e-government. On the other hand it is very important for the regulators to recognize such evolutionary nature of this approach, and necessity to follow different approach once the knowledge society reaches certain level of maturity.

3 Holistic Approach: An Evolutionary Step?

Second way to regulate the e-governance is to generalize and formalize fundamental legal principles, needs and requirements for development of e-government and its processes [4, 5].

Legal acts of European countries that regulate the area of e-government are relatively new; therefore it is still difficult to evaluate the practical problems of their application. Also it is not always the case that they follow the same framework of principles, needs and requirements for development of e-government and its processes [6].

Legal research which may provide the base for coherent principles for legal environment of the e-government is also relatively new, and may be limited to the specialists of the field. Jurisprudence of the knowledge society is also only taking its first steps, especially in countries where knowledge society is rather young.

The application of information communication technologies to government may encounter legal or policy barriers. Legislatures must ensure that laws are updated to recognize realties of the knowledge society. They must take proactive steps to ensure that regulatory policies support rather than impede e-government. Policymakers implementing e-government must consider the impact of law and public policy. Otherwise, any initiative will encounter significant problems. The effort may incorporate a holistic view, one that is not just focused on technology. Archaic laws, old regulatory regimes, overlapping and conflicting authorities can all greatly complicate or altogether halt the e-government undertakings. As already shown by the limited examples, the legal reforms and new policy directives based on uniform principles, may have to be adopted before the online world can function smoothly [7].

Assuming the above premises, the governments of some countries, which according to the indicators of the development of information society are the leaders in the field (e.g. in UK, Germany, Sweden and Finland, etc.), state initiatives for the development of e-government, which are usually implemented by means of special programmes or plans (e.g. the U.K. E-Government programme, German BundOnline 2005 programme, which is aimed at creating electronic government in Germany by 2005 utilising the Internet etc.). Such all-embracing programmes or plans may be considered a first step into the direction of developing coherent e-government legal principles framework.

One possible approach to implement such coherent legal framework and specialised uniform e-government legislation may be adoption of the law on the fundamentals of the development of e-government. Such law should be the basic legal act that would regulate the development of e-government in the state. The main objective of the law must be to define and specify the basis for necessary for the successful development of e-government legal regulation in order to ensure legal stability and continuous state policy on the process of creating the e-government [8, 10].

This law should also identify the key tasks of the state and the main implementation measures thereof, the law also must provide for the state administration bodies responsible for the development of e-government and their competence, the procedure for drafting and approval of the documents on legal regulation and the financial sources of the development of e-government. Issues such as facilitation of e-commerce, protection of intellectual property rights, open source solutions may also be addressed through such legislation. The law would specify, what functions of state administration will be carried out by which governmental institutions, defining their competence, rights and obligations. as well as the principles of strategic planning.

General background principles of this law could be:

Acknowledging of fundamental rights and freedoms. The commonly recognised rights and freedoms shall be unambiguously extended to the cyberspace, along with new extensions, which are made available by emergence of cyberspace and e-government (e.g. access to internet, electronic information and knowledge).

Coordinated approach. Legal and regulatory issues are part of a wider, "holistic" approach - a set of complementary initiatives in the legal, technological, business and other areas.

Minimalist regulation. The one of general principles of e-government regulations is: "No regulation for regulations sake!"

Technological neutrality of e-government initiatives and processes. No discrimination of any of communication channels technology between government and society shall be tolerated.

Relevance to all group of users - G2C, G2B, G2G as well as minorities (disabled, elderly, etc.). Any framework shall be universally accessible, trustworthy and non-discriminatory.

Transparency and openness are major cornerstones of modern democratic society, hence of e-governance of such society.

Access to public information. Notably, information in the public domain should be easily accessible. Information is the basis of a well-functioning and transparent decision-making process and a prerequisite for any democracy. Knowledge is the key agent for transforming both our global society and local communities.

Protection of privacy and data security. E-government is not possible without respect for privacy of its citizens, as well as secure information infrastructure. If this principle is not ensured, the important reliability and trust in e-government will never be achieved.

Increased role for self-regulation and co-regulation. These instruments also confirm the central role of self-regulation in a number of key areas (content, liability of operators, notice and take down procedures, consumer protection, electronic media, etc.).

Government and public cooperation. E-governance allows increased involvement of the general public into governmental processes, what shall be recognized legislatively.

Promoting universal access at affordable cost. Community-led development is a critical element in the strategy for achieving universal access to information and knowledge. Community access centers and public services (such as post offices, libraries, schools) can provide effective means for promoting universal access in particular in remote areas, as an important factor of their development.

It is noteworthy that common e-government legal principles framework may greatly benefit knowledge societies, at a certain level of development, also may facilitate the unification and improvement of existing programmes and plans, also assist in the process of practical implementation thereof [4, P. 225-227]. Based on practical examples, it also seems to the authors that it is the natural stage of advancement of e-governance regulations.

One of the latest practical initiatives to implement the uniform legal framework approach is undertaken in the United States by means of 17 December 2002 Electronic Government Act [9]. It does not include all of the above suggested elements and principles of coherent e-government legislation, however may be considered more advanced step than above outlined e-government strategies and plans, i.e. represents further evolution of approach to the legal environment of the e-government.

4 Conclusions

Practical benefits of the late coherent legislation initiatives in the United States and elsewhere, which to date are the most comprehensive undertaking of the holistic approach, remain to be seen, however the existence of the above identified two approaches for regulation of e-government, already now raises the implications for the countries following the fragmented regulation approach. It may also be suggested that e-government regulation based on coherent framework approach is the more advanced evolutionary step in comparison to the fragmented approach; on the other hand, the holistic approach may allow benefits only at a certain level of maturity of the knowledge society.

References

1. Hanz van Zon, Brian Dillon, Jerzy Hausner, Dorota Kwiecinska. Central European Industry in the Information Age. Aldershot: Ashgate, 2000. P. 54–67.
2. Legal framework for the information society. http://www.unizar.es/DERECHO/FYD/lefis/index-legal.htm
3. Designing e-government on the crossroads of technological innovation and institutional change. The Hague: Kluwer Law International, 2001.
4. Global Networks and Local Values: A Comparative Look at Germany and the United States. Washington D.C.: National Academy Press: 2001.
5. Ahti Saarenpaa. Privacy and the harmonization of law in Europe.//Function and future of European law : proceedings of the International conference on the present state, rationality and direction of European legal integration. Helsinki, 1999 P.147–157.
6. Fernando Galindo: Self-regulation in e-Government: A Step More.//Electronic Government, Proceedings of First International Conference, EGOV 2002, Springer, 2002, P. 411–418.
7. Elaine Ciulla Kamarck, Joseph S. Nye, Jr., eds. Governance.com: democracy in the information age. Washington, D.C.: Brookings Institution Press, 2002.
8. Nick Moore, Rights and Responsibilities in an Information Society, The Journal of Information, Law and Technology (JILT). N1, 1998. http://elj.warwick.ac.uk/jilt/infosoc/98_1moor/
9. US E-Government Act of 2002. http://www.cdt.org/legislation/107th/e-gov/020325s803analysis.pdf.
10. Petrauskas R. Informacinių technologijų taikymas viešajame administravime. Vilnius: LTU, 65 p. (2001).

A Federative Approach to Laws Access by Citizens: The "Normeinrete" System

Caterina Lupo[1] and Carlo Batini[1,2]

[1] Autorità per l'Informatica nella Pubblica Amministrazione
Via Isonzo, 21b
00198 ROMA, Italy
{lupo,batini}@aipa.it
[2] Università di Milano "Bicocca"
Via Bicocca degli Arcimboldi 8
20126 Milano, Italy
batini@disco.unimib.it

Abstract. The paper presents an e-government project set up in Italy to build the portal "Normeinrete" (i.e. "laws on the net"). It offers a co-operative information service to citizens providing unified access to Italian and European Union legislation published on different institutional web sites. The system is based on a co-operative technological architecture, resulting in a federation of legislative data bases developed on different platforms. Co-operation is achieved by means of suitable application gateways that provide "loose" integration by adopting two standards to identify the resources and to represent document structure and metadata by XML mark-up according to ad-hoc DTDs. The adoption of these standards allows automatic dynamic hyperlinking among laws and semi-automatic building of legislation in force. The approach adopted allows a good level of integration among different systems while maintaining the autonomy of institutions.

1 Introduction

The Normeinrete project, promoted by the Italian Authority for Information Technology in Public administration (AIPA) and the Ministry of Justice, aims to fulfill the citizens' right to acquire knowledge of legislation and to support Public Administration (PA) in managing the legislative documentation life-cycle efficiently. These objectives are pursued through the following actions:
- implementation of a specialized portal for legislative documents retrieval;
- definition of standards to represent data meaningful in the legal domain;
- software distribution to support legislative document management and publishing;
- training and knowledge sharing among Public administrations.

The system is based on a federation of legislative data bases developed with different platforms and it is built upon a co-operative technological architecture.

The paper is organized as follows: section 2 contains a general description of the project, section 3 describes the standards; section 4 describes the system's architecture; section 5 deals with current developments and future directions.

R. Traunmüller (Ed.): EGOV 2003, LNCS 2739, pp. 413–416, 2003.

2 The Normeinrete Project (NiR)

The Normeinrete project (NiR) aims to improve accessibility to legislation by providing a unique point of access to Italian and European Union legal documents published on different web sites through a specialized portal (www.nir.it).

The portal runs a search engine that operates homogeneously on distributed data sources. Its full-text search index is selectively built detecting only legislative documents [2]. The achievement of a higher level of cooperation relies on the adoption of two standards, defined within the project by ad hoc working groups in which major PA and research institutions have taken part. The standards have been issued as Aipa technical norms and published as regulatory acts in the Italian Official Journal. The definitions make use of IETF Uniform Resource Names (URNs) (RFC 2141) and eXtensible Mark-up Language (XML W3C Recommendation) standards. Another project goal is to support PA in the tasks related to law consolidation. Its achievement is also based on the standard definitions provided, since they allow to identify the norms in a distributed environment and to track the modifications, thus allowing semi-automatic consolidation. The project also aims to create a virtual space for knowledge sharing within the PA community, also offering dedicated services, such as e-learning tools and opensource software download. Thus far more than 40 public institutions have taken part in the project with more than 140.000 documents indexed. The site supplies about 150.000 search sessions monthly.

3 Unifying Standards

3.1 Uniform Resource Name (URN)

Each law contains several references to other laws. The whole legislative *corpus* can be seen as a net, each law being a node linking, and linked by, several other nodes through natural language expressions. Manual activity is required in order to build an hypertext through the usual web link mechanism based on the physical addresses. The disadvantages deriving from URL approach include the significant editorial work that must be carried out before publishing a document and the subsequent activities needed to prevent or to limit broken links. The URN is a persistent, location-independent, resource identification mechanism. URNs are defined as a combination of elements according to a specific grammar [4]. The basic elements are: name of the promulgating authority, type of law, date, number and a set of more detailed specifications when needed. The adoption of a scheme based on URN allows an automated distributed hypertext to be built according to a model similar to the DNS (Domain Name System) used to resolve the self-explaining web sites names into numerical HTTP addresses. This opportunity relies on the following considerations:

- the natural language expressions used in the quotation of laws usually contain repetitive patterns, making references automatically detectable;
- the URN is built by combining data (almost) always included in the reference;
- the cross reference between each URN and the list of corresponding URLs, needed for the resolution service, can be built automatically.

3.2 Document Type Definition (DTD) of Italian Legislative Acts

XML representation of legislative documents allows the improved effectiveness in managing, publishing and retrieving norms by electronic means [1] [3]. Normeinrete had defined Document Type Definition (DTD) for Italian legislation, considering the peculiarity of legislative documents and other significant useful information. Italian legislative and regulatory acts can be divided into three categories:
– documents with a well-defined structure (i.e. state laws, regional laws, etc.);
– documents partially structured (i.e. regulation act, decrees, etc.);
– generic documents (i.e. any kind of non-structured acts, enclosures, etc.).
To avoid a proliferation of DTDs, it has been considered more convenient the definition of a single DTD containing many elements capable of representing all the types of documents. Given the variations in the structure of Italian legislative documents, the mark-up language is very complex and the resulting DTD has three different versions, containing the same set of elements to represent all kinds of documents with different constraints. Documents validated against strict rules are also valid against looser ones. The DTD elements defined can be classified as follows:
– structural elements, identifying the parts in which the document is structured (heading, preamble, articles, etc.);
– special elements identifying meaningful parts of the text in the legal context, (for instance references to other laws) or associating a formatted representation to text-embedded relevant entities (institutions, dates, places);
– elements containing metadata (for instance subject-matter classification, publication data, procedures to enact a bill, etc.).
Mark-up must be carried out using only elements relevant to the kind of document being considered.

4 The Architecture of the NiR Systems

The main components of the system are:
– NiR-nodes: components belonging to administration domains containing legal database systems and related application gateways. Documents can be stored in the file-system or within database/full-text management systems. They are all accessible through the internet.
– Central registries: components in the co-operative layer publishing information needed to allow effective co-operation; they include:
1. standards repository (XML DTD and URN grammar definitions and tools);
2. the registry of official authority names, needed to standard URN adoption;
3. the registry of NiR-nodes, containing information needed to allow interaction between NiR agents, and domain application gateways;
4. the norms catalogue, containing, for each norm: title, basic classification, URN and the list of known physical addresses (URL) where it is published.
– The co-operative system NiR, that is the component in the co-operative layer that runs all the specific applications, including the URN resolution service (at the moment managed centrally) .

5 Current Developments and Future Directions

New developments are being carried out in the current stage. Some of these concern new software tools to support the administrations in the adoption of NiR standards; in particular, a specialized editor is being developed, that will be distributed as opensource software. XMLSchema definition is being developed. A parsing service will be available, that will return submitted documents with references to other legislative acts suitably marked and with the corresponding URN inserted. A working group is being constituted to investigate additional metadata representation and automatic document classification. Future initiatives will include the implementation of distributed URN resolution. In the next stage it will be evaluated the opportunity to define the access services to norms in terms of web services. This opportunity could become more attractive in the event of a more extended adoption of standard languages and models, such as WSDL and UDDI, within the Italian public administration co-operative model. The other major theme to be addressed concerns the certification of acts authenticity through digital signature technology.

References

1. Boer, A., Hoekstra R., Winkels, R., *MetaLex: Legislation in XML* , Legal Knowledge and Information Systems – JURIX 2002
2. Lupo, C. *Norme in rete: un progetto di cooperazione per l'informatica giuridica* Iter Legis - luglio-ottobre 1999.
3. Marchetti A., Megale F., Seta E., Vitali F., *Using XML as a means to access legislative documents: Italian and foreign experiences,* ACM SIGAPP Applied Computing Review, 10(1), ACM Press New York, 2002, pp. 54–62
4. Spinosa P.L., *Identification of legal documents through URNs (Uniform Resource Names)* in: O. Signore and B. Hopgood (eds.), Proceedings of the Euroweb 2001 Conference "The Web in Public Administration" (18- 20 dec. 2001), Pisa, Felici Editore, 2001

Constitutional and Technical Requirements for Democracy over the Internet: E-Democracy

Patricia Heindl[1], Alexander Prosser[2], and Robert Krimmer[2*]

[1] Institute for Constitutional and Administrative Law
Vienna University of Economics and Business Administration
Althanstrasse 39-45, A-1090 Vienna, Austria
Phone +43 (1) 31336 4079
patricia.heindl@wu-wien.ac.at
[2] Institute for Information Processing and Information Economics
Vienna University of Economics and Business Administration
Pappenheimgasse 35/5, A-1200 Vienna, Austria
Phone +43 (1) 31336 – 5615
{alexander.prosser,robert.krimmer}@wu-wien.ac.at

Abstract. In this paper the authors discuss the legal and technical implications of enabling democracy over the Internet (short e-Democracy) would have. Which requirements does the law, respectively the constitutional law, define for internet-based political communication, especially for computer-aided voting procedures? Which technical procedures and algorithms do fulfil these requirements?

1 Introduction

Democracy means a form of political decision-making. Article 1 of the Austrian Constitution defines: "Austria is a democratic republic. Its law emanates from the people." Austria[1] has an indirect parliamentary democracy, with some additional instruments of direct democracy. That means that the laws are not made by the people themselves, but by elected representatives, the parliamentary bodies. **Voting** is the most important but indirect act in political decision-making by the population.

Beside that the people can take part in the political decision-making process by three legal instruments of direct democracy:

- **Referendum** (Volksabstimmung)
  With the – facultative or obligatory – referendum the people can accept or reject parliamentary resolutions at a constitutional level. The results of a referendum are binding.
- **Public consultation** (Volksbefragung)
  With the public consultation the parliament merely collects public opinion on a special issue. The results of a public consultation are not binding.

---

* The work of Krimmer was supported by the City of Vienna under grant number JUB0109.
[1] For the situation in the Switzerland and in Germany see [1]

R. Traunmüller (Ed.): EGOV 2003, LNCS 2739, pp. 417–420, 2003.
© Springer-Verlag Berlin Heidelberg 2003

- **Popular initiative** (Volksbegehren)
  With the popular initiative a qualified number of people can raise a law-making initiative, which has to be discussed in parliament upon passing a certain mark of supporters, who would have the right to vote. Still parliamentary discussion decides whether an initiative is followed or not. A further difference of Election and the named elements of direct democracy are the legal instruments in the process of people's decision-making. They constitute the basic democratic instruments. In a wider sense these also include the pre-forming of political decision-making, particularly performed by political parties, organizations and pressure groups.

2   Constitutional Issues

The constitutional law defines clear and strict rules for voting and the instruments of direct democracy. If one wants to use computer-aided communication in these fields, the techniques eventually used must fulfil the relevant legal requirements.

Starting with the instrument of Voting, the electronic variant would have to fulfil the requirements the law defines for traditional voting. These requirements are the principles of general, immediate, equal, personal, secret and free voting:

- Regarding the principle of general voting computer-aided communication does not seem to cause particular problems, given that e-voting is used alongside traditional voting.
- The principle of immediate voting demands that the cast votes have to reach the central voting-teller directly and non-altered. The principle of equal voting demands that each individual can cast her/his vote only once.
- With parallel e-voting and traditional voting there is also the requirement for equality between the two voting instruments. For instance there must be no different information on either of the two voting-"ballots" (eg: programmes of the political parties or information about the candidates). Also different error-filtering procedures might be problematic from the aspect of equality between electronic and traditional voting. Furthermore e-voting also requires the possibility to cast unvalid votes.
- Much more problems are in the principles of secret, personal and free voting. e-voting poses similar problems like postal voting. In both the votes are not given within a secure polling booth, but the voters themselves must look for the secret and free voting act. Therefore postal voting is allowed only in some countries and also there only in exceptional cases.

The special challenges with e-voting are twofold. On the one hand, the techniques must guarantee that only legally entitled people can cast their votes and this only once. On the other hand, the techniques must guarantee that identification of the voter is impossible. In other words: both must be guaranteed: identity of the elector and authenticity of the cast vote and at the same time strict anonymity of the ballot paper.

Furthermore e-voting, like traditional voting, must be also be fully auditable (allow ex-post examination of the Election result): therefore the Election-data have to stay accessible after the Election Day in an adequate way.

As mentioned above the direct democracy elements referendum and public consultation differ from traditional voting only in the field of initiation and impact, therefore the same arguments apply to e-Referendum and e-Public consultation as they apply to e-voting.

The requirements for a popular initiative are a subset of those for e-voting in what the act of supporting a popular initiative is to sign it publicly and therefore the requirements for anonymity and secrecy do not apply.

3 Technical Issues

From a technical point of view, the following three criteria for conduction Elections over the Internet can be derived from the Austrian constitution as well as from the Internet Voting workshop [IPI01]:
1. Unambiguous and doubtless identification of the eligibility of the voter,
2. Absolute anonymity and
3. No possibility for the Election administration to break the anonymity or to change and fake votes.

In complying with these criteria lies the basic problem of a working e-voting system and researchers in the whole world have been working on solutions for that since the 80s. In a basic publication Nurmi, Salomaa and Santean [NSS91] identified the following two processes:
1. the identification (registration) process during which the voter is identified unambiguously
2. the anonymous voting process itself

When developing the e-voting system, the identification process is the more challenging. The voters can be identified using three methods (i) PIN, (ii) TAN or (iii) smart cards with digital signatures. Whereas the first two methods cannot link the physical person and the digital identity this is possible for smart cards, when they are equipped with a so called person identification file (Personenbindung). This is a combination of digital identity (the digital signature of a citizen) and the physical person. Such a link is only possible if a central register of all citizens exists (this means, that every citizen has a unique personal identification number).

While central databases are prohibited in some countries like in Germany, the Austrian registration law (Meldegesetz) of 1995 installed the central citizen registry (ZMR) and set it into service in 2002. This ZMR is also the basis for the Election register. Therefore using a person identification file allows the unique allocation of a signed voting application to the eligible voter entry in the ZMR. This also guarantees that each voter can only be identified once (even if she uses different smart cards).

The solution for the second task, the anonymity required for the vote casting, can be solved by using a technology called blind signature by David Chaum [Chau82]. It allows signing a document without knowing it. This can be compared with signing on a carbon-coated envelope which then lead to a signature on the contained document.

The implementation of this technology requires algorithms that fully guarantee the anonymity of the voter. In Germany [2] and Japan [3] researchers have developed a one-phased algorithm using the blind signature method of Chaum. Still in an electronic process it is not possible to change the status of being identified and anonymous during one session due to IP-tracing et. al. This requires to physically separate those two tasks in a two-phased Election process. An example how this can be realised was proposed by [4] and is being implemented for a mock-Election in Vienna.

4 Resume

Internet-based political communication is conceivable in all the above mentioned fields of democracy. Web Pages of political and parliamentary parties or political discussion-forums in the internet are a case in point. But such type of communication is also possible with institutionalised instruments of decision-making. The buzzwords here are e-voting and e-Referendum. Clearly the latter case calls for a more stringent legal framework than the former.

From the technical point of view all three Election-style democracy elements - **e-voting (representative Elections), e-referenda** and **e-public consultations** – with their requirement of anonymity can only be e-enabled using a two-phased system with blind-digital-signatures. Especially this is very challenging for e-referenda and e-voting as they are binding in contrast to the public consultation.

The legal requirements for an **e-popular initiative** seem comparatively easier to fulfil. Here only authenticity, but not anonymity is required. Also this makes it easy to realize using a one-phased-system with the identification via digital signatures and the personal identification file. From the political point of view computer-aided political communication in this element of direct democracy might have the most practical relevance. Election collection of digital signatures is far less costly than the traditional type of signature collection and hence, this might not only lead to more frequent use of this instrument, it might also give smaller and less institutionally organized groups better opportunity to raise political initiatives.

5 References

[1] N. Braun, P. Heindl, P. Karger, R. Krimmer, A. Prosser, and O.-R. Rüß, "e-voting in der Schweiz, Deutschland und Österreich: ein Überblick", Wirtschaftsuniv., Wien 2003.
[2] Forschungsgruppe Internetwahlen, http://www.internetwahlen.de, accessed on 2002-05-23.
[3] A. Fujioka, T. Okamoto, and K. Ohta, "A Practical Secret Voting Scheme for Large Scale Elections," presented at Advances in Cryptology - AUSCRYPT92, Berlin, 1993.
[4] A. Prosser and R. Müller-Török, "Electronic Voting via the Internet," presented at International Conference on Enterprise Information Systems ICEIS2001, Setùbal, 2001.

An XML Editor for Legal Information Management

Monica Palmirani and Raffaella Brighi

C.I.R.S.F.I.D
University of Bologna
via Galliera 3
40100 Bologna, Italy
{palmiran,brighi}@cirfid.unibo.it

Abstract. *e*Government is an opportunity to improve the public service delivery, increased productivity and reduced costs using Internet-based technology. On the other hand the eGovernance should go beyond: to enhance the citizen's access to government information and provide new ways to increase citizen participation in the democratic process. For this reason a Legislative Management System is a fundamental IT System for providing the basic inputs to a good governance. Without a clear understanding of the normative system in force in a country is not possible to build correct polices, to stimulate democratic debate, to build concrete economic strategies. Norma-System is an integrated web-based system that is able to manage all the cycle of the law production: back-office and front-office sides.

1 Assumption: The Knowability of Law in the E-Governance

The White Paper on European Governance, COM(2001) 428 final, defines eGovernance as the use of the electronic technologies in order to realise the complex concept of "good governance" taking in account the emergent new form of governance in Europe (federalism, new member states, European Constitution). On the other hand for "good governance" we means a body of principles, norms, technical rules, best practices, that must serve as the reference framework for concrete strategies (policies). eGovernment refers indeed to these specific policies the State decides for restructuring itself and electronically reorganising, and, as such, constitutes the moment of the implementation and diffusion of an instrument: let us say the telematic-informatic one. We observe, therefore, that a gradual shift is in course from a model based on the mere delivery of information and services via Internet to a more conscious manner of exploiting online computer-based devices for the task of a "good governance" [7]. We are assisting to the passing from the Information Society to the Knowledge Era, where the citizen/customer pretends to the public administration not only a mere information and services, but moreover to participate to the decision-maker process.

This appears to be even more true when one devotes attention to the issue of the knowability of the law and, thus, puts online the legislation in force and makes available the tools through which it is possible to access it (COM(2002) 278 final, "Simplifying and improving the regulatory environment"; COMM(2002) 275 final "Better lawmaking"). For this reason a Legislative Management System is a

R. Traunmüller (Ed.): EGOV 2003, LNCS 2739, pp. 421–429, 2003.

fundamental IT System for providing the basic inputs to a good governance. Without a clear understanding of the normative system in force in a public administration is not possible to build correct polices, to stimulate democratic debate, to build concrete economic strategies.

Norma-System [6] is an integrated web-based system that is able to manage all the cycle of the law production: back-office and front-office sides. Norma-System is now based on four Web software modules that make it possible to: (1) Norma-Editor that supports practitioners of the law in drafting normative acts and helps users create unified texts; (2) Norma-Database that traces the history of the normative documents, stores all the versions of the document in the time and manages the coherency rules to apply to the electronic law system; (2) Norma-Interface that publishes in Internet the databases content including all the normative texts consolidated, original texts and intermediate texst (versioning function) (4) Norma-Search that permits advanced searches on the temp display data along the temporal lines of the force, and efficacy of norms. The aim of this article is to present in detail the XML editor module and a particular case study of application in the Italian Supreme Court of Cassation. The normative XML editor is the core part of the back-office side and the instrument on which the public administration could perform eGovernance policies in order to favor the comprehension and the access of the law system to the citizens.

2   Accessing Normative Texts: A Representation Standard

The lawmaking system in Italy and Europe is facing a normative overproduction problem, so we need to make it possible for everyone to access norms readily, at the same time bringing information systems to account in reordering the mass of legislation presently in force. The main problem in putting up systems of this kind is finding a uniform way of representing normative texts. By a method of this kind, we can uniform all the points of access to online legislation and set up functions for searching and connecting norms and partitions. XML (for Extensible Markup Language) has now come into wide use in the legal domain, among others, as the basic standard with which to describe and exchange data. This language makes it possible to separate the interface layer on which data is represented from the data itself, and so use this data for further processing and automation. Extensibility enables you to work out your own set of tags, a feature that endows the standard with wide applicability in just about any discipline.

Many initiatives now underway in Europe and around the world are framed to encourage using XML to represent legal texts. A standout case among these is LEXML, a network of websites put up by countries like Austria, Germany, Netherlands, and Sweden, essentially an open forum for exchanging ideas and experiences and ultimately arriving at XML models for legal applications. Likewise in the USA, where OASIS (Organization for the Advancement of Structured Information Standards) is running a legal XML project of longer standing.

In Italy, the Ministry of Justice launched in 1999 a project called NormeInRete [1], and subsequent to it, all public administrations received two circular notices [4][5] laying out a set of guidelines for representing legal texts in XML. This is because digitally processed legal texts cannot be shared and exchanged without a common set of DTDs (Document Type Definitions). The DTDs worked out define structures for different types of legal provision: these structures can be made more or less rigid, making it possible to describe a variety of provisions having different or irregular formats. Also for NormeInRete, a set of rules have been designed with which to give each legal provision an accurate name (URN, Uniform Resource Name) specific to it, so that the norms making up a body of law can be linked up effectively. But we cannot implement these standards unless we edit legal texts marking out their partitions and relevant data in such a way as to enable a subsequent XML conversion.

This paper presents a word-processing prototype editor designed to take text-format documents and give them an XML format valid for the DTDs worked out for NormeInRete. This editor is part of a wider project aimed at helping legal drafters bring out consolidated texts linked up to one another by the cross-references (here, normative references) they contain. This prototype, developed under an agreement with the Center for Electronic Data Processing (EDP) of the Italian Supreme Court of Cassation, is conceived to help legal drafters (i) mark up legal texts in XML, (ii) reframe them as the law actually in force, and (iii) integrate them into the legal database NewItalgiurie-Find (NIF).

3   Case Study: EDP of the Italian Supreme Court of Cassation

In the 1970s the EDP of the Italian Supreme Court of Cassation started providing remote computer access to legislation, jurisprudence, and doctrine, now an online collection of 47 archives containing over four million documents [2]. The first version of its search tool, Italgiure-Find, presented users with a command-driven interface requiring them to master a specific syntax. Then in 1988 a system called Easy Find was introduced that opens up a user-friendly search window. There is little doubt that this system—for all its limitations: a pay service requiring a multiphase search procedure—has from the very outset provided the fullest, most effective access to online legislation and jurisprudence in Italy. Now an effort is underway, in cooperation with the Italian Ministry of Justice, to redesign Italgiure-Find for improved capability and for passing to Web approach. The new system, NIF (enabling natural-language search strings, too) is entirely based on XML-formatted document management and so made it necessary to use batch procedures to convert the documents accordingly.

ALEA, the software now in use for processing normative texts as back-office tool, works with the plain version of Italgiure-Find, which is now not in line with the new XML requests because based on old data-collection models. In the process of bringing out the NIF, some legal drafters have been interviewed to obtain a picture of the way their work is currently set up. It was found out that the process of marking up a single legal provision is laborious, requiring the drafter to memorize numerous markers that have to be inserted manually before the software can partition the text correctly, and the markup procedures are not always intuitive. Drafters have to edit each document in separate batches, losing sight of the overall framework, and the algorithms for detecting normative references and text partitions are found to be lacking in performance. These shortcomings were such that the developers decided to make over that Italgiure-Find almost from scratch, retaining little of the old architecture.

It was thought best to base the new editor on a word processor (Microsoft Word XP) rather than use an XML editor such as XML SPY. This course was decided on out of the need to present public-administration personnel with a software and interface they can already use (without having to retrain), making the XML markup process functional and transparent.

In addition, new algorithms for automatic text recognition are being developed that will spare legal drafters from much of the manual procedures now required and so speed up the editing process. Indeed, the legal drafters at EDP have a mass of documents to go through quite disproportionate to what other personnel have to process at the lawmaking bodies we have done projects with in the past. This makes it all the more necessary to speed up the process by which text partitions are marked up, so that the greater effort can go into the data entry and sorting of normative references that gets the texts ready for consolidation. Lastly, it emerged from the interviews that a new classification of normative references is in order: the current system is not sufficiently specific and granular, and it fails of uniformity besides, finding different modes of application in different archives. We cannot, in any automated fashion, bring out a valid texts enforceable as law unless we identify accurately the way it stands affected by the normative references made to it. In the sections that follow we illustrate the functions built into the prototype and present the DTDs valid for NormeInRete.

4   Analysing ad Extending the NIR DTDs

In designing the functions to be built into the editor we focused on the DTDs specific to the NIR project. To this end, we looked at the partitions of a normative text that need to be extracted and mapped out to have documents that are valid and interchangeable under NIR standards, and we also looked at the elements that needed to be added to the existing DTDs to enable text versioning, a further function sought for the prototype. Four kinds of element have been introduced to bring out DTDs for NIR.

(1) Structural elements. These serve to define a layout for the normative text, describing all the partitions that make up its structure and the rules for giving the text a format (heading, opening formula, division into articles, closing formula, annexes).

A number of questions to be worked out came up in this process. First, there is at present no element with which to mark up a text for partition names (like "art." and "article"). So this label cannot be printed without an accompanying stylesheet, which of necessity causes the processed text to fall out of line with the original text on the public record. Also a key point here is the way to go about managing IDs. ID numbers need to get built in accordance with a syntax specified in an instructions document attached to the DTD (for example, rewrite "article 1, section 2" as "art1-sec2"), in such a way as to enable cross-referencing. This function, therefore, is not effected by an X-patch device designed to move up and down the text's tree structure along designated axes, but rather by way of the ID number assigned to each text partition. A lawmaking body that should ignore this convention will find it impossible to carry out a core function the NIR project is designed for, namely: the linking up of different bodies of law in such a way as to make possible hypertext navigation by clicking on normative references.

(2) Special elements. These serve to detect anywhere in the text given types of information, normative references in particular. The NIR elements designed to mark up normative references fall short of what is required to process a normative text for consolidation. To this end, we need to apply to the initial text the changes consequent on a normative reference. Thus, each reference needs to be classed according to the change it lays onto the norm it refers to: For example, does it integrate, abrogate, or limit its scope (as through a saving clause)? Some of these changes make it necessary to intervene in the initial text; others affect the purview of the norm and consequently require comments to be added as notes. Each normative reference must therefore be completed with all such additional information, indicating what kind of reference it is we are dealing with, the date the modification was entered, any comments added, etc. In working to align the editor with the NIR project specifics and DTDs, we defined some meta-elements connected by ID number to the elements Mod and Rif, each of which carries information on the normative reference in question. The DTDs contain so-called owner elements that each lawmaking body can use to add different kinds of information a document. There is still, however, the problem that Rif elements do not require ID numbers.

(3) Meta-information. This information is not part of the normative text proper but something that users can look up to learn more about the same text. Thus you can insert here owner information necessary for processing a text to extend the NIR DTDs. The prototype editor will use the data entered in this text field to manage the consolidation and versioning of legal provisions. Let us note, however, that text enrichment by owner elements is only limited, and does not follow the course the scientific community is taking in the effort to make information systems inter-operable all-around, as to technology, syntax, and semantics (content). Owner elements (and the system of codified references they make up) hand over entirely to the editor the task of reading text contents, and in addition make it difficult for legal drafters to understand the resulting XML format.

(4) Generic elements. These make it possible to mark up text parts meeting no specific content description, but which drafters choose to highlight for some purpose, as to format that text in a particular way.

5 Norma-Editor: An XML Editor for Marking-Up Legal Text

5.1 General Architecture

As mentioned earlier, Norma-Editor brings out XML documents (having past or present force) that are valid for NIR DTDs. The documents so processed will be ready to go into the NIF system. But the editor cannot bring out a consolidated text without a database module to lean on: this module, which we call Norma-Database (NDB), makes it possible to create, in a coordinated and congruent fashion, legal texts enforceable as law; so, too, it provides the NIF search engine with new search options, such as searching according to the chronology by which a group of texts has come into force or according to the versioning a single text has gone through over time. Figure 1 shows how the editor and the NDB enter into the different phases by which a normative text is processed, laying out at the same time the system's overall architecture.

Phase 1 brings out an XML-formatted text: the editor acquires unmarked text-format documents (input) and yields XML documents (output) aligned with NIR DTDs. The editor's XML markup enriches the DTDs currently in use with additional tags and information necessary for producing consolidated texts, which, too, will be XML-formatted. This XML document gets validated for NIR DTDs and then is parsed and entered into the NDB before being sent to the NIF system. The editor and the NDB work in constant connection. In order to favor the end-user, Norma-Editor utilizes a parser module able to identify in the automatic way the main structured parts of the legal text and to mark them directly in XML. The end-user could in any time correct the automatic inference made by the editor.

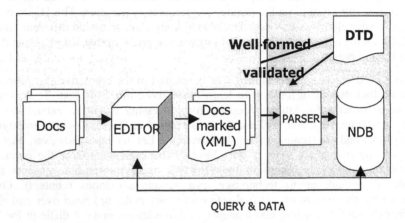

Fig. 1. Phase 1: markup of a legal text having lapsed out of force.

Phase 2 generates the consolidated text. The editor takes as input two XML documents generated in Phase 1—one is a text to be updated and the other a norm by which it gets modified. The text is then modified (updated) accordingly and a new document is yielded (output) that goes through the same checks and passages carried out in Phase 1. Here, too, the editor operates in connection with the database.

5.2 Macro Tasks in Processing a Legal Text

Getting into greater detail, we illustrate now the macro tasks the prototype editor performs when a user marks up a text and enters it into the NDB database.

(1) Importing into an editing environment the document to be processed. At this point the legal provision will already be on digital support and can be downloaded from other databases, or it can be scanned or again sourced from other government offices. The editor can acquire all the (unmarked) formats that MS Word can read (ASCII, RTF, TXT, etc.), as well as XML-format documents marked up for NIR DTD validity. This latter function imports all preexistent markups and checks and inserts them in the Word document, making it possible for legal drafters to further

mark up the document with all the information which Norma-System needs for its processing, and which the NIR DTDs do not carry.

(2) Managing the attachments. Here the editor runs through the texts automatically to detect and take out any attachments it may contain, thus managing them as separate files connected with the file they come from.

(3) Marking up the document structure. Here the heading, opening formula, closing formula, and conclusions get marked up, as does the document layout into articles, sections, and normative references. Each such text partition or segment can be marked up manually or automatically. Manual markup is enabled by a toolbar button that you simply click on to markup a text you selected on the screen. The editor checks your markup for coherence, looking at the kind of data you marked up, its placement in the document layout, and any previous markups. Automatic-detection functions can be enabled for each kind of text partition. A parser could infer the structured parts of the legal text on the base of a set of general and specific rules.

(4) Marking up and classifying normative references. We know from experience that no task weighs down on the legal drafter more than that of managing normative references. For each normative reference detected, the drafter must specify its destination point, the kind of provision referred to (or the partition of it, with all the data necessary for identification), and the type of reference it is, that is, the way the provision referred to impacts on the provision the reference starts from. The new prototype editor has been designed for automated detection of normative references, thereby taking some of the burden off the legal drafter. So in this phase the editor detects automatically the normative references found in a text (internal and external references as well as references to attachments), and then the drafter can check the process and bring it to completion. With this done, the references are classed according to the type of provision referred to and supplemented with the information coming therefrom. This task is effected in connection with the NDB database to check that the norms referred to actually exist, and then completing the reference if necessary.

(5) Inserting meta-information. The task here is to supplement the XML text with meta-information, meaning by this all the data required for the NIR DTDs which is not written directly into the text. Examples of such information are the date the provision referred to (or a section thereof) takes effect, and all the data identifying its enactment. Meta-information is inserted by way of input fields that pop up on request by clicking on designated toolbar buttons.

(6) XML Conversion. The editor enables the conversion of an MS Word document into an XML document. The markups written into the document make it possible to pick out all the text elements defined and required for NIR DTD operation. An automated procedure uses these elements to build an XML text. In addition to performing text-structure checks throughout the editing process, the editor runs the XML document through a final validation. Every document that fails this validation test is submitted to the legal drafter, who will intervene manually to align the document with NIR DTDs. The validated text is then fed to the database.

Norma-Editor, in addition to managing all the phases in the editing process, makes available functions with which to consolidate the texts so edited. A key part of consolidation consists in using the editor to supplement an edited text with all the changes consequent on the references made to it, but before this versioning process can get underway we need to download from the database the entire body of documents to be consolidated (the norm-changing documents and the documents receiving such changes). With this document base ready, the editor proceeds with consolidation, updating (and so versioning) each document to its current legal validity and enforceability. Finally, the documents so updated can be sent back to the database and so entered into its chains of legal validity and efficacy.

6 Conclusion

To provide law in force (or better *applicable*) and in the same time to reduce the *law corpora* dimension for improving the economic and political national and European environment is an evident priority for all the Member State, but in particular of the European Commission. Inside of the recently Communication of the Commission "Updating and simplify the Community acquis" (COMM(2003) 71 final) is settled a Action Plan including five main objectives able to control the overproduction of the law systems: simplification, consolidation, codification, removing obsolete documents in the body of law, ensure transparency, establish inter-institutional collaboration. Indeed the European Commission aims to "set a good example" to all the Member States in order to encourage them to implement proper strategies of securing a reliable, up-to-date and user-friendly body of Law to the benefit of citizens, workers and businesses. This is more true considering the accession of ten new Member States in May 2004 and the consequential amplified necessity of law harmonisation, law knowledge, clear access to valid legislation. Instruments as Norma-Editor, moreover Norma-System, are based on these principles and they are able to manage totally these objectives. The case study of the Court of Cassation confirms also the feasibility to reorganise the entire National and Regional *law corpora* in the direction settled by the European Commission. Finally the lesson learned from the major European and National experiences in the legal drafting sector stresses the key role of the *interoperability* and *standardisation* issues: vertical interconnection between different layers of law (European, National, Regional, Local) is essential, as well as the horizontal inter-linking inside of the same *corpora*. Only an accurate attention to the standardisation, reinforced with semantic web technologies (meta-data and ontologies), could guarantee a durable results of the legal text marking-up operation with the aim to build in the future, with appropriate web services, an effective and usable *valid law corpora* in support of the eGovernance.

(The contributions of this paper are assigned as following: M. Palmirani par. 1, 3, 5.1, 6; R. Brighi par. 2, 4, 5.2.)

References

1. AA.VV. , Studio di fattibilità per la realizzazione del progetto "Accesso alle norme in rete", Informatica e Diritto No. 1, 2000.
2. BIN R., LUCCHI N., 2002, Informatica per le scienze giuridiche, pp.48–141, CEDAM, Padova.
3. BOER A., HOEKSTRA R., WINKELS R., MetaLex: Legislation in XML, in the proceeding of JURIX2002: the Fifteenth annual conference of Legal Knowledge and Information System, IOS Press, Amsterdam, 2002.
4. Circolare 22 aprile 2002 n. AIPA/CR/40, "Formato per la rappresentazione elettronica dei provvedimenti normativi tramite il linguaggio di marcatura XML", Gazzetta Ufficiale n. 102, 3 maggio 2002.
5. Circolare 6 novembre 2001 n. AIPA/CR/35, "Assegnazione dei nomi uniformi ai documenti giuridici", Gazzetta Ufficiale Serie generale n. 262, 10 novembre 2001.
6. PALMIRANI M., BRIGHI R., NORMA-SYSTEM: a legal document system for managing consolidated acts, Database and Expert System Applications, in the proceeding of the13[th] International Conference, Dexa 2002, Aix-en-Provence, Berlin, Springer, 2002.
7. TRAUNMÜLLER R., LENK K., Electronic Government: Where Are We Heading?, Electronic Government: first international conference, EGOV 2002: Aix-en-Provence, France, September 2-6, 2002, Springer, Berlin, 2002.

Information Technology as an Enabler for Innovation in Government-to-Citizen Processes

Luiz Antonio Joia

Brazilian School of Public and Business Administration – Getulio Vargas Foundation
and Rio de Janeiro State University
Rua Presidente Carlos de Campos 115/503, BL 02
Rio de Janeiro, RJ, Brazil, 22231-080
luizjoia@fgv.br

Abstract. The scope of this paper is to analyze the extent to which Information Technology can be used as an enabler in the transformation of productive processes associated with the activities of government organs, with an emphasis on the use of Internet technology, in government-to-citizen processes in the Brazilian context. For this purpose, the process of issuing and renewing driver's licenses coordinated by the Department of Transport of the State of Rio de Janeiro in Brazil is presented so as to show how redesigning the former production process with the assistance of Information Technology brought about improvements for the citizen.

1   Introduction

The scope of this paper is to analyze the extent to which Information Technology (IT) can be used as an enabler in the transformation of productive processes associated with the activities of government organs. For this purpose, the process of issuing and renewing driver's licenses coordinated by the Department of Transport of the State of Rio de Janeiro (DETRAN-RJ) is analyzed. By means of this work, the intention is to study how redesigning the former production process with the assistance of Information Technology brought about improvements for the citizen and gave greater agility to the government organ itself, namely within the scope of a typical e-Government G2C (Government-to-Citizen) undertaking.

Consequently, the following questions are analyzed and tackled in this paper *vis-à-vis* the case under scrutiny:

– To what extent did the new process for issuing and renewing driver's licenses, with the assistance of Information Technology, provide benefits for the citizen?
– To what extent did the new process for issuing and renewing driver's licenses, with the assistance of Information Technology, provide benefits for the partners in the logistical chain of services of DETRAN-RJ?
– To what extent did the adequate use of Information Technology provide benefits to the internal administration of DETRAN-RJ?

Single, descriptive case study methodology focusing on the experience of the implementation and use of a G2C undertaking in DETRAN-RJ was used to answer these questions, according to Yin's approach [4].

R. Traunmüller (Ed.): EGOV 2003, LNCS 2739, pp. 430–433, 2003.

2 Case Study

The DETRAN-RJ case sets out to show, empirically, how IT via the Internet made it possible to innovate the procedures of the organ, transforming a highly verticalized logistical chain of services - Venkatraman's level 2 [3] - into a logistical network in which the organ itself took over the role of performing functions which essentially involved the integration and regulation of the activities as a whole -Venkatraman's level 4 [3]. The considerations raised within the scope of this analysis are the result of a project conducted together with the Driver's License Department of DETRAN-RJ during the period from 1999 through 2001, which resulted in the innovation of its processes by means of the implementation of the State Network for Driver Training and Qualification for the State of Rio de Janeiro (REFOR-RJ).

From 1998 onwards, the Transport Departments (DETRANs) have been obliged to incorporate changes in order to comply with the provisions of the new Brazilian Highway Code - CTB, which has forced the state transport organs to alter their traditional model of management and operation. With respect to services relating to training and qualification of candidates for driving vehicles in particular, the new CTB recommends that the DETRANs turn themselves into units essentially dedicated to performing the function of regulation and coordination of the processes, within their areas of jurisdiction, according to [1]. In order to adapt themselves to this new profile, the activities of an essentially operational nature of the executive transport organs – the DETRANs – needed to be transferred to specialized organizations, using a model for outsourcing of services. The adoption of this new operational model in DETRAN-RJ, covering the whole of the geographical extension of Rio de Janeiro, involving the participation of more than 800 accredited companies and attendance of 4,000 candidates per day, requiring the performance of services of a high quality standard, only became feasible after implementation of ITresources on a broad scale, principally involving the Internet.

2.1 Case Environment

The organization in question is the Department of Transport of the State of Rio de Janeiro (DETRAN-RJ), and the unit under scrutiny is the Driver's License Department (DIHAB), responsible for providing services to vehicle drivers and candidates wishing to qualify for or renew their national driver's licenses, within the State of Rio de Janeiro. Among its many attributions, DIHAB is responsible for compliance with the regulations of the Brazilian Highway Code – CTB and all complementary normative aspects, with regard to aspects relating to vehicle drivers.

Lastly, it is responsible for the regulation and supervision of all services and procedures connected with the Driver's License Qualification Service, statewide, including checking all obstacles to qualifying for or renewing permission to drive vehicles. This also includes the theoretical and practical training of candidates, medical and psychological examinations, monitoring the theoretical and practical examinations for driving vehicles and issuing driver's licenses. From a systemic standpoint, DIHAB is represented through the State System for Qualification of Drivers of Motor Vehicles (SEHAB), the mission of which is the management and operation of all procedures relating to qualification of candidates wishing to apply for a National Driver's License, within the whole of the State of Rio de Janeiro. SEHAB is regulated by directives related to the Brazilian Highway Code – CTB, stipulated by The Brazilian Transport Council – CONTRAN and The Brazilian Transport Department – DENATRAN.

2.2 Logistical Chain of Services

The logistical chain of services of the State Driver Qualification System is structured around five main processes and their respective activities: (1) providing information to candidates about available services; (2) receiving applications and beginning the processing of forms in the Attendance Stations; (3) screening the qualification/aptitude of the candidate; (4) issuing the driver's license and delivering it to the candidate; (5) administration of the driver training system. The heavy concentration of the activities of the chain of services at internal units of DETRAN-RJ before the changes resulting from implementation of the REFOR-RJ network meant that it was characterized as being highly verticalized.

The critical points, which justified a structured intervention for the transformation of the existing operational model, were as follows:
– The inadequacy, from a medical and psychological standpoint, of criteria for assessment of the qualification of candidates at DETRAN attendance stations to meet the standards demanded by the Brazilian Highway Code;
– The lack of systematic follow-up by DETRAN, as the regulatory entity for the activities and performance of Driver Training Centers, with respect to training of candidates;
– The absence of more rigorous controls in some internal processes of DETRAN, especially with respect to activities related to the scheduling, screening and registering of results of practical exams for motor vehicle driving;
– The deficiency in procedures for providing information, receiving application forms and beginning to provide the services for candidates wishing to obtain their first operator license or renewal of their existing national driver's license, due to overloading of the telephone answering services of the organ.

3   Concluding Remarks

3.1   Benefits Directly Perceived by Service Users

The enhanced process incorporates new links in the chain of services, chief among which is the www.detran.rj.gov.br site by means of which the user has access to information on legislation and procedures relating to the services rendered, making the whole process more straightforward and user-friendly. Furthermore, the new process makes it easier to obtain the required service. One of the major problems in the previous system lay in the difficulty encountered by the user to schedule an appointment to go to the Attendance Stations and start the process.

3.2 Benefits for the Partners Integrated in the Logistical Chain of Services

The partners integrated in the logistical chain of services, especially the medical/psychological clinics and the driver training centers, now have straightforward access to the REFOR system under the enhanced process. In order to be included in the REFOR network, via an extranet connection, the partners only need to have access to a microcomputer and a link-up with an Internet service provider. The procedures for operation are available using online transactions, incorporated to the system, and information is transmitted to the database of the REFOR system in real-time by electronic means. Connection via the Internet network involves lower operational costs and the security of the data is guaranteed by adopting transmission procedures through virtual private networks (VPNs) and firewalls.

3.3 Benefits Related to Internal Administration

Among the instructions contained in Administrative Ruling N. 47 of DENATRAN, one of the central requirements involves the integration under a single system of all of the procedures and information relating to training, qualification and performance of the candidates, making it possible to monitor the training and supervisory entities and organizations simultaneously. These specifications involve the need for control procedures and systems which were not available within the scope of the DETRAN-RJ under the former system, and which only became viable by using a computerized system, in view of the scale and complexity of the network of operations to be monitored. Another relevant aspect which justified the adoption of the new model of administration and operations was the rationalization of internal procedures and the link-up with external entities, especially with the elimination of the flow of paperwork during the process [2]. Since the adoption of the enhanced process using the REFOR network, DETRAN-RJ effectively assumed the role of regulatory and supervisory organ of the Brazilian Transport System, in line with the recommendations of the Brazilian Highway Code (CTB).

References

1. BRASIL (1999). Portaria N. 47, CTB, March 18, 1999.
2. Joia, L. A. (1998). "Large-Scale Reengineering on Project Documentation at Engineering Consultancy Companies", *International Journal of Information Management, Elsevier Science Ltd*, 18 (3) June, pp. 215–224.
3. Venkatraman N. (1994) "IT – Enable Business Transformation: From Automation to Busines Scope Redefinition", *Sloan Management Review,* Cambridge, , v 35, n 2. pp. 73–87
4. Yin R. (1994) *Case Study Research and Design,* SAGE Publications, Thousand Oaks, California.

Life-Event Approach: Comparison between Countries

Anamarija Leben and Mirko Vintar

University of Ljubljana
Faculty of Administration
Gosarjeva 5
1000 Ljubljana
Slovenia
{anamarija.leben,mirko.vintar}@vus.uni-lj.si

Abstract. Designing user-friendly public e-services is one of the prime concerns of most e-government initiatives and programmes. In this context a life-event based approach seems to be one of the most promising. There are several research projects and several live-event description and design methodologies under development, most of them still in an early stage. In the paper we are trying to focus and compare three selected methodological approaches to designing live-events. Main aim of our research was to compare the selected approaches and outline their main characteristics as well as differences between them.

1 Introduction

A life-event approach in designing public services has proved to be one of important initiatives in e-government programmes in Europe and worldwide. Many public web portals use this approach. At University of Ljubljana, this approach was employed in the project 'Development of an Intelligent Life-Event Portal' [5,6]. Within this project, the concepts of an active life-event portal were introduced. The core system of such portal is a knowledge-based system that uses a pre-defined structure of particular life-event to form an active dialog with the user and in this way helps him to identify and solve his problem related to a particular life-event. The development of an adequate methodology for description of life-events was one of the major tasks in this project. When evaluating the developed methodology, we found out, that in some other European countries similar methodologies were introduced. We find two projects especially interesting: 'Life Event Access Project' in Great Britain [2] and 'An Integrating Platform for Realising Online One-Stop Government' [1], which is a joined project of three countries (Austria, Greece and Switzerland). Our main aim in this paper was to compare these approaches and point out some differences between them.

R. Traunmüller (Ed.): EGOV 2003, LNCS 2739, pp. 434–437, 2003.

2 Life-Event Methodologies

LEAP – Life Events Access Project is a partnership project within a group of Councils in Great Britain [2]. It aims to utilise knowledge management in order to improve service provision to customers. LEAP combines services around life-events. The LEAP project applications will query the user about their needs and requirements and steer them to the processes and information they require.

eGOV – An Integrating Platform for Realising Online One-Stop Government has as a main objective the provision of an open, extensible and scalable platform for realizing online one-stop government [1].

ILEP – Development of an Intelligent Life-Event Portal aims to develop a prototype of an intelligent life-event portal [5], a language for description of life-events, life-events models, an on-line repository of life-events and supporting system for managing this repository.

LEAP Methodology

LEAP concentrates on developing knowledge about local services, which are typically organized under service headings. For different reasons [2], services are broken down into discreet processes. Sets of these processes are then aggregated under particular life-event. A service can comprise one or more functions and a function one or more processes. A function can also be described as a branch process, a branch process usually comprises one or more leaf processes and a leaf process is an operation or a group of related activities. *Branch processes* are high-level processes. *Leaf level processes* are self-contained; they should contain all the functionality to allow them to operate as self-contained units. The same leaf level process can be used in different branch processes. The model of branch process indicates its hierarchical structure.

The project requires agreeing a standard methodology for mapping life events and services. Expert knowledge about how specific services are delivered is captured in the process maps to enable non-expert front-line staff to make correct decisions and give expert advice. The chosen method for process mapping is required to capture *customer-facing processes* in order that they may act as a guide to generic staff and also to be transposed into rule based software systems. Decision tree diagramming method was selected with some additional features from standard flow chart diagrams [2]. Only leaf level processes are modelled as decision trees [3]. The end-points of a process map presents information whether a customer is eligible to certain public service or not with additional information about process. The depth of a process map depends on the depth of customer involvement. A map stops when the customer involvement ceases.

eGOV Methodology

Within this project, a framework including a terminology that links "life events" and "business situations" with "public services" and "processes" was developed [4]. A public service consists of one or more processes. A particular process may be a part of different public services. In a further decomposition, a process may be composed of several process steps and operations. The methodology proposes two types of public services: an *elementary public service* is public service produced by a single public organisation, a *composite public service* is composed of one or more elementary public services and addresses a specific need of a user.

Life events indicate the overall semantic content to facilitate the customer's navigation, orientation and search through the complete public authorities' offers. However, the customer does not consume a life-event but public services as the concrete products. Therefore, public services are the core concept to be handled by the eGOV integrated platform. Life-events and public services present an external viewpoint, while processes and process steps present an internal viewpoint of public administration functioning.

In literature, available about eGOV project on Internet, diagramming methods for modelling basic concepts of presented framework are not especially defined, although in some examples UML use case diagrams and sequence diagrams are used [4].

ILEP Methodology
According to the ILEP structural design, an intelligent guide through life-event has three levels [6]: (1) level of topics, where life-event is identified; (2) level of life-events that results in a list of generic administrative procedures required to solve a life-event (also a sequence and/or parallelism of these procedures must be apparent) and (3) level of procedures, where a variant for each generic administrative procedure is identified (for each variant, required documents and guidelines are defined). A life-event is understood as a whole process of solving a particular user's problem.

An implemented methodology for description of life-events captures these three levels. For each level, different diagramming techniques were selected for modelling. A model of a main *topic* is a tree, presenting its hierarchical structure. Leafs of these tree are composed life-events. To model the decision-making process related to the execution of a *life-event*, the concepts from eEPC (extended event-driven process chain) diagrams where used. A function (an element presenting an action in eEPC diagrams) can present a life-event, an elementary life-event or generic administrative procedure depending on the level of particular life-event. The model of *generic administrative procedure* that aims to identify parameters to define a variant of the procedure is based on AND/OR graph.

3   Comparison of the Methodologies

The comparison of described methodologies (Table 1) is based on different features.

A *design method* refers to a process of structuring and describing life-events. Within LEAP project, processes are starting points of this analysis what indicates that mainly bottom-up approach was implemented. Within other two projects, a top-down approach is implemented. The BPR feature indicates whether a *business process reengineering* is implemented or not. LEAP project especially instruct that no BPR is allowed [3], while eGOV project particularly requires BPR [4, Pg. 20]. In ILEP project, only redesign of processes is planned. There are two *viewpoints* of PA functioning: external refers to characteristics important to customer, while internal viewpoint refers to characteristics important for PA itself. In eGOV project, both viewpoints are considered, while LEAP project deals only with external point of view [3]. ILEP methodology is focused manly on external viewpoint with some internal aspects to identify all procedures and their parameters for a particular life-event. Public service could be divided in four phases [4]: (1) information and intention building phase, (2) contracting phase, (3) service delivery and payment phase, and (4) aftercare phase. Therefore, a next compared feature indicates, which *phases of public services* are considered in particular methodology. A very important aspect is, whether a *life-event is regarded as a process* or not. In a broad sense, a life-event presents a concept, where processes are combined in one complex process. On the other hand, a life-event can be only regarded as a topic, under which all corresponding processes are gathered. Whether implemented methodology *enables to depict a parallelism* in process or life-events execution or not, is a very important aspect if we want a methodology to be comprehensive enough to describe all types of processes involved in a public service delivery. This aspect suggests also *diagramming techniques* applied to model processes and life-event.

Table 1. Comparison of presented methodologies for description of life-events

		Methodology for description of life-events		
		LEAP	eGOV	ILEP
compared features	Design method	mainly bottom-up	top-down	top-down
	BPR	no	reengineering	redesign
	Viewpoint	external	external and internal	mainly external
	Phases of public services	information	all phases	information
	Life-event as a process	no	partly	yes
	Parallelism	no	yes	yes
	Diagramming techniques	Decision trees	UML tools	eEPC, AND/OR graphs

A comparison of presented methodologies indicates that the comprehension of implemented methodologies corresponds to the scope and objectives of particular project. The intention of this comparison is not to criticize one methodology or another or to point out which one is the best. The results of comparison should encourage the developers and designers to consider different aspects of life-events, which are important if we want to achieve real benefits from life-event approach for customers as well as for public institutions and organisations.

References

1. eGOV – An Integrating Platform for Realising Online One-Stop Government. http://www.egov-project.org/default.htm (February 2003)
2. LEAP – Life Event Access Project. http://www.leap.gov.uk. (February 2003)
3. LEAP – The LEAP Process Mapping Guide (released on January 2001). http://www.leap.gov.uk/xpedio/groups/public/documents/training/000063.pdf
4. Tambouris E., Spanos E., Kavadias G. (Eds.), eGOV Services and Process Models Functional Specifications (Jan 2002). http://xml.coverpages.org/eGOV-D121.pdf
5. Vintar et all. Development of the Intelligent Life-Event Portal, Year Report. School of Public Administration, Ljubljana, November 2002. (in Slovene)
6. Vintar, M., Leben, A. The Concepts of an Active Life-event Public Portal. In: Traunmüller, R., Lenk, K. (Eds.), Electronic Government, Proceedings of the First International Conference, EGOV 2002, Aix-en-Provence, France, September 2002. Springer-Verlag. Pg. 383–390.

For the Good of the Public – What Can We Do for You? Effective Partnering between Local Government and Business for Service Delivery

Katja Andresen

University of Potsdam
Professorship for Public and Business Information Systems
Postfach 900327
D-14439 Potsdam
kandres@rz.uni-potsdam.de

Abstract. Portals do help communities to expand its level of government services providing a frame to implement e-government and the opportunity to revitalize local government. Hereby, partnering is particularly relevant in today's rapidly changing world and its focus on the needs of citizens and communities. In this article current factors and trends are presented focussing on the situation in Germany.

1 Status Quo – The Best Is Yet to Come

The international study "Government-online 2002"[1] analysed the penetration of electronic government services by country. It shows an average usage of 30 percent of citizens positively responding to local online public services.

For Germany, the study stated 24 percent what means an increase of seven percent in total. Also, the access to information currently is the most important for German citizens. Germany is ranked the 18th place in the community compared with the 13th place the year before. Obviously, the usage is rising though the usage degree has risen slower than in other countries. The study also pointed out the main barriers to use electronic government for the citizenship namely, security concerns[2].

So far most of the effort in electronic government was directed at presenting information hence most of its potential for improved service the business transformation point on the stage of transactions is to be expected.

2 Organisational Structures – Form Follows Function

Portals have recently become the most popular way of presenting local areas and public service to the community. Nowadays, cities tend to offer public services and

---

[1] TNS EMNID. Government Online 2002 – Global Report.
[2] 82% in Germany against 65% average value.

R. Traunmüller (Ed.): EGOV 2003, LNCS 2739, pp. 438–441, 2003.
© Springer-Verlag Berlin Heidelberg 2003

electronic commerce activities such as virtual market places within the portal. Beyond information more "advanced" cities carry out transactions online. The online handling of public service involves the integration of back-end processes "behind" the portal, the seamless usage of the electronic support to establish the electronic workflow. [1]

The technical realisation is accompanied by organisational changes. To realize these complex issues cities are confronted with the issue on how to manage and maintain the city portal. To open the domain for private investors is one solution to optimize personnel as well as financial recourses. Currently the trend points towards cooperation between the public and the private sector (Public-Private Partnerships) in this field.[3] Partnerships have been used in a variety of programs. However, in the realm of city portals concrete models for successful PPPs do not yet exist. [2]

From an organisational point of view two significant groups can be identified. The first group takes a rather institutional and non commercial point of view. For issues related to the virtual town hall as eGovernment, eVoting, eCommunity the public administration holds the complete responsibility whereas eCommerce activities are delegated to private partners[4]. For this group it is common that a public agency enters a contract with a private-sector organisation to complete the tasks mentioned (outsourcing of functions). Sometimes, this division deploys different domain names per area[5]. Clear structures and responsibilities can be seen as advantage of this type. Additionally, the public administration concentrates on its core competences.

The second group is characterized by focussing on activities to optimally present all aspects of life events in the portal. This approach emphasizes user friendliness as major design goal. Activities which are related to city portal access, the technical platform or public services are bundled and performed by a single body under private law which is usually founded for this purpose. The centralisation of the city portal management leads to a complete integration of public and private services into one technical platform. It is the preferred structure by major cities as Bremen, Hamburg, Hanover and Berlin for instance.

Cities preferring the institutional point of view (first group) require the customer to get into the detailed bureaucratic set-up. The portal presentation follows the motto: "This is what we do! This is who we are!". However, a common customer of a public service wants to get some sort of task done. Therefore the navigation should be based on the intentions of the user as the service-oriented city portals do following the design approach "How can we serve you?".

Besides a couple of mixed forms do exist comprising cities that can not be assigned to either group[6]. In fact, the majority of municipal areas and cities are to be found in neither group. The reason may be of temporary nature as many of them are in the process of planning a convenient structure.

Nonetheless, since customer-oriented, citizen-friendly presentations are major factors to increase the usage it is to assume the integrative design approach might become more popular over the next years. From a structural point of view this type of cooperation leads to challenges we will look at now.

---

[3] In the context of this paper a Public-Private Partnership (PPP) is based on a contractual agreement between a public agency and a private (for profit) body. Through this agreement skills, know how, recourses are shared in order to deliver some service to the general public.

[4] As Saarbrücken, Hagen.

[5] As Cologne (Köln): www.koeln.de and www.stadt-koeln.de.

[6] As Leipzig, Dortmund, Essen.

3 The Berlin Model

Derived from the national eGovernment program "BundOnline 2005"[7] the Land
Berlin defined its initiative on electronic government. In April 2002 the so called
"Master Plan"[8] was published. Like many other regions too the *Land* Berlin is
considered at the threshold to continuously automate its business processes what this
is to become a big and expensive plan. Although the external appearance of public
institutions is getting the most attention (e.g. the service of portals) the redesign of
work-flows allowing data sharing across agencies, tele-cooperation and knowledge
management might lead to the biggest effect of electronic government inside the
governmental apparatus. However, as the internal structure directly affects the ability
to deliver advanced service as web based transactions the degree of systematisation of
business processes is reflected in the relationship government to its external
customers[9]. This may explain the focus of attention.

The City Portal berlin.de
Since 1998 the *Land* Berlin cooperates with a private partner. The partnership was
established after a public invitation to bid undertaken in 1995 – 1997 to set-up
maintain and develop the city portal under the domain www.berlin.de.
   A new (self-financing) body under private law was founded for that purpose. The
expectations of the partnership were part an agreement clearly describing the
responsibilities of both the *Land* Berlin and the private partner.[3] Key Points of the
contractual agreement include financial issues, the deployment of modern and
standardised technology as the digital signature along with the establishment of
interactive public services. In Berlin profitability has to be realised without public
funding. Also, IT consulting, programming know-how and maintenance of the web
presentation is to be assured by the partner. Additionally, marketing activities to
attract citizens, customers, visitors are expected. The *Land* Berlin contributes by
exclusively announcing the usage of the attractive domain name www.berlin.de for all
Berlin related public services and presentations. Along with that the domain can be
used for commercial purposes by the private partner. Due to a tight budget circle the
Land Berlin did not invest in the partnership body – hence the economical risk is
completely delegated to the private partner.[10] After four years of experience the
collaboration is seen positively. The city portal is one of the leading city portals in
Germany[11] – gradually more services are integrated.
   As there was very little experience the initial partnership started on experimental
grounds. The abovementioned positive results naturally were accompanied by
challenges. The identified areas comprise competence, orientation and budget issues.
   During the first for years the partnership faced major changes as seven new
partners emerged associated with seven new managing directors to appoint. Very
optimistic business plans, competition among Berlin city portals followed by the
break-down of the internet market led to uncertainty on the government's side. As the

7   BundOnline2005 started in 1999. It aims to offer 376 public services online by 2005.
8   Senatskanzlei (Berlin). E-Government im Land Berlin – Masterplan 2002.
9   Government to Citizen (G2C); Government to Business (G2B).
10 Other major German cities as Bremen, Hamburg, Hanover do share a limited finacial risk.
11 Please see up to date figures on page-impressions, click rates at URL: http://www. ivu.de.

frequent changes of different partners might indicate the basis for a stable relationship was difficult to establish. What the pace of change in partners does not reflect is the staff situation. From the perspective of key staff it can be considered stable until 2002. Because of this some negative effects of the company take-overs were outbalanced as contact persons were the same over a longer period of time.

Although the project Berlin.de faced difficult challenges – the partnering model is considered a success. The concept was taken over by Hamburg, Schleswig-Holstein, and Frankfurt/Main. Among future candidates are Brandenburg, Munich, Stuttgart and the virtual market place of Austria.[12]

4 Conclusions

A Public-Private Partnership is a long-term relationship that should be established carefully. Identifying the right partner should be related to experience in the area of interest. The development of a partnership is an ongoing process based on trust and stability. As Berlin.de has shown the public sector was to approve different for-profit corporation, affecting various stakeholders within its first four years. All stakeholders develop opinions and positions which influence the image of the partnership, its value to the pubic. To avoid misconceptions and potential resistance of stakeholders it is important to communicate openly. Also, every service provided by public institutions per se is suspected more expensive and less professional than a comparable service given by private companies. In that sense PPP are also a means to improve the reputation of public agencies. Nonetheless the partnership needs to establish a winwin situation for either site to work out successfully.

There is not an absolute flawless technique or a set formula for a successful PPP to implement government/city portals. However, the benefits of a well chosen partnership provide the unique opportunity to newly define and realize public services to be offered to citizens, employees, and businesses, from a customer perspective.

References

1. C. Baron. Public-Private-Partnership-Konzepte für den IT Markt, Wiesbaden 1999.
2. B. Grabow. Städte auf dem Weg zum virtuellen Rathaus. 2001.
3. H. Ullrich (Senatskanzlei, Berlin). Das Stadtinformationssystem „berlin.de", E-Government-Forum Niedersachsen, 2002.

---

[12] Source: E-Government im Land Berlin, Version 1.4, 13.08.2002, page 25.

Implementing E-Government in Spain

José Luis Bermejo Latre

University of Zaragoza
c/Pedro Cerbuna 12
50009 Zaragoza
Spain
berlatre@unizar.es

Abstract. The main aim of "e-Administration" programmes in Spain is to regulate and to implement administrative procedures that enable e-documents to be telematically processed, recorded and filed in a unified system that may be used by various entities. S. 45 of the 30/1992, of 26 November, Administrative Common Procedures Act is the general basis for the regulation of the specific demonstrations of computer and telematic techniques in Administrative procedures, such as the management of e-documents, the use of e-signature, the handling of administrative databases or general records on computer means, the issuance of e-mail notices and the management of administrative information by telematic means, either displaying it on administrative websites or by subscribing to e-lists. For those purposes are noteworthy Tax regulations, which establish the general conditions and regulate the procedure for telematically presenting declarations of different tax models over the Internet.

1 Introduction

The use of new ICTs has brought about a noteworthy transformation in the way the Administration relates to citizens, (the phenomenon called *e-Government*). The implementation of *e-Government* gives rise to a series of important challenges: to define the appropriate legal framework capable of arranging the "information society"; to select and to use the various telematic and computer utilities that are most suitable for public management; and to train civil servants on how to use these computer utilities. Furthermore, the dynamic nature of the technological market makes it necessary to readapt the administrative ICT systems, to train public employees properly and to choose the most suitable utilities to enable users to directly readapt to new issues.

The range of technical transformations creates a constant interactive flow of information on administrative action proposals, which in turn demands special attitudes from administrative services. Furthermore, the reception of integrated administrative services demands an effective implementation of inter-administrative coordination and cooperation standards, as administrative entities can share information [1]. The administrative information is now more easily accessed than ever, the use of ICTs for administrative procedures makes the decision-making processes more immediate and standardised: in few words, the public management is no longer subject to limitations for which the current procedural legislation was

R. Traunmüller (Ed.): EGOV 2003, LNCS 2739, pp. 442–447, 2003.
© Springer-Verlag Berlin Heidelberg 2003

conceived. However, we are currently at an initial stage of uncertainty and expansion, inasmuch the society is still learning the new "e-language"[1]. Also, the use of ICTs by the Administration gives rise to problems that should be kept in mind, regulated by the Personal Data Protection Organic Act 15/1999 of 13 December and by Royal Decree 994/1999 of 11 June, regulations that should soon adapt to what is stipulated in the Directive 2002/58/EC of the European Parliament and of the Council of 12 July 2002 concerning the processing of personal data and the protection of privacy in the electronic communications sector ("Directive on privacy and electronic communications").

2   The Requirements for Developing E-Government in Spain

In Spain, the *e-Government* phenomenon is known as *e-Administration,* expression that refers to public authorities' plans to extend the use of ICTs in relations with citizens, providing administrative services through Internet-based technologies. To satisfy this aim, it is necessary to create telematic administrative procedures that enable e-documents to be telematically processed, recorded and filed in a unified system that may be used by various public entities (State, Autonomous and Local). These procedures should also allow telematic consultations of administrative files and provide the possibility of receiving the information needed to carry out private transactions that require administrative documents.

Implementing *e-Administration* initiatives could be broadly considered handling administrative procedures over the Internet [2]. In this sense, computer and telematic technologies within the field of administrative procedures are exclusively used to transfer traditional physical document supports onto electronic supports when processing procedures. The essence of administrative procedures and the principles they support would remain unaltered; only processing techniques and means would vary [2]. Thus, the challenge when using new technologies for administrative procedures is based on certain rules about the use of computer and telematic systems for processing procedures. These rules are already present in our Administrative law system: s. 45 of the Administrative Common Procedures Act 30/1992, of 26 November (LAP from here on) is the cornerstone for the process of incorporating automated techniques in the Civil Services' legal production. This section proposes the introduction of ICTs for administrative management, responding to the main problems appearing in the use of ICTs before the citizens, guaranteeing the validity and publicity of computer and telematic applications for administrative use and guaranteeing complete security of telematic administrative procedures. For these purposes, LAP was amended by s. 57 of the Fiscal, Administrative and Social

---

[1] Here are some statistics on the penetration of the "information society" in Spain: nearly 12.000.000 Spaniards consider themselves to be Internet users. According to studies carried out for 2001 by OCDE and the Ministry of Science and Technology (own elaboration and data taken from EUROSTAT -Eurobarometer 103, June 2001-), 35% of the Spanish population over the age of fourteen use a PC, approximately 27 % of Spanish homes are equipped with a PC and 24 % of Spanish homes have Internet access. Nearly 45% of Internet users visit official websites, of which 38% of users do so to search administrative information. Moreover, in Spain there are some 1.200 SSL ("secure web servers").

Measures Act 24/2001 of 27 December, which intended to boost telematic administrative registries and records, telematic presentation of requests, applications and communications addressed to the State Administration, and telematic administrative notices.

LAP clearly and specifically aims to overcome the lack of formal recognition towards the validity of automated means and techniques, intending to boost telematic administrative registries and records, telematic presentation of requests, applications and communications addressed to the State Administration, and telematic administrative notices (a regulation of e-Notices having been completed by Royal Decree 209/2003, of 21 February).

2.1 ICTs for a New Administrative Management Culture

The validity and publicity of the software used to exercise administrative power is guaranteed by LAP s. 45 and Royal Decree 263/1996, of 16 February (RD 263/1996 from here on), whose ss. 5, 9 and 11 stipulate that the software needed for information processing, whose results are used to exercise State Administration power, must be approved by the competent administrative entity to resolve the procedure, and published in the State Official Gazette[2]. Approval Regulations should, at least, name and describe the application, determine its scope, indicate the rules that regulate them and specify the system and means to access the application, keeping industrial and intellectual property rights in mind if dealing with licensed software. Publicly broadcasting elements of programmes and applications used by the Administration simplifies the control of administrative actions' legality while it exercises its power. Within an open technological field that is constantly growing, it is necessary to ensure compatibility of computer systems and languages for communications.

2.2 Procedural Rights and the Use of ICTs

The citizen's procedural rights held in LAP s. 35 must be kept in mind when using computer and telematic means for developing the *e-Administration*. Thus, administrative websites should contain utilities that inform citizens of their procedure's processing status. Each procedure's table-summary should also identify the authorities and administrative staff responsible for processing the procedure, and contain support utilities such as FAQ menus or an online help utility for answering questions (guidance on legal or technical requirements) or queries on how to use the computer or telematic utilities that are available to the citizen. Each administrative website must also place registries and files thereon and must include automated and secure access utilities, while respecting both the limits of access rights to

---

[2] I.e. the Resolution of 27 June 2002, by the Tax Computing Department of the State Tax Agency (Agencia Estatal de la Administración Tributaria, AEAT from here on), *which publicises serial numbers and digital fingerprints of AEAT server certificates*. It publishes "AEAT Server Certificate" specifications, an electronic document issued by RSA Data Security, Inc. which enables users to verify that they really are accessing AEAT secure servers: the certificate encryption capacity, its expiry date, serial number expressed with hexadecimal notes and its digital print with MD5 and SHA1 hash algorithms.

administrative files and records and the personal data protection regulations. Neither does there seem to be any obstacles for sending documents through telematic means. *E-Documents* can be received manually by the civil servants that are responsible for the procedure, or directly through automated means on the administrative website. In both cases, it is necessary to guarantee the follow-up and correct filing of the documents presented, which would become part of the procedure list to prevent duplicity, banned by LAP s. 35. f). It is also necessary for the *e-Administration* to issue digitally sealed copies of the documents presented and those contained in the files, by electronically superimposing on the documents an intervention act.

One of the problems arosen by the *e-Administration* in the field of procedural rights is the adaptability to the various Spanish co-official languages (basque, catalan and galician) of computer systems and programs used for processing procedures. Therefore, all computer and telematic applications addressed to the public should provide interfaces in those co-official languages, regardless of the high costs that this measure entails.

2.3 Specific Demonstrations of ICTs in Administrative Procedures

e-Documents, material basis of the telematic procedure, embraces two realities: computer and magnetic supports (diskette, CD-ROM, DVD) for physical processing and telematic supports for on-line document registration over the Internet, usually XML utilities [3]. Regulation for issuing, copying and storing *e-Documents* is currently stipulated in RD 263/1996 ss. 6 and 8, which grant identical value to electronic and physical documents. Nonetheless, communications between the Administration and citizen on *e-Documents* requires another computer technique -the *e-Signature*- that should endow the process with integral security by enciphering *e-Documents* [4]. The *e-Signature* is currently the only mechanism that can guarantee complete security in e-document exchanges, at least in conditions comparable to ordinary document processing. *e-Signatures* are now regulated by Royal Decree-Act 14/1999, of 17 September, but a new Electronic Signature Act is drafted (based on Directive 1999/93/EC of the European Parliament and of the Council of 13 December 1999, on a Community framework for electronic signatures), whose aims are to extend the use of digital signatures as a security tool for transactions, inasmuch it gathers the knowledge and advances experienced since the current Royal Decree-Act came into force. Two new aspects that will help increase the availability, utility and accessibility of *e-Signatures* have been included in this draft: the digital National Identity Card and the issuance of digital certificates for companies and other entities [4].

LAP s. 38.3 regulates the installation of general records on computer mediums as the natural destination for telematically processed electronic documents. To that end, s. 7.4 of RD 263/1996 recognises telematic communication systems (usually, web servers) as auxiliary records, with accessibility from units in charge of the corresponding general records. Within this context, LAP s. 38.9 allows for the creation of telematic records for receiving and issuing requests, documents and communications transmitted by telematic means, and is subject to LAP s. 38.3 general requirements, twenty-four hours a day all year round. In accordance with this article, the 18th Additional Disposition of the LAP regulates the telematic treatment of requests and communications sent to the State Administration and its public entities, allowing the replacement of tax or Social Security certification contributions for the cession of data to the managing organ by competent entities.

With regard to telematic notices, the new LAP s. 59.3 stipulates that "for the notice to be made through telematic means, the user must previously select that means as preferential or give express consent, also stating his e-mail address, which should meet established requirements. In these cases, the notice will be legally completed when the contents are accessed at the e-mail address. If there is evidence that the notice has been received at the e-mail address, and ten days have passed without accessing its contents, it will be understood that said notice has been rejected (...), unless it is legally proven that the address was technically or materially unable to access" [5]. One of the first applications thereof is s. 29.3 of the Spanish Brands Act 17/2001, of 7 December, which, although, allows notices to be sent (by request from interested party) by fax or e-mail by the Spanish Patent and Brand Office, among other means.

The last *e-Administration* challenge to keep in mind is much less problematic than the previous ones, and refers to the spreading of administrative information by telematic means, either displaying it on administrative websites or by subscribing to information lists sent on demand by e-mail (*e-lists*) [6]. Internet is also the ideal means for for displaying public notices, organising online public enquiries and proposing public hearings.

2.4 The Regulation of Telematic Administrative Procedures

Tax regulations have pioneered in the field of telematic procedure regulations, to the point that its example has been followed when designing regulations aimed at establishing a telematic framework for managing their own procedures. In this sense, it is worth considering the Ministerial Order HAC/573/2003, of 13 March, which approves the forms for the Income Tax 2002 and regulates its telematic administrative procedure; establishing the general conditions for telematically submitting declarations of different taxes over the Internet, with rules that are usually descriptive and perform a simple regulation.

Apart from the high quality and functionality of regulations brought forward by the State Tax Agency, there are other regulations much simpler than tax ones, due to the fact that they refer either to concrete issues of specific procedures, such as the Directive of 20 March 2002, from the General Bureau of Registries and Notaries, concerning telematic reception and issuance of certification requests in Registry offices; Resolution of the Commission's Tobacco Market, of 11 April 2002, regulating the general criteria for processing telematic applications and e-documents, e-requests and e-communications before this entity; Ministerial Order ECO/1101/2002 of 13 May, regulating telematic applications for foreign trade requests; Resolution of 23 July 2002, by the President of the State Tax Agency, creating telematic registries; Ministerial Order ECO/97/2003, of 22 January, establishing general criteria for telematic applications in competition proceedings for civil servants; Resolution 2/2003, of 14 February, by the State Tax Agency, on issues related to on-line billing.

References

1. AGUIRREAZKUENAGA, I.; CHINCHILLA, C.: "El uso de medios electrónicos, informáticos y telemáticos en el ámbito de las Administraciones Públicas" ["Using Electronic, Computer and Telematic Mediums in the Field of Civil Services"], *Revista Española de Derecho Administrativo* no. 109, January-March 2001, pp. 35–59.
2. BAUZÁ MARTORELL, F.J.: *Procedimiento administrativo electrónico*, [*Electronic Administrative Procedure*] Granada, 2003; and LAFUENTE BENACHES, M.: "El soporte electrónico y telemático en el procedimiento administrativo", ["Electronic and Telematic Medium for Administrative Procedures"], from the collective volume *Nuevas perspectivas del régimen local. Estudios en homenaje al Profesor J.M. Boquera Oliver* [*New Perspectives in Loal Government. Studies Honouring Professor J. M. Boquera Oliver"*], Tirant lo blanch, Valencia, 2001, pages. 331–348.
3. DAVARA RODRÍGUEZ, M.A.: "El documento electrónico en la vigente Ley de Régimen Jurídico de las Administraciones Públicas y del Procedimiento Administrativo Común", ["The Electronic Document in the Current Civil Services and Common Administrative Procedure's Act"] *Revista de Adminsitración Pública* n. 131, 1993, pp. 355-491; andTORRES LÓPEZ, M.A.: "El documento electrónico en las relaciones jurídico-administrativas: especial referencia a los actos de comunicación" ["Electronic Documents in Legal-Administrative Relations: Special Reference to Communication Acts"], *Revista Vasca de Administración Pública* no. 55 (1999), page 253 onwards.
4. GARCÍA INDA, A.: "Firma electrónica y servicios de certificación. El Real Decreto 14/1999, sobre firma electrónica", ["Electronic Signature and Certification Services. Royal Decree 14/1999 on Electronic Signatures"] *Revista Vasca de Administración Pública* no. 55, 1999, pp. 313 ss.
5. GAMERO CASADO, E.: "La notificación por correo electrónico tras la Ley 24/2001, de 27 de diciembre" ["The Notices made by e-mail after the 24/2001 Act, of 27 December"], *Revista española de Derecho Administrativo* no. 116, 2002, pp. 501-528; and ALVAREZ CIENFUEGOS, J.M.: "La nueva Administración electrónica y las notificaciones efectuadas por medios telemáticos" ["The New e-Administration and Notices made by Telematic Means"], *Revista Jurídica de Navarra* no. 32, julio-diciembre 2001, pp. 77–96.
6. BEATO ESPEJO, M.: *Cauces de comunicación de las administraciones con los ciudadanos: tecnologías de la información: efectos técnicos y jurídicos*, [*The Administration's Communication Channels with Citizens: Information Technology: technical and legal effects*] Madrid, 2002.

Citizens and *E*-Government: An International Comparison of the Demand-Side of *E*-Government

Maarten Botterman[1], Emile Ettedgui[2], Irma Graafland[1], and Andreas Ligtvoet[1]

[1] RAND Europe
Newtonweg 1
2333 CP Leiden, The Netherlands
sibis@rand.org
http://www.randeurope.org
[2] RAND Washington Office
1200 South Hayes Street, Arlington
VA 22202-5050, United States
sibis@rand.org
http://www.rand.org

Abstract. Existing studies of e-government concentrate on the supply-side, focusing on the availability and level of sophistication of online services and usage. This study addresses the demand-side of e-government - not only usage, but also perceptions and barriers to utilisation that have not been treated previously. Indicators to measure acceptance and adoption of e-government were used to build a survey that was then piloted among members of the 'general population' in the 15 EU Member States, Switzerland and the US. A second survey was used to study 10 Accession States. The results of the surveys indicated a preference for online services that do not require users to provide a great deal of personal information. Reasons for preferring online services to their traditional counterparts include added convenience and increased efficiency. Attitudes toward e-government tended to vary by country, although reasons for this are not clear at this time.

1 Introduction

The public sector, like the private sector, has been struggling with how to use information and communication technologies to build relationships with citizens. This electronic facilitation of relationships between governments and the users of their services has become known as e-government. Ideally, the development of an e-government strategy is based on a thorough understanding of how users perceive e-government, how well they can complete expected transactions, and what barriers stand in the way of successful adoption.

Previous studies concentrated on the supply-side of e-government, availability and level of sophistication of online services and usage[1]. This study[2] [6] complements

---

[1]   See references [1][2][3][4][7][8]
[2]   SIBIS (Statistical Indicators Benchmarking the Information Society) project funded by the
European Commission in the IST program (1998-2002). http://www.sibis-eu.org.

R. Traunmüller (Ed.): EGOV 2003, LNCS 2739, pp. 448–451, 2003.

these existing studies by addressing the demand side of e-government; not only usage, but also perceptions and barriers to utilisation, which have not been treated previously. To better understand what factors may influence the acceptance of and participation in e-government, several indicators were piloted in a survey. This survey was targeted to citizens and thus this study focuses on government-to-citizen (G2C) services. The outcomes can help policy-makers target their e-government strategy more.

2 Methodology

In 2002 a 'general population survey' using computer-aided telephone interviews in the EU, Switzerland and the US was used to query citizens about their views on the Information Society. In 2003 a personal-aided personal interviews in the 10 Accession States[3] were used to query those citizens about their views. All respondents are persons aged 15 and over, living in private households in the respective countries and speaking the respective national language(s). Almost 12,000 interviews were successfully completed in the EU, Switzerland and the US. More than 10,000 interviews were successfully completed in the Accession States. Target households were selected at random in all countries, either by random dialling techniques such as permutation of final digits, by multistage stratified random-route sampling or by drawing a random sample from official sources. In most cases, a geographical stratification was implemented beforehand. For the selection of the target person common random keys were applied in all countries.

As part of the survey, regular Internet users[4] were asked about their perception of e-government compared to traditional modes of interacting with government. The government services addressed in the survey originated from the report "e-Government Indicators for Benchmarking e-Europe" of the European Commission [5].

The survey examined respondents' preferences for, access to, usage of and attitude toward e-government. The government services included in the general population survey are tax declarations, job search services at public employment agencies, requests for personal documents (e.g. birth certificate, passport, driving license), car registrations, declarations to the police (e.g. for reporting theft), searches for books in public libraries and announcements of change of address.

3 Some Results

The preference for online or traditional access to government services varies across services. In this study, the results of the survey shows that citizens are interested in some aspects of e-government and show a significant preference for some e-government services over their traditional counterparts. For example, the online

---

[3] Bulgaria, Czech Republic, Estonia, Hungary, Lithuania, Latvia, Poland, Romania, Slovenia and Slovakia.

[4] Respondents who have used the Internet in the 4 weeks prior to the survey.

search for books available in public libraries, rates a high preference. The use of job search services also tends to be rated highly by respondents.

Generally, it appears that services that do not require users to reveal a great deal of personal information about themselves are popular while those that do, are less likely to elicit a positive response. To better understand the factors that may influence acceptance and usage it is important to correlate the responses to variables such as age, employment status, time spent online and level of Internet know-how. While this may not explain why particular factors influence the affinity of respondents for e-government, it may suggest ways to enhance its acceptance and usage.

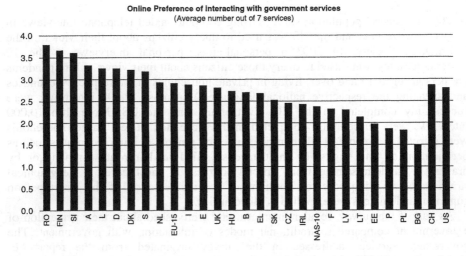

Fig. 1. Preferences for online access to government services in the EU, Accession States (NAS), CH and US. Preference for public services: average numbers out of seven services. Source: SIBIS, GPS 2002 and 2003. N= 5944 for EU-15, CH and US; N= 3025 for NAS-10

The cultural variety of the countries in the survey may combine with other factors to influence the interest in e-government of citizens in each of the countries. For example, respondents from the northern countries of Europe show a greater preference for interacting with government using Internet than the EU average. Romania shows a very high ranking and scores well above the average of the Accession States (NAS-10), indicating that the regular Internet users in Romania are very willing and enthusiastic about the possibilities the Internet can create for them in the future[5] (Figure 1).

Many externalities that vary from one member state to the next may influence the preference of respondents for e-government. These were not considered in the survey. Therefore, differences that are seen across the countries cannot be analysed immediately. However, the results suggest that further study may prove fruitful in understanding why citizens may opt for or against e-government.

Among respondents who indicated a preference for online government services, citizens were not always aware of which government services were available online.

---

[5] Further research learns that current availability and usage of online services is low.

The general pattern appears to be that citizens were well aware of e-government services requiring little or no personal information while they were not sure of whether those requiring a great deal of personal information were available to them. The exception to this pattern was tax declaration, which over half of respondents identified as available to them.

The attitudes of citizens toward e-government point to convenience of time and location as factors that strongly favour e-government over traditional government. In addition, citizens felt that e-government is faster than traditional government. Nearly half of the respondents did not feel that e-government services are difficult to use.

4 Conclusions

The indicators developed in this project are a first attempt to get a clearer picture about the use of electronic public services by citizens, their preferences and assessment of these services. The G2C survey of citizens shows that e-government services requiring little personal information are better perceived than those requiring a great deal. In addition, attitudes toward e-government vary with the level of familiarity with the Internet. An understanding of regional variations in the acceptance of e-government will require more in-depth investigation.

It is clear that the current study does not cover every single aspect of the demand-side of e-government and future research is essential to get a more complete picture of the perceptions and attitudes of the users of e-government services. Analysing why results per service or per country differ is of great interest for policy-makers.

References

1. Accenture, Rhetoric vs reality – Closing the Gap (April 2001)
2. Accenture, eGovernment leadership – Realizing the Vision (April 2002)
3. Bertelsmann Stiftung & Booz, Allen & Hamilton, Balanced e-Government (2001)
4. Cap Gemini Ernst & Young, Summary Report Web-based Survey on Electronic Public Services (2001 and 2002)
5. European Commission, e-Government Indicators for Benchmarking e-Europe (Feb. 2001), http://europa.eu.int/information_society/eeurope/action_plan/pdf/egovindicators.pdf
6. SIBIS, RAND Europe, Topic Report No. 8: e-Government (2003), http://www.sibis-eu.org/sibis/reports/results.htm
7. United Nations, DPEPA, Benchmarking e-government: A global perspective (2002)
8. World Markets Research Centre, Global e-Government Survey (Sept. 2001)

Ten Factors for Success for Local Community E-Government

Tina Siegfried, Busso Grabow, and Helmut Drüke

MEDIA@Komm accompanying research
German Institute of Urban Affairs
Strasse des 17. Juni 110
10623 Berlin
Tel.: ++49+30 39001-201
siegfried@difu.de
http://www.mediakomm.net

1 Introduction

What is local community e-government? What is needed to be successful in setting up virtual town halls? Many different answers are given to this question. For some it is a successful and useful Internet presentation by a municipality, for others it is a new initiative for modernisation in the public administration enhanced by the technological development. But all too often, local community e-government is reduced to on-line services such as the provision of forms on the Internet, possibilities for participation in municipal websites or the availability of electronic interaction and transactions.

The basis for the "Model for success in local community e-government" developed in the accompanying research of MEDIA@Komm (cf. www.mediakomm.net) is a comprehensive understanding of e-government. This includes *all* aspects of government and administration (determining public opinion, decision-making, creation and provision of services, public participation) insofar as they can be supported and enhanced by the use of information and communication technology.

The long-term success of local community e-government is determined by far more factors than are often assumed. On-line applications and their benefits are only one aspect. One of the main insights of Administrative Science on the subject of e-government is that the technology or the applications on their own are not the key to successful e-government. In fact, there is a whole range of factors such as organisational measures, strategic procedures, qualifications, communication, partnerships, obtaining resources and much more.

2 Ten Factors for Successful E-Government

The accompanying research of MEDIA@Komm separated the following 10 factors (including more than 50 sub-factors, cf. overview) for successful E-Government:

R. Traunmüller (Ed.): EGOV 2003, LNCS 2739, pp. 452–455, 2003.

- Designing visions and strategies is essential. Strategies and measures should be guided by political assistance of city mayors or city councils to emphasize the importance of municipal E-Government.

- The new orientation towards the users requires an extensive modernisation of the administration. In connection with the creation of a virtual town hall, administrative structures must be fundamentally changed. E-Government requires project management skills and experience in change-management-processes. Important inner-administrative questions are "who are in charge of designing E-Government-strategies, projects and action plans"? Co-operation between different departments has to be implemented.

- Applications are at the "heart" of local community e-government. There are four dimensions of applications: information, communication, transactions and participation. Successful E-Government does not mean to simply offer existing services electronically via the internet. The challenge is to integrate different kinds of applications and to combine information with communicative elements and transactions. The technical aspect of transformations via the internet shows only one dimension, a series of organisational and strategical measures is necessary to create "new" applications in a virtual town hall.

- Costs and benefits have to be calculated. In doing so, municipalities should be aware of their targets and several target groups. Multiple targets are possible when offering online services: an increase of administration's efficiency or economies of scale, the improvement of services for the customers etc. An analysis of costs and benefits using defined and common criteria is absolutely necessary.

- The use of the right technology and the organisation of the technical equipment used are major elements of the virtual town hall – and more than that: they are a central requirement before e-government can be implemented at all. The necessary steps for planning and implementation include creating the technical infrastructure with in-house networking of workplaces, and implementing suitable software solutions for effective network-assisted cooperation. The introduction of electronic signatures requires a decision about which signatures should be used, and to what extent. In addition, a concept must be prepared and implemented for the necessary technical and organisational framework for the use of electronic signatures. Standards have to be developed and secure transactions require minimal security standards and data protection. E-government is often associated only with access to the Internet. This is an over-simplified view. One of the major hallmarks of the virtual town hall is the variety of possible forms of access: Internet, call centres, citizens' advice centres, kiosks, "voice government", mobile access, TV access and more. Which of these options is selected is a question of preference and the access which is available to the "customers".

- The qualification of staff, management, heads of departments and members of the city council is indispensable. Education and training of these groups is essential. If necessary they must be motivated to support the e-government-project. The citizens and the owners and managers of small and medium-sized businesses must not be forgotten: Here, additional measures to provide qualifications and greater competence can help to overcome the "digital divide" within society.

- Acceptance for E-Government has to be created. To heighten acceptance by councillors and the administrative staff, a wide variety of information channels can be used (e.g. Intranet, notice boards, information meetings, workshops). This must all be based on a communication strategy which, in a goal-oriented and detailed manner, defines what messages are to be communicated through which channels – and what feedback is desired. Citizens and local business companies are customers who have different interests. They also have to be approached in a specific way to make sure that the municipal E-Government–project will meet great acceptance.

- Co-operation among authorities and public-private-partnerships are further important factors for successful E-Government. Municipal administrations often have low experience in dealing with big IT-projects and have to decide the "make or buy"-question: "do we have enough knowledge" or "do we need external specialists"? Furthermore municipalities often are simply not used in cooperating with the private sector and have to learn how to conduct negotiations; management skills are not very common but required.

- E-Government is not a short-term-project. A sustainable implementation of E-Government-projects must guarantee sufficient budgets for personnel costs and capital investments. Knowledge management is one of the future skills.

- Municipal E-Government requires special legal knowledge. Sufficient budgets to ensure legal advice and/or specially trained employees should be available.

Table 1. Overview: factors for success and their sub-factors (Source: compiled by the German Institute of Urban Affairs)

	Factor for success	Sub-factors
1	Guiding principles and strategy	– Guiding principles for e-government – Overall strategy "Virtual town hall" – Integration of the guiding principles and strategy into wider guiding principles and strategies – Dealt with by the top leadership – Political support – Priorities and long-term planning for the project "Virtual town hall"
2	Organisation, project and change management	– Project organisation – Combination with administrative reform – Re-engineering of the procedural organisation, transaction process analysis and optimisation – Re-engineering of the structural organisation – Organisation of cooperation – Evaluation and monitoring of results
3	Applications	– Information – Communication – Transactions – Integration – Participation

Table 1. (continued)

	Factor for success	Sub-factors
4	Benefits and costs	– Citizens – Business companies – Guests – Administration – Politics
5	The right technology and organisation of the use of technology	– Workplace design – IT networking – hardware – Network-based software solutions – Core services and infrastructure – Electronic signatures – Technical platform – Access – Standards – Security
6	Competence, motivation and qualifications	– Staff – Management – Council/senior administrative staff – Users
7	Creation of acceptance, marketing	– Internal communication – External communication
8	Cooperation and partnerships	– Cooperation with other public authorities – Partnership with business companies – Cooperation with associations and initiatives – Exchange with science and research
9	Sustainable resources	– Financing – Personnel – Knowledge
10	Legality	– Legal competence – Permissibility of portal services – Operating structure of the portal – Integration of private expertise – Compliance with general obligations for portal operation – Legal provision of information services – Legal provision of communication services – Legal provision of transcription services – Changes in the law

Cross-Cultural Factors in Global E-Government

Edith Denman-Maier and Peter Parycek

Donau-Universität Krems
Abteilung Telekommunikation Information und Medien
Dr.-Karl-Dorrek-Straße 30
A-3500 Krems, Austria
{edith.maier,peter.parycek}@donau-uni.ac.at

Abstract. Today's Western democracies where most e-Government initiatives are being launched tend to be far from culturally homogeneous political entities. Most of them harbour large minorities who may not only speak different languages, but have different religions, use different scripts and differ in their cultural values, traditions and attitudes. We assume that these factors have an influence on their understanding of information distributed by public authorities and on their cognitive approach to knowledge representation.

1 Introduction

Apart from cultural background, factors such as education and training, profession, age and gender play an important role in the cognitive approach to information and knowledge. In our paper, however, we shall focus on (inter-)cultural factors. Our basic approach is one that regards cultural diversity as a source of enrichment rather than as a barrier to overcome which is why we consider intercultural competence as an important asset in information and knowledge management.

If traditional forms of information dissemination by the public sector are to be supplemented by electronic tools and methods, cultural customisation will have to be integrated into the design, presentation and delivery of information.

1.1 Cultural Customisation of Public Sector Information Portals

As far as design issues are concerned, those who develop and implement public sector web portals offering electronic services to citizens can refer to a growing number of publications, mostly in the HCI (human-computer interaction) and usability literature on internationalisation and localisation. These reflect an increasing awareness that developing truly effective interfaces for an international or multicultural audience requires more than just translating text. Interface elements affected by culture, such as colour, images, symbols, must be adjusted for cultural differences. Images, symbols and icons like words can raise problems because they can be understood differently by culturally diverse people when they do not share the knowledge of the context in which they are rooted. Even functionality is determined by social and cultural factors. Certain features, e.g. for encouraging interaction, might be taken for granted in one society, but met with disapproval in another.

R. Traunmüller (Ed.): EGOV 2003, LNCS 2739, pp. 456–459, 2003.

The European Union (EU) like other multinational organisations both in the public and private sector invest heavily in the cultural adaptation of their communication and dissemination products and activities. The EU has clearly recognised that a quest for harmonisation and coherence within the EU does not rule out preserving the cultural heritage of its member states. Instead we would like to argue that the two aspects complement each other because only if we respect the cultural values and traditions of our European neighbours, are we ready to cooperate with them more closely.

However, in most cases the smaller entities such as municipalities, regions or provinces of a country cannot afford to develop web offerings in a range of languages. But even those maintained by larger entities tend to be monolingual. Whether this shows a lack of awareness concerning the cultural diversity of the citizens they want to address or whether it is a deliberate choice because they consider a command of the national language(s) a sine qua non for successful integration, is really of no relevance. In either case the developers will want to reach the widest possible audience and will therefore endeavour to create websites, which are also accessible to people whose mother tongue is different from the official language(s) or who belong to a cultural minority.

2 Acessibility of E-Government Websites

Before the information relevant for e-government websites can be presented on-line it has to be captured, structured and organized. It tends to be derived from a great variety of sources mostly in the public sector. How can one classify and structure information in a way that it becomes accessible to people from all walks of life as well as to people from different cultural backgrounds?

It is comparatively easy to find guidelines and recommendations with regard to the compatibility of technical platforms or systems. When it comes to knowledge organisation and presentation we can observe a lack of standardisation and harmonisation. This was no problem at a time when the reach of local or regional authorities did not go beyond "natural" borders. However, faced with the growing mobility of citizens this is becoming an increasing problem or – rather – challenge even for municipal authorities. It is no longer sufficient to adhere to technical standards to exchange data and information with one's partners, but they are called upon to take into account the requirements and needs of new target groups to make the information widely accessible. Inclusivity, i.e. enabling all citizens to participate in public decision-making, has become one of the keywords in this strive for standardisation in the non-technical field. The accessibility guidelines developed by the World Wide Web Consortium (W3C) mark a first step in this direction (see below).

2.1 Background

As already mentioned, harmonisation in the structuring and presentation of information is essential for facilitating access to e-government websites. The problem arises at all administrative levels, but the higher the level the more intercultural the audience tends to be. Unfortunately, all the member states have been developing their own systems and approaches, which will make transnational coordination very difficult. Although we find similar e-government projects and initiatives at national as well as European level, there is a lack of coordination and harmonisation. Furthermore, any recommendations or quality standards which might be proposed cannot be enforced legally.

However, since Resolution No. 1720/1999/EC extends the interoperability objectives to include the service and application layers of trans-European telematics services, it might be necessary to adapt the national public sector information gateways. National and European experts are therefore called upon to work on harmonising current projects so as to conform to the above resolution.

Like most national administrations the EU administrative units are usually oriented towards national governments, administrations and corporate bodies rather than towards citizens. For the sake of democracy, the access of citizens to EU information will have to be improved and EU administrative processes and procedures will have to be made more transparent and easier to understand. This leads us to the next paragraphs, i.e. the accessibility of public websites.

2.2 Different Aspects of Accessiblity

Discussion about accessibility commonly refers to access for users with disabilities which tends to include visual, hearing and motor impairments. The number of people with disabilities is normally estimated to lie between 15 and 30 per cent of the total population.[1] It is more difficult to find figures on the numbers of people whose "disabilities" might be defined as cognitive which is probably due to a lack of generally accepted definitions or criteria with which to measure the phenomenon.

Today's democracies are far from being homogeneous nation states but tend to boast a culturally highly diverse range of different groups. Even though citizens might be expected to be proficient in the language(s) of their home or host country, it can be assumed that their varied cultural values, traditions and attitudes have an influence on their understanding of the content on web sites and their cognitive approach to knowledge presentation.

But the principles that guide web design to improve accessiblity for disabled users are equally applicable for improving the online experience of users coming from different cultural backgrounds.

The World Wide Web Consortium (W3C), an organisation that develops common protocols and promotes interoperability across the web, advises that web designers should be aware that many users are operating in contexts that are different to their own:

Apart from users not being able to see, hear, move or process some types of information easily or at all, the W3C also recognises that certain users

– may have difficulty reading or comprehending text
– may not speak or understand fluently the language in which the document is written.[2]

---

[1] A report by the US Census Bureau published in 1997 states that 19.6 per cent of the US population have a disability. (www.census.gov/hhes/www/disable/sipp/disab97/ds97t1.html)
[2] Web Content Accessibility Guidelines (WCAG) 1.0 World Wide Web Consortium (W3C) Web Accessibility Initiative (WAI). (www.w3.org/TR/WCAG10/) (working draft of version 2 available at: www.w3.org/TR/WCAG20/).

Guidelines, standards and legislation are being developed across the world to try to improve the accessibility of websites. The most influential to date is Section 508 of the Rehabilitation Act in the US.[3] In the UK, the Office of the e-Envoy has published *Guidelines for UK Government Websites* to help public sector organisations provide user-friendly and accessible websites.[4]

Since government websites are supposed to provide quick, easy, low cost access to services and information, it would be unfair to exclude some citizens from this additional means of communication. Besides, representatives from ethnic minorities might benefit even more from the range of employment and educational opportunities usually offered by government web sites. For example, women whose movements are restricted due to certain cultural values or traditions, might appreciate it if they can enjoy the advantages of finding out about such opportunities without having to leave their homes.

2.3 Practical Implementation

How to ensure universal access? There are a number of other considerations to be taken into account apart from following the guidelines for accessible design. Even if one follows accessibility recommendations, it is essential to involve real people. This is normally referred to as usability testing and focuses on observing how actual users interact with a site when completing a task. Rather than rely on an automated accessibility checking tool, web designers should therefore obtain the feedback from representatives from different cultural backgrounds.

Successful integration of minorities is only possible, if they are allowed to participate fully in the democratic decision-making process. This presupposes free and easy access to information about all aspects of public life. Even though public bodies are not (yet) legally obliged to take cultural diversity into account when delivering public sector information, it will pay off to do so in the long run since being excluded from democratic processes can lead to discontent and finally revolt against the decisions taken.

---

[3] Section 508 (www.section508.gov/).

[4] *Guidelines for UK Government Websites.* Office of the e-Envoy (www.e-envoy.gov.uk/weguidelines.htm).

Experiences of Take-Up of E-Government in Europe

Charles Lowe

e-Forum Working Group on Take-up and Benefits, e-Forum Association,
51 Rue du Moulin a Papier, B-1160 Bruxelles, Belgium
Tel: +44 20 8840 2397, Fax: +44 20 8840 2397
charles.lowe@btinternet.com

Abstract: This paper examines the experiences of driving take-up of eGovernment applications in Europe. It develops ten key actions that, if followed, result in a dramatic increase in eGovernment usage. The work breaks new ground in a number of areas including the recognition that the factors affecting take-up fall into two distinct groups. The first of these is a vital set of preconditions. The second of these is a set of factors all of which have been shown individually to raise take-up dramatically but only when the first set are in place. The biggest single factor is sharing of benefits with users.

1 Introduction

Public sector organisations across Europe have spent fortunes on eGovernment, but as yet have seen little benefit: citizens and organisations are still not using them much, as demonstrated for example by the Taylor Nelson Sofres 2002 survey [1]. This lack of usage in depth is hurting both the European public sector, which is suffering the cost of delivering an additional access channel and European citizens and organisations.

A Working Group [2] was therefore set up by e-Forum [3], the EC-sponsored European eGovernment association, to understand the key factors driving successful take-up of eGovernment applications and develop a set of guidelines for implementers on the best ways of rapidly achieving high take-up.

2 Methodology

A key finding of the Group is that there are two types of factor that influence take-up. The first set of factors is referred to as Necessary Conditions. Without these Necessary Conditions, services are unlikely to be much used, but they only work up to a threshold. Thus, people will not share sensitive information with the public sector unless they are comfortable about the security of their connection; once they are comfortable, further efforts to improve security will have little impact on take-up.

The second set of factors is referred to as Potential Drivers. These are factors that are key to achieving high take-up. When the right Necessary Conditions are in place, these Potential Drivers take over to determine usage. Thus, to extend the previous example, once users are comfortable about the security of their connection and other

R. Traunmüller (Ed.): EGOV 2003, LNCS 2739, pp. 460–463, 2003.

similar factors, they will only make the odd transaction. However if they perceive, say, a financial benefit to using eGovernment services, they will use them more intensely – double the benefit and take-up will grow substantially.

3 Necessary Conditions

A primary requirement is for *infrastructure*, to deliver the connectivity. Once the connectivity is adequate for the use though, any further increase in bandwidth has only a marginal impact on take-up, as was very evident when attempts to roll-out broadband preceded the applications that needed the extra bandwidth.

Unless users have *awareness* of any service, usage is bound to be low, as it will be until users have *acceptance* that an electronic service can deliver what they require.

The issue of *trust* is often quoted as the main reason why people will not access government services electronically, which feels intuitively correct: you worry what government will do with information that, now it is electronic, can be sent anywhere, accessed by anyone. Misuse somehow seems much easier than with paper. Add to that the seemingly ever-lower overall level of trust in which the public sector – across much of Europe – is held and you have a potent cocktail discouraging usage.

Yet intriguingly the statistics are at best equivocal on this. For example, the Taylor Nelson Sofres survey quoted earlier [1] found that the take-up of eGovernment, say in the UK in 2002 by citizens, was just 13%, whereas that for, say France was 25%. However 26% of people in the UK trusted electronic communications with the public sector as measured by the same survey whereas only 15% in France did. This very much supports the Group's contention that trust is a Necessary Condition

The need for security is often over-exaggerated by some public sector organisations, perhaps seeking justification to avoid modernisation. Support for this comes for example from a recent ICM/Hedra survey [4] that found that only 38% of UK citizens "would prefer not to use the Internet for public services because it is not secure", whereas an even more recent survey of senior UK public sector employees by the eGovernment Bulletin [5] found that 57% considered that "security concerns are impeding the public take-up of electronic services".

Because successful eGovernment relies on a fundamentally different delivery structure to paper government, a *process change* is often required anyway. Thus departments – and administrations – need to work together in ways they rarely have in the past to deliver services that centre round the citizen or organisation being served. This is a major change management challenge, needing a strong, high-level champion to resolve the many issues inevitably raised by changes in the balances of power.

User focus is the last of the necessary conditions the Group has identified, one element of which is interface design & navigation. With over 3000 [6] public sector websites in the UK and many more than that in more decentralized countries like Germany, the scope for confusion is high – with up to six layers of government in some countries, even those in the public sector get confused, so a post code-driven portal is essential. There is one now in the Netherlands and the UK [7].

The Group found only one serious 'repeller' – a factor that on its own reduces eGovernment take-up: credit cards, which selectively discourage the less well-off part of society (that will of course also benefit most from eGovernment).

Another element of user focus is appropriate education and skills, although studies have shown [8] that just giving people secure connectivity and good competence still does not drive up usage. Potential Drivers are needed, to encourage usage.

4 Potential Drivers

An essential – and obvious – requirement is *content* that users want to access. For example, eGovernment programmes initially focused on benefiting the sponsoring government/department, not the user, like tax collection. Where tax authorities have also subsequently implemented applications for returning money to citizens in the form of grants or allowances, take-up has been much higher though. For example, the percentage of applications for the UK's Child Tax Credit and Working Tax Credit received online is already far higher than the percentage of those in the UK filing tax returns online, even though the tax credit application has only recently gone online.

Another way of increasing take-up is *cultural alignment*. In Sweden & Denmark, one easy way of overcoming security concerns is to send people government-completed tax returns (on paper) for them to confirm (electronically, ideally) their correctness. There it is culturally acceptable; in the UK it probably would not be.

A major usage driver that is also strongly culturally related is *alternative channels*. Intermediaries are especially well placed to deliver eGovernment services. For example in Italy all tax returns are filed electronically through financial intermediaries. Intermediaries can also integrate the public sector elements into a more appealing whole – thus, again as in Italy, the filing of the tax return is just a small part of an overall financial service. With the loss of trust in the public sector, intermediaries can be used too to lend their trustable image to eGovernment services.

Another way of getting people to use new services is *communication* of benefits, yet it seems to have had very mixed results so far in the realm of eGovernment - eg in France it encouraged many more visits to the public sector portal, but no significant increase in transactions. Online advertising is impacted by three factors. The first is premature marketing, where the service is advertised before it is fully mature, permanently damaging peoples' perceptions. The second is the big difference between browsing and doing – if you've driven to a tax office, then a short wait is ok, but if you've gone there in the click of a button, the same time spent on authentication can be a turn-off. The third is that online products are almost unique in being deliverable half-built – advertisers have little experience of selling such products.

In short, advertising of online services will only work if the service being advertised fulfils a real need, and does it now. This view is supported by the finding that advertising of good eGovernment services to select groups of people – for example the legal community in Bremen – has produced spectacularly good results.

The final element that the e-Forum Working Group has identified is *sharing benefits*. Examples abound elsewhere in the world; in Europe, one example is the Belgian social security system (where those eligible for additional benefits are automatically sent cheques for these by the system), the French Vitale healthcare card (that has eliminated one billion paper claim forms, to date) and the UK tax credit system mentioned earlier. Such incentives, if they truly reflect a sharing of benefits, are considered by the Group to be the most effective way of motivating take-up.

However such sharing is considered by many as inappropriate to the current European culture. "Just think what the papers would say" is a common response.

Once citizens see real benefit from eGovernment in the form of cash and time saving, take-up will grow very rapidly – perhaps this is one public sector cultural issue that we should work to change. Certainly in the poll quoted earlier [4], citizens look to be very supportive of the idea, with 81% agreeing that they "would use the Internet to access public services more if it saved me money".

5 Results

From our work to date, ten key actions emerge that, if added to activities already in hand, will significantly increase take-up of eGovernment services in Europe:
1. Minimise the level of access security you need;
2. Work hard to be seen to be appropriately trustworthy by users;
3. Recognise that the hard part is organisational change;
4. Make it easy for users to find the services they want;
5. Research the most attractive content; prioritise delivery;
6. Recognise the cultural constraints;
7. Provide alternative payment methods if you must have credit cards;
8. Consider other channels for delivery of eGovernment services
9. Only advertise services that are fit for purpose; target advertising carefully;
10.Share benefits with users.

References

1. Government Online – An International Perspective, Taylor Nelson Sofres, November 2002 http://www.tns-global.com
2. The e-Forum Working Group consists of a mix of public, private and academic sector people, from across the EU. Those who have also made a significant contribution to this article include Doug Holmes (Author of "eGov"), Andre Wilkins (Ogilvy), Julian Hubbersgilt & Staveley Ferguson (London Borough of Hammersmith & Fulham), Prof. Francois Heinderyckx (Univ. Libre de Bruxelles), Prof. Herbert Kubicek (Univ of Bremen), Emilie Normann (office of the e-Envoy), Luis Ballester (Instituto de Economica, Publica), John Shaddock (Yorkshire & Humberside Assembly) and Tim Anderson (Norfolk CC).
3. www.eu-forum.org
4. ICM/Hedra poll December 2002 www.icmresearch.co.uk
5. Security Counts, a report by eGovernment Bulletin, April 2003, www.headstar.com
6. UK Public Accounts Committee August 2002 http://www.parliament.uk/commons/selcom/pachome.htm
7 www.UKVillages.co.uk
8. See for example Everybodyonline at www.citizensonline.org.uk

The Development of Electronic Government: A Case Study of Thailand

Wanchai Varavithya and Vatcharaporn Esichaikul

School of Advanced Technologies
Asian Institute of Technology
Pathumthani, Thailand
{St018576,Vatchara}@ait.ac.th

Abstract. This paper examines the development of electronic government (e-government) in Thailand. The development of information technology (IT) projects in Thai public agencies was initiated in the early 1990s, albeit without developing a national IT master plan or establishing a national IT agency. However, when many problems arose in the use of IT in public agencies, the Thai government formulated in 1996 the first national IT master plan to cope with e-governance problems. This case study illustrates the Thai e-government's development experiences and examines e-government strategic approaches. The lessons may be relevant to and may be a learning experience for countries at similar stages of development.

1 Introduction

Electronic government (e-government) development strategic approach can be classified as distributed and centralized [1]. In distributed strategic approach, the government encourages each agency to develop its own information technology (IT) systems without intervention but will consider linking those systems after completion. For the centralized strategic approach, the government plays a central role in the development of IT projects in public agencies.

In the past decade, Thailand has experienced with both strategic approaches. Studying the Thai governments' e-government development experience, other developing countries may learn to avoid failure and be able rationally to apply the e-government development approach.

2 IT Development in Thai Public Agencies

The development of IT projects in Thai public agencies was initiated in the early 1990s, albeit without developing a national IT master plan or establishing a national IT agency, such as the population database by the Ministry of Interior and tax computerization by the Ministry of Finance [2]. In the mid 1990s, the government promoted the use of Electronic Data Interchange (EDI) to increase efficiency and effectiveness of the government services in various public agencies, such as the

R. Traunmüller (Ed.): EGOV 2003, LNCS 2739, pp. 464–467, 2003.

Customs Department and the Port Authority of Thailand [3]. The first national IT master plan "Towards Social Equity and Prosperity: Thailand IT policy into the 21st century" was introduced in 1996 [4] and in 2001, "the Thailand Vision toward a Knowledge-based Economy" was formulated to pursue the knowledge-based and sustainable economy/society [5].

3 The Development Experience

It is imperative to understand that in the development of IT projects in the early 1990s, Thailand followed the distributed strategic approach, under which each public agency individually initiated and developed its IT projects. This approach has bred many problems, to name a few [6]:

- Different types of legacy systems
- Different types of data standard
- Inability to directly exchange data because of differences in data formats
- Each public agency collects duplication data with other existing database systems
- Multiple efforts in software development, etc.

With the national IT master plan in place since 1996, public agencies have gradually adopted the "whole picture" approach to their own IT master plan (i.e. ministry level and department level). The main driving force of the evolution is the active role of the National Information Technology Council (NITC) and the National Electronics and Computer Technology Center (NECTEC), which serve as a catalyzed agency. The integration of various government IT systems and the sharing of IT resources such as applications, network, information, and knowledge, has become a top priority in the development process. The expected outcome of integration, such as a one-stop service portal, government data exchange, government information services aim to increase the efficiency and effectiveness of government services and decision-making, and reduce investment costs. With the formation of the national IT master plan, the e-government objectives and missions became well defined and has directed IT development in public agencies toward an integrated-government objective. The relationship between IT projects and the IT master plan can be illustrated in figure 1.

Guided by the IT master plan, the government used both distributed and centralized strategic approaches together with the central IT agency to the e-government development.

The government took the distributed strategic approach with well-established e-government projects by forming a workgroup e-government project development with the national IT master plan model and linking those systems together to consolidate information and services using EDI or XML. This approach is proven to be a cost-effective approach, as public agencies can consolidate their own systems, and share resources and knowledge in pursuing the same objectives.

The government has also attempted to utilize the centralized strategic approach, especially on the national data network infrastructure and software applications. This approach intends to reduce IT investment cost and create a common standard of IT use amongst public agencies. The national IT agency has played an active role in this approach.

It is not feasible to describe all the e-government projects in Thailand in a single paper. Nevertheless, the e-government projects in compliance with a national IT master plan can be categorized into three groups: a) individual e-government projects (for example, the Thairegistration.com initiated by the Department of Commercial Registration); b) group of e-government projects (for example, the agriculture information project by the Department of Agriculture); and c) national e-government projects (for examples, Government Information Technology Services, and Government Data Exchange Center).

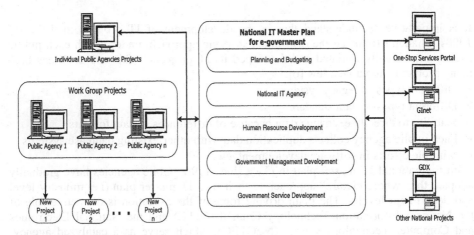

Fig. 1. The relationship between IT projects development and the national IT master plan.

4 Lessons Learnt

There are three main lessons learnt from Thailand's experience.

- Firstly, an individual e-government development without the national IT master plan and the establishment of the national IT agency can cause a chaotic mess. The national IT strategy provides a road map of where the e-government is at present and where it will be in the future. The wide range of subjects covered in the high-level national IT master plan must include all critical issues starting from vision, strategy, IT plan, re-organization framework to budget allocation scheme, human resource development, government management, and government services. The e-government developments must be routinely assessed to evaluate the impact of the national IT master plan and adjust it accordingly.

- Secondly, the catalyst role played by the national IT agency is vital to the process of e-government development in public agencies. The central national IT agency should be mandated and equipped with a power equal to ministerial level. Without such power, the national IT agency will not able to accomplish the tasks, which requires full co-operation with other public agencies. The national IT agency must also work closely with agencies and provide guidance so that the agencies explore their own innovative and creative potential in redesigning their own work processes using IT as a means to achieve the end.

- Finally, the formation of IT projects needing collaboration between various public agencies must start with a clear objective and vision together with advice and guidelines from the national IT agency. The collaboration tasks are not only in the area of technology but also in altering and updating the outdated laws that each of the public agency has or enacting new electronic support laws and regulations that facilitate the proliferation of e-governance, such as electronic signature, and security protection law.

5 Conclusions

This paper has shown that the e-government development approach used together with the national IT master plan and the national IT agency is the correct mix that supports and sustains the e-government project development, particularly in the context of a developing country. In Thailand, there are many individual autonomous, independent legacy systems located in various public agencies, which resulted from an absence of a national IT master plan. The need to integrate those systems has become a top national policy agenda. It should be noted that, the formation of the national IT master plan and the national IT agency is vital to the success of e-government development. Eventually, Thailand adopted the hybrid e-government project development with the central IT agency, which integrated both the centralized and distributed approach to the e-government development [1].

References

1. Chutimaskul, W.: E-Government Analysis and Modeling. 3rd International Workshop on "Knowledge Management in e-Government" KMGov-2002 proceeding, Schriftenreihe Informatik, volume 7, (2002) 113–124.
2. Durongkaveroj, P.: Computerization development in the public sector in Thailand. Economic and Social Commission for Asia and the Pacific, (1995) http://www.unescap.org.statgc/EGM/thailand.html
3. Thailand EDI Council: EDI Implementation in Thailand, (1997) http://www.nectec.or.th/bureaux/tedic/index.html
4. National Information Technology Committee of Thailand: Towards Social Equity & Prosperity: Thailand IT policy into the 21st century: IT 2000, (1996) http://www.nitc.go.th/document/publications.html
5. National Information Technology Committee of Thailand: National Information Technology Policy: IT 2010, (2002) http://www.nitc.go.th/itpolicy.html
6. National Electronics and Computer Technology Center: IT for Good Governance, ISBN 974-7577-13-5, (1999)

The Service to Businesses Project: Improving Government-to-Business Relationships in Italy

Marco Bertoletti[1], Paolo Missier[2], Monica Scannapieco[3],
Pietro Aimetti[1], and Carlo Batini[2]

[1] Gruppo Clas
{m.bertoletti,p.aimetti}@gruppoclas.it
[2] Università di Milano "Bicocca"
pmissier@acm.org
batini@aipa.it
[3] Università di Roma "La Sapienza"
monscan@dis.uniroma1.it

Abstract. The paper describes the main ideas and results of a project improving the government to business relationships in Italy by a cooperative architecture based on a Publish & Subscribe communication paradigm.

Keywords: e-Government, data quality, electronic service delivery

1 Introduction

In 1999, the Italian Public Administration started a pilot project, called Services to Businesses, which involves extensive data reconciliation and cleaning, as well as business process re-engineering, aimed at enhancing the relationship between citizens, businesses and the government agencies.

The initial focus was on simplifying the large number of transactions required for a business to register itself with various agencies, as well as to update their existing registry entries. Complicating the project is the fact that similar information about one business is likely to appear in multiple databases, each autonomously managed by different agencies that, historically, have never been able to share their data about the businesses. Furthermore, many errors were present in those databases, causing mismatches among different records that refer to the same business.

Because of these complications, the comprehensive approach chosen for the project followed two main strategies, aimed at improving the state of existing business data and at maintaining correct record alignment for all future data:

1 A "one stop shop" approach was followed to simplify the life of a business and to ensure the correct propagation of its data. In this approach, one single agency is selected as a front-end for all communication with the businesses. Once the information received by a business is certified, it is made available to other interested agencies through a Publish & Subscribe (P&S) mechanism.

R. Traunmüller (Ed.): EGOV 2003, LNCS 2739, pp. 468–471, 2003.

2 Extensive record matching and data cleaning was performed on the existing business information, resulting in the reconciliation of a large amount of business registry entries.

2   The Services to Businesses Project: A Cooperative Architecture

The Services to Businesses project, currently under development as part of the Italian e-Government initiative, aims at offering businesses a way to interact efficiently with central and local agencies in the Italian Public Administration (PA). Three central agencies are involved, namely the social security agency called INPS in the following, the accident insurance agency, called INAIL, and the chambers of commerce, called CoC. Agencies operate autonomously and they usually require accessing each other's data and services in order to fulfill business goals. Although this calls for inter-agency cooperation, the complexity of their organization and of their legacy information systems makes the migration to new and open systems impractical. The approach to cooperation among agencies followed in Italy to address this problem is based on the concept of Cooperative Information Systems (CIS), i.e., systems capable of interacting by exchanging services with each other. The general cooperative architecture for the Nationwide CIS network of the Italian P.A., is specialized to the Services to Businesses project in Figure 1. Besides transport and basic services, a cooperative services layer is shown, including application protocols, repositories, gateways, etc.. Each administration defines the set of cooperative interfaces that include data and application services available to other systems. The general architecture supports cross-administration applications that are assembled using those interfaces. In addition, for the purpose of the project, two specific features have been implemented. First, a central database (DB) has been created to manage all the records resulting from linking the identifiers of independent business records that pertain to individual agencies. This new repository provides agencies with a unified view of Italian businesses. The process of creating this new repository from the existing databases is sketched in the upcoming section. Second, an event notification service has been deployed in order to guarantee synchronization between the new unified view and the independent views that each administration still maintains. The event notification service has been implemented according to a Publish&Subscribe communication paradigm. The combination of these two extensions results in a clean base of business data whose high quality can be sustained over time. A number of administrative processes were re-engineered in order to take advantage of this architecture, following the main criteria of moving away from multiple front end transactions (business-to-agency), and towards a single front end transaction plus a number of back end transactions (agency-to-agency) that are supported by the cooperative architecture. In particular, specific agencies have been selected as front end entry points to businesses. Once these selected agencies accept and certify the quality of the incoming information, the messaging service (e.g., notification) is used to propagate it to other interested

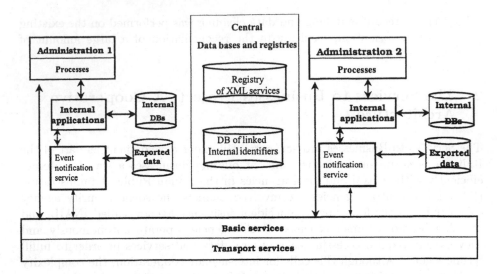

Fig. 1. A cooperative architecture for the Services to Business project.

domains. Results have been achieved in terms of reduction of per-transaction cost, reduction in the total number of transactions, and increased quality of the information acquired by the agencies.

2.1 Building the DB of Linked Internal Identifiers: Data Integration and Cleaning

In this Section we provide an overview of the steps followed to produce the DB of linked internal identifiers. Similar to what is done in the context of data warehousing, the project includes both schema and data integration, the latter requiring a complex record linkage activity. Six databases were included in the project. INPS provides four different databases, each representing a different view on the collection of all the owners and employees that are subject to Social Security regulations. INAIL contributes its single database of employees that are subject to work insurance obligations, and finally the CoC database is the official registry of all Italian businesses.

In order to determine the project scope and to identify the useful database pairs, the following key assumptions were used in the project. The main assumption is that all entities (and the corresponding extensions) in the CoC are considered in the integrated schema, since the database of the CoC is considered the official registry of businesses by law. Second, it was decided that an entity (and the corresponding extension) is within the scope of the project, if it appears in at least two of the schemas.

The general strategy for record linkage is the following. For each record, our goal is to determine which entity in the integrated schema it belongs to, by linking it to records in the other DBs. When linking is not feasible, it may still be possible to *explain* the record, i.e., to determine that it refers to a valid business. Thus, *unexplained* records are those that cannot be traced at all to a real business. The overall methodology consists of the following steps:

1 Build the conceptual schemas of INPS, INAIL, CoC;
2 Build the integrated conceptual schema, that, due to the above assumptions, results from the integration of the CoC conceptual schema and the common part between INPS and INAIL conceptual schemas;
3 Perform the record linkage activities, in order to identify and link all records that potentially refer to the extension of the integrated conceptual schema.

Figure 2 reports the final results of the record linkage process. The first column shows the total amount of records, that are then broken down into deleted (i.e., no longer active) and active Economic Agents. The fourth column gives the number of matched records, while the fifth one reports the unmatched but explained residuals, and the last column reports the unexplained residual records. It may be noted that the percentage of unexplained residuals is fairly low. The CoC database contains no unexplained records because it is considered as the benchmark. For the other databases, the number of unexplained residuals ranges from 0,15 millions to 0,2 millions in both INPS and INAIL databases.

	# of records	# of records deleted	# of active records	# of matched records	Residual records explained	Residual records not explained
CoC Business DB	6.6	0.7	5.9	3.2	2.7	0.0
INPS Business DB	2.5	0.2	2.3	1.95	0.2	0.15
INPS Owners DB	4.0	0.0	4.0	3.5	0.3	0.2
INAIL Business DB	7.1	3.7	3.4	3.1	0.15	0.15
Total	20.2	4.6	15.6	11.75	3.35	0.5

Fig. 2. Final results from the linkage process.

3 Conclusions

The major contribution of the paper is a solution for improving G2B relationships, that has been adopted in a real project and implemented in the context of an e-Government initiative. The idea of putting specific agencies in charge of the quality of specific information, and then having them propagate the information using a P&S system, can be generalized and adopted in similar contexts.

It Takes More than Two…
Developing a TANGO Arena for Regional Cooperation around E-Government

Sara Eriksén[1], Yvonne Dittrich[2], Markus Fiedler[3], and Marie Aurell[4]

[1] Department of Human Work Science, Media Technology and Humanities
[2] Department of Software Engineering and Computer Science
[3] Department of Telecommunications and Signal Processing
[4] Department of Business Administration and Social Sciences
Blekinge Institute of Technology
Box 520
SE-372 25 Ronneby
Sweden
{Sara.Eriksen,Yvonne.Dittrich,Markus.Fielder,Marie.Aurell}
@bth.se
http://www.bth.se

Abstract. The TANGO e-government arena is an on-going project in Southern Sweden, funded by the Innovative Actions of the European Regional Development Fund. The aim of the project is to establish cooperation between the public sector, private enterprise and university-based research in designing public e-services. Our starting point is e-government understood as co-construction of technology, society and citizenship in everyday life. This approach is based on the Scandinavian Tradition of Participatory Design, but also motivated by on-going technological development. In cooperating around development of new, integrated services, catering to various categories of users as well as to a growing diversity of mobile technologies, we are aiming to establish feedback channels between practice and theory, between use and design, and between different academic disciplines where we see a need to synchronize the models and methods we work with. Our current research questions focus on exploring and managing multi-perspectivity as a resource for design.

1 Introduction

This is a position paper about developing a regional arena for cooperation around e-government. The authors are involved in research and teaching at four different departments at Blekinge Institute of Technology, a university in Southern Sweden with a profile in applied IT. Among us, we represent five different scientific disciplines: business administration, telecommunications, computer science, informatics and human work science.

Although we represent different research traditions and approaches, we all share the belief that it is crucial for design and development of technology to be grounded in an understanding of *actual, everyday use of technology*. In cooperating within the

R. Traunmüller (Ed.): EGOV 2003, LNCS 2739, pp. 472–475, 2003.
© Springer-Verlag Berlin Heidelberg 2003

arena for e-government around design and development of new public services, many
of them integrated and catering to various categories of users as well as to a growing
diversity of mobile technologies, we are aiming to establish long-term mutual
feedback channels between practice and theory, between use and design, and between
different academic disciplines, where we see a growing need to synchronize the
models and methods we work with. [1]

Our current shared research questions are, given this background, pragmatic but
not trivial; we are focusing on exploring and managing multi-perspectivity as a
resource for design of e-government. In this paper we briefly describe some of the
dimensions of multi-perspectivity that we are working with, and how.

1.1 Background – Developing a Case for Multi-perspectivity

During the past three years, two of the authors, Dittrich and Eriksén, have developed
interdisciplinary research cooperation around design of IT in the area of e-government, mainly within the framework of the DitA project (*Design of IT in Use –
supportive technologies for services to the citizens*, funded by the Swedish Agency for
Innovation Systems, VINNOVA, 2000-2002). Although coming from different
disciplines, we share an interest in the Scandinavian Tradition of Participatory Design
and evolutionary systems design. The DitA project focused on computer support for
front office employees in one-stop shops and the integration of municipal intranet
applications with public service provision via the Internet.

It was during this research cooperation that we discovered, on the one hand, the
rich complexity of on-going design activities that are part of emerging e-government
technologies and work practices, and, on the other hand, how combining perspectives
from different disciplines helped us to seriously challenge our own assumptions and
develop new understandings of IT in use and the implications these might have for
design and development of IT. [2]

2 Thematic Arenas Nourish Growth Opportunities – TANGO

During the autumn of 2002, the DitA project was phased into a new, up-starting
project, the TANGO e-government arena. This is one of five arenas within TANGO
(*Thematic Arenas Nourish Growth Opportunities*), an on-going regional project
partially financed by the Innovative Actions of the European Regional Development
Fund (ERDF).[1] The region, in this case, consists of the two southernmost counties in
Sweden, Skåne and Blekinge.

Within each thematic arena, the ambition is to establish concrete, problem-based
and development-oriented cooperation between the public sector, private enterprise
and university-based research.

---

[1] http://europa.eu.int/comm/regional_policy/innovation/index_en.htm

2.1 Coordinating Different Rhythms and Rationales

The TANGO arenas are being co-funded by ERDF for two years. During this time, the aim is to run several specific, short-term research and development projects together with different municipalities and ICT companies on each arena. Currently, three different research and development projects, chosen, rigged and owned by three different municipalities in the region, are in process on the e-government arena. These projects are being run in parallel during 6-12 months.

Thus, as researchers, we are being forced to 'dance to a faster rhythm' on the TANGO arenas than we are used to, and to keep pace with external partners in real life design projects. Paradoxically, this clearly and collectively enforced rhythm may help us researchers step beyond our own disciplinary boundaries and find ways to cooperate between departments, not only in the short-term problem-oriented projects, but also around building a platform for long-term multi- and interdisciplinary e-government research. [3]

3 Co-constructing E-Government

Our starting-point is e-government understood as co-construction. In order to link theory and practice, and enhance mutual learning, in discussions between disciplines and across organizational boundaries, we use a simple figure of on-going design-oriented interactions (fig.1) to highlight shifting foci on relationships of co-development of services, citizenship and technology. The figure, albeit simple, helps explicate concrete examples of this on-going everyday co-development, presented from the different perspectives that we, as researchers from different disciplines and traditions, and practitioners from different organizations and groups, represent in the project. In this way, we are able to explore and discuss working relations of technology production and use that we see as central to what is actually making e-government happen - or not happen. [4] The main challenge in this area, as we see it, concerns making visible, and developing supportive infrastructures for, the continuing local adaptation, development and design in use of integrated IT and public services. [5]

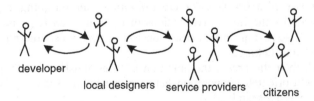

developer   local designers service providers   citizens

Fig. 1. A simple figure of on-going design-oriented interactions in co-development of e-government

Another way to deliberately make use of multi-perspectivity as a resource for theory-building within the e-government arena, is by exploring - in depth, and using concrete examples from our projects - shared concepts of relevance for design and development of e-services. Accountability and accessibility are two such concepts that we are currently working with. Accountability in an ethnomethodological sense, taken seriously as an issue for design of e-services, may drastically change both the way we understand information and communication in organizations and society, and the way we design technology to support it. [6], [7], [8] At the same time, accountability and accessibility in telecommunications research rely heavily on mathematical models for optimization, yet are beginning to spill over into tentative discussions about users' experiences of e-services, and how much users need, or want, to know about the infrastructure in use. Surely, we could learn from these differences in 'shared' concepts?

4 Concluding Remarks

We have briefly sketched some of the ambitions, ideas and explorative methods with which we are currently working within the TANGO e-government arena. In parallel with on-going research and development, we are planning an interdisciplinary program for higher education in e-government. That, however, is another story.

References

1. Dittrich, Y., Eriksén, S.: Situated Innovation. Exploring new forms of co-operation in innovation and design between researchers, user-groups and ICT providers. Paper presented at the Nordic R&D Conference on University and Society Cooperation, Ronneby, May 2003.
2. Dittrich, Y., Eriksén, S., Hansson, C.: PD in the Wild; Evolving Practices of Design in Use. In: Proceedings from PDC'2002, Malmö, Sweden (2002), pp.124–134.
3. Dittrich, Y., Eriksén, S., Wessels, B. :From Knowledge Transfer to Situated Innovation. Cultivating spaces for co-operation in innovation and design between academics, user-groups and ICT providers. Paper presented at the conference Innovations in Europe: Dynamics, Institutions and Values, Roskilde, Danmark, May 2003.
4. Suchman, L.: Working Relations of Technology Production and Use. In: Journal of Computer Supported Cooperative Work 1994 (2), 21–39
5. Dittrich, Y., Ekelin, A., Elovaara, P., Eriksén, S., Hansson, C.: Making e-Government Happen. Everyday co-development of services, citizenship and technology. In: Sprague, Jr., R.H. (ed.): Proceedings of the Thirty-Sixth Annual Hawaii International Conference on System Sciences, HICSS-36, Hawaii, January 2003.
6. Dourish, P.: Where the Action is. The Foundations of Embodied Interaction. MIT Press, Cambridge, MA, USA (2001)
7. Eriksén, S.: Designing for Accountability. In: Berthelsen, O., Bødker, S., Kuutti, K. (eds.), NordiCHI 2002 Proceedings of the Second Nordic Conference on Human-Computer Interaction, October 19th–23th 2002, Århus, Denmark (pp.177–186).
8. Eriksén, S.: (2002), Mobile Services – a Different Way of Seeing. Organizations as on-going activities and cultivation of relationships. (In Swedish) Paper presented at the Nordic Radio seminar on mobile services, Gothenburg, October 10th –11th 2002. http://nrs.s2.chalmers.se/

Towards a Semantic E-Community

Youlin Fang, Weihua Zhang, Dongqing Yang, and Shiwei Tang

Department of Computer Science and Technology,
Peking University,
Beijing, China
{ylfang,zwh,dqyang,swtang}@db.pku.edu.cn

Abstract. With the extensive application of the World Wide Web, an important application is community management, many governments have built district-oriented websites to serve the citizens who live, work in the community, named as e-community. The e-community should be up-to-date, personalized and flexible to provide information. Furthermore, they should be embedded with knowledge that can be utilized for content analysis and marketing intelligence and above all with minimal administrative overhead.

In this paper, we first systematically review major problems existing in the e-community, then we we show an practical project designed for the municipality of Ningbo, China, exploiting the currently emerging data exchange and metadata representation standards of the web to address such kinds of problems. And finally and we could see that inhabitants may benefit more from the e-community while constructing a semantic e-community under our methodology.

1 Introduction

For many governments, an e-community provides regional and location-based information which the citizens living in a community needs. Such websites are used to register various organizations, companies, hospitals etc., and various services they provide, and also to provide citizens with online help. The success of an e-community direct affects and reflects the efficiency of the municipality. As the e-community enables the municipalities entirely new ways of administration (e.g. town functionality planning), it revolutions the way the government interact with citizens and companies in the district. E-community face many problems [1,2,3]:

- Plenty of services and multiple service catalogs are very common, making it difficult to maintain a unified website thus giving the citizens a unified portal;
- The problem of responsive online services support (Most electronic catalogs and online shops do not capitalize the interactivity available on the Web.);
- The difficulty of maintenance such complex e-community and the cooperative problem among different divisions in maintenance;

R. Traunmüller (Ed.): EGOV 2003, LNCS 2739, pp. 476–479, 2003.

- Most websites give (many) pages with few relevant to a given topic and even unrelated to the topic the user is interested in.

As a natural consequence, we have developed the E-Community Management System (ECMS). The founding idea of ECMS is to provide an open way to cooperatively build an e-community and to update its contents. The main aim of this paper is to describe our experience of how to fully utilize RDF (Resource Description Framework) and RDF schema for use in describing Web documents so as to make the website into an semantic web infrastructure. The contributions of this paper are (a) a detailed specification of metadata infrastructure model that well support resource discovery and thus make a semantic e-community, (b) how to make an e-community easier to manage knowledge, and (c) how to make an e-community more valuable to service promotion, municipal service and solutions.

2   Designing a Semantic E-Community

In this section we address four major kinds of resource descriptions needed in the constructing and maintenance of e-community as we do in implementing Haishu E-community management system.

2.1   Descriptions of Information Resources

We utilize RDF(Resource Description Framework)[4] as the basic script to describe resource information. When RDF is used as a resource descriptor, it includes assigned (or, non-derived) metadata and content (or, derived) metadata. Assigned metadata includes metadata values as signed by external users and which are not derivable from the actual content of the data object. Examples include name of the author, title, and pixel resolution for images. Content metadata examples include number of pixels in an image, size of a file, and aspect ratio.

such site semantics denotes various kinds of formal description of the 'meaning' of an community's different URLs. Many kinds of RDF schemas for classifying the site's URLs have been proposed in the ECMS. Such information is useful for implementing diverse goals of analysis as identifying association rules between purchases of goods, requiring service, or site administration improvements such as determining differences between site designers' goals and visitors' actual behavior, identifying semantically meaningful navigation episodes, improving the interface, and characterizing the workload of a site.

2.2   Descriptions of Business Resources

Business resources are a wide area of assets. In the same way as information resources they have to have a structured description to make them maintainable, usable, and reusable. Business resources are described through a vocabulary that captures what citizens talk about and act upon in their everyday life. The descriptions of business resources have traditionally been captured using entity-relationship representations and conceptual modeling languages. However, in ECMS, structured document representations such as XML have been favored. In these cases DTDs (Document Type Definitions) and XML schema have been used to structure the documents, business objects and their relations.

2.3 Descriptions of Knowledge

in ECMS, we use our own with a multitude of metadata representations. The e-community widely exploits many-to-many data-interchange medium, and it poses new requirements for the exchange format:

- *Universal expressive power.* Because it is not possible to anticipate all potential uses, a Web-based exchange format must be able to express any form of data.
- *Syntactic interoperability.* Applications must be able to read the data and get a representation that can be exploited. J2EE Software components like parsers or query APIs, for instance, should be as reusable as possible among different applications. Syntactic interoperability is high when the parsers and APIs needed to manipulate data are readily available.
- *Semantic interoperability.* One of the most important requirements for an exchange format is that data be understandable. Whereas syntactic interoperability is about parsing data, semantic interoperability is about defining mappings between terms within the data, which requires content analysis.

2.4 Internet Electronic Service Catalogs

The growing importance and potential of the Internet for new electronic means of conducting community management has motivated many companies to offer their services and products online through electronic markets. By offering a multimedia representation of services, combined with classification and retrieval support, in addition to interfaces to other market services, companies registered in Haishu E-community management system are the suppliers of products and services, interacting with their potential customers in the district through the service catalogs.

The different types of information relevant for an IESC can be summarized as follows:

- *Structured service information* enables a quick search for services especially in a large number of homogeneous services registered in the service catalogs. Usually the most important features of services are organized as well-structured data sets. Examples of such features are price, service identification number, name, service time, etc. The structured information is stored in relational databases and can easily be offered online.

- *Unstructured product information* such as multimedia presentations, extensive textual and graphical service descriptions and information as well as company backgrounds enhance structured service information. The form of the unstructured information varies from documents to complex multimedia data structures.
- *Customer-generated information* appears in different forms: ratings of services and products, contributions to discussions, citizen's testimonials or comments. Some of the customer-generated information is direct related to specific services as for example ratings, testimonials and comments and must be linked to other information about the service. Another type of customer-generated information such as discussions or communities is unstructured and topic oriented. This makes it more difficult to connect them to a specific service, compared to service-related information.
- *External information* is relevant information, which is produced by independent, external sites. It can have any of the above-mentioned forms of internal information.
- *Intermediate search results* are a selected subset of the whole service catalog. As these results reflects the most common concerns, they may be listed according to the search frequency with the same search condition.

The above information pools can be available in different forms and might have various reasons of importance for particular branches.

3 Conclusions and Future Work

We have presented techniques how to build a citizen-friendly E-community that support resource discovery. Our experiences are very promising. We employ RDF as the main metadata description language and have developed many metadata specification to make the E-community more useful special for the citizens in the district who use the E-community. The practical project designed for the municipality of Ningbo, China seems working well, and inhabitants may benefit more from the e-community while constructing a semantic e-community under our methodology.

References

[1] Sheng, Q.-Z., Benatallah, B., Dumas, M.: SELF-SERV: A Platform for rapid Composition of Web Services in a Peer-to-Peer Environment. In VLDB2002.
[2] Martin, P., Eklund, P.: Embedding knowledge in Web documents. Computer Networks, 31 (1999):1403–1419
[3] Nakayama, T., Kato, H., Yamane, Y.: Discovering the gap between Web site designers' expectations and users' behavior. Computer Networks, 33(2000):811–822
[4] Brickley, D., Guha, R.-V.: Resource Description Framework (RDF) Schema Specification. W3C Proposed Recommendation, 03 March 1999,
http://www.w3.org/TR/PR-rdf-schema

Governing Internet in Korea: NEIS and Domain Names

Chan-Mo Chung

Korea Information Strategy Development Institute
cmchung@kisdi.re.kr

Abstract. During the last few years there have been many confrontations between the government and the private sector over Internet governance in Korea. Two cases are examined: NEIS and domain name governance. The case of NEIS shows that the public interest concerns should be given serious consideration at the early stage of building e-strategies. For the case of domain names it is suggested that the respective role of the government and the private sector in Internet regulation should be complimentary rather than exclusive.

1 Introduction

As of the end of 2002, Korea has about 26million Internet users (59.4% of the total population) who regularly surf the Web. Over 10 million households are hooked up to the high-speed Internet network based on xDSL technology. The figure represents 70 percent of Korean households, suggesting that the country is at the forefront of the broadband service in the world. A Brown University study (Global e-Government, 2002) ranked Korea second among the 198 nations in e-government performance.

The growth of the Internet community produced not only virtues such as the expansion of e-commerce and e-government but also vices that include the circulation of indecent Internet contents and computer viruses. Some form of order is required for the sustainable development of the Internet community. In setting laws and principles for Internet usage, conflict of interest and divergent beliefs among actors have been revealed. Two cases of conflict that attracted public attention are examined: NEIS and domain name governance.

2 National Education Information System (NEIS)

The Korean government introduced NEIS as part of the e-government project to connect 10,870 primary and secondary schools to 16 educational boards to handle educational affairs electronically. Under the existing computing system, CS, information about students is collected and managed directly by school principals on separate school servers in each school.

Since 2000 the government has injected about 52 billion won towards the establishment of NEIS. It is expected that NEIS will have a return of 1.4 trillion won during the next five years. The system enables information sharing among parents, graduates, schools and education agencies. In addition, it significantly reduces the need for paper documents. Even when paper documents such as diplomas, academic transcripts are required, it can be applied for online. At the time, the system is in its final stage of completion. Most schools have already established the information database and have begun to utilize the system.

However, the teachers union opposed to the system, threatening to go on massive strike. The union requested that the government give up the program, arguing that it would pose a threat to the privacy of students and teachers. On May 12 2003, the National Human Rights Commission gave support to the opposition by deciding 6-to-4 that three categories of information (school management/ students' academic performance, health and enrollment records) required constitutional protection of privacy. The Commission recommended that each school revert back to the use of an intranet to store such private information, while enhancing the security level of the system. The Commission claimed that inestimable damage could result if hackers managed to break into the network.

Counter-criticism also exist over the Commission's decision:

1. the old system isolated within a school is far more vulnerable to security breaches than NEIS, although damage may be limited in scope. Enhancing security would significantly raise costs.

2. the benefits of the project is expected to be significant. Privacy protection may be upgraded to the extent that cost permits when the new system is in operation

This case shows a typical type of confrontation between privacy groups and the IT efficiency proponents. The government has failed to persuade each side to a compromise or to present its own position consistently. Korea still has to go a long way to find out a win-win solution.

3   Governing Domain Names

3.1 .KR Governance

The Ministry of Information and Communication (MIC) founded the Korea Network Information Center (KRNIC) to manage the allocation of Internet domain names and IP addresses. KRNIC is composed of about 50 staff members headed by the president under the guidance of a board of directors. Within the organization, KRNIC hosts the Number & Name Committee (NNC) and Korea Domain Name Dispute Resolution Committee (KDDRC).

The NNC claims that it inherited the tradition of private pioneership that initially introduced Internet into Korea. The committee studies, reviews and recommends regulations and policies for .KR domain names. As of December 2002, the number of .KR registered domain names is approximately 500,000. This number is expected to double when KRNIC rolls out a 'Korean letters.kr' service and foreigners are allowed to register .KR domain names.

The KDDRC was officially launched on January 4, 2002 to resolve the disputes involved in .KR domain names. The committee is an alternative dispute resolution mechanism that was established to efficiently settle a rapidly increasing number of disputes related to registration and use of domain names. In 2002, there were 54 filings, 20 transfers, 7 cancellations, 12 withdrawals, 6 dismissals and 9 pending cases.

The KRNIC Board is composed of the KRNIC President, the NNC Chair, the KDDRC Chair, the .KR administrative contact, the MIC Director General for Internet Policy and some honorable professionals. The Minister for Information and Communication appoints the Board Chair-elected and the KRNIC President-elected.

3.2 The Dynamic Market and the Consumer

A host of companies are operating Internet domain businesses, and relatively new technologies such as keyword, voice recognition and graphic-based addresses are competing with each other in the fledgling market. The keyword service allows users to access web-sites by just entering the name of a company, individual, or other keyword. It employs search engines like Lookup, CNRP and LDAP. Netpia is the leading company providing the Korean character keyword service.

The current domain name system is based on the English ASCII code. Various multi-lingual domain names have been experimented with. VeriSign started to provide 'Korean letters.com' and 'Korean letters.net' services in January 2003. KRNIC's 'Korean letters.kr' service will be underway sometime this year. KRNIC also developed a number domain and keyword service for mobile Internet users. Number domain subscribers can enter a set of numbers to access a web site registered under the mobile number address system. ENUM, a protocol that converts a telephone number into a URL, is being tested for operation.

Consumers and businesses, however, do not seem to benefit much from these new services. Some quasi-domain name service providers, even without any preparation for the stable resolution of their services, were eager to collect pre-registration fees in advance. In addition, trademark holders are perplexed with the increase and variety of cyber-squatting of their names. Furthermore, consumers are often misled to unexpected and even offensive sites.

3.3 Internet Address Management Bill

Faced with these market developments, the MIC formally proposed a Draft of Internet Address Management Bill in September 2002. The bill finalizes a set of regulations that will control and manage the country's Internet address system, a move that aims to discourage individuals and enterprises from abusing Internet addressing resources.

The bill is intended to manage the Internet IP and domains systematically. It contains measures to enhance the stability of the Internet addresses management. As well, it obliges the MIC to set up comprehensive plans for managing and developing online addresses periodically. Furthermore, it provides a mechanism and criteria for settlement of domain disputes, and the protection of Internet address users.

The bill, once enacted, will guarantee that all Internet users, related private organizations and government agencies can voice their opinions equally. To that end, an Internet Address Policy Review Committee will be established. The KRNIC will be transformed into the 'Korea Internet Promotion Agency,' taking on greater responsibility to push for the development of next-generation Internet addresses. As the market and technology develops, the bill leaves the possibility that some different agencies may take charge of IP, domain addresses and other next-generation Internet address systems.

In response to the concerns that the expansion of regulatory power of the government or semi-governmental agencies for controlling the Internet address system could lead to over-regulation, the bill ensures a minimum involvement approach in the value added name services. A voluntary certification system among private service providers would be supported.

Lastly, the draft law makes sure that the rightful domain name owners maintain their web sites while at the same time blocking cyber-squatters from abusing the Internet address system. This would give more credibility to the decision of the KDDRC and reduce the rate of appeal to the court.

The initial response from the private sector to the bill however was not a warm one. The professional domain name dealers and registras worried that the bill would introduce stricter regulations on their businesses. Civil activists and members of the NNC feared that they would lose their voice in the decision making process. And academics warned that the law was premature since there are only a few precedents overseas and the present situation is not so bad enough to require an overhaul.

However, the situation has changed slowly in favor of the bill. The number of consumer complaints has not been reduced. Quasi-domain names have raised far greater concerns over cyber-squatting. There is growing consensus that limited government intervention is necessary to keep consumer confidence on the Internet address system as a whole. The bill is expected to pass the parliamentary procedure by the end of this year.

4 Conclusion

During the last few years there have been many confrontations between the government and the private sector over Internet governance. Generally speaking, government regulation sneaks in wide areas of Internet activities where private actors have traditionally set rules among themselves. This was caused partly by the increased social importance of the Internet and partly by the failure of the private sector to effectively regulate Internet misuse.

On the other hand the case of NEIS reveals that the government has taken a few missteps in pursuing e-government projects. The effect on public interest including human rights has not been seriously tested at the early stage of building e-strategies.

As a result, role defining and confidence building is necessary. The respective role of the government and the private sector in Internet regulation should be complimentary rather than exclusive. The government should focus on the area of private sector failure and strategic planning. Both sides need to be more receptive to the other's opinion.

ICT in Belarus

Mikhail Doroshevich and Marina Sokolova

Republic of Belarus

Abstract. Major developments of the years of 2001-2002 prove that the ICT sector consisting of various sub-sectors (e.g., telecommunications, electronics, software, hardware, services, etc.) is expanding and infiltrating business, administration, education in Belarus. While awareness of these dynamics is growing, Belarusian government is already pursuing an array of ICT-related laws and regulations. Overview of the governmental ICT initiatives shows that the key focus is the development of telecommunication infrastructure, widespread introduction of information technology to government in order to collect and process data and information security which are regarded as a step of transition to information society. "Electronic Belarus" is oriented generally to organizational and technological upgrading of the public administrations. Issues of wide public electronic access to information and participation in democratic process, transparency of public administration are not mentioned in the programme. But the fact that e-government is proclaimed as a perspective creates opportunities for further work in this direction.

ICT has very quickly come to play important role in Belarusian society being used by companies and private individuals to engage in business, research, the collection of information and, more generally, communications in the country. According to the results of a poll conducted in 2002 by the Institute of Sociology and Social Technologies of the National Academy of Science and published by Belorusskaya Gazeta 40 per cent of Belarus' population is computer literate. More than a quarter (27 per cent) of respondents have access to the internet but only one tenth of them access the internet daily. More than one fifth (22 per cent) of those who access the internet do it more than once during the week, 29 per cent access the net several times a month, while 39 per cent go online less than once a month. One tenth of those polled said they were unaware of the internet. 62 % of Belarusian internet users live in Minsk, the capital of the country. Regional centers make up 23 per cent of internet users.. Meanwhile, cities with over 10,000 inhabitants, claim 13 per cent of Belarus internet users, up from 11 per cent last spring. The most active internet visitors are between 17-22 years old, comprising 40 per cent of Belarusian internet users. 23-29 year olds, meanwhile, make up 28 per cent of users, while 30-39 year olds make up 15 per cent. The 16 year old and younger crowds make up only 8 per cent of Belarusian internet population. 40-49 year olds make up 6 per cent of internet users, while 50-59 and 60-over make up 2 and 1 per cent of Belarusian internet users respectively. Students and young people, therefore, continue to make up two-thirds of internet users. Currently, however, about 3000 elderly people use e-mail, generally to correspond with their relatives abroad. The majority of users are men, at 75 per cent. 41 per cent of internet users have a higher education, while 28 per cent have an unfinished higher education.

R. Traunmüller (Ed.): EGOV 2003, LNCS 2739, pp. 484–487, 2003.
© Springer-Verlag Berlin Heidelberg 2003

At the same year the Information Technologies Enterprise and the Institute of Technical cybernetics together with the University of Mannheim have taken part in the international TeSIAC (Telemedicine System for Image Analysis and Consultation) project to create a system for the analysis of and consultations on thyroid cancer cases in Belarus. TeSIAC is intended to interconnect the Radiation Medicine and Endocrinology Institute, the Minsk city cancer clinic and Tumor Center and the Radiation University of Wurzburg. The TeSIAC database will contain 3D ultrasound images of every patient's thyroid glands before and after operating.

Icetrade.by, the website of the National Marketing and Market-Determined Prices Centre is offering information on international government tenders and auctions. The site is intended to provide Belarusian Ministries and government organisations with updates on more than 5,000 tenders and auctions all over the world. It lists specialized bulletins and reports of trade delegations abroad, along with a review of 600 websites. Icetrade.by also maintains information on national tenders by Belarusian companies and government

In 2001 Priorbank was the first bank in Belarus to issue Visa internet cards for virtual payments. In the end of 2002 Belarusian portal Tut.by has recorded a profit, and return on investment (100KUSD) is expected in 2-5 years. More than 20,000 users visit the portal daily. TUT.BY offers internet, educational, cultural and other resources. Services offered by Tut.by include information on job openings and pager messages. In addition, Tut.by offers hosting and e-mail services to 300 companies and organisations. Furthermore, the scope of the portal's advertising services is constantly growing. Online advertising sales on Belarusian sites reached E39,986 by the end of 2002, according to a report by BelarusMedia agency. This figure doubles 2001 online advertising sales which totalled E19, 993. Belarusian online shopping service shop.by has launched an internet payment system, EasyPay.by, for customers to pay for products bought through its service. Shop.by began two years ago and now has 60 independent shops using its services. The company said the most popular items bought online include electronics, CDs, books and GSM mobile phones through the internet. On average, customers spend more than $100 (E111) on a single purchase. Last year, the company said overall turnover exceeded $2.6m (E2.9m), and $400,000 (E445,000) at Christmas. Combined, all the shops belonging to the system generate about 20,000 hits daily and last year, customers made 27,000 purchases

But in general Belarusian companies are still slow to see the benefits of the interne to raise awareness of their business and connect with companies, but e-mail and electronic accounting systems are well-established. Websites are used by 29.6 per cent of companies in Belarus, according to a recent survey by the Institute of Privatization and Management in Minsk, in cooperation with CIPE in Washington. PCs are used by 88.4 per cent of the 378 respondents, and 70.4 per cent of managers have introduced electronic business accounting systems in their enterprises. The survey also reports that electronic documents are used by 40 per cent of the companies, and that 70.4 per cent of managers use the internet and e-mail services

By the end of 2002 a number of governmental portals were created in Belarus. The Supreme Court for Economic Affairs in Belarus has launched a new website (http://court.by/), which details the procedures and operating principles of the economic courts. On the website questions about bankruptcy procedure are dealt with in detail and the order of the reference in economic courts of Belarus is described. Visitors to the site can also view the responses of judges of the court to questions about bankruptcy procedures. President Lukashenko of Belarus has signed a decree on the creation of a "national legal internet portal"(http://ncpi.gov.by). According to the decree, the portal created under the authority of the National Centre for Legal Information of the Republic of Belarus is to become the main governmental e-resource on legislation and the government's "Information Programme". The portal is aimed at providing citizens with information about legislation and to improve governmental judicial activities. The Belarusian Ministry of Defence has launched a new military website (http://www.mod.mil.by/) with information about the Office's tenders, recruitment practices, and the military dog-breeding center. There is also a special feedback page for users to get answers to questions about serving in Belarusian army.

This list of major developments of the years of 2001-2002 proves that the ICT sector consisting of various sub-sectors (e.g., telecommunications, electronics, software, hardware, services, etc.) is expanding and infiltrating business, administration, education in Belarus. While awareness of these dynamics is growing, Belarusian government is already pursuing an array of ICT-related laws and regulations. In 1991 Council of Ministers of the Republic of Belarus adopted the *Programme of Informatization of the Republic of Belarus for 1991-2000 years*. At the same time Belarusian Found for Informatization was established by the government. But because of the lack of funding and political will only few projects were accomplished and in 1993 the programme was suspended. The real basis for the present government policy in the ICT sphere was laid by the *Law on Informatization adopted in 1995*. In this document such concepts as "data", "information resources", "information network", "information product", "information services" were defined as subjects for law for the first time. In 1998 inter-departmental commission on informatization was organized. The strategy worked out by the Commission was adopted by the Presidential decree in 1999. The *Concept* states that transition to the information society is the major objective of the Belarusian government strategy in the sphere of informatization. Development of infrastructure and security of information are pointed out as the basis for the transition. National *telecommunications* policy is based on the following legal acts: Concept of the development of telecommunications of the Republic of Belarus (1993); Programme of telecommunications development 2001-2005 (2001). In 2000 Law on Electronic Document was adopted in the Republic of Belarus.

According to the Concept and Programme "in order to ensure effective state control over telecommunications and in order to create appropriate technical and financial conditions for their development … it is necessary to preserve sate monopoly" for primary telecommunications networks; long distance and international fix phone and fax services and for telegraphy; radio and television transmitters; mail services.

In 2001 President of the Republic of Belarus, has signed a decree that will see the establishment of an association of companies involved in the development and export of IT. Membership in the association, which will be an affiliate of the state university in Minsk, will only be available to those with a legal background, and all members are to be engaged in IT development. Foreigners and enterprises with foreign investments can also be members of the association. The government is expected to give unprecedented tax concessions - VAT amounts of five per cent and immunity from taxation. In February of 2003 the Council of Ministers of the Republic of Belarus published its programme for the widespread introduction of information technology to government from 2003 to 2010. "Electronic Belarus" is aimed at developing governmental ICT infrastructure and the co-ordination of the introduction of ICT into administrative practice at all levels - from local authorities to ministries. The programme also provides measures for the promotion of e-commerce and e-learning in the country. Various e-government initiatives are also mentioned as possible next steps after a successful implementation of the programme. In 2003-2005 the government will allocate E15m (BYR32bn) for the implementation of the programme. The government hopes that implementation of the programme will result in growth of ICT exports of between five and ten per cent annually, and a reduction in the cost of internet access of 50 per cent. The programme highlights the existence of many monopolies in the IT sector in Belarus as one of the main obstacles for the successful implementation of an 'e-Belarus'.

At present more than 50 Ministries and governmental structures have their websites. 16 institutions update their sites on the daily basis. These are the sites of the President of the Republic of Belarus (http://www.president.gov.by), the governmental portal (http://www.main.gov.by) and the web site of the Council of Ministers Council (http://www.government.by/), sites of the ministries: http://www.mfa.gov.by (Ministry of Foreign Affairs), http://www.nalog.by (Tax administration), http://www.mod.mil.by/ (Ministry of Defence), http://www.mininform.gov.by (Ministry of Information) http://mvd-belarus.nsys.by/ (Ministry of Internal Affairs); web sites of National Centre for Legal Information of the Republic of Belarus (http://ncpi.gov.by), of the National Olympic Committee (http://www.noc.by), of the the Supreme Court for Economic Affairs (http://court.by/) and of the State Committee on Aviation (http://www.avia.by/). Sites of local administrations should be added to the list

(http://www.minsk.gov.by/, http://www.gorod.gomel.by,
http://www.region.mogilev.by, http://www.brest-region.by/).
Most of the sites have two versions – Russian and English.

This short overview of the governmental ICT initiatives shows that the key focus is the development of telecommunication infrastructure, widespread introduction of information technology to government in order to collect and process data and information security which are regarded as a step of transition to information society. "Electronic Belarus" is oriented generally to organizational and technological upgrading of the public administrations. Issues of wide public electronic access to information and participation in democratic process, transparency of public administration are not mentioned in the programme and do not form the core of ICT activities of the majority of the governmental structures. But the fact that e-government is proclaimed as a perspective creates opportunities for further work in this direction.

E-Governance in India: Models That Can Be Applied in Other Developing Countries

Aneesh Banerjee and Sachin Jain

Graduate Students of Management
XLRI Jamshedpur, India
{aneeshb.04,sachinj.04}@astra.xlri.ac.in

Abstract. Gone are days when every thing related to "e" must be western or related to developed countries. There were times not long ago, when India was considered a country of snake charmers. With technological revolution, India has been the front runner in the area of Information Technology. India's matured and robust educational system provided the much-needed backbone to IT manpower needs in country and abroad. Implementation of Information Technology is not only in the industrial sector as thought, but also in the area of governance. Information Technology has became a new tool for "Democracy". Although e-governance is there on priority for every state government, some have taken a lead and developed effective models from which others can take a lead.

1   What Is E-Governance?

e-Governance is much more than just a government website. Many definitions exist for e-governance and several other terms are interchangeably used with e-governance. Some of these terms are e-business, e-democracy, e-democracy. E-government is the use of information and communications technology (ICT) to promote more efficient and cost-effective government, facilitate more convenient government services, allow greater public access to information, and make government more accountable to citizens[1]. No observation on e-government can apply to all countries in such a diverse region, ranging in terms of population size from the People's Republic of China (PRC) to Nauru, and in terms of per capita GDP from Singapore to Nepal.

Therefore, a common definition for e-government could be:
Electronic Government is a form of organization that integrates the interactions and the interrelations between government and citizens, companies, customers, and public intuitions through the application of modern information and communication technologies.

---

[1]   Some define e-government more restrictively, making it the public sector equivalent of e-commerce, see World Bank, "E*Government" (Online). Available:
<http://www1.worldbank.org/publicsector/egov/index.htm>.
Others take a broader approach, see Economist. "Survey: Government and the Internet". June 22, 2000. This article takes the broader approach to reflect the many benefits that can result from other ICT applications in the public sector. Major English dictionaries do not yet list the word "e-government" or the phrase "electronic government."

R. Traunmüller (Ed.): EGOV 2003, LNCS 2739, pp. 488–491, 2003.

2 Indian Reality

E governance in India and perhaps where ever it is in a nascent state, in third world countries would have three essential problems to tackle. These can be summarized as
1. Scale
2. Standards
3. Reusability
In the case of Andhra Pradesh governments e-seva initiative these problems come out clearly. As the endeavor is the first of its kind in India the identification and subsequent elimination is possible.

In developing countries like India even though the service providers are available it seems to be unlikely that any one of them would be able to match up to the scale at which the initiate is being taken up. Hence the problem of scale leads to a typical problem of not being able to entrust a solution provider with a part of e governance.

The second problem finds its roots in the first, however has a completely different bearing on the project. It is that of maintaining the same standard across the service as well as services. As each service provider would use its own technology, data schemes and standards integration becomes a challenge.

The third problem is to encourage the development of portable or replicable solutions that can re-used in applications for other government agencies, states etc. The reason behind this is that just as in businesses, around 85% of the processes are same across companies within the same industry, it is expected that 85% of the processes should be similar across different governments. Thus, it should be possible to use the solutions developed for one government, in another government. Reusing the e-Governance asset across different governments can substantially bring down the cost of governance

Gartner, an international consultancy firm, has formulated a four-phase e governance model. The four phases of maturity, in a nutshell are

1. Information   Presence
2. Interaction   Intake Process
3. Transaction   Complete Transactions
4. Transformation   Integration & change

This model does not imply that an institution has to go through all the phases at the same time. On the contrary in the western world government institutions are in 1, 2 or 3. From a value to citizen point of view the value chain would be 4>3>2>1 and on the complexity scale it would also be 4>3>2>1, 4 being most complex. This serves as a template for governments to put their projects on track, and point at parts of the value line taking into consideration the complexity.

3 E-Seva: A Role Model

The e seva model is designed on 4 layers. These layers are as follows

Implementation Framework   6 C model
Prioritization Framework (the big picture)   PPP model
Technology framework   ICT Architecture

The ICT structure would enable the government to prioritize its projects, implement them in phases. It would also help in avoiding duplication and ensure interoperability. As part of the continuum of the framework it enables PPP to achieve sustainability.

The Private Public Partnership addresses lots of issues. It caters to the need to provide high quality services. Accounts for shrinking budget support. Ensure a steady pace of implementation. It also controls the risk of technology obsolescence. It provides cost effective solutions and also delivers to the system efficiency and accountability.

There are certain prerequisites of PPP. The participant government must be a proactive government. There should be abundant IT skills in the private sector. Connectivity should be cost effective. There should be administrative reforms to enable the IT architecture for e government. A foolproof framework for security of the system must be in place.

The PPP methodology for e governance can be put into 8 steps. These are
1. Identify partner for project development and management
2. Establish project development processes
3. Identify 5 core to 50 pivotal projects
4. Invite proposals
5. Shortlist
6. Develop prototypes
7. Enter into appropriate partnerships
8. Evaluate results through third party audits

The 6 C model looks into the following aspects of an e governance project. They are
1. Content
2. Capital
3. Competencies
4. Connectivity
5. Cyber laws
6. Citizen interface

As part of content identification and definition the project manager must prioritize his applications, System study. Get Ownership/involvement/inclusion in the project. Set standards of data, hardware, software and networking. Set the local language interface. Define the architecture of e government and security of the system.

The next part of the 6C structure is capital. This includes budget support, public private partnership. Leasing Vs. Purchasing. Sustained stream of revenue and user charges.

Connectivity is the essence of any e governance project. The project requires National/ state backbone of optical fiber cables. Satellite based communication networks. Campus area networks and most importantly affordable access

While setting up projects the government must be aware of Cyber laws that include IT Act 2000 Digital signatures Encryption Evidentiary value of electronic records Privacy issues Need for specific legislation/rules (Registration Act & Rules)

The citizen interface includes integrated citizen service centers. Internet based applications and Community Internet infrastructure, Smart cards and electronic payment gateways.

4 Conclusion

The overall model suggested in the paper about scale, standards and reusability was conceptualized through our interaction with the department if information and technology, Government of Andhra Pradesh, the service providers and also a section of the people who are availing the services of e-seva. The difficulties faced by us while using the system have further strengthened our framework. The layered structure is the right template that can be applied to e governance projects across developing countries as again verified through our interactions. Thread of problems in implementation of e-governance projects runs through all developing countries. The 4-layered structure tackles these problems in a structured, sequential manner. This structure has been developed after studying the shortcoming and success of Indian e-government projects and can be extended to other projects beyond of political boundaries.

Santa Catarina Information Technology Nucleus NECATI

Hugo Cesar Hoeschl, Érica Bezerra Queiroz Ribeiro, Louise Barcia Ramos Reis,
Thais Helena Bigliazzi Garcia, Andre Bortolon, Filipe Corrêa da Costa,
and Irineu Theis

Instituto Jurídico de Inteligência e Sistemas
Trindade – Florianópolis – Brazil – 88036-003
Tel: 55 48 3025-6609
digesto@digesto.net
{erica,louise,thais,andre,filipe}@ijuris.org
irineu@wbsa.com.br

Abstract. This paper deals with an Electronic Government project that has as objective the creation of the Santa Catarina Information Technology Nucleus – NECATI, due to the importance that CITs have in the State of Santa Catarina, in Brazil. It has as objective the R&D in CITs fomentation, offering legal and commercial specialized assistance. NECATI is structured in two sub-nuclei: the Copyright Support Nucleus – NAPI, that has as objective to give technical assistance to the generating technology entities, and the Knowledge Management Nucleus – NUGESCO, that has as target the commercialization of new Knowledge Management technologies. It still has as objective the creation of a web portal. NECATI will be organized by the Juridical Institute of Intelligence and Systems – IJURIS, having as co-executor FUNCITEC, counting on the support of the State Educational Foundations Association – ACAFE.

1 Introduction

The increasing dissemination of information on copyright in the Internet is of extreme importance for the social clarification and the enhancement of business-oriented technologies.

The increasing dissemination of information on copyright on the Internet is of extreme importance for the social clarification and the enhancement of business-oriented technologies.

In Brazil, the State of Santa Catarina is presented as strong producer of innovative technologies through its knowledge generating centers, deserving prominence in national and international ambit in terms of Science and Technology.

The State, however, presents difficulties to identify innovative technologies developed by the research institutions, due to inexistence of an infrastructure of support to the protection of the intellectual production. Many innovative technologies are restricted to the academic level, generating a deficit in the market. The result is the weakness of the economic and legal protection of the developed products.

R. Traunmüller (Ed.): EGOV 2003, LNCS 2739, pp. 492–495, 2003.

The lack of register and regularization of innovative technologies are pointed as the main problem, due to the unfamiliarity with the legal system that regulates the copyright and questions associates and, mainly, the lack of an institution in the State to guide the defense of copyright and the of an structure to stimulate the commerce of these technologies developed in the academic ambit.

2 The Santa Catarina Information Technology Nucleus

To solve this demand and to stimulate CITs R&D the Santa Catarina Information Technology Nucleus – NECATI is considered, offering legal and commercial specialized assistance.

The NECATI will guide the defense of innovative technologies copyright. The nucleus will also propose policies for R&D produced by technology generating centers, stimulating the development of innovative technologies in the market, that promote sustainable development through the promotion of bio-business, for example.

NECATI intends to become a reference center in promotion of Knowledge Management and CITs innovations thus stimulating the businesses related to these technologies. Creating and consolidating a nucleus specialized in copyright in Santa Catarina.

To reach its goals, NECATI received support from Green and Yellow Fund, which was created to stimulate university-company interaction for innovation support.

NECATI creation will be coordinated by the Juridical Institute of Intelligence and Systems – IJURIS, having as co-executor the Santa Catarina Science and Technology Foundation – FUNCITEC, who will co-ordinate the efforts of the main generating knowledge centers of the State aiming at the university-company integration. counting on the support of the State Educational Foundations Association – ACAFE.

3 NECATI Structure and Functioning

NECATI is structured in two sub-nuclei: the Copyright Support Nucleus – NAPI, that has as objective to give technical assistance to the generating technology entities, and the Knowledge Management Nucleus – NUGESCO, that has as target the commercialization of new Knowledge Management technologies.

It will be also developed a Portal that will contain a database modeled with information regarding to Intellectual Property, which will serve as support to consultations and decision taking for NAPI, avoiding waste of investments in research. It will also help NUGESCO to develop an efficient e-commerce policy on knowledge management technologies, facilitating the access to information for institutions that are distant from urban centers.

NECATI web portal allows an unified vision of the information, applications and services. Through the database, important information is published on Intellectual Property and technologies. This database also allows a statistical rising on P&D in Information Technology and Knowledge Management.

4 Experiences with E-Government

Prof. Hugo Hoeschl, Ph.D., gave the first post-graduate course on Electronic Government in Brazil in the ambit of the Post-Graduate Program of Production Engineering - PPGEP of the Federal University of Santa Catarina – UFSC, in the beginning of year 2001. It possesses, since its implementation, a multidisciplinary character. It materializes direct connection between detached aspects of two great areas: Social Applied (mainly Law, Administration and Economy) and Technology (mainly Engineerings and Computer Science).

Inside this context UFSC was chosen to develop for the National Antidrugs Secretariat, agency of the Institutional Security Cabinet Agency of the Presidency of the Republic, the OBID web portal and, therefore, the management model of the Observatory itself since 2002. The Health department was responsible for its fund raising and the University Research and Extension Support Foundation in UFSC managed the project. The Laboratory of Distance Learning – LED in UFSC and the Juridical Institute of Intelligence and Systems – IJURIS were responsible for the development and implementation of the Observatory.

The team was awarded, in December 2002, with General Honor Mention for Social Relevance to the Excellency in Electronic Government Prize, instituted by the Brazilian Association of Data Processing State Companies, Brazilian School of Public Administration and Companies of the Getúlio Vargas Foundation and the Ministry of the Planning, Budget and Management of the Federal Government.

In 2003, it was developed by IJURIS the, first Brazilian MBA in Electronic Government, totally offered as distance learning. Besides the conceptual modeling and the scientific discussion the course will contemplate important useful pragmatic aspects to the public and private sections involved in the electronic government's context.

Researches from the Law and Intelligence Systems Research Institute – IJURIS and from the Federal University of Santa Catarina jointly many government entities, especially the Consumers and Human Rights Commission of Florianópolis' Municipal Chamber and the State of Santa Catarina Consumers Rights Public Office, developed "Consumers SC – The Santa Catarina's Consumers Portal" to offer consumers unprecedented protection while strengthening confidence in the marketplace.

Consumer SC (www.ijuris.org/consumidor.sc) is the first Portal in the country to congregate scientific and academic researches; e-gov services; a software – the Aletheia v and free virtual legal assistance in the consumer's rights matter.

Aletheia is an intelligence system that allows the citizen to write a query in natural language – describing a customary situation – responding to this with the legal solution to the case. The system is a strong enforcement mechanism designed to be available on the Internet, for free download, in order to help Brazilian consumers make informed decisions.

5 Conclusions

Santa Catarina presents itself as a strong producer of innovative technologies through its knowledge generating centers. In spite of all that production, the great majority of the developed technologies don't have the capacity to enter in the market in a competitive way. The industrial section presents an enormous lack in relation to innovative technologies. Those technologies are considered factors of competitiveness in the corporate markets for the companies and factor of socioeconomic development for the State. The creation of the Santa Catarina Information Technology Nucleus - NECATI,, with the intention of assisting the regional demand of technological innovations, will benefit, without a doubt, the State, because, in Santa Catarina, an institution that guides the defense of the intellectual property rights doesn't exist.

The link among different sections of the society, will promote the increase of the dissemination of important information for the social explanation and enhancement of technological businesses. Promoting the fomentation and support to the accomplishment of partnerships among NECATI, public and private organizations, research institutions, reference centers and companies, it will also be contributing with the generation of employments and increasing of their technological capacity.

All those impacts will turn NECATI into a Reference Center in business fomentation in the ambit of Knowledge Management and Information Technology with prominence and leadership, in state ambit, of the development, production and commercialization of technologies.

References

1. HOESCHL, H. C., BUENO, T. C. D., MATTOS, E. S., BORTOLON, A., RIBEIRO, M. S., THEISS, I., BARCIA, R. M. Structured contextual search for the UN Security Council. In: ICEIS - 5th International Conference On Enterprise Information Systems, 2003, Angers. Selected Papers Books: Enterprise Information Systems IV. Kluwer, 2003.
2. HOESCHL, H. C., BUENO, T. C. D., BORTOLON, A., MATTOS, E. S., RIBEIRO, M. S. AlphaThemis - from Text into Knowledge In: 1st worksohp on Automatic Deduction and Artificial Intelligence (IDEIA), in the 8th Iberoamerican Conference on Artificial Intelligence (IBERAMIA), 2002, Sevilha. Proceedings of the IDEIA, 2002. v.1. p.91 – 100.
3. HOESCHL, H. C.; BUENO, T. C. D.; BARCIA, R. M.; BORTOLON, A.; MATTOS, E. S. Olimpo System. In: 8th International Conference on Artificial Intelligence and Law, 2001, St. Louis. Proceedings of 8a. ICAIL. 2001.
4. BUENO, T. C. D., HOESCHL, H. C., MATTOS, E. S., BARCIA, R. M., WANGENHEIM, C. G. V. JurisConsulto: Retrieval in Jurisprudencial Text Bases using Juridical Terminology In: The 7th International Conference on Artificial Intelligence and Law, 1999, Oslo-Norway. Proceedings of the Conference. New York: ACM, 1999. v.1. p.147 – 155.
5. HOESCHL, H. C., BUENO, T. C. D., BARCIA, R. M., BORTOLON, A., MATTOS, E. S. Olimpo: Contextual structured search to improve the representation of UN security council with information extraction methods In: 8th International Conference on Artificial Intelligence and Law, 2001, St. Louis-EUA. ICAIL 2001 Proceedings. New York: ACM SIGART, 2001. p.217 – 218.

E-Government Requirement Elicitation

Wichian Chutimaskul

King Mongkut's University of Technology Thonburi
91 Suksawasd 48, Bangmod, Tungkru
Bangkok 10140 Thailand
wichian@it.kmutt.ac.th

Abstract. The quality and productivity of e-Government is measured by its successful usage for country development. The e-Government requirement is one of the most important features, which must be elicited from related stakeholders. The e-Government crisis normally comes from the shortage or unqualified IT Man, Machine, Money, Methodology, and Management (5M framework). The e-Government requirement elicitation requires a good management of 5M. This paper introduces the requirement process that is a super set of requirement elicitation and modeling. The e-Government architecture, which is classified into three layers, is discussed.

1 Introduction

e-Government, a tool for good, efficient and distributed governance which has the concepts of transparency and openness, requires the use of information communication and technology (ICT) [1]. Proper management of e-Government leads to country development, budget saving, efficient government, and knowledge economic system [2]. Hence, e-Government can be claimed as a process, which needs a good management to reduce both financial and political risks. If e-Government is not properly implemented, invested resources will be wasted.

e-Government requirement elicitation is a process of capturing the e-Government needs, which come from government, business, and citizen. The changes of government administrators, an insufficient IS Development skill, incompetent vendors, and less business and citizens' participation lead to a poor requirement. To solve these problems, the 5M framework (Man, Machine, Money, Methodology, and Management) must be properly managed. Man must know his or her role and must give good support to the system. Machine and Money must be sufficient. Furthermore, Methodology and Management must be considered. Many e-Government projects underestimate the important of requirement process. The shortcut of eliciting requirement makes requirement creeping or the e-Government project unsuccessful.

Requirement elicitation involves all related stakeholders. A good e-Government specification should be flexible and dynamic and should support the future needs. It is clear that truly understanding requirements will increase the quality and productivity of e-Government. Requirement prototype and requirement testing must also be employed during the requirement process to ensure the completeness of specification.

R. Traunmüller (Ed.): EGOV 2003, LNCS 2739, pp. 496–499, 2003.

2 E-Government Problem Consideration

e-Government can be used to provide the political transparency. Its successful usage can be measured by the improvement of standard of living, knowledge society, and world peace. However, these can be suffered from e-Government development due to poor management of 5M. In Thailand, a half of national budget was wasted due to poor management and corruption [3]. The government agencies with poor work indicator are an incubator of corruption. Compared to product development, knowledge development is important since it is used to solve this severe problem.

The problem analysis of e-Government projects can concentrate on the 5M framework as follows:

- Man. Government, business and citizen should get involved in e-Government projects. The conformance of each government agency strategy helps building good e-Government. Government officers are always rotated, therefore the responsible persons for e-Government development are often changed. The shortage of IT personal can be solved by the outsource concept.
- Machine. Machines are resources for e-Government development, which must be shared among government agencies. Such resources are hardware, network, software, and information. Many government agencies do not utilize their resources.
- Money. Some e-Government projects are created without truly understanding their needs. The false expectation always causes the broken promises. Furthermore, the mistake of accepting e-Government projects with poor specification causes the country damage.
- Methodology. The methodology is concerned with the right activities for e-Government development. The standard processes, deliverable and document need identify to make a concise development.
- Management. Management concerns the political issues. Bureaucracy should be reformed to support efficient government. The collaborative work is created to replace an individual work. Special inspection must keep an eye on each private benefit. A good leadership must also be found.

The 5M can be considered as a framework for e-Government projects. The return of investment on e-Government must be declared. The e-Government assessment, such as knowledge availability, service level, and operational efficiency, must also be identified. Finally, the citizen relationship management (CRM) must be constructed.

3 E-Government Requirement Process

e-Government requirement should be elicited from government, business and citizen to improve the public services and to give a high level of coordination and integration. The requirement pattern must be built to help stakeholders understand the requirements. The requirement elicitation cannot be completed without real needs. e-Government projects must be initiated with full responsible personal and management support. Having the clear goal is not enough, the process of elicitation must also be declared.

3.1 E-Government Project Management

To implement e-Government projects, some aspects must be considered in order to make the most of the money value and to make e-Government truly work. They are the national e-Government master plan, strategy and policy, information and knowledge, human resource management, financial management, development methodology, information technology management, standard and security, citizens' and business satisfaction, and e-Citizen society.

Many e-Government projects fail during development. It makes one wonder how transparency can be achieved if the beginning of e-Government project is not transparent. Not only the sufficient and competent human resource but also the honesty is required to make e-Government usable to citizens [4]. Controlling and monitoring of e-Government progress is compulsory. Note that developing countries always have an unusual high investment on e-Government due to imported technology, poor management, and corruption [5]. Furthermore, each government agency uses different technology and standard on e-Government development, which makes it hard for integration. The trust can be achieved by transparency and openness.

The good e-Government investment must reduce waste. To gain benefits of e-Government resource sharing, each government agency requires a top-down approach, e.g. the need of centralize e-Government master plan. The central government must invest on IT infrastructure, e.g. telecommunication and networking that can be shared for all. In addition, the basic software such as human resource management, financial and accounting system, and document flow system must be uniquely built and be deployed many times. Failure to control IT investment causes waste, over-time development and poor e-Government quality. Unique investment on IT infrastructure, basic application software, and national data-information-knowledge are claimed to be good; however, it is hard to be achieved.

3.2 Requirement Elicitation

Stakeholders must get involved for e-Government requirement elicitation. They are government, business and citizen, vendor, and IT personnel, e.g. system analyst, system designer, software engineer and software tester, application expert or consultant, requirement architect and pattern architect. Requirement must be correct and complete for further development; therefore, application experts or consultant, and pattern architect need to participate on this requirement elicitation. The pattern architect deals with the reuse of models for requirement gathering. Patterns, well-understood good solutions to a common problem in context, help novices to learn by example to behave more like expert. Having the outsourcing concept, care must be considered since government knowledge will be transferred to outsource companies.

e-Government requirement elicitation is a process for capturing the real needs. Requirement architect must identify the details of actual e-Government requirements and future needs, an ongoing technology guideline, e-Government users, e-Portal, e-Service and e-Application, and requirement process.

4 E-Government Architecture

e-Government architecture must be created as a blueprint for better understanding. This architecture, which behaves as a plug-and-play model, contains three layers namely e-Portal, e-Service and e-Application. Prototyping is a technique for improving better understanding of the e-Government requirement. It can reduce risks, time and cost of e-Government development. Requirement must be tested to ensure that e-Government requirement is complete and correct. Working on good requirements is a sign of producing good products, which are delivered on time, within budget, and meet the real needs. To develop a practical e-Government, requirement specification must be clearly defined, flexible, traceable, consistent and correct. The requirement specification should be signed-off for common understanding before further development.

The e-Government application contains both front- and back-office e-Application. They are citizen registration, education, health care, military, social security and welfare, judicial system, tax, transportation, political election, human resource management, financial and accounting management, document flow system, e-Payment, e-Procurement, and e-Card. e-Application must have a standard, citizen-centric, and shared resource and data. e-Service provides a one-start service. A simple way of getting e-Service is to employ Internet technology.

5 Summary

e-Government requirement elicitation, an important phase of e-Government development process, is discussed. Most requirement faults come from requirement creeping and shortcut system development. Stakeholders play an important role for requirement elicitation. Thus, e-Government requirement must captured from government, business, and citizen. e-Government specification contains not only the present needs but also the future business operation. Such a specification must be flexible and dynamic. Requirement process and e-Government architecture are also addressed. Requirement prototype and requirement testing must be included to ensure that all elicited requirements are complete and correct. The efficient e-Government, which is a vehicle of democracy, can be measured by fast service, minimum cost, high performance, and decentralize government agencies. Experience gained from e-Government requirement elicitation leads to future knowledge elicitation.

Reference

1. Sweeney, J.: e-Government Challenge the Case of Thailand, Bangkok (2002)
2. Suebwonglee, S., ICT Minister: *Thailand e-Government Project* (2003)
3. http://www.manager.co.th/politics/PoliticsView.asp (2003)
4. Thailand e-Citizen in http:\\www.ecitizen.go.th (2003)
5. Chutimaskul, W.: e-Government: Can It Solve Serious Problems? Workshop on Knowledge Management and e-Government, IFIP, Siena-Italy (2001) 39–44

E-Government: Assessment of GCC (Gulf Co-operating Council) Countries and Services Provided

Mahmood A. Awan

Dubai University College
Dubai, UAE
mawan@duc.ac.ae

Abstract. Just like other parts of the world, governments of Gulf Co-operation Council (GCC) countries are also in cut – throat competition with each other to attract inward investment, make their products and services competitive on a global scale and create an in-country atmosphere that will attract the brightest minds. The current research assesses major government websites of GCC countries. The criteria for ranking included, online information, foreign language access, communication, services provided, and use of advertisements on government websites. The study reveals that all GCC countries have made some strides towards placing information and services online, however there is considerable variation across GCC countries in how much material is on these government websites. Further, among the GCC countries, UAE Government websites were ranked as highest in all the criteria researched. Kingdom of Saudi Arabia was rated as the lowest.

1 Introduction

The Internet is changing the way people work, live and communicate. It is changing the way business is conducted. Citizens around the world are also demanding the same kind of changes from their governments. Citizens demand that governments be more open in their interaction with the civil society. Access to information and knowledge about services, about political process, and about choices available, is characteristic requirement in all good governance systems. E-Government refers to government's use of technology, particularly web-based Internet applications to enhance the access to and delivery of government information and services to citizens, business partners, employees and government entities.

The Gulf Co-operating Council (GCC) was created in 1981 by six Gulf States – Bahrain, Kuwait, Saudi Arabia (KSA), Oman, Qatar and United Arab Emirates (UAE). All these countries have high per capita income levels, and the region itself posses many traits common to emerging markets. A SWOT analysis done in Arabian Business (2000), of Arab countries regarding E-government, indicated that all governments of GCC countries have placed a wide range of materials on the Web from publication to database. However no extensive research has been done to compare GCC countries in offering online services.

Thus the purpose of this paper is twofold, firstly to evaluate over 150 GCC government websites, for various features available online, explore what kind of

R. Traunmüller (Ed.): EGOV 2003, LNCS 2739, pp. 500–503, 2003.

variations exist across countries, as well as how e- government sites respond to citizen requests for information. Secondly, we looked at the number and type of online services offered. The sites were ranked by the score provided and the average score per site was compared with other countries.

2 Literature Review

David (2002) has mentioned that numerous possibilities exist for countries to use the Internet and Web – based technologies to extend government services online. It allow citizens to interact more directly with government, employ customer – centric services, and transform the provision of traditional government services. Federal Government websites are capable of providing fast, cost – effective access to an abundance of government information stored in a variety of electronic formats. Yet to enhance the overall usefulness and impact of Federal Websites (Eschenfelder 1997) believes that careful consideration should be given to the purpose, structure and operation of Federal Websites, and that federal information policies should be re-examined. They should determine whether eliminating paper publications and disseminating information via the Web actually would result in significant social inequities. They should ensure the privacy rights of the citizens being protected.

In terms of information availability, many countries have made considerable progress in putting publications, forms and databases online for citizen access. Government agencies have discovered that it is very efficient for the general public to be able to download common documents rather than having to visit or call the particular agency. Darell (2001)has also included the countries in his evaluation of global evaluation, but no attempt has been made to compare the countries. The similarity in exclusive economical and political background makes it important to evaluate them on their own.

3 Methodology

In our analysis of websites, we looked for material that would aid an average citizen logging onto a governmental site. This included contact information that would enable a citizen to find out who to call or write at an agency to resolve a problem, material on information, services, and databases, features that would facilitate e-government access by special populations such as the disabled and non-native language speakers, interactive features that would facilitate outreach to the public, and visible statements that would reassure citizens worried about privacy and security over the Internet.

Services provided online benefit both government and its constituents, as it lowers costs and makes services more accessible. All the GCC government websites chosen for evaluation of features, were also evaluated and scored for services. Services included, complaint filing, paying parking violation tickets, service request, permit application, job applications, document request, report of crime and paying taxes. The ranking was also done based on the score awarded for each service.

In order to examine responsiveness to citizen requests, we sent an email to the address provided, asking the information about how to get to the particular office, and directions, to get there. Email responses were recorded based on the time it took for the agency to respond.

4 Findings

In our analysis of over 150 government websites of six GCC countries, we looked at the material that would aid an average citizen or business logging onto a governmental site. This included contact information that would enable a citizen to find out who to call or write at an agency to resolve a problem, material on information, services, and databases, features that would facilitate e –government access by non-native speakers, interactive features that would facilitate outreach to the public, and visible statements that would reassure citizens worried about privacy and security over the Internet. We used the same criteria utilized by Darell (2001) for his global E-Government survey.

Evaluating for the information stage, loading times for most countries was moderate to good. However, the range of information varied from country to country. UAE topped in providing quality and quantity information online. The most frequently found service on GCC websites was service request, followed by document request, complaint filing and job applications. Applying for passport and renewing vehicle licenses was only found on UAE websites.

In order to see how the six countries ranked, we created an index for each website based on twelve important features centering on citizen contact material, services and information, addresses, publications, databases, foreign language access, privacy policies, email contact information, and search capabilities. The index measured the presence and absence of the features on each website.(Table 1) While UAE received the highest score for features, KSA received the lowest score for features online.

Table 1. GCC Countries Websites Assessment Average Results per Site & Ranking

	Features	Site Analysis	Services	Response Time	Total	Rank
KSA	5	7.3	0.67	0.27	13.24	6
UAE	5.8	11	1.03	0.7	18.53	1
Qatar	5.5	10	0.67	0.5	16.67	2
Oman	5.3	7.5	0.7	0.4	13.9	5
Bahrain	5.7	9.2	0.8	0.33	16.03	3
Kuwait	5.8	9	0.6	0.43	15.83	4
Max. Possible	12	27	10	5	44	

Enabling conversation between citizens and government is not the only way to bring citizens and government closer together. Making governments more easily accessible is another component of this endeavor(Osorio, 2002). There are a few features that make it possible. The first thing we examined was the ability to search the particular website. More than half of the GCC government websites evaluated, had this feature. This information is important in that it makes the information available on the website more easily accessible by allowing a visitor to search for information he or she desires.

We only got response of a total of 10% of all the Emails sent to government officials of GCC countries. Responses received from UAE sites were the highest, 18%, followed by Qatar 16%. Overall, this low response shows that the agency does not want to be contacted. Lack of communication and interaction in this study, was considered a serious problem and a big hindrance in moving the GCC countries to the next phases of E-government

5 Conclusion

Citizens bring diverse perspectives and experiences to e-government, and agencies benefit from citizen suggestions, complaints, and feedback. Even a simple feature such as a comment form empowers citizens and gives them an opportunity to voice their opinion about government services they would like to see. Governments should consider market research, public opinion surveys, or focus groups that would provide them with information on how citizens feel about e-government websites and what features would attract them to use these sites. This would help them design updates and service enhancements that would satisfy the interests of their particular users.

The results found are in line with the E- government SWOT Report (Arabian Business, 2000) which stated that Dubai is expected to surge ahead in the race of E-government, while because of low Internet penetration in KSA, it will take time. It is recommended that all GCC countries improve website organization and structure, post all means of contact information i.e. phone, address, and Email contact information and finally, increase website accessibility. Such study is planned for every year to monitor progress of E-government in the region.

References

1. Arabian Business.com Magazine "E-government SWOT Report", June 2000, Pg 39 – 44.
2. David Noack, Government Websites – A status report, Link – Up, May / Jun 2002
3. Dawes Sharon and Lise Prefontaine, Delivering the Government Services, Communications of the ACM, Jan 2003, Vol 46, No 1
4. Darell M.West, Global E-government Survey, World Markets Research Center, Sep, 2001
5. Dempsey, James X, How E-government Interacts with its Citizens, Working Paper, World Bank, 2003
6. Eschenfelder, Kristin. R, Assessing U.S. Federal Government Websites, Government Information Quarterly, 1997, Vol 14, Issue 2
7. Osorio, C , Alignment of Readiness Factors for E-government, Working Paper, Information Technologies Group, Center for International Development, Harvard University, 2002
8. Robert M. Lloyd, Electronic Government, Business and Economic Review, Jul – Sep 2002

South African E-Government Policy and Practices: A Framework to Close the Gap

Jonathan Trusler

Faculty of Commerce
Department of Information Systems
University of Cape Town
Private Bag
Rondebosch
7701, Cape Town
South Africa
jon@wpf.co.za

Abstract. E-government in South Africa has a particularly important historical and social context due to the legacy of apartheid. As a result, a ten year e-government implementation horizon has been created from tested world wide practices. Thus far the plan is not being realised and a gap is appearing between what the policy says should be happening and what is actually happening. This gap is most likely a result of a lack of government capacity to meet the policy objectives. In this paper the author puts forward a framework – drawing on actor network theory (ANT) and the due process model – which aims to improve the current e-government implementation process and close the gap between policy and practices in South Africa.

1 Introduction

South Africa held its first multi-racial, democratic elections in 1994. This event can be seen as a watershed in the lives of South Africans. Before 1994 South Africans lived under the system of Apartheid which created a deeply divided society along racial lines. Post-1994 South Africa is home to the "rainbow nation" and a government that has the very difficult task of "addressing apartheid's legacy of inequality and poverty." [1]

The issue of e-government in South Africa has a very important historical and social context; consequently, any e-government initiatives have to contend with a number of realities. These include: a high level of inequality; a weak Information Communications Technology (ICT) infrastructure (particularly in rural areas); a general lack of government ICT readiness; and other (apparently) more pressing demands in the public service which make ICT development a lower priority in budgetary terms. [2]

This paper briefly outlines the current policy of e-government in South Africa. It then looks at current practices and how these fall short of the policy objectives. Finally, an e-government implementation framework is proposed that could aid in rectifying the situation.

R. Traunmüller (Ed.): EGOV 2003, LNCS 2739, pp. 504–507, 2003.
© Springer-Verlag Berlin Heidelberg 2003

2 E-Government Policy in South Africa

The Department of Public Service and Administration (DPSA) drafted South Africa's *E-Government Policy* in 2001 after an extensive two year consultation process with various private sector representatives, community organisations and public service officials. [2] The policy outlines a ten year implementation plan for implementing e-government in South Africa. According to the authors, the implementation plan draws on tested world wide practices and seeks to avoid the mistakes, and improve on the successes of other governments implementing e-government initiatives. [2]

2.1 The "Batho Pele" Principles

In 1997 the DPSA released a White Paper on the Transformation of the Public Service. In this paper, the concept of Batho Pele was introduced:
   "Batho Pele is Sesotho for 'People First'. The name was chosen to express the key message [...] that the purpose of the Public Service is to serve **all** the people of South Africa." [3]
   Batho Pele can be seen as South Africa's (rather poetic) way of moving towards a "citizens as consumers" approach.

2.2 Ten Year Implementation Horizon

The political party landscape of South Africa is very stable compared to most other countries. The *African National Congress* (ANC) is the ruling party and is likely to stay in power for the foreseeable future due its strong support in the country. Thus, a ten year implementation horizon for e-government is entirely feasible.
   The plan follows six stages in chronological order: information provision; two-way transactions; multi-purpose portals; personalized portals; clustering of services; and comprehensive corporate transformation. (see [2] for definitions)
   Currently the government is seeking to achieve three main objectives through its e-government initiatives: increased productivity; lowered costs; and increased citizen convenience. This indicates a strong focus on service delivery improvement. Very little mention is made however, of any fundamental transformation objectives except for a vague but inevitable restructuring that begins in stage 5 of the implementation plan above. However, there is an implied overall aim of the e-government implementation to undergo a "comprehensive corporate transformation" i.e. to see the plan through to its final stage.

3 Current Practices of E-Government in South Africa

There is little consolidated information available with regards to the progress and current practices of e-government in South Africa. However, a brief scan of the "South Africa Online" website (www.gov.za) shows that some progress is being made. Almost all individual government departments have their own websites. A comprehensive resource of government documents including White Papers, Green Papers, speeches, annual reports, legislation, policies and other information is available for download.

This is consistent with the first phase of the implementation plan namely, "information provision". However, this should not be seen as an automatic improvement in service delivery. "Creating a Web site may be a benchmark, but it does not guarantee performance or customer usage." [5]

According to the targets set out by the plan, initiatives in "two-way transactions" (at least in the G2G arena but also starting in the G2C and G2B arenas) as well as in "multi-purpose portals" (mainly G2G at this stage) should be taking place.

However, there is little evidence that initiatives in either of these stages are currently being entered into by any government websites. There are several promising initiatives underway such as the *Gateway Project* [2], aimed at providing a central portal to government services, but none are as yet operational. Thus, it seems that the ten year plan is already experiencing some significant setbacks. A gap is developing as a result of practices failing to meet the targets set out by policy.

Furthermore, there seems to be a major lack of coordination between government departments with regards to the overall e-government policy. A key feature of the policy is that it relies heavily on the individual departments to come up with their own strategies and projects. At best the departments do not seem to be initiating e-government projects at the rate that is expected; at worst they are not initiating e-government projects at all.

4   What Is Causing the Gap?

It is difficult to pin-point why the ten year plan is not going according to schedule. It is still in its infancy but things are definitely not going well as evidenced by the already large gap between policy and practices. The lack of adequate progress is probably due largely to the obstacles outlined in the first section of this paper. There is an apparent willingness to pursue e-government but a lack of capacity to follow this through. Evidence from other studies such as Wastell [4] indicate that public sector organisations are often characterized by a profoundly defensive "discourse of dependency", with services being seen as the prerogative of a professional elite who define what the community needs and take largely unilateral control over planning and delivery. The professionals "know best" what the community needs and the community "gets what it is given". This subtle, but powerful resistance to change by public officials could be a further reason for the existence of the gap.

5   A Proposed Framework for E-Government Implementation

As a result of the problems being experienced in the implementation of e-government in South Africa and in other countries, the author proposes a new framework to guide the implementation processes. The framework is based on concepts from ANT and follows a due process model. The author intends to study the framework's ability to successfully guide an e-government implementation process.

In particular, the framework shows how to overcome the resistance to change of public officials through its fundamentally inclusive approach to implementation that goes beyond mere consultation. Using the framework as an implementation guide could also improve alignment between policy and practices through its more integrated approach to these two processes.

The proposed framework will be discussed in more detail at the conference presentation and can be obtained by emailing the author.

6 Conclusion

The Batho Pele principles provide an excellent foundation for successful e-government in South Africa. Unfortunately, it appears that capacity is a major limitation to implementing e-government initiatives in South Africa. Therefore, a gap is developing between the espoused e-government policy and actual practices. It is envisioned that the proposed framework could provide a way of managing the implementation of e-government in South Africa so that true progress in this arena could become a reality.

Acknowledgement. The financial assistance of the National Research Foundation of South Africa (NRF) towards this research is hereby acknowledged. Opinions expressed and conclusions arrived at, are those of the author and are not necessarily to be attributed to the NRF.

References

1. South African Government, (2002) Overview on Government's Programme of Action. *South Africa Yearbook.* Available online at: http://www.gov.za/yearbook/2002/overview.htm.
2. DPSA, (2001) *E-Government Policy.* Second Draft, Version 4.13. Available online at: http://www.gov.za/documents/index.html
3. DPSA, *Batho Pele Frequently Asked Questions.* Available online at: http://www.dpsa.gov.za/projects/batho-pele/faqs.htm.
4. Wastell, D.G. (2002) Organizational Discourse as a Social Defense: Taming the Tiger of Electronic Government. *Global and Organizational Discourse about IT Working Conference Proceedings,* December 2002, Barcelona, Spain. Kluwer, pp. 181–194.
5. The Working Group on E-Government in the Developing World, (2002) *Roadmap for E-government in the Developing World.* Available online at: http://www.gov.za/reports/2002/e-govfinal.pdf.

Author Index

Lecture Notes in Computer Science

For information about Vols. 1–2698
please contact your bookseller or Springer-Verlag

Vol. 2734: P. Perner, A. Rosenfeld (Eds.), Machine Learning and Data Mining in Pattern Recognition. Proceedings, 2003. XII, 440 pages. 2003. (Subseries LNAI).

Vol. 2735: F. Kaashoek, I. Stoica (Eds.), Peer-to-Peer Systems II. Proceedings, 2003. XI, 316 pages. 2003.

Vol. 2739: R. Traunmüller (Ed.), Electronic Government. Proceedings, 2003. XVIII, 511 pages. 2003.

Vol. 2740: E. Burke, P. De Causmaecker (Eds.), Practice and Theory of Automated Timetabling IV. Proceedings, 2002. XII, 361 pages. 2003.

Vol. 2741: F. Baader (Ed.), Automated Deduction – CADE-19. Proceedings, 2003. XII, 503 pages. 2003. (Subseries LNAI).

Vol. 2742: R. N. Wright (Ed.), Financial Cryptography. Proceedings, 2003. VIII, 321 pages. 2003.

Vol. 2743: L. Cardelli (Ed.), ECOOP 2003 – Object-Oriented Programming. Proceedings, 2003. X, 501 pages. 2003.

Vol. 2744: V. Mařík, D. McFarlane, P. Valckenaers (Eds.), Holonic and Multi-Agent Systems for Manufacturing. Proceedings, 2003. XI, 322 pages. 2003. (Subseries LNAI).

Vol. 2745: M. Guo, L.T. Yang (Eds.), Parallel and Distributed Processing and Applications. Proceedings, 2003. XII, 450 pages. 2003.

Vol. 2746: A. de Moor, W. Lex, B. Ganter (Eds.), Conceptual Structures for Knowledge Creation and Communication. Proceedings, 2003. XI, 405 pages. 2003. (Subseries LNAI).

Vol. 2747: B. Rovan, P. Vojtáš (Eds.), Mathematical Foundations of Computer Science 2003. Proceedings, 2003. XIII, 692 pages. 2003.

Vol. 2748: F. Dehne, J.-R. Sack, M. Smid (Eds.), Algorithms and Data Structures. Proceedings, 2003. XII, 522 pages. 2003.

Vol. 2749: J. Bigun, T. Gustavsson (Eds.), Image Analysis. Proceedings, 2003. XXII, 1174 pages. 2003.

Vol. 2750: T. Hadzilacos, Y. Manolopoulos, J.F. Roddick, Y. Theodoridis (Eds.), Advances in Spatial and Temporal Databases. Proceedings, 2003. XIII, 525 pages. 2003.

Vol. 2751: A. Lingas, B.J. Nilsson (Eds.), Fundamentals of Computation Theory. Proceedings, 2003. XII, 433 pages. 2003.

Vol. 2752: G.A. Kaminka, P.U. Lima, R. Rojas (Eds.), RoboCup 2002: Robot Soccer World Cup VI. XVI, 498 pages. 2003. (Subseries LNAI).

Vol. 2753: F. Maurer, D. Wells (Eds.), Extreme Programming and Agile Methods – XP/Agile Universe 2003. Proceedings, 2003. XI, 215 pages. 2003.

Vol. 2754: M. Schumacher, Security Engineering with Patterns. XIV, 208 pages. 2003.

Vol. 2756: N. Petkov, M.A. Westenberg (Eds.), Computer Analysis of Images and Patterns. Proceedings, 2003. XVIII, 781 pages. 2003.

Vol. 2758: D. Basin, B. Wolff (Eds.), Theorem Proving in Higher Order Logics. Proceedings, 2003. X, 367 pages. 2003.

Vol. 2759: O.H. Ibarra, Z. Dang (Eds.), Implementation and Application of Automata. Proceedings, 2003. XI, 312 pages. 2003.

Vol. 2761: R. Amadio, D. Lugiez (Eds.), CONCUR 2003 - Concurrency Theory. Proceedings, 2003. XI, 524 pages. 2003.

Vol. 2762: G. Dong, C. Tang, W. Wang (Eds.), Advances in Web-Age Information Management. Proceedings, 2003. XIII, 512 pages. 2003.

Vol. 2763: V. Malyshkin (Ed.), Parallel Computing Technologies. Proceedings, 2003. XIII, 570 pages. 2003.

Vol. 2764: S. Arora, K. Jansen, J.D.P. Rolim, A. Sahai (Eds.), Approximation, Randomization, and Combinatorial Optimization. Proceedings, 2003. IX, 409 pages. 2003.

Vol. 2765: R. Conradi, A.I. Wang (Eds.), Empirical Methods and Studies in Software Engineering. VIII, 279 pages. 2003.

Vol. 2766: S. Behnke, Hierarchical Neural Networks for Image Interpretation. XII, 224 pages. 2003.

Vol. 2769: T. Koch, I. T. Sølvberg (Eds.), Research and Advanced Technology for Digital Libraries. Proceedings, 2003. XV, 536 pages. 2003.

Vol. 2776: V. Gorodetsky, L. Popyack, V. Skormin (Eds.), Computer Network Security. Proceedings, 2003. XIV, 470 pages. 2003.

Vol. 2777: B. Schölkopf, M.K. Warmuth (Eds.), Learning Theory and Kernel Machines. Proceedings, 2003. XIV, 746 pages. 2003. (Subseries LNAI).

Vol. 2779: C.D. Walter, Ç.K. Koç, C. Paar (Eds.), Cryptographic Hardware and Embedded Systems – CHES 2003. Proceedings, 2003. XIII, 441 pages. 2003.

Vol. 2782: M. Klusch, A. Omicini, S. Ossowski, H. Laamanen (Eds.), Cooperative Information Agents VII. Proceedings, 2003. XI, 345 pages. 2003. (Subseries LNAI).

Vol. 2783: W. Zhou, P. Nicholson, B. Corbitt, J. Fong (Eds.), Advances in Web-Based Learning – ICWL 2003. Proceedings, 2003. XV, 552 pages. 2003.

Vol. 2786: F. Oquendo (Ed.), Software Process Technology. Proceedings, 2003. X, 173 pages. 2003.

Vol. 2787: J. Timmis, P. Bentley, E. Hart (Eds.), Artificial Immune Systems. Proceedings, 2003. XI, 299 pages. 2003.

Vol. 2789: L. Böszörményi, P. Schojer (Eds.), Modular Programming Languages. Proceedings, 2003. XIII, 271 pages. 2003.

Vol. 2790: H. Kosch, L. Böszörményi, H. Hellwagner (Eds.), Euro-Par 2003 Parallel Processing. Proceedings, 2003. XXXV, 1320 pages. 2003.

Vol. 2794: P. Kemper, W. H. Sanders (Eds.), Computer Performance Evaluation. Proceedings, 2003. X, 309 pages. 2003.

Vol. 2796: M. Cialdea Mayer, F. Pirri (Eds.), Automated Reasoning with Analytic Tableaux and Related Methods. Proceedings, 2003. X, 271 pages. 2003. (Subseries LNAI).

Vol. 2803: M. Baaz, J.A. Makowsky (Eds.), Computer Science Logic. Proceedings, 2003. XII, 589 pages. 2003.

Vol. 2810: M.R. Berthold, H.-J. Lenz, E. Bradley, R. Kruse, C. Borgelt (Eds.), Advances in Intelligent Data Analysis V. Proceedings, 2003. XV, 624 pages. 2003.

Vol. 2817: D. Konstantas, M. Leonard, Y. Pigneur, S. Patel (Eds.), Object-Oriented Information Systems. Proceedings, 2003. XII, 426 pages. 2003.